THE UNSEEN WAR IN EUROPE

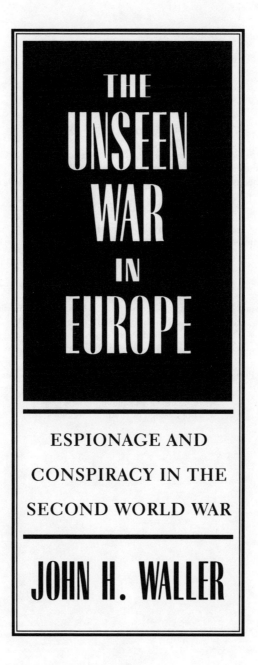

THE UNSEEN WAR IN EUROPE

ESPIONAGE AND
CONSPIRACY IN THE
SECOND WORLD WAR

JOHN H. WALLER

RANDOM HOUSE

NEW YORK

Library of Congress Cataloging-in-Publication Data

Waller, John H.
The unseen war in Europe: espionage and conspiracy in the Second
World War/John H. Waller.
p. cm.
Includes bibliographical references and index.
ISBN 0-679-44826-8
1. World War, 1939–1945—Secret service—Europe.   2. Subversive
activities—Europe—History—20th century.   I. Title.
D810.S7W35   1996
940.54'85—dc20   95-32723

Printed in the United States of America on acid-free paper
2 4 6 8 9 7 5 3
First Edition
Book design by Jo Anne Metsch

For
the men and women of the OSS

Acknowledgments

I wish to give my thanks to the following persons who were of particular help to me in researching and writing this book: Samuel Halpern, the late William Henhoeffer, Maria Waller, Vladimir Kabes, Neal H. Petersen, John Taylor, Lawrence H. McDonald, Cordelia Hood, George Constantinides, Timothy Naftali, Christof Mauch, Elizabeth McIntosh, Nicholas Scheetz, Roger Goiran, Paul Smith, the late Jaroslav Kašpar-Páty, Gillian Mueller, Mme. Jacques Teissier, Anthony Cave Brown, John V. Lanterman, Russell Holmes, Mechtild von Podewils, Theodore Prochazka, and Dan T. Moore.

Contents

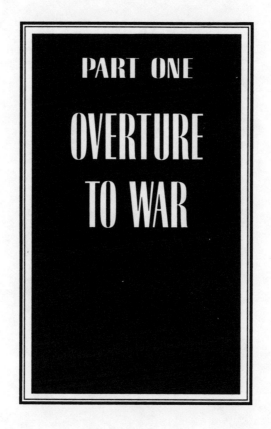

PART ONE

OVERTURE TO WAR

PART ONE

OVERTURE
TO WAR

ONE

Genesis

IT WAS TWO-THIRTY IN THE MORNING WHEN GERMAN U-BOAT CAPTAIN VON Arnauld de la Perière, cruising off the east coast of Spain, surfaced in Salitrona Bay near Cartagena. His mission was to rescue Captain Lieutenant Wilhelm Canaris, German secret agent in Spain, who was being pursued by French counterspies in a little-known drama of World War I. The French were particularly anxious to apprehend Canaris because of his intrigues among the French Moroccan tribes. Arnauld was uneasy since his Morse recognition signals evoked no reply, nor was there any other sign of the fishing smack whose special passenger, Canaris, was waiting apprehensively for his rescuers. But the U-boat captain's instructions were explicit: He was to rendezvous at this specific spot at this specific time on September 30, 1916.

The captain cruised silently on the surface in the direction of the Tiñoso light, then back again along a previously arranged line hoping to receive signals indicating that the fishing boat carrying Canaris was nearby. By six forty-five, as dawn came, there was still no response. It was dangerous to loiter longer in daylight so Arnauld remained submerged, surfacing only once to charge the U-boat's batteries. In his official report of the mission Captain von Arnauld wrote that he realized that his submarine might be observed if he were to remain long on the surface, but "the risk had to be taken" as he "had to be operative on the rendezvous line from late afternoon till dusk."

As he waited, Canaris had a close call when his boat came under scrutiny from another craft nearby. He later described how the trawler rapidly approached: "We hid ourselves in the sand ballast inside our boat.

The trawler stopped close by our stern. When it saw only our Spanish crew, it proceeded on, slowly travelling toward another vessel, now coming into sight." That the trawler, no common fishing boat, was in fact an official boat probably searching for Canaris seemed obvious since "The crew . . . wore French naval uniforms."[1]

At 2:10 A.M. the next day, October 1, when Arnauld again surfaced, he saw the dimmed lights of some small craft, which began sending Morse signals. Fearing this to be a trap, the captain plunged into Salitrona Bay. It was dangerous to persist in his hunt since the French were presumed to be prowling about, but before giving up, Arnauld finally picked up the right contact signals from the fishing boat on which Canaris waited. On the following morning Canaris's craft was visually spotted by Arnauld against the rising sun. The captain surfaced some fifty yards from it and within five minutes was able to take on board Canaris and two companions. Mission accomplished.

Arnauld's instinct had been correct; a French trap had been set. In addition to the trawler there had in fact been two French submarines, the *Topaze* and the *Opale*, lurking in the vicinity to spoil the operation and capture Canaris. A leak to Allied counterespionage had provided the tip-off, but the French submarine did not have time to close in before the German rescue craft made its getaway with Canaris on board. The frustrated French officer in charge of the two submarines, Captain Pradeau, described in his official report how he had been blinded by the sun at the crucial moment, thereby enabling Canaris to board the German U-boat and get away.

Much later, after World War I, fate would find French Captain Pradeau at some function where he met both Arnauld and Canaris. He was much impressed by the man who had been his quarry. In an article, "*Souvenirs Maritimes Sociaux et Politique d'un Ancient Officier de Marine*," the French officer wrote of his satisfaction at having "been prevented from destroying so gallant an enemy."[2]

The story of how and why Canaris had found himself in this predicament, from which he had to be rescued at great risk by a specially dedicated German submarine in 1916, is typical of a man whose extraordinary career, spanning two world wars, is no less exciting than the plot of a good spy novel. Escaping from a Chilean internment camp after scuttling the German warship *Dresden* to avoid its capture by the British, Canaris served German naval intelligence in Spain as an undercover operator. With the assumed name Reed-Rosas, he not only intrigued among North African tribesmen,*

---

*In early 1915 a British naval intelligence officer, better known as the pre–World War I novelist A.E.W. Mason, had been in Morocco consulting with French General L.H.G. Lyautey on a problem bedeviling the French. German intelligence, it seemed, had incited an anti-French riot by the Moors. This rebellion had been the handiwork of Wilhelm Canaris, alias Reed-Rosas.

trying to incite them to rebellion against their French masters, but was a problem for the British since he collected intelligence on their naval movements in the Mediterranean.

The Allied effort to capture Canaris in World War I must certainly have been closely watched by British Army Captain Stewart Graham Menzies, who then served as counterintelligence chief—spy catcher—for the British Expeditionary Force in France.* Destined to be in charge of the British Secret Intelligence Service (MI-6) in World War II, Menzies found his and Canaris's professional lives very much entwined. In a curious twist of fate, Menzies prevented Canaris from being assassinated by vetoing an operational proposal submitted by a British intelligence officer, Harold A. R. "Kim" Philby. It would be many years before Philby was unmasked as a secret Soviet agent within MI-6. In retrospect it is likely that the idea to murder Canaris originated with Philby's Soviet controllers, whose objective had been to hinder British efforts to collaborate with the German Resistance. In his retirement Menzies, who during World War II had reason to want Canaris alive, not dead, was quoted as saying that he "did give me assistance; I liked and admired him. He was damned brave. . . ."[3]

Canaris's submarine rescue in 1916 became necessary since he was a wanted man. A bout of malaria had caused him to attempt a risky overland escape to Germany. Because of close French scrutiny at their borders, Canaris had traveled in disguise to Italy as a religious pilgrim bound for the shrine of St. Francis of Assisi, his story being that he was seeking a miracle cure for tuberculosis. To make this more believable, he would bite his tongue so he could spit out blood as he was being questioned by border guards.

Canaris successfully crossed southern France and reached Italy only to be jailed by the Italians, who had obviously been tipped off by Allied counterintelligence. Thanks to strong diplomatic intervention on the part of the Spanish government, Canaris was spared an Italian trial that could have brought him a conviction as a spy and possibly a death sentence. Spanish friends were willing to intercede for a "tubercular" Reed-Rosas "near death" in a situation in which the German government was powerless to intervene for a naval intelligence spy. Released by the Italians, Canaris made his way back to Spain, luckily evading British and French agents who were hot on his trail. This is why a German U-boat had dashed to his rescue.

THE YEAR 1916 WAS ALSO FATEFUL FOR WILLIAM "WILD BILL" DONOVAN, who later led New York's "Fighting Irish," the famous 69th Division. Be-

---

*Stewart Menzies reported for duty to the Intelligence Section of the General Staff of the British armies in France on December 16, 1915, to become chief of counterespionage and security for the British armies in France.

fore the United States became involved in World War I, a civilian Donovan had a ringside seat at the "war to end all wars." Wild Bill was active in Poland with Herbert Hoover's American War Relief Commission and in occupied Belgium with the Rockefeller Foundation's relief efforts. Behind the lines he was able to observe military placements and developments of interest to the British, who took advantage of his ability to roam about the German-occupied Lowlands. This experience, however brief and casual, was an exhilarating apprenticeship for the man destined to become founder of U.S. strategic intelligence in World War II.

As his assignment with the War Relief Commission came to an end, Donovan happened to meet in London a young Canadian officer from Winnipeg, Manitoba. As captain in the Royal Canadian Engineers this twenty-one-year-old lad had twice been gassed while attacking German lines in France and invalided out of action. But hiding this fact, he had talked his way into the Royal Flying Corps and qualified as pilot after relatively few hours of training. Before the war ended, he had become a much-decorated British ace.

Donovan was much impressed with this young Canadian, whose name was William Stephenson. As coincidence would have it, the same Bill Stephenson, upon becoming the New York–based British intelligence representative in World War II, worked closely with Donovan during the crucial early months of the Battle of Britain to convince the U.S. government that the British were not beaten and deserved American help. This intelligence marriage nearly a quarter of a century after their chance meeting in 1916 produced a full-grown offspring named the Office of Strategic Services.[4]

If Donovan had his first taste of spying in World War I, the British intelligence mentor assigned by Stephenson to help him create the Office of Strategic Services (OSS) in World War II was a seasoned professional who had been immersed in the most complex of intelligence operations since the First World War. He was Charles Howard Ellis, an Australian who had worked in tandem with a Captain Reginald Teague-Jones, stationed in General Sir Wilfred Malleson's British intelligence mission in Meshed, Iran, gateway to Central Asia. Ellis became thoroughly immersed in the Caucasus and the Trans-Caspian underbelly of Russia as World War I came to an end. These two operatives, remnants of the Great Game that had dominated British-Russian relations in Asia during the nineteenth century, risked their lives trying to deal with czarist terror and Bolshevik revolution in the oil-rich Caucasus, not to mention a German-backed Turkish invasion of the Caucasus, an Armenian vendetta against their Muslim Azerbaijani neighbors, and Persian tribal insurgency.

Teague-Jones, Ellis's colleague, mysteriously disappeared in 1922. It would come out only many years later in 1988, as Teague-Jones lay dying, that for thirty years he had served as a British secret agent living and working under an assumed identity as Ronald Sinclair. Teague-Jones/Sinclair had been hidden under this deep cover by MI-5 — Britain's domestic and empire security service — in order to protect him from assassination by the Soviet secret police, who (wrongly) were convinced that he had murdered twenty-six Bolshevik leaders in the infamous massacre at Krasnovodsk in 1918.[5]

While Teague-Jones remained for the most part in or about Central Asia, Charles Ellis also continued to work against the Bolsheviks, this time among the Russian émigrés in Paris who seemed to constitute a rich vein of conspiratorial talent worth mining. German military intelligence would also try to thread its way though this miasma of intrigue. Russian émigré circles consisted of duplicitous, vainglorius, even genuine conspirators working against the Bolsheviks, only to discover how badly the White Russian colony in Paris had been penetrated and controlled by an omnipresent Soviet secret police provocation scheme known as the Trust.

Somewhere in this maze Ellis seemed to have lost his way. Long after World War II it was alleged that during these confusing interwar days Charles Ellis had been recruited by German military intelligence — the Abwehr — as a spy for Germany. He confessed to this charge not long before his death in the 1980s, according to a former British MI-5 senior officer, Peter Wright, in his controversial 1987 best-seller *Spy Catcher*,[6] although there were lingering suspicions, unacknowledged by Ellis before his death, that he was really a Soviet agent used to penetrate both the Abwehr and British Secret Intelligence (MI-6). Thus Charles Ellis, while serving as deputy to William Stephenson, the man called Intrepid (after his wartime New York cable address), may have provided a window on the OSS as well as MI-6 for both the Germans and Soviets.[7] Stephenson, however, denied his guilt, as did onetime MI-6 chief Maurice Oldfield.

A YOUNG AMERICAN VICE-CONSUL NAMED ALLEN DULLES ALSO HAD HIS BAPtism as a secret agent in 1916 and 1917 while serving as ad hoc intelligence officer for the U.S. Legation in Switzerland. One day—April 11, 1917, to be exact—he received a telephone call from an accented German-speaking man introducing himself as Vladimir Ilyich Lenin and urgently requesting a secret meeting. He said he would arrive in Bern in the afternoon and must make contact with someone in the American Legation. Young Dulles declined on the excuse he was "busy" (euphemism for having a date for tennis with a young lady named Helene Herzog, who had caught his eye), but he tried to make an appointment with the mysterious-sounding Mr. Lenin for the next day. But "tomorrow" would not do, it would be "too late," the caller explained in a despairing voice. Dulles learned later that on the fateful day following the call Lenin was indeed "unavailable": He had been shipped off to Russia in a sealed railway coach by the German intelligence chief Colonel Walther Nicolai (chief of Section III-b of the German General Staff, predecessor of the Abwehr). Military intelligence, which had been clandestinely supporting Russian Bolsheviks in German exile, was eager to knock Russia out of the war and saw the revolutionary Lenin as the one man who could arouse the Russians to revolt under the red banner of Bolshevism and end the czar's war with Germany.[8]

By a curious twist of fate, Dulles returned in World War II to Switzerland, where he served as the OSS chief of station and maintained an indirect, unacknowledged relationship with Canaris, a successor of Colonel Nicolai. This contact was maintained initially through an Abwehr officer in Zurich—and Resistance activist—named Hans Bernd Gisevius.

Dulles's principal assistant in Bern at this time was Gero von Schulze-Gaevernitz, who was to help cast the OSS's net widely and through whom the OSS chief would, among other achievements, secretly negotiate the unconditional surrender of German forces in Italy. That magic year 1916 was the year in which Dulles first met Gaevernitz.

A few years after World War II Dulles became director of the OSS's successor, the Central Intelligence Agency, leading its Cold War warriors against the heirs of Lenin, the man with whom he had not had time to speak in Bern.

The Soviet Union also sowed early the seeds of its World War II European intelligence apparatus, referred to by the Gestapo as the *Rote Kapelle*, or Red Orchestra. But first priority had to be given to protecting Lenin's Revolution against counterrevolutionary machinations by ill-wishers, principally the devotees of the Romanov dynasty, the so-called White Russian émigrés who had found refuge in Paris and other capitals of Europe. How the Revolution survived its birth trauma and the efforts of the émigrés, with British and American help, to destroy it are the story of the Trust, one of the greatest deceptions of all time. This was an operation that set the style of Soviet counterconspiracy and counterespionage for the decades of precarious interwar peace, World War II, and the Cold War ahead.

Communism, as defined by that troika of prophets Marx, Engels, and Lenin, erupted from its ideological cocoon in 1917 as the Bolshevik Revolution and became an official, practicing political-economic religion whose holy see was Russia, but whose followers, downtrodden masses and intellectual theorists alike, sprang up most everywhere that dissatisfaction ran deep. In a world dislocated by war, where the poor now seemed poorer, and the rich, richer, the gospel according to Marx had an irresistible appeal to many. That this "sublime" system, this would-be panacea for the common man's woes, crumbled seventy-two years later and took with it to an ignominious end a superpower that for so long sang its siren song is a profound milestone of history.

It is symbolic that in 1991 a Russian foundry in what once again is known as St. Petersburg found itself stuck with a four-ton fifteen-foot statue of Lenin that its commissioner, the Black Sea city of Krasnodar, no longer wanted and sold to an American antiques dealer, who then discovered that he did not know what to do with such an unwanted supericon. Equally evocative of what went amiss in the Soviet Union is the demise of another foundry creation, the statue of Felix Dzerzhinsky, grandfather of the KGB and inspiration of Soviet police power. This statue was torn down in passion by Moscow street mobs after the abortive coup d'état against Gorbachev in 1991. If Stalin had corrupted the dreams of Marx, Engels, and Lenin by creating a regime of terror devoted to preserving his own power, Dzerzhinsky had proved himself a brilliant, if ruthless, midwife to the process.

The Trust, a provocation of astonishing proportion, was designed to lure counterrevolutionary enemies into a trap that, unknown to them, was controlled by Dzerzhinsky. The Trust's achievement was not only to expose enemies of the new Soviet regime and neutralize them but to serve as an object lesson, a deterrent to future would-be plotters against the state. Felix Dzerzhinsky successfully defended the Soviet Union from its enemies within and without, but in so doing, he created a ruthlessly efficient security system that smothered the very freedoms for which Marx had cried out.

The labyrinthine details of the Trust's activities were hard to understand, even when finally exposed. To put it simply, the Trust served as a secret holding company that enveloped most of the Russian antiregime and royalist émigré organizations without their knowing it. In this way it manipulated them and, when necessary, did away with them in some subtle way. For skill and effectiveness it was without parallel in the annals of provocation and can probably be credited with saving Bolshevism at its most vulnerable time. It also set a standard for later KGB manipulation and control of the Soviet population. This great deception fooled and dismayed several foreign intelligence services, including that of the British, which had secretly involved itself in the nascent politics of the Bolsheviks, even plotting Lenin's downfall. Sidney Reilly, the later publicized British superspy, is believed to have been killed by the Trust in 1925 for his activities in behalf of what he believed to be the anti-Soviet Monarchist Association of Central Russia. Could he too have been a Soviet double agent? That thought has occurred to several students of deception mesmerized by the paranoic spell cast by such convolutions.

In April 1927, as a Trust officer who secretly reported to the Bolsheviks' GPU, predecessor to the KGB, one Edwards Upeninsh—alias Opperput—appeared to defect to the West and expose in detail the great deception. This marked the end of the Trust's effectiveness, yet some believe that Upeninsh's act was still another GPU maneuver, a ringing down of the curtain on the Trust to dramatize the GPU's omnipotence and thus deter future dissidents from plotting against the regime.

The U.S. Central Intelligence Agency's historical postmortem of the Trust, written many years later, sums up its accomplishments: "It gained a clear picture of White émigré organizations, their character, membership and objectives; it was able to deepen the antagonism existing in these organizations and discredit the various groups inside the USSR; it succeeded in duping foreign intelligence services, particularly the Poles, Estonians and Finns." But, concludes the CIA study, "Its most striking and lasting success was psychological. . . . From this point on, Russian intelligence became a force to be reckoned with world wide."[9]

If Lenin was worried about enemies abroad bent on the destruction of Bolshevism, his successor, Joseph Stalin, was concerned about his own power and person threatened by domestic enemies within the party. Provocation techniques used by the Trust to rid the USSR of its political opposition in exile foreshadowed the purges of the 1930s targeted inward to eliminate good party members whose misfortune was to have been distrusted by Stalin.

The murder of Sergei Kirov, Bolshevik leader of Leningrad, arranged by the NKVD in December 1934, triggered the Great Terror, in which millions of innocent party members were jailed or killed. This in turn led to the massive purge of the Red Army in which Stalin wiped out the senior leadership of his army on the eve of World War II in his ruthless efforts to stifle potential opposition at all cost. In Stalin's paranoic view of life, the original sin, is man's propensity to betray.

TWO

Interwar

AT THE END OF WORLD WAR I CANARIS TRIED TO CREATE THE HAVEN OF A home while at the same time plunging himself into a cauldron of politics in a crippled and demoralized Germany. In 1919 he married Erika Waag, daughter of a well-off industrialist. Fräulein Waag brought grace and culture to the new Canaris household. Music was her passion; she played the violin well and delighted in having musicales at her home. In due course Frau Canaris bore two daughters. She was not part of her husband's world, however, and constantly strove to keep her home uninvolved in his politics and intrigues. Canaris was consumed by his work. He seemed to be moved by two professional passions: his love of the traditional, monarchial Germany, now jarred from its moorings, and the game of espionage and political action.

The year 1919 also brought a bid from the left for power in Germany: the Communist Spartacus revolt. The would-be revolution fizzled. Germany would not follow Lenin's call for workers everywhere to rise. In this drama of left versus right, Socialists Karl Liebknecht and Rosa Luxemburg were murdered by counterrevolutionary, right-wing Freikorps officers, members of a paramilitary vigilante organization dedicated to fighting bolshevism.

Canaris's name became linked with these events when he was accused by the left of helping the murderers escape. (One of his accusers was the prominent Socialist Dr. Julius Leber, who in World War II allied himself secretly with Canaris and others of the anti-Nazi Resistance.) While

Canaris was sympathetic with Freikorps efforts to curb Communism, he did not have anything to do with the escape of Liebknecht's and Luxemburg's assassin.

The year 1920 saw a bid for power from the right, a short-lived monarchist coup in Berlin led by Wolfgang Kapp. Like many of his fellow naval officers, Canaris saw merit in what seemed to be a patriotic regime that promised to return Germany to its former glory. But the new nationalist government soon revealed its frailty and collapsed when it failed to suppress a general strike.

Canaris's sorties into politics landed him in jail for a few days when the Kapp putsch failed, but otherwise his nimble footwork saw him through the crises facing Weimar Germany. What in normal times might have been tantamount to mutiny on the part of officers like Canaris who became too entangled in politics was now part of widespread upheavals caused by Germans trying to assert themselves in the power vacuum left by the end of an era. The military services with their built-in power bases and relatively disciplined organization were inevitably swept into the maelstrom. For military and naval officers, their services provided a definable focus for loyalty in a still-ambiguous state reeling in defeat from deep economic depression and even deeper humiliation. Canaris was intent on re-creating German military prowess, particularly naval prowess. He and like-minded naval officers dreamed of building a new grand fleet despite the restrictions imposed by the Versailles Treaty.

Canaris for a while kept out of trouble by immersing himself in naval matters. He served two years on the admiral's staff of the Baltic Squadron. In 1922 he was transferred to the cruiser Berlin, a naval training ship where fatefully he befriended a maladjusted cadet named Reinhard Heydrich, later to become infamous as a leading architect of the Holocaust and the "Butcher of Prague." But the lure of intrigue and dark doings drew Canaris away from mainstream naval duties.

In the late 1920s Canaris was again in Spain or visiting its offshore islands, where he played a shadowy role arranging for naval shipbuilding in behalf of the Weimar Republic in circumvention of the Versailles Treaty. Canaris often visited Vigo on the northwestern coast of Spain, where he arranged for cooperating shipyards to produce ships for Germany's illegal navy. Tenerife in the Canary Islands, off the coast of Morocco, was another site for clandestine shipbuilding, but Vigo's well-covered operations were Canaris's great successes.[1]

The German Navy's Division of Marine Transport devised a special cover organization under whose auspices Canaris now operated. When financial irregularities surfaced in this most irregular of industrial enter-

prises, Canaris inevitably became involved, although the officer principally responsible was a Captain Walter Lohmann of the Transport Division. While Lohmann was the son of a respected director of the North
German Lloyd shipping line and had made a good name for himself in
naval circles, he mishandled the navy's "black" funds used for clandestine
purposes after being entrusted with the command of the Naval Transport
Division in 1920.

In the period from 1923 to 1927 Lohmann's office clandestinely set up a
complicated array of projects for the navy, but by 1926 Lohmann was in
trouble, having used extremely bad judgment in trying to establish dubious cover mechanisms with which to fund the navy's secret shipbuilding
operations. He quickly found himself over his head in various deals, particularly one that involved financing the Phoebus Film Company, a major
German movie producer that in turn was expected to serve as a secret
funding channel to shipbuilders. He also used bad judgment in providing
a make-work job in Phoebus for a lady friend, Else Ektimov, whom he had
met in Moscow and brought to Berlin. However trivial, this added to the
appearances of impropriety in the Phoebus affair.

The Phoebus company went bankrupt, and Lohmann's principal
source of indirect funding for his clandestine naval projects was gone.
Lohmann's Naval Transport Division, now suddenly unfunded for reasons
too complicated to explain publicly, was in jeopardy of having its secret
operations exposed as well. When the whole affair was publicized by Kurt
Wenkel, an enterprising financial writer on the liberal daily newspaper
Berliner Tageblatt, influential shareholders of Phoebus, angry bankers,
and the general public reacted badly, not only because of the financial irregularities that were exposed but because it revealed serious German violations of the Versailles Treaty.

In papering over this messy situation, Chancellor Wilhelm Marx named
an official Cabinet inquiry board. Lohmann was hastily retired, and a Su-
pervisory Commission for the Secret Tasks of the Armed Forces was set up
as a permanent oversight group. Lohmann, a broken man who did not appear to have benefited financially from his misbegotten enterprises, soon
died of a heart attack.[2] Nothing further was heard from Else Ektimov.

Because of his association with Lohmann, Canaris also suffered from
the adverse publicity stirred up by the Phoebus scandal. A clever parody of
the scandal appeared in the form of a hit play entitled *Tale of the Canary
Islands*, a pun on Canaris's name. Canaris was whisked out of Germany by
the navy and told to cool off in Spain.[3]

While in Spain Canaris made many good friends and cemented his
relationship with Major Francisco Franco, whom he had first met in

Morocco in World War I.[4] Destined to become the Caudillo (dictator) of Spain, Franco was to prove helpful to Canaris. Conversely, Canaris's assistance proved crucial to Franco by helping him gain German and Italian support in the Spanish Civil War. Later, while serving as chief of German military intelligence (Abwehr) in World War II but secretly collaborating with the German Resistance, Canaris was to be instrumental in stiffening Franco's resolve to resist Hitler's plan to occupy Spain and attack the strategically vital British bastion of Gibraltar.

In 1934 British naval intelligence's secret agent in Spain, Juan March, whose relationship with the British had begun in World War I, sized up Canaris as a German Navy man to be reckoned with. This former Spanish smuggler had since the First World War risen in prominence and could count among his friends many of Spain's political and military luminaries.* He saw in Canaris a kindred soul who seemed to be working the same side of the street in Madrid. March and the sometime British intelligence agent Basil Zaharoff, legendary international arms merchant, had become friendly with Canaris in Madrid and shared with him his admiration for Franco, who even then was a rising star in the Spanish Army.[5]

That year March allegedly told his British naval intelligence contact in Madrid that Canaris "does not love nor trust his new masters [Hitler and his Nazi clique] and is our best ally in Europe at the moment."[6] Believing that Canaris would be amenable to secret contact with British intelligence, March urged his service contact to keep an eye on the German agent and consider bringing him secretly into camp as a "sleeping partner."[7]

Since Canaris was about to become head of German military intelligence at the beginning of 1935, March's suggestion was better than he knew. For nearly a decade, until he was hanged as a "traitor," Canaris led a double life as a secret adversary of Hitler and a patron of the German Resistance, but the available record goes blank before it can be seen what specific British follow-up there may have been at the time.

Fabian von Schlabrendorff, an Abwehr officer who became prominent in the anti-Hitler Resistance, recalled after the war that Canaris once mentioned to a friend that he had considered the advisability of working with the British Secret Intelligence Service in his struggle against Hitler. He did not, however, trust the faction within the British service that, like Chamberlain, favored reaching an accommodation with Hitler. Canaris was also canny enough to recognize the dangers of exposure through German intercepts of British cable traffic or other penetrations of the British service.

---

*Juan March, who had become wealthy from his tobacco monopoly in Spain, may have brokered in 1936 a deal by which certain London bankers backed Franco.

Schlabrendorff described Canaris as a lone plotter who kept all the reins in his own hands.[8]

PERHAPS THE MOST FATEFUL EVENT IN CANARIS'S CAREER OCCURRED ON January 1, 1935, when as rear admiral he assumed charge of the Abwehr, the military intelligence arm of the German Ministry of War. How this came about was a sign of the times, a dropping of the pilot, to use a naval term, bred in a pre-Hitler Germany, and the installation of Canaris in his stead. Canaris was an officer no less ancien régime than his predecessor but thought to be, at least, manageable. How wrong the Nazis were.

Canaris's predecessor, a career naval officer, Captain Konrad Patzig, had survived as Abwehr chief but a short while. His failing was to have stood up to Heinrich Himmler and his SS security intelligence (RSHA, or *Reichssicherheitshauptamt*) chief, Reinhard Heydrich, who were determined to control all security and intelligence matters without interference or competition from the Abwehr. Patzig loathed both men. The ambitious Heydrich, handpicked by Himmler, would brook no opposition from Patzig. When Patzig persisted in running intelligence operations against the Poles contrary to Hitler's orders, Heydrich seized the opportunity to get rid of him. What had really worried Heydrich was what he knew to be Patzig's intention of compiling a dossier, recording all his "atrocities." But as a pretext Heydrich accused Patzig of conducting aerial reconnaissance over Poland in violation of the German-Polish nonaggression pact.

The Polish government officially protested, and Heydrich complained about Patzig to Minister of War Field Marshal Werner von Blomberg. Blomberg discussed the matter with naval chief Admiral Erich Raeder, repeating Heydrich's claim that Patzig's presence as head of the Abwehr was "not compatible with the aims of the National-Socialist Party."[9] That constituted an order endorsed by Himmler that Blomberg dared not ignore. Patzig was, in fact, glad to return to line duty. He could not work with Heydrich any more than Heydrich could work with him.

The choice of Canaris to head the Abwehr may have been influenced by kindnesses shown to Heydrich when the fledgling naval officer had been Canaris's charge on the training ship *Berlin*, before Heydrich's SS career began. And when Heydrich had been fired by the head of the navy for conduct unbecoming an officer and a gentleman, Canaris had taken pity on him and had some of his service privileges restored.

Hitler himself had remembered Canaris's sympathy with the Freikorps in its early struggles against the Socialists and his hatred of Soviet Bolshevism. Admiral Raeder did not particularly like Canaris—that "secretive, clever, manipulator," whose abilities seemed out of place in a naval setting. He did not oppose Canaris's candidacy for long, however; at least Canaris was a sailor, and the navy wanted to keep some control of the Abwehr within the War Ministry by having it led by one of its own.

In fact, Canaris was not only experienced in intelligence matters but smart and resourceful, and he could manage men. His subordinates invariably liked him. Most important, he could handle Heydrich, and he somehow seemed invulnerable to Himmler's intrigues. "Old Whitehead," as his men affectionately referred to the forty-seven-year-old veteran, would build an intelligence empire staffed at the top with men whom he trusted, officers who, like him, would dedicate their lives to trying to rid Germany of Hitler!

THE SPANISH CIVIL WAR PROVIDED CANARIS AS CHIEF OF MILITARY INTELligence, with a drama of intrigue, a challenge for his Machiavellian inclinations. This situation warranted and got his official attention. Spain, his spiritual home and a place he knew so well, would consume much of his time. His client was General Franco, a good personal friend whose portrait always hung in his office.

As often happens, the assassination of a politically important figure can set in motion calamitous events that dwarf the single act of terrorism in importance. So it was in Spain on July 16, 1936, when the Conservative politician José Calvo Sotelo was found murdered. Two days later a cabal of aroused Spanish generals, including Franco, then posted in the Canary Islands, revolted. Franco was called upon to take command of the Army of Africa and flew to Tetuán in Morocco on July 19 as the military uprising occurred on the mainland under the command of General Emilio Mola Vidal. After considerable maneuvering behind the scenes, Franco with his military power base in Morocco emerged as preeminent leader of the military junta. On October 1, 1936, he was named head of state to lead the bloody civil war that left Spain prostrate before it ended on the eve of World War II.

Franco knew that he could not win without outside help. It would fall to his friend Canaris to see that this was provided. The admiral brought Nazi Germany and Fascist Italy into this war by proxy to combat Soviet involvement and what he considered the evil influence of international Communism.

One source on the Abwehr chief's role in Spain was Major Rudolf Bamler, of the Abwehr military Security Section posted to Madrid. Bamler, who was distrusted by Canaris (and who defected to the Soviets in 1945 as the Red Army approached Berlin), was nonetheless well informed on Abwehr actions in this strategically important country at the time.[10] According to Bamler, two German Nazi party zealots living an expatriate life in Spain, Adolf Langenheim and Johannes Bernhardt, rushed to Berlin when civil war broke out in Spain. They bore an urgent plea for help from Franco and instructions to seek out Canaris for counsel and support. Franco needed military assistance and most immediately needed air transport to carry troops from Morocco to Spain so that they could engage the Republicans. Bamler recalled that "Canaris brushed aside all other questions and spared neither time nor effort to have the top leaders of Germany and Italy become interested in his plans."[11] Canaris made the case for intervention in Spain directly to Hitler.

Tending to confirm Bamler's account, a Reich Chancellery document of July 5, 1939, proposed that the two expatriate Germans, Langenheim and Bernhardt, be decorated for their services in the Spanish Civil War. The document recounts how in late July 1936 they delivered to Hitler in Bayreuth a letter from Franco appealing for assistance. At a meeting that thereafter took place with Hitler, Göring, War Minister von Blomberg, and "an admiral"—almost certainly Canaris—it was agreed that Germany would comply with Franco's requests.[12] In the next four months some 868 flights carrying fourteen thousand Spanish troops from Morocco, and forty-four artillery pieces, not to mention other lesser items of equipment, were airlifted to Spain for Franco's army.

Canaris then flew to Italy to enlist his friend General Mario Roatta, head of Italian intelligence, in convincing Mussolini to help Franco as well. Canaris met directly with Mussolini to plead the case, then closed the deal: Il Duce committed Italy to Franco's cause. It then became Canaris's task to orchestrate the Axis aid efforts. Among other things he set up a purchasing commission called Rowak, headed by Bernhardt, to act as the agent for providing German military assistance. Hitler awarded Bernhardt a decoration for services to the Third Reich, but Franco, more materially, later bestowed on this expatriate a large estate in Spain in appreciation of his services to Spain.[13]

Another contribution Canaris made to Franco's cause was his secret role in arranging indirectly for the Republican forces to receive arms as well. But these arms, relics of World War I, were doctored to prevent them from functioning properly in combat. Canaris had a German arms dealer named Josef Veltjens buy up such antiques, many of which were German arms that Canaris himself had been responsible for having sold abroad for the German Navy soon after World War I. This devious plan of sabotage, carried out secretly under Hermann Göring's aegis, was apparently very successful in hampering Republican soldiers at critical moments of combat.[14]

In still another way Canaris proved himself Franco's benefactor. As point man for Germany's and Italy's intervention in the Spanish Civil War, Canaris oversaw a military aid program worth some five billion reichsmarks without extracting from Franco any binding quid pro quo. Franco remained an internationally uncommitted leader, a fact for which he was grateful as World War II threatened to engulf Spain. Looking at the record, one can sense Canaris's influence in the September 1938 Czech crisis in which Franco refused to involve himself or take a stand in favor of Germany, an act Hitler deeply resented. And Canaris's advice to Franco during the latter part of 1940, advice that ran directly contrary to Hitler's wishes and Nazi Germany's policy, kept the Caudillo out of the war,[15] prevented German troops from entering Spain, and saved the critically important British bastion of Gibraltar from being attacked by the Germans.

The Spanish Civil War also served as an espionage proving ground for Kim Philby, posing as a pro-Franco British foreign correspondent for the *Times* of London. In reality Philby was a Soviet spy, first contacted at Cambridge University, where he became one of the Cambridge Five Communist fellow travelers, then recruited as a committed Soviet agent with instructions to burrow into Britain's intelligence establishment. During the summer of 1940 Philby indeed metamorphosed as an officer of the British Secret Intelligence Service (SIS) and began his rise to become one of Menzies's top officers in World War II and afterward.[16]

IN 1936, THE YEAR THE SPANISH CIVIL WAR BROKE OUT, MENZIES NOW A senior officer in British Secret Intelligence, again encountered Canaris's traces. Like many of his colleagues, Menzies spent the weekends in the country. His estate was near the village of Luckington. One day he noted with interest that the venerable Guilsborough House at Luckington Manor had just been rented by a Latvian-German baron named Robert Treeck, who was accompanied by his Chilean mistress, Baroness Violetta de Schroeders. A brief glance at SIS files soon made it apparent to Menzies that his new next-door neighbor was an agent of Canaris's Abwehr, who presumably found the stylish Beaufort Hunt a good hunting ground for influential contacts. The Prince of Wales, sometimes seen at the Beaufort Hunt, may even have been of interest to Treeck. The prince had various connections with Germany, including blood ties with Germany's former royal family. His close American friend and soon-to-be-bride Wallis Warfield Simpson was rumored to have been on particularly good terms with Hitler's foreign affairs adviser, Joachim von Ribbentrop. To watch a German agent in red hunting jacket riding with the hounds in the company of Britain's best families was a dimension of the Abwehr worth noting, but was Treeck performing his chores for the Abwehr or for Canaris, who by then was secretly in determined opposition to the Nazis and was laying the groundwork for an extensive network of influential foreign contacts abroad potentially useful to the Resistance?

During the summer of 1939, on the eve of war, Treeck suddenly decamped, leaving behind most of his belongings and an aura of mystery. Whatever he was doing and whatever success he may have had or what he did next seem to have escaped public knowledge.

On November 4, 1939, when the head of MI-6, Admiral Hugh Sinclair, died, Stewart Menzies was the logical successor. Despite vigorous opposition by Winston Churchill, who associated Menzies with Neville Chamberlain's antiwar philosophies and the dismal record of appeasement, the majority of the War Cabinet gave him stewardship of MI-6. The intelligence battle lines between Britain and Germany were taking shape, but they would be strangely configured. Menzies would face Admiral Canaris, his dueling partner in the netherworld of intelligence. Both had been seasoned intelligence operators since World War I; both were convinced that Bolshevism and Russia were really the prime enemy; each loved his country. But Canaris, as head of the Abwehr, protector of the state, was charged with supporting a German war effort of which he had not approved, and was in fact secretly committed to bringing about Hitler's downfall. From an intelligence point of view, the dice was loaded in Britain's favor. All this promised a curious scenario, one that produced strange consequences as the war progressed.

DESTINED TO HEAD THE UNITED STATES' FIRST STRATEGIC INTELLIGENCE service, William Donovan, like Canaris and Menzies, began his involvement in international affairs in World War I. During the interwar period he had become part of an informal Anglo-American roundtable of eminent men dedicated to preserving close U.S.-British relations and keeping abreast of world developments following World War I. During the boom times of 1927 the Room came into being in New York. It was a loose assemblage of powerful Ivy League Americans and establishment Britons brought together by Vincent Astor, scion of the American branch of the great British Astor family. The group believed fervently in Anglo-U.S. solidarity in a still-troubled world. As giants of international business and men of infinite social connections as well, the members of the Room generally knew what was going on in the world—and sometimes made it happen. At monthly meetings they shared their knowledge and insights with one another, doubtless for corporate benefit but also for Anglo-American wellbeing as they saw it. Through Sir William Wiseman, a senior member of the banking house Kuhn, Loeb, who had been a representative of the British Secret Intelligence Service in the United States during World War I, the wisdom of the Room reached the British government, and through American members of this exclusive club, it reached U.S. policy makers and was to prove valuable to President Franklin Roosevelt.

Close associates of Wild Bill Donovan saw to it that he was brought into this privileged circle. The Room not only provided Donovan with an informal structure in which to indulge his interest in foreign affairs but also brought him in touch with men of influence, including his old law school classmate at Columbia University President Roosevelt. Donovan's law partner John Lord O'Brian became for a while Roosevelt's adviser on intelligence affairs and helped bring Donovan and the president closer together despite their political party differences. At a time when isolationism inhibited dynamic involvement in the affairs of the world, talented amateurs such as O'Brian and Donovan were useful to Roosevelt as discreet agents of an unpopular cause.

In 1936 Donovan, acting as informal fact finder for President Roosevelt, took on the Ethiopian problem. As the Italo-Ethiopian war got under way, Donovan volunteered to conduct an impartial evaluation of the situation from the Italian side of the lines. Europe had been outbluffed by Benito Mussolini, who had shouted to his people, "To sanctions of a military nature we will reply with war." Sir Samuel Hoare, Britain's representative at a League of Nations session on the Ethiopian crisis, had exhorted the assembled delegates to follow Woodrow Wilson's advice and, if necessary, punish aggression. He brought a deafening round of standing applause when he said, "Britain stands for steady and collective resistance to all acts of unprovoked agression." But Hoare did not mean what he said. His bluff was a terrible failure, and Mussolini's army marched into Ethiopia.

Just as Donovan arrived at General Pietro Badoglio's headquarters, Ethiopian Emperor Haile Selassie was unleashing his chieftains in a massive counterattack to cut off an Italian advance south of Mekele. The tribesmen pounced on Italian tanks, shoving their spears through the turrets and fouling the tank treads with logs. Badoglio, however, described to Donovan a brighter picture. Explaining his strategy to the American fact finder, he was the soul of confidence. The villain, according to the Italian general, was Great Britain, which was pushing for, at least, a League of Nations oil embargo against Italy. What Donovan did not discover at the time was that a hard-pressed Badoglio was resorting to mustard gas sprayed from aircraft to keep the Ethiopian tribal levies at bay. With great difficulty the Italians finally defeated the Ethiopians and entered Addis Ababa triumphantly on May 5, 1936.

Donovan was also unaware of the reasons for a visit to Ethiopia at that time by the Italian genius of radio Guglielmo Marconi, who was conducting field experiments in his effort to perfect radar as a defensive weapon of war, although exaggerated rumors had it that he was working on a "death ray" that could down enemy aircraft.

On his way home Donovan stopped off in England to visit Alfred Duff Cooper, the British secretary of state for war, and Sir Robert Vansittart, senior secretary of the Foreign Office, who presided over a political intelligence group known informally by some as Vansittart's Dectective Agency. Neither official was taken in by Donovan's overoptimistic estimate of Italy's intentions.

Donovan was more persuasive with Roosevelt. After he returned to Washington, no more resolute about stopping aggression than Hoare had been, he convinced the president not to seek an oil embargo against Italy. The League of Nations was also of this mind and voted against the embargo. Mussolini had described as his objective in conquering Ethiopia: "to make Italy great, respected and feared." While it would take more than the killing of spear-throwing Ethiopian tribesmen to accomplish this, Mussolini's adventures in aggression had shown up the impotence of the League. So had Haile Selassie in his own, very different way revealed the weakness of the West by a brave but futile plea for help in a long-remembered address delivered to the League of Nations and repeated worldwide in poignant newsreels.

Perhaps the most significant result of the Italo-Ethiopian war and the failure of Western Europe to take action in defense of Ethiopia was what it taught Hitler: He was now convinced that he could pursue his own destiny in Europe with impunity.[17]

THREE

Enigma

IF MEMBERS OF THE GERMAN RESISTANCE IN WORLD WAR II, FOR REASONS
of conscience and motives they considered patriotic, would believe it necessary to seek help from the Western Allies to save Germany from Hitler's
megalomania, faceless spies driven by less noble motives found new opportunities in a tense Europe as the threat of war loomed ever larger. They
were the nook-and-cranny feeders that thrived on the detritus of troubled
places but whose value should not be judged by the taudriness of their
motives.

One such spy stands out in history as being of very special value to the
Western Allies in winning World War II. He was a minor German bureau-
crat named Hans-Thilo Schmidt, who sold German military secrets, including cipher secrets, to the French. As Schmidt's purloined documents
were subjected to the genius of Polish cryptanalysts between the world
wars, then improved upon and systematically exploited by British intelligence in World War II, there would be very few moves made by the German war machine that were not known in advance by the Western Allies.
And because of a remarkable effort by the British to exploit intercepted
German cipher traffic for the purpose of doubling German agents and
through them playing back misinformation, the German High Command
unknowingly depended on intelligence fabricated in Britain. But the story
begins much earlier, in the 1930s, before Hitler came to power.

Hans-Thilo Schmidt, lackluster son of a highborn German mother and
respected father, entered the French Embassy in Berlin on June 8, 1931, a

fateful day. His offer was startling, an opportunity so exciting that at first it was rejected as suspect. Schmidt described himself to a French intelligence officer, Maurice Dejean, as an employee of the German Army's cipher center, the *Chiffrierstelle,* whose job it was to distribute new ciphers and destroy old ones when their term of use had ended. In a sentence, Schmidt was willing to make available German military secrets and cipher keys that would satisfy France's highest intelligence priorities. It seemed too good to be true. Fearing provocation, Dejean turned him away but gave him a Paris post box number to which he could write and explain his offer more fully. Schmidt followed these instructions, urging the French to reply before October 1, 1931, to an address he gave in Switzerland. He suggested a rendezvous "in Belgium or Holland near the German border."[1]

On November 8, 1931, French intelligence officer Rudolf Lemoine, known by the cryptonym Rex, met Schmidt in room 13 of the Grand Hotel in Verviers, Belgium. Indicative of the importance put on this operation, Lemoine was joined a week later by Captain Gustave Bertrand, chief and founder of Section D of the French intelligence service—*Service de Renseignements*—whose tasks were to steal foreign cryptographic materials and intercept foreign cipher traffic. The samples provided by Schmidt were startling.

Schmidt's motive was simple: He needed money to support a lifestyle he craved. A high-living bachelor, the German cipher clerk lusted for good wine and lovely women, one of the oldest clichés in the world of espionage. He wasted no time in concocting more noble-sounding rationalizations for his treason.

Captain Bertrand had a working arrangement with Polish intelligence, which, like the French, had a stake in monitoring the German military establishment lest it tried to evade constraints imposed on it by the Versailles Treaty following World War I. The Poles had been most proficient in cracking German ciphers, but they had been stopped in mid-1928, when the Germans suddenly introduced a radically new system based on a cipher machine called Enigma that defied Polish cryptanalytical efforts.

Hans-Thilo Schmidt in 1934 had been promoted to a new, particularly secret cryptographic unit in the German Army, the *Forschungsamt,* founded by Nazi air force leader Hermann Göring that same year.* In his

---

*Hans-Thilo Schmidt owed his progress in the service to his older brother, Rudolf Schmidt, who in 1926 had become head of the German Army Signal Corps unit handling cryptological matters. Rudolf Schmidt went on to earn distinction as commander of the XXXIX Panzer Corps in the Russian campaign, and in December 1941 he replaced Germany's famous tank warfare expert General Heinz Guderian as commander of Germany's 2d Panzer Army.

new position Schmidt had ready access to what was needed to break the new German cipher. Of particular interest to Polish cryptanalysts were details of the new German cipher machine. A talented Polish mathemetician named Marian Rejewski would come close to breaking Enigma with his own mathematical cerebration, but with Schmidt's data he could confirm his own calculations and would find the solution to the missing equations.*

Schmidt and his French spymasters settled into a clandestine relationship for the next seven years—well into World War II. Sometimes described as the most valuable spy of the War, Hans-Thilo Schmidt was an asset to be treasured and protected. For security reasons, meetings with "Asche," his code name, were infrequent and elaborately plotted in such different locations as Belgium, Denmark, Czechoslovakia, and Switzerland.

Schmidt's case officer, or handler, M. Lemoine, was known as the Monk. His real name was Richard Stallman-Korff-König. He was a German by origin, who, like Schmidt, loved the good life. Before World War I Lemoine had indeed lived well in Berlin as a gambler and card shark. His idyll ended, however, when he was caught cheating at cards and forced to flee to Paris, where he became a French citizen and found employment in a precarious new profession as a spy for French intelligence.†

On rare meetings with his case officer, Schmidt would unpack his bag of stolen classified documents like some miscast Santa Claus passing out presents at Christmas. He would pull such treasures as the German Army's mobilization ciphers from the bag. On one occasion Schmidt danced a little jig of joy to celebrate a particularly good "take." But the greatest trea-

---

*Rejewski had a master's degree from Poznań University and had studied actuarial mathematics in Germany, but no amount of training could account for his natural genius. As early as 1930 he worked part-time at the Polish Cipher Bureau on German codes and ciphers. Two years later, working with two cryptologists, Henryk Zygalski and Jerzy Rozycki, Rejewski broke a German naval code. Wisely Polish intelligence required Rejewski and his colleagues to break the German Enigma ciphers with their own efforts, without the crutch of Schmidt's keys. In this way they honed their skills for the day they would not have Schmidt's product.—Richard A. Woytak, *On the Border of War and Peace: Polish Intelligence and Diplomacy in 1938–39 and the Origins of the Ultra Secret* (New York: Columbia University Press, 1979), P. 52.

†Working out of his Paris cover office as arms merchant at 44 Rue de Lisbonne, Lemoine met with other star performers, such as a Hungarian chemist who produced in 1936 the secret formulas used by Germany to make poison gas weapons.

It says something about the prewar French intelligence service that Lemoine was permitted to make money by exploiting his intelligence affiliation. Specifically he was allowed to sell French visas, passports, and work permits for personal gain. Such profiteering had become common before the fall of France, and more than one scandal had to be swept under the rug.

sures of all were the bimonthly keying manuals of the Enigma machine, which French cryptologists kept hoping would enable them to break the German cipher system.

Bertrand of French intelligence shared much of the cryptographic material produced by Schmidt with Commander Wilfred Dunderdale, British intelligence representative in Paris, although London seemed only mildly interested at the time.[2] What both the French and British wanted was the kind of information that would permit them to reconstitute the Enigma machine itself.

When Bertrand went to see Colonel Gwido Langer of the Polish crypt-analyis department in mid-December 1931, Langer had confided: "Thanks to your documents, we now know the descriptions of the machine and how it works,"[3] but not until the end of 1932 had Rejewski been able to "solve the machine." After Schmidt had given the French the necessary keys, the Poles were able to read German Army traffic from 1933 until the end of 1938. But this miraculous achievement was not yet revealed to either the French or the British.[4] The more who knew such secrets, the more chances of leakage.

On January 24, 1936, Bertrand and Lemoine met with Schmidt to receive new documents on a variety of subjects. Schmidt's brother, Colonel Rudolf Schmidt, then commanding officer of the 13th Infantry Regiment, had given him a bundle of papers in a trash bag with instructions to throw it away. The colonel was cleaning out his office preparatory to his transfer to the Army General Staff in Berlin and was not careful about what he included in his trash bag, therefore providing his brother with a bonanza of useful cipher material for his French masters.[5]

One particularly interesting item produced by Schmidt concerned Hitler's secret announcement to his generals that the German Army would occupy the Rhineland in March 1936. Schmidt's brother, now a general, was also the unsuspecting source of a later report dated June 23, 1936, concerning the mobilization of the German armed forces.[6] The implications of this were inescapable: Hitler was preparing for military action in contravention of the Versailles Treaty.

In early 1937 Schmidt brought news that Enigma was now used by all military services, and within eight months Enigma messages were spotted in police and Nazi security intelligence (*Sicherheitsdienst*, or SD) traffic as well. The Poles were becoming the best-informed country in Europe as far as German actions were concerned. Even though French intelligence had not yet broken Enigma, its documentary intelligence obtained from Schmidt provided it with a good view of German military intentions. Much of this was shared with its ally, the British.

On November 6, 1937, Schmidt called an emergency contact with French intelligence. The burning subject was the landmark meeting that Hitler had with his top military leaders on November 5, only the day before. At this top secret session Hitler outlined his strategic plans for the next decade, including, high among his priorities, the invasion of Austria and Czechoslovakia. It was the substance of this meeting that German Resistance leaders had also believed important enough to pass indirectly to the French and British, so the Allies had good confirmation.

The special importance of Schmidt's information was that the enciphered message sent via the French ambassador in Berlin to Paris describing Hitler's secret speech had been intercepted and deciphered by the *Forschungsamt*. Within twenty-four hours the German cryptanalytical organization was able to present the deciphered message to Hermann Göring. Schmidt had learned the import of the meeting the same day it occurred from his brother, who in turn had heard it from Hitler's aide-de-camp. Two things were revealed by this intercept: First, the Germans learned that from somewhere within the inner circle there had been a leak, although a subsequent investigation did not find the culprit; second, the French were able to conclude from Schmidt's report that the *Forschungsamt* was regularly breaking their diplomatic ciphers.[7]

On June 9, 1939, a letter from Schmidt to his French masters mentioned Hitler's specific plan to invade Poland. He had scribbled: "Watch out, it's for the end of August."[8] During July and early August Schmidt sent a large number of messages to the French written in secret ink describing the German order of battle in preparation for the invasion of Poland.

With independent indications of Poland's impending peril, the chief of the Polish General Staff ordered the intelligence office to summon French and British intelligence representatives to a meeting to reveal its mastery of Enigma, a secret he believed must be passed on to allies who were standing by Poland. In a series of meetings, conducted between July 25 and 27, Colonel Langer of Polish intelligence held spellbound his French and British counterparts, Colonel Gustav Bertrand and Commander Alistair Denniston, as he divulged how the Poles had exploited Schmidt's intelligence to fathom the secrets of Enigma. The Poles, who had even been able to reconstruct working models of the Enigma machine, presented the French and British with copies for their own use.*

---

*British Secret Intelligence officer Frederick W. Winterbotham in his book *The Ultra Secret* concedes that this account of how Britain received the Enigma machine from the Poles "may well be true," but he claims that he had been officially told at the time that an Enigma machine was retrieved from a downed German aircraft off the coast

The French also made arrangements to remove the Polish cryptanalysts to France for safety.[9]

Thanks to the Polish-reconstituted Enigma cipher machine and the accumulated data provided by Bertrand's agent Hans-Thilo Schmidt, the British were thenceforward able to enhance their own cryptanalytical capabilities. As war approached, Bletchley Park, a converted country estate outside London known as Station X within the service, had become Britain's cryptological center. Despite its cover, Government Code and Cipher School, it was no academic institution. A team of talented men and women, several thousand by the end of the war, were engaged in deciphering Enigma and other systems and devising ways to exploit the product for tactical and strategic advantage. They contributed to saving Britain during the air Battle of Britain, protected the crucial Atlantic supply lines from German submarine attack in the Battle of the Atlantic, provided information regarding preparations being made by the Germans for Operation Sea Lion—the invasion of England—enabled General Claude Auchinleck to gain tactical advantage in his North African battles with Rommel's Afrika Korps, thus saving Suez and Cairo, and provided intelligence in August 1944 to enable the Allies to win the critical Battle of Falaise, in which General Günther Hans Kluge's German force was decisively defeated in France. Through a related but parallel program called ISOS,* they supplied vital cryptographic services to British intelligence, enabling it to mount the so-called Double-Cross counterespionage operations in which Abwehr spies abroad were induced to deceive their masters with deception material calculated to mask the real Allied landing areas first in North Africa during Operation Torch, then in Normandy for the definitive Allied invasion of Europe.[10]

British Ultra intelligence gained from intercepting German ciphers and the Double-Cross system used to gain control of German spies were the greatest secrets of the war. Bletchley Park with its riddle-solving geniuses, so essential to Allied victory, was kept secret for three decades.[11] Churchill called the Bletchley people "the geese that laid the golden eggs and never cackled."[12]

---

of Norway, and in May 1941 the Navy retrieved an Enigma with its keys intact from a captured German submarine.—Frederick W. Winterbotham, *The Ultra Secret* (London: Weidenfeld & Nicolson, 1974), pp. 16, 28.

*ISOS stands for "Intelligence Service, Oliver Strachey," after the officer whose team broke the Abwehr ciphers. In January 1941 the Twenty Committee (XX, hence the phrase *Double-Cross*) was formed within MI-5 to determine what information and misinformation should be passed to the Germans to mislead them.

FOUR

German-Soviet Relations:
Friendly Enemies

THE RELATIONS BETWEEN GERMANY AND RUSSIA FOLLOWING THE BOLSHE-
vik Revolution, particularly after Hitler came to power in 1933, are important in fathoming the shifting diplomatic maneuvers that culminated in
the Hitler-Stalin nonaggression pact of 1939 on the eve of war and the 1941
German invasion of Soviet Russia in cynical violation of that equally cynical agreement. The unfortunate coincidence of two such malign leaders'
emerging simultaneously from history's dark wings backstage to positions
center stage at the World Theater—enter right, enter left—to play leads in
this ghastly drama of World War II was bad luck for the human race. It is
worth searching backstage for clues to how and why it all came to pass.

The history of Russia between the two world wars was neither a story of
propagating the Communist faith as Marx would have had it, despite the
formation of the Third International in 1919, nor Russian nation building
under the red flag of Communism. It was a tale of political mayhem in
which Stalin, by destroying those whom he considered his enemies, almost destroyed his nation. And in foreign affairs as in domestic affairs,
Stalin was concerned primarily with his own power; he was more pragmatist than Communist ideologue.

The Soviet dictator recognized the importance of improving relations
with Nazi Germany, at least for the time being, despite the chasm dividing
their ideologies. And Hitler, for his part, was not yet ready for war with the
Russian giant to the east, particularly since he had an intrinsically hostile
and numerically large French army on his western border.

Following World War I, the Russians and Germans were in different ways victims of the Versailles Treaty. The two countries, one a Bolshevik revolutionary outcast from the Western European capitalist family of nations, the other a defeated, economically ruined, and humiliated enemy of the West, could find common cause in their frustration. Germany discovered that the Russians were willing to help it clandestinely rebuild its armed forces in contravention of the Versailles Treaty. The Soviets could begin to emerge from their political isolation with the 1922 Treaty of Rapallo* and, beyond the terms of the treaty, secretly learn much about the art of modern warfare from the technically advanced Germans.

With the failure of the 1919 Spartacist uprising in Berlin, Communist revolution in Germany seemed remote. In fact, a secret German courtship of Soviet Russia began in the most unlikely place, the Moabit jail in Berlin, which was playing host to Karl Radek, the Bolshevik agitator who had been incarcerated because of his role in the Berlin rebellion. This spasm of discontent, a product of the chaos that characterized defeated Germany in 1919, had brought to the streets German leftists who sought relief from their despair in what they hoped would be a brotherhood of the proletariat. When the uprising fizzled, the far left had to find another solution.

Confined for the time being in his prison suite, Radek could nonetheless look forward to an early release and repatriation to the USSR. Now he was at least permitted to receive guests, including German Communist leaders. Because of his close ties to Moscow, he attracted Germans who saw advantages to a German-Russian alliance. Even the Weimar foreign minister, Walther Rathenau, consulted Radek on establishing a so-called Industrial Study Commission to examine the possibilities of détente with the Soviets. Such senior German military figures as General Hans von Seeckt held discreet discussions with him about military collaboration. Ernst Niekisch, once a German Social Democrat, who had become the mainspring in a movement to promote German-Russian friendship, also met with Radek, by now back in Moscow, at the behest of the German Army High Command.[1]

Toward the end of 1920 Seeckt, as head of a German War Ministry frustrated by restrictions imposed by the Versailles Treaty, formed a highly secret unit called Special Group R as a vehicle for clandestine German-Soviet military cooperation. World War I Air Force ace Colonel von der Lieth-Thomsen and his deputy, Oskar von Niedermayer, World War I

*In the Treaty of Rapallo, signed in 1922, the Germans extended de jure recognition to the USSR. The two countries canceled prewar debts and concluded several trade agreements.

leader of a secret paramilitary mission to Afghanistan, established an aircraft manufacturing plant near Moscow.[2]

The German Luftwaffe can be said to have been born in Russia when the Germans in 1925 established an air-training facility some 250 miles southeast of Moscow. Squadron 4 of the Soviet Air Force, masquerading as a private Russian flying school, was in reality the founding cadre of the Luftwaffe.[3]

According to a secret Soviet-German agreement of 1926, the Red Army assisted the Germans with other training camps and supply channels beyond the prying eyes of the Western Allies. The vaunted German panzer force, for example, was born in Russia. The so-called Kama Project, named for its birthplace, the town of Kasan on the Kama River, began in 1926 as a Heavy Vehicle Experimental and Testing Station, cover euphemism for tank school.

British intelligence seemed only vaguely aware of what was going on. A leak to the *Manchester Guardian* brought down the German Cabinet, but Colonel James Cornwall, British military attaché in Berlin, reported helplessly in 1931: "The relations between the German and Soviet Russian authorities remain something of a mystery."[4]*

By 1926 the Locarno Treaty and Germany's entry into the League of Nations had made the Western countries less concerned with German rearmament violations although German airpower remained worrisome. The Soviet Union, isolated from Europe by the Locarno Treaty, was intent on keeping—even increasing—military cooperation with Germany. Marshal Kliment Voroshilov was the prime mover in this policy although Marshals Mikhail Yegorov and Mikhail Tukhachevsky played important roles as well. Despite Hitler's rise to power in 1933, the Reichstag reaffirmed the 1926 Berlin treaty, which called for Russia and Germany to remain neutral if one of them was attacked, and each power promised not to join in any political or economic coalition harmful to the other.

One in a series of intelligence failures on the part of both Soviet Russia and the Western democracies concerned the underestimation of Hitler. The highly respected British historian Arnold Toynbee, for example, discounted the importance of Hitler, predicting that the Nazi party would never win the government of Germany.[5] British intelligence was no more prescient. It was at first difficult to take seriously the street brawler with the

---

*The *Guardian*'s source was Gustav Hilger, high-ranking officer in Germany's Moscow embassy, who later figured in efforts to warn Stalin of the imminent German invasion in 1941. Hilger also became a member of the German Resistance.—Klemens von Klemperer, *German Resistance Against Hitler* (Oxford: Oxford Clarendon Press, 1992), p. 151, fn. 334, regarding Hilger's Resistance connection.

funny little mustache. Not until he replaced the Weimar Republic, gripping his country in an iron fist of control and force-feeding the Germans with a spirit of imperial revival, did the West really take serious notice.

One exception, at least, in the somnambulant Britain of the early 1930s was Winston Churchill. As early as September 1930, well before Hitler came to power, Churchill saw handwriting on the wall invisible to most. On one occasion, over dinner at the German Embassy in London, the German counselor of embassy took note of remarks made by his guest Churchill and sent a report on them to Berlin. "Hitler, of course, declared he does not intend starting a world war," wrote the German diplomat, "but Churchill believes that Hitler and his followers will grasp the first chance to resort to arms again."[6]

Doctrinaire Russian Bolsheviks were slow to see in Hitler the threat he would become; they were blinded by their ideological convictions. As guardians of the Communist faith in an international class struggle, party theoreticians expected revolution in Germany from the left, even if the Berlin Communist uprising of 1923 had failed. The more Hitler postured and ranted against Communism, they reasoned, the closer Germany would come to revolution. But German Communists tended to underplay the evils of Nazism in their parochial zeal to defeat the Social Democrats. By the time they saw their tactical mistake and tried to form a popular front against Hitler with their Social Democrat rivals, most of their leaders were in jail. Soviet Foreign Minister Maxim Litvinov seemed to reflect official Soviet views when he said to Hitler in the mid-1930s, "We don't care if you shoot your Communists."[7]

Radek, whose role in the 1923 Spartacist rebellion was still remembered, at his Moscow treason trial in 1937 was to pay for having said in a previous lapse into nostalgia recalling earlier German help to the Soviet Army, "In the faces of brown-shirted German students we see the same dedication and inspiration that once brightened the forces of Red Army officer candidates and volunteers of 1813," referring to Prussian volunteers in the war of liberation against Napoleon.

Some of the Soviet military leaders seemed to want to cling to their German ties despite the cooling of relations at the top. In May 1933, the year Hitler came to power, Soviet Marshal Voroshilov hosted a dinner party for German General von Bockelberg, head of German Army ordnance, and toasted continuing ties between the two armies, although soon afterward Stalin ordered the Soviet Army to cease all military cooperation and close the German aviation training center at Libetsk. The Soviet-German military collaboration was officially at an end, even though Marshal Tukhachevsky in a farewell speech to German Embassy Counselor von Twardovsky on October 31, 1933, said warmly that the Red Army command would forever remember the German Army's valuable assistance in building up Russian forces.* "Don't forget," he went on, "it is politics, your policy alone that separates us and not our feelings, our most friendly feelings toward the Reichswehr."[8] But was either country yet prepared to vent its hostility toward the other?

There is considerable evidence suggesting that the seemingly rapid deterioration of relations between Hitler and Stalin may have been illusionary. Soon after World War II, in 1948, a former prominent German Communist, Ruth Fischer, claimed to have new insight on German-Soviet relations following Hitler's rise to power in 1933. Despite the Nazi-staged and -manipulated trial in Leipzig, during which Stalin's friend the Bulgarian Communist Georgi Dimitrov stood in the dock on charges implicating him in the Reichstag fire, rumors were circulating that there had been a top secret agreement made between Hitler and Stalin. Adding substance to rumor, scapegoat Dimitrov was unexpectedly acquitted in the rigged Nazi show trial. In the course of Ruth Fischer's early investigations into this phenomenon, she had interviewed such persons as the Communist Wilhelm Pieck, destined to become president of East Germany, and Rudolf Diels, with Nazi ties at the time, and had concluded that the rumors were true. There had been covert collaboration on certain matters between Stalin and Hitler dating from 1933, the very year of the Führer's accession to power and Stalin's cancellation of secret joint military projects.

In 1989 the Columbia University scholar Stephen Koch told of his interview with the aging widow of Willi Munzenberg, who had been Stalin's agent to organize the massive Comintern propaganda campaign in the wake of Dimitrov's trial vilifying Hitler and the Nazis. Munzenberg's widow, Babette Gross, confirmed Ruth Fischer's earlier theory that some kind of secret deal had been struck. Koch, in a *New York Times* article of January 22, 1994, described new material unearthed when Comintern files were opened in

---

*Sir Robert Vansittart of the British Foreign Office, whose intelligence group flourished in the 1930s—thanks in large measure to the efforts of Group Captain Malcolm Christie—seemed to have gained some insight into lingering friendly contacts between Red Army officers and German Army officers well into the 1930s. The Christie papers, preserved at Churchill College, Cambridge, England, contain information pointing to Reichswehr-Red Army connections in 1936–37, suggesting that certain officers of the German High Command under Hitler tried to keep a "Soviet option" open, but there seems to have been no real confirmation of this.—Donald Cameron Watt, "British Intelligence and the Coming of the Second World War in Europe," *Knowing One's Enemies*, ed. Ernest May (Princeton, N.J.: Princeton University Press, 1984), p. 247. Also Paul Blackstock, *World War II: Soviet Versus Western Intelligence, 1921–1939* (Chicago: Quadrangle, 1969), p. 262.

1991 that pointed to considerable continuing contact between German Army officers and Soviet officials in the 1930s. These files also divulged more details of Dimitrov's exoneration. Koch specifically referred to conversations with a former high-level Bulgarian Communist, Peter Semerdjiev, who provided additional data on the so-called Dimitrov Conspiracy.

In his analysis of all this material, Koch believed that for all the bitter propaganda exchanges of the 1930s, neither dictator wanted to precipitate armed conflict prematurely. Both benefited by providing each other with evidence, real or forged, which could be used to prosecute their respective domestic enemies. If Gestapo forgeries were used by Stalin to attack Field Marshal Mikhail Tukhachevsky and many others during the Red Army purges of 1937 and 1938,* Hitler similarly used Communist charges invented by the imaginative Soviet propagandist Willi Munzenberg to justify his purge of the Nazi SA (*Sturmabteilung*, or storm troopers) and the execution of its leader, Ernst Röhm, during the Night of the Long Knives on June 30, 1934. Passages in the memoir of Walter Krivitsky, former high-ranking Soviet intelligence officer in Europe who defected to the West and was mysteriously murdered in a Washington, D.C., hotel room in December 1939, are revealing in this connection.[9] Krivitsky claimed that the secret Soviet-German détente preceded the German-Soviet pact of August 1939 by six years. The Dimitrov conspiracy was perhaps the earliest manifestation of a secret understanding between Stalin and Hitler, as Koch asserts in his article, and determined the course of events a decade before the Second World War broke out.[10]

The Tukhachevsky case also provides insight into the modus operandi and evil genius of Sicherheitsdienst (SD) chief Reinhard Heydrich.

KNOWING THAT THE OFFICER CORPS OF THE WEHRMACHT LOOKED ON HIM with suspicion, Hitler had created the Waffen SS, first as a bodyguard, then as a Nazi military force on which he could rely. Stalin too had feared that there were seditious stirrings within the senior ranks of his army. Just as he had launched the Great Terror of the 1930s to rid himself of rivals and dissidents within the party, so he now targeted the senior ranks of the Red Army in a purge of frightening proportions.

Stalin realized that disaffection in the armed forces could pose a serious threat to his policies and his person. The army had guns, but there was

---

*According to Pavel Sudoplatov, former high-ranking Soviet KGB official, in his controversial book *Special Tasks*, Stalin was not responsible for Kirov's death, nor was his death political. Nonetheless, Stalin used Kirov's death as a pretext for the purges. — Pavel Sudoplatov and Anatoli Sudoplatov with Jerrold and Leona Schecter, *Special Tasks* (New York: Little, Brown, 1994), pp. 50–56.

more to it than that. British hostility toward Bolshevik Russia in the wake of Lenin's Revolution had provoked a reciprocal reaction of hostility toward the British. This probably played a part in Stalin's obsessive and chronic fear of an Anglo-German rapprochement at Soviet expense. This fear remained even after the British and Americans allied themselves with the Soviets against Nazi Germany. The fear became the fact after the war in a different kind of war, the Cold War, when a prosperous West Germany became NATO's anchor in common defense against a perceived Soviet threat to the Atlantic Pact powers.

To forestall any British-German agreement at Soviet expense, Stalin planned to bind Hitler to him in an alliance until he became strong enough to challenge him. Stalin could not, however, risk an agreement that might be exploited by Russian-German military camaraderie in a dangerous replay of the Rapallo era any more than he could tolerate Communist party zealots in his midst who, out of ideological conviction, would attack him for his dialectical heresy in reaching agreement with Hitler.

Hitler too needed détente with Russia as a temporary expedient, but only until he could secure his western frontier against France and Britain. Stalin certainly had ample warnings of Hitler's eventual intentions toward the USSR, but there was not much the Soviet leader could do about it except hope that the Führer could be kept from attacking by negotiations, ending in economic concessions, if necessary. Stalin was reluctant to accept the likelihood that Hitler wanted a conquest, not a deal; wanted Lebensraum carved from Soviet territory, not more generous import agreements with Stalin.

Before the great Soviet purges of the late 1930s, there had been strong opinions voiced within the party about how to view Hitler. The great revolutionary Nikolai Bukharin at first saw Hitler's rise to power in Germany as only a passing episode in the chaotic German political scene. Capitalist-imperialist Britain and France, he believed, would not tolerate Hitler's political survival for long. But as events unfolded and Bukharin could see that the Western Allies would not stop Hitler in time, he opposed Stalin's policy of appeasement toward Germany.

The intellectual old guard of Bolshevism, epitomized by Bukharin, approached the problem of Hitler dialectically. Fascism/Nazism was an ideological anathema that must be eradicated by a German anti-Fascist popular front supported by the USSR. As the editor of *Izvestia* and the leading party theoretician Bukharin was outspoken in his hostility toward Hitler and the Nazis until he was silenced by execution in the great party purge.

Unlike traditional Bolsheviks committed to an anti-Fascist struggle, Stalin was unmoved by ideological, much less moral, reasoning. In his address to the Seventeenth Party Congress in 1934, he had explicitly stated that he was "not enthusiastic" about the Fascist government in Germany, but "ideology was no problem."[11] Despite the Soviet-French agreement in March 1936, Stalin did not seem to have given up hope of reaching détente with Germany. In that same month Soviet Foreign Minister Vyacheslav Molotov was quoted in *Le Temps* as saying that Soviet Russia "thinks that improvement in Soviet-German relations is possible."[12]

However bothersome Soviet Communist ideologues might prove to be, Stalin would not be swayed from his policy of expediency. He would act upon his conviction that Germany must be appeased and at all costs dissuaded from joining with the West against the USSR. In seeking a Soviet-Nazi alliance, Stalin would not brook troublesome internal opposition, particularly within the Red Army. He conceived an ornate plan to accomplish his purposes. The story is an ugly one, one in which the Nazi SD, strangely enough, played a role and its leader, Reinhard Heydrich, later to gain infamy for his role in the Holocaust, first exhibited his evil genius.

TO UNDERSTAND HOW HEYDRICH'S PLOT WORKED, IT IS NECESSARY TO DESCRIBE the fatal trap that Soviet Marshal Tukhachevsky, deputy chief of the Red Army Commissariat of Defense, fell into. The marshal attended King George V's funeral in London as official Soviet representative in February 1936. This provided the disaffected Tukhachevsky with a convenient cover under which to conspire with émigré White Russian counterrevolutionaries in France and Germany.

Marshal Tukhachevsky paused in Berlin en route back to Moscow from London and there held secret discussions with Russian émigré conspirators. Because of the thorough penetration of the émigré groups by the Soviets through the Trust network, specifically by General Nikolai V. Skoblin, a leader of the Union of Czarist Veterans, but secret NKVD provocateur, word of these talks reached the ears of a German Communist agent named Blimiel, who promptly passed it on to the Soviet Embassy in Berlin. Skoblin, however, was also a German SD agent and revealed to Heydrich that Tukhachevsky and his fellow conspirators were in secret collaboration with certain senior officers of the German General Staff, who were similarly plotting against Hitler.

Upon returning to Moscow, Tukhachevsky was shunted off to a lesser command on the Volga River, where he could be closely watched. In the meantime Skoblin's story, as transmitted to Reinhard Heydrich, set in motion an intense investigation by the SD in Germany. While Skoblin could not be trusted, the nature of his information gave Heydrich ammunition with which to ingratiate himself with Hitler by revealing subversive links between German and Soviet officers. And on the basis of Skoblin's information Heydrich could offer Hitler an audacious scheme to drive a wider wedge between Stalin and the Red Army. Heydrich assigned his best officer, Walter Schellenberg, to the case and engaged a skilled intelligence adviser, Kurt Jahnke, to flesh out the report by additional research into post–World War I connections between German and Soviet army personnel. Jahnke shrewdly and accurately suspected that Skoblin was a double agent who had planted the information on the Germans at Stalin's behest, hoping to alienate Hitler further from the German officer corps. According to Jahnke's reasoning, Stalin also anticipated that the information he planted on the Germans would be fed back to him with embellishment, thereby providing him with more credible-sounding evidence with which to prosecute Soviet officers whom he already considered disloyal. Before proceeding with the prosecution of suspect generals, Stalin wanted incriminating evidence he could present as a source to the Germans rather than simply provide dubious Russian evidence that might appear to have been cooked up for self-serving political reasons.

Jahnke's theory was unwelcome to Heydrich; it meant that Stalin was manipulating the Germans rather than vice versa. Heydrich suspected—or rationalized—that Jahnke was also an agent of his rival, Canaris, whose objective was to protect German General Staff officers from such plots. In an effort to muzzle Jahnke, Heydrich had him temporarily jailed.*

Heydrich had the Abwehr archives burgled for documents that could be doctored to make them more startling. By copying the signature of Tukhachevsky from the old but still-secret military agreement between

---

*According to Schellenberg's postwar memoir, *Hitler's Secret Service*, 2d ed. (New York: Harper & Row, 1956), pp. 28–30; Kurt Jahnke's intelligence career went back to World War I. Before that he had moved to the United States, where he joined the U.S. Immigration Service border police. He left Immigration's employ to try to get rich in an ingenious enterprise in which he shipped the bodies of dead Chinese from America back to their homeland for proper burial, according to their custom. With the outbreak of World War I, Jahnke joined German intelligence, becoming active in fomenting strikes in the United States and committing other forms of sabotage on East Coast docks and forwarding facilities. Jahnke was part of the Toms River Gang that blew up several ammunition barges in New Jersey harbors during the First World War.

After the war Jahnke formed a private intelligence service in Germany, selling his services principally to the Nazis. He became Rudolf Hess's adviser on intelligence matters and later served in the same capacity for Ribbentrop and the German Foreign Ministry. Schellenberg believed that Jahnke had been a British agent as well as an Abwehr agent within the SD.

the Soviet Union and the Weimar Republic in 1926, Heydrich was able to create a particularly convincing and damaging document incriminating the Soviet marshal with invented details of his anti-Stalin plotting. Upon discovering the violation of his files, Canaris was furious. The incident told him that his onetime friend Heydrich would stop at nothing in winning Hitler's favor and humbling his rivals in the Abwehr in the process.

When Heydrich presented Hitler with his partly accurate, mostly doctored dossiers incriminating senior Soviet generals, including Marshal Tukhachevsky, the Führer considered whether he should sit on the report, even back Tukhachevsky in getting rid of Stalin, or give the Soviet dictator the material permitting him to destroy his military opposition. Hitler decided to do the latter. If there was to be a temporary détente with Stalin freeing the Wehrmacht to conquer Western Europe, he must for the time being preserve the Soviet leader and protect him from any Red Army plot.[13] Moreover, to allow, much less encourage, a Red Army plot linked to his own dissident Wehrmacht generals would obviously be a recipe for disaster.

It was May 1937 when Heydrich with Hitler's endorsement had the explosive dossier passed to Stalin by way of President Eduard Beneš of Czechoslovakia, who had been taken in by the fraud. Stalin, startled by what appeared to be a treachery even greater and more imminent than he had thought, planned to use the forged documents as needed to cinch the guilt of his perceived enemies within the army.*

In a Stalin-bashing speech before the 1956 Twentieth Congress of the Supreme Soviet almost two decades later, Nikita Khrushchev reported that a special investigation of Stalin's military purge revealed that the alleged counterrevolutionary conspiracy had never existed,[14] something long suspected in the West. U.S. Chargé d'Affaires Loy Henderson in Moscow reported on June 23, 1937, that no foreign observer "believed that the executed Red Army officers were guilty of the crimes attributed to them." The trials were based on evidence trumped up or exaggerated by the NKVD—with or without Heydrich's creative contribution.

The casualty statistics of the purge were staggering. One estimate put at 35,000 the number of senior officers who were killed,[15] and thousands of lesser officers, quite innocent of any crime, were unjustly executed. The only marshals to survive were Semyon Budenny and Kliment

---

*Canaris biographer Heinz Höhne believed that the dossier was not used against Tukhachevsky in his trial.—Heinz Höhne, *Canaris* (Garden City, N.Y.: Doubleday, 1979), pp. 229, 250.

Voroshilov. Only 5 members of the Military Soviet of 1934 were allowed to live. Every one of the 11 deputy commissars for defense was executed, and every commander of a military district was shot. An estimated 57 out of 85 corps commanders, 110 of 195 divisional commanders, and 220 of 406 brigade commanders were killed.[16] The leadership of the Red Army was destroyed.

Göring believed that the Soviet Army "had ceased to exist as a fighting force." In view of the state of the Red Army, French Premier Léon Blum despaired of the Soviet Union as a credible deterrent to German aggression.[17] Three months before the Munich crisis, Soviet Foreign Minister Litvinov gave as his country's opinion that the Czech government should "find reasonable limits for concessions."[18] This amounted to a Soviet version of appeasement in the Czech issue more craven than Chamberlain's. By May 1938, as the Czech crisis was coming to a boil, the British prime minister convinced himself that neither the USSR nor France could be expected to fight in defense of Czechoslovakia. This surely must have influenced his position and provided him with a rationale for his own actions.

If Stalin in his mass purge of the Red Army had wielded a meat-ax, Hitler adopted different approaches to gain control of the Wehrmacht. One technique had been to establish and carefully to nourish a parallel armed force, the Waffen SS, made up of reliable Nazis and headed by party faithful Himmler. The SA street brawlers had outlived their usefulness. More important, the SA, which had developed delusions of grandeur, posed a threat to Himmler and his SS force and to Göring with his own delusions of power. Taking a page from Stalin's book, Hitler destroyed the SA, assassinating its top officers, including its leader, Hitler's old friend Ernst Röhm, in a sudden bloodbath, the so-called Night of the Long Knives. As for the German Army, Hitler relied on pseudolegal trials to get rid of officers whom he did not trust and showered favors on those willing to bow to him.

Encouraged by Himmler, Hitler believed that the German High Command was in fact maintaining secret contact with high Soviet officers. On Himmler's orders, Heydrich brought to trial a score of German officers whose only sin had been to conduct the official, but secret, liaison with their Soviet counterparts during the period of cooperation in the late twenties. The principal defendant was Ernst Niekisch, who had been involved in drafting the 1926 military cooperation accord with Russia. In these trials, futile fishing expeditions, the Gestapo without sufficient evidence failed to make a convincing case and abandoned the prosecution.

Himmler and Heydrich now designed a more insidious scheme, one intended to discredit the widely respected commander in chief, Colonel General Baron Werner von Fritsch. Fritsch was in line to succeed Blomberg as minister of war; seen through Nazi eyes, this was a risky place for a conservative general known to have monarchist leanings. His removal would make way for a military leader more congenial to the Nazis.

FIVE

Exit General von Fritsch

IT WAS NOT EASY TO DISCREDIT GENERAL WERNER VON FRITSCH IN THE
eyes of his fellow officers. He was admired by his peers, the ranking generals,
and his record was flawless. Moreover, the aged hero of World War I, Reich
President Field Marshal Paul von Hindenburg, had been personally responsible for choosing the general as chief of the Army Command in 1933.
Charged with illegal homosexual behavior, he was found not guilty by a military tribunal despite the framed evidence introduced by Himmler and his
hatchet man, Heydrich, during the February 1938 trial. Fritsch's reputation
was nonetheless tarnished by the proceedings, and he lost his position. As intended from the beginning, Hitler took over active command of the army
with Fritsch's removal, but in doing so, he provoked many senior military officers, driving a number of them into a resistance movement.

Both Fritsch and his superior, War Minister Field Marshal Werner von
Blomberg, had disagreed with Hitler's policies leading to the Czech crisis,
but it was their objections to the master plan revealed by Hitler in a historic
secret briefing of senior officers on November 5, 1937, that determined their
fate and led Hitler to become supreme in matters of war strategy. In his November remarks the Führer stressed Germany's need for more living space,
Lebensraum. The armed forces of Germany must move to accomplish this
before their equipment became obsolete. The army might be called upon
to act soon if it became apparent that France, because of internal problems,
was unwilling or unable to oppose Germany. It was also Hitler's opinion
that neither France nor Britain was willing to come to Czechoslovakia's

defense if Germany invaded. There were even implications in Hitler's remarks that he saw Germany's eastern approaches as the promised Lebensraum when he said that an opportunity might present itself for Germany to
invade Czechoslovakia and Austria as prelude to "the improvement of
our politico-military position . . . to remove the threat to our flank in any
possible operation against the West."[1] Both Blomberg and Fritsch argued
that Germany could not afford to have France and Britain as enemies;
the French Army, at least on paper, was superior to that of Germany. Moreover, Germany's fortifications against invasion from France were inadequate while Czechoslovakia's defenses against a German attack were
strong. Such talk was unwelcome; in his commanders Hitler wanted com-
pliance, not argument. Blomberg and Fritsch had defied him and would be
made examples of what befell dissenters.

It did not take much prodding from Göring, who reveled in Blomberg's
heresy and humiliation, for Hitler to remove the war minister from office.
Blomberg's marriage to a woman of dubious reputation provided a handy
pretext. To make matters worse, Hitler had attended the wedding without
knowing that the bride had been a woman of low repute. The Führer was
furious at Blomberg's poor judgment in marriage but overjoyed to have a
pretext to get rid of him.

It would be General von Fritsch's turn next to pay for his criticism of
Hitler. Rather than be promoted to take Blomberg's place in logical succession as minister of war, he was jettisoned, permitting Hitler himself to
assume undisputed control of the armed forces.

Himmler, like Göring, had ambitions for himself in the denigration
of the old-line army officer corps. The *Reichsführer* welcomed anything
that would discredit the army and thus enhance the power of his SS, so
he became the very willing instrument of Fritsch's fall from grace.
Himmler's precocious deputy Heydrich saw this as an opportunity to
shine, to show off to Hitler his political acumen. This fast-rising star of
SS intelligence saw in this operation another success similar to his fram-
ing of Tukhachevsky.

To make a spurious case against Fritsch, Himmler showed Hitler a
dossier that Heydrich had discovered in the Gestapo files. The dossier was
meant to prove that the general was a practicing homosexual, but in fact it
was that of someone with the same name who had a police record for male
prostitution but had nothing to do with Fritsch, chief of Army Command.
Himmler, moreover, tried to link Fritsch with an alleged sexual partner
who, as it turned out, had been bribed by the Gestapo to support the totally fabricated story in court. Fraud and corruption on the prosecution's
part was bad enough, but those in the court were treated to a weird exhi-

bition of Himmler's mysticism in which spirits and extrasensory perceptions were invoked to get at the "truth."

Even Himmler's own star security intelligence officer Walter Schellenberg was aghast at what he saw. "During the Fritsch case I witnessed for the first time some of the very strange practices resorted to by Himmler through his inclination toward mysticism," explains Schellenberg in his postwar memoir. "He assembled twelve of his most trusted SS leaders in a room next to the one in which von Fritsch was being questioned and ordered them all to concentrate their minds on exerting a suggestive influence over the General that would induce him to tell the truth." A dozen SS officers sitting in a circle "in deep and silent contemplation" was indeed "a remarkable sight," writes Schellenberg.[2]

The misbegotten trial fizzled to an end after a three-week interruption caused by the crisis in German-Austrian relations. The Anschluss provided Himmler and Heydrich with a fortunate distraction from their embarrassing effort at a show trial that did not bear further showing. Hitler nonetheless removed Fritsch from office and ejected him from the service even though the general's innocence had been amply proved by the defense. Fritsch's disgrace—truth never catches up with accusations—ignited a storm of indignation among the senior officers who saw through Himmler's frame-up. The officer corps particularly resented the fact that Hitler took the occasion not only to arrogate to himself direct supreme command over the Wehrmacht but also to extract by trickery an oath of loyalty to his person from the entire German officer corps, a sacred commitment of loyalty traditionally reserved for the fatherland, not for its leader.

Thanks to the backstage maneuvering of a cabal of men intent on rescuing Fritsch from the consequences of conviction, the general was spared imprisonment, but his public reputation and his career were ruined. Fritsch's particularly active benefactors were Abwehr Chief Canaris; Canaris's chief of staff, Hans Oster; Chief of the Army General Staff, Colonel General Ludwig Beck; a Justice Ministry officer assigned to the case, Hans von Dohnanyi; and the military court judge Dr. Carl Sack. By their tireless and dangerous efforts to disprove the evidence produced by the prosecution and because the army had in the first place been able to insist on holding the trial in a military court of honor rather than agree to a Gestapo drumhead hearing, these men had bested Himmler and Heydrich.

The trial's venue within the military system had not been foreseen by Heydrich, who was infuriated with the way it turned out. He doubtless suspected that it was Canaris who had outwitted him. Himmler had given in without serious protest rather than push the already outraged army any further.

The Fritsch affair disgusted many in the army. A respected fellow officer had been falsely accused and shamed. More seriously, the usual avenues of respectful dissent on matters of military strategy traditionally open to the General Staff were now closed. Hitler now had unquestioned control of the Wehrmacht and would not tolerate, much less welcome, advice. The military could henceforward expect a policy of unbridled aggression—a recipe for disaster.

Stunned by what seemed the probable consequences of the Fritsch affair, Canaris and Oster were determined from this time onward to work toward the overthrow of Hitler. This was high treason, the most dangerous of conspiracies in Nazi Germany. The whole affair had at least served a purpose in giving focus to anti-Hitler sentiment within the officer corps and providing the stimulus for a small but determined resistance movement whose members would devote the rest of their all-too-short lives to trying to rid Germany of Hitler. The time was ripe for action.

While there were other groups beginning to coalesce in opposition to Hitler, such as the Foreign Ministry, the clergy, university students, labor, and even one or two in the Gestapo, the Abwehr and army were to provide the initial cadre for action. During the emotional aftermath of the Fritsch affair, Canaris, who later remained in the background as patron of the Resistance, providing invaluable Abwehr services and enlisting foreign contacts, plunged aggressively into the shrouded contest.

Canaris had nursed doubts about Hitler since before he took office as head of the Abwehr in January 1935. In the beginning he had applauded Hitler's efforts to revive Germany, whose people's pride had suffered from humiliating sanctions imposed by the Treaty of Versailles and whose economy had been shattered by war damage, burdensome reparations, and the Great Depression. But he was at heart a monarchist who believed in the rule of law and legitimacy, not street brawling, as the right road to office.

The Night of the Long Knives, the massacre in which the SS cut down in cold blood such Nazi leaders as SA chief Ernst Röhm, Kurt von Schleicher, and Gregor Strasser, who threatened Hitler's leadership in one way or another, sickened Canaris. An old friend of the admiral's, Franz Maria Liedig, said under interrogation after the war, "events of June 1934 [the purge of the SA] proved to Canaris that Hitler was and would remain a confirmed revolutionary to whom the exploitation of trust, decency and truth was a mere instrument of policy. Hitler was ready to deny today what he swore yesterday provided that his plans and aims were thus served."[3]

The German occupation of the Rhineland in 1936 and the absorption of Austria in 1938 bespoke a policy of military adventurism and flagrant duplicity that Canaris believed was doomed eventually to destroy Germany.

The treatment of Fritsch made obvious to him and others in the armed services Hitler's disregard of individual life, liberty, and loyalty, as well as his
megalomaniacal insistence on running the Wehrmacht as a personal fief-
dom to be used recklessly for unprovoked aggression.

A longtime friend of Canaris's, Colonel General Ludwig Beck, had
been a General Staff officer since 1911 before becoming general chief of
staff of the army in 1935. Like Canaris, Beck had served in World War I and
in the Weimar Republic and had survived in office under Hitler. He had
argued strenuously against Hitler's Czechoslovakian policy on the ground
that it would provoke war with France and Britain. He predicted that this
in turn would lead to a world war for which Germany was unprepared and
could not hope to win. Beck did not believe that Germany's need for
Lebensraum should be gratified by force. Total war "cannot lead to a good
peace," he said. Moreover, a "political leader must be a moral person who
must ultimately submit to his own inner ethical code, his conscience."[4]

In 1938, as a result of the Fritsch affair as well as the baleful unfolding
of the Czech drama, Beck had hoped that his fellow generals would join
him in forcing Hitler to abandon his war plans. If the Führer refused, Beck
believed that the general officers should show their opposition by resign-
ing en masse from the service. This entreaty did not succeed, leaving only
Beck to resign in protest, as he did on August 18, 1938. He continued to
work with the Resistance and was thereafter accepted as the military head
of the conspiracy.[5]

Canaris's chief of staff, Hans Oster, had served in combat during World
War I and been rewarded by a General Staff appointment in 1917. He
served in the Reichswehr Ministry, then in the High Command of the
Wehrmacht as a senior officer of the Abwehr. When Chancellor von
Schleicher was murdered on June 30, 1934, by the SS, Oster's hopes that
Hitler could be politically defeated evaporated, and he became a convinced and an active member of the Resistance. With the approval of Canaris, who generally shared his sentiments, Oster proceeded to organize
the Abwehr so that its considerable facilities and files could be used for
purposes of the Resistance. As chief of the Central Department of the Abwehr, Oster could provide invaluable services for the Resistance. Abwehr
officer and Resistance member Liedig testified to the Allies after the war
that without Oster, "Canaris would have been unable to build and defend
the unity of the Abwehr in its struggle against the ever-increasing claims
to power of the RSHA [Reichssicherheitshauptamt, or SS security-
intelligence arm] under Himmler and Reinhard Heydrich."[6] While there
were doubtless some pro-Nazi officers in the Abwehr, it remained essentially an organization that was either apolitical or essentially anti-Nazi in

makeup so long as Canaris and Oster were in charge—an astounding situation in a country preparing for a major war.[7]

Oster had been outraged by the Fritsch affair in the spring of 1938 and worked closely with Canaris and Beck to produce evidence that Himmler had framed the general. This was for Oster an introduction to conspiracy; with a devotion sometimes bordering on recklessness he then launched himself into the underground struggle against Hitler. There were those who said that from the beginning he did not expect to survive. The cause was all.

The Fritsch case also brought Hans von Dohnanyi together in secret collusion with Canaris, Oster, and Beck and determined his underground career as a member of the Resistance. Son of a well-known German composer, Dohnanyi was born and brought up in Austria. He was trained as a lawyer and in 1929 joined the Ministry of Justice, where he specialized in constitutional law with a particularly keen interest in matters of treason and high treason, a curious foreshadow of his own future efforts to overthrow Hitler. From his vantage point in law and justice he learned enough about the excesses of the Nazis to compile a monumental secret archive on the crimes of Hitler and of Hitler's leaders that he had hoped to use to discredit them and bring about their downfall. The Gestapo later described him as "the author and the intellectual head of the movement to remove the Führer."[8] This may have overstated his role, but he might have appreciated the accolade.

In the Fritsch trial Dohnanyi adroitly helped organize the general's defense. It was then that he became close to Canaris, who later brought him into the Abwehr as his political adviser, providing him with cover for his Resistance activities.

Another secret benefactor of Fritsch was the military court judge Dr. Carl Sack, who played an important role in the preliminary investigations as well as during the trial. Recognizing the legal fraud being perpetrated by Heydrich, Sack was able to keep Canaris, Oster, and Dohnanyi aware of the prosecution's bogus case as it unfolded, making it easier for the defense to discredit it.

Sack and Canaris thereafter were good friends. Sack was useful in steering military tribunal cases away from matters that might endanger the Resistance. He was also a valuable source of information for Canaris in the latter's artful dodging of Gestapo traps.

The Canaris-Oster circle of resistance within the Abwehr was the first group within the General Staff to work systematically against Hitler. Canaris's old navy friend, Commander Franz Maria Liedig, head of the Abwehr's naval intelligence branch, described the group as the "center of gravity" for resistance within the German military.[9] Having been aroused by the Fritsch affair, Canaris now saw Hitler's overthrow by a military putsch as the only solution to the Führer's dangerous leadership. He also saw the trial as an opportunity to discredit Heydrich, a dangerous rival, by reminding senior commanders that his acts in the Fritsch case were acts against the German Army.[10] One friend of Canaris's much later referred to the Fritsch affair to a British journalist, saying, "If you're looking for one specific event that shook Canaris's allegiance to Hitler, there you have it."[11] He threw himself into this cause with such intensity that a more cautious Beck feared that he might set off an ill-prepared, premature mutiny bound to fail. Or if nothing as dramatic as that happened, he could at least get himself into a lot of trouble. While Beck had also been busy agitating among his officer friends, he was not ready for action and warned Canaris to calm down.

The army, while infuriated by the Fritsch affair, was not ready to rise by any stretch of the imagination. But rumors had spread and talks of a putsch had put Heydrich and his minions in a high state of alert. Heydrich's deputy Schellenberg tells a strange tale in his memoir. He describes a private dinner he had with Heydrich in which the SD chief seemed to be having a severe attack of nerves. The jittery man had apparently heard through his informants that officers of the General Staff, inflamed by the Fritsch trial, were considering a coup that night. He expected them to burst in and seize him at any minute. That was in fact why he had invited Schellenberg to dinner. Noted for his sharpshooting skills, Schellenberg realized that his role would be to keep at bay any army raiding squad bold enough to strike.

No putsch occurred, but word of Heydrich's panic somehow got around. Schellenberg, for one, was disillusioned by his boss's cowardice.[12] Fortunately Heydrich had been frightened by rumor, not fact, and he did not have the evidence he needed to move against any real or imagined army plotters. Putsch planning, inspired by the Fritsch case, was embryonic; the new Resistance would soon conceive of a more serious plot to prevent Hitler from moving against Czechoslovakia, one meant to provoke the French and British to threaten to come to Czechoslovakia's defense. The Resistance believed that this was the time to take a stand since Germany was not yet prepared for war. This would be perhaps the last occasion when Hitler's bluff could be called, but more to the point, a strong stand by the Western Allies would provide the army members of the plot with the motive they needed to question Hitler's judgment and move against him. But there were surprises along the road to Munich, as the Resistance began to realize that the Western Allies were intent upon keeping peace at any cost.

SIX

Munich

HITLER'S AGENDA FOR CZECHOSLOVAKIA PROVOKED SERIOUS RESISTANCE from several quarters, particularly the military. Army Chief of General Staff Beck had dared speak up to Hitler in the presence of the service chiefs, warning against the invasion of Czechoslovakia on the ground that it would almost certainly bring about serious retaliation from the British, French, and Russians. When Hitler's response was to scoff and rail against officers who had no faith, nascent Resistance groups coalesced to plan seriously for a putsch against the Nazi regime.

Professional army officers, with their heritage of service and tradition, generally looked down upon Nazi newcomers, whose leaders were considered boors and bullies. The Third Reich made a mockery of Germany's well-ordered society and rule of law. The army establishment had seen the Nazis and had taken note, during the purge of 1934, when the SS massacred Ernst Röhm and his fellow SA leaders, of the street thugs who had helped bring Hitler to power. This had taught a lesson: The SS could one day strike again at any group that threatened the regime, including the army. The Blomberg and Fritsch affairs revealed the extent to which Nazi leaders would go to discredit and depose senior army officers so that Hitler could appoint in their places more malleable officers through whom he could exercise absolute control. While the Wehrmacht, smarting from the humiliation of the Versailles Treaty following World War I, had welcomed Germany's military revival under Hitler, the ambitious plans unfolded by the Führer shocked the army, which did not consider Germany ready for such adventures.

The military prime mover of the secret Resistance was General Beck. As chief of the Army General Staff since 1935 he had held out hope that Hitler's rash beginnings would be modified by events and, as he explained, Nazism "would grind itself to pieces on the flinty good qualities of the German people."[1] But Hitler's twin sins, humiliating Fritsch on false charges of homosexuality and dashing headlong toward military disaster, had disillusioned him, as it had Canaris and many others. When it became apparent that Hitler intended ultimately to seize Czechoslovakia by force, Beck knew he could no longer serve as a Wehrmacht officer; he resigned. He rationalized his disregard for the sacred oath that all German officers had taken and his conspiratorial role within the Resistance on the ground that Germany was faced with "[a]bnormal times that require deeds that are also out of the ordinary."[2] The shadow government plotted by the Resistance cast Beck as regent in a post-Hitler regime. There were others outside the military who secretly joined the movement, most notably Carl Goerdeler, who was named to head a new government as chancellor.

Dr. Carl Friedrich Goerdeler, the former lord mayor of Königsberg and later the mayor of Leipzig, was highly respected and readily accepted as one of the leaders by most members of the Resistance. Well before the war Goerdeler had found Hitler and his fellow Nazis distasteful, but when SA brown-shirted street mobs tore down the statue of Jewish composer Felix Mendelssohn in Leipzig, he was deeply angered and resigned his position as mayor in protest. From then on he devoted his considerable energies to fighting national socialism. Conservatives not only saw him as their political leader in the *Widerstand* (Resistance) but looked upon him as the leading candidate to guide Germany in a post-Hitler era. Goerdeler's Resistance circle, while mainly consisting of conservatives, also included Catholic trade unionists and moderate leftists.

The pedestal on which his admirers placed him was in one way a liability. He attracted too much attention. Unfortunately he was also sometimes indiscreet. His bravery and self-confidence made him disdainful of the Gestapo, not a wise thing in Nazi Germany, although his very outspokenness tended to mask his conspiratorial role. Moreover, his public prestige caused the Nazis to be wary of attacking him.

If Goerdeler found underground plotting alien to his frank nature, Admiral Canaris was the consummate conspirator, who carried on his anti-regime plotting from the cloistered back rooms of the Abwehr on the Tirpitzufer. As head of military intelligence, an integral part of the High Command, he was relatively well protected from the usual Gestapo harassment. He could provide invaluable organizational facilities and cover for the Black Orchestra, a name for the Resistance originally coined by the

Gestapo. A master of intrigue, schooled in intelligence and counterintelligence since the First World War and in possession of voluminous files on the misdeeds of Nazi leaders, Canaris was, in an inconspicuous way, enormously powerful. He brought to the Resistance a knowledge of Nazi inner workings, the jealousies, ambitions, and vulnerabilities of Hitler's macabre entourage. And as head of one of the few organizational entities in the Third Reich with license to engage in secret, sometimes convoluted activities, such as double agent operations and provocations, he could hide the clandestine activities inherent in the conspiracy or assuage suspicions inevitably aroused from time to time by his or his staff's actions.

Canaris operated in the shadows. He provided more a support service than an active leadership role. He must have recognized that in his position it would be irresponsible to do otherwise. If he were caught, it could mean the end of the Abwehr and its vital contribution to the Resistance. Goerdeler became the major inspiration for the Resistance, and General Beck the hands-on organizational talent, particularly with military collaborators, but Canaris was the protector. He provided the insulated Abwehr cocoon from which it could mount its operations. His Abwehr facilities also enabled him to provide communications and channels for foreign contact, indispensable requirements of the Resistance. The Abwehr also had its own passport office, which could issue documents required for travel abroad.

Within the Abwehr circle it was Canaris's deputy Colonel—later General—Hans Oster who was principal activist. He maintained the contacts and coordinated the activities of the different circles of the Resistance. Without Oster the clandestine machine would not have run as efficiently as it did. It was also Oster who collected the kind of information the Resistance needed to protect itself. He was well connected with the Gestapo, the regular uniformed police, and the SD, from whose files he could usually discover what he needed to know. Oster also maintained secret contact with two Resistance collaborators, Count Wolf Heinrich von Helldorf, the head of the Berlin Police, and Arthur Nebe, a Gestapo man who led the Criminal Investigation Department.

Beck had become progressively disillusioned by Hitler. The humiliation of Fritsch had disgusted him. When in August 1938 he resigned, he was replaced by General Franz Halder, who also feared Hitler's headlong dash to disaster but was more discreet about expressing himself.[3] With Halder's secret collaboration, Beck now devoted himself to the military resistance program with the full cooperation of Canaris as well as Oster. Beck and Oster played the leadership roles in this risky endeavor, while Canaris and Goerdeler devoted themselves to arranging secret foreign contacts.

It was not the intention of the Resistance at this time to assassinate Hitler. The idea appealed to neither Canaris nor Beck; the Führer should be tried in court so that all his crimes could be paraded before the German people, rather than risk his going down in history as a martyr. The institution of the People's Court had been devised by Hitler to serve Nazi party needs by summarily prosecuting enemies of the regime. In 1934, following the Reichstag fire, special courts had been hastily created to try cases under an edict "Against treason to the German nation." It would be a form of justice in itself if Hitler could be tried by this judicial device, which he himself had designed to contravene the traditional courts of the land.

The specific plan that evolved on the eve of the Munich crisis called for Hitler's arrest by a cabal of army officers. Hans von Dohnanyi, whom Canaris had made head of the Department of Military Intelligence in the Abwehr, used his new position to augment his secret file of Hitler's crimes, which he had begun while working in the Ministry of Justice. These data would be vital in prosecuting Hitler at a People's Court once the putsch was successful.

Hjalmar Schacht, former president of the Reichsbank and minister for economic affairs who had resigned over differences with Hitler in August 1937, was also in on the plot.[4] Professor Karl Bonhoeffer, a well-respected neurologist, after examining Hitler, would testify in good conscience that Hitler was insane.[5] According to the plan, however impractical, the Führer would spend the rest of his days in an insane asylum under close guard.* Other influential sympathizers, on whom the Resistance could rely, included General Karl Heinrich von Stülpnagel, the quartermaster general, and, best of all, General Franz Halder, who, as chief of staff, was the second most important military figure in the German Army.

Field Marshal Erwin von Witzleben, commander of the 3d Military District of Berlin and Brandenburg, was also a key military player who was to work in close collaboration with Count von Helldorf, head of the Berlin Police, and his deputy Count Fritz-Dietlof von der Schulenburg, once the putsch began. General Erich Höpner and his 1st Light Division, poised on the Czech frontier, would head back to Berlin for support when the signal was given.

*Among the mounds of documents seized by the American forces in Germany at war's end in 1945 was a top secret file, dated January 23, 1944, personally handled by Himmler himself and given to Martin Bormann. The investigation and report, which may or may not have been requested by Hitler, linked the Führer and his parents with a Josef Veit, whose descendants included a very high percentage of neurotic and psychotic persons. — Ben E. Swearingen, "Hitler's Family Secret," *Civilization* (March–April 1995).

The conspirators also needed the support of Britain and France. No putsch, they believed, could succeed unless the Resistance justified its actions by accusing Hitler of rushing headlong into war. The Allies must therefore be prodded into credibly threatening war over the issue of Czechoslovakia; this would provide the rationale needed for the plotters to arrest Hitler in the interests of European peace. Several emissaries of the Resistance therefore conveyed in secret their pleas to selected British officials urging that Britain firmly protest German aggression against Czechoslovakia.

The first to plead the Resistance's cause and take the temperature of British resolve was Dr. Goerdeler, who visited London secretly in July 1938 to see Sir Robert Vansittart, chief diplomatic adviser to the British government who ran a Foreign Office intelligence organization. One sour note, however, prejudiced their talks. Vansittart, predisposed to distrust Germans of any kind, could not accept Goerdeler's stand on the Sudetenland, which favored German hegemony over the German-speaking enclave so long as it could be negotiated without violence.* Goerdeler's comments only reinforced Vansittart's skepticism. However threatening Hitler seemed, it was not easy for the British Foreign Office to rattle the sabers enough to provoke a war-threatening situation, but not a war, just to give the German Army an excuse to stage a coup d'état, then reward it with the Sudetenland.

Beck and Canaris then chose Major Ewald von Kleist-Schmenzin, a close friend of the admiral's, as another secret emissary to the British. As Canaris put it in nautical terms, "England must lend us a sea anchor if we are to ride out the storm."[6] Equipped with false travel documents prepared by the Abwehr, Kleist-Schmenzin arrived in London on August 18, 1938. To pave the way, he had first met in Berlin with Ian Colvin, then British correspondent of the *News Chronicle,* to convey to the British Embassy the need for Britain to oppose resolutely any warlike move by Hitler against Czechoslovakia. Colvin wrote an account of his talk with Kleist-Schmenzin and gave his own appraisal of the atmosphere at the time: "It seemed to me that Admiral Canaris was using every oblique means in his power to beset and confound the cocksure demagogue [Hitler] and that one of the highest officers in the state [Canaris] was Adolf Hitler's secret

---

*To put Vansittart's views in perspective, however, it should be noted that he repeatedly warned that Hitler and Stalin were on the verge of reaching détente. According to British author Tom Bower's recent biography of MI-5's (and later MI-6's) postwar chief Sir Dick White, Vansittart's reliably sourced warnings were generally ignored by both the Foreign Office and MI-6.—Tom Bower, *The Perfect English Spy: Sir Dick White and the Secret War, 1935–1990* (London: Heinemann, 1995), p. 31.

enemy."[7] But by dealing with the enemy behind Hitler's back, the conspirators were playing with fire. As he left for England, Kleist-Schmenzin told his wife: "Remember that you have never heard me mention the names Canaris and Oster."[8]

In London, Kleist-Schmenzin first went to see Vansittart, as Goerdeler had just done. He told Vansittart bluntly that "war [with Czechoslovakia] was a certainty" unless the British stopped it.[9] "Von Ribbentrop," Kleist-Schmenzin said, "keeps telling [Hitler] that when it comes to the showdown, neither France nor England will do anything." He described the Resistance movement in the German High Command, emphasizing that "it could do nothing without assistance from outside, particularly help in the form of speeches by England's leading statesmen emphasizing the inevitable general catastrophe to which Hitler's aggression would lead."[10]

In his report to Chamberlain, Vansittart confessed he felt uneasy about the Czechoslovakia situation, but he remained concerned about the Resistance's own intentions of keeping the Sudetenland for Germany should it be successful in removing Hitler from power. He also thought that Kleist-Schmenzin's demarche had to be "discounted a good deal" in view of the emissary's violently anti-Hitler sentiments.

Winston Churchill, whose influence as a member of Parliament was at that time limited, also met in secret with Kleist-Schmenzin. Churchill seemed fairly sympathetic, although Kleist-Schmenzin, like Goerdeler, prejudiced his presentation by intimating that the German Resistance favored the peaceable return of the Sudetenland and the creation of a German-controlled Polish Corridor. The future prime minister nonetheless responded in a limited but important way to the Resistance envoy's entreaties: He wrote a letter, which he cleared with Foreign Secretary Lord Halifax, that the Resistance was free to use as it saw fit. The key phrase in Churchill's letter states: "I am sure that the crossing of the frontier of Czechoslovakia by German armies or aviation in force will bring about a renewal of the world war."[11] In his monumental war memoir *The Second World War*, Churchill's initial sympathy for the Resistance, destined to wither as unconditional surrender became Allied doctrine, is suggested when he writes: "Several visitors of consequence came to me from Germany and poured out their hearts in their bitter distress."

Kleist-Schmenzin's mission came to nothing. Prime Minister Chamberlain had decided to beard Hitler in his lair and try to reason with him. Aside from the futility of this course of action, it telegraphed Britain's weakness. Chamberlain was set against a preventive war or even posturing in a threatening manner and was confident he could find "peace in our time." While his policy was a historic failure and Chamberlain's name would forever be synonymous with the word *appeasement,* the prime minister's actions were not those of a coward or a fool; he knew that Britain was pitifully unprepared for war. He may have been buoyed by false hope, but he was also fighting for time. There was not yet enough known about the Resistance to bet everything on the promises of a few senior officers to stage a coup d'état against Hitler if he moved against Czechoslovakia. Above all, Chamberlain still believed he could reason with Hitler.

Sir Ivo Mallet of the British Foreign Office echoed Chamberlain's sentiments when he said that this was no time to negotiate with "treasonous factions who had never given us any reason to suppose that they would be able or willing to take action such as would lead to the overthrow of the regime."[12] As it happened, General Beck resigned his post on the day Kleist-Schmenzin returned to Germany from Britain, hardly an auspicious omen for the Resistance, even though Beck's replacement, General Franz Halder, was also secretly committed to the movement against Hitler.

The German Foreign Ministry also harbored critics of Hitler who viewed the planned Czech adventure with alarm. It is not strange that Foreign Ministry experts resented Hitler's seemingly off-the-cuff, often mystical approach to foreign affairs. Nor is it difficult to understand why Ribbentrop, as pretentious as he was unqualified, exasperated the professionals when he took over the ministry in February 1938.

The number two man in the German Foreign Ministry, State Secretary Baron Ernst von Weizsäcker, was a good friend of Canaris's and collaborated with Oster in Resistance matters. A respected professional, he disapproved of Hitler's warlike foreign policy and hated Ribbentrop. Weizsäcker's official responsibilities nevertheless required him to take actions in support of Hitler's foreign policies and otherwise associate himself publicly with a regime that was anathema to him. By choosing to oppose Hitler from within the Nazi establishment, he would suffer the disapprobation of those who hated Hitler but were not aware of his secret cooperation with the Resistance. Another professional diplomat, Erich Kordt, strategically placed in the Foreign Ministry as head of the Ministerial Bureau for Information, was an active member of the Resistance, as was his brother, Theo Kordt, then serving as German chargé d'affaires in London.

Ribbentrop was presumably oblivious of Resistance activities within his ministry. He was unaware that with Oster's urging Weizsäcker and Erich Kordt had drafted a moving appeal to the British to take a hard line with Hitler at Munich and had it delivered to British Foreign Secretary Lord Halifax by Erich's brother, Theo, on September 7.[13] German Chargé Theo

Kordt secretly asked the British government for an "energetic declaration" against German action in Czechoslovakia. On his own initiative he told Lord Halifax that elements of the German military under Beck's secret orders "would know how to prevent an outbreak of war," euphemistically adding, "In that case there would be no Hitler."[14] This was stretching his Resistance instructions since at this time assassination, strongly implied in his words, was not part of the plan.

Theo Kordt, when he met with Halifax after slipping in through the garden door at 10 Downing Street, was explicit. Speaking as a member of the Resistance and reflecting a careful briefing by Oster that went further than Weizsäcker had intended, he requested a British public radio statement beamed at the Germans that would justify "the leaders of the Army to move against Hitler's policies by force of arms."[15]

But Kordt's presentation also failed to move either Halifax or Chamberlain. Plans for Munich were too far advanced. The prime minister had set his course. With advice from the ad hoc Committee on the Czechoslovakia Question, which consisted of appeasement-minded leaders, such as Lord Halifax, Sir John Simon, and Sir Samuel Hoare, Chamberlain was committed to peace, however much he must sacrifice for it. The torrent of intelligence pointing ominously at Hitler's plans and intentions had not really made much of a dent. What had made a large dent was British intelligence's overestimation of German military strength.[16]

The Resistance had perfected its blueprint for action, the so-called Halder-Witzleben-Oster Plan. With Generals Witzleben and Halder on their side, the Resistance was confident that it could muster enough military muscle in the Berlin area to stage a successful putsch. Oster had formed a small commando strike force headed by an Abwehr officer, Lieutenant Colonel Friedrich Wilhelm Heinz, a staunch monarchist, whose mission would be to capture Hitler. Despite plans made to put Hitler on trial, giving a patina of legality to the affair, Heinz fully intended to assassinate him so that he could not be used as a totem around which the Nazis, particularly the SS, could rally in a countercoup.[17]

The missing ingredient was still assurances by the British and French that they would set the stage by denouncing Hitler's plans for Czechoslovakia and make it clear that German invasion would trigger Allied intervention. The putsch could then be billed as saving Germany from Hitler's mad schemes of conquest and preventing a war for which the Third Reich was not prepared.

Weizsäcker's role at this time was useful because of his foreign contacts. He could, for example, count Carl J. Burckhardt, the League of Nations high commissioner in Danzig, as among his closest friends and collaborators in his secret strivings for peace. Contact between them was maintained by a German Foreign Ministry officer, Count William Ulrich Schwerin von Schwanenfeld, also a member of the Resistance.

Another accomplice in these matters was Italy's ambassador to Germany, Bernardo Attolico, a friend of Weizsäcker's. It is startling to realize that Germany's second-highest Foreign Ministry official, Baron von Weizsäcker, the Italian ambassador to Germany, Bernardo Attolico, and Ulrich von Hassell, the German ambassador to Italy, all were conspiring against Hitler's aggressive policies. Specifically they were consciously trying to undermine relations between Nazi Germany and Fascist Italy, central to Hitler's strategy as he veered toward a break with France and Great Britain.[18] Weizsäcker and Attolico had concluded that Mussolini and Hitler must be dissuaded from joint foreign adventures that could provoke a European war. During 1938 and 1939 Mussolini did, in fact, exercise caution in allying Italy with Hitler's actions in Czechoslovakia and Poland; it was likely that Attolico deserved some of the credit for this. The Italian ambassador was later quoted as complaining bitterly, "... here in Berlin we must deal with dangerous fools who have no idea of the world. . . . In Italy things are not much better."[19]

Attolico confided in Burkhardt that Weizsäcker uniquely understood how to meet the challenges facing the conspiracy. But with the military particularly in mind, he complained that others lacked "patience, knowledge of men, psychology and tact." He added that "the one thing that could become dangerous for him is the carelessness, the naïveté and indiscretion of the so-called conspirators." He specifically warned Weizsäcker that by being "in communication with Fritsch, with Beck, [and] with Witzleben," he had dangerous cohorts who in extremis would sell him out. The Resistance members, he predicted, will "all be locked up, disappear in camps. . . ." Attolico added admiringly that Weizsäcker, to the contrary, "does everything to prevent war with a dedication worthy of admiration. No one is able to catch him at anything."[20]

After the Munich crisis Weizsäcker continued to work for peace, trying to persuade Hitler not to seize Prague itself. To quote again his admirer Attolico: "He went as far in frank speech as it is at all possible with the monomaniac, this tyrant [Hitler] who talks on the verge of raving."[21]

DETERMINED TO FIND A FORMULA FOR PEACE THROUGH ACCOMMODATION, Chamberlain flew to Munich on September 15, then motored up the mountains to meet Hitler at his retreat above Berchtesgaden. News that the British prime minister in the role of supplicant was on his way to meet with Hitler, even before the results of their meeting could be known, filled

Canaris with despair. The Abwehr chief was dining with a few of his trusted officers when he learned of Chamberlain's fatal sally forth to treat with the devil. Canaris's friend and Abwehr associate the Austrian Erwin Lahousen remembered vividly how Canaris paced the room, leaving his food untouched and muttering about Chamberlain: "What, he—visited that man?" Canaris now knew without doubt that Great Britain was determined to capitulate on the Czechoslovakia issue; the generals would not have the excuse they needed to rise against Hitler. He feared specifically that Halder under the circumstances would waver.[22]

On September 22 Chamberlain had a second session with Hitler. In a dramatic midnight meeting Hitler confronted Chamberlain with what was in effect an ultimatum. The German leader was determined to seize the Sudetenland by October 1, 1938. Behind Chamberlain's back Hitler talked more ferociously; he promised to "smash the Czechs."

On September 28 General Halder and Witzleben agreed that Hitler had set a course for war; it was now or never that the Resistance must act. Despite his qualms, Halder saw Walther von Brauchitsch, commander in chief of the army, whom he thought he had convinced to move against the German leader. But at this crucial moment the picture changed; the putsch had to be postponed.

September 28 had been a crucial day. The ultimatum given by Hitler was due to expire at 2:00 P.M. In desperation Chamberlain had played an Italian card by telegraphing Mussolini and appealing to him to intervene in the interest of finding some peaceful solution. Hitler did in fact step back from the brink of war to convene a meeting of the principals when Il Duce suddenly announced his intention to visit and discuss with him the fate of Czechoslovakia. Chamberlain could now tell a cheering Parliament, "Herr Hitler has just agreed to postpone his mobilization for twenty-four hours and to meet me in conference with Signor Mussolini and M. Daladier at Munich."[23]

Mussolini's sudden self-insertion in the Czech crisis may have been influenced by Weizsäcker's and Attolico's "quiet" diplomacy. Even quieter, though perhaps more deft, were actions of Canaris. The Abwehr chief, who was close to the Italian intelligence chief General Roatta, had secretly convinced him to use his considerable influence with Mussolini to dissuade Hitler from provoking Britain and France to the point of war over the Czech crisis.[24] While Canaris and others in the Resistance wanted Britain and France to stand up to Hitler—certainly to make no agreement giving Czechoslovakia away to Germany—he did not want Hitler to provoke the Western Allies actually to go to war, engaging the Wehrmacht in combat before the Resistance could marshal its military forces to act.

On September 28, 1938, Mussolini arrived in Munich to convey Italy's views and informally to represent Hungarian and Polish interests as well. Quite full of himself, he expected to mediate an agreement on Czechoslovakia. The next day all concerned except the Czechs assembled to meet with Hitler. Mussolini's hastily conceived plan, drafted mainly by Hermann Göring, called for British and French acquiescence in a "peaceful" German occupation of the Sudeten. On September 30 a fragile peace had been secured, but at the price of Czechoslovakian territorial integrity. Germany now had license to occupy the Sudeten and would soon seize Prague as well.

The agreement signed in the small hours of the morning on September 30 but dated the day before, when discussions had begun, specified that the Czechs must evacuate the Sudetenland by October 10. An international arbitrator would decide when a plebiscite should be held and what the borders of a truncated Czechoslovakia would be. Poland would also receive a three-hundred-square-mile piece of the Czech corpse in Silesia.

The German chargé d'affaires in Prague was received by Czech Foreign Minister Kamil Krofta at 6:20 A.M. on September 30 and presented the text of the Munich agreement. France and Britain both urged Czech acceptance. Chamberlain's terse instructions to the British minister in Prague left no doubt about his attitude: "There's no time for agreement; it must be a plain acceptance."[25]

Krofta had the unenviable job of presenting the humiliating agreement to the Czech cabinet. He declared: "In theory, it is possible to reject it, [but it] would be followed by a German invasion, by a war in which nobody would join us, and by a Polish aggression. It is doubtful whether in such a situation the Soviets would wish to help us. . . ."[26] Czechoslovakia stood alone. Beneš and his cabinet had no choice but to accept a "solution" in which the Czechs had become another victim of Hitler's rapaciousness.

Hitler had been given everything he wanted, yet the Allies' capitulation depressed him. "Chamberlain spoiled an entry into Prague," he complained. The Führer would have preferred a triumphant military takeover of the whole country to a negotiated settlement. France's Premier Édouard Daladier, who understood the import of the agreement and was ashamed of it, was apprehensive about his homecoming. Would he be met in Paris by a public display of derision? (He was not.) Beneš of Czechoslovakia, who had not been consulted, gave in reluctantly but was understandably bitter and would soon have to seek exile. Only Chamberlain exulted.

Britain and France had crumpled in the face of Hitler's will rather than risk war—as the Führer had predicted, contrary to his generals' dire predictions. By appeasing Hitler, Chamberlain had sold out Czechoslovakia, a historic mistake that made war a certainty. After the Second World War the Czechoslovakian representative at the Nuremberg trials asked German Marshal Wilhelm Keitel, "Would the Reich have attacked Czechoslovakia in 1938 if the Western powers had stood by Prague?" The former chief of staff's answer from the dock was: "Certainly not. We were not strong enough militarily." Generals Fritz Erich von Manstein and Alfred Jodl both agreed that had Czechoslovakia appeared ready to defend itself and had France taken a more warlike posture in Czechoslovakia's support, Germany would have had to back down.[27]

CHAMBERLAIN HAD FRUSTRATED THE GERMAN RESISTANCE, WHOSE FORMULA for action was predicated on the Western Allies' holding the line on Czechoslovakia. Hitler could savor victory while the Resistance watched their last good opportunity to get rid of him evaporate. The eloquent Churchill, reminiscing about the Munich affair, stated that the "Führer's leadership had triumphed over the obstruction of the German military chiefs" and in fact "overawed them. Thus did Hitler finally become undisputed master of Germany. . . . The conspirators lay low and were not betrayed by their military comrades."[28]

German General von Kleist-Schmenzin, who had no sympathy for the Nazis, gave his opinion more briefly: "Hitler may be a swine, but the swine is lucky."[29] General Halder, in the heat of the Munich crisis, took the events very personally: He collapsed over his desk when he heard the news of Chamberlain's capitulation. Hans Bernd Gisevius, at one time affiliated with the Gestapo but now an Abwehr officer and Resistance fighter, reached a conclusion generally shared by other Resistance members: "Chamberlain saved Hitler." And in the cool light of retrospection, one of the papers presented at a 1958 seminar at Chatham House, the prestigious foreign affairs gathering place in London, pointed out the "bitter irony" that the "Western Allies virtually co-operated, not with the German Resistance, but with Hitler."[30]

When we look at the tragedy of Munich with the benefit of hindsight and untold volumes of latter-day analyses, we see that Chamberlain's brief, illusory peace was an inevitable culmination of Britain's and France's long toleration of Hitler's rise to power. In democracies the decibels of alarm bells must become shrill if people and governments are to be stirred to action. Resort to war is a difficult decision, not one to be taken lightly, particularly when only twenty years had elapsed since the "War to End All Wars" had ravaged Europe and at a time when Britain and France were woefully unprepared for another one. But in 1938 procrastination only meant that Poland, instead of Czechoslovakia, would serve as flash point for the Western Allies. Hitler's grab for Czechoslovakia did at last stiffen Allied resolve regarding Poland, even if the latter was one country too late and the wrong place to have taken a stand.

Britain's generally inhospitable reception to German Resistance overtures and its refusal to face the reality of Hitler's actions was not caused by ignorance; accurate intelligence may have been sparse, but the real problem was poor analysis of the intelligence that was in hand and the situation that faced it. Chamberlain's administration was riven by policy disagreements and internecine frictions while Whitehall lacked the machinery for central overall assessment. According to the authoritative book *British Intelligence in the Second World War*, Permanent Undersecretary Alexander Cadogan issued a minute explaining that secret agents who report somewhat indiscriminately "exercise a certain amount of discrimination themselves, but do not take the responsibility of too much selection. . . ." He admitted that it was Whitehall's "job to weigh up the information . . . and try to draw more or less reasonable conclusions from it."[31] In fact, the Secret Intelligence Service (MI-6), as well as other services, such as Vansittart's group within the Foreign Office, did produce considerable raw intelligence, but they all were inclined to withhold dissemination of items of doubtful credibility, and judgments on what was credible were not always correct.

Still, the underlying problem was Chamberlain's wishful thinking. He could not yet believe that Hitler was intent on conquest. The English poet John Dryden long ago diagnosed this disease of statesmen: "With how much ease believe we what we wish!"[32]

PART TWO

WAR

SEVEN

Case White:
Hitler Invades Poland

IN A CLOUD OF SELF-GENERATED EUPHORIA, PRIME MINISTER CHAMBERLAIN in February 1939 seemed to believe that everything he had seen pointed "in the direction of peace." And Foreign Secretary Halifax as late as March 13 found satisfaction in his perception that "rumors and scares had died down." Hitler "was not planning mischief in any particular quarter."[1] Two days later Hitler's forces occupied Prague.

Chamberlain's public optimism did not agree with more pessimistic messages sent to Washington in January. With Chamberlain's approval, Foreign Secretary Halifax provided Washington with a comprehensive situation analysis dated January 24, 1939, in which he tells of "a large number of reports from various reliable sources." Apparently an effort was now being made by the British to analyze available intelligence; at least Halifax's message was an effort to do so. The foreign secretary suggested that Hitler in his rage over Munich, which deprived him of war with Czechoslovakia, considered Britain "the chief obstacle . . . to the fulfilment of his further ambitions." Peace through negotiation, Hitler believed, lessened the warlike ardor of the German people, making it more difficult to stir them to the martial fervor necessary for larger-scale military aggression.[2] Earlier reports from November 1938 cited abundant evidence that Hitler was planning some "further foreign adventure." The question was, Where? At first it seemed as though he were looking eastward, even considering creating an independent Ukraine. But more recently advisers, such as Ribbentrop and Himmler, were pushing him to attack Western powers "as a preliminary to subsequent actions in the East."

In surveying the various possibilities, Halifax in his January message to Washington suggested that Hitler's motive would be economic: The dictator might see a foreign campaign as providing Germany with scarce commodities and distracting the people from domestic deprivation. Then, as an interesting item of speculation, Halifax gave another possible motive: insuring the loyalty of the army by keeping it busily engaged.

Halifax predicted that the danger period would begin in February, by which time the German mobilization would be completed. But for all its plausible argumentation, Halifax's seminal analysis in January prepared for President Roosevelt emphasized the dangers of an attack against Western powers and gave no inkling of either a nonaggression pact with Russia or a campaign against Poland. Halifax's language, while "not wishing to be alarmist," was just that: ". . . it is remarkable that there is one general tendency running through all the reports. . . . Hitler's mental condition, his insensate rage against Great Britain, and his megalomania . . . are entirely consistent with the execution of a desperate coup against the Western Powers."[3] Shining through Halifax's message was an impression that British sources were good, but Chamberlain and Halifax still found it difficult to abandon their hope, if not conviction, that Hitler had been bound over to peace at Munich.

Well warned by adequate intelligence, Chamberlain had had no basis for euphoria. His fantasies of peace unfolding leap from the pages of history like lines from Tweedledee's rendition of "The Walrus and the Carpenter" in *Alice in Wonderland*:

> The sun was shining on the sea,
> Shining with all his might:
> He did his very best to make
> The billows smooth and bright—
> And this was odd, because it was
> The middle of the night.[4]

Faith in Chamberlain's Munich as a magic wand of peace rapidly faded. Hitler paraded through Prague enveloped in an evil aura of triumph as he gave the Nazi salute to the dispirited Czechs from his open Mercedes staff car. Now it was obvious: Hitler's promises to Chamberlain at Munich had been empty. It was the twilight of a very long and dark night of war.

By March 30 some thirty leading Conservatives in the British Parliament, including Winston Churchill, were demanding a new government that could more effectively negotiate the shoals of mounting crisis. Churchill thundered: "This is only the beginning of the reckoning . . . the first foretaste of a bitter cup which will be proffered to us year by year unless, by a supreme recovery of moral health and martial vigour, we arise again and take our stand for freedom as in the olden time."[5] First Lord of the Admiralty Duff Cooper resigned; the rest of Chamberlain's shaken and disillusioned government could only wonder and worry. Where would Hitler strike next?

On the day following the fall of Prague, Viorel Virgil Tilea, the Romanian minister in London, rushed to the Foreign Office claiming that German panzers would soon slice through Hungary to invade Romania and seize its rich Ploesti oil fields to fuel Hitler's *Drang nach Osten*. Whatever his sources, the Romanian Foreign Ministry denied the rumors, but this flurry of alarm added to the confusion in Whitehall. All too real was the dismemberment of Czechoslovakia. Poland, about to be Hitler's next victim, grabbed the Czech frontier area of Teschen—an odd way to court friends such as Great Britain and France in Warsaw's hour of peril. Hungary too played the scavenging jackal when its troops moved into the eastern province of Czechoslovakia, the Carpatho-Ukraine.

Chamberlain seemed to have been surprised by Hitler's seizure of Prague. Despite intelligence warning, he had not expected it so soon and in such blatant disregard for the Munich agreement. Cadogan's diary comments suggest that Whitehall's problem was too much intelligence, or noise, as it is known in the trade, and too little analysis of the plentiful harvest of information. For months there had been much speculation that Hitler's next move would be to invade Poland, but as Cadogan describes it, "we were daily inundated by all sorts of reports. It just happened that these were correct; we had no means of evaluating their reliability at the time of their receipt. (Nor was there much that we could do about it!)"*

Now, in an abrupt about-face, the shocked prime minister excoriated Hitler in a speech delivered in Birmingham, accusing him of a flagrant breach of faith.

Intelligence reports beginning in mid-December 1938 described Hitler's ambitions, his dream of Lebensraum in the East.[6] By sending word

---

*By late 1940 British Lieutenant Colonel Kenneth Strong was forming up within the intelligence division of the War Office known as MI-14 a small unit (some twenty officers) dedicated to assessing more systematically German strategy and intentions. Another division of MI-14, which was headed by Brian Melland, focused its attention on the German intelligence and security organizations, the Abwehr, Sicherheitsdienst, and Gestapo. In this context it is unsettling to be reminded by former MI-14 officer Noel Annan in his recent book *Changing Enemies* that this group included Leo Long, a student of Soviet agent Anthony Blunt at Cambridge who had himself been recruited by Soviet intelligence.—Noel Annan, *Changing Enemies* (London: HarperCollins, 1995), p. 3.

through various secret emissaries, Admiral Canaris and his deputy Hans Oster were desperately trying to warn the Western Allies that they must prepare for war. Information originating with Canaris and meant for the British did in fact influence Britain to accelerate its preparations for hostilities. On March 29, after Hitler had annexed Bohemia and Moravia and occupied Prague, Chamberlain announced that he planned to double the Territorial Army.

In his wrap-up of events transmitted to the United States Halifax's rhetoric may have been useful in helping convince doubters there that Britain needed and deserved assistance, but there were lingering reservations about the accuracy of available intelligence since most of it came from the German Resistance, still viewed with some suspicion. Halifax seemed to have drawn the conclusion that what Canaris and others in the Resistance were reporting was exaggerated in an effort to encourage a more resolute British posture in opposition to Hitler's aggression. This may have been true, but if Canaris on occasion exaggerated information concerning imminent German attacks, his motive in prodding the Western Allies into taking a stand against Hitler and preparing for an onslaught that was sure to come was laudable, and the British should have been grateful, as events would soon show.[7] Reports in early 1939 that Hitler would soon attack Britain and France had been premature, but they were not exaggerated. They did in fact help convince the Allies to bestir themselves—and that was not a bad thing.

Poland's jeopardy now seemed inevitable, and the Western Allies certainly had advance word of "Case White," as the Wehrmacht referred to the coming Polish invasion, finally scheduled for September 1. There had been "plentiful intelligence about Germany's plans"[8] according to the monumental semiofficial British history published after the war. Throughout the spring of 1939 reports flowed in that Germany was specifically preparing for an attack on Poland,[9] even though Halifax chose not to mention it in his long report to Washington. Resistance activists Carl Goerdeler and Theo Kordt, particularly, confided in their British friends about German plans and exhorted them to stand firm against Hitler on the issue of Poland.[10]

One of Great Britain's best sources in this crisis was an Abwehr officer who had offered his services as a spy to the Czech Intelligence Service as early as February 1936. When Prague fell to the Germans, British intelligence took control of the case, working through the Free Czech organization in London. Paul Thümmel, alias A-54, would thereafter run up an enviable record of accurate predictions on every major event in wartime Europe, including the Czech invasion, the forthcoming Polish invasion, the invasion of France and the Lowlands, and the German invasion of Soviet Russia. Having come recommended by Heinrich Himmler, who had befriended him in the late 1920s, he was working in Dresden for Canaris's Abwehr when he made his treasonable arrangement with the Czechs. He was clearly one of the most valuable Allied spies of the war.

While Thümmel always claimed to have been willing to spy against the Nazi regime on his own volition, there remains the possibility that Canaris had put him up to it. This point was never resolved, but he was a good friend of the admiral's, and for all his dislike of the Nazis, he would have been unlikely to deceive him. He did not seem to want money for his information, so that is ruled out as a motive. Moreover, his services for the Czechs fitted the pattern of other Abwehr agents secretly dispatched by Canaris to provide Hitler's victims or potential victims with valuable forewarning as to Nazi intentions, as we shall see when the war progresses.

ALTHOUGH SOVIET RUSSIA HAD BEEN LEFT OUT OF THE CZECH CRISIS, IT could not be ignored in the Polish problem. The British Foreign Office and Soviet Foreign Commissar Maxim Litvinov had begun talks on Poland in mid-April. On April 16, 1939, Litvinov formally proposed a mutual assistance pact among the USSR, Britain, and France with provisions to include Poland. Its objective was to guarantee the states of Eastern and Central Europe against German aggression.

Since countries such as Poland, Romania, Finland, and the Balkan states feared the Soviet Union as much as they feared Germany, the Western Allies ultimately felt constrained to reject the offer. This was unfortunate since a tripartite alliance of Britain, France, and the USSR would have faced Germany with formidable two-front foes.

The Allied rejection contributed to souring the Soviet Union on the Western Allies, although talks continued. The negotiations became a charade; Stalin saw advantage in drawing them out simply to improve his bargaining position with the Germans. He was well aware that Whitehall, chronically wary of the Bolshevik "bogey," had little enthusiasm for an alliance with the Soviet Union. Unknown to the British, the Italian Intelligence Service had gained access to the British ambassador's safe in Rome; all correspondence was photographed daily by an agent who gave one copy to the Italian service—and a second copy to the Soviets. In this way Stalin had been able to read telegrams from British Foreign Secretary Halifax to the British Embassy in Berlin but passed to the British Embassy in Rome for its information. One of Halifax's messages made it clear that he would prefer reaching some modus vivendi with the Germans rather than the Soviets.[11]

An announcement from Moscow on May 3 that Litvinov was being replaced by Vyacheslav Molotov should have signaled a basic change in Soviet policy. In Stalin's opinion, Litvinov had not delivered the Western Allies, so must be replaced. The Soviet Union would now ally itself with Germany rather than risk war with Hitler; in the bigoted world of nazism it would not do to have such critical negotiations conducted with Germany by Litvinov, "a Jew."

While the British government could speculate that Litvinov's removal meant a new approach to Germany, Soviet overtures to Whitehall suggested that Stalin might still be amenable to a rapprochement with Great Britain if that were possible. The Soviet dictator's true intentions were enigmatic. The British were blind to developments in Moscow during most of the fateful summer of 1939, even though British intelligence did learn about the German side through spies and Resistance emissaries.[12]

The situation became clearer when, on August 21, Stalin announced the arrival of German Foreign Minister von Ribbentrop in Moscow to sign a nonaggression pact.[13] By the terms of this agreement Hitler could now gain access to vitally needed Soviet raw materials, such as oil, and Poland would be divided between the two powers. Germany would no longer have to fear Russian hostility on its eastern front.

What Stalin did not know then was that on the next day, August 22, 1939, an exhilarated Hitler gathered together top officials at his Berghof mountain retreat and cynically confided in them: "My pact was meant only to stall for time. . . . We will crush the Soviet Union."[14] Crushing Russia would mean war on two fronts in disregard of time-honored German Army doctrine, although Ribbentrop had solemnly assured Hitler that the British would not fight. The German foreign minister had always been better at telling Hitler what he liked to hear rather than arriving at sound judgments.

There was a secret annex to the German-Soviet pact assigning spheres of influence. This important document was kept from the Western Allies until a copy was discovered in the German archives soon after the war's end. It began to leak to the world in 1987, when the question of its release became an item of historical contention within the Soviet Communist party Politburo. The agreement bearing Molotov's and Ribbentrop's signatures was finally openly acknowledged as authentic in 1992 during Constitutional Court proceedings concerned with the legal status of the Communist party—all part of Boris Yeltsin's efforts to discredit his predecessor, Mikhail Gorbachev, and all other former Communist leaders.

The agreement was also relevant to the efforts of the Baltic states, Finland, Bessarabia, and Poland to free themselves from the Soviet grip in the

1980s since their capture by the USSR in World War II had been the result of this secret German-Soviet protocol drafted by the long-discredited wartime leaders of the two countries.[15]

When Chamberlain rashly guaranteed Poland's territorial integrity without getting a similar commitment from Stalin, the USSR seemed to gain protection from German aggression at no cost, but Canaris pointed out that there were drawbacks to such a Faustian deal. As head of the Abwehr Canaris was responsible for preparing an intelligence estimate for Hitler—really a warning—that was disseminated within the inner sanctum of the Nazi establishment in the wake of the German-Soviet pact. The admiral warned of the danger that Germany could become an "adjunct of the Russian world revolution" by allying itself with Stalin.[16]

Canaris had tried hard to convince Keitel that war with the West would be the consequence of invading Poland, but the field marshal remained confident that Britain and France would not fight on this issue any more than they had in the case of Czechoslovakia. While most of Canaris's diaries were lost or destroyed by war's end, a revealing account of the admiral's discussion about this with Keitel on August 17, 1939, survived because a copy had been made by Canaris's friend and colleague Erwin Lahousen. According to the diary, Canaris argued with Keitel that the British would at least blockade Germany and sink Germany's merchant shipping. The German Navy, he wrote, was able to put only ten submarines in the Atlantic at this time. Keitel minimized the effects of such a blockade on the ground that the Russians would supply the most vital commodity, oil.

Keitel did, however, believe that while it would be a good thing if Mussolini told Hitler Italy would not fight in the event of war with Poland, the Italian leader would in the end fight all the same. Canaris disagreed, citing a recent Ciano-Ribbentrop meeting and quoting Abwehr intelligence to the effect that the Italian king would not even sign a mobilization order. Canaris also warned Keitel that the British would respond to a Polish invasion by initiating action in the Balkans.[17]

Canaris exulted in news reaching the Abwehr on August 25 that Hitler had last-minute qualms about Case White and had withdrawn Halder's orders to march, thus suspending the attack on Poland. The admiral crowed to some of his Resistance colleagues: "Peace has been saved for the next twenty years." He could hope that perhaps his lobbying had had some impact on Hitler after all. Resistance activist Gisevius was more cynical and predicted that the warmongers Himmler and Ribbentrop would again prevail and that Hitler's hesitancy was only temporary.[18] Gisevius was right: The Führer would not temporize for long.

IN THE MEANTIME STALIN WAS UNAWARE OF HITLER'S SECOND THOUGHTS. Surrounded by a few of his top functionaries, including Nikita Khrushchev, Nikolai Bulganin, Anastas Mikoyan, and Kliment Voroshilov, Stalin had dined at his dacha late in the evening of August 24, 1939. The dictator was in high spirits according to Khrushchev. Having just agreed to a draft agreement negotiated by Molotov and Ribbentrop, Stalin believed he had pulled a fast one on the British and French, whose representatives had simultaneously been laboring in vain to reach an accord with the USSR. Stalin had what he considered a good deal.

Long after the war Khrushchev analyzed Stalin's motives in his memoirs. He believed neither Stalin nor Hitler considered the treaty a definitive or lasting reflection of Soviet-German relations. Both leaders had their own objectives: Stalin hoped he could delay an attack by the German Army in this way and direct Hitler's aggression against the West instead.[19] The treaty would give the Soviets access to the Baltic Sea and permit annexation of Latvia, Lithuania, and part of Poland. It would also provide the Soviets with stategically important territorial advantage in Bessarabia, Romania, and eastern Finland as well as eastern Poland. Above all, it would buy Stalin time to build up the Red Army, crippled by the Great Purge and divided between Europe and the Far East by the Japanese threat. Khrushchev also believed that Stalin, influenced by the disastrous Finnish campaign, had lost confidence in his army's ability to fight.[20]

Hitler's emotional harangue of August 22, in which he had revealed the German-Soviet pact, had been top secret and strictly off the record, but Canaris, sitting in the back of the room, recognized its importance and discreetly took notes.[21] He had several copies of his notes made for judicious distribution. A Resistance fighter, Hermann Maass, a Social Democrat in the Weimar government, received a copy on August 24, one week before the German Army was scheduled to roll over Poland. At Beck's suggestion, Maass rushed a copy to the American journalist Louis Lochner, bureau chief of the Associated Press in Berlin.

On August 25, Lochner called on the U.S. chargé d'affaires in Berlin, Alexander Kirk, and offered him the electrifying document, which not only signaled the imminence of World War II but revealed Hitler's intention of allying Germany with the Soviet Union. Kirk, known as "the man in gray" (famous in the Foreign Service for his philosophy: Nothing is black and white in this world, only shades of gray) had a wardrobe exclusively in gray, from socks to hat. His reaction to Lochner's story was, however, a brooding black. Kirk called the report "dynamite" because he knew that Hitler was at that moment in negotiations with British Ambassador Sir Nevile Henderson in an effort to find a peace accord. Perhaps fearing that Lochner's information, by uncovering Hitler's deception, would cause the British to break off negotiations, Kirk refused to have anything to do with it, much less send it on to Washington, where it might get wide distribution.[22]

With Kirk's apparent display of uninterest as Europe teetered on the brink of war, Lochner rushed his treasure to a British friend, Sir George Ogilvie-Forbes, who saw to it that it was passed to the Foreign Office.[23] The Foreign Office was of course not surprised. News of the historic meeting that Hitler had held with his top military chiefs outlining his schedule of aggression had been already passed indirectly to the British by Canaris.

The ever-alert *News Chronicle* Berlin correspondent Ian Colvin had picked up the news from Resistance leaders Beck and Oster, both of whom had passed it on with Canaris's knowledge.[24] Colvin flew to London on March 28, 1939, to discuss it personally with Sir Alexander Cadogan and Lord Halifax. The Germans, Colvin also learned, might not have yet moved troops to the border, as Beck reported, but had stored military rations for an invasion of Poland, scheduled originally for March 31. When Colvin talked with Chamberlain himself, describing the imminence of a German invasion, the prime minister listened attentively and was moved. He announced almost immediately a declaration guaranteeing British defense of Poland in the event of a German attack.[25]

Chamberlain's speech to Parliament on March 31 was strong in its condemnation of Hitler, with whom he was now utterly disillusioned. It put the Führer on notice: "In the event of any action which clearly threatened Polish independence . . . His Majesty's Government would feel itself bound at once to lend the Polish Government all support in their power."[26] The British prime minister added that the French stood with Great Britain on this matter. Chamberlain's sudden hawkish stance on Poland was perhaps as misbegotten as his previous capitulation on Czechoslovakia. As Duff Cooper remarks in his war memoir, "Never before in our history have we left in the hands of one of the smaller powers the decision whether or not Britain goes to War."[27] This was a recipe for war; all the ingredients were in the pot, and the pot was beginning to bubble over.

Chamberlain's about-face came as a rude shock to Hitler. According to Canaris, who by chance was in Hitler's presence when the Führer received the news of the prime minister's challenge, Hitler became almost apoplectic with rage. As he pounded the table, he screamed, "I'll cook them a stew they will choke on."[28]

Five Resistance leaders—General Beck; the former mayor of Leipzig, Dr. Carl Goerdeler; the German ambassador to Rome, Ulrich von Hassell; the Army chief of economic warfare, General Georg Thomas; and Colonel Hans Oster—collaborated in sending a secret letter to Field Marshal Keitel, chief of the German High Command, protesting plans to invade Poland on the ground it would ignite war with Britain and France. Keitel was unmoved.

The British Foreign Office was still in close touch with the German chargé in London Theo von Kordt, who, as a member of the Resistance, had earlier discussed the Czech crisis with Vansittart of the Foreign Office. As war clouds gathered, Kordt was about to be transferred to Switzerland, thanks to Resistance influence within the German Foreign Ministry. His loss in London would be felt, but he would at least remain in secret contact with the British in Switzerland.

Goerdeler and Schacht in late March had discussed Hitler's plans for Poland with notables in London. Then, on May 6, Goerdeler told the Foreign Ministry of a "new and unexpected offer from the Soviet Union [to the Germans] which might entirely change the situation."[29] In June 1939 Canaris had sent still another Resistance agent, Colonel (ret.) Hans Böhm-Tettelbach, to London for secret meetings with Sir James Greg. Weizsäcker of the German Foreign Ministry was in touch with Vansittart of the British Foreign Office, whom he kept current on the secret German-Soviet negotiations and forthcoming invasion of Poland throughout the summer of 1939. Adam von Trott zu Solz, an Oxford graduate and Count Helmuth von Moltke, who were the inspiration for the so-called Kreisau Circle of civilian intellectuals working with the Resistance, continued to meet with influential friends in England.[30] And in mid-August Ulrich von Hassell talked with British Chargé Henderson in Berlin, who assured him that an invasion of Poland would trigger war. "Now," as Henderson put it, "it was impossible for Chamberlain to fly here again with his umbrella."[31] If Resistance sources were not enough to convince the British of impending peril, Soviet GRU (military intelligence) defector Walter Krivitsky had told Britain's internal security organization, MI-5, of the possibility of a German-Soviet pact.[32]

Despite this avalanche of alerts, the British were strangely reluctant to believe that Hitler and Stalin would actually join hands. The reports were suspected of being either a form of Soviet pressure to bring the British to reach agreement with them or a ploy by the Germans to disrupt the Anglo-Soviet negotiations. The British, whose negotiations with the Soviets had not progressed—understandably in view of what had occurred—could only await developments, fearing the worst but still hoping for the best.

Recognizing Mussolini's differences with Hitler, the Western Allies had earlier hoped to bring about Italy's defection from Germany's camp. But when Chamberlain and Foreign Secretary Halifax paid a visit to Il Duce on January 11, 1939, the Italian dictator had not been impressed; his reaction after they had left was perhaps summed up in his quip "These men are not made of the same stuff as Francis Drake."³³ Mussolini had his own plans of aggression. In a venomous speech on March 16 he pressed Italian claims in the Mediterranean, most of which were at French expense. Behind the scenes he soon planned to take Albania, a springboard for invading Greece. He could see in Hitler's explosive plans, certain to ignite a European war, disruption of his own, more modest blueprint for glory.

Ironically, while the American ambassador to Great Britain, Joseph Kennedy, unashamed defeatist, was trying to convince Chamberlain's top adviser Sir Horace Wilson that Poland could not be saved and its resistance to Hitler could only "plunge all of Europe into destruction," Mussolini was making a last-ditch effort to convince Hitler not to march against Poland for fear of starting a war. Mussolini wrote Hitler on August 25, stating, "This is one of the most painful moments of my life, but I must tell you that Italy is not ready for war."³⁴ Canaris, who had an extremely close relationship with the head of Italian intelligence, may well have played a role in forming Mussolini's attitude.

Even Reichsmarschall Hermann Göring, for his own reasons, was against invading Poland and had made his voice heard well before war broke out. Göring's aide General Karl Bodenschatz testified at the end of the war: "Six months before the War, Reichsmarschall Goering and I met [at Göring's seaside house near Sylt-Westerland] some influential English industrialists [concerning] the madness of waging war on each other."³⁵ Göring also began a strange dialogue with the British through a neutral Swedish businessman, Birger Dahlerus, apparently with peace as its objective but with an undercurrent of self-preservation.

Göring had quailed at the thought of a war involving Great Britain and France. Besides its being a dangerous gamble for Germany, which, Göring believed, would ultimately be forced to face the United States, his own fortunes would be inextricably bound up with those of a defeated Germany. How much better to live the good life of personal indulgence and power uncomplicated by a war that might not come out right. Göring, like the Resistance but with more selfish motives, could wonder if Hitler was right in believing that the Western democracies would not fight a war over Poland. Was the Führer plunging toward catastrophe by provoking them? Hitler, the gambler, enjoyed defying the odds but, like all gamblers, did not always win. Although he was convinced that Chamberlain, beset by his Munich mentality, would anyway accept Germany's conquest of Poland rather than risk war, Hitler was not averse to dangling tempting propositions that would satisfy German objectives yet formally commit the British to accepting Germany's invasion of Poland—and ultimately an invasion of Soviet Russia itself. How much better to put the British out of play on Poland, as in the case of Czechoslovakia, in exchange for some face-saving provisions (probably later to be ignored), such as German recognition of the inviolability of Britain's overseas empire. If Britain were willing to agree to something along these lines, France would follow suit. After the Soviet Union had been dealt with in a single-front war, there would be time enough to force neutralized France and Britain into vassalage. Hitler never scrupled over breaking his word.

Hitler tolerated, even encouraged Göring's efforts through Dahlerus to neutralize the British while Case White, the subjection of Poland, went forward. This provided Göring with the perfect cover under which to deal with the British for more daring, self-serving proposals, such as securing peace with a Germany *minus Hitler*. Göring's confidant, General Bodenschatz, certainly with Göring's complicity, had secretly informed the British of the Soviet-German talks pointing toward a nonaggression pact between the two countries. Although this highly classified disclosure could have been simply a gambit to upset ongoing British-Soviet talks, it seemed to have been something else,[36] perhaps an effort by Göring to ingratiate himself. And significantly, Swedish pro-German industrialist Axel Wenner-Gren reported to Göring that Chamberlain had recognized some of his secret démarches as being "out of step with Hitler."[37] The *Reichsmarschall* was playing a dangerous game through Dahlerus. But just who was this Swedish intermediary, and what was his role?

EIGHT

The Göring Connection

WHILE MUNICH WILL STAND AS AN LONG-REMEMBERED OBJECT LESSON IN the folly of making deals with perfidious statesmen, Hermann Göring's effort in behalf of Hitler to con Chamberlain once again into acquiescence as Germany prepared to invade Poland is less well known.

Chamberlain was faced with a dilemma: He desperately wanted peace because Great Britain was not prepared for war. On the other hand, he now knew he could not trust Hitler's word. Perhaps because hope is the only antidote to despair, Chamberlain seemed at least willing to hear Göring's siren song, as rendered by a well-meaning devotee of peace, a Swedish businessman named Birger Dahlerus. This neutral intermediary shuttled secretly between Göring and Whitehall in what proved a vain effort to commit Britain to peace while Hitler prepared to seize part of Poland—this, despite strong intimations reaching the British of an impending German-Soviet pact that would doom Poland and the rest of Eastern Europe. Uttered sotto voce by Göring in the course of his negotiations were innuendos that he, as heir apparent, would be willing to oust Hitler and rule a more peaceful Germany himself if the British thought they could not deal with the Führer. This drama is worth noting as another example of duplicity within Hitler's court and reveals an atmosphere of desperate frustration within Whitehall.

BIRGER DAHLERUS'S FRIENDSHIP WITH HERMANN GÖRING BEGAN IN November 1934, when the Swedish machine tool manufacturer sought the

German's help in getting the necessary permits from the Nazi bureaucracy for marriage to his German fiancée. In May 1935 Göring asked Dahlerus to do him a favor in return. The *Reichsmarschall's* stepson in Sweden, Thomas von Kantzow, needed a job, and Dahlerus was more than happy to oblige his influential friend by fixing the boy up with a suitable position.[1]

As the thunderheads of war became ever more ominous, Dahlerus, whose ties with Britain were strong, became involved in a plan to organize informal meetings between prominent British business friends and influential German officials. Dahlerus claimed that the idea originated with him, as it may well have. But it is also possible that he was encouraged in it by the British. At least Foreign Secretary Halifax in early July 1939 endorsed the idea that Dahlerus travel to Berlin and take soundings of his German contacts. Dahlerus had gained the impression that the British would be willing to go "so far but no farther" toward assuring peace, but they would not seek it "at any price," unlike the case of Munich. To kick off this ambitious undertaking, Dahlerus had first invited several of his British friends to a dinner on July 2, at the Constitution Club.

The specific problem under discussion concerned Poland: How could war be avoided when Germany was demanding the port of Danzig and a corridor linking Danzig with Germany, while Britain had guaranteed Poland's territorial integrity? The consensus of Dahlerus's friends was that Britain wanted peace but that Hitler's aggressive ambitions were exasperating; he seemed intent on holding the line on Poland. A German seizure of Danzig would force the British to honor their commitments to Poland and, if necessary, enforce them by war. However desirable peace may have been, Britain would not buy it at the expense of Poland.

With the benefit of an official, though highly informal, endorsement of these views from Foreign Secretary Lord Halifax, Dahlerus met Göring at Karinhall, the *Reichsmarschall's* estate near Berlin, and presented him with what he described as a likely British position. More practically he convinced Göring that a preliminary conference should be held in which representative members of the British business establishment would meet with responsible Nazi officials in an informal effort to find a formula for reconciliation—one that might be acceptable to Hitler and Chamberlain. The meeting would take place at an estate at Sonke Nissen Koog in North Friesland on the west coast of Schleswig-Holstein owned by Dahlerus's wife. Lord Halifax gave Dahlerus his blessing while emphasizing that the conclave should not in any way implicate the British government. Hitler similarly agreed to such an informal gathering but insisted that it be kept strictly secret.

Dahlerus's meeting did in fact take place in early August. Supporting Göring on the German side were his friends Adjutant Ministerialrät Gornnert, Four-Year Plan chief Paul Körner, and General Bodenschatz, whom Göring used to maintain liaison with the Führer's office. The British representatives included Brian Mountain, Sir Robert Renwick, Charles Maclaren, T. Mensforth, A. Holden, Charles Spencer, and Stanley Rawson.[2] Dahlerus believed that this amiable group had at least agreed that a more official conference should be held to defuse the tense situation. The Germans in attendance even nodded yes to the British idea that such a meeting should be a four-power conference with Britain, Germany, France, and Italy participating.

What the British contingent, and presumably Dahlerus as well, did not know was that Göring was fully aware that Hitler and Stalin were on the verge of signing a pact that would doom Poland. At the meeting Göring never went beyond saying, "We still have many friends in Russia." A few days later, however, on August 12, an apparently frustrated Göring confided in a British guest at Karinhall, the son of British Lord Runciman, that if his English were only better, he would visit London and impress upon the British: "If there were war between us now, the real victor would be Stalin."[3] On that same day, as British negotiations with the USSR became hopelessly mired in disagreement, Stalin agreed to hold talks with Ribbentrop.

Only two days later, on August 14, at a landmark meeting, the Führer informed Göring and the other German service chiefs that he had made the decision to invade Poland on August 25. Hitler was confident that the British and the French would not fight.

Army Chief of Staff General Franz Halder, a Resistance accomplice, left a diary record of Hitler's decision to risk war by invading Poland. He quotes the Führer stating his opinion that Britain stood to lose by war. "This is the key to an understanding of the actions of men of less than heroic cast," he said. Moreover, British armaments were inadequate for waging war; the British "armament program [was] being pushed in too many areas, with resulting mutual interference." As for France, Hitler dismissed its army as "limited" and hopelessly outdated.

Halder's diary comments on what Hitler conceived to be Britain's reluctance to field an army in defense of Poland: "If Britain had made any positive commitments, the Poles would be much more cocky." Halder in an enigmatic aside writes: "Tapped telephone conversations! *Führer is concerned lest Britain hamper showdown by last-minute offers*" (Halder's italics)—shades of Munich. Relevant to this, Halder in an August 26 diary entry refers to a contrary assessment made by Canaris, again in italics for emphasis: "*Positive evidence that Britain will strike.*"

In summing up, Hitler said: "The last weeks have brought increasing convictions of [Poland's] isolation." Anyway, "Poland will be polished off in six or eight weeks even if Britain should step in." As for Stalin, Hitler believed that "Russia has no intention of pulling Britain's chestnuts out of the fire. Stalin has to fear a lost war as much as he would a victorious army." Halder interestingly interpreted Hitler's summary conviction with a question mark. "Central problem is Poland. Must be carried off at all cost?"[4] "All cost" could be very expensive.

On August 18 Sir Robert Vansittart telephoned Lord Halifax, who was relaxing in Yorkshire, and in guarded language let it be known that there was a crisis looming that made it imperative the foreign secretary return to London. One of Vansittart's mysterious sources, a "German diplomat" in The Hague, had reported that a German attack on Poland was almost definite within two weeks. Sir Alexander Cadogan of the Foreign Office added his voice to convince the foreign secretary of the urgency, even though "it was impossible to feel certain about Van's [Vansittart's] information."[5] Halifax, Cadogan, and Vansittart met and agreed that Mussolini should be asked to use his relationship with Hitler to keep Hitler from invading Poland.

On August 22 Hitler's nonaggression pact with Stalin was signed. That was the day Hitler briefed some fifty of his top military men of this momentous decision at a secret Berchtesgaden meeting.[6] A despairing Canaris, sitting inconspicuously in the rear, jotted down Hitler's words, including the phrase "I have only one fear: that at the last moment some *Schweinhund* may offer to mediate"—again this obsession to avoid another Munich-style stand-down.

Dahlerus went to see Göring at Karinhall on August 24, despite a warning from a Swedish banker friend in Berlin, Allan Weltermark, that he would be "risking arrest if he discussed peace plans with Göring against Hitler's will." Göring urged his friend to advise the British quickly that it was important that they initiate negotiations as soon as possible—the very thing that Hitler had made clear he did not want if that meant a Munich solution. The only kinds of negotiations Hitler wanted would be those leading to British acceptance of his invasion of Poland. The charade continued: The British ambassador to Germany, Sir Nevile Henderson, was called in to confer with Hitler with regard to opening official channels for negotiations or at least discussions.

British MI-6 deputy chief Stewart Menzies reported to Halifax that he had been approached by Dahlerus with the suggestion that Göring come to London to talk with Chamberlain. (This suggests that Dahlerus was a SIS contact, if not agent, whose role as intermediary with Göring may have been arranged in the first place and handled by Menzies.) The British were agreeable, and the necessary arrangements were made for him to fly secretly to London on August 23. The visit never occurred, but the fact it was proposed dramatized the seriousness of the times.[7]

Dahlerus saw Lord Halifax on August 14 and briefed him on the August 7 meeting at Sonke Nissen Koog. Of greater importance, Dahlerus conveyed Göring's sense of urgency as revealed in a recent phone call to him. The *Reichsmarschall* feared war at any minute, blaming his pessimism on news that Chamberlain had signed a pact with Poland at almost the same time that Henderson had been meeting with Hitler. Hitler, turning things upside down, believed this action gave the lie to British protestations that they wanted peace.[8]

At Dahlerus's recommendation, Halifax drafted a personal letter to Göring reiterating Britain's genuine hope that a peaceful settlement could be made. Chamberlain approved the letter, and Dahlerus duly delivered it to Göring at Karinhall on August 27. Dahlerus impressed on Göring how resolute Britain was with respect to its promise to stand by Poland in the event of German aggression and how important it was for Germany to avoid actions that could trigger war. According to Dahlerus, Göring was moved by Halifax's letter and dashed back to Berlin to show it to Hitler even though it was in the middle of the night and the Führer had to be roused from deep sleep.

Göring sent for Dahlerus to join him with Hitler. As the Swedish businessman–cum–British "friend" entered the Führer's study after marching through the "long gallery" of the chancellery, he came face-to-face with Hitler for the first time. After a brief acknowledgment of Dahlerus's presence, the Führer launched into a monologue about German aims and his hope of reaching an understanding with Great Britain. As he warmed to the subject, his criticism of the British became more strident; he blamed them for not having any genuine desire to cooperate.

Dahlerus found Hitler's demagogic effort to "force his point" emotional and increasingly tedious. Seizing an opportunity to interrupt, Dahlerus said he could not agree with the harsh criticisms of the British. Having once worked as a common laborer in England, he said he had developed a high respect for the British workingman and the British people in general. This seemed to hit a responsive chord in Hitler, who switched gears and spent a half hour questioning Dahlerus about the British lower classes. Hitler concluded that anyhow there was a multitude of less estimable plutocrats in England.[9]

Dahlerus recalls that suddenly Hitler "stopped in the middle of the room and stood there staring. His voice became blurred and his behavior was that of a completely abnormal person . . . and finally one could not follow him at all."[10]

Dahlerus describes Hitler's "mental equilibrium as patently unstable." The Führer was highly agitated and nervous, repeating again and again his conviction that Germany was irresistible and that he could win by means of a rapid war. "If there should be war," he said, "*dann werde ich U-boote, U-boote* [then I will become a U-boat, a U-boat]." According to Dahlerus, Hitler's voice "became more indistinct. . . . He seemed more like a phantom from a story book than a real person." Dahlerus was shocked; he could only think, "Here is the man who holds not only the fate of his own people in his hand, but those whose actions can influence a whole continent, the state of a whole world, the weal or woe of millions of people. . . ."

Dahlerus remembers Hitler's eyes as glassy, his voice unnatural as he uttered inane homilies such as "If there should be no butter, I shall be the first to stop eating butter—eating butter." When he finally stopped his strange monologue, he asked Dahlerus for his analysis of the British attitude. The Swede frankly replied that the difficulties posed by the British "are founded on a lack of confidence in you, personally, and in your government."[11] This provoked an outburst from Hitler: "Idiots. Have I ever told a lie in my life?" In ending the interview, Hitler exhorted Dahlerus to go to England at once and give the British the benefit of his views, adding: "I do not think that [British Ambassador] Henderson understood me. . . ."

Dahlerus protested that he would need a clear definition of Hitler's position, particularly his stand on Danzig. This made Hitler smile—the only time he ever smiled in Dahlerus's presence. Göring at this point reached for an atlas on a nearby table and, turning to a map of Europe, tore out the page on Poland and hastily ringed in red pencil the territory that Germany wanted.[12]

Dahlerus committed to memory Hitler's terms so that he could pass them on accurately to Halifax. Germany wanted to sign a pact with Great Britain resolving all their difficulties. Britain must agree to back Germany's efforts to gain a free port in Danzig, accessible by a land corridor, although Poland would be awarded a corridor to Gdynia and Germany would guarantee Poland's borders. Hitler insisted that agreement must be reached about Germany's former colonies, and there must be guarantees for protecting German minorities in Poland. Lastly, in a show of "magnanimity," Hitler pledged Germany to defend the British Empire with the Wehrmacht, wherever necessary.[13]

Dahlerus was delivered to England by a German aircraft with his vital communication committed to memory rather than entrusted to the written word, which could be compromising to Hitler if it fell into the wrong hands. Dahlerus's heady mission filled his thoughts; he could be the instrument of achieving peace in a world threatened by a war potentially more destructive than any war in history, or, he wondered, was he merely "a pawn in a game of intrigue?" He writes in his memoir of his role as go-between: "I realized that I was dealing with a person who could not be considered normal."

In London Dahlerus was received by Chamberlain, Halifax, and Cadogan at 10 Downing Street immediately upon his arrival. They were dubious about the proposals he brought, but the Swedish go-between was struck by Chamberlain's determination to "avert a catastrophe"—i.e., avert war—for all his distrust of Hitler. The prime minister told Dahlerus that his government was about to send Ambassador Henderson back to Berlin with an official communication to Hitler but agreed that Dahlerus should see Hitler first to "test the water."[14] As Chamberlain bade Dahlerus farewell, Cadogan described Britain's feelings toward Germany in a phrase: "This gangster policy will have to cease. Britain would have to formulate her demands and proposals so as to put a stop to Hitler's advance along the road leading to disaster for the whole of Europe."

Cadogan's specific points entrusted to Dahlerus for delivery were informally keyed to Hitler's proposed terms. The British agreed in principal to try to reach agreement through special negotiations. The questions of Danzig and the Polish Corridor should be solved by negotiations between Germany and Poland. The British held that Hitler's promise to guarantee Poland's borders was inadequate; the borders must be guaranteed by the USSR, Italy, France, and Britain as well as by Germany. Two of Hitler's points were predictably rejected as totally unacceptable: the restoration of Germany's pre–World War I colonies and Germany's presumptuous and condescending offer to defend the British Empire.

The peripatetic Dahlerus rushed back to Berlin. Göring was pessimistic; the British position, he thought, would be unsatisfactory to Hitler; moreover the situation was "highly precarious." Hitler's reaction, however, was surprisingly positive. He would respect Britain's insistence on a five-power international guarantee of Poland's borders and agreed that Germany and Poland should settle the Danzig matter through direct, bilateral negotiations. On the face of it this seemed to mean that Hitler would shelve his plans to invade Poland, a development of major significance. Hitler insisted only that when Ambassador Henderson arrived with Britain's formal response, his démarche be consistent with the informal points presented by Dahlerus. Moreover, Hitler made it clear that Henderson's note must not yet be made public, nor should mention be made of any exchange of views the British might have had with the United States.[15]

Dahlerus was optimistic when he reported his conversation with Hitler to Sir George Ogilvie-Forbes, British chargé in Henderson's absence, for transmitting to London. Yet Göring remained the picture of gloom. He re-iterated that the situation was serious and the hour late. The Polish Army, he reported, was ready to march, and the German mobilization was com-plete. Dahlerus also gained from Göring's remarks that Hitler was being buffeted by a battle of wills between the *Reichsmarschall,* on one hand, and other Nazi leaders, such as Himmler and Ribbentrop, on the other.

For another point of view, it is interesting to note the comments of For-eign Ministry official Ulrich von Hassell to the infighting going on around Hitler as his senior lieutenants jockeyed for favor during this crisis. In his diary entry of August 7, 1939, Hassell accuses Ribbentrop of behaving "like a lunatic—unbearable in the office." The foreign minister, adds Hassell, "is in bad with Goering."[16]

At 1:00 A.M., August 29, Dahlerus heard from Colonel Conrad of the British Embassy in Berlin that Henderson's note had been received by Hitler. The message submitted by the British ambassador was indeed con-sistent with the points made informally in advance by Dahlerus.

When Dahlerus saw Bodenschatz and Göring at 11:00 A.M., there was an atmosphere of unbounded euphoria. Bodenschatz was "delighted" with developments, and Göring fairly yelled with joy: "We'll have peace. Peace has been assured!" Göring confided in Dahlerus that at his meeting with Hitler the Führer had turned to Ribbentrop and said mockingly, "Do you still believe that Dahlerus is a British agent?" The German foreign minister allegedly mumbled acidly that "perhaps this is not the case."

Dahlerus met with Henderson, who looked tired and somehow older. He was pessimistic, reporting: "Under no circumstances could one believe a word of what Hitler said." The ambassador was also skeptical of Göring's word. The *Reichsmarschall* had often lied, although Henderson admitted that he was easier to deal with than other German leaders. In Henderson's last meeting with Ribbentrop, for example, the session had turned into a shouting match. Ribbentrop's attitude had "increased in violence" with each point Henderson made in his démarche as he "kept jumping to his feet in a state of great excitement."[17]

In fact, Hitler had no intention of abandoning his plans for Poland. Late in the evening of August 29, when Henderson met with Hitler, the talks had gone sour when the Führer demanded that if peace was to be preserved, a Polish delegate must arrive in Berlin for negotiations on August 30—within hours. This was a new, unexpected barrier. Henderson called the German demands, as phrased, outrageous and tantamount to an ultimatum. This in turn caused Hitler "to fly into a tantrum, painful and violent."[18]

Göring, who had spoken with Hitler after Henderson's departure, gave Dahlerus the bad news. The *Reichsmarschall* was upset and nervous. He blamed Henderson for the row and saw it as proof that the British did not want an agreement with Germany. In a tirade of vituperation against the British, he told Dahlerus that "sixty German divisions are waiting [on the Polish border] — that means about one million men, so settlement must be reached without delay."[19]

Göring said good-bye to Dahlerus in such a way as to cause the Swedish intermediary to conclude that they might never meet again. The *Reichsmarschall* explained ominously, ". . . certain people are doing what they can to prevent you from getting out of this alive!"[20] According to Dahlerus's memoir, Ribbentrop had tried to arrange for his aircraft to develop "motor trouble" and crash; this had accounted for Göring's somber comments. As a rabid Anglophobe Ribbentrop had, in Dahlerus's opinion, convinced Hitler that aggression against Poland would not provoke war with France and Britain,[21] a cataclysmic misjudgment typical of the German foreign minister.

Even at this late hour Dahlerus would not give up. Time was running out, however, and any new moves must be made quickly. Dahlerus urged Göring to fly immediately to London and attempt himself to reach some sort of agreement forestalling war. The *Reichsmarschall*, having recently been designated heir to power in Germany by Hitler, was impressed with his new importance and still intrigued by the dream of "saving the world from war." Ribbentrop had so far spoiled his hopes of being architect of a successful peace plan, depriving him of the prestige that would have crowned his career, but perhaps there was still time to find a formula for settlement with the British. Göring instructed Bodenschatz to prepare an aircraft to stand by for a flight to London.[22]

At first Hitler appeared to have agreed with this idea, provided the British would receive Göring, but Chamberlain would not consider it unless Hitler responded to the British ultimatum by calling off the invasion of Poland. And the tenor of Hitler's response to this would determine whether or not Halifax would receive Göring for further talks.[23]

Göring joined Dahlerus at a picnic table set up under the trees beside the *Reichsmarschall*'s private command train to break the news of Hitler's negative response. The Führer was clearly not interested in having Göring fly to England; the time for negotiations had passed — if it had ever existed. Shortly after the deadline set for 11:00 A.M., September 2, a somber Chamberlain went on the radio to announce that Great Britain was at war with Germany.

SS CHIEF HEYDRICH HAD SOUGHT THE SERVICES OF THE ABWEHR TO PROvide Polish uniforms in which to dress a group of SD agents and German concentration camp inmates to simulate dead Polish soldiers in creating an incident on the Polish border at Gleiwitz. This was meant to provide an excuse for invasion.[24] Canaris could not refuse the request but when he learned of the intended purpose of the uniforms, he had alerted the *Oberkommando der Wehrmacht* (OKW) chief of staff, General Keitel, describing the deliberate violation of international rules of engagement in war, and complained that the Abwehr had been duped. But in an August 17 meeting, Keitel, known within the Resistance as the Rubber Lion, predictably would do nothing to interfere with Hitler's plan for a fabricated casus belli.

Canaris and others in the Resistance had done all in their power to prevent Hitler from going to war. As the invasion approached, Canaris sent a warning to the British through their military attaché in Berlin, Major Denis Daly, that an air raid on London was scheduled for September 3. (However well intentioned, Canaris's tip proved wrong; the raid was postponed.) The admiral and a few of his closest colleagues in the Resistance listening to the BBC World Service had been deeply depressed when Neville Chamberlain announced that Britain was in a state of war with Germany.

At this fateful moment in his country's history Canaris commented to his friends: "National defeat would be disastrous, but victory for Hitler would be a catastrophe."[25] He added: "The Abwehr would do nothing to prolong conflict by one day," his way of saying that the Abwehr would not stretch itself to win the war for Hitler's greater glory. In fact Canaris was convinced that Germany could not survive this war, particularly if the United States joined the Western Allies.* The invasion of Poland deeply depressed Canaris. Hassell, who visited him in late November, gained the impression that Canaris had "given up all hope of resistance from the generals, and thinks it would be useless to try anything more along this line."[26]

GÖRING MAY NOT HAVE BEEN AS CONVINCED AS CANARIS THAT HITLER would lose the war, but he was sorry it began. War did not deter him in his

---

*After the war Hungary's wartime regent, Admiral Miklós Horthy, remembered that he and his "good friend" Canaris agreed that Germany was doomed if the United States joined Britain and France. Canaris, Horthy claimed, had warned him as early as September 1938 against allying Hungary with Germany. —Ian Colvin, *Canaris, Chief of Intelligence* (Maidstone, England: George Mann, Publishers, 1973), p. 67.

pursuit of either peace or personal advantage, the two, in his mind, being closely linked. Göring, like most others in the Nazi inner circle, blamed Ribbentrop for precipitating the conflict. When Chamberlain made his historical announcement of hostilities, Göring had rushed to the telephone and screamed at Ribbentrop, "Now you've got your war!"

As so often is the case, Canaris's shadow could be seen behind the scenes. Allen Dulles, on the basis of his OSS experience in Bern, later ventured a well-founded observation that Canaris had for a while tried to bolster Göring's prestige within the Nazi hierarchy in 1939 by appealing to his vanity. Knowing that Göring thought Germany should not risk war until 1941, when it would be better equipped, Canaris had encouraged the *Reichsmarschall* in his peace-seeking efforts by providing him with intelligence showing how ill prepared Germany was for a European war against the Allies. The Abwehr chief also did all he could to encourage the dissension between Göring and his archrival Himmler; the more the Nazi leaders worked at cross-purposes, the better the chances would be for the Resistance to move successfully against Hitler.[27]

Canaris's old friend Franz Maria Liedig, who headed the Abwehr's naval intelligence section, told a revealing story during Allied interrogation after the war. Since the spring of 1939 he had been busy preparing for Canaris's use reports calculated to convince Hitler and his principal military commanders of the "absolute certainty of war with England and France" in the event of a German attack on Poland. In the autumn of 1939 Liedig was tasked by Canaris to verify and gather additional proof of Göring's efforts to enter into secret negotiations with the British *that were known to neither Hitler nor Ribbentrop*. According to Canaris's dossier on Göring as compiled by Liedig, the *Reichsmarschall* had on occasion discussed the possibility of a coup against Hitler in which the Führer would be declared insane and Göring would be his "successor [and] preserver of the peace."[28]

Former Economic Minister Hjalmar Schacht, also secretly active in the anti-Hitler Resistance, was convinced that Göring saw himself one day replacing Hitler. The Abwehr Resistance plotters in 1938, on the eve of Munich, had even considered designating Göring as Hitler's temporary replacement following a putsch to play the role of "preserver of the peace." Schacht, however, had little regard for Göring, whose vanity and ambition were fueled by his insatiable lust for "personal enrichment and good living."[29]

In other testimony given at the Nuremberg trials after the war, Schacht stated that in his opinion, Göring was "immoral and criminal." Schacht thought him "the most egocentric being imaginable. . . . His greed knew no bounds." Comparing him to Nero, Schacht related a story in which Göring appeared at a tea party wearing a Roman toga, "his hands bedecked with jeweled rings . . . his face painted and lips rouged."[30]

Johannes Popitz, Prussian finance minister under Göring, had been recruited into the embryonic resistance movement by the Abwehr officer Hans Oster in 1935 and had developed a conspiratorial relationship with Göring on the eve of the Munich crisis in 1938. Shortly before the Munich agreement was signed, the *Reichsmarschall* had gone so far as to promise Popitz that he would break off with Hitler, "if given comfortable sanctuary abroad as compensation."[31]

As a "moderate," a very relative term in discussing Nazis, Göring inevitably was invoked from time to time among the resistants. The hardcore members of Hitler's opposition wanted to have nothing to do with Nazis of any stripe. The Canaris/Oster Abwehr Resistance circle did not want to ignite civil war within Germany by declaring war on all who had worked with Hitler, but it had discarded Göring from consideration for any position in a post-Hitler government. As a remnant of the Nazi regime he would be unacceptable under any circumstances. But there were those in the Resistance, such as Weizsäcker of the Foreign Ministry, who wanted peace at almost any price and could see the usefulness of Göring's "legal" claim to power in the event of Hitler's death or removal. While not to their liking, Göring might be acceptable to this faction so long as he proved himself willing to abandon Hitler's war agenda.[32]

The diaries of Resistance activists Ulrich von Hassell and Hans Groscurth refer to Göring several times. While not making a case for him, neither diary flatly rejects the idea of some form of collaboration with him if that proved necessary to construct a viable post-Hitler government.[33] Even an army member of the Resistance, General Thomas, let his fellow dissident Chief of Staff Halder know that Göring was sending out peace feelers to the British via Sweden—i.e., Dahlerus—and suggested that the *Reichsmarschall* should perhaps be co-opted by the Resistance to work with it in the interests of peace. Halder rejected the idea on the ground that Göring could not be trusted.[34]

Canaris had early abandoned any idea that Göring should be an ally of the Resistance, although from time to time he considered his usefulness as a counterforce to Himmler in a divide-and-conquer approach to destroying Nazi leadership. The Abwehr chief's mind worked that way; guile always appealed to him more than frontal attack.

Sir Francis d'Arcy Osborne, British envoy to the Vatican, notified the Foreign Office that "Goering was said to share the 'apprehensions of conservative military circles' concerning the rapid growth of Communism in

Germany and to 'accept the idea of secret negotiations for a fair and honorable peace' over the heads of Hitler and Ribbentrop."[35] In sum, Göring on one hand was busy currying favor with Hitler while his other hand furtively waved at the British behind Hitler's back just in case the Führer was ousted from power in an army putsch or clearly began to lose the war.

Dahlerus was devastated by events and angry with Göring. "My blood boiled," he writes in his account of this drama, "as I saw the hopelessness of this powerful man unable to exert any influence on the contents of [Hitler's] reply to Great Britain's ultimatum. Was it really possible that a man, who through a caprice of fate, had obtained such power and position could be so completely in the hands of a crazy individual . . . or was he playing a double game"? But Göring too harbored doubts about Hitler's sanity. One of his closest friends was quoted by Hassell as saying that Göring agreed with him that Hitler was mentally ill and "should be removed from office."[36]

At the end of the war, with the benefit of hindsight, Dahlerus realized that "Goering's aim all along had been to get Great Britain's consent to the German seizure of Poland"[37] and testified to this effect during the Nuremberg trials. "Had I known what I know today," he said, "I would have realized that my efforts could not possibly succeed."[38] Hitler did not want to be cheated out of his target by a peace agreement, as he had been at Munich.

In a foreword to Dahlerus's memoir, *The Last Stand*, Sir Norman Birkett offers the opinion that Göring was not "a single-minded seeker of peace" but was trying to "isolate the opponent," which means "make the task of destruction easier and more certain." The Nuremberg tribunal itself, after hearing all the evidence, arrived at the solemn conclusion that "Goering's aim all along had been to get Great Britain's consent to the German seizure of Poland."[39]

Göring's motive in taking the lead in these secret ill-starred negotiations for a peaceful settlement was almost certainly self-serving. Had he succeeded in keeping Britain at peace while Germany invaded Poland, he would have improved his own standing in the Führer's medieval court, a collection of jealous privilege and power seekers. He also saw peace as an end in itself. War was an event that would eventually upset his carefully perfected way of life: a wardrobe of gaudy uniforms to flatter his vanity; a luxurious country estate; a fabulous, albeit stolen, collection of Europe's best art; an air force under his command too grand to be wasted as a casualty of war and continuing control of the Forschungsamt, Germany's signals intercept and phone tap unit on which he could rely to monitor his fellow courtiers and their devious designs to unseat him as heir apparent to Hitler's throne. And of course he had a pretty wife and child to complete the tableau of contentment that would be shattered by war.

There was also personal advantage to be gained by cultivating his image in Great Britain as the most reasonable man among Hitler's zealots. Should the British choose the more devious path to victory, secret alliance with Resistance plotters intent on overthrowing Hitler, he would be a logical candidate to replace the Führer as legally designated heir—or so he wrongly thought.

THE POLISH CRISIS CULMINATING IN WAR HAD PROVOKED ELEMENTS OF THE Resistance to renew planning to depose Hitler. On this occasion General Kurt von Hammerstein, rabidly anti-Nazi, roused himself from obscurity to plot against the Führer. Hitler had retired him in 1934 because of suspicious contacts with leftist labor groups, but with war looming he had been called back to duty and now held command of an army defending the Rhine.

Hammerstein plotted Hitler's undoing in collaboration with other Resistance leaders, including Fabian von Schlabrendorff, former chief of staff under General Ludwig Beck; Ulrich von Hassell, former ambassador to Rome; General Georg Thomas, economic warfare chief; Carl Goerdeler; and Hans Oster, Canaris's number two in the Abwehr. Hammerstein hit upon a simple scheme: He would invite Hitler to visit his headquarters on the Rhine, arguing that such a visit would dramatize the military power of the Third Reich in the West. Hammerstein had it arranged that he would arrest Hitler on arrival, which act, he hoped, would trigger a general army rebellion. Perhaps because Hitler sensed a trap, he canceled the proposed visit and soon relieved the general of his command. Before that happened, on the very day war would begin, Schlabrendorff's assignment in preparation for Hammerstein's putsch was to inform the British of the plan. He found Sir George Ogilvie-Forbes at the Adlon Hotel in Berlin as the ambassador and the other members of the British Embassy were being assembled in preparation for their evacuation. Schlabrendorff was able to pass on his message to Forbes despite the presence in the Adlon lobby of a large number of SS security officers milling about.[40]

HITLER'S RELUCTANCE TO BELIEVE THAT BRITAIN AND FRANCE WOULD GO to war over Poland had been a failure to understand the British character as much as it had been an intelligence failure. Canaris's advice against invading Poland, along with the advice of other military officers, had been ignored by Hitler. Ribbentrop, eager for war, had been the one to encourage the Führer in his calamitous misunderstanding of British character. But Chamberlain too had been guilty of epic bad judgment.

Winston Churchill, waiting in the wings to become prime minister, eloquently summed up Chamberlain's mistake: "There was sense in fighting for Czechoslovakia in 1938 when the German Army could scarcely put half a dozen trained divisions on the Western Front, when the French with nearly 60 or 70 divisions could most certainly have rolled forward across the Rhine or into the Ruhr . . . yet, now at last, the two western democracies declared themselves ready to stake their lives upon the territorial integrity of Poland."[41] He might have added that taking a stand on Czechoslovakia and threatening war to preserve that country's territorial integrity might have triggered serious dissension within the Wehrmacht command that, incited by the nascent Resistance movement, could well have struck at Hitler. It could not do so now.

The invasion of Poland was an exhibition of Hitler's willingness to use atrocity as an instrument of war. Canaris's disillusionment with Hitler as a leader of Germany reached a new intensity with what occurred in Poland. Testimony given at the Nuremberg trial by Canaris's friend and collaborator in resistance Erwin Lahousen was telling. Lahousen described how Canaris during a meeting in Poland on September 12, 1939, with Keitel and Ribbentrop protested against "extermination measures against the Polish intelligensia, the nobility and clergy and the Jews." The outraged Abwehr chief warned: "One day the world will also hold the Wehrmacht . . . responsible for such methods." Keitel's response was to dismiss the indiscriminate bombing of Warsaw and the wanton shooting of the Polish intelligentsia and Jews as necessary "political house cleaning." Keitel then formally ordered Canaris "to instigate in the Galician-Ukraine an uprising aimed at the extermination of Jews and Poles." Ribbentrop confirmed this order, specifying that "all farms and dwellings of the Poles would go up in flames and all Jews be killed."[42] Canaris flatly refused.

These terrible orders had been inspired by Hitler himself at the fateful August 22 meeting with his top officials. He had ranted: "Now we can strike at the heart of Poland." He added, "I have ordered to the East my Death's Head units [SS] to kill without pity or mercy all men, women and children of Polish race and language." The elephantine Göring, who for British benefit had posed as an apostle of "peace," leaped on a table and danced about "like a savage" as he toasted Hitler's "bloodthirsty tanks and bloody promises."[43]

The SS was assigned the dirty work that Hitler promised, sparing the army at least this dishonor. Even parts of the SS were shaken by the enormity of the orders they were forced to carry out. Count Wolf Heinrich von Helldorf, president of the Berlin Police and a member of the Resistance, told Oster that the SS chief in Krakow was having trouble keeping his troops in line. Before carrying out the atrocities assigned them, they were making themselves blind drunk.[44]

War and genocide were marching hand in hand. What Canaris had seen in Poland, particularly the mayhem and destruction in Warsaw itself, left him for a while "utterly shattered."[45] He was nonetheless very able to help a Polish lady in distress by putting her and her daughters out of harm's way in Switzerland. The lady would prove to be very useful.

NINE

A Polish Lady

THE ROLES OF MARIAN REJEWSKI AND OTHER POLISH MATHEMATICAL GE-
niuses from Poznań University who solved the German Enigma code machine and broke the German ciphers earned for them prominent places in
the Allied pantheon of World War II heroes. Their work made it possible
for the British throughout the war to exploit with devastating effect the intelligence derived from intercepted German messages in the now-famous
Ultra program at Bletchley Park in England. According to some, Ultra
made it possible to end the war in Europe some two years earlier than
would otherwise have been the case. Some even claim that without the genius that made Ultra possible, Hitler might well have won the war.

Another Polish refugee from Nazi aggression, Halina Szymanska, also
made a unique contribution to her homeland and the Allied cause. Her
services did not shorten the war, much less win it, but the spirit that motivated her was the same as Marian Rejewski's; the risks she ran were greater.
Her story involved Admiral Wilhelm Canaris. He planted trusted personal
contacts in several key capitals abroad, not to serve the Abwehr but,
through him, to serve the purposes of the Resistance movement, by providing information to the Western Allies. One of these contacts was
Madame Szymanska.

Canaris's anguish at the treatment meted out to Poland and its people by
the Nazis and the revulsion he felt when Hitler allied Germany with Soviet
Russia reinforced his determination to undermine Hitler in every way he
could. One move was to arrange secret, indirect contact with Great Britain,

without whose resolute determination to defeat Hitler the Resistance would find it difficult to remove the Führer from power and restore peace. For this purpose he arranged that his good friend Madame Szymanska, wife of the former Polish military attaché in Berlin, be sent to Switzerland with an understanding that she seek contact with British intelligence.[1]

When the Red Army invaded Poland, the Russians captured and imprisoned Madame Szymanska's husband, Colonel Antoni Szymanski, a German specialist on the Polish General Staff. This left his wife and three young daughters in political jeopardy and without any means of support. The nature of Canaris's relationship with Halina and her husband had been such that he could trust her to maintain a clandestine arrangement with the British in Bern without incriminating him. But he was concerned for her well-being as well. Using the facilities of the Abwehr, Canaris saw to it that Madame Szymanska and her children were given safe passage from Poznań across Germany to Switzerland[2] and would be provided with an Abwehr contact in Bern to whom she could turn for help.

Lieutenant Colonel Claude Edward Majoribanks Dansey, one of the most active and important officers of the British Secret Intelligence Service during the interwar period, had served in Switzerland. Some have claimed that Dansey inspired the character of Colonel "R" in Somerset Maugham's World War I spy story *Ashenden*. In real life it was Dansey who made the arrangements for Madame Szymanska to be in contact with SIS officer Count Frederick vanden Heuvel in Bern in 1939. Dansey equipped Szymanska with a false identity: that of Marie Clenat holding French ID card 596, forged by the SIS.[3]

By late December 1939 Syzmanska had made contact in Bern with the Polish government-in-exile's intelligence chief in Switzerland, Captain Szczesny Chojnacki. Within two months she was also in contact with vanden Heuvel. Her visible life was spent modestly as a typist at the "Free" Polish Legation; in reality she served secretly as a unique link between Abwehr chief Canaris and MI-6 chief Menzies. Canaris sent Abwehr officer Hans Bernd Gisevius to Switzerland under vice-consul cover to provide support for Madame Szymanska. Gisevius, a member of the German Resistance, who had been a Dansey contact in early 1939, was to provide her with intelligence to pass on to the British through the vanden Heuvel link, although Canaris himself met with her on a few occasions in Switzerland, France, and Italy.[4]

Ian Colvin, a British Foreign Office German expert during the war and one of Canaris's early biographers after the war, wrote about this case, although he withheld her name, referring to her only as Madame J. Colvin describes how he met her after the war in Surrey, where she had settled.

She acknowledged having known Canaris from the days when she and her husband had been assigned to Berlin.[5] In response to queries from Colvin about "espionage" work, Madame J, or Halina Szymanska, denied having been a "spy" and explained the subtleties of her role. Canaris on his visits to her never asked for any information concerning the Allies, but he would volunteer information about Hitler's classified plans. This was the way she put it: "I don't suppose you could call Admiral Canaris an indiscreet man, but he could be very outspoken." Canaris visited Madame Syzmanska the winter of 1940, to keep her abreast of war developments. Then, in October 1941, when he saw her again, he confided in her: "The German front had run fast [but] bogged down in Russia and . . . would never reach its objective." To Colvin she revealed something else: "By then I was asked to relate our conversations to the British." When Colvin asked her directly if Canaris considered her a link with the British, she described the admiral's comments to her as "calculated indiscretions"; Canaris was well beyond being just "outspoken." But she added, "All his conversations were in the sphere of high politics. . . . He would not have told me of petty military matters—small treason such as agents deal in." She admonished Colvin to "make it plain . . . that [Canaris] did not give away ordinary military secrets—otherwise the Germans will say he was a British spy."[6]

More than forty years later, with its curiosity aroused by the Canaris-Syzmanska-British connection described in Nigel West's book *MI-6*, the *Sunday Times* of London extracted an interesting comment from a retired British intelligence officer named Andrew King.[7] King told the *Times* that "Canaris had tipped off Szymanska in the late autumn of 1940 about Hitler's plans to invade Russia the following year." He added, "Canaris and Szymanska had an understanding that this information would be relayed to London."[8]

Nigel West in another book he wrote, *A Thread of Deceit*,[9] relates how he again found Halina Szymanska, now age seventy-seven, in 1983. By then she was living with a grandson in Mobile, Alabama. She graciously told him more about her strange wartime role and her relationship with Canaris.

The significance of this indirect, closely held link between Canaris and the British is that the Abwehr chief established and ran it personally, a departure from his usual practice of staying in the background of the Resistance. The relationship was a commentary on his trust in Halina Szymanska. Abwehr officer Hans Gisevius, her German contact in Switzerland, was to figure prominently in German Resistance affairs, including the July 20, 1944, bomb plot against Hitler, and to become a secret contact of OSS officer Allen Dulles in Switzerland.

That Canaris was willing to take the risks involved in this dangerous operation is indicative of his despair in the wake of Poland's tragedy. His worst fears had been realized when Hitler rushed headlong into war and joined Stalin in an unholy alliance. His disgust had been aroused by witnessing unimaginable Nazi atrocities in Poland. His fear of what lay ahead, invasions of Norway, the Lowlands, France, and Britain, drove him and others in the Resistance to devise a daring plan to enlist the secret help of the Pope as an intermediary with the British in ridding Germany of Hitler and bringing peace to a Europe teetering on the brink of a world war.

TEN

Operation X:
The Vatican Connection

WITH THE SUCCESSFUL INVASION OF POLAND BY GERMANY AND THE occupation of Danzig, the Resistance found itself in a quandary. In this hour of
victory and public euphoria the Wehrmacht was not eager to be party to
a putsch. Hitler seemed to have been right in predicting that Britain
and France would not intervene militarily to stop German aggression in
Poland; the generals had been wrong. If at this time German military officers were to support a revolt against Hitler, it would, they feared, serve as
an invitation for the Western Allies to exploit Germany's vulnerability by
attacking.

The course that appeared most useful to the Resistance now was to
work for peace and convince the Western Allies that they should restrain
themselves from aggressive moves in Europe in the hope that all-out war
could be avoided. Only if German public apprehension about Hitler's future plans replaced the euphoria of present victory could the Resistance
hope to enlist Wehrmacht cooperation for a coup. The Resistance again
dispatched secret emissaries to the Western Allies, this time to plead for
peace.

The man sent to make contact with the Western Allies by the Resistance was the German Foreign Ministry officer Adam von Trott zu Solz, a
person whose background seemed ideal for the task. Trott could be described as a man of passion. His biographer, Christopher Sykes,[1] notes that
he frequently gave in to temptation and had numerous affairs with devoted
women. If Trott was passionate about love, he was equally so about the fate

of his country, and he did not like the direction in which the Nazis were taking it.

Trott studied law in Munich, Berlin, and Göttingen, where he also immersed himself in philosophical exploration. While a critic of the feckless Weimar Republic, its successor, Hitler's National Socialist regime, offended him deeply. Undecided whether he should remain in Nazi Germany or flee its tyranny, he sought advice from his old British friend Lord Lothian, the secretary of the Rhodes Trust and a member of the Clivenden set. Heeding Lothian's advice to get out of Germany for a while, Trott spent a year in China, where he wallowed in the wisdom of Confucianism far from the problems of his homeland. But Trott was drawn back to Germany, where he threw himself into the Resistance cause. Peace had become his obsession.

Trott, who joined the German Foreign Ministry, visited London in June 1939 on an official mission to explore British attitudes toward Germany. By then he was also working underground, leading a double life with the German Resistance in opposition to Hitler's war-oriented policies.[2] General Beck, head of the military Resistance movement, had briefed him to warn the British against giving in to Hitler's demands; appeasement would only whet the Führer's territorial appetite.

Trott met with Prime Minister Chamberlain and Foreign Secretary Halifax among others. Upon his return he officially reported to the German Foreign Ministry that British hard-liners would push for Allied military intervention if Hitler insisted on new territorial acquisitions. But if Hitler showed himself sincerely opposed to war, the considerable body of opinion that favored "appeasement" would express itself as being opposed to hostile acts against Germany. He added that Germany could win over British public opinion and "paralyze its enemies" in the U.K. if Hitler would withdraw German occupation forces from Bohemia and Moravia.[3]

Trott reported secretly to the Resistance that he had impressed upon Lord Halifax the importance of not giving in to Hitler's aggressive threats and warned that there were strong indications that the Nazis were on the verge of some new and hostile initiative. This ominous reference to what soon was revealed as the Hitler-Stalin pact made little impression on Halifax. Trott reported to Beck that Chamberlain was "half dead" and unconvinced that the Resistance, with or without British backing, could overthrow Hitler.

Perhaps because of his double mission, secret emissary of the Resistance as well as Foreign Ministry representative, Trott had not been fully trusted by Halifax; this was all too Machiavellian for the foreign secretary's taste. The more resolute anti-Nazis such as Winston Churchill were suspicious of Trott because of his links with the appeasement-minded Cliven-den set, some members of which he had seen during his visit. In all, Trott's mission in behalf of the Resistance had been unsuccessful. For all his good intentions, he had found little sympathy in England.

Within the German Foreign Ministry Resistance circle another idea bubbled to the surface: Engage the still-neutral United States in a peace process. The job of trying to convince President Franklin Roosevelt that he should become peacemaker in this crisis fell to Trott. He was from an aristocratic Hessian family, but his mother was half American, and his ancestors included John Jay, chief justice of the United States. Reared as a devout Calvinist by his mother, Trott was a man of staunch Christian ethics. He was an Anglophile because of his education; in 1929 he had won a Rhodes scholarship to Oxford University, where he enjoyed good times and made good friends. Nonetheless, he cherished his American heritage and had a variety of close contacts in the United States.

Trott's trip to the United States in September and October 1939 was made under the auspices of the Foreign Ministry. On this occasion he served as delegate to a conference hosted by the Institute of Pacific Relations in Virginia Beach. Again this served as cover for a secret Resistance mission. The substance of his message in behalf of the Resistance drew on Woodrow Wilson's 1917 plea that military victory should not be considered a valid basis for future peace.[4] It was Trott's hope that the Western Allies would consider the present German regime not as a natural one, but as an aberration born of the Versailles Treaty. To avoid another unfortunate postwar situation, Germany should be integrated into a new Europe once it had rid itself of its Nazi raiments rather than be ostracized as an incorrigible.[5]

These views were expressed to Assistant Secretary of State G. S. Messersmith and, through him, to Secretary of State Cordell Hull and Undersecretary Sumner Welles. The British ambassador to the United States, Lord Lothian, Trott's good friend, was also entrusted with a copy of his paper.

On November 20 Trott stressed in his discussion with Messersmith that he had found a strong element in Great Britain that still wanted some kind of settlement with Hitler. This he deplored, pointing out that such a course of action would undermine Resistance efforts to depose the Führer, a requisite for avoiding a major war in Europe.

Messersmith respected Trott yet was suspicious: How could a Foreign Ministry representative trusted with a mission to the United States be in the secret underground movement? Even Supreme Court Justice Felix Frankfurter, an acquaintance of Trott's from Oxford days, could not quite accept him as a bona fide Resistance leader. The FBI, unaware of the true nature of the German Resistance, was particularly distrustful of Trott and kept him under close surveillance. President Roosevelt also had his doubts; he wrote a note chiding Frankfurter: "For Heaven's Sake! Surely you did not let your Trott friend get trotted out of the country without having him searched by Edgar Hoover. . . ."[6] Not only was Trott's mission to the United States a failure, but his efforts at lobbying in Washington increased the risk of the Gestapo's discovering his activity in behalf of the Resistance.

Hitler's speech before the Reichstag on October 6, 1939, was meant to be an offer of peace on Nazi terms—that is, British and French capitulation. Peace would be possible, he repeated, if the new Reich frontiers, based on history, ethnography, and economics, were accepted and if German colonies, taken away by the Treaty of Versailles, could be restored. When this less than good-faith "offer" was ignored by Britain and France, an exasperated Hitler issued Directive No. 6, describing his intentions to invade the West, a decision known by the military High Command since September 26. After France and Britain were defeated, he planned to turn his attention to the East, where he would seek Lebensraum and the attendant economic resources that would flow to Germany and its people at the expense of the Soviet Union.

As shocking as this directive was, it confirmed the Resistance's estimate of Hitler's objectives and provided the underground leaders with a badly needed argument for action, an argument that had been lacking since Hitler's successful seizure of Poland conspicuously uncontested by France and Great Britain. The specific date set for the invasion of France, November 12, was made known to the army leaders on October 27.

Chamberlain's reply to Hitler's "peace" offer, delivered before the House of Commons on October 12, was ambiguous. In a more specific vein, Sir Robert Vansittart sent private word to Resistance member Theo Kordt in Bern through British agent T. Philip Conwell-Evans that Chamberlain and Halifax wanted it understood that the British government could not negotiate with "Hitler or his like," so that the German opposition's job was "to produce a German government capable of negotiating and on whose word the British could rely."[7] Vansittart's message was a hopeful one from the Resistance's point of view, even if it placed the burden of action on them, but Chamberlain's discouragingly weak message did nothing to arouse the German military to action. Nonetheless, the Resistance, energized by what it considered Hitler's catastrophic plans to invade France, found new heart and hope in spurring the British on to support them.

It was now important to dissuade the Western Allies from mounting an offensive in Europe. For the Wehrmacht to back a coup it would be essential that it not be seen throwing down its arms in the midst of battle, an image that would revive World War I accusations that the military was capable of stabbing the fatherland in the back.

It would be necessary for the Resistance to convince the Western Allies of its credibility, of its backing within the military and its support from other influential segments of German society. It would also be important to find an eminent figure, internationally respected, who would be willing to be patron of their cause of peace. What better symbol of all that was good and right, what more trustworthy intermediary could there be than the Pope? And what better Pope to enlist for their endeavor could the Resistance have hoped for than Pius XII, who in 1917 had been Archbishop Eugenio Pacelli, nuncio to Munich, then elevated to nuncio at Berlin in the 1920s. His Holiness was a friend of Germany but an opponent of Hitler for all his façade of political neutrality. Moreover, he knew and respected both Beck and Canaris from his days in Berlin.

It was in late 1939 that Admiral Canaris and his deputy Hans Oster conceived of an ambitious plan, code-named Operation X, to enlist the Pope's help. They would use a newly recruited Resistance activist, Munich lawyer Josef "Joe the Ox" Müller, to maintain contact with friends in the Vatican, particularly the Pope's close advisers Father Robert Leiber and Monsignor Ludwig Kaas, former leader of Germany's Center party. Dr. Müller's challenging assignment was to convince Pius XII, newly ascended to St. Peter's throne, to serve as patron of Resistance efforts to reach secret détente with the Western Allies. The objective was to negotiate a peace with Great Britain and France calling explicitly for Hitler's removal from power and the formation of a non-Nazi German government. Müller reached Rome in October 1939, and by November he saw glimmerings of hope.

Müller had been a leader within the Bavarian People's party and a close associate of the premier of Bavaria, Heinrich Held, during the period of the Weimar Republic. A true friend of the Roman Catholic Church, he had known Cardinal Pacelli, when he was secretary of state of the Vatican. Somehow the rumor had spread that Pacelli had officiated at Müller's marriage in St. Peter's crypt. This was not true, but the myth flourished in German Catholic circles and was perhaps what saved his life during the 1944 roundup of Resistance members following the July 20 attempt on Hitler's life.[8] SD chief Kaltenbrunner, and perhaps Bormann as well, conceived of him as a possible hostage to be used in negotiating with the Vatican for asylum in the event of a final collapse of Nazi Germany.

Müller was a particularly good friend of Father Leiber, SJ, principal aide to Pius and an official of considerable influence within the Vatican. The value of their relationship became apparent at the outset. Father Leiber informed Müller in a memorandum dated November 6, 1939, that the Pope, profoundly upset by German atrocities in Poland, would cooperate in the role planned for him "when conditions justify it"⁹—i.e., when the German Army had removed Hitler from power. (How he would be removed was not established.) Müller's report was passed on to Oster and Dohnanyi, who showed it to Canaris before giving it to Army Chief of Staff Halder.

Sir Francis d'Arcy Osborne, British minister to the Vatican, was made aware of Resistance overtures by the Pope through Father Leiber. As the Pope put it, "The German opposition must be heard in Britain."¹⁰ But Pius would involve himself only on condition that the British and French promise neither to interfere in internal German politics once Hitler and his henchmen were removed nor to take advantage of the inevitable turmoil to occupy Germany.

London had given Osborne authority to listen to Resistance overtures made through the Vatican, but his report aroused only mild interest in Whitehall. Until members of the Resistance themselves jettisoned Hitler, Whitehall was not eager to dicker with them, particularly since the generals still insisted on keeping the Sudetenland for Germany and holding a plebiscite in Austria to determine that country's future.¹¹ Giving greater authority to Osborne's position, Foreign Secretary Halifax made London's views public in a speech on January 20, 1940, although this was in response to official, though muted, Nazi peace feelers. Halifax made it clear that the only reason why peace could not be made was that the Germans had as yet given no evidence of their readiness to repair the damage that they had wrought upon their neighbors.

In early February Pius told Osborne that the German Army was prepared to move against Hitler so long as the union of Austria and Germany would not be undone. British Foreign Minister Halifax responded on February 17 with a message saying that Britain must act in concert with France and both powers would insist on a definite program that guaranteed reparations to Germany's neighbors and that Austria would be permitted to choose whether or not it would stay within a German union.

Sir Alexander Cadogan, permanent undersecretary of the British Foreign Office, was apparently neither impressed by nor optimistic about the Vatican's role. His diary remarks for February 21 spared only a parenthetical reference to the Pope's efforts: "Had talk with H. [Foreign Secretary Halifax] who hadn't much to tell me that I didn't know (except communications from Pope to which I don't pay much more attention than I do to all these stories)."[12]

In fact chances of the German Army's overthrowing Hitler were by then remote. Hitler's popularity had grown in the wake of his relatively effortless conquests of Austria, Czechoslovakia, and Poland. The German High Command could not be relied upon. The X report blueprint for peace, to be negotiated through the good offices of the Vatican, had been received as coolly by General von Brauchitsch when put to him by Resistance collaborator General Halder, as it had been by the British Foreign Office.

Drafted by Müller, Dohnanyi, and General Thomas, the X report, with tacit approval of the Pope, had gone forward to the High Command through Halder. It had been carefully drafted to make clear that peace negotiations were contingent on the removal of Hitler and the Nazi regime. But it would still be found objectionable by the British since it called for a plebiscite to determine Austria's future and insisted on the Sudetenland's remaining within Germany.

Now committed to prosecuting the war and probably afraid of becoming involved in such dangerous plotting, Brauchitsch reacted in anger when Halder presented him with the document: "You should never have shown me this. . . . This is pure treason against the State."[13] Halder was shaken by Brauchitsch's negative attitude and was reluctant to argue the issue with his commander in chief in the midst of war. Halder himself was losing faith in the Resistance. He once broke down in tears while defending his own reluctance to take a sterner action against Hitler, suggesting that the strain of plotting had temporarily unstrung him. Treason against a chief of state to whom he had sworn allegiance was not an easy thing for a German army officer, whatever the justification.

One sign of Halder's state of mind was an odd suggestion he made that Hitler's astrologer be bribed to warn the Führer from mounting any offensive in the West that did not enjoy an auspicious arrangement of the stars! At the end of November Canaris had a long talk with Halder. Once a pistol-packing activist who had prayed for an opportunity to shoot Hitler, a broken and frightened Halder now told Canaris that he could not go down in history as the first German General Staff officer to participate in treasonable actions. Nor did General Beck have any more success in strengthening Halder's resolve. Halder took refuge in the excuse that the Wehrmacht was rapidly approaching a state of readiness that would ensure success in the forthcoming invasion of France; in other words, Hitler was not as foolhardy as the military had believed him to be. The fault, Halder argued, was with the British and French, whose procrastination and lack of will would enable Hitler to triumph easily despite the Allies' greater military strength.

The real problem was that the Vatican connection had become known to Heydrich's Sicherheitsdienst (SD), the SS security intelligence arm; Müller, specifically, was under suspicion. Heydrich's interest in Müller's Vatican contacts had begun well before the war, but in 1940 details of Operation X had been leaked to the Swiss press by a loose-lipped Benedictine monk, Hermann Keller, with SD ties.

Canaris, acting quickly, conducted an Abwehr "investigation" that he made sure cleared Müller. The canny admiral argued that Müller's actions were justified as those of an Abwehr double agent assigned to spy on the Vatican.[14] Heydrich probably did not believe Canaris's excuses but lacked evidence to proceed further against Müller. Moreover, his boss, Himmler, did not appear to want the matter pursued further. As had been the case with other evidence implicating Canaris, the file on this case was squirreled away by a frustrated Heydrich for a more auspicious time to make his move against the Abwehr.

ULRICH VON HASSELL, FOREIGN MINISTRY DIPLOMAT WITHOUT A NEW appointment since his removal as German envoy to Italy, kept busy with Resistance matters. He now tried his hand at negotiating with the British for a peace without Hitler and the Nazis. In February and again in April 1940, Hassell met secretly in Switzerland with J. Londsdale Bryans, a close friend of Halifax's. The foreign secretary, however, had only reluctantly given Bryans license to talk with the Resistance about peace; his constraints left Bryans little room for maneuver.

Hassell was not aware of the Resistance initiative with the Vatican until mid-March, when he met with fellow conspirators Beck, Oster, and Dohnanyi. They now wanted him to try his hand at returning a backsliding Halder to the fold. The general, however, had a bad case of cold feet and avoided Hassell. The rivers of war were now flowing faster than the subterranean conduits of peace; German generals were conditioned to fight, not to intrigue in treasonous causes in violation of their sacred military oath. In any case, by April Hitler had invaded Denmark and Norway, distracting the generals from their plotting. Again there was the British government to blame. Hassell was not a little disappointed as he wrote in his diary: "I cannot understand how the English managed to be taken by surprise again."

Ulrich von Hassell had struck out twice, first with Bryans, then with Halder. With the Resistance's insistence on keeping Austria and the Sudetenland in union with Germany, the British were not in any mood to reach agreement. But a wholly unexpected event occurred in Holland on November 9 to put a damper on Operation X. Known as the Venlo incident, this occurrence not only affected the Vatican negotiations adversely but was a catastrophe for the British Secret Service. It also inhibited British willingess to deal with the German Resistance, whatever face it presented, for the remainder of the war.

ELEVEN

The Venlo Incident

THE ONSET OF WAR, EVEN ONE CALLED A PHONY WAR BECAUSE OF ITS LACK of ground combat, gave a new sense of urgency to the British MI-6 outpost in The Hague, where Major Richard Stevens and a colleague, Captain S. Payne Best, were feverishly working on the German target.[1] Stevens's MI-6 station in the Netherlands had just taken under its wing the European part of a hitherto separate and highly secret parallel organization called the Z network. This latter apparatus had been the brainchild of Claude Edward Majoribanks Dansey, appropriately known as Colonel Z. Sigismund Payne Best was one of its best operatives in Europe.*

These parallel segments of British MI-6 had been brought back together in the interests of better coordination in wartime. But the British Foreign Office, riven by factions, still suffered from misunderstandings and lack of coordination. Prime Minister Chamberlain had thought it necessary to take the reins of foreign policy largely into his own hands. Ivan Maisky, then Soviet ambassador to Great Britain, put it accurately: "The Prime Minister

---

*Over the years MI-6 had fallen into an easily recognized cover pattern in which its staff personnel had been housed in British consulates around the world identified as "passport control offices." In the interest of creating a less visible, more secure organization that could function in the event operations of a "passport control" office were hopelessly compromised, Claude Dansey had won over the service to his concept of a separate network in which a special cadre of British agents under various nonofficial covers—usually business covers—could continue to operate securely.—Anthony Read and David Fisher, *Colonel Z* (New York: Viking Press, 1985), pp. 208–210.

usurped control of British foreign policy, and reduced the Foreign Office to the condition of a mere diplomatic chancery attached to his own person. To avoid complications, the important post of Permanent Undersecretary, taken from Sir Robert Vansittart, was given to Sir Alexander Cadogan, who could be relied upon not to provide any unexpected surprises."

Vansittart, now chief adviser to the Foreign Office, but still operating his so-called private detective agency,[2] or cadre of handpicked agents and informants, managed to keep his hand in. Sir Robert circulated convincing-sounding but not always accurate reports from his own agents, or quoted "telling phrases . . . attributing them to 'a *very* secret source.' " During 1938 and 1939 he turned several messages from private informants into "insistent minutes . . . to influence the decisions of the Cabinet."[3] According to F. H. Hinsley's official British war history of intelligence, these practices could be traced to Whitehall's "lack of adequate arrangements for central and considered assessments of such intelligence as was available. . . ."[4]

Following the German invasion of Poland that triggered war, Chamberlain had become desperate to find some formula for peace before Europe was totally lost to Hitler. If peace could not be found, he knew war would likely take on catastrophic dimensions. Direct negotiations with Hitler would raise the specter of another Munich, and Chamberlain had learned to be wary of the indirect overtures being made by Göring through Dahlerus. Maxim Litvinov, who had been the foreign minister of the Soviet Union until his removal by Stalin in 1939, was convinced that Chamberlain, frustrated in his efforts to reach an acceptable agreement with Hitler, "would conclude that only by encouraging a German-Russian conflict could Great Britain survive."[5] This was going too far, but the prime minister was beginning to believe that only the Wehrmacht, working from within, could rid Germany of Hitler without need of a general war.[*]

---

[*]Sir Arthur Rucker, Chamberlain's principal private secretary, six weeks after war broke out, discussed the situation with Chamberlain's other secretary, John Colville. Colville noted the conversation in his diary, providing some insight into Chamberlain's views, as reflected in Rucker's analysis at this time:

> Arthur Rucker says he thinks Communism is now the great danger, greater even than Nazi Germany. All the independent states of Europe are anti-Russian, but Communism is a plague that does not stop at national boundaries, and with the advance of the Soviet into Poland the states of Eastern Europe will find their powers of resistance to Communism very much weakened. It is thus vital that we should play our hand very carefully with Russia, and not destroy the possibility of uniting, if necessary, with a new German Government against the common danger. What is needed is a moderate conservative reaction in Germany: the overthrow of the present regime by the army chiefs.
>
> —John Colville, *The Fringes of Power: 10 Downing Street Diaries, 1939–1955*
> (New York: Norton, 1986), p. 40.

With its intelligence estimative resources wanting and its foreign policy being guided by a prime minister whose judgments were based on his conviction that war must somehow, even at this late hour, be avoided, Britain was vulnerable to epic trickery. Enter the consummate intriguer Walter Schellenberg of the SD with an imaginative deception operation. Having accumulated evidence that the British had been making contact with Resistance members, Schellenberg believed that they would fall for his scheme. He had gained some inklings of British efforts to reach dissident German military figures from Project X, the Vatican connection, as well as from other bits and pieces that the SD and Gestapo had picked up. His boss, Reinhard Heydrich, had in fact opened a dossier called Black Orchestra, chronicling the Resistance and its suspected British contacts.

Schellenberg planned to dangle before the British an enticing "opportunity" to arrange contact with Wehrmacht Resistance officers eager to oust Hitler and negotiate for peace. He was confident that the British would rise to the bait. Unfortunately for the British, Chamberlain's desperation to find a solution to the crisis facing his country and his government, reflected by Menzies and Dansey of MI-6, dovetailed neatly with Schellenberg's plan.

Responsive to the prime minister's desires, MI-6 had stepped up its efforts to find and evaluate genuine German Resistance groups capable of staging a revolt against Hitler, but with little result to date. Secret emissaries from the Resistance, including those who were making contact through the Vatican, were difficult to deal with because for all their hatred of Hitler, they did not want Germany to relinquish such ethnically German enclaves as Austria and the Sudetenland, popular prizes seized by the Wehrmacht. Yet because of pressure from Chamberlain, the SIS proved to be receptive to still another overture from unknown persons as Schellenberg's deception plot unfolded. Stewart Menzies, in line to succeed the ailing Admiral Hugh Sinclair as head of MI-6, was particularly eager to respond favorably to what seemed to promise direct contact with the German General Staff.

A key actor in Schellenberg's play was "a big bluff, self-confident fellow . . . inclined to talk as big as he looked,"[6] who called himself Solms and described himself to Best as an adjutant to a senior Luftwaffe general. In fact Solms was a former operatic tenor and consummate actor named Johannes "Hans" Travaglio. His calculated name-dropping with Best included no less a personage than Field Marshal Gerd von Rundstedt, whom he alleged to be a collaborator with the Resistance.

Best, an old pro in the intelligence business, was suspicious of Solms (Travaglio) since he had been introduced by a man with an unsavory background named Franz Fischer. But Best's words of caution were ignored as

Menzies urged him on in the hope that it would lead to better contacts within the Wehrmacht and ultimately some action to prevent an invasion of France.

Chamberlain watched this operation closely; he had high hopes that there might still be some quick fix by which to restore peace.* The Stevens-Best negotiations with Solms not only had prime ministerial and Foreign Office approval, but senior officers of the Foreign Office closely monitored its progress.[7]

British Undersecretary Cadogan referred cryptically to the Netherlands connection from time to time in his diary. On October 17 he wrote: "Admiral [Sinclair, Chief of SIS] has a story from his two German Generals that they will be in Holland today! . . . [but] it's always 'tomorrow.' " Indications of the kind of hardly credible misinformation that Heydrich and Schellenberg were passing through this channel to dramatize their notional German Resistance can be seen from Cadogan's diary entry: "Hitler has 'bad news' from Italy: is in an excitable state: has given orders which Goering refuses to carry out: and that latter has been dismissed! We shall see!"[8] On October 23 Cadogan's growing skepticism became even more evident when he wrote: " 'C' [Sinclair] has got report on interview with his German General friends. I think they are Hitler agents."[9] But Cadogan put aside his suspicions and, like Chamberlain, Halifax, Sinclair, and Menzies, accepted the German generals as genuine.

Albeit with the wisdom of hindsight, Best was to claim after the war that he had soon begun to have serious doubts about Solms.[10] The captain had become annoyed when Solms refused to divulge more information about his "Resistance" principals despite the fact that Best had proved his own bona fides by arranging with the BBC to broadcast a specific text supplied by Solms at a specific time. Menzies, however, would not allow Best to drop the contact despite his reservations.

---

*John Colville, Chamberlain's secretary, noted in his diary:

> Once it was realized that the Germans had no immediate intention of bombing London or Paris, and that the expected offensive on the Rhine was delayed, there were lingering hopes in some breasts that the full impact of war might even yet be avoided for all but the unhappy Poles, whose spectacularly gallant but tragically ill-equipped army had been smashed and whose country was systematically devastated by Germans and Russians alike.
>
> These hopes were expressed in the Cabinet by Lord Halifax and found a strong echo in the staff at 10 Downing Street. . . . Chamberlain, to whom the very thought of war was abhorrent, would have gone further than Churchill in making concessions to a new German Government, even if it had contained some of the Nazi leaders! [Colville, *The Fringes of Power*, p. 34].

On October 20 Best and Stevens through Solms met two new players at Dinxperlo on the Dutch frontier: Captain von Seidlitz and Lieutenant Grosch, aliases for two officers from the SD counterespionage section claiming to represent a General von Wietersheim. A new dimension of the operation began in late October, when Solms actually produced in person and introduced to Best a "member" of the German General Staff, one Major Schämmel of the General Staff's Transport Service. Schämmel in fact was Schellenberg himself, lead player in his own play. The major, hiding behind a monocle to the fascination of Best—also a monocle wearer— appeared with two other Germans: Grosch, who drove his car, and a friend, Colonel Martini, allegedly a high-ranking member of the Resistance.

Stevens and Best listened intently as Major Schämmel described the Resistance plan, which called for jailing Hitler and forcibly, if necessary, extracting from him written authority for the army to take power and initiate peace negotiations. In return the German "conspirators" insisted on being told what terms the British could offer for a "just and honorable" peace.[11]

Chamberlain, Halifax, and Cadogan took this overture seriously enough to devote the evening of October 31 to drafting a reply that could be conveyed to Schämmel. The message had to be redrafted, however, when the cabinet, which had been kept mostly in the dark about the whole affair, raised objections.[12] Churchill, in particular, insisted that the Resistance must first remove Hitler before peace negotiations could be discussed.[13] Nonetheless, grasping at straws, Chamberlain optimistically commented on November 5: "I have a hunch that the war will be over by Spring."[14]

CHAMBERLAIN WAS AT THE SAME TIME STILL RECEIVING SECRET PEACE feelers from the Nazi government as represented by Hermann Göring through the latter's Swedish friend Birger Dahlerus. Adding to the confusing picture was Dahlerus's scarcely veiled tip that while Göring had Hitler's authority to talk with the British about peace, the *Reichsmarschall* had his own secret agenda, which went further than Hitler would ever countenance. Implied was the likelihood that Göring might consider finding peace by overthrowing Hitler and taking control of the government himself.[15] The pro-German Swedish industrialist Axel Wenner-Gren, who occasionally cooperated with Dahlerus's efforts, was of the opinion that Chamberlain had been more than interested in the implications that Göring might be pursuing his own course, contrary to that of Hitler.[16]

Dahlerus was not Göring's only back channel to Chamberlain. In July 1939 the prime minister turned to his friend the economist Helmut

Wohlthat. In early June Wohlthat, at the prime minister's behest, held discussions with Chamberlain's close advisers Sir Horace Wilson and Sir Joseph Ball concerning possible means of economic cooperation with Germany. Then Robert Hudson, secretary of the Department of Overseas Trade, told Wohlthat to pass on to Göring that not only Great Britain but the United States as well might be prepared to help Hitler if only he would disarm; perhaps the Western democracies might even return to him Germany's former colonial holdings. This was too much for certain anti-Hitler elements in the British Foreign Office, who leaked this startling conversation to the press. On July 23, 1939, the *Daily Telegraph* trumpeted that Chamberlain's government had offered Nazi Germany a "billion pound credit" by way of buying off Hitler. Since Göring could be seriously embarrassed by any authentication of his disclosure, he indignantly labeled the Wohlthat-Hudson proposals "rubbish."[17]

Göring's "official" but secret initiatives with the British, while known in general by Hitler, had been taken behind Ribbentrop's back. On the stand at Nuremberg after the war Göring was questioned about what he had hoped to accomplish by his British contacts. He replied: "it was not a question of accomplishing something. If I wanted to influence the Führer, that was possible only if I had something in my hand." Göring added that he wanted to be able to tell the Führer: "On my own responsibility, but with your knowledge and without committing you and your Reich policies, I am conducting negotiations in order, circumstances permitting, to create an atmosphere which will be able to facilitate the official negotiations in a direction of a peaceful solution."[18]

The likelihood of Hitler's overreaching, trying for a still-riskier prize in Western Europe, alarmed Göring as it portended his own ultimate doom as well as that of Nazi Germany. Even before the Polish campaign was concluded, Göring reinvigorated his secret peace initiatives, however fraught with danger. He seemed willing to press to the limit, even overstep the line between peace overtures that Hitler approved of and those that required the Führer to do what he would never do: give up some of his recent conquests.

What exactly was the "honest peace" Göring described to Dahlerus on September 8 as a basis for negotiations with Chamberlain? Now that German troops had defeated much of the Polish Army, how far would Britain tolerate Hitler's new gains and how much give would there be on the Führer's side?[19] Certainly, not all of Göring's messages passed through Dahlerus would have met with Hitler's approval. Throughout the uneasy days preceding the offensives against Scandinavia, the Lowlands, and France, Göring again hinted to Chamberlain through his Swedish friend that he was willing to replace Hitler as Germany's leader, delegating the Führer to some kind of ceremonial position, to evacuate German troops from non-German parts of Poland, and to halt the persecution of the Jews.[20]

At the same time that Göring was dealing with the British, he tried to open a channel to President Roosevelt. In a simply coded "double-talk" telegram dated September 8, Göring's go-between, Dr. Joachim Hertslet, Germany's Four-Year Plan representative in Mexico, urged his well-connected American friend William Rhodes Davis to come to Germany on September 26, to meet personally with Göring, who he claimed was "ready to become boss here." Hertslet's astonishing message promised that Göring "can assure absolute appeasement after Poland war if new combination here [i.e., Göring-headed government replacing Hitler] is assisted by neutral U.S.A. Government."[21]

Through the good offices of Hertslet's friend labor leader John L. Lewis, the message was given to Davis and passed to Roosevelt. Davis was able to answer that Roosevelt was "in perfect agreement," and "this side [is] ready providing flexibility with you."[22] But nothing came of this curious contact; Davis reported that he had not found confirmation that anything like this would occur. State Department officer Adolf A. Berle's diary entries of October 5 and 6 state that "Roosevelt now withdrew, apprehensive about falling for a Göring or Himmler trap." And in his October 7 diary entry Berle says: "So FDR has evidently ordered the whole [Davis] mission squelched."[23]

British Undersecretary Cadogan was at this time receiving a varied assortment of visitors. One of them, German Duke Karl-Alexander of Württemberg, Queen Mary's religiously inclined cousin, excitedly told Cadogan about a plot headed by Generals Halder and Beck to oust Hitler. Rather than see this as significant in the context of Stevens's and Best's ongoing contacts in Holland with alleged General Staff secret emissaries, Cadogan wearily recorded in his diary on December 13, "He [Württemberg] was very nice, but I should think rather credulous." Cadogan added: "We went to see the Marx brothers in 'At the Circus'—I don't see why I shouldn't relax sometimes and damn the work."[24]

To return to the drama being played out on the Dutch border, Schellenberg, under his alias, Captain Schämmel of the Army Transport Service, had prepared himself well for his first encounter with Stevens and Best on October 21. He brought with him to the meeting an officer calling himself Captain von Seidlitz, otherwise known as Sturmbannführer Salisch, and a Lieutenant Grosch, whose real name was Christiansen.

Stevens and Best brought with them a Dutch intelligence officer, Lieutenant Dirk Klop, who was documented as an Englishman. Klop was provided by Major General J. W. van Oorschot, the friendly chief of the Dutch Intelligence Service, whose cooperation had been enlisted by the British.

The rendezvous took place over an amicable lunch at a roadside café near the border village of Zutphen. From there the group went to Arnhem for more serious discussions. The meeting was cut short when their safe house seemed to be the object of Dutch police curiosity. Lieutenant Klop could have quietly fixed that problem, but the Germans did not feel secure and called it a day. October 25 was set as the date for a second meeting.

The October 25 meeting date was postponed to the thirtieth. This time Schellenberg brought an old friend, Professor Max de Crinis, Berlin University director of psychiatry, who used the alias Colonel Martini and played the role of a close aide to the leader of the opposition group in Germany. Christiansen, known as Grosch, again came along.

There seemed to be another hitch in the plans when at the prearranged border rendezvous Stevens and Best failed to appear. Dutch policemen watched the Germans inquisitively and took them off to the nearest Dutch police station for closer scrutiny. As Schellenberg recalled, "To all appearances, it seemed that we had fallen into a trap."[25] Their luggage was thoroughly searched. To his horror, Schellenberg spotted in Christiansen's toilet kit a roll of aspirin tablets that was wrapped with a German SS label. Only by a deft move was he able to grab the partly used roll and swallow it whole, label and all, before this telltale SS identification could come to the inspector's notice.

Klop, sent to meet the Germans at the border, finally showed up and cleared them through. When the Germans glumly described their ordeal, Stevens apologized profusely, claiming the driver had gone to the wrong pickup place, but Schellenberg/Schämmel was convinced that the interception had been deliberately planned to throw them off-balance.

Stevens and Best still felt uneasy about the whole thing, but it rated only a perfunctory note in Cadogan's diary, in which the undersecretary referred to the often promised but never produced "live generals." On October 23 Cadogan's diary read: " 'C' [Sinclair, head of the British Secret Service] has got report on interview with his German General friends [albeit indirectly through Schellenberg]." The next day he added: "C's Germans have put two questions and I discussed with H. [Foreign Secretary Halifax] answer to give them."[26]

On October 28 Cadogan made reference in his diary to two genuine Resistance overtures received through other channels: "Talked with H. [Halifax] and Van [Vansittart] about messages which Van had received from

'K'* and Max Hohenlohe [Max Eugen zu Hohenlohe-Langenburg]."
David Dilks, editor of Cadogan's diary, thought "K" probably stood for
Kanaris, a sometime spelling of Admiral Canaris's name. In the same diary
entry Cadogan says that he, Halifax, and Vansittart "decided on answers to
give—much on lines of that given to D. [Dahlerus] and the Generals
[Stevens's and Best's imaginary contacts with the General Staff]." It is significant to note that long after the war (June 26, 1953) Dahlerus visited
Cadogan and produced evidence that made the former undersecretary
conclude: "Canaris turned against Hitler long before we knew he did."[27]
The questions that this poses are how and when did Dahlerus learn this and
in 1939 did Göring know it as well.

SCHELLENBERG WAS ROUSED FROM A DEEP SLEEP BY A PHONE CALL FROM
Himmler, who gave him some details of a bomb plot against Hitler in
Munich. On November 8, only twenty minutes after Hitler had delivered
an emotional address at the historic beer hall celebrating the anniversary
of the abortive 1923 Nazi putsch, a powerful bomb went off, killing and
wounding several of the faithful who had gathered for the occasion. In
Nazi eyes, the scene of destruction was a shocking tableau of what might
have been had Hitler not left the hall early.

The American Embassy on November 9 telegraphed the Department
of State that the Nazis were blaming the British Secret Service for the incident.[28] A week later American Chargé Alexander Kirk gave further details. Hitler, it seemed, had two engagements in Munich that day; one was
a visit with Unity Mitford, a Nazi sympathizer belonging to the well-
known British Mitford family, who was recovering in a Munich hospital
from an attempted suicide. The other appointment, scheduled for 8:00
P.M., was the fateful Nazi beer hall reunion.[29]

German press claims that the British were responsible for the outrage
were vague and unconvincing. The actual perpetrator, Georg Elser, was
an obscure German cabinetmaker known for his Communist sympathies,
who had constructed a remarkably sophisticated bomb device. Links to
the banned Communist party of Germany could never be proved, nor,
from a propaganda point of view, would this have been helpful since
Goebbels was intent on blaming the British and their allies the Dutch in
order to create an incident justifying German invasion.

Himmler told Schellenberg that there was no doubt that the British
were behind the plot: the Nazi party line. Though not true, this provided

---

*Klemens von Klemperer, in his *German Resistance Against Hitler*, p. 201, fn. 61, says
that "K" most likely stood for the German chargé in London, Theo Kordt, a member
of the Resistance.

a reason for ordering Schellenberg to kidnap the two British agents Best and Stevens on the morrow. Himmler made it clear that these were Hitler's orders, not to be questioned, even though this might spoil Schellenberg's plan to achieve a more profound penetration of British intelligence networks and Resistance contacts within Germany.

The November 9 meeting was to take place at the Café Backus near the Dutch border town of Venlo. At 10:00 A.M. the two Englishmen set forth from The Hague in their big Buick automobile, hoping, but doubting, that the promised "generals" would put in an appearance. Again Klop of the Dutch service was with them. Another Dutchman, Jan Lemmens, was their driver as they headed for the border.

This time Schellenberg would have an SS detachment of twelve men nearby to capture the Englishmen, preferably before they entered the café. With them was an SS expert at "muscle" operations named Alfred Naujocks. He had been the man who staged the Gleiwitz operation on the eve of the Polish invasion, in which German prison inmates in fake Polish uniforms had been shot to create an illusion of Polish violence, thereby providing the Germans with a pretense for invading. (Journalists, always alert for catchy phrases, sometimes referred to Naujocks as "the man who started World War II.") It was an exaggeration to think that any incidents staged on the Dutch border could provide Hitler with a plausible excuse to invade the Netherlands. Even Goebbels would only halfheartedly try to sell that line.

Schellenberg remembered that he was growing nervous as his wait for the two British agents stretched into more than an hour. But finally, at 3:20 P.M., their auto pulled in and parked behind the café. Schellenberg ran out of the café to wave at them. The wave was a signal to Naujocks, whose Mercedes, filled with handpicked men then roared through the border barrier, firing wildly as they screeched to a halt in front of the café.

Stevens and Best raised their hands as ordered. Klop made a break for it, dashing toward the bushes, firing behind him over his shoulder as he went. One of the SS men returned his fire and brought him down, seriously wounded. In the confusion another SS goon tried to capture Schellenberg, mistaking him for the equally monocled Englishman Best. Schellenberg shook him off with appropriate oaths and sped off in his own car while Naujocks and his men bundled the Englishmen into the Mercedes; they were not seen again by British intelligence until the end of the war. Klop was taken as well but soon died of his wounds in the Düsseldorf hospital. The whole operation lasted only minutes; the Dutch border guards, taken by surprise, had had no time to react.[30]

On November 10 Cadogan noted cryptically in his diary: "Our men, who met, or were to have met [the generals] yesterday, [were] bumped off on Dutch-German frontier. Discussed [it] with 'H' [Halifax] and Menzies."[31] The next day, November 11, Dahlerus's efforts at mediation were halted; the British had rejected all terms put forward. The Venlo incident also brought to a temporary halt Müller's communications on behalf of the Resistance with British Minister Sir Francis d'Arcy Osborne via the Pope's good offices at the Vatican.

To add to the confusion, the MI-6 chief, Admiral Sinclair, had died on November 4, four days before the Munich bombing. This had created succession problems, but Menzies was the leading contender for the job and, despite Winston Churchill's doubts about his competence and politics, was appointed. Newly seated as chief, Menzies was said to have been ashen with shock when he first heard the news from Venlo. His head of MI-6 Air Intelligence Group, Captain Frederick Winterbotham, was witness to the grief revealed as the stricken man muttered, "What the devil are we going to do now?"

Hugh Trevor-Roper, the highly respected wartime MI-6 officer, in a commentary on the British intelligence organization written more than twenty years after the war, states: "How we used to sympathize with Menzies. He held a most invidious position, responsible to an exacting Prime Minister [Churchill]."[32] Referring to the Venlo incident, Trevor-Roper also notes: "Colonel Dansey's 'agents' in Europe were mopped up and swept away." Presumably on the basis of the hostile interrogations by the Gestapo of Stevens and Best, Himmler in a public speech "named all the chief officers of the SIS [MI-6] from 'C' [Menzies] downward."[33] And later the German press published exhaustive details of the MI-6 apparatus in Europe.[34]*

The Munich bomb incident remains something of an enigma. Whatever Georg Elser's motives may have been, they provided a propaganda

---

*If Venlo resulted in the near total destruction of the SIS networks, as claimed by Trevor-Roper and several other historians, it may not have been all a result of Stevens's and Best's capture and rigorous interrogation. Best, who wrote his memoirs after the war, freely admitted that he had told his interrogators what they clearly knew already, as could be judged by the questions they asked. The German SD, in his opinion, had good information about all operations in Holland, including his own. How could that have happened?

One guess is that their earlier source was an Australian, Charles Ellis—that is, if the accusations, sometimes disputed, made by former senior officer Peter Wright of MI-5 (internal security intelligence) are true. Wright in his long-banned-in-Britain book *Spy Catcher* (New York: Dell Publishing, 1988. First published by Viking Press, 1987), pp. 411–416, claims that when Ellis was faced with the interrogation report of an Abwehr officer who named him as an Abwehr spy and revealed other incriminating evidence, he confessed. He admitted giving the Germans detailed order of battle plans for

peg on which to hang conspiracy charges against Stevens and Best and an opportunity to interrogate them thoroughly. According to Resistance player Otto John, a Lufthansa official, the linkage of the bombing with the British agents at Venlo had been a brainchild of Schellenberg's friend Professor de Crinis.[35] As a propaganda effort to whip up more anti-British sentiment, the bombing in the beer cellar was not a success; the general public was not particularly aroused. The episode had the attributes of an opposition plot—if not Communist, then some other form of opposition. Nonetheless, Hitler awarded Crinis the Iron Cross in gratitude.

Elser, apprehended and held for the crime, never came to formal trial. Cynical observers, wise in the ways of the Nazis, suspected he was kept out of the public courts because the plot had been staged by Heydrich with encouragement from Himmler and Hitler himself. Within the Abwehr it was widely believed that Heydrich was responsible for the bombing, and according to plan, Elser had to take the fall.

Resistance activist Ulrich von Hassell revealed in his diary entry of November 16 that he guessed it to be "the act of dissatisfied elements within the [Nazi] Party," but this was only intuition. He was certain, however, that Goebbels's propaganda had not convinced the public that it was part of a British plot. "All Germany is discussing the attempt on Hitler's life at the Bürgerbräu," he writes, but "many people quite openly express regret that the explosion came so late [after Hitler had left the hall]." Hassell reported that people were whispering about the explosion, and speculation was rife that it had been a provocation staged by the Nazis to whip up anti-British sentiment on the eve of Hitler's expected campaign in the West. He too was inclined to believe the affair could be traced to ambitious or dissatisfied party leaders.[36]

Within the Abwehr circle of Resistance, it was widely believed that Heydrich had been responsible for the Elser actions. It was the kind of thing that Heydrich would do—either to make it appear that there had been British plot without killing Hitler or, some would believe, actually to get rid of Hitler so that his boss, Himmler, could take over and he could become number two. Arthur Nebe, president of the Criminal Police, Branch V, RSHA, who played a role in investigating the crime,

British intelligence during the war and betraying a British tap on the Hitler-Ribbentrop telephone link when the latter was Nazi ambassador in London (*Spy Catcher*, p. 415). Since Ellis worked for the better part of the war in New York as Sir William Stephenson's deputy, his German connection was of interest to the United States, even in retrospect. What makes the Peter Wright story all the more intriguing is his allegation that Ellis, while serving the Abwehr, was a triple agent under Soviet control.

seemed to have found no credible evidence linking it to the Communist party or any other opposition organization. Nebe's instincts led him to suspect Heydrich as being behind this diabolical scheme, but evidence was lacking, and anyway, it would have been foolhardy to have tried to indict him. Whatever the case, the plot did not inflame public opinion against Britain as Nazi propagandists would have it; this had not been another Reichstag fire.

Nebe's views were shared with the Resistance, with which he collaborated, but there would be those who had doubts about him.* As a Gestapo officer, he had in fact been associated with anti-Jewish atrocities during the early stages of the war, but he claimed to have secretly broken with the Nazis and joined the Resistance because of the revulsion he felt. Whatever his past and his motives, he proved valuable to the Resistance in his position as chief of the Criminal Police with access to Gestapo files, and he ultimately died on the gallows after being charged in connection with the July 20, 1944, bomb plot against Hitler.

André Brissaud, a French chronicler of the Resistance, writes that Himmler was outraged that Nebe could not come up with a case implicating the British with Elser. In his frustration Himmler brought to Munich a well-known medium, who went into a trance to find the "truth." Both Nebe and Gestapo Chief Müller watched the medium writhing on the sofa when he suddenly blurted out the name Otto. This enigmatic utterance, perhaps meant to incriminate Otto Strasser and his alleged British patrons, proved nothing. Nebe could only conclude that his boss, Himmler, was "incurably credulous" and the medium was a fraud. Enraged by the failure of this experiment in the occult, Himmler vented his anger by kicking the hapless Elser, who still protested that he had worked alone without accomplices.[37]

---

*The Austrian Wilhelm Hoettl, prominent SD official (Branch IV), considered Nebe an opportunist whose loyalty to the Resistance was questionable (Wilhelm Hoettl, *The Secret Front*, [New York: Praeger, 1954], pp. 61, 62), but the risks he took and the fate he met on the gallows belie this opinion. It should be noted that after the failure of the July 20 bomb plot against Hitler, Nebe incriminated himself by fleeing and going into hiding rather than be forced to give testimony demanded of him by Gestapo chief Kaltenbrunner that would implicate his friend and fellow Resistance fighter Berlin Police Chief Helldorf. This act of loyalty to a friend and to the Resistance was used against him during his trial and served as basis for his being hanged—Roger Manvell and Heinrich Fraenkel, *The Canaris Conspiracy* (New York: David McKay, Inc., 1969), p. 24.

Hans Gisevius, contact of the OSS station chief in Bern Allen Dulles, with the insight afforded him as having been a Gestapo officer before switching to the Abwehr, vouched for Nebe's credentials as a genuine anti-Nazi worthy of the Resistance's trust.

Elser spent the rest of the war in solitary confinement, although he was treated reasonably well, even given a workroom in which he could continue to craft his beloved zithers. It should be noted that he was incarcerated in the same prison as British officers Best and Stevens after their capture at Venlo.* He was never put on trial despite his confession, but as Germany came crumbling down during the last days of the war, he was hanged. Perhaps he knew too much.

*For glimpses of Captain Best during the last few trying days of the war, as seen at close range by another Nazi victim, we are indebted to the wartime memoir of Fey von Hassell (Pirzio-Biroli), daughter of the Resistance martyr Ulrich von Hassell (*Hostage of the Third Reich*, ed. David Forbes-Watt [New York: Charles Scribner's Sons, 1989]). Fey von Hassell, incarcerated toward the end of the war only because she was her father's daughter, writes with evident admiration of her fellow prisoner Captain Best. Other prisoners in the group included such luminaries as Dr. Martin Niemöller, who gained fame as a Christian voice against Hitler; ex-French Premier Léon Blum; German industrialist Fritz Thyssen; Dr. Josef Müller, Canaris's Vatican contact, who had been finally cornered; Resistance member General Franz Halder; and former Chancellor of Austria Kurt von Schuschnigg. Having been subjected to five years of solitary confinement, Best remarkably recovered to assume a very useful role among the captives. His courage and strong will helped the others to maintain a semblance of unity and good spirits during the critical last days before the final fall of Germany when their lives hung in the balance; the Gestapo wanted no witnesses to its inhumanity. This tall, monocled figure of an English gentleman saved Fey von Hassell and the others from execution by his influence over their guard, Untersturmführer Edgar Stiller. Stiller, curiously dominated by Best, refused to carry out an execution order long enough for American troops to rescue them — Fey von Hassell, *Hostage of the Third Reich*, pp. xii, xiii, 183, 203, 207, 209.

TWELVE

Hitler Goes West

THE STAKES HAD BEEN HIGH AT VENLO. SCHELLENBERG TOOK A CHANCE, fraught with the personal risk of capture or death, but the gamble paid off: He made a score—and won a promotion. One wonders why a fairly well-known personage in Germany such as Schellenberg, disguised only by a monocle, had not been recognized by British intelligence. Also puzzling was why the British did not pay more attention to inconsistencies between an offer presented by Schellenberg at Venlo and offers made by Müller through the Vatican in Project X, when both ostensibly originated with the Resistance.[1]

It is unfortunate that the Venlo overtures, suspicious at best, had been so enthusiastically embraced by Chamberlain, Sinclair, and Menzies when a parade of obviously authentic Resistance emissaries who had pleaded for help from the British, had been rebuffed. Adam von Trott, an object of unwarranted suspicions, had no success in either Britain or the United States, perhaps because it was difficult for American and British officials in their naïveté to understand how a German Foreign Ministry representative, an employee of the despised Ribbentrop, could at the same time be a secret spokesman for the Resistance.[2] Ewald von Kleist-Schmenzin, despite his friendship with Ian Colvin, the well-connected British journalist in Berlin who became a Foreign Ministry expert on Germany when war broke out, also left London without reaching any understanding with the British. The German chargé d'affaires in London, Theo Kordt, a member of the Foreign Ministry Resistance circle, had long discussions with British go-between Conwell-Evans but could not resolve the Polish problem. If it was contact with the German military that the British wanted, it is difficult to understand why some responsible Whitehall official did not take a greater interest in Chief of Staff Halder's secret emissary, Colonel Hans Böhm-Tettelbach, in early September 1938. Then there was the international lobbying of the peripatetic Carl Goerdeler, good friend of Vansittart's, who was highly respected; he sent several messages to the British that promised a revolt by the Wehrmacht. And State Secretary Ernst von Weizsäcker of the German Foreign Ministry, a tireless champion of peace, worked through Erich Kordt, his chief of the Ministerial Bureau, in a vain attempt to interest the British in peace without Hitler.* Hans Ritter, star informant of Vansittart's ace operative in Europe, Group Captain Malcolm D. Christie, kept the British foreign secretary informed.[3] With such an array of past contacts and with the current Vatican link to General Beck, Canaris, and other impressive Resistance figures, how was it that Chamberlain and his intelligence advisers put so much faith in Best's and Stevens's mysterious "generals" at Venlo, whose sting created such havoc?

As useful as Venlo had been to Heydrich and Schellenberg, it was inevitable that the SD and Gestapo would also get wind of Britain's flirtation with the real opposition. Admiral Canaris, given no advance notice of Venlo by Schellenberg, was infuriated by his rival's operation. He was also justifiably worried that Best and Stevens, under Gestapo-style interrogation, would disclose incriminating information about Britain's various Resistance contacts. Despite several requests made by Canaris, Heydrich never disseminated to the Abwehr the Englishmen's interrogation reports, an ominous indication that the SD had learned more than it wanted Canaris to know.[†]

---

*To the distress of the Soviet prosecution team at the Nuremberg war crimes trial, Weizsäcker testified that the Soviets had offered Murmansk as a submarine base to the Germans during a critical period of the Battle of the Atlantic as a case in which Stalin was willing to render help to Hitler at British expense. It may or may not have been a coincidence that N. D. Zorya, an assistant prosecutor on the Soviet team, shot himself a few days after Weizsäcker's testimony—Robert E. Conot, *Justice at Nuremberg* (New York: Carroll & Graf Publishers, 1984), p. 420.

Noel Annan, British officer in wartime MI-14 assessing German intentions and strategy, alleges in his 1995 book *Changing Enemies* (London: HarperCollins), p. 111, that the British Foreign Office "suppressed documents" and "manipulated evidence" at the close of the war; it specifically "tampered with evidence "that might have helped Ernst von Weizsäcker when "Americans put him on trial" at Nuremberg.

†Resistance activist Groscurth recorded in his diary entry of November 15, 1939, that Heydrich had not given Canaris information gained from the interrogation of Best and Stevens despite three requests—Klemperer, *German Resistance Against Hitler*, p. 162, fn. 66; Harold Deutsch, *The Conspiracy Against Hitler in the Twilight War* (Minneapolis: University of Minnesota Press, 1968), p. 247, from Groscurth's diary entry of November 15.

Canaris could reason that Heydrich's motives with regard to the Venlo operation were, on one hand, to discover more about Resistance circles and the extent to which they had established contact with the British and, on the other, to gain insight into British-Dutch secret collaboration that could provide Germany with an excuse to invade neutral Netherlands.[4] Canaris had been disturbed by Keller's allegations concerning Müller's role in the Vatican and hard pressed to explain them to the SD. But outspoken criticism of Nazi policies, long voiced by such opposition leaders as Schacht, Weizsäcker, Beck, Goerdeler, and Hassell, was enough to focus Heydrich's attention on the Resistance underworld. Heydrich also had definite suspicions about his old friend Canaris, whom he would half-admiringly, half-accusingly refer to as "an old fox with whom one has to be on the watch."[5] Hitler himself described Beck as the one general who "might attempt something."[6] Whatever Heydrich learned from Stevens and Best under interrogation, either fresh information or confirmation of what he had already extracted from other spies, he knew enough to provide a basis for a thorough investigation of the Abwehr and military circles of the Resistance. The mystery is why Heydrich did not move against them more aggressively than he did.

Venlo had set back the Resistance's negotiations with the British through the Pope's good offices. Some five or six weeks were lost as both parties, British and Resistance, reexamined their situations. It was demoralizing for the Resistance and British intelligence alike. Müller's role at the Vatican, already suspect in the eyes of the SD because of the Keller affair, was made more risky by Venlo. In the meantime Müller had to act with extreme caution.

Burned at Venlo, the British also worried that Müller might be another provocateur although the Pope never wavered in his confidence in the Abwehr agent. His Holiness again vouched for Müller and his Resistance principals when pressed for reassurances by British Ambassador Osborne at the Vatican. For security reasons, however, Müller moved from the Vatican to San Bellarmino.[7]

Josef Müller's effective efforts at the Vatican had come close to producing a mutually acceptable agreement with the British when they were interrupted by Venlo, but the Resistance itself, only loosely allied in its crusade, was probably at fault for having fielded such a variety of uncoordinated emissaries to the British. The Pope certainly thought that the other Resistance channels to the British, of which he was vaguely aware, had confused and vitiated the Vatican's efforts.[8]

NEWS IN EARLY FEBRUARY 1940[9] THAT U.S. UNDERSECRETARY OF STATE Sumner Welles would undertake a fact-finding visit to Europe for President Roosevelt and Secretary of State Hull had an unsettling effect on some members of the Resistance. Goerdeler confided to a friend that Welles's mission could convey to the generals an impression "that the other side was ready after all to negotiate with Hitler. . . ."[10] According to Hassell's diary, Resistance sources had reported: "The sole purpose of Sumner Welles's visit was to talk Hitler out of a Western offensive."[11]

At a suggestion made by Hassell to American Chargé d'Affaires Alexander Kirk, Welles met with Hjalmar Schacht and Ernst von Weizsäcker, both collaborators of the Resistance. As number two man in the German Foreign Ministry, Weizsäcker had to be circumspect in what was billed as an official meeting with Welles on March 1, but in hushed tones, meant to foil audio devices in his office, the German state secretary made it clear that he differed greatly with Hitler's foreign policies. Upon parting, Weizsäcker had tears in his eyes,[12] which said more than any words to describe his anguish and frustration.

Schacht was more outspoken, confiding in Welles that there was a movement led by certain generals dedicated to removing Hitler from power who needed assurances from the West that Germany would be allowed to regain its "rightful place in the world." Welles was cautious, but Schacht was heartened by the undersecretary's expressed wish that they both stay in touch and by his assurances that the United States had no intention of ever dismembering a defeated Germany. For the second-ranking foreign affairs official of a still-neutral United States to discuss the treatment of a defeated Germany after the war gives some idea of the tenor of their conversation and must surely have sent a signal that the United States intended to join France and Britain as belligerents if Germany attacked them. Welles argued that the prevention of an offensive in the West would be in Hitler's best interests since the Führer could survive only by abandoning his agenda of conquest; to invade Western Europe would surely lead to his destruction.[13] While Hitler's refusal to let Schacht travel abroad prevented him from following up on Welles's suggestion that they meet again, the American chargé in Berlin kept his own lines out to the Resistance through his good friend Helmuth von Moltke, leader of the so-called Kreisau Circle of the Resistance. When Kirk left Berlin, he turned his Moltke contact over to First Secretary George Kennan[14] (later to become prominent as the architect of containment, keystone of the U.S. Cold War policy toward the USSR).

By the spring of 1940 new military developments also interfered with Resistance efforts to reach an agreement with the British by way of the Vatican. German military campaigns in Norway and Denmark killed whatever hopes survived the Venlo catastrophe. German officers, upon whom plans for a putsch depended, found it difficult to violate their oaths, much less commit high treason against the state while engaged in combat. Once committed to military action, most German officers would not sell out their comrades-in-arms.

On April 9, 1940, military Resistance leader General Beck instructed Müller to tell the Pope through Father Leiber that "his friends in Berlin" regretted that the negotiations were at an end. Müller's message also revealed to Pius XII the still-classified secret of Hitler's planned aggression in the West: "In the name of the decent Germans we repudiate this breach of neutrality, and we are convinced that the greater part of the German people, if it could decide freely, would condemn this violation of international law."[15]

If Hitler's military plans in the West temporarily upset Resistance plans to remove him, they did not keep certain Resistance leaders from secretly alerting his would-be victims of their imminent danger by selected leaks of top secret German invasion plans. This was treason, but treason justified by the hope that Western democracies, particularly France and Britain, informed of their peril, would prepare themselves to resist the Nazi onslaught convincingly enough and soon enough to deter Hitler from committing national suicide. Hitler's first target, however, was Norway.

OPERATION WESER-EXERCISE, AS HITLER'S PLANNED INVASION OF NORWAY was known in code terminology, meant gambling the entire German surface fleet. German intelligence regarding British intentions toward Norway was to prove crucial to German success. Although Germany's action in Norway had been part of Hitler's strategic concept, standing on its own merit, its timing was in response to specific British plans as reported to Hitler.[16] The Abwehr was naturally tasked with intelligence support for the German invasion of Norway and Denmark. Canaris reported in mid-March that the British Home Fleet had been transferred to Scapa Flow to be nearer the Norwegian coast. His agents had also been able to observe a buildup of British troops and transports along the northeast coast of England, a good indication that the British intended to occupy Narvik and Trondheim.[17]

Hitler's decision to move against Norway was made on April 2, 1940, primarily on the basis of information acquired in March by Göring's code-cracking Forschungsamt unit, which had intercepted a Finnish diplomatic message transmitted from Paris to Helsinki. The Finnish Embassy message stated that Winston Churchill had passed to the French in a secret meeting information that a British expeditionary force was about to invade Norway. Abwehr information provided the details that Britain would make landings in Narvik and Trondheim.

On the same day that Hitler made his decision to strike, Admiral Canaris's deputy Hans Oster sought out his old friend Colonel Gijsbertus Jacobus Sas, Dutch military attaché in Berlin, to warn him that a German invasion of Norway was imminent. On that date three German steamships filled with troops kept below to avoid observation sailed for Narvik.

As Oster intended, Sas informed his colleague in the Norwegian legation in Berlin, but astonishingly, the information seemed so unbelievable that the legation refused to report it to Oslo. The story, however, quickly leaked out. The Swedish press reported that German troops were boarding invasion craft in Baltic ports.

According to Colonel Erwin Lahousen, Abwehr senior officer and Resistance conspirator, his organization had learned that despite advance notice of Weser-Exercise, the British could not believe that the Germans would risk their navy in a contest with the Royal Navy. After the war Lahousen told British Foreign Service officer Ian Colvin: "Foreign Consuls had reported the movements of German shipping and the Abwehr had records of their telephone conversations [reporting it]."[18] In fact, the British had received a firm report from Oslo on April 7, two days before the invasion, that the Germans intended to take Narvik, and there were abundant sightings of German ship movements toward Norway to confirm this. But Whitehall believed this indicated only a raid of limited scope. Not until April 9, when the invasion of Norway began, did the British belatedly recognize that the Germans intended to invade all Norway.[19]

The British official history *British Intelligence in the Second World War* strangely concludes that the Germans "achieved total surprise by their invasion of Norway"; the history adds that it had been a British intelligence failure caused by inadequate collection and faulty analysis.[20] The Germans suffered heavy casualties but succeeded in placing most of Norway under Nazi control. The British, who woke up to what was happening too late, had failed to repel the invasion. It may have been a failure in intelligence analysis, but it did not seem to have been a failure of collection.

During the German occupation of Norway Canaris in his Resistance role was well served by an agent in Norway named Theodor Steltzer. Steltzer had been in opposition to Hitler from the beginning. In 1933, the year Hitler came to power, he found himself charged with high treason for writing and distributing seditious material vilifying the newly declared Führer. Somehow, in the confusion of the times, he was let off without a trial, but his anti-Nazi ardor had not been cooled by this close call. He continued to work underground against Hitler, although this time more discreetly in association with Moltke and the Kreisau Circle of intellectuals.

Steltzer's earlier indiscretions had been forgotten when he was accepted by the army after war broke out. When he looked up Canaris, probably at the suggestion of Moltke, he was recruited for the Abwehr—and the Abwehr circle of the Resistance. In 1940 Canaris assigned him to Norway, where his main task was to establish secret liaison with the Norwegian anti-Nazi underground intent on harassing the invading German Army. Steltzer led a double life at great risk to himself. Overtly he served General Nikolaus von Falkenhorst as chief of Army Transport. Covertly he worked with the Norwegian underground against his own army, helping it to survive. He was best remembered by his underground cohorts for protecting Bishop Berggrav, one of Norway's wartime underground heroes.

GÖRING, IN THE MEANTIME, WAS STILL USING DAHLERUS AS HIS AGENT IN backdoor diplomacy. During the hard-fought naval battle for Narvik, Göring had Dahlerus offer to negotiate at Narvik an armistice in which neutral Sweden, which was refusing to allow critically needed German supplies to reach Norway, would administer the area until the war was over.[21] Nothing came of this sortie into high politics, but the Luftwaffe had acquitted itself well in the Norway campaign, boosting Göring's sagging esteem in Hitler's eyes.

The air marshal now prepared for the next campaign, Case Yellow, the invasion of France. This was being done with considerable haste since the secret was beginning to leak out to the dismay and undisguised anger of Hitler.[22] Göring's Forschungsamt code-cracking unit intercepted a message dated May 7 from the Belgium representative at the Vatican stating that a "German traitor" had arrived from Berlin on April 29 and revealed to the Vatican the precise date set for Case Yellow.*

---

*Despite the failure of Project X negotiations and evidence that the SD and Gestapo had suspicions about the Vatican, Admiral Canaris maintained secret indirect contact with the Holy See until he lost his position in 1944—National Archives, Record Group 226, Entry 17, Box 1.

THIRTEEN

Case Yellow:
German Invasion of France

FRANCE, GERMANY'S TRADITIONAL ANTAGONIST, NOW KEY TO ITS PREEMI-
nence in Western Europe, was an inevitable Nazi target. Exhilarated by
his victories in Czechoslovakia and Poland, Hitler would not listen to any
formulas for peace except his own uncompromising terms, which meant
the vassalage of France and at least the neutralization and isolation of
Britain. Only with full control of Western Europe could he proceed with
his grand plan for the defeat of Russia.

Hans Oster, like most of his coconspirators in the Resistance, feared
that a German invasion of France would prove disastrous for his country.
Statistically the British-French Allies outgunned Germany. Confident
that his sentiments were shared by his chief, Admiral Canaris, and others
in the Resistance, Oster systematically set about warning Hitler's next victims, hoping that German defeat in Western Europe would end the war
and bring about the downfall of Nazi power in Germany. Oster described
his self-assigned mission to his friends: "It is my hope and my duty to rid
Germany . . . of this scourge [Hitler]."[1]

Almost certainly the "German traitor" identified by the Belgian envoy
to the Vatican in his intercepted message of May 7, concerning the imminent invasion of Denmark and Norway, was Josef Müller, but it was Oster
who had passed to Müller the invasion alert for secret dissemination to the
Western Allies. Similarly, Oster tried to warn France and Britain, as well as
the Netherlands and Belgium, of the coming German invasion of the
Lowlands and France. He worked through his friend Colonel Gijsbertus

Jacobus Sas, Dutch military attaché in Berlin, whom he had used as a conduit for the warning prior to the Denmark invasion.[2] In an act for which he could have been shot if caught out, Oster disclosed to Sas in October 1939 that Belgium and the Netherlands would be invaded to distract the Allies from the major attack on France.* The problem was that Sas's superiors would not believe him. Having refused to reveal his source out of concern for Oster's safety, Sas was accused of sensationalizing his reports. The Netherlands supreme commander, General Reynders, dismissed the report and forbade its further dissemination to the Dutch government hierarchy, frantic for news of possible invasion.

Despite his rebuff by Reynders, Sas confided his news to two highly placed friends and even tried to reach the queen to alert her to the imminent danger. When the invasion was postponed and nothing happened on the day predicted, Sas's credibility was further damaged as far as Reynders was concerned. When Sas argued his case, the supreme commander angrily accused him of wasting his time with idle gossip.

As it had done before Munich and again before the invasion of Poland, the Resistance believed it must again try to arouse the German High Command if it hoped to topple Hitler. While it was important to convince the British and French that the German threat was real and that only a strong line backed by credible military preparedness could hope to deter Hitler from another rapacious adventure, it was even more urgent to galvanize the German Army through its senior officers to take a stand against Hitler's aggressive plans. The letter from Resistance leaders to Field Marshal Keitel, urging him to protest Hitler's intentions to invade Poland had fallen on deaf ears. The Polish campaign succeeded, but the Western Allies were aroused to the point of war even though no military action in defense of Poland was taken. Now the question was, Could the Army command, faced with the certainty of all-out war with France and Britain if France were invaded, be convinced to move against Hitler? An attack on France would mean real war, not a so-called phony war.

As chief of the Army General Staff, Franz Halder had the responsibility for planning the German invasion of the Lowlands and France. This had

*Sas, using a self-devised simple code, had telephoned electrifying news on April 3 to Captain Kruls, adjutant of the Dutch secretary of war, that the German invasion of Denmark and Norway would take place on the revised date of April 9 and the invasion of the Lowlands and France would follow soon thereafter. Sas also passed the word to the Danish naval attaché, van Kjolsen, and the Norwegian attaché, Stang. (Later it was discovered that Stang had not forwarded the vital information. Roger Manvell and Heinrich Fraenckel in their book *The Canaris Conspiracy*, p. 85, allege that Stang in fact was a German agent.)

placed a strain on him since he did not believe in his mission, nor did he agree with Hitler's outmoded battle strategy, which he described to intimates as an "unimaginative replica of the [World War I] Schlieffen Plan."[3] He also disagreed with the timing; as planned, the attack could last well into the winter—not a season in which to wage offensive warfare in Western Europe.

Not only faced with planning responsibility for a war he did not want and harassed by unrealistic demands levied on him by Hitler, Halder was being constantly prodded by his Resistance colleagues to assure army support for a putsch against Hitler. The Resistance plotters had burdened Halder with a call to action contained in a memorandum given him in late October. Pressure for peace coming from the Foreign Ministry Resistance circle headed by State Secretary Ernst von Weizsäcker was matched by similar pressure exerted by the Abwehr circle that had updated the 1938 blueprint for military action against Hitler.

Halder was so unsettled by the risks he was being asked to take and by the fact that his subordinate General Karl Heinrich von Stülpnagel was already positioning troops for maximum advantage in support of a coup that he could not hold back tears of frustration when he discussed his problems with Abwehr resistance leader Groscurth. On top of all his problems, Halder's rebuff by an angry Brauchitsch when the field marshal's cooperation was solicited was more than he could bear. Halder thought that Brauchitsch agreed with Resistance aims and was taken by terrible surprise when the field marshal, whose cooperation was central to the plan, erupted in anger and accused him of high treason. During a Resistance damage control meeting held at the Abwehr's Zossen headquarters, Canaris announced the startling news that Halder had suffered a nervous collapse.[4]

Halder, it seemed, lost his nerve completely when Brauchitsch quoted to him an angry outburst by Hitler in which the Führer ranted about the "spirit of Zossen," which he promised to eradicate. Mistakenly taking this to mean that the plot had been compromised, Halder collapsed with fear and was thereafter in no state to take part in any putsch.

Oster's assumption that his leaks to Sas telling of the Western invasion would reach Britain and France had been wrong. The Abwehr officer had not known about Reynders's refusal to allow dissemination of this critical information to his allies. Whitehall, however, found out about German plans in other ways.[5]

On January 10 the complete German invasion plans were found in a German aircraft that had crash-landed in Belgium. In the papers found by the Belgians in the wreckage, the Ardennes Forest was described as the major point of thrust.[6] Oster, who had the same information from the Abwehr, passed it to the Allies, this time through Müller and his Vatican contact, Father Leiber; it was this message that Belgian envoy Nieuwenhuys retransmitted to Brussels, only to have it intercepted by the Germans. It must not have been too difficult for the SD to track back the Vatican's source to Müller, already under suspicion because of the Benedictine monk Keller's earlier indiscretions. Initially, however, suspicion was directed toward the Belgian military attaché, known to have good connections in the German High Command.

At a January 20, 1940, conference with his military leaders, Hitler bemoaned the aircraft crash, admitting that it had revealed "everything to the enemy." Because of the aircraft incident, he became furious about security laxity in general[7] and called in both Canaris and Heydrich, to demand that they investigate their respective organizations and apprehend anyone found responsible for the leakage. Lieutenant Colonel Joachim Rohleder took over the general investigation, while Canaris busied himself with damage control within the Abwehr, taking steps to protect his men Müller and Oster, who he feared were already under suspicion. Müller, when questioned by Rohleder, told a concocted story pinning the leak on the Italian ambassador at the Holy See, who he claimed had learned of the invasion date from a source on German Foreign Minister von Ribbentrop's staff. Rohleder's investigation nonetheless pointed directly at Müller as the guilty party and even extended into another case implicating Oster, but Canaris with his usual wizardry managed to sweep it all under the carpet. Gestapo chief Heinrich Müller and presumably his immediate superior, Heydrich, probably on Himmler's orders, bowed out of the case on the ground that it was an Abwehr internal disciplinary matter not demanding further SD investigation or prosecution.[8] Again Canaris had survived a close call and managed to protect his sometimes careless staff, thanks to a reluctance that Himmler seemed to have when it came to investigating suspicions concerning his rival. Nonetheless, Canaris was badly shaken by the whole affair.

If Canaris was upset by the consequences of the security investigation, Hermann Göring was no less distressed that one of his aircraft had aroused Hitler's concern over security. The disastrous accident, permitting the Allies to seize and study the German invasion plans, made Göring and his Luftwaffe look bad. The *Reichsmarschall* was distraught as the full facts about the accident became known to Hitler. At first Göring had hoped that the compromising documents had been consumed by fire when the aircraft struck the ground. He even consulted a clairvoyant to reassure him that the critical documents had not fallen into Allied hands. And as a test, he tried burning some papers in his fireplace to prove that the invasion file could not have survived the fire upon impact. The only result of his home-made simulation was badly burned hands. Nothing assuaged Hitler's anger, and Göring, diminished in standing, was ordered by the Führer to get rid of the Luftwaffe commander and his chief of staff, who had ordered the ill-fated flight. Hitler also postponed the invasion date.[9]

Göring again tried his hand at secret talks with the British, this time involving negotiations calculated to achieve Hitler's objectives in Western Europe without having to run the risk of further conflict. Success in achieving a bloodless victory would perhaps improve his diminished standing with Hitler as well as avoid war with the Western Allies. On two occasions in December 1939 he tried to make contact with the British. First he used a Count Eric von Rosen; then he worked through a Norwegian Air Force officer, Major Tryggve Gran, but they were no more successful than Dahlerus had been.[10]

If human intelligence sources were considered fallible by skeptical Allied intelligence analysts, and the unmistakable evidence contained in the captured invasion plans ignored, the British Radio Security Service (RSS) monitoring German military traffic should have rung alarm bells when it revealed a sudden surge of activity in the Ardennes region. And German air reconnaissance over the Lowlands and France made invasion plans obvious.[11] When the indications were added up, there could now be little doubt about what the Germans intended to do and when they would do it. Where they would do it also seemed conclusive. Most of the evidence pointed to an Ardennes invasion, but the French Army refused to believe it since it ran counter to accepted military doctrine.

As early as March 25 British/Free Czech agent Paul Thümmel (code alias A-54), the doubled Abwehr officer, had reported that the principal German invasion thrust would be through the Ardennes Forest with the panzer divisions crossing the Meuse north of Sedan.[12] Yet Thümmel also reported an attack through Belgium and the Netherlands. The answer to this apparent inconsistency was that both routes would be used.* Aware that France's defensive strategy was based on a German attack according to the old Schlieffen Plan of World War I—a dash through the Lowlands—the German High Command obliged by overrunning both Bel-

---

*Wartime British MI-14 (strategic estimates) officer Noel Annan in a recent book (*Changing Enemies* [London: HarperCollins, 1995], p. 10) perhaps incorrectly states that British-Czech agent Paul Thümmel had not warned of the Ardennes invasion route. He mentions, however, that "a woman of the Polish underground" did warn of this attack. The anonymous woman fits the description of Admiral Canaris's friend Halina Szymanska in Switzerland, who on guidance from Canaris was reporting to the British.—Colvin, *Canaris, Chief of Intelligence*, pp. 85–92. Also see Nigel West, *A Thread of Deceit* (New York: Random House, 1985), pp. 36–38.

gium and the Netherlands. Army Group B's thirty divisions launched a four-pointed invasion into these two hapless countries, causing French and British forces to concentrate on holding a line along the Dyle River in Belgium. In the south movements by the German Army Group C with its nineteen divisions served as a feint. What the French had failed to foresee was the main German invasion force, Army Group A, forty-five divisions strong, consisting mostly of hard-hitting panzer units, which struck through the Ardennes and part of Luxembourg, then dashed toward the English Channel to cut off Allied forces, taken by surprise.

The British and French forces seem to have been caught completely off-balance and were appalled to discover that the main German invasion force had attacked on May 10 through the "impenetrable" Ardennes Forest as though it were a parade ground. How could this have happened? Certainly, massive German redeployment required to accommodate General Erich von Manstein's plan could not have been hidden from the French. German infantry divisions were increased from twenty-five to fifty-seven, and seven out of ten panzer divisions were poised to strike south of Liège—hardly an augmentation easily disguised.

General Alphonse Georges, commander in chief of Allied forces on the western front, had predicted the German strategy but could not persuade the French commander in chief, General Maurice Gamelin, that the German buildup in the north was only a diversion and that the main attack would take place between the Meuse and the Moselle. On March 8 King Leopold of Belgium also warned Gamelin that the Germans would make the main thrust through the Ardennes, thereby trapping Allied forces covering the Belgium front.[13] This information had originated with Oster, who signaled an urgent meeting with Sas on November 8, two days before the German invasion, to tell him that the tanks were about to roll and that Hitler, "that swine," had already left for the front. Sas hurriedly met with the Belgian military attaché to pass on the news and rushed to phone his own War Office in The Hague. While the unbelieving Netherlands High Command refused to disseminate this information, King Leopold at least notified the French.

On May 1 the French military attaché in Switzerland received reliable intelligence, consistent with Leopold's report, confirming that Sedan would be the German invasion's "center of gravity."[14] Despite such warnings, Gamelin did nothing to adjust France's defenses or mount air reconnaissance of the area. French tank patrols actually encountering German tanks in the Ardennes did not even trigger an alarm. Gamelin, completely resistant to the obvious evidence, allowed Allied forces to fall for the German ruse when Hitler's armies struck on May 10.

The British officer Frederick W. Winterbotham, a key man in the Ultra cipher-breaking operation at Bletchley Park outside London at the time, found it hard to believe that Gamelin could have been so blind. In his authoritative book *The Ultra Secret*, Winterbotham goes so far as to write: "To the intelligent onlooker, it appeared that he was deliberately allowing the Germans a quick victory. . . ."[15]

In *The Gathering Storm* Winston Churchill describes how "the decisive stroke of the enemy was not a turning movement on the flank [i.e., the Lowlands] but a break through the main front. This," he admitted, "none of us or the French, who were in responsible command, foresaw."[16] As late as May 8, two days before the invasion, a British War Office intelligence summary stated: "Still no sign that an invasion of Belgium and France [is] imminent."[17] In view of the good intelligence available, how could this have been?

France had been a victim of rigid preconceptions on the part of its military leaders, who saw the German threat through the lens of a Maginot Line mentality. Chief of Staff Gamelin's theory of the "Power of Defense" had become the military bible of France. "Fortress France" would, unfortunately, prove useless against fast-moving, deep-thrusting panzer strikes. The age of tank warfare had arrived, but France did not know it. Gamelin's General Staff was unmovable and his defenses, in reality as well as figuratively, were cast in concrete—almost as unmovable. The French could not conceive of an Ardennes offensive; their greatest sin, however, was to rush troops into Belgium when it happened—to fall into the German trap set for them. There had, in fact, been an Ultra intercept containing a German order for a full panzer corps to move south from its position on the Belgian frontier and join the Sedan attack.[18]

It had been German General von Manstein's idea to strike hardest though the Ardennes, but if this strategy fooled the Allies, it had worried many of the German generals, who feared it would not work. Only by going over their heads to Hitler was Manstein able to get his innovative idea adopted. Hitler liked it, even claimed it as his own, yet at the last moment it was nearly abandoned.

The General Staff argument raised against Manstein's plan was based on German air photography that had spotted strong French fortified emplacements guarding the approach to the Meuse River at Sedan. An alert Austrian photo interpreter took another look at the pictures and noticed that the French defensive fortifications were not yet operational; they were still under construction. This would enable Lt. General von Kleist's tank column to advance without dangerous interference. As it turned out, the German armored columns could cross the Meuse and with strong air support race forward without having to wait for the infantry to catch up.

The French were stunned as they saw defeat facing them. The British too were shocked, but now fighting for survival, the two allies were drawn closer together in common cause. With their fortunes in doubt, but with hope still strong and determination even stronger, it was no time to negotiate with the enemy. Hard-liners such as Vansittart had always believed that German "militarists," once shed of Hitler, would not so easily abandon his territorial gains. Moreover, the multivaried peace overtures, to which Britain had been subjected, were not only confusing but bespoke a lack of coordination and perhaps disarray in the ranks of the Resistance. Further confusing the situation had been the "semiofficial" feelers sent out by Göring, which had only teased the British with innuendos of his own willingness to jettison Hitler. The Venlo sting had not only been a terrible operational failure for the British but had made Chamberlain look the fool. Astonishingly, however, Chamberlain continued to hope for some last-minute vindication of his search for German generals willing to make a deal right up to the invasion of Western Europe, when Churchill replaced him.

Defeatist Lord Lothian, British ambassador in Washington, apparently still marched to Chamberlain's drummer, out of step with Churchill's new policies. On his own authority he wrote his good friend Adam von Trott, exhorting him to work toward British-German peace. Lord Lothian did not specify "peace without Hitler" and left Trott confused about whether his friend was addressing him as a Foreign Ministry man or as a Resistance fighter. Trott did nothing, letting this unclear and untimely entreaty die quietly without referring it to anyone either in Ribbentrop's office or in Resistance circles.

Operation X had been the best effort by the Resistance to reach an agreement with the British. But by the spring of 1940 it had become apparent to the Vatican that the British would not meet Resistance terms. Realizing that a German invasion of the Lowlands and France was inevitable, the Vatican leaders feared that the Pope would be at serious risk if his role as intermediary between the Resistance and the British became known to Hitler. Mussolini too could pose a problem if it all came out, by accusing the Pope of violating the Lateran Pact when he took part in behind-the-scenes political action. The Vatican scrambled to destroy any written records of the secret negotiations and hoped that the British would do the same since there was always the possibility that the Germans would invade Britain and, in the process, come across documentary evidence of Project X. More immediate was the good possibility that Paris would be overrun, putting French intelligence records of Resistance activities in jeopardy.

With this in mind, Oster, no less concerned than the Vatican, made plans to be on hand when Paris fell so as to rescue any incriminating papers.[19]

Then there was the bureaucratic solution: create a new agency to address any opportunities for harnessing anti-Nazi Resistance movements everywhere. The British minister of economic warfare, Hugh Dalton, reassigned by Churchill to be head of a new paramilitary arm of British intelligence, Special Operations Executive (SOE), talked with optimism of helping the anti-Nazi Resistance "set Europe ablaze" in the crusade against Hitler. But consistent with his posture of optimism and staunch, unyielding opposition to the enemy, Churchill soon found no merit in trying to strike a deal with the Germans' Resistance, much less in listening to the hybrid "semiofficial" propositions still being peddled by Hermann Göring.

When one of Göring's Swedish intermediaries, Count Knud Bonde, appeared at the British Legation in Bern, reiterating an earlier message of "peace" from the *Reichsmarschall,* Churchill issued a directive (dated January 20, 1941), making it clear that the British reaction to peace inquiries from whatever quarter should be absolute silence.[20] While Churchill cannot be faulted for his valiant—and successful—effort to inspire hope and confidence in Britain at this dark hour and to prove to the United States that his country was not a lost cause and should be helped in its struggle with the Nazi threat, his cold shouldering of the Resistance meant an opportunity lost. It was perhaps unfortunate that Churchill could not have found some formula to encourage the Resistance without compromising Britain's insistence on undoing Hitler's acts of foreign aggression.

While Churchill, an English "bulldog," defied Hitler despite the frightening odds facing him, Hitler, with larger designs on Russia in fulfillment of his dream of Lebensraum, began to perfect his Eastern strategy. Britain could be militarily dealt with later. In the meantime, negotiating from strength, he would try to neutralize the British as a European player by peaceful agreement, rather than now try to occupy the British Isles by force, facing Germany with the prospect of a two-front war and possibly provoking U.S. intervention.

First, however, Hitler had to conquer France to protect Germany's western approaches. French defenses proved to be no match for the German panzers, and the submission of Britain's ally was only a matter of time—not much time by all indications. Of immediate concern to the British, however, were their expeditionary forces in France, which would be sorely needed to defend Britain if France fell. The only thing that could now stop the German lightning advance to the Channel and save the French and British troops trapped on the beaches of Dunkirk came in an unexpected way: Hitler cried halt.

FOURTEEN

France Falls;
Britain Stands Alone

IF NEITHER THE FRENCH NOR THE BRITISH COULD EXPLAIN WHY ON MAY 23, 1940, Hitler's armies were suddenly stopped in their race to trap the British Expeditionary Force and elements of the French Army before they could be rescued from certain destruction from the beaches of Dunkirk, the attacking German panzer forces were even more mystified. The Führer's unexpected decision was one of the most damaging military blunders of World War II.

The German OKW had urgently phoned Field Marshal von Rundstedt, commander of Army Group A, ordering him to halt German forces at the Aire–St.-Omer Canal, only twenty miles from Dunkirk. The generals directly involved questioned the orders but received no satisfaction. When Lt. General von Kleist, commander of the 5th Panzer Division, attached to Army Group A, allowed some of his tanks to proceed, he received a blistering order to pull them back. General Wilhelm Ritter von Thoma, close enough to Dunkirk to see the town, erupted in frustration when he got the word, shouting, "You can never talk to a fool. Hitler spoilt the chance of Victory."[1] Germany's top tank officer, General Heinz Guderian, observed that Dunkirk was not good tank country; there were too many canals. Anyway, he rationalized, "Infantry forces are more suitable than tanks for fighting in this sort of country." Rundstedt later complained: "My hands were tied by direct orders from Hitler. . . . If I had had my way, the English would not have got off so lightly at Dunkirk."[2]

After the war Lt. General von Kleist recalled that he had received an order from Hitler to withdraw his forces and send them southward to attack the French Army along the Somme: "It was left to the infantry forces, which had come down from Belgium, to complete the occupation of Dunkirk—after the British had gone."[3]

Hitler explained that he had wanted to keep a maximum number of tanks ready for the big push through France; many of the tanks needed repair after rumbling at top speed through the Ardennes Forest. Then there was the story that Göring wanted the victory over the British Expeditionary Force to go to the Luftwaffe, not the panzers.[4] But such explanations do not really answer the riddle posed by Hitler's sudden decision. The halt order permitted the British to complete their epic naval evacuation, a remarkable achievement in which every seaworthy craft afloat along the English side of the Channel was pressed into service to evacuate nearly the entire force: 337,000, 110,000 of whom were French, the balance, British.[5]

Perhaps Hitler's real reasons for halting the panzers and letting the British escape can be found in his frank talk with Generals Gerd von Rundstedt, Sodenstern, and Günther Blumentritt at Army Group A's Charleville headquarters on May 24. Britain's talented but sometimes controversial military analyst B. H. Liddell Hart, who talked with Blumentritt after the war, relates the general's revealing account of this meeting. Hitler surprised the generals "by speaking with admiration of the British Empire, of the necessity for its existence and of the civilization that Britain had brought into the world. . . . He compared the British Empire with the Catholic Church, saying they were both essential elements of stability in the world." Hitler asserted that all he wanted from Britain was that it should "acknowledge Germany's position on the Continent. . . ." Blumentritt explained to Liddell Hart: "If the British Army had been captured at Dunkirk, the British people might have felt that their honour had suffered a stain which they must wipe out."[6]

General Halder's journal of May 21, 1940, confirms the general thrust of Hitler's remarks, as remembered by Blumentritt. Halder, secretly in league with the German Resistance, quoted in sarcastic parody Hitler's presumptuous dream: "We are seeking to arrive at an understanding with Britain on the basis of a division of the World." General Halder writes wistfully in his diary, "[I]f only our armour had not been held back." In his diary entry of May 24, he describes his frustration with Hitler's orders regarding Dunkirk: "The left wing, consisting of armored and motorized forces, which had no enemy before it, will be stopped dead in its tracks upon direct orders of the Führer! Finishing off the encircled enemy is to be left to the air force!!"[7] Luftwaffe strafing could have been a problem in good weather, but according to General Halder, bad weather greatly helped the evacuation.

The reasons for Hitler's halt order, granting the Allied forces two days' respite from attack and an opportunity to conduct an almost total evacuation, are less certain and have been the subject of much debate. But it is clear that the rescue of the expeditionary force, heart of the British Army, permitted the British to fight another day and made a German invasion of the British Isles a more risky proposition from the German point of view. It is possible that the ultimate outcome of the war turned on this decision by Hitler.

One explanation of the phenomenon is that Hitler simply never anticipated that the British could rally their jerry-rigged rescue armada so quickly as to effect a total evacuation. By keeping the British Expeditionary Force bottled up at Dunkirk, not totally destroyed but forced to surrender, Hitler hoped to extract peace on his terms, permitting him to husband all his resources for a Russian invasion. Had the British not had the secret advantage of Ultra, the massive rescue effort might not have been attempted. The British Y organization, whose function was to jam German Air Force communications and confuse the Stuka dive-bombers strafing the beaches, had intercepted a clear-text message stating that the attack on the line, Dunkirk–Hazebrouck–Merville, was to be "discontinued for the present."[8] But the profound significance of this providential message was perhaps not fully grasped at Dunkirk. In the confusion on the Dunkirk beaches General Henry Royds Pownall, General John Gort's chief of staff, read the message but dismissed it as "too much to hope for."[9] But Ultra reports confirmed to the British Hitler's halt order. Knowing that Britain had a little more time, London had therefore been encouraged to mount a major evacuation effort at Dunkirk.

The Dunkirk halt order provided a clue to Hitler's thinking, though one not thoroughly understood at the time, but a series of events leading up to Hitler's abandonment of Operation Sea Lion—the plan to invade Britain—explains more fully why Britain was spared the fate suffered by France. To put it simply, Hitler wanted peace with the British on his terms, ensuring that they would remain neutral while the Wehrmacht destroyed the Soviet Union. In this way Hitler would not have to take the risks of invading the British Isles or expend the manpower and resources necessary to police a captive enemy on its own territory. Total defeat of Britain would come later.

British secret contacts during the phony war, particularly the Dahlerus-Göring connection, not to mention intelligence service secret dalliance with the mythical generals at Venlo, must have impressed the Germans with Chamberlain's devotion to peace at any price. After all, Chamberlain's performance at Munich had established his determination to find peace; at least that was the impression gained by Hitler, who misjudged British resolve and stamina on more than one occasion. Hitler had not believed that Britain would go to war over Poland, but even when Chamberlain unexpectedly took a stand and declared war, the Western Allies did not immediately initiate military action against Germany.

Hitler also overestimated the strength of Britain's so-called peace party in Parliament, made up of defeatists who had favored appeasement. Foreign Secretary Halifax's various public statements of themselves must have persuaded Hitler that the British government was eager to negotiate. And it is noteworthy that a secret November 1939 assessment prepared by Secretary von Weizsäcker of the German Foreign Ministry concluded that important members of the British cabinet and several members of Parliament would be willing to make concessions to reach a negotiated peace.[10] But with Churchill's accession to power on May 10, 1940, the day Hitler struck in the Lowlands in a diversion to distract the French from the invasion of their own country, things would become very different.

CHURCHILL'S MOST DIFFICULT TASK WAS TO KEEP DEFEATISM AND APPEASEment at bay within Britain. Not only was high public morale essential to its defense, but it was important for him to convince Germany that Britain had the will and strength to defend itself and, in making that case plausible, convince President Roosevelt that this was a viable cause worth major assistance, that the British people had not given up.

Upon taking office as prime minister, Winston Churchill faced not only the prospect of defeat on the Continent as the British Expeditionary Force fell back toward Dunkirk to await what seemed to be its inevitable destruction but the discouraging sight of a disintegrating French Army as well. At home he would have to cope with those of little faith, the harbingers of doom, who believed that a humiliating negotiated peace with Hitler, if that was what it would take, was better than a crushing defeat and German occupation of the British Isles.

Churchill clung to the hope that he could get eleventh-hour relief from Franklin Roosevelt in the form of help at sea and access to America's engines of production despite the blanket of isolationism covering the United States. It must have been discouraging for Churchill to read such things as an American United Press dispatch on June 27 stating that Chamberlain was trying to unseat him and form a new government to begin peace negotiations with Hitler. Similar reports springing up around the world caused the Foreign Office to instruct its chanceries to deny categorically all such baseless rumors. When the papal nuncio in Switzerland, presumably on his own initiative, made an offer to British Ambassador Sir David Kelly in Bern to serve as a peace mediator, Churchill was provoked to send stern instructions to his envoy: "I hope it will be made clear that we do not desire to make any inquiries as to terms of peace with Hitler."[11]

Churchill's rejection of all German peace overtures was driven by his need to squash dissent from his policies on the part of defeatists within the Conservative party still imbued with the spirit of Munich and still convinced that Russia was the greater enemy. As for the Resistance, Churchill basically believed there was neither enough will nor strength within the leadership of the army to overthrow Hitler. Moreover, he could not accept Resistance insistence on Germany's retaining Austria, the Sudetenland, and Alsace-Lorraine.

Kelly's activities as British ambassador in Switzerland almost certainly would have rubbed Churchill the wrong way once he became aware of them. Political gadfly Prince Max von Hohenlowe, who seemed to play on both sides of the street, told Ribbentrop that Kelly had described Butler and Halifax as "our mutual friends in England, who have a following." According to Hohenlowe, Kelly agreed with him that the British must continue to fight "for the honor of the Empire until they were in a position to make a reasonable peace." The British ambassador described Churchill in what he considered pejorative terms as being of another mind, "a bull running his head into a wall."[12]

Churchill could get no encouragement from American Ambassador Joseph Kennedy, a confirmed defeatist. The pessimism exuded by the U.S. ambassador was particularly galling to Churchill. Kennedy lost no opportunity to remind the British government that America had little confidence in Britain's ability to survive. One of his more memorable comments during Britain's days of trial was made on July 1, when he told the newly ousted Chamberlain, "Everyone in the U.S.A. thinks [Great Britain] shall be beaten before the end of the month."

If this were not enough, Ambassador Kennedy's sievelike embassy in London permitted the most damaging of Allied secrets to escape to German intelligence at a most critical moment of the war in Europe. On May 18, 1940, London's Scotland Yard found it necessary to confront Kennedy with the discovery that his confidential code clerk, Tyler Kent, was a German spy and would be charged with violating the British Official Secrets Act. Kennedy waived diplomatic immunity to permit a trial to proceed in strictest secrecy; Kent was duly found guilty and jailed for the duration of the war.

At the time of his arrest a search of Kent's apartment uncovered a collection of some fifteen hundred copies of highly classified cables in clear text going back to October 1939. It also became clear that he had made it possible for German intelligence to break the best American diplomatic cipher system. His excuse for doing what he did, perhaps a rationalization rather than a motive, was that he wanted to spoil Roosevelt's efforts to bring the United States into war. By revealing to the Germans in all its stark detail the cable correspondence between Churchill and Roosevelt, he had given Hitler a ringside seat from which to watch Churchill's impassioned efforts to solicit American help and to see with clarity Kennedy's efforts to undercut these efforts.

Kennedy, in an interview with the *New York World-Telegram* in 1944 — long after he had been relieved of his post in Britain but while the war in Europe still raged — spoke frankly: "The result was that for weeks right at the time of the fall of France, the U.S. Government closed its confidential communications service and was blacked out from private contact with American embassies and legations everywhere." Kennedy commented that this meant that at a time when critical decisions had to be made, "no private message could be sent or received from the President or Mr. Hull or anyone else."[13]

In his interview with the *World-Telegram*, Kennedy was explicit in his estimate of the damage done:

> This . . . raised the question of whether Kent had been giving the Germans copies of our Embassy's secret cables to the President and the State Department ever since October 1939, which means throughout the war. So long as that was true, the Germans did not need any secret service in Europe; they didn't have to guess about anything. They could just read the facts about Great Britain and America and most European countries by reading the secret London–Washington diplomatic dispatches and cable traffic since the London Embassy was the clearing point for nearly all European matters on the continent.

Kennedy added, perhaps to justify his own pessimism during those dark days in Britain: "In the period after England declared war Prime Minister Churchill was very complete in revealing to me, and through me to President Roosevelt, England's unpreparedness. Mr. Churchill and other high officials gave me the whole picture — the figures on Britain's land, sea and air forces, the disposition of British units everywhere, England's home inventory of war materials, her prospective war production and the fundamentals of Great Britain's plans."[14]

Kent's partner in espionage had been a "White" Russian émigré in England named or at least known as Anna de Wolkoff, who had been involved with the ultraconservative Right Club, suspected of pro-German activities. Wolkoff, it seemed, had Italian connections as well, through which Kent met a man who called himself Mr. Marcaroni, but in reality was Colonel Duke Antonio del Monte, Italian assistant military attaché. Del Monte was the link to German intelligence. Making things more complicated, however, were later allegations that Kent may have been ultimately controlled by Soviet intelligence.[15]

CHURCHILL'S VEHEMENT DENIALS THAT PEACE TALKS WERE IN THE OFFING were not as convincing as his action in sinking the Vichy French fleet at Oran, Algeria, on July 3, 1940. While this act, code-named Operation Catapult, inflamed the French, it denied to the Germans an enhanced navy with which to invade Britain. Perhaps even more important, it conveyed to the world at large and to the United States in particular that Churchill intended to fight, not to sue for peace. His actions, he told Parliament in ringing rhetoric, would get rid of "all the lies and rumors which have been so industriously spread by German propaganda . . . that we have the slightest intention of entering into negotiation in any form." (This may have been disturbing to the German Resistance, which still hoped to arrange peace with the British.) Churchill assured the members: "We shall, on the contrary, prosecute the War with the utmost vigour." At this the House of Commons erupted with deafening cheers, but the prime minister's action at Oran impressed another vitally important audience: the president of the United States. Franklin Roosevelt later told Churchill that Oran was the most important event in convincing him that Great Britain would "stay in the fight alone and, if necessary, for years."[16]

GREAT BRITAIN'S SURVIVAL DEPENDED ON GAINING THE UNITED STATES AS an ally. Churchill would do everything in his power to bring Roosevelt into camp and overcome the inertia bred of deep-seated isolationism that kept the U.S. people at arm's length.

In the 1930s one key to American public opinion was found in Hollywood, the place where tinsel-festooned dreams were produced to cheer the depression-laden public. Clouds of war gathering over the United States were an irritation for some in Hollywood. While reviewing a biography of Louis B. Mayer by Charles Higham, aptly titled *Merchant of Dreams*, the *Economist* alleged that the great cinemogul had film scripts sometimes tailored "so that they would not offend Axis powers," and actress Myrna Loy was once restrained from criticizing Hitler on film because Mayer thought "there was still money to be made from the German market."[17] Of course, once America was at war, Mayer was in the front ranks pounding the drums for victory and producing a number of super-patriotic films.

Short of a Pearl Harbor, unimaginable in the 1930s, only Hollywood could pack a media punch capable of denting America's isolationist mindset. The British were on to the propaganda value of the movies. Ronald Colman, star of countless romantic epics and sauve film lover of such stars as Claudette Colbert, had in real life been encouraged by the British to make certain that Britain would look its best on the screen. Such early wartime films as *That Hamilton Woman* and other films produced by the British-Hungarian producer Alexander Korda, who had been co-opted for the British Secret Intelligence Service by Lieutenant Colonel Claude Dansey,[18] all were designed to make Americans feel more sympathetic toward their British cousins' predicament.

Lord Cadogan noted in his diary on August 8, 1941, while cruising with Churchill on HMS *Prince of Wales*, that the prime minister, who was seeing *Lady Hamilton* (as the film was titled in Britain) for the fifth time, had been moved to tears. After it was over, he announced to the little shipboard gathering, "Gentlemen, I thought this film would interest you, showing great events similar to those in which you have been taking part."[19]

The British MI-6 officer H. Montgomery Hyde, working for the British New York MI-6 office, known as British Security Coordination (BSC), was assigned to Hollywood to assist Alexander Korda. Hyde recalled that he had passed the time agreeably, socializing with the likes of Charlie Chaplin, Greta Garbo, Errol Flynn, Noel Coward, and Mary Pickford. He writes in his memoir, *Secret Intelligence Agent,* that Korda was, in effect, "a clearing house for British Intelligence."[20] On Churchill's recommendation, Korda was awarded a knighthood when honors were passed out at George VI's birthday observance in 1942.[21]

U.S. Senator Gerald Nye, a staunch isolationist, was less charitable toward British filmmakers in the United States. At an America First rally held in St. Louis on August 1, 1941, Nye claimed that "Hollywood is a raging inferno of war fever" and demanded that "America be freed of foreign propaganda." Samuel Goldwyn was accused by Nye of turning out films that were "engines of propaganda." Nye referred to British actors and filmmakers as "the British Army of occupation." During a Senate investigation of Hollywood's alleged foreign-sponsored propaganda role on the eve of Pearl Harbor, Nye testified that interventionist propaganda films have served "to change, if not warp, a lot of clear thinking in American minds."[22]

The British were understandably concerned by the America First organization, prime standard-bearer of isolationism. In the autumn of 1941 Stephenson's BSC had amassed considerable evidence that, it claimed, revealed clandestine links between Nazi Germany and the America Firsters. In BSC-sponsored press campaigns, U.S. Representative Hamilton Fish was accused of accepting Nazi financial support for his isolationist activities. This may or may not have been true, but it badly damaged the credibility of the America First movement. The BSC also saw to it that the suspected abuse of congressional mail franking privileges in support of isolationist lobbies was publicized.

The BSC could not be accused of lacking imagination. It somehow found a Hungarian astrologer named Louis de Wohl who allegedly had once read the stars for Adolf Hitler. In midsummer 1941, de Wohl publicly shared with a credulous American public his predictions of things to come—all intimations of disaster facing the Nazis.[23]

BY MID-1940 DEVELOPMENTS IN EUROPE POSED URGENT PROBLEMS FOR the British. Winston Churchill needed desperately fifty overage American destroyers, known to be available, if Britain was to survive the U-boat onslaught that he dubbed the Battle of the Atlantic. Britain also needed American help in providing additional North Atlantic antisubmarine patrols. In February 1941 the United States increased naval patrols as a function of a newly constituted Atlantic Fleet under the command of Vice Admiral Ernest J. King. The carrier *Yorktown* and a group of destroyers were moved from the Pacific to the Atlantic for this purpose.[24] Despite American neutrality, U.S. naval patrols did become involved in the U-boat war taking place in the U.S.–declared "neutrality zone."

The BSC chief—i.e., MI-6's representative in New York—was the Canadian businessman William Stephenson, whom William Donovan had first met in World War I. Stephenson did a herculean job of promoting closer U.S.-British relations in general—i.e., nudging the United States toward war—and, more specifically, forging closer cooperation between U.S. and British intelligence. After the war Stephenson became known as Intrepid because of his wartime New York cable address and a book about him titled *A Man Called Intrepid*.[25] If Intrepid's techniques sometimes seem devious from the perspective of half a century later, it must be remembered that Great Britain was alone and fighting for its life in 1940. The United States, moreover, had a stake in preserving Europe from Nazi domination, even if Americans did not quite realize it yet. For all their isolationist instincts, the American people were soon shocked into the war by Pearl Harbor, but for the present survival drove the British to press in every way they could for U.S. intervention. Not only must Roosevelt himself be encouraged to act swiftly in Britain's behalf, but the American people on whom Roosevelt depended for his mandate must be encouraged to crawl out of their cocoon of isolation.

If U.S. Ambassador to Great Britain Joseph Kennedy was an American influence for defeatism during the dark days when England reeled under Luftwaffe attacks, William Donovan was, to the contrary, an apostle of faith. "Wild Bill," as he was affectionately known, was still remembered for his heroism while serving in New York's 69th ("Fighting Irish") Division in World War I and was much respected by President Roosevelt, who had given him a variety of intelligence odd jobs on the eve of U.S. participation in World War II. Firmly convinced that the British would survive and that Britain's cause was worthy of all-out backing by the United States, Donovan was an ideal person for Stephenson to turn toward in Britain's hour of need. "Big Bill" and "Little Bill," as the pair were sometime called, were soon the coarchitects of a wartime U.S.-British intelligence partnership that made a vital contribution to ultimate Alied victory.

FIFTEEN

A Friendly Connection

BOTH DONOVAN AND CANARIS, AS WE HAVE SEEN, HAD BEEN DRAWN INTO the service of their countries long before World War II for patriotic reasons, and both in very different ways pursued what they believed to be their respective nations' best interests. In these pursuits both made significant contributions to the war against Nazism. Each at critical times in World War II took actions that helped Britain survive in the face of what seemed imminent defeat. Each, very differently, had what may be called a "friendly connection" with Great Britain.

"Friendly connection" is a translation of a Soviet intelligence term of art, *doveritel' naya svyaz'*, which is particularly apt in describing someone, often of high rank, whose national loyalty is unquestioned but whose objectives run parallel to those of another country—the cobeneficiary. Such a helpful "friend" with mutual interests should never be considered an agent, but is often more useful.

In Canaris's case the friendly connection with the British was indirect and unspoken, motivated by a desire to save the fatherland from Hitler's rush to national self-destruction, a Nazi Götterdämmerung that could only benefit the Soviet Union. In Donovan's case, the connection was proudly acknowledged as contributing to what inevitably would be a U.S.-British partnership in a crusade against Nazi Germany and, of course, was entered into with the approval and encouragement of his president and commander in chief, Franklin Roosevelt.

The beginnings of Donovan's involvement in World War II began well before America went to war. In the late summer of 1938 the peripatetic

Donovan had been watching German Army maneuvers as the Czech crisis came to a boil. Typical of itinerant fact finders, who are usually at the mercy of information handouts and forced to rely on purely impressionistic judgments, Donovan came away from Germany with inflated estimates of its weapons-manufacturing capacity. He had not, however, been impressed with the "fifth column" threat in Britain, which was often talked about but which seemed to have been based on the fallacious assumption that German sympathizers had significantly contributed to the rapid collapse of France. Donovan did not believe that a so-called fifth column would be a problem in the defense of Britain.

Unlike the American Chiefs of Staff,[1] the American ambassador in London, and other pessimists, Donovan had faith in the staying power of Churchill's Britain. He believed, however, that the British would need massive American help immediately if they were to survive a German assault. Influence exerted on Roosevelt by Donovan, a strong advocate of U.S. intervention, compensated for the defeatism of U.S. Ambassador Joseph Kennedy in London. A CIA retrospective monograph published in 1992 describing *The Intelligence War in 1941* went so far as to claim that Donovan "let himself be used" by Stephenson, then head of British Security Coordination, the MI-6 station in New York, as a British channel for influencing not only Roosevelt but also the American public.[2] This is unfortunate phrasing since it does not grasp the nuances of Donovan's role. The official British history of intelligence during World War II refers to Donovan more accurately as "predisposed in Britain's favor,"[3] rather than imply that he was a dupe. Donovan saw his actions as being in the U.S. national interest and mandated by a like-minded president. As history bore out, Donovan was right even though he was on the wrong side of American isolationist sentiment. Polls indicated that prior to Pearl Harbor 83 percent of Americans wished to remain neutral in the war, but Donovan's interventionist views had significant impact on official U.S. attitudes at the very top, where it counted the most. Donovan was respected and liked by Roosevelt, who looked upon him as an intelligence and foreign affairs expert. He knew his way around Washington's corridors of power. It was not surprising that the British would look to him for help in those desperate times.

On June 10, 1940, Roosevelt articulated his true foreign policy convictions when he inserted some last-minute editorial changes in an address he gave to a University of Virginia graduating class. Neutrality, a politically useful stance in light of an isolationist American popular attitude, was ignored when he said, "Some indeed hold to the now obvious delusion that we of the United States can safely permit the United States to become a lone island in a world dominated by the philosophy of force."[4]

Nine days later Hitler made an equally important public speech in which he held out to Britain the possibility of peace based on a German guarantee of the British Empire in exchange for Britain's acceptance of a "Europe for Europeans," which meant German hegemony in Europe.

Against the background of these two very different responses to Britain's predicament, one of hope, the other of threat wreathed in deceptive peace, Stephenson on June 21, 1940, was entrusted with a special mission in the United States: gain for Britain much-needed war supplies, particularly the fifty overage American destroyers that Churchill had long had an eye on. In his campaign to convince Americans that Britain's war with Hitler was their war as well, he was also to enlist Donovan in a campaign to counteract the malign influence of American isolationists and defeatists.

In a meeting at the St. Regis Hotel Stephenson invited Donovan to visit Britain and inspect the intelligence and defense organizations there. This was a euphemistic way of asking him to see for himself that Britain could survive—given help from the United States. Roosevelt approved the mission, recognizing that he could benefit by an independent assessment of Britain's chances of survival.

The British were ready for Donovan when he reached London in mid-July.* The American's tour had been set up by MI-6, whose chief, Stewart Menzies, had personally made the arrangements.[5] Donovan immediately met with Menzies in the latter's offices at 52 Broadway in London across from St. James's Park. On the day following Donovan's arrival the permanent undersecretary of state, Sir Alexander Cadogan, sent a revealing message to Foreign Secretary Anthony Eden:

> Menzies tells me that Mr. Stephenson, who traveled over with Colonel Donovan, has impressed upon him that the latter really exercises a vast degree of influence in the administration. He has Colonel Knox in his pocket and, as Mr. Stephenson puts it, has more influence with the President than Colonel House had with Mr. Wilson. Mr. Stephenson believes that if the Prime Minister were to be completely frank with Colonel Donovan, the latter would contribute very largely to our obtaining all that we want of the United States.[6]

Indicative of the importance that the British attached to the mission, Prime Minister Churchill had lunch with Donovan within two days of his

---

*Toward the end of July 1940 three U.S. military officers of high rank, calling themselves the Standardization of Arms Committee, visited Britain. They too had been sent to assess Britain's ability to survive.

arrival.[7] What was uppermost in his mind was reflected in a recent personal cable to Roosevelt: "It is now most urgent for you to let us have the destroyers, motor boats and flying boats for which I have asked." It can probably be assumed that Churchill's words to Donovan reflected this anguished plea.

Escorted by Ronald Tree, private secretary to Duff Cooper, then minister of information, Donovan was artfully steered through an impressive cast of British leaders and fed a rich diet of upbeat information calculated to show Britain as invincible, an assessment at odds with what Ambassador Kennedy claimed Churchill had given him. Menzies saw to it that Donovan was given broad access to the world of British intelligence. Only the secret-of-secrets, Ultra, was for a while kept from the OSS.[8]

Donovan "scurried about London . . . inspecting many of the military naval and air installations then girding for the defense of the islands." Rear Admiral John H. Godfrey, British director of naval intelligence, was especially attentive to Donovan. Discouraged by the U.S. naval attaché's defeatist attitude, Godfrey welcomed Donovan's positive approach. In his diary the British admiral wrote that Donovan "quickly became aware of the spiritual qualities of the British Race and [decided] that there was still time for American aid, both material and economic, to exercise a decisive influence on the War."[9]

By the time Donovan left England on August 3, he was fully prepared to plead Britain's case and present a long list of badly needed armaments headed by the fifty destroyers, B-17 Flying Fortress bombers, and a highly effective U.S. aircraft bombsight. Even before Donovan returned, Roosevelt had made the decision to grant the British requests in principle, and by August 22 Donovan could send word to Menzies via Stephenson that forty-four of the fifty destroyers, which had been approved, were ready for delivery. Donovan's influence on Roosevelt had been important in this decision; moreover, his law firm had found the legal loopholes that made the transaction possible. Wild Bill had proved his worth to Roosevelt—and to Churchill.

Donovan's mission undoubtedly influenced Roosevelt's later decision to make him his strategic intelligence chief. Admiral Godfrey, in another diary entry following a mission he had made to the United States in June and July 1941, writes: "Colonel Donovan was persuaded to increase his personal interest in intelligence, and details as to how U.S. intelligence could be improved in the common cause were worked out in collaboration with him. . . . The question was also discussed with the President direct, and Colonel Donovan's qualifications as Co-ordinator of Intelligence were advocated to Mr. Roosevelt."[10]

Donovan was clearly the British choice to conduct America's overseas intelligence effort, and Churchill himself had worked hard to ensure his appointment. More to the point, Donovan was Roosevelt's choice; on July 11, 1941, the president formally established the position, coordinator of information, predictably naming Donovan to it. Soon the COI, coming of age, metamorphosed into the Office of Strategic Services, whose ambiguous-sounding name cloaked a wide-ranging repertoire of dark arts. The announcement creating the COI stated: "Mr. Donovan will collect and assemble information and data bearing on national security from the various departments and agencies of the Government."[11] What Roosevelt's spokesman, Stephen Early, did not specify when he made the announcement was that the executive order empowered Donovan to conduct subversive operations, political warfare, guerrilla warfare, psychological warfare, and espionage. This was a large order.

Stephenson immediately telegraphed London the good news of Donovan's impending appointment. As Stephenson put it, "He will be coordinator of all forms of intelligence including offensive operations equivalent [to] SOE," Britain's paramilitary organization. The "intrepid" Canadian had accomplished an important assignment; his proprietary attitude toward Donovan can be seen in the concluding line of his telegram: "You can imagine how relieved I am after three months of battle and jockeying for position in Washington that our man [Donovan] is in a position of such importance to our efforts."[12]

The existing U.S. intelligence establishments—State, Army, Navy, and the FBI—concerned with protecting existing empires, were not as enthusiastic. Donovan encountered political opposition from various quarters, and there were inevitable quarrels with giants of the military such as Secretary of Navy Frank Knox, Secretary of War Henry Stimson, Chief of Staff General George Marshall, and Chief of Naval Operations Admiral Harold Stark. Donovan had to win the Battle of Washington before he could take on the enemy, but Roosevelt firmly backed him at every turn. Donovan, in a remarkably short time, performed the miracle of creating from nothing a strategic intelligence and clandestine espionage service that made an important contribution to winning the war.

Donovan was forever grateful for the help received from the British. After the war, exaggerating a bit, he told an interviewer, "Bill Stephenson taught us everything we ever knew about foreign intelligence operations."[13] British liaison became especially useful when the OSS was given limited access to Ultra material gained from intercepting and breaking German radio signals. There was more than altruism involved in sharing Ultra; the British wanted the fruits of the American Magic program, in which Japanese ciphers were systematically broken. While most of Magic was oriented toward the Far Eastern war with Japan, extremely important intelligence on the European war against Germany was gleaned from intercepting the messages sent by Japanese Ambassador Hiroshi Oshima to Tokyo.[14] Oshima, significantly, was a very close friend of Canaris's. Soon the Double-Cross system, by which German intelligence was fed deception material through double agents, proved invaluable to both countries. It would have been disastrous for the Americans and British to have fished separately in the murky waters of espionage and counterespionage without close coordination. The British were understandably afraid that an uncontrolled U.S. intelligence service, long on enthusiasm and short on experience, could inadvertently upset the all-important Double-Cross system, ruining the deception program designed particularly to cloak the North African landings and later the true landing area in France for the final invasion of Europe.

Then there was the Soviet factor. While Stalin's intelligence apparatus had remarkably good penetrations of Hitler's army and government through the war, it targeted the United States and Great Britain as well — a harbinger of the Cold War to come. The long-term enemies of the Soviet Union never ceased to be the capitalist countries of the West. Stalin was obsessed by his concern that the Western Allies would secretly seek a separate peace with anti-Nazi elements of the German Army at Soviet expense.

Soviet intelligence was aware of the close intelligence agreements made between the British and Americans; it could rely on Soviet spy Kim Philby and others to keep Stalin informed of this. Stalin never trusted Churchill and looked with grave suspicion at the close British-American intelligence liaison as evidence of a hidden policy. Donovan particularly worried him as a force for anti-Soviet sentiment within the American government—which he was.

Not everyone in the U.S. intelligence and foreign policy hierarchy saw merit in Donovan's close arrangements with British intelligence. In normal circumstances the vision of the first U.S. strategic intelligence service's being born with the help of a foreign midwife, however friendly, would have been unthinkable. World War II, for all its ominous precursors—reoccupation of the Rhineland, Spanish Civil War, Munich, Hitler-Stalin pact—found the United States placidly isolationist. Yet there were those who could see the approaching war and realize that it concerned the United States as well as Europe. Franklin Roosevelt was one; William Donovan, another. That Roosevelt was right to guide his country toward accepting the idea of helping the British in their time of need became clearer when Pearl Harbor ruptured the American cocoon, but at the time his interventionism was viewed with suspicion by many Americans. Pearl Harbor almost instantly convinced Americans that this was their cause as well as Britain's and that they should fight and die for it.

Menzies of MI-6 always looked upon the OSS as a bumptious upstart that needed close watching. The wartime service relationship nonetheless endured and prospered even though William Stephenson's New York outpost of British intelligence, the British Security Coordination office, did on occasion abuse American hospitality and exceed the rules of cooperation. J. Edgar Hoover's FBI found a good deal to grumble about as Stephenson tried independently to ferret out German spies and saboteurs. It is ironic that it was later discovered that Hitler had at this time instructed Canaris not to conduct sabotage in the United States for fear it would provoke America to enter the war. In fact, fifth column activities would never assume dangerous proportions despite the pathetic posturing of such lunatic-fringe groups as the German-American Bund.[15]

Certain methods used by Stephenson to influence U.S. public opinion and nudge it toward war were indeed questionable. The case of the Belmonte papers in which the British pulled the wool over American eyes, reminiscent of the famous Zimmermann telegram in World War I, is perhaps the best example.

It began in May 1941, when FBI chief J. Edgar Hoover caught Stephenson's attention with reports that Major Elias Belmonte, Bolivian military attaché in Berlin, was intriguing with the Germans against Bolivia's pro-American president, Enrique Peñaranda. The United States was particularly concerned because this could threaten U.S. access to wolfram, essential to aircraft manufacturing. German machinations to deter Latin American participation in economic agreements, revealed in 1940 at the Pan-American Conference in Havana, had been worrisome, but the new FBI information suggesting the Nazis were planning a power play in Bolivia was alarming.[16]

BSC chief Stephenson dispatched agent H. Montgomery Hyde to Bolivia to investigate this threat to a very strategic material that was understandably important to the British as well as to the Americans. Hyde, according to his description of what then occurred as contained in his postwar memoir,[17] was creatively inspired to craft a misinformation operation calculated to provoke the United States into the war. With considerable ingenuity and diligent research, he fabricated a convincing but fake letter from Belmonte, describing his plot. He contrived an equally notional scenario in which a German courier from La Paz to Buenos Aires was robbed by a British agent. When the contents of this supposedly purloined letter were passed by Stephenson to J. Edgar Hoover for Secretary of State Hull's reading, alarm bells rang. President Roosevelt himself read the report and reacted strongly.

Hyde's imaginative letter "from Belmonte," addressed to the German minister to Bolivia, Dr. Ernst Wendler, contained such eye-catching phrases as "the coup should take place in the middle of July" and, following the coup, "We must rescind the wolfram contract with the U.S." The bogus letter concluded with an earnest hope that the work of the conspirators "will save Bolivia in the first place and afterwards the whole South American continent from North American influence."[18]

The United States notified the Bolivian government, which promptly proclaimed a state of siege and arrested all suspected pro-Nazi activists. President Roosevelt took to the airwaves on July 19, 1941, to expose the dastardly Nazi plot described in the Belmonte letter.[19] Hyde, author of this disinformation masterpiece, reflected on his handiwork in his memoir, praising it for having "averted a revolution in Bolivia . . . caused the closing of the German Legation in La Paz . . . denied Germany further exports of wolfram and prepared the climate for the Pan-American Conference at Rio six months later when Bolivia and 18 other Latin American States broke with the Axis powers and banded together in a common scheme of hemisphere defence."[20] U.S. Undersecretary of State Súmner Welles, with the wisdom of aftersight and despite the knowledge of how the United States had been deceived, had warm praise for the operation's results and called the Latin American break with the Axis "the decision that saved New World unity."[21]

The British BSC in New York also seemed to have pulled the wool over Donovan's eyes more than he realized at the time. A CIA monograph published more than fifty years later,[22] describes what purported to be a secret German map of the Western Hemisphere dated 1941, given to Donovan by Stephenson. President Roosevelt cited it in a radio speech to the nation in October 1941, alleging a "Nazi design, not only against South America, but the [neutral] United States as well." Roosevelt, in one of his famous "fireside radio chats," claimed in good faith that the map proved that the Nazis intended to seize the Panama Canal and planned to absorb Latin America, joining its fourteen republics into "five vassal states."[23] This map was, however, another Stephenson forgery meant to inflame U.S. public opinion against the Nazis and help goad the United States into the war.

The State Department's Adolf Berle was highly critical of BSC's operations. With help and encouragement from the FBI's Hoover, Berle railed against BSC's freewheeling intelligence and propaganda operations. Both men were highly critical of BSC's close liaison with Donovan's OSS. Berle went so far as to accuse BSC chief Stephenson's deputy Charles "Dick" Ellis of running the fledgling OSS.[24] Berle did not then know that Ellis's liaison with OSS, which he so disapproved of, would sound much more sinister nearly a half century later, when the SIS veteran was accused of being a wartime Nazi spy—perhaps a Soviet agent as well—by MI-5 senior official Peter Wright.[25]

BSC's tricks were insignificant in their impact compared with Pearl Harbor, the ultimate affront that instantly solidified American public opinion against Japan and its ally, Hitler. But before that day of infamy changed history, Great Britain, shocked by the fall of France, braced for a German invasion of the British Isles and the possibility that Hitler's armies might march through Spain and seize Gibraltar, suffocating the empire by cutting its Mediterranean lifeline.

SIXTEEN

Felix Foiled:
How Gibraltar Was Saved

FOR MANY GERMANS THE VICTORY OF THE PANZER-LED LEGIONS OVER THE
French Army was an event to be savored. Taking on an enemy that many
believed to be stronger had been risky. But France had simply collapsed;
Germany was now on the English Channel, a vantage point from which
its soldiers could actually see what they assumed to be their next victim.

Admiral Canaris did not share this general euphoria, nor could he consider the fall of France a victory. "Should Hitler win," he told his trusted
subordinate Colonel Heinz, "this will certainly be the end of us, and also
the end of the Germany as we love it and desire it to be. If Hitler loses," he
added, "this will also be the end of ourselves for having failed to get rid of
him."[1] What must have seemed to Heinz to be undue gloom was more justified than he could know. Canaris's flashes of insight sometimes made
him despondent; now was such an occasion. After inspecting defeated
France in the company of Colonel Walther Nicolai, long-retired military
intelligence chief in World War I, he sought solace in Spain—always his
refuge from an overburden of worry—and stayed there for a few days with
his nephew Abwehr officer Joachim Canaris.

For quite different reasons Hitler's High Command now also looked toward Spain. Göring counseled Hitler to occupy Spain and North Africa,
rather than invade Britain. As early as June 1940, before an armistice had
been signed in France, General Guderian, commander of the 19th Panzer
Corps, also argued for seizing Britain's strategic bastion of Gibraltar. The
general even urged Hitler to postpone the armistice so he could rush on

through Spain with two panzer divisions, take Gibraltar, and from this springboard invade French North Africa. General Alfred Jodl, chief of OKW operations, presented the Führer with a formal plan to cut off Britain from its Eastern empire by invading Spain, Gibraltar, North Africa, and the Suez Canal as an alternative to invading the British Isles.[2]

The plan, soon to be called Operation Felix, targeted Gibraltar but also made provisions for occupying Spanish possessions in North Africa: Spanish Morocco, Río de Oro, and the Canary Islands, where Spanish ports could be used by Germany as bases for its U-boats in the Battle of the Atlantic. If successful, Felix would deal a crippling—possibly fatal—blow to the British.

The plan, however, clearly went against the wishes of General Franco. Despite Nazi Germany's critical assistance during the Spanish Civil War, Franco had his own view of what now constituted Spain's best interests. On June 12, 1940, he announced a state of "nonbelligerency"; then two days later with British and French agreement—but not German—he sent troops in to occupy Tangier.[3]

The British, of course, had been worried that Spain could be persuaded by Hitler to become a belligerent, with all that would mean for the Allied war effort. Sir Samuel Hoare, archapostle of appeasement, was dispatched to Spain on a special mission to persuade Franco to resist German pressure. So pessimistic was Hoare about succeeding in his mission that he kept an aircraft at the ready to fly him out if Spain suddenly entered the war.

Hoare's discussions with the Spanish government, beginning in mid-June 1940, would be critical, so critical that the British War Cabinet had given him authority to promise, if necessary, that Britain would "be ready to discuss after the war any matter of common interest to Spain."[4] This perhaps innocent-sounding statement would almost certainly be recognized by the Spanish as meaning that the British would be willing to discuss giving up Gibraltar to Spain. Hoare refrained from holding out any promises, implicit or explicit, to discuss Gibraltar after the war because as the meetings progressed, Franco for his own reasons made no demands concerning this British bastion and seemed "determined to keep out of the war."[5] Despite eruptions of bravado early in the talks made for the record, such as "Why don't you end the war; you cannot win it,"[6] the Caudillo was surprisingly accommodating. It was reported that Franco had informed Hitler that before he would join him in war and open his country to German troops, Germany must reward Spain with French Morocco and Algeria.[7] Such bargaining annoyed Hitler, particularly since Franco's demands were so unrealistic.

On July 10 Field Marshal Keitel asked Canaris, the acknowledged expert on Spain, to examine the operational feasibility of investing Gibraltar. Within ten days the admiral, shedding his depression over France, was on his way to Spain. He was accompanied by Abwehr officers Hans Piekenbrock, Lieutenant Colonel Hans Mikosch, and Captain Hans-Jochen Rudloff, as well as the Abwehr station chief in Spain, Captain Wilhelm Leissner. He was, however, able to get off alone long enough to look up his old friends General Juan Vigón, chief of Spain's General Staff, and General Carlos Martínez Campos, chief of Spanish intelligence, whom he urged to discourage Franco from going along with Hitler's requests. It is significant that his relationships with these men permitted such astonishing frankness; it strongly suggests that Canaris had long ago brought them into his fold as "friendly connections" in Spain. One of Canaris's biographers, Dr. K. H. Abshagen, probably got it right when he described the admiral's relationships with Vigón and Martínez Campos as being based on "mutual confidence."[8]

On July 18, Franco claimed Gibraltar, not that he expected the British to give it to him but to keep Germany from trying to take it. Britain's special envoy, Samuel Hoare, whom Secretary Cadogan once referred to as "that little blighter,"[9] became very agitated at this, apparently not realizing the game Franco was playing to keep Gibraltar out of Hitler's hands.

Being honest with himself, Canaris saw no reasons why Germany militarily could not seize Gibraltar if enough resources were dedicated to doing so, but because he was opposed to this latest adventure of Hitler's as still another vainglorious initiative, his report was negative. He claimed that heavy artillery and strong air support would be required.[10] Specifically, he wrote that without fifteen-inch heavy assault cannon—which he knew were not available—Gibraltar could not be taken.[11] When he reported to Keitel, he gave his opinion that even if Germany with Spain's cooperation were able to take Gibraltar, the British would land in Morocco and French West Africa, perhaps with the help of French General Maxime Weygand and even Admiral Jean Darlan in command of North African–based French troops.[12]

In August Canaris talked with Franco's brother-in-law Ramón Serrano Súñer, about to be made foreign minister. The admiral urged Serrano Súñer to do what he could to convince Franco that Spain should stay out of the war—a surprisingly frank conversation. Franco sent Serrano Súñer to Berlin shortly afterward to get an independent feel for Hitler's attitude since Canaris had insisted that Germany would not forcibly intervene in Spain. At a meeting with Serrano Súñer on September 16, Hitler did not seem to press very hard on the issue of Spain's involvement in the war,[13] perhaps because he had decided to save stronger persuasion for an upcoming meeting with Franco himself at Hendaye on the Spanish border with France.

In a private meeting at which Canaris was supposed to urge Franco to cooperate with Hitler in taking Gibraltar, Canaris did just the opposite. He warned Franco that if he allied himself with the Axis, not only would Spain suffer economically, but the Spanish islands—even the peninsula itself—would be at risk from British attack. Canaris stated that his own considerable research had led him to conclude that Spain should not risk war with Britain.[14] Moreover, Hitler's war plans did not anticipate troops for the defense of Spain.

Franco might have considered acquiescing in Hitler's request so that he could share the spoils of victory if the Germans won—and at this point it looked as though they probably would. But convinced by Canaris that Hitler's cause was doomed, he saw greater virtue in remaining on the sidelines. As Winston Churchill expressed it, he thought it better to keep "his exhausted people out of another war."[15]

Knowing that Franco feared a hostile German invasion of Spain if he refused to cooperate, Canaris used his most telling argument: Hitler had no intention of invading Spain by force. Revealing the Führer's closest-held secret, he told the Caudillo about Barbarossa, Hitler's ambitious plan to invade Russia. This was why Germany could not spare troops for a Spanish campaign, much less for garrisoning the country afterward. The Abwehr chief startled Franco by expressing his conviction that Hitler could not win the war; therefore Spain, as an active German ally would certainly invite postwar vengeance by the victorious Western Allies.

On August 8, emboldened by Canaris's most secret assurances, Franco presented extortionistic terms to German Ambassador Eberhard von Stohrer. The Caudillo stated that he would join Hitler only if Spain were promised Gibraltar and French Morocco as his spoils of war. Germany must also promise military assistance as needed and provide wheat and oil to bolster his lagging economy. In the most important demand of all, Hitler's forces must first land on the English coast in a full-scale invasion before Spain would join the war.[16]

Such presumption provoked Hitler to rush Canaris off to Spain again in an effort to convince Franco to join the Axis and, at least, soften his "outrageous" demands. This of course Canaris did not do in conversations with his old friend. To the contrary, he again reminded Franco of the folly in joining the side doomed to lose the war. General Halder's August 9 diary entry cryptically quotes Canaris upon his return: "Spain will not do anything against Gibraltar on her own accord. . . . Drawing Spain into War, desired by Führer, will be difficult. Economic problems!"[17]

By the end of August Halder was quoting Canaris as presenting a very gloomy picture of Germany's chances of gaining Spanish cooperation. "Franco's policy from the start was not to come in until Britain was defeated for he is afraid of her might," he said. Moreover, "The consequences of having this unpredictable nation [Spain] as a partner cannot be calculated. . . . We shall get an ally who will cost us dearly." By mid-September Halder's diary again revealed cryptic traces of the consummate spoiler: "Canaris's report on Spain. Spanish demands with respect to arms and fuel. Troop requirements for Gibraltar."[18]

Determined to reach an understanding with Franco, Hitler himself would take him on. A meeting was called for October 23 at the French border village of Hendaye to discuss Operation Felix. On October 20 Himmler was feted in Madrid. He had come at Serrano Súñer's invitation for the ostensible purpose of dealing with security matters attendant to Hitler's imminent arrival at Hendaye. In fact, he discussed a wider range of subjects, including long-term cooperation between Spain's and Germany's police organizations. Himmler, taking advantage of Hitler's visit, was obviously trying to move in on Canaris's preserve.

Hitler arrived at Hendaye in his private train accompanied by Foreign Minister von Ribbentrop; Marshal Keitel, chief of the High Command; and Marshal von Brauchitsch, commander in chief of the German Army. Conspicuous by his absence was Admiral Canaris. Disliking Canaris in general and fearing that as Franco's close friend he would steal the spotlight, gaining the credit for bringing the Caudillo into the Axis as a cobelligerent, Ribbentrop had managed to exclude the admiral. It was the one thing Ribbentrop need not have worried about.

General Franco was accompanied by his brother-in-law Foreign Minister Ramón Serrano Súñer,* and General Eugenio Espinosa de los Monteros, Spain's ambassador to Germany.[19] What Hitler expected was an exercise in protocol with enough pomp and panoply to flatter Franco. A German brass band was even brought along to entertain the gathering and create a proper martial ambiance. To help make the point that Hitler could take Spain easily by force if Franco did not willingly grant transit rights, a large contingent of German troops had arrived in the French

---

*According to Canaris's biographer Ian Colvin, British Foreign Office wartime expert on German intelligence, Canaris had instructed his Vatican agent, Josef Müller, to approach Spanish Foreign Minister Serrano Súñer during one of the latter's visits to Rome and convey to him in strict confidence the following: "The Admiral [Canaris] asks you to tell Franco to hold Spain out of this game at all costs. It may seem to you now that our position is the stronger. It is in reality desperate, and we have little hope of winning the war." — Colvin, *Canaris, Chief of Intelligence*, p. 128.

Pyrenees near the Spanish border on June 26, 1940, four months before the Hendaye conference.

Hendaye was meant to be a diplomatic ritual in which Franco would graciously accede to Hitler's wishes concerning Gibraltar, thereby allying himself fully with a Germany in the war and placing himself under German protection in the event of British retaliation. Instead Hitler found Franco unyielding in his refusal to compromise his nonbelligerency and to permit German troops on Spanish soil.

On the day before his arrival at Hendaye Hitler had paid a visit to Vichy leader Pierre Laval near Tours in France. He also planned a call on Marshal Henri Pétain himself the day following the Hendaye conference, in order to talk France into abandoning its neutrality and collaborating with Germany against Britain.[20] Franco, finding himself sandwiched between the two Vichy leaders, was not pleased. When Hitler made it clear that he could not ignore France's needs and desires, Franco realized that he would have nothing to gain territorially by entering the war on Germany's side, and much to lose.[21] Canaris's warnings of British reprisals now seemed all the more telling.

For his part, Hitler seemed to realize the futility of pushing too hard for Spain to become a belligerent when he could not hold out Morocco as a prize if he was to make his vassal, Vichy, France, a cornerstone to his planned southwestern Europe bloc. Hitler had been warned by Canaris (with good reason) not to expect much from Franco at Hendaye. Moreover, German State Secretary von Weizsäcker (a secret collaborator of the anti-Hitler Resistance and a friend of Canaris's) had told the Führer: "In my opinion Spain should be left out of the game; Gibraltar is not worth it. Whatever England lost there would soon be made up with the Canary Islands [implying that Britain would surely take them]."[22] Army Chief of Staff Franz Halder (also a secret Resistance collaborator) in his October 11 diary entry mentioned telling Brauchitsch for Hitler's benefit: "Spain's domestic situation is so rotten as to make her useless as a political partner. We shall have to achieve the objectives essential to us [meaning Gibraltar] without her active participation." And at the October 15 Brenner Pass conference, in conversation with General von Etzdorf, Halder reported in his diary: "Gibraltar is tied up with the French question. Bringing in Spain raises the issue of French colonial possessions and entails collaboration with France in North Africa."[23] Halder correctly pointed out that if France heard that its North African possessions might go to Spain, "She would cease defending her colonies and play them into British hands."[24]

Franco's and Pétain's demands were incompatible, and that fact, in essence, doomed Hendaye. Franco, for his own reasons, did not want to accede to Hitler's demands, but he feared that if he did not cooperate, Germany would forcefully take Spain—and Gibraltar. It was this point that made Canaris's lobbying with Franco important. The admiral had stressed that Germany would not open a Spanish front when Britain was still a factor, particularly at sea, and, above all, when Germany needed all the power it could muster for the impending, but still very secret, invasion of the USSR.

Hendaye broke up when Hitler took umbrage at Franco's expressed doubts concerning a German victory in the war. The Caudillo pointed out to the Führer that even if the British Isles were conquered, the British government and fleet would continue to fight from Canada with American support.[25] This line, incidentally, sounds very much like Canaris. After the war Hungary's wartime regent, Admiral Miklós Horthy, quoted Canaris as predicting as early as September 1938 that Germany would be doomed in any war if, as would be likely, the United States joined Britain and France. Canaris had said this as part of his warning to Horthy that Hungary should try to stay out of war.[26]

Although a meaningless memorandum of understanding was signed by Hitler and Franco at Hendaye, the Führer did not get what he wanted out of Franco, and Franco could not get what he wanted out of Hitler. An angry Hitler is supposed to have later told Mussolini, "I would rather have four teeth out than go through that again!"[27]

Despite Franco's attitude, Hitler kept Operation Felix alive. He was convinced that an attack on Gibraltar to seal the Mediterranean, coinciding with a major assault on the Soviet Union toward the end of 1940, would be more effective in forcing Great Britain into submission than a risky cross-Channel invasion. Not until December did Hitler lose complete faith in Spain.

Franco's later refusal to have anything to do with German plans to occupy Vichy France (Operation Attila) provoked Hitler to consider voiding his existing agreements with Spain. Then Franco answered negatively still another request from Hitler to join the war, received on February 6, 1941, using as an excuse Spain's precarious economy. Ribbentrop, in one of his few correct assessments, told Hitler that in his opinion, Franco had "no intention of joining the war."[28]

When the peripatetic Bill Donovan arrived in Madrid on February 26, 1941, fact-finding for Roosevelt, he was a visual reminder that the powerful United States was in the wings. In his conversation with Franco and Serrano Súñer, Donovan made it clear, implicitly at least, that the United States would not stand by and watch the demise of Great Britain.* British Am-

---

*It is possible that Franco was also influenced by William Donovan's visit to Madrid in February 1941 as an informal fact finder for President Roosevelt. British Ambassador Sir

bassador Hoare commented in a message to London: "Public opinion [in Spain] immediately deduced that, far from coming to an end, the war was soon to enter a new phase with the formidable participation of the U.S."[29]

Had Hitler known that his head of military intelligence, Admiral Canaris, had all along been an inspiration for Franco's incorrigible behavior, he would no doubt have exploded with rage and Canaris would have immediately, rather than some four years later, paid with his life. Canaris had taken a tremendous risk by his actions. Vague rumors inevitably leaked from the Spanish side, but fortunately for Canaris, Himmler apparently did not follow up; hence such stories either did not reach Hitler himself or were presented in such a way as to cloak the real significance of the matter.

Spanish Foreign Minister Serrano Súñer, was reported to have muttered darkly to Franco that in Berlin Canaris had spread "confused ideas on the Spanish problem."[30] In his postwar memoirs, *Between the Pyrenees and Gibraltar*, Serrano Súñer was still discreet about the Gibraltar affair, making no reference to what actually transpired at the Hendaye conference, but he did admit enigmatically, "Anything to do with Spanish affairs was utterly confused," and, "[O]ne of the reasons for the confusion was the somewhat singular role played by Admiral Canaris."[31]

After the war, when General Reinhard Gehlen, head of West Germany's new intelligence organization, and one of his senior officers, Captain Eric Waldman, visited Franco to revive liaison with him, the Spanish intelligence chief (G-2) revealed the story of Canaris's role in persuading the Caudillo not to give in to German pressure and join the Axis in war, saying that Hitler, despite his successes to date, was certain to be defeated. The chief of G-2 also stated that in order to show his gratitude, Franco after the war had offered Canaris's widow a home in Spain and other assistance.[32]

General Muñoz Grandes, commander of the Spanish Blue Division, which fought with German troops in Russia, accused Canaris outright of persuading Franco to stay out of the war. Other sources alerted Gestapo senior officer Walter Huppenkothen to Canaris's actions. The Gestapo certainly passed these reports on to Himmler. But Canaris, not for the first

---

Samuel Hoare writes an interesting paragraph in his postwar memoir, describing a conversation Donovan had with Franco and Spanish Foreign Minister Serrano Súñer: "He [Donovan] spoke to them with a frankness that did not bother with precautions. . . . Using his juridical glibness of speech, he built up on his premises a long indictment which left no doubt as to the reasons for his protestations—but what was by far the most important was that the different circles in the Spanish capital soon knew that Colonel Donovan had not hesitated to show firmness and determination"—Jacques de Launay, *Secret Diplomacy of World War II* (New York: Simmons-Boardman, 1963), p. 44, from Samuel Hoare, *Ambassadeur en Mission Speciale* (Paris: Vent du Large, 1946), p. 157.

time, survived mere suspicions. And not for the last time Himmler, faced with evidence implicating Canaris in high treason, refrained from further investigations. Himmler seemed to fear the Abwehr chief.[33]

The British were obviously relieved by Franco's posture toward Hitler. Although somewhat peeved by Spain's occupation of Tangier, Cadogan at the Foreign Office seemed to realize that this action did not mean that "they [the Spanish] are in with the Germans."[34] And the British Joint Intelligence Committee in December 1940 reported authoritatively that Franco would not cooperate with Hitler and the Germans would not try to invade Spain "by force."[35] At about the same time in December German Ambassador von Stohrer, who may have felt bad about not being able to deliver Spain, reported that Franco continued to plead lack of arms and food shortages in rejecting the idea of entering the war.[36]*

Hitler told Mussolini later that Franco's objectives were "absolutely out of proportion to [Spain's] strength," a pompous way of saying that the Caudillo's demands had been presumptuous. Franco's demands, in fact, seemed to increase with time. His ultimate list included: a correction of the Spanish frontier with France in Spain's favor, outright gifts of French Catalonia, Algeria, from Oran to Cape Blanco, and almost all of French Morocco, plus as a precondition a successful German invasion of Great Britain as well as an Axis seizure of Suez. Franco surely knew that such terms could never have been met.[37]

In *The Second World War* Churchill writes, "Thus by subtlety and trickery and blandishments of all kinds, Franco succeeded in tiding things over and keeping Spain out of the War, to the inestimable advantage of Britain when she was all alone."[38] In a "Former Naval Person" private communication with President Roosevelt on December 23, 1940, Churchill wrote that "an offer by you of food month by month so long as they [the Spanish] keep out of the war, might be decisive. . . . The occupation by Germany of both sides of the Straits would be a grievous addition to our naval strain, already severe. . . . The Rock of Gibraltar will stand a long siege, but what is the good of that if we cannot use the harbour or pass the Straits?" With his usual nice turns of phrase, Churchill says in his memoir: "It is fashionable at the present time to dwell on the vices of General Franco, and I am therefore glad to place on record this testimony to the duplicity and in-

*Winston Churchill, still concerned by the possibility that Hitler would try to take Gibraltar, was relieved when in early January 1941 his good friend Captain Alan Hillgarth, British naval attaché in Madrid, reported: ". . . it is becoming increasingly unlikely that the Spanish government will give Hitler passage [to Gibraltar] or join the war against us"—Winston Churchill, *The Second World War*, vol. 3, *The Grand Alliance* (London: Cassell, 1950), p. 22.

gratitude of his dealings with Hitler and Mussolini. I shall presently record even greater services which these evil qualities in General Franco rendered to the Allied Cause."[39]

Too discreet to mention Canaris's secret role so soon after the war, Churchill left it to later historians to reveal the whole story behind Operation Felix. The British government–sponsored history of *British Intelligence in the Second World War* mentions only that German pressure on Spain to "declare war and join in the capture of Gibraltar was resisted." But a U.S. Central Intelligence Agency monograph, *The Intelligence War in 1941: A 50th Anniversary Perspective*, published its author's view that, as a consequence of Canaris's actions, the "Canaris Factor," "Franco decided that Spain should remain, in effect, neutral."[40]

HITLER, WHILE PREPARING FOR A CROSS-CHANNEL INVASION, WAS SIMULTA-neously extending peace feelers to Britain. And neutral Spain, an active playground for espionage operations on both sides, would again be the site of dark doings by Germany. It would feature the Nazi security intelligence star operator Walter Schellenberg of the SD, the man who choreographed the Venlo incident. On orders of Foreign Minister von Ribbentrop, Schellenberg would be involved in a surrealistic operation involving the attempted subornation or kidnapping of the former king of England, the Duke of Windsor.

SEVENTEEN

A Reluctant Sea Lion and
an Errant Duke

GERMAN GENERALS, RELUCTANT TO RISK WAR IN THE FIRST PLACE, fought tenaciously once they engaged the enemy, while Adolf Hitler, who had recklessly plunged Germany into war, procrastinated when faced with the challenge posed by Britain. The missed opportunity to destroy the British Expeditionary Force at Dunkirk was a symptom of the Führer's reluctance to attack the British Isles. Certainly, in light of subsequent developments, the question that cried out was, with France defeated, the Soviet Union restrained by its treaty with Germany, and Britain reeling from aerial attacks, why did Hitler hesitate, then abandon altogether Operation Sea Lion, the long-expected invasion of Britain? And what did he hope to gain by extending peace feelers to the British?

On July 2, 1940, Hitler called on the Wehrmacht to perfect its plans for Sea Lion. Two weeks later he told his commanders that preparations must be completed by mid-August. Yet Hitler seemed reluctant. At a conference between Hitler and Admiral Raeder, on July 11, the navy commander in chief gave as his opinion: "An invasion should be used only as a last resort to force Britain to sue for peace." Hitler agreed, adding that he thought air superiority over the Channel must also be a prerequisite to invasion. An operational directive incorporating these views was issued on July 16, and on the nineteenth Hitler's hesitancy was reflected publicly in a speech to the Reichstag.

Aware that Mussolini would be put in an awkward position by a negotiated peace between Germany and Great Britain, Italian Foreign Minister

Count Galeazzo Ciano, warned of Hitler's dovish speech: "I believe that his desire for peace is sincere." The next day Ciano talked directly with Hitler, then recorded in his diary his impressions of the Führer's thinking: "He would like an understanding with Great Britain. He knows that war with the British will be hard and bloody. . . ." Mussolini by now was dedicated to defeating Britain; he never forgave the British for their attitude toward his Ethiopian campaign. Hitler's apparent loss of heart now concerned him.[1]

Hitler's hesitancy to proceed with Sea Lion was ostensibly based on military considerations. He believed it to be an exceptionally hazardous undertaking because the Channel "is dominated by the enemy; . . . operational surprise cannot be expected; without complete mastery of the air the supply lines would be impossible."[2]

Again the hand of Admiral Canaris intruded behind the scenes. Abwehr intelligence estimates were distinctly pessimistic, giving an excuse for Hitler's hesitation, if not helping to cause it in the first place. In view of Canaris's wrecking role as a member of the Resistance and his specific opposition to a military invasion of Britain, his reports were almost certainly exaggerated on purpose.

The Abwehr estimated British forces at thirty-four and a half divisions on September 17. There were in fact only twenty-nine divisions, most of which were understrength, not combat-ready and many shown by the Abwehr to be in the wrong place.[3] This inflated estimate was soon further increased by the Abwehr to thirty-seven divisions, which seemed to count the independent brigades as divisions.

Most Abwehr agents in Britain were ill trained and hastily dispatched. Virtually all of them were quickly captured.* German naval intelligence may have done better; at least it had broken British naval ciphers. But even that advantage disappeared when the British changed their compromised naval ciphers in August. Only Göring could keep his spirits up, but his Luftwaffe would soon begin to take unacceptable casualties in its air war over England.

The British had from the beginning overestimated the Luftwaffe; the Nazis maintained an unjustified illusion by masterful propaganda. The truth was that there was a shortage of German reserves, spare parts, munitions, and construction facilities. Moreover, the British had a tremendous advantage in their technological triumphs: radar and Ultra.

---

*According to General Ulrich Liss, head of the German Army's intelligence operations: "In SEA LION, although Canaris appeared to be trying to be efficient, he was not doing his job against England with conviction"—James T. Rogers, *The Secret War: Espionage in World War II* (New York: Facts on File, 1991), p. 34.

But there was more to Hitler's hesitancy than fear of Britain's defenses: By the time France capitulated, Britain was in such disarray that a German invasion could probably have succeeded. Göring, at least, was confident that it could have. While the British Expeditionary Force in France had been successfully evacuated from Dunkirk, it had left behind most of its equipment, and it had not yet been fully redeployed or fully retrained to meet an invasion.

Hitler, however, preferred to neutralize Great Britain without having to fight for it or destroy it. A totally defeated Britain would benefit only the United States and Japan, Hitler reasoned, but the British Empire as his junior partner in Europe, if not complete vassal, could help contain the Soviet Union or even defeat it and destroy communism while the United States continued to slumber in blissful isolation. Moreover, Hitler, whose power had been demonstrated in Poland and France, should be able to convince Britain to come to agreement on German terms. The Führer concluded that with Britain's back to the wall and with little prospect of the United States' coming to its rescue, even Churchill might listen to his peace offers. If not, there were others in Britain who would. The actions and antics of a few freewheeling but prominent British defeatists encouraged him in this hope. Hitler's peace offensive began in high gear during the first week of July 1940.

Sir David Kelly, British ambassador to the Vatican, who had already fielded peace feelers from the papal nuncio, met Dr. Carl Burckhardt, acting president of the International Red Cross, in Switzerland. Burckhardt had come directly from Berlin, where he had ostensibly discussed relief for refugees in France. In fact, he had discussed a peace proposition that he passed on to Kelly. Hitler had ideas of some kind of European federation or a general peace treaty with Britain such as that which Prussia had made with Austria in 1866.

Within a week another German caller talked with Kelly. Introduced by Spain's minister to Switzerland in Bern, Prince Max Eugen zu Hohenlohe-Langenburg, of defunct royal nobility (who also had contacts with the German Resistance), quoted Hitler as saying he was "prepared to accept an agreement with the British Empire, but time was very short and England must choose."[4] A postwar examination of German archives revealed that Hohenlohe claimed that it had been British Undersecretary of State Richard Austin Butler who instructed Kelly to feel out the Germans on peace terms. While Butler must have had Halifax's authority, his initiative did not represent British policy, nor was it Churchill's wish. This was a dangerous game that Butler and Kelly were playing; had it leaked out, Britain's urgent efforts to get U.S. aid might have been delayed or spoiled altogether.

Sir Frank Roberts of the Foreign Office, a hard-liner who had himself re-buffed earlier indirect peace feelers from Göring sent through the latter's Swedish businessman friend Birger Dahlerus, commented on Kelly's report by warning: "Any conversations with Germany on such a basis as peace terms at the expense of France and Belgium would enable Hitler at once to unite Europe, including France, against us and deprive us of growing American sympathy and support."[5]

Roberts's fears were well justified. President Roosevelt was genuinely alarmed at the political maneuvers of defeatist Lord Halifax, who might even have become the Conservative party's choice for prime minister instead of Churchill. Even Chamberlain, the archetypical appeaser of Munich, was appalled to realize that Lord Halifax in the summer of 1940, with war only a year along, seemed capable of conspiring against Churchill and discussing peace with Hitler. Roosevelt was so desperate to stop the British from concluding a "soft peace"—that is, capitulation permitting the British Navy to fall into German hands—that he secretly tried to enlist Canadian help to prevent Britain from caving in.[6]

German peace feelers were also sent through Washington: British Ambassador Lord Lothian had already received German overtures through the Italian ambassador in Washington when, on July 19, the day of Hitler's speech to the Reichstag, Lothian heard the same thing directly from the German chargé d'affaires. In reporting to London, Lord Lothian advocated a positive response to these overtures: "We ought to find out what Hitler means before condemning the world to 1,000,000 casualties." Back in London Lord Halifax, no less a pessimist about Britain's chances of winning the war, expressed himself as favoring the German peace initiative. Churchill, however, would have none of it[7] and canceled Halifax's instructions to Lothian encouraging the British envoy in maintaining contact with the Germans.

Lord Lothian paid little heed to Churchill's unambiguous instructions and, without immediately telling London, encouraged the intermediary efforts of Malcolm Lovell, executive secretary of the Quaker Service Council in New York, who had also become involved with peace feelers put out by the German chargé.[8]

Another unauthorized effort to promote peace with Germany encouraged by Lord Lothian almost defies belief, yet as the bizarre plot unfolded, Hitler's persistence in keeping peace hopes alive can perhaps be better understood. This complicated scenario involved in various degrees of complicity, duplicity, or unsuspecting innocence a large number of people. There were Captain Fritz Wiedemann, German consul general in San Francisco, who had in better days been Hitler's adjutant; Sir William

Stephenson, British intelligence chief in New York and liaison contact with Wild Bill Donovan of OSS; Sir William Wiseman, Kuhn, Loeb financier who had been head of British intelligence in the United States during World War I; Princess Stephanie von Hohenlohe-Waldenberg of the former German royal family, who was finally deported by the FBI as a suspected German spy; James D. Mooney, European vice-president of General Motors; Francis Cardinal Spellman; and British Ambassador Lord Lothian, despite Churchill's explicit prohibitions. Lothian's unquenchable zeal in trying to find peace at any price was stifled only by his death from a kidney ailment on December 12, 1940.[9]

The significance of this opera buffa was that it further misled Hitler into believing that the British were interested in peace or at least that there was a significant group of British defeatists ready to talk. It was an unfortunate coincidence, not lost on Hitler, that both the U.S. ambassador to Britain, Joseph Kennedy, and the British ambassador to the United States, Lord Lothian, during these crucial early months of the war, when so much depended on whether the United States would provide critical help to the beleaguered British, were defeatists at odds with the war policies of their respective leaders. This episode, really a non-event despite all the work it probably caused the FBI, pales into insignificance compared with the Nazi plot to co-opt—or kidnap—the Duke and Duchess of Windsor in the interest of reaching a peace on Hitler's terms with British defeatists.

In case there were any doubts about Hitler's intentions to extort peace from the British, if necessary, and cast Great Britain in a vassal's role similar to that of France, Operation Willi, a clumsy effort to subvert the Duke and Duchess of Windsor and place them on the British throne, should dispel them. Of all those out of step with their homeland, few caused more anguish than the Duke of Windsor, Great Britain's abdicated monarch whose longing for proper recognition, if not restoration, sometimes affected his judgment.

The frenzy of the international press covering the 1936 abdication of King Edward VIII "for the woman he loved" was a wonder to behold; it was a story with the ingredients of a latter-day fairy tale. Yet the "handsome prince" and twice-divorced would-be "beautiful princess" did not live happily ever after, and it was left to others to save the kingdom from the folly of this once-admired heir apparent who found being king too great a burden. Having slipped from grace, he had become a mere duke—not the right ending for a proper fairy tale.

Secrecy enveloped a Nazi plot during the summer of 1940 to subvert—kidnap, if necessary—the Duke of Windsor, and his ambitious American bride, the former Wallis Simpson, as they waited in Lisbon for transport to the Bahamas. Humiliated by his removal from the British throne and stung by the refusal of the British government to permit him to reside in Britain or recognize his wife with a royal title, the duke and duchess seemed dangerously vulnerable to the flattery of Adolf Hitler. Add to this formula for disaster the duke's long-held conviction that Hitler, a potential ally against Russia and Bolshevism, was someone with whom Britain could work on honorable terms, particularly if he were once again to become king.

Britain's darkest hour, the Battle of Britain with its terrifying aerial blitzes, suddenly seemed a little darker to British security officials as news of the Duke of Windsor's pro-Nazi, defeatist indiscretions in Spain and Portugal reached London from their all-seeing, all-hearing agent A-54, Abwehr officer Paul Thümmel in Prague. Worse, this drama coincided with the German preparations for the October Hendaye meeting in which Hitler was to seek Franco's cooperation in a German assault on Gibraltar, also reported by agent Thümmel.

Fed by German-stimulated propaganda, the Spanish press trumpeted the allegation that the Duke of Windsor and British Ambassador Sir Samuel Hoare were secretly seeking peace with Germany. This was an embarrassment to Britain and specifically to Hoare, who urged that the duke be recalled to London. The Germans, to the contrary, wanted him in Spain, where they could manipulate him and lure him into their camp. German Ambassador Eberhard von Stohrer cajoled the Spanish Foreign Ministry into offering him a suitable castle as enticement. Stohrer had high hopes when he reported to Hitler: "Windsor has expressed himself in strong terms against Churchill and against this war."[10]

The Duke of Windsor was frankly an embarrassment to the British government wherever he was. At the beginning of the war he had been given a meaningless liaison job attached to the British Military Mission at the French Army GHQ. When France fell in June 1940, he and the duchess had fled to Spain, then Lisbon, to await transport home—much against his wishes. Although the Duke of Windsor finally agreed to proceed to London, Churchill on July 4 found a solution and offered him a sinecure, governor-general of the Bahamas—hardly a prize. While awaiting a ship for the Bahamas in Lisbon, an embittered duke realized his new appointment was a "solution," not a serious job. In a black mood he told almost anyone who would listen that Britain's cause was hopeless and a negotiated peace with Hitler was the only way out. An American diplomat in Lisbon, H. Claiborne Pell, reported to Washington that the "Duke and Duchess are indiscreet and outspoken against the British Government"[11] and recommended he not be permitted to visit the United States.

German Minister to Portugal Baron Oswald von Hoyningen-Hüne,* had picked up similar gossip. He reported to Ribbentrop in the Foreign Ministry on July 10 news of the Duke of Windsor's state of mind: "He is convinced that had he remained on the throne, war could have been avoided, and described himself as a firm supporter of a peaceful compromise with Germany. The Duke believes with certainty that continued heavy bombing will make England ready for peace."[12]

Ribbentrop, having been German ambassador to London, fancied himself an expert on the British. In fact he had long held unfounded, wildly inflated views on the political importance of the British royal family. He saw merit in the Duke and Duchess of Windsor that very few others in Britain saw. In his fevered mind—fevered by the prospects of this imminent "catch"—Ribbentrop saw himself gaining favor with Hitler. While Hoyningen-Hüne's report was little more than gossip about a disgruntled, disgraced ex-king who, in his misery, was often indiscreet, Ribbentrop packaged the information for Hitler, making it appear to be just the opportunity Germany needed to reach a negotiated settlement with Great Britain. With Hitler's blessing in hand, Ribbentrop bypassed Himmler and Heydrich to enlist their ace operative Walter Schellenberg, head of the counterespionage section of the RSHA, in the plot against the Windsors.

Canaris and the Abwehr were also pointedly left out of the operation. Ribbentrop hated and mistrusted Canaris, who he feared would use his reputation as expert on Spain to scuttle the plan, as he surely would have done. Always solicitous of his friend Franco, Canaris indeed soon counseled the Caudillo to avoid actions that could seriously provoke the British. For that matter, Canaris at roughly this time was in Spain on his fact-finding mission for Hitler, preparatory to Operation Felix, the plan to seize Gibraltar from the British and deed it over to Franco in return for Spain's joining him in the war. Having contrived to slip Hitler one of his greatest diplomatic defeats of the war by artful manipulation of Franco, Canaris could be grateful for having been spared involvement in Ribbentrop's misbegotten plans for the Duke of Windsor.

Tempted to return to Spain from Lisbon, as suggested by the Germans, rather than proceed to the Bahamas, the Duke of Windsor finally agreed to obey orders. Churchill had Sir Walter Monckton to thank for this. This old friend of the duke's had been rushed to Portugal to reason with him.

---

*Hoyningen-Hüne until 1934 had been on German President von Hindenburg's staff. Half English, he was not a member of the Nazi party, nor was he sympathetic toward the Nazis in political conviction.

Ribbentrop's instructions to Ambassador von Stohrer were thorough, if nothing else, but they revealed an astonishing lack of reality. Had the Windsors been lured back to Spain from Portugal, "if necessary by force," the duke would have been told "Germany wants peace." If this could be achieved, Germany "would be prepared to accommodate any desire expressed by the Duke, especially with a view to the assumption of the English throne by the Duke and Duchess."[13] But if this was pushing things too rapidly, Ribbentrop was willing to have the duke simply recruited as a secret German agent of influence. "Should the Duke have other plans, but still be prepared to co-operate in the restoration of good relations between England and Germany, we would assure him and his wife any existence which would enable him, either as a private citizen or in some other position to lead a life suitable for a king."[14] In the event the duke refused to co-operate in any way, Ribbentrop had planned to force Franco to intern him as a "deserting military refugee" and exploit him under duress.[15]

Franco anticipated further pressure from Hitler to become involved in the German cause, and this worried him. He must proceed with caution. While he made a pretense of being helpful to the Germans, he had no intention of risking Spain's relations with Great Britain over such a harebrained scheme.[16]

Ambassador von Stohrer was clearly in over his head, so Ribbentrop had SS General Walter Schellenberg, expert in such matters, flown into Spain to perfect the plan for gaining control of the duke and duchess. Time was important, as the British were doing all they could to speed up the Windsors' departure for the Bahamas, where he would assume his new duties as governor-general of the island colony. Schellenberg's account of his briefing by Ribbentrop is illuminating. The German foreign minister had obviously convinced himself and Hitler that the Duke of Windsor would welcome liberation from the constraints of being an ex-monarch under constant surveillance by British intelligence and enduring the humiliation of being snubbed by the royal family. To sweeten the deal, Ribbentrop gave Schellenberg authority to offer the duke, still in Portugal awaiting ship, considerable amounts of money—perhaps fifty million Swiss francs, although more would be forthcoming if necessary. For this sum the duke must agree to denounce the British royal family and reside in an exile approved by Hitler, one such as Switzerland, within Germany's sphere of influence. If the duke rejected the German offer, he would be kidnapped![17]

In his memoir Schellenberg remembered being puzzled by Ribbentrop's logic. If the duke was pro-Nazi, why would he have to be kidnapped, and if he was taken against his will, wouldn't he cease being so well disposed toward the Nazis? The foreign minister explained weakly that the duke would ultimately be grateful even if at first he resented being taken against his will.[18]

Just what happened in Lisbon as the Germans tried to lure the Duke of Windsor back to Spain, where they could better isolate him from British persuasion and protection, is not clear. Almost anything authoritative about the Duke of Windsor is in top secret British files sealed until well into the twenty-first century. But an intriguing story by Peter Allen in his book *The Crown and the Swastika*,[19] documented in part by German records, has the Duke of Windsor in earnest conversation with no less a person than Rudolf Hess, deputy Führer, in Lisbon on July 28, 1940. They were allegedly discussing a plan of action in which the duke, under the cover of a "hunting party" near the Spanish border, would slip across into Spain and, as a guest of Franco, distance himself from British war policy. A telegram to Berlin sent by Schellenberg on July 28 described his own discussions with SD Chief Reinhard Heydrich, who apparently felt his presence in Lisbon was required to look after Hess's security and cover. Schellenberg in his message made mention of the fact that "Victor" (Hess) was with "Willi" (Duke of Windsor) and that the duke had asked for forty-eight hours to think over the proposition presented to him.[20] And, according to author Allen, Schellenberg also sent a private message to "A. H. [almost certainly Hess's friend Albrecht Haushofer] on July 28, assuring the recipient, "Our friend 'Tomo' [nickname used by Haushofer for Hess] met with 'C' [Heydrich's code designation] and Willi [Duke of Windsor] this morning." Allen, however, probably jumped to a false conclusion in identifying "C" as Heydrich even though the SS officer used to sign himself as "C" in his intraoffice correspondence, probably in imitation of the head of MI-6, who did the same. According to another author, Leo Kessler, "C" in this case referred to Captain José Catela, deputy chief of the Portuguese Secret Police.[21]

Schellenberg's message to Haushofer referred to a seven points plan, "which had been discussed in detail at a meeting held on July 29."[22]

The plan, whose basis was to invite the duke and duchess to a hunting party near the Spanish border, where he could be spirited away to German captivity, was never executed. Schellenberg, who had the duke and duchess's residence in Portugal under intense surveillance, concluded that despite the duke's quarrel with Churchill and the royal family, he would not cooperate, and to kidnap him would be to defeat the purpose of the operation: The Germans would lose a valuable sympathizer who might still prove useful.

Ribbentrop nonetheless pressed Schellenberg to act. The foreign minister sent an extraordinary telegram to the duke in Lisbon to be delivered by German Ambassador Hoyningen-Hüne. Informing the duke that Germany was on the verge of invading Great Britain, Ribbentrop in his message stressed that there must be a change of government in London if an honorable peace were to be made. Germany would restore the crown to the Duke of Windsor, who would play an important role in bringing peace to the two countries. That was the carrot. The stick was a heavy-handed harassment campaign simultaneously orchestrated by Schellenberg but meant to be attributed to the British Secret Service. Rocks were thrown through the duke's windows, anonymous threatening letters were sent to him, and other unconvincing but annoying gambits were aimed at the couple. Schellenberg claimed after the war that he had not liked the operation and had wanted to stop it without seeming to defy Ribbentrop's orders.

Ribbentrop's message to the Duke of Windsor, delivered on July 31, was remarkable for its effrontery but nonetheless elicited a response from the duke that was even more remarkable for its innuendos of serious indiscretion. While declining Hitler's offer lest it bring about a scandal, he expressed his appreciation for it and implied that if the state of affairs changed, he would reconsider his position.[23] This compromising document left the door open for further German intrigues with the duke.[24]

In the end Schellenberg had the sense to circumvent orders and take no action to kidnap the Duke and Duchess of Windsor. He received from Ribbentrop grudging approval to abandon the operation. With much relief, Schellenberg watched through high-powered binoculars from the safety of the tower room in the German Legation in Lisbon as his quarry sailed into the sunset for the Bahamas.* In his memoir Schellenberg writes: "Since the Duke was so little in sympathy with our plan, an abduction would be madness."[25]

One can easily guess that Ribbentrop's pipe dream filled Canaris with contempt. (Almost anything Ribbentrop did filled Canaris with contempt.) As the German expert on Spain the Abwehr chief could see what the consequences to German-Spanish and German-Portuguese relations at this critical point in the war might have been if Schellenberg had not abandoned it. Franco must have been relieved that Operation Willi had died of its own impracticality; he had not had to act to squash it himself and incur the wrath of Hitler or to cooperate with the Germans and incur

---

*After the war Prime Minister Churchill tried unsuccessfully to ensure that all derogatory material concerning the Windsors would be kept from publication, at least until many years had passed. But when certain reports began to leak out in 1957, the British government declared that the duke had "never wavered in his loyalty to the British cause."

the wrath of Great Britain. But the Caudillo's problems with Ribbentrop and Hitler were not over. Hitler still coveted Gibraltar, and German Ambassador von Stohrer was ordered to spare no effort in bringing Spain into the war on Germany's side.[26]

Rudolf Hess's visit with the Duke of Windsor in Lisbon, if such a meeting did in fact take place, could have further misled him to believe that there was a significant constituency in Britain for peace at almost any price. But even without such an encounter, Hess was convinced that there was still hope to end the state of war between Germany and Great Britain.

The British had not seen the last of bizarre efforts by Nazis to arrive at peace on their terms with the British. The strangest effort would be that of Hitler's deputy Rudolf Hess himself.

EIGHTEEN

The Hess Mission: Quixotic Adventure, Secret Diplomacy, or British Sting?

FIGHTER GROUP 13 OF THE ROYAL AIR FORCE, AT TURNHOUSE, WEST OF Edinburgh, had the mission of scrambling to intercept intruding enemy aircraft along the Scottish coast in its defense of Scotland and northern England. Its commanding officer was wing commander the Duke of Hamilton. David Douglas-Hamilton, as he was more simply known, had led a varied career. He had been the first person to fly over Mount Everest and had served as a Conservative Member of Parliament. Before the war he had the reputation of being well disposed toward Germany and belonged to an organization known as the Anglo-German Fellowship Association. Now he served the RAF in its time of trial, the Battle of Britain.

None of this prepared him for the night of May 10, 1941, when Rudolf Hess, Hitler's trusted deputy, parachuted to earth on his estate in Scotland. Hess had flown solo to Scotland in a Messerschmitt 110 equipped with extra gas tanks. His intention was to land on the Duke of Hamilton's private airstrip. Unable to spot the field in the darkness after circling the area for half an hour, Hess bailed out. He was found nursing a wrenched ankle by a Scottish farmer, David Maclean, and taken into custody at the village of Turnhouse. He would only explain to the police and home guard who detained him that he was carrying out a "special mission" and had to see the Duke of Hamilton.

In a report prepared by the duke describing his first interview with Hess on the morning after the unexpected landing, Hess reminded him that they had met at the 1936 Berlin Olympic Games and had lunched together. (For the record the duke reported that he had no recollection of this.) Hess described his act as a mission of mercy, saying, "The Führer did not want to defeat England and wished to stop fighting [the English]." He said that it had been Albrecht Haushofer (son of the well-known German geopolitician Karl Haushofer) who had recommended Hamilton as "an Englishman who . . . would understand his [Hess's] point of view." Earlier efforts by Haushofer to arrange a meeting between Hess and Hamilton in Lisbon had failed. In his report Hamilton denied any inkling that Haushofer's invitation to meet him in Lisbon had anything to do with Hess.[1]

Hess revealed to the duke that he had tried to fly to Scotland on three previous occasions, but each time the weather forced him to turn back. He had purposely not set out on his mission at a time when Britain was enjoying victories in Libya so that his actions would not be construed as a sign of weakness on Germany's part. Instead he chose a time when Germany had achieved successes in North Africa and Greece. The Führer sincerely believed that Germany would win the war, if not soon, within three years. He wanted to stop unnecessary slaughter, which would surely occur.

Hess asked the Duke of Hamilton if he could assemble leading members of his political party "to talk things over with a view to making peace proposals." On such an occasion Hess promised to describe what Hitler's terms would be. Hess insisted on a basic stipulation that there must be "an arrangement whereby our two countries would never go to war again," and "Britain would give up her traditional policy of always opposing the strongest party in Europe." Hess then asked that the King of England grant him a "parole," as "he had come unarmed and on his own free will."[2]

Some two and a half years later Hess, still a prisoner, was interviewed by Lord Beaverbrook. In response to the question why Hitler had invaded the USSR, Hess replied to the effect that Hitler feared that eventually the Soviets would attack Germany, particularly if Hitler was engaged in fighting a war with Britain. Such answers led Beaverbrook to conclude that Hess was not crazy. He also decided that Hess not only reflected Hitler's hope that peace with Britain would give him a free hand against Russia but had received Hitler's permission to meet with the Duke of Hamilton—with the understanding that Germany would disavow the contact if anything went wrong.

Hess volunteered that after his meeting with Hamilton he realized that he had been duped by the British; he would not be given a meaningful opportunity to have his proposals heard. This is why, Hess said, he had tried to commit suicide by throwing himself down a stairwell early during his stay in England. Only because his foot was caught in the banister was he spared a probably mortal plunge to the bottom of the stairwell.[3]

Hess's unceremonious arrival in Scotland began one of the greatest mysteries of World War II, one that is not yet completely solved and probably will not be solved until the British War Office files on Hess are declassified and released. A few tantalizing reports, long held classified by the former Soviet Union, were finally released by the KGB,[4] possibly shedding further light on the matter. But despite their allegations that Hess's mission was approved in advance by Adolf Hitler, this thesis has not been proved, nor does it seem likely.

One key to the mystery may be Hess's relationships with the Haushofers, father and son. Karl Haushofer, famous as the author of a German school of geopolitics whose theories influenced the Nazis, had once been Hess's professor. Dr. Haushofer's son, Albrecht Haushofer, who in mind and conscience broke with the Nazis (and much of his father's philosophy), collaborated secretly with the Resistance even though he became a very close friend of Hess. In the 1920s Karl Haushofer had made a name for himself for his views on economic determinism and Germany's requirement for Lebensraum. He also believed that war was a natural pursuit of mankind. Albrecht, however, was offended by Nazi brutality and disturbed that because his mother was half Jewish, the family was an object of Nazi suspicion. He was brilliant and emotional but too impulsive to make a good underground fighter. He found himself drawn to the Resistance for ideological reasons, yet intent on making an impact on German foreign policy, he played a risky double role, overtly as a member of Hitler's foreign policy establishment in the Information Section of the Auswärtige Amt (Foreign Ministry) and covertly as an activist in the Resistance. He could count on secret support from Canaris and his deputy Hans Oster, of the Abwehr, for his clandestine efforts to find a formula for peace with the West that did not include the Nazis, while at the same time being protected within the Nazi establishment by Rudolf Hess, a genuinely close friend of the Haushofer family.

Within the Resistance, Albrecht Haushofer knew Carl Langbehn, who was Himmler's attorney and sometime confidant—an interesting connection. Haushofer was also associated with the Kreisau Circle of the Resistance, including its leader, Helmuth von Moltke—a six-foot-seven-inch giant of a man—Ulrich von Hassell of the Foreign Ministry, and Johannes Popitz, former Prussian finance minister. The tireless Haushofer even had contact with Harro Schulze-Boysen, head of the widely ramified and effective Soviet spy net in German-occupied Europe known as the Rote

Kapelle, or Red Orchestra. Determined to convince the Nazis that Great Britain and the United States would defeat the fatherland and anxious to prod Hitler into abandoning his war with the West or, that failing, to overthrow the Führer, Haushofer took extraordinary risks.[5]

Rudolf Hess's quixotic act of flying to Scotland may well have had its origins in a fateful conversation with Karl Haushofer at an Austrian spa in August 1940. It was then that Hess described to Haushofer senior his hope that Germany would reach a peace agreement with Great Britain rather than invade it. Encouraged by Hess's interest in this matter, Haushofer wrote his son, Albrecht, on September 3, urging him to mount "the larger stage" and then, referring to the pending invasion of the British Isles, "stop something which would have such infinitely momentous consequences."[6]

Armed with his father's letter, Albrecht Haushofer went to see Hess on September 8. In an amazingly frank discussion he described for Hess's benefit the almost universal British opinion of Hitler as a "representative of Satan on earth" and accused Ribbentrop, whom he hated, of having seriously misjudged and misreported the British while he was German ambassador in London. Haushofer then proposed certain Britons who, in his opinion, would be receptive to German peace overtures if Hitler were out of the picture. He mentioned in this connection Sir Owen O'Malley, British ambassador to Hungary; Sir Samuel Hoare, ambassador to Spain; and Lord Lothian, ambassador to the United States. At the top of his list was his friend the Duke of Hamilton, who he claimed was well connected and, more specifically, had access to Churchill and the king.

Haushofer saw himself as the German peace envoy. Having in mind Resistance objectives, he would use Hess's endorsement to legitimize his mission but, in fact, would talk secretly to the British about peace without Nazi participation, which he knew was the only kind of peace that the British would consider. He wrote to his various British contacts in confidence, outlining his ideas "for an understanding with Britain" in which the Germans would evacuate all western and northern territories under occupation. Germany would be granted special interests in southeastern Europe, but not sovereignty. The eastern frontier would be settled bilaterally between the Germans and the states in question. Haushofer also suggested a European Economic Council, calling not only for the abolition of customs barriers but for a European police force and joint air command. The German and other European navies would come under British command.[7] Haushofer's plan to see Hoare in Spain to discuss peace along these lines did not materialize although Hess may have authorized him to undertake such a mission.[8]

Confident of Hess's protection, Haushofer was not as careful as he should have been in his Resistance activities. When the Gestapo became suspicious, he was arrested on May 12, two days after Hess's flight to Scotland. His timing had been unfortunate since without Hess present to protect him, he was extremely vulnerable. SD chief Schellenberg's report to Hitler on Hess's flight stated that Hess had been long "influenced by agents of the British Secret Service and their German collaborators, and they played a large part in bringing about his [Hess's] decision to fly to Scotland."[9] This suggests that Albrecht Haushofer, because of his Resistance contacts, was one of the "agents" whom Schellenberg had in mind, although he mentioned specifically a Professor "G," gland specialist in Upper Bavaria.

After two months of detention and interrogation, Haushofer was released by Himmler. His release suggests that either his hidden Resistance role was not proved and his activities were interpreted as simply an excess of zeal in trying to bring about peace between Britain and Germany or, more likely, that Himmler thought he might later prove useful. It may also have resulted because of Haushofer's connection with Karl Langbehn, Himmler's lawyer, who was collaborating with the Resistance.

Himmler was no stranger to the subterranean world of peace plotting. He, at least, knew of Albrecht Haushofer's energetic efforts to bring British friends together with his patron Rudolf Hess to talk peace. Himmler probably also knew that Carl Burckhardt, the Swiss Red Cross representative who was spreading the story that the British would consider peace without Hitler, was seeking contact with Haushofer.[10] But Himmler was both practical and ambitious; if the war went badly, or even before that happened, he might need men like Haushofer, who had contacts with the West.

Reichsführer Himmler, in fact, was not above thinking in terms of jettisoning Hitler and assuming power himself with the aid of the SS and perhaps even the army, so that he could conclude a peace with the Western Allies—a hidden agenda that he held in reserve. On May 10 Burckhardt in Zurich passed along an interesting piece of information to Ilse von Hassell, wife of Ulrich von Hassell, member of the Foreign Ministry Resistance circle. The Red Cross president claimed to have been sought out by a go-between in touch with Himmler (possibly Prince Max Eugen zu Hohenlohe-Langenburg, who, among others, later contacted OSS's Allen Dulles in Bern[11]), whose mission was to see if Britain would consider reaching peace with Himmler on condition the Führer was no longer in the picture.[12]

Hassell himself talked to Burckhardt in February, shortly after the latter had returned from London, where he had taken peace soundings in behalf of the Resistance. Burckhardt had gained the impression that many in Great Britain, among not only the Halifax-Hoare peace-minded clique but even persons close to Churchill, believed that some modus vivendi with Germany had to be found.[13]

Blindly loyal to Hitler and knowing Hitler's hope to neutralize Britain by negotiation rather than invasion, Hess likely was moved by Albrecht Haushofer's ideas although he seems to have ignored Haushofer's all-important warning that the British, even the defeatists, would not do business with Hitler. While in British detention, Hess is supposed to have testified to the effect that he had hoped to make peace with the British — albeit a peace in which Churchill would forgo his position as prime minister — and return to Germany swathed in public acclaim. Hitler would smile on him, he believed; his waning prestige in Nazi circles would be restored, and the Führer could proceed safely with his crusade against the Soviet Union. Resistance activist Hassell believed that Hess may have had another motive: He feared "a move against him" by other top leaders of the party.[14]

Almost certainly Hess's choice of the Duke of Hamilton as point of contact was because of Albrecht Haushofer's friendship with the Scotsman. A message dated September 23, 1940, from Haushofer to Hamilton was intercepted by British security intelligence. Intimately phrased, Haushofer's letter opened with the salutation "My dear Douglo," followed by an assurance that his attachment to Hamilton "remains unaltered and unalterable."[15]

For their own reasons British intelligence officers waited five months before delivering the message to Hamilton. Finally the Secret Service proposed to Hamilton that he travel to Portugal, where Haushofer had suggested a meeting, and find out what his friend wanted to discuss. This proposal does not seem to have been implemented. For one thing, it seemed apparent that Haushofer was intent on discussing peace, and this was something that Churchill had banned. Another reason may have been that the Secret Service was baiting a trap without the duke's knowledge. By the time the intelligence people got around to discussing it seriously with Hamilton, Hess had landed in Scotland.[16] How much Hess's decision had in the first place been the result of correspondence between Haushofer and British intelligence in the guise of the Duke of Hamilton — and perhaps without the duke's knowledge — can at this time only be guessed, although much later Hamilton confided to his son that the British Secret Service (MI-6) had attempted to enlist him as a "catspaw" in a "peace" initiative involving Albrecht Haushofer. Hamilton claimed that even Prime Minister Churchill did not know about this.[17] If this is true, one may speculate that MI-6 had devised a sting in an effort to get back at the SD for its sting at Venlo and benefit from an interrogation field day with Hess, just as the Germans had benefited from their exhaustive interrogations of Best and Stevens.

Hess's wife, in her postwar book *Prisoner of Peace*, described Albrecht Haushofer's efforts to establish contact with the British as having been undertaken with Hitler's knowledge. Haushofer himself wrote that Hess had given him the impression that he had discussed with Hitler the matter of seeking out British friends. But even if this is true, it is of course unlikely that Hess had shared with Hitler Haushofer's pessimistic opinion that there was "not the slightest prospect of peace" and his conviction that there was not the least possibility of making British contacts.[18] Otto Dietrich was also under the impression that Hess had had a conversation with Hitler about peace contacts, and Hassell had no doubt that Hess "frequently attempted to revive contacts with England, in most cases with Hitler's approval."[19] Wilhelm F. Flicke, a veteran cipher officer, commissioned by Chief Army Signals Officer General Erich Fellgiebel, during World War II to write a history of German cryptography, made brief reference in his memoir to the Hess incident. He stated that Hitler's deputy had flown "unofficially" to Scotland, but with "Hitler's knowledge."[20] This, however, was an assumption, not something Flicke knew with certainty.

The big question remains: Did Hitler have any idea that Hess would go so far as to fly to the British Isles himself? For Hitler to agree to a black flight to Britain, technically difficult, politically dangerous, and altogether unnecessary, strains credulity, particularly at that time since Hess had knowledge of the imminent German invasion of Russia, a secret he might be forced to divulge. Hess's secretary, Ingeborg Sperr, in commenting on this subject, said nothing of Hitler's being privy to the plan, confining herself to the opinion that Hess undertook the flight "in his fanatic love for the Fatherland; he wanted to make the greatest sacrifice of which he was capable to Adolf Hitler . . . to leave nothing undone to bring the German people the desired peace with England."[21]

The weight of evidence seems to suggest that Hitler knew and approved of Hess's trying to "make contact with" British defeatists to discuss peace— i.e., peace on Hitler's terms. The term *make contact with* is where the ambiguity arises: Did it mean physical contact on British soil—the enemy camp? Or did it mean indirect contact through intermediaries? Just as Hitler encouraged Göring to establish contact with the British through the Swede Dahlerus during the Polish crisis but vetoed the *Reichsmarschall's* plan to fly to England to meet with Chamberlain, he probably would have vetoed Hess's plan had he been given the opportunity.

If Hitler knew in advance of Hess's flight, he was a consummate actor. Chief of Staff General Franz Halder, wrote in his diary on May 15, 1941, that the "Führer was taken completely by surprise by Hess's flight."[22] After an emergency meeting with Hitler that day to discuss this electrifying development, Halder summed up his views: Hess was depressed by the "fratricidal struggle between the two Germanic nations," Germany and Britain, and genuinely sought peace between them. Driven "by some mystical sense of mission,"[23] Hess had become upset by what he believed to be his lessening importance in Nazi circles.

Ribbentrop's man at Hitler's headquarters, Walter Hewel, described in his diary the scene of utter confusion and dismay at Hitler's mountain retreat, Berghof, when news of Hess's strange adventure became known. When Göring arrived, having been hastily summoned, Hitler exploded with the news: "Hess has flown to England." He waved the letter in which Hess had explained his willingness to place his life in jeopardy by making peace with Great Britain. Hans Frank, one of sixty or seventy Nazi leaders present when Hitler discussed the Hess crisis, reported later that he had not seen the Führer so grief-stricken since the suicide of his adored niece, Geli, ten years before. Frank said it was obvious that the Hess matter had taken him by surprise.

Schellenberg writes in his memoirs that Hitler had been "momentarily filled with such consternation that he was hardly capable of any reaction." Called upon to investigate the matter, Schellenberg reported that Hess had devised his flight plan on the basis of advice from an astrologer. This news was enough for his boss, Heydrich, to order the arrest of most of the astrologers, mediums, and assorted mystics in Berlin for questioning. "With satanic glee" Heydrich told his boss, Himmler, an astrologist himself, that one who worries about "stars in heaven" is no worse than one who worries about "stars on the epaulettes."[24]

Whatever the truth of this strange case, Stalin seems to have concluded that Hess's actions meant that Russia was about to be victimized by a peace conspiracy between Great Britain and Germany. In November 1990 the Soviet KGB released for publication by a British historian certain wartime NKVD reports on the Hess affair, which had been originally prepared for Stalin. These reports quoting Soviet spies revealed that Hess had been "lured to Britain as the result of a MI-6 plot." A British intelligence report, forwarded to Moscow by the NKVD resident agent in London, who had in turn received it clandestinely from Russian spy Kim Philby, described Hess as having brought peace offers from Hitler.[25] Specifically, the report claimed that Hess had Hitler's full consent to initiate peace negotiations since Hitler could not do so openly without harming German prestige. As authentic as this may seem, Philby's information must have come from the interrogation of Hess; therefore, it was based on Hess's implied claim to having been sent by Hitler. But he could not have claimed otherwise and still have worn the mantle of Hitler's approved emissary. Genrikh Borovik, the Russian author of *The Philby File* (1994), writes that within eighteen months of Hess's flight NKVD chief Lavrenti Beria informed Stalin that the London NKVD resident had "reliably" reported (presumably from Philby) that the British SIS had enticed Hess to Britain in an effort to create confusion in Germany.[26] This could be true but does not prove, or even suggest, that Hitler sent Hess to Britain.

Still another NKVD report, this one allegedly originating with a Soviet agent in Washington with contacts within the German OKW, was explicit in claiming that Hess's flight was taken "with full approval from Hitler for the purpose of beginning a peace process with Britain."[27] Then reports from Soviet espionage networks within Germany, including the effective Rote Kapelle group, also painted Hess's flight as part of a "Nazi conspiracy" to make peace with Great Britain as a prelude to invading the Soviet Union.[28] Here the word *conspiracy* leaps out. Hitler may have endorsed Hess's efforts to find a contact with the British, but it would have taken two parties to make a "conspiracy," and while the SIS may have encouraged Hess to establish a contact with a British representative like the Duke of Hamilton for intelligence purposes—such as probing for confirmation that Hitler intended to invade Russia—one cannot easily believe that there could have been British participation in a "conspiracy" against the USSR, involving British appeasement zealots willing and able to defy hard-liner Churchill.

However specific some of the old NKVD reports seem to have been on Hitler's prior awareness of and agreement with the Hess mission, such reports were from fallible agents, perhaps quick to leap to wrong conclusions. The Soviets knew about Hitler's peace campaign and the apparent willingness of some British defeatists and appeasers from Chamberlain's administration to agitate for a peace deal despite Churchill's strong opposition, but this was a long way from a German-British agreement to join forces and attack the Soviet Union.

Churchill had never been reticent in expressing his strong opposition to a negotiated peace with Germany, which even during Britain's darkest hours struck him as an act of national blasphemy. Any negotiations at this point would have been negotiated under implied duress, casting Britain virtually in a vassal's role. While there were defeatists in Britain, even in the government, who may have sent misleading signals to the Germans, the likelihood of their unseating Churchill and forming a new government willing to capitulate, as France had done, is not credible.* For an official of Hess's exalted rank and propinquity to Hitler to have flown to Scotland presupposes that he at least believed he had been duly invited by the British, however secretly, but that does not mean that it was anything more than a British trap—if that. His crash landing in Scotland and his rigorous internment upon arrival must have made him see the light: He had been had.

It was true that Hitler had become increasingly unreasonable in his demands for more raw materials from the Soviet Union, and current negotiations over this and other provisions of the Russo-German trade agreement had already cast a shadow on the alliance. So Stalin, steeped in his own conspiracy ethos, may have sincerely believed Hess to have been an authorized German emissary to Britain blessed by Hitler. Three years after these events Stalin, still obsessed by the Hess case, had the occasion to ask Churchill about it. In his war memoir Churchill recalled that Stalin was exceedingly suspicious; he still seemed to believe "there had been some deep negotiation or plot for Germany and Britain to act together in the invasion of Russia, which had miscarried." When Churchill vehemently denied any such thing, Stalin "with a genial grin," said, "[T]here are lots of things that happen, even here in Russia, which our secret services do not necessarily tell me about."[29]

Former *Sunday Times* of London correspondent and writer on the Philby case Phillip Knightly, alleges in his book *The Master Spy* that Churchill kept SIS officers "away from Hess" because he thought the service still favored a "peace pact" and "alliance" against the Soviet Union.[30] While Churchill had sternly admonished the SIS to avoid contact with a German opposition after the disastrous Venlo incident, it is difficult to be-

---

*Ultra produced an intercepted message dated November 29, 1941, sent by the Japanese ambassador in Berlin to the Japanese Foreign Ministry, which must have interested Churchill when he read it on December 4. At least, he made a mark in the margin with his famous red-ink pen highlighting a Ribbentrop statement to the effect that Hitler was convinced that Britain would be beaten without need for a German attack because of a deep division within the Conservative party. But this was probably Ribbentrop's view attributed by him to Hitler. Since Ribbentrop had often been wrong in his assessment of British resolve, this may have amused Churchill more than upset him.

Perhaps more important was another paragraph in the message describing Germany's intention to wrest Gibraltar from the British and throw them out of the Middle East and Africa. This kind of intelligence must have disturbed the empire-minded Churchill. It may have also have contributed to his insistence on invading North Africa as an early order of business once the United States had joined the war—John P. Campbell, "A British Plan to Invade England, 1941" *Journal of Military History* (October 1944), p. 672.

lieve that he conceived of the service's being willing to make secret peace overtures behind his back.*

It was, however, equally difficult for a conspiratorial man like Stalin to believe that Hess, moved only by misguided zeal, made the flight on his own initiative or that British Secret Intelligence, if involved, was involved in no more than some deception or harassment operation calculated simply to embarrass the Germans. It was particularly difficult for Stalin to dismiss the possibility, at least, of an anti-Soviet, Anglo-German entente, with Hitler absent, in the aftermath of a military putsch when Stalin was almost certainly aware of German Resistance efforts to interest the British in such a plot. Stalin, moreover, was well aware that there existed appeasement-oriented British officials at odds with Churchill's policies, who in varying degrees believed that Britain would lose the war with Germany or that the Soviet Union was the more dangerous adversary—or both. It may be no wonder that Stalin, realizing Russia's military weakness, seemed paranoiac. He would in fact never cease to distrust the British and later the Americans as well; to the last hour of the war he feared that the Western Allies would join with the Germans and turn on Russia. In 1941, when it became evident that Hitler had indefinitely put off an invasion of Britain and reports that Germany was instead looking eastward poured into the Kremlin, Stalin could not help suspecting Anglo-German complicity. Indeed, while the British in fact had no dark role in Germany's decision to invade the Soviet Union, he could not help reasoning that there was more to Germany's decision to abandon the Battle of Britain than readily met the eye.

*There have been other conspiracy theories. One was described by British spy writer Richard Deacon in his 1984 biography of the late Sir Maurice Oldfield, former head of MI-6. As fanciful as it may sound, Deacon quotes Sir Maurice as asking him if he knew that Hess had his own spy service whose head had been an NKVD agent. Oldfield wondered if this agent could have been behind Hess's flight to Scotland—Richard Deacon, "C": A Biography of Sir Maurice Oldfield, Head of MI-6 (London: Macdonald, 1985), pp. 86, 87.

Oldfield probably had in mind a German named Franz Pfeffer von Solomon as Hess's intelligence man. Solomon, a former SA officer, served Hess as head of a somewhat amorphous diplomatic intelligence network consisting mainly of relics from the Imperial Intelligence Service of World War I—Peter Padfield, Hess: Flight for the Führer (London: Weidenfeld & Nicolson, 1991), pp. 61, 62. Among other tasks performed by Solomon was denigration and harassment of Christian churches in an effort to rid Germany of an ideological rival of Nazism. And in preparation for the Anschluss, he manipulated a German fifth column within Austria (ibid., p. 100). He also followed the political eddies within Britain, particularly those swirling about Chamberlain, including the military expert Basil Liddell Hart, Menzies of MI-6, and the Duke of Hamilton. It was not made clear by author Padfield what Solomon and Solomon's master, the NKVD, could have had as a motive.

WHILE HITLER'S PEACE OVERTURES TO THE BRITISH, UNAPPETIZING CARrots at best, had failed, the Luftwaffe stick might have succeeded if Hitler had kept at it a little longer. But he did not, and the Battle of Britain was lost by Germany.

The Battle of Britain, code-named Operation Sea Lion, with its heavy air attacks, was assumed by the British to have been a prelude to German invasion. It began on August 8, 1940, when Göring's Luftwaffe flew 1,485 sorties from German bases in France. By August 15 the number of sorties per day had risen to 1,786, an awesome pounding by any standard.

Britain's Air Marshal Sir Hugh Dowding's fighter command with only 650 fighter planes kept command of the air despite Luftwaffe numerical superiority. Aside from superior tactics, the RAF could thank modern technology for its success. British pilots, guided by an efficient ground command, could better defend themselves by newly developed radar techniques, while Ultra, the fruit of Britain's ability to break the German Enigma ciphers, also came to the RAF's rescue.

A German Air Force navigational aid system that could locate a target with intersecting beams was deciphered at the British government code and cipher facility at Bletchley Park in early July 1940. With this critical information, the British could devise countermeasures to confuse German bombers and lead them off course.[31] The second phase of the Battle of Britain occurred between August 24 and September 5, 1940, when Göring changed tactics, now targeting the principal RAF bases so as to destroy airfields and communications and control facilities as well as aircraft. Some 450 British fighters were destroyed, and 103 pilots killed.

In the midst of the Luftwaffe's damaging campaign against the RAF, Göring committed a blunder. On August 24 the Luftwaffe sent 200 German bombers to attack targets ranging as far afield as Wales. Aircraft factories and oil depots on the edge of London were also bombed, but for the first time there was what appeared to be wanton attacks on residential areas as well. This was later determined to have been unintended, but at the time it provoked Churchill to order retaliation.

RAF bombers in a night raid were sent over Berlin, where they dropped their bombs for three hours without serious interference. While the damage inflicted was small, the psychological effect on the Germans was immense. When on August 28 and 29 the RAF struck Germany's capital again, as well as Düsseldorf and Essen, Hitler was badly shaken. Göring had promised him that bombs would never drop on Berlin. Trying to regain face, Hitler ordered the Luftwaffe to concentrate its attacks on the city of London. While this caused hardship for Londoners, it increased their resolve to withstand Hitler's attacks; morale was never higher. But more important, by concentrating on London, the Luftwaffe abandoned its attacks on RAF stations, which had almost driven the Spitfires and Hurricanes from the skies. The RAF Fighter Command was saved from imminent destruction.

Hitler's mass bombing of London reached a peak on September 15. Wave after wave of German planes—some thousand bombers and seven hundred fighters—attacked the beleaguered city that day. Luftwaffe casualties were so great, however, that Göring thereafter abandoned daytime bombing of London. The RAF Bomber Command, by contrast, went on the offensive, destroying more than two hundred invasion barges in French and Belgian Channel ports poised for action against Britain—or put there to deceive the British.

Operation Sea Lion, scheduled for September 27, was suspended. Having failed to gain air control of British skies, Hitler canceled the invasion for the foreseeable future on October 12. On December 5 Army Chief of Staff Halder noted in his diary that Sea Lion could be possible only "when the English fighters are totally eliminated. . . . That cannot be expected."[32] Glancing into the future, he added pessimistically, "Sea Lion cannot be considered." Halder assessed the situation accurately when he noted in his diary: "Britain did not sacrifice her fighter strength over London; she is sacrificing London instead. . . . This enabled Britain to conserve and increase her fighter planes. We were forced to change over to night attack."[33] Commemorating the end of the Battle of Britain, Churchill in a moving address uttered his now-famous phrase "Never in the field of human conflict was so much owed by so many to so few."

Without minimizing the valor and skill exhibited by the British, warriors and civilians alike, they had an unintended ally in Hitler's bad judgment. Had Germany invaded almost immediately after Dunkirk while the British were still reeling from the shock of the German panzer attack on France and their own retreat from the Continent, they could probably have conquered the British Isles. The British had been forced to leave in France almost every first-line tank. General Montgomery's 3d Division was the only battle-ready division available, and the RAF was badly crippled. While the British Navy commanded the Channel, a German airlift could probably have established a bridgehead and supplied it even though German intelligence estimates at the time were pessimistic and counseled caution. Hitler was so determined to invade the Soviet Union, key to Continental dominion, that he could ill afford to take serious risks or, even if successful in Sea Lion, tie up the troops necessary to police an occupation of the British Isles.

After the war Gerd von Rundstedt, one of the army's top generals, confirmed that the German Navy had felt unsure of its ability to contest the

Channel and North Sea with the British Navy, and the Air Force had not yet perfected air supply techniques such as those that were used successfully in Russia during the winter campaign of 1941. Only Göring favored attempting an invasion of the British Isles, even though he had failed to gain air superiority over the Channel.[34]

Hitler never seemed to have had his heart in Sea Lion. Not without reason, he had seemed to prefer reaching détente with a viable Britain, not a morose band of occupied people, whose government and navy would have fled to exile stations in Canada, India, and Australia with massive help from the Commonwealth and probably the United States to continue the war. As reflected in *Mein Kampf*, his long-range objective was to make Germany master of Europe in some kind of arrangement in which fellow Nordic Britannia would rule the waves and nourish its empire. Of course, that achieved, he would have had the British Isles and much of the empire within his grasp whenever he found it expedient to seize them.

Having failed to reach a peace agreement with the British and then not having been able to risk a crossing of the English Channel for want of air superiority, Hitler was determined to attack Soviet Russia and fulfill his Eastern strategy to gain Lebensraum—and Russian oil. Once Russia had been conquered with lightning panzer attacks along a broad front, Britain, he believed, would have no choice but to reach an accord with the German victor, master of the Continent. The Führer could reckon that even though he had not subdued the British, they were now in no position to attack him on the Continent.

On the heels of the campaign in the West, Hitler on July 21, 1940, announced in secrecy to his generals that he now intended to destroy Russia. On December 18 Hitler approved a comprehensive plan of attack that was to be known as Barbarossa after the twelfth-century emperor of the Germans, Frederick I Barbarossa, the "red-bearded one." But what Hitler hoped would be a monthlong victorious campaign against Russia lasted for four years, dragging Hitler and Germany to a humiliating defeat. Barbarossa was Hitler's greatest mistake.

PART THREE

WORLD
WAR

NINETEEN

Barbarossa: "Sparrows Chirped About It at Every Crossroad"

A WARTIME ARMENIAN JOKE HAD IT THAT HITLER WAS THE ONLY MAN STALIN ever trusted, a commentary on how trusting the Soviet leader was in his apparent belief that the Germans would not attack Russia. In fact, Stalin trusted no one, certainly not Hitler, nor did he seem to respond to a deluge of warning intelligence that flowed to him from a wide variety of sources. There was, however, more to account for his deaf ear than distrust of his intelligence sources. But whatever it was that caused the Soviet leader to take so little action in preparing his country for the coming German onslaught despite the chorus of warnings, Hitler's armies, as predicted, invaded the Soviet Union on June 22, 1941, just before dawn along a two-thousand-mile front. Barbarossa was, perhaps, the most massive attack ever launched by an army in the history of war. This is the story of intelligence early warning and in some cases its disregard: who knew what, when did they know it, and what did they do or not do about it.

Throughout the war Stalin was wedded to the conviction that not only had Churchill seen Germany's invasion of the USSR as the salvation of Great Britain but that thereafter Britain's Prime Minister Churchill would watch the terrible battles for Russia's survival with morbid satisfaction, hoping that in the end both countries, Britain's traditional rivals, would be ruined in the process. The procrastination of the Western Allies to launch a second-front invasion of France was interpreted by Stalin as a calculated strategy to let the Red Army and the Wehrmacht destroy each other before British and American troops joined the continental land battle to reap the fruits of victory.

   Stalin so distrusted Winston Churchill that when the British prime minister warned him of the impending German invasion, he thought it was a
trick. He reasoned that Hitler could not be unwise enough to risk war on two
fronts; Churchill's warning, he feared, was deception designed to sow dissension between Germany and the USSR. In fact, Churchill had learned
from Ultra intercepts that the Germans had transferred armored units to
southern Poland from Yugoslavia. After disguising Ultra as its source,
Churchill, on April 3, instructed British Ambassador Sir Stafford Cripps in
Moscow to give this highly significant indicator of invasion immediately to
Stalin. For reasons not clear, Cripps delayed passing the message until April
19, 1941. The delay did not matter, however, since Stalin ignored it.
   British intelligence had received hints of a German plan to attack the
USSR as early as August 1940, only a week after Hitler in great secrecy had
informally approved Operation Barbarossa. German planning for the invasion had begun on July 29 at a conference of key military officers chaired
by chief of staff of the OKW Jodl. Even as Molotov was visiting Berlin for
"friendly discussions," Directive No. 21, entitled "Operation Barbarossa,"
was formally issued on November 18 to a select few who had a need to
know. Hitler's cynicism was explicitly revealed in the passage of the directive that reads: "Irrespective of these discussions [with Molotov] all preparations for the East which have been verbally ordered will continue."[1]
   Chief of Staff Halder's cryptic notes, made after a meeting with Hitler
and other top military officers on July 31, 1940, suggest the thinking that lay
behind the invasion of Soviet Russia. Since a German invasion of Britain
had been put on ice, "our action," he wrote, "must be directed to eliminate
all factors that let England hope for a change in the situation. To all intents
and purposes, the war is won. France is no longer part of the setup protecting British convoys. Italy is pinning down British forces." And, Halder
underlined for emphasis, *"Britain's hope lies in Russia and the United
States,"* but, "If Russia drops out of the picture, America too is lost, for
elimination of Russia would tremendously increase *Japan's power* in the
Far East." According to Halder's notes, Hitler emphasized: "Russia is the
Far Eastern sword of Britain and the United States pointed at Japan. *Russia is the factor on which Britain is relying the most. . . . With Russia
smashed, Britain's last hope would be shattered.* Germany then will be master of Europe and the Balkans."[2]*

*According to a Magic decipherment of a message sent by the Japanese Embassy in
Berlin to Tokyo, Hitler had confided in Ambassador Oshima at the end of March 1942:
"I know that if I left Russia alone and continued my fight against England, Russia
would stab us in the back when we were least able to resist"—Bruce Lee, *Marching Orders* (New York: Crown Publishers, 1995), p. 29.

Churchill's warning to Stalin, indeed Churchill's own convictions as to what Hitler would do, had not been based on any formal estimating process within the British government. To put it simply, after the fall of France Churchill's own intuition, based on raw intelligence, proved more accurate in divining Hitler's intentions than the formal estimates put together by his political analysts. The vital question had been, What next? Would Hitler attack the British Isles, or would he first turn eastward and try to knock out the Soviet Union? The prevailing wisdom of the "wise" in the Foreign Office, General Staff, and intelligence agencies was that Britain would be the next target for German assault.

This conclusion was based on fallacious, simplistic preconceptions. Because most Britons considered Germany their most urgent enemy, they assumed that Germans reciprocated the honor and considered Great Britain its principal foe. That was probably not true. Hitler did not believe it to be the case. Despite his pact with Stalin, a purely expedient maneuver to gain time, the Führer feared and loathed the Communist behemoth to the East for geopolitical as well as ideological reasons and had long thought a German-British entente was a more natural alliance—provided, of course, that Germany would control continental Europe while Britain contented itself with its overseas empire. He also saw Eastern Europe and the western Soviet Union as the area from which he must carve out Lebensraum, with resources needed to satisfy his people and his own vaunting imperial ambition. In the short run he realized that the German Army, not to mention German industry, needed the oil of Romania and the Caucasus. Without oil Germany would have neither army nor air force.

Another British preconception was that Germany, on the advice of its generals, would not be foolhardy enough to risk a two-front war. That may have been the classical doctrine of the German Army, but it was not accepted by Hitler, who did not rely on his generals for advice as much as the British thought he did. Hitler believed that with France under German occupation, a militarily unprepared Britain could not hope to invade the Continent in time to interfere with a lightning German blitzkrieg against an ill-prepared Soviet Union, whose army was still divided between the Far East and Europe and whose officer corps had been decimated by Stalin's Great Terror. Hitler reasoned that a negotiated peace would be the best way to neutralize Great Britain. That failing, the British would still be unable to invade the Continent, much less launch an offensive against Germany's western front so long as defeated France remained under Nazi control. He also believed that isolationist America was not now, if ever, ready to join the European war. Britain's best hope would be a military alliance with the Soviet Union, pinching Germany in the middle—reason enough why Russia had to be knocked out of action before it could join hands with the British.

A third preconception, plausible on its face but also wrong, was that Germany considered Britain an easier target than Russia; the lightly defended British Isles would lend themselves to a quick German victory. The defeat of Russia would, in the opinion of British analysts well read on Napoleon's catastrophic invasion of imperial Russia, take longer and be infinitely more costly in manpower. This reasoning was flawed. The British in 1940–41 did not fully realize that Hitler's euphoric self-confidence, excited by victories in Poland and France, would lead him to folly. At the same time Hitler, respecting British naval superiority, shied away from a cross-Channel invasion unless he had complete air superiority over Britain. The Luftwaffe, contrary to Britain's inflated view of its prowess, had not convinced Hitler that it had that superiority. German generals also had an aversion to invasions by sea. Land war was what they knew best.

Perhaps the most basic mistake made by Britain's military analysts was to assume that Hitler would act "rationally"—that is, act as they would in his circumstances. To assume that he would follow a logical course of action in Germany's best interest was always a mistake, one for which Chamberlain had paid dearly at Munich. The several secret emissaries sent to Britain by the German Resistance based their case on just this point: A megalomaniacal Hitler was leading Germany to disaster; logic had nothing to do with his judgments. British officialdom should have listened more closely.

An effort by the British to improve their estimates of Hitler's true intentions after the several grievous failures to call the shots right did not succeed. FOES, short for the clumsy title Future Operations Enemy Sections, was founded in August 1940 and staffed with the best and the brightest, who were enjoined to "think like the Germans." It was a brave effort at anticipating the enemy's moves, but it proved no better than the unfocused, ad hoc approach that preceded it. FOES was soon abandoned.[3]

Bureaucratic adjustments were not the answer, nor could anyone think quite like Hitler, a man with a troubled mind whose judgment, despite flashes of insight, was obsessive and unpredictable. The raw intelligence reaching British analysts was remarkably good. The Ultra product has been unequaled in the annals of intelligence. Other reporting sources also warned the British of Barbarossa with remarkable accuracy. Barbarossa was a badly kept secret.

Fortunately Churchill was willing to rely on Ultra for facts and his own intuition for judgments. In his war memoir he mentions having heard an intelligence report in late March 1941, describing German armor movements by rail from "Bucharest to Cracow. To me," he writes, "it illuminated the whole Eastern scene like a lightning flash. The sudden movement of so much armour needed in the Balkan sphere could only mean Hitler's intention to invade Russia in May." To keep the great secret, Churchill attributed the Ultra data vaguely to "one of our most trusted sources."

Churchill had the benefit of good sources other than Ultra, thanks to Canaris and the Resistance circle within the Abwehr, who saw to it that warnings of critical development reached the British. And there was the British/Free Czech spy Paul Thümmel, A-54, the senior Abwehr officer in Prague, who was able to report to the British through the Czech Intelligence Service that the Abwehr had hired specialists on the Crimea and Caucasus in preparation for a German invasion of the USSR planned for the end of May 1941.[4] A-54's record of reporting had been exemplary, so this news was taken seriously.*

British inability to make an early, definitive prediction of the German invasion of Russia, a matter of great relevance to them, was summed up by one Barbarossa historian, who accused British intelligence of being "slow,

---

*A former Free Czech intelligence officer questioned by the author on October 31, 1994, remembered that A-54's information was always good; only once was there reason to question his facts. The Czech analysts studying A-54's apparently good information on Barbarossa were disturbed by other information he produced at roughly the same time describing German plans to transit Spain and attack Gibraltar. The Czechs found it difficult to believe that Hitler would tempt fate by doing battle with the British over Gibraltar while he stretched his capabilities to the limit in Russia.

Apparently the Germans thought that they could invest Gibraltar if they had Spanish cooperation despite their great commitment to Barbarossa. There are those world war scholars who believe that the Gibraltar operation, Felix, was simply saber rattling in the West to camouflage Germany's plans against Russia in the East, but existing evidence does not support this. Hitler seemed to have gambled that the British were at the time in no position to fight, even to preserve Gibraltar, particularly since they were fully engaged in Libya and had no nearby land base from which to support the defense of Gibraltar. Moreover, it would have been unwise for the British to denude the British Isles themselves of the thinly stretched defense force for the sake of Gibraltar. The critical factor that caused the Germans to abandon Felix, at least for the time being, was Franco's refusal to cooperate. And while Franco had his own reasons for not wanting to become involved in the German adventure, it was Canaris's assurances that the Germans would not force the issue if he demurred because of their upcoming Barbarossa campaign and perhaps his faith in Canaris's judgment that Germany was doomed to lose the war in the longer run. After all, Canaris was a longtime friend whom he felt he could trust, and what judgment on Germany's chances was better than that of the head of German military intelligence?

vacillating and quite fragmented despite access to information even more detailed and accurate than that received by the Russians."[5] The British official history of intelligence in World War II, less stark in its condemnation, conceded that British intelligence suffered from "weakness in organization," which accounted for the fact that it was only three weeks before the German attack that it fully realized what was about to happen in the East.[6]

Churchill surmounted the inadequacies of his intelligence analysts by using his own intuition, but Stalin, whose judgment may have been warped by paranoiac preconceptions, had his own reasons for not acting more dynamically on the eve of Barbarossa. Certainly, good intelligence, which spoke for itself without aid of analytical massaging, was plentiful.

Stalin had very detailed reporting from the widely ramified Soviet espionage net in Germany known by the Gestapo as the Rote Kapelle (Red Orchestra). One of the network's most talented agents, Arvid Harnack, code-named Corsican, gave to his Soviet control officer, Korotkov, an extraordinary report on September 26, 1940. Because of the confusion in the NKVD ranks caused by Stalin's great purge, Harnack had been out of contact with Moscow for five years; this first offering upon recontact must have suggested to Moscow how much intelligence it had missed during the long interregnum.

The report, as it appeared in the NKVD's archives reads: "An officer of the Supreme Command of Germany has told Corsican that by the beginning of next year, Germany will be ready for war with the Soviet Union. . . . The objective of the campaign will be to occupy Western European Russia along the Leningrad-Black Sea line and the creation of a German vassal state."[7]

One of the more puzzling phenomena of the intelligence war in Europe was the Lucy ring, within the Rote Drei spy ring operating out of Switzerland into Germany as an extension of the Rote Kapelle apparatus. Unsubstantiated postwar allegations claimed that the British had a penetration within the Rote Drei—unknown to the Soviets—through whom they could insinuate Ultra reporting, cleverly masked as to source but meant for Soviet consumption. Why would they want to do this? Because Stalin distrusted British intelligence openly passed to him through Moscow liaison, which he believed was designed simply to sow discord between the Germans and Soviets. The Lucy operation, therefore, was one way to disguise the British origin of Ultra, making it credible and thus helping Stalin despite himself, while helping themselves as well since Britain's own survival depended on German engagement with the Soviets. While an ingenious idea, it was not true. But aside from how and where

Lucy (Rudolf Roessler) later acquired his amazingly accurate information on German military plans and actions, it was not available before Barbarossa took place so could not give credible warning to Russia of the German invasion. (Alexander Foote, Lucy's radio operator, who claimed to have been a British-controlled penetration of the Rote Drei, stated in his exposé *Handbook for Spies*,[8] that "for three vital years of the war" he "sent back much of the information that enabled the Russians to make their successful stand before Moscow." This boast, however, has never been confirmed by the British.

Stalin had the benefit of American information. Sumner Welles, U.S. undersecretary of state, gave Soviet Ambassador Konstantin Oumansky in Washington an emphatic warning in March 1941. This was based on a U.S. intragovernmental "alert memo" that stated: "The Government of the United States . . . has come into possession of information which it regards as authentic, clearly indicating that it is the intention of Germany to attack the Soviet Union."[9]

Considering the disarray of U.S. intelligence at this stage of the war, the State Department's advance notice of Operation Barbarossa, first-rate intelligence by any standard, was a remarkable achievement. The story behind the alert memo and its passage to Oumansky did not involve William Donovan, nor did it involve U.S. military intelligence. It was the handiwork of an inconspicuous U.S. commercial attaché serving in Berlin named Sam Woods. A clever ferret, Woods had good friends within Nazi circles. His prime source for Barbarossa seemed to have been one Erwin Respondek, who, before the Nazi period, had been a well-connected liberal Catholic of the Center party. As he watched with horror the burgeoning Nazi movement, Respondek established contact with German military Resistance figures who were plotting against Hitler on the eve of the Czech crisis. Through a Jesuit Resistance friend, Hermann Muckermann, Respondek was able to tap no less an authority than Chief of Staff General Franz Halder for critical details concerning Barbarossa. In August 1940 Respondek told his friend Woods of "conferences taking place at Hitler's headquarters concerning preparations for war against Russia." This was a reference to Hitler's secret meeting on July 31, 1940, with his military leaders concerning the forthcoming Russian campaign.

At a time when Hitler's attention seemed to be directed toward Great Britain, this intelligence was difficult to believe although Woods's ultimate source, General Halder, explained that the continuing "air raids against England served as a blind for Hitler's plan for a sudden, devastating attack on Russia."[10] Another deception plan called for westward troop movements.* By November 1940 Halder, in touch with the Black Orchestra Resistance, had indirectly provided Respondek with a windfall of valuable details, including the basic strategy of the attack.[11]

Sam Woods's intelligence was met with skepticism by the U.S. War Department because the army attaché in Berlin, Colonel B. R. Peyton, had dismissed it as just one of the "wild rumors" circulating in Berlin, devoid of "real military information."[12] Another naysayer, U.S. Chief of Mission Berlin Leland Morris, pompously commented that it was not the proper business of U.S. diplomats to "run around Berlin digging up secrets." Assistant Secretary of State Breckinridge Long, more imaginative, took a lively interest in Woods's reports and saw in them an opportunity to "incite Russia against Germany."[13]

President Roosevelt and Secretary of State Hull agreed that the gist of the report should be given to the Russians; Sumner Welles accordingly notified Ambassador Oumansky.[14] Simultaneously a State Department message with perhaps a few more details was sent to Molotov in Moscow, unequivocally informing the Soviet foreign minister of Germany's intention "to attack the Soviet Union in the not distant future."[15] Stalin's reaction to the American warnings was expressed in a single word scribbled on the telegram: "Provocation!" He did not want to be "incited" against Germany. While the usefulness of the report to drive a wedge between Hitler and Stalin was not overlooked, Washington's principal motive was to help Stalin, faced with certain war, defeat the Germans, thereby saving Britain, France, and the rest of Europe from Nazi dominance as well as serving as a force for control over Japanese ambitions in the Far East.

The visit of Japanese Foreign Minister Yosuke Matsuoka to Berlin in late March 1941 caused a flurry of enciphered Japanese messages between Ambassador Hiroshi Oshima in Berlin and Tokyo. The first of a series of meetings between Matsuoka and Hitler was reported by Oshima on March 17. When American cryptanalysts, engaged in the top secret code-breaking operation Magic against the Japanese Purple ciphers, deciphered Matsuoka's messages, probably on April 1, a startling nugget of intelligence leaped out from the text: a comment by Hitler hinting that a German-Soviet war might break out.[16] There followed several messages on this theme sent by Oshima from Berlin, including a mid-April message broken by the United States discussing Hitler's specific plan of attack. The Amer-

---

*In a conversation with Göring in early April 1941, with regard to the upcoming German invasion of the USSR, Goebbels stated: "It is being very carefully camouflaged and only a handful of people know about it. It will begin with extensive troop movements to the West. We shall divert suspicion to all sorts of places. . . . A mock invasion of England is in preparation."

ican cryptanalyst noted in his log, "I was too excited for sleep that night," then added significantly, "We and the British informed the Russians about [the invasion plan] but they were too dumbfounded to believe it at first."[17]

As seen above, Rudolf Hess's strange flight to Scotland on May 10, 1941, reinforced Stalin's conviction that the British and Germans were about to gang up on him. According to the Russian historian A. M. Nekrich, writing just before Hitler's invasion of Russia, Stalin was certain that Britain not only was aware of the impending invasion but "was inciting Germany to attack the USSR; that secret negotiations were taking place in London with Rudolf Hess." Given this distorted assumption, it is little wonder that the Soviet dictator considered Churchill's warnings "a British provocation."[18] Soviet spy Kim Philby in one of his reports to Moscow[19] claimed that Hess "had brought peace offers."[20] Philby also quoted Hess as saying, "Germany has certain demands of Russia, which would have to be satisfied either by direct negotiations or *as a result of war* [author's italics]."[21]

The NKVD scrambled to confirm Philby's reports[22] and produced information that drew the disturbing conclusion that Hess's flight had not been the act of a deranged man, as some in Britain were claiming but was symptomatic of "a Nazi conspiracy to reach a peace agreement with Britain before attacking the Soviet Union."[23]

In a letter to G. E. Millard of the British Foreign Office dated April 7, 1945, written as the war was ending, Churchill stated: "The Russians are very suspicious of the Hess episode," and Stalin "steadfastly maintains that Hess had been invited over by our Secret Service."[24] Philby's reporting to his Soviet masters disclosed that before Hess's flight a letter from him to the Duke of Hamilton was "intercepted by the British counter-intelligence service."[25] Assuming Stalin heard this from such high-level NKVD penetrations of the British, we should not find it surprising that he leaped to the conclusion that the Hess flight was part of a British-German conspiracy rather than simply a British Secret Service provocation sting.

Certain U.S. files, declassified in 1989, are revealing. In a letter of November 5, 1941, from American officer Raymond E. Lee to Brigadier General Sherman Miles, assistant chief of staff, G2, Lee states that Hess "gave warning of Hitler's intentions to invade Russia." Lee's source had apparently been British Major Desmond Morton, Prime Minister Churchill's aide with whom he talked over lunch on October 26. Lee also quoted U.S. Ambassador John G. Winant—Ambassador Kennedy's replacement—as saying, "There was only one thing I did not know and that is that Hess came over here [Britain] to tell the British that the Germans were about to attack the Russians."[26] (This may have been a misunderstanding on Winant's part or a loose interpretation of what he heard, since it is most unlikely that the prime purpose of Hess's flight was to tell the British about Barbarossa even though he may have mentioned it as relevant to his pitch for Anglo-German détente, in which Britain would acquiesce in Germany's plan to invade the USSR.)

According to KGB archives, Morton's information was acquired through an informant in London, who of course could have been Kim Philby. And Philby could have overinterpreted Hess's comments.

Stalin would never be satisfied with the official explanations given him by the British on the Hess flight and insisted on linking it with imagined German-British peace talks. NKVD records, recently opened by the KGB, also made reference to a wartime Soviet agent within the Deuxième Bureau of the Vichy French General Staff who reported that the British Secret Intelligence Service had a part in encouraging Hess to make his famous flight to Scotland.[27] Such reports, however inaccurate about British objectives, were probably persuasive to Stalin and could have caused him to jump to the false conclusion that Hess had been specifically "invited" for the purpose of negotiating a peace.

Lending credence to reports that the British Secret Intelligence Service had invented an imaginary group of Scottish and English conspirators seeking peace with Germany and, in the name of the Duke of Hamilton, had tried to lure Hess's friend Albrecht Haushofer, or some other emissary, to Portugal or Spain were reports from British Ambassador Sir Samuel Hoare in Madrid. Hoare in his war memoir recalls: "Throughout the summer individual Germans made several attempts to enter into relations with the British Embassy." He adds, "Although their credentials seemed good, my staff and I were extremely cautious in our response. . . ."[28] Cautious perhaps, but was there response? Prince Max Eugen zu Hohenlohe-Langenburg, scion of one of Germany's princely houses and someone who professed to have sympathies with the British, had made peace overtures to them through Switzerland during the latter part of October 1939 and was remembered by the Chamberlain government for his interesting suggestion that it would be more useful to negotiate for peace with Göring than with Hitler,[29] implying that Göring had his own plans, which did not include Hitler. Again in mid-November gadfly Hohenlohe appeared, this time in conversation with British Group Captain Malcolm Christie of Vansittart's Foreign Office intelligence unit, whom he tried to interest in a general disarmament scheme.[30] In June 1940 Hohenlohe told Ribbentrop that Richard Austin ("Rab") Butler, Undersecretary at the British Foreign Office, was trying to meet him through International Red Cross Director Carl Burckhardt. The peripatetic, self-appointed — and not altogether unreliable — peace envoy reported that David Kelly, British minister to Switzerland, had tried to convince him that Halifax, Butler, and Vansittart were representative of a group of British leaders who disagreed with Churchill's hard line against Germany. Contrary to orders from Churchill, Kelly had allegedly gone so far as to tell Hohenlohe that peace with Nazi Germany was still a possibility.[31]

Now, on March 5, 1941, Hohenlohe, one of those Germans who Sir Samuel Hoare remembered had "made attempts to enter into relations with the British Embassy," surfaced in Madrid. Hohenlohe made contact and was featured in a memorandum Hoare sent to Cadogan in the Foreign Office on March 6. Somewhat defensively Hoare wrote Cadogan that he hoped the Foreign Office would "approve his decision" to meet with Hohenlohe, knowing full well that such meetings were in contravention of Churchill's insistence on "absolute silence" and would not be approved.[32]

Hoare's memorandum to Cadogan described Hohenlohe as nervous. The thrust of Hohenlohe's message to Hoare seemed arrogant in tone: "Germany could never be defeated; the only result of continuing the war would be the end of European civilization and the 'Communization' or 'Americanization' of the world, whereas, if peace were made now, Hitler would be very reasonable; he had never wanted to fight Great Britain."[33] Hoare reported dutifully that he had not risen to the bait; he claimed to have said to Hohenlohe flatly that he saw no basis for peace negotiations.

The Italian ambassador in Madrid learned of the meeting, presumably from Hohenlohe, and reported to Rome quite another verson of what transpired. He claimed Hoare had confided in Hohenlohe that Churchill could "no longer rely on a majority" in Parliament, and "sooner or later he [Hoare] would be called back to London to take over the Government with the precise task of concluding a compromise peace."[34]

In learning of such intrigues, Soviet intelligence was undoubtedly served by its British penetrations, not least of whom were Philby and top secret cryptologist John Cairncross.* Backdoor overtures such as the one made by Hohenlohe, even if not taken seriously by the British, must have

---

*John Cairncross was recruited by Guy Burgess at Cambridge University in the 1930s for service as a Soviet spy and turned over to Soviet intelligence case officer James Klugman. He was briefly employed by the British Treasury before joining the most secret Government Communications Headquarters (GCHQ), or cryptological service, at Bletchley Park, in 1940. There he had access to closely held Enigma secrets and Ultra production that proved invaluable to his Soviet masters. In 1944 Cairncross joined Section V, the counterespionage department, of MI-6, giving him access to many other secrets of intense interest to the Soviets. Cairncross was not conclusively exposed as a Soviet spy until March 1964, when under MI-5 interrogation he admitted his long career as a Soviet spy—Nigel West, *MI-6, British Secret Intelligence Service Operations, 1909–1945* (New York: Random House, 1983), p. 242.

excited suspicions in Stalin's mind. The Soviet dictator's fear of an Anglo-German peace deal at his expense, with or without Hitler's involvement, was to become an obsession that preyed on him throughout the war.

Stalin, through fear of a German invasion, was ready to make concessions to Hitler, even if it meant promising to provide more critical supplies for Hitler's armies or even ceding territory to Germany. The Red Army was simply not ready for war. The Finnish War had proved this conclusively; Stalin needed to stall for time. In the meantime he would be careful not to provoke Hitler.

Stalin's suspicions of Churchill made it impossible for him to turn to the British for help immediately. Aside from the Hess affair, he was still smarting from a misbegotten French-British plan in early 1940 involving Finland that had died aborning, but not before Stalin's ire had been aroused. The plan called for the Western Allies to send a small expeditionary force to help the Finns in their spirited defense against the faltering Soviet invasion—even if it meant war with Soviet Russia as well as Germany.[35] This did not take place because of Finland's capitulation to the Soviets.

The Germans were aware of this development as well as another curious action by the Allies. Franz von Papen, German ambassador in Turkey, reported to Chief of Staff Halder that the French were eager "to relieve Finland by an attack on Baku in the Caucasus."[36] In fact British reconnaissance aircraft did overfly Soviet oil installations at Baku and Batum and drew antiaircraft fire. It is difficult to understand such a provocative act by the Chamberlain government. One wonders how the British chargé d'affaires in Moscow could in January 1940 have written the foreign secretary in the following foolish vein: "The effective and continuous bombardment of Baku should . . . present no great difficulty to us and it alone should be sufficient to bring Russia to its knees within a very short time."[37]

Robert Bruce Lockhart, remembered for his intrigues against the Bolsheviks in Moscow after the 1918 Revolution and head of the Political Warfare Executive in World War II, made brief reference to this little-known episode in his war diary of May 25, 1943, on the occasion of the anniversary of the Anglo-Russian Treaty. He wrote that within the Foreign Office proposals had been discussed calling for a declaration of war against the USSR in relief of the Finns during the Finnish-Russian War. Lockhart mentioned a specific proposal to bomb by air the Russian Caucasus oil installations in Baku. He identified a few Foreign Office men who had favored such an absurd scheme.[38]

Part of Soviet Russia's problem was that much of its army was in the Far East. It was critical for the Soviets to monitor closely German-Japanese relations. While the Russian-Japanese neutrality treaty had eased tensions between the two countries, Moscow still feared that Japan might turn on its traditional Russian enemy in the event of a German attack on the USSR from the West.

One of the Soviet Union's most valuable secret agents in World War II was Richard Sorge operating in Tokyo. In recent times his memory has been resurrected as a Russian folk hero by a commemorative stamp bearing his dour face. Sorge, a German, was born in Russia but schooled in Berlin. He became a Soviet agent in 1925. Having arranged his own cover as a correspondent for the *Frankfurter Zeitung,* he established an espionage organization in Tokyo. Working in tandem with a brilliant Japanese journalist named Hotsumi Ozaki, he set about establishing a ring of spies whose tentacles reached deep into the Japanese government. Sorge also ingratiated himself with the German Embassy in Tokyo and in the mid-1930s became a trusted friend of German Military Attaché Eugen Ott, made ambassador in 1938, from whom he received valuable intelligence on German-Japanese developments.

In April 1941 Ott told him in confidence that Germany had completed preparations to attack the USSR. This was electrifying information, which was confirmed by a German military visitor to Tokyo in May who explained in more detail Hitler's plans. At about the same time Sorge learned the invasion date from another visiting German officer who had been introduced to him by Ott. June 20 was the date he gave although it actually took place two days later on June 22. It was most unlikely that Stalin would completely ignore Sorge's crucial reports.[39]

The stream of intelligence pointing to the likelihood of war between Germany and the Soviet Union was becoming a torrent. Hitler's ambassador to the USSR Count Friedrich Werner von der Schulenburg even joined the chorus. Ambassador in Moscow since 1934 and one of the chief negotiators of the Ribbentrop-Molotov pact in August 1939, Schulenburg was on good terms with Stalin. Disturbed by hearing of Hitler's intention to violate the pact by invading the Soviet Union and by its consequences, the German ambassador at great risk to his life now took an action that, had it been known by Hitler, would have been considered treasonous. Schulenburg and his counselor of embassy for commercial affairs, Gustav Hilger, divulged to Stalin the date of Hitler's planned invasion of Soviet Russia. Because of their hate for Hitler, the two men would be drawn to the German Resistance and "deliberately incur the greatest danger for the purpose of making a last effort to save the peace."[40] On May 5 Schulenburg warned the Soviet ambassador in Berlin, Vladimir Dekanozov, of mortal dangers facing the Soviet Union and advised him to take "as fact" the invasion rumors going around. The Soviet diplomat, perhaps because he was confused by these highly irregular confidences, was strangely unresponsive. Stalin did, however, finally learn of Schulenburg's indiscretions from Dekanozov; his ungrateful, even contemptuous reaction was summed up in the remark: "Now faked information has reached the level of Ambassadors."[41]

ABWEHR CHIEF CANARIS WAS OPENLY CRITICAL OF THE RISKS HITLER WAS taking in invading the Soviet Union. In performance of his duty as chief of military intelligence, he repeatedly warned such Nazi leaders as Schellenberg of the SD and Chief of Staff Keitel that it was not possible to defeat the Soviet Union. So persistent was Canaris that Keitel, tired of hearing this litany of gloom, reprimanded him. Canaris had to satisfy himself by indirectly planting on the German High Command doctored intelligence exaggerating the strength of the Red Army just as he had in the case of Britain while Operation Sea Lion was still under consideration.

Canaris made efforts to warn the British of the forecoming invasion of Russia. According to Ian Colvin of the British Foreign Office, the admiral sent word to them through his agent, Müller, at the Vatican, the same person who conducted secret liaison with the Pope in behalf of the Resistance and whom he had used on at least one occasion to make discreet contact with Franco. Canaris also arranged for his agent Nicholas von Halem, a German "businessman" who frequently traveled to Russia, to let an officially connected British friend know in Moscow.[42] And, in the late autumn of 1940 Canaris visited Switzerland to give the important news of Barbarossa to Halina Szymanska, the Polish lady whom he had settled in Switzerland and was using as a link with the British Secret Service. He could rely on her to pass his comments on to the local British SIS representative.[43] Unfortunately the British were then inclined to treat Canaris's information as "plants" calculated to demoralize them.[44]

GÖRING AT FIRST APPEARED TO BE OPPOSED TO BARBAROSSA AND AMONG close friends expressed dismay at the prospect of a two-front war. But unable to talk Hitler out of his ill-omened project, Göring dutifully joined the chorus endorsing Hitler's bold plan. He seemed particularly pleased that Germany planned to seize Romanian oilfields since his Luftwaffe badly needed fuel. Yet where did Göring really stand? Was he playing both sides? On March 25, 1941, in an act that must surely qualify as being a purposeful breach of security amounting to disloyalty, he confided in his Swedish friend Birger Dahlerus the scope and date of Barbarossa. This intelligence was, of course, intended for the British, and indeed, in early June Dahlerus informed the British envoy in Stockholm that according to Göring, Germany would attack Russia sometime around June 15.

Dahlerus similarly tipped off the American Legation in Stockholm.[45] At about the same time the exiled Polish foreign minister in London told Anthony Drexel Biddle, Jr., former American ambassador to Poland, that Göring had confided in a "close Swedish friend" that "he might expect Germany to launch an attack against Russia on Sunday, June 22. Dahlerus had been a busy man whispering the word of this secret of secrets.[46]

CANARIS INVOLVED HIMSELF IN THE "EASTERN QUESTION" IN QUITE ANother way in his efforts to forestall Nazi aggression in the East. He saw the Balkans as a weak spot in Hitler's master strategy, so he tried his hand at stirring that cauldron of discontent. The Balkans were strategically important as a buffer between Russia and Germany. They would be particularly important in a German invasion of Soviet Russia. Stalin too understood the importance of the Balkans, which were high on the Soviet agenda during Molotov's talks with Hitler in November 1940. Hitler had then made all the right remarks to Molotov, but on December 18, a few weeks after the Soviet foreign minister's departure, he cynically gave the order for Operation Barbarossa to proceed.

King Boris of Bulgaria was content to remain neutral and quailed at the thought of having his quiet, intellectual life disturbed by the dogs of war. Hitler had summoned him for discussions, however, and he knew that a crisis was approaching. The Nazi dictator's intentions were made clear when he sent troops into neighboring Romania.

George Earle, the flamboyant U.S. minister to Bulgaria, tried hard to convince Boris to keep his country neutral. Earle was, in fact, more than the usual diplomat. Having been the Democratic governor of Pennsylvania and a onetime aspirant for the presidency who had withdrawn his bid in favor of Franklin Roosevelt, he had been given first an Austrian, then the Bulgarian diplomatic post as consolation prizes. He served as President Roosevelt's personal eyes and ears in the Balkans, bypassing the usual State Department machinery in his reporting. Boris liked the gregarious Earle and for his own reasons would probably have stayed out of the war but for his position in Hitler's path of aggression and his fear of Soviet Russia.

Earle's war with the Germans predated the U.S. state of war with Germany. One memorable evening at the Astoria Hotel in Sofia a nightclub brawl erupted between tipsy German officers out on the town and anti-German Bulgarians. Earle became involved in what turned into a bottle-throwing contest requiring police intervention. President Roosevelt later referred to Earle as a veteran of World War II's "Battle of the Bottles." This was diplomacy with a difference!

Another figure who counseled King Boris to remain neutral was his good friend Admiral Canaris. The admiral, however, had to be circumspect in pushing this line too far. He knew that Hitler's planning for an eastern invasion required Bulgaria as a staging point for operations to secure the Balkans.

On March 2, 1941, Bulgaria, under German pressure, signed the Three Powers Pact, and Boris watched helplessly as German troops prepared to enter his country. Romania, which signed the treaty as well, had been under German occupation since mid-October 1940. This left Yugoslavia as a conspicuous holdout, but finding itself surrounded by German and Italian troops, it signed the pact with Germany on March 25.

The pro-German party of Croatian partisans, the Ustashi, under the leadership of Dr. Ante Pavelič, had long agitated for Croatian independence with secret German connivance and now constituted a German fifth column. The predominantly Serbian officer corps and most of the Serbian population, however, were opposed to close ties with Germany. Before the Yugoslavian delegation reached Belgrade after signing the Three Powers Pact, the government under Regent Prince Paul was overthrown by a military coup d'état hostile to Germany. Hitler erupted in rage. The Yugoslavian upheaval was a nasty fly in the Barbarossa ointment, a fly that had to be swatted even if it meant postponing Germany's invasion of Russia, scheduled for May 15.

Admiral Canaris, who secretly applauded Yugoslavia's national revolution, was aware of Hitler's intention to invade the hapless country. He sent a secret warning to the new Yugoslav government, which prompted it on April 3 to declare Belgrade an open city to avoid its being destroyed. Canaris had done his best, but his warning was of no use. In the German attack on April 8 an estimated seventeen thousand people were killed by aircraft or artillery bombardment.

Canaris was one of the first Germans to reach the stricken city. He was appalled by what he saw: rotten corpses protruding from the ruble; zoo animals wounded by the explosions, hobbling about pathetically in search of food; and a populace stunned and maimed by the disaster. This experience caused Canaris to have a virtual nervous breakdown. Profoundly upset by the carnage, he flew off to Spain to find peace in what he considered his spiritual home. Had they known, the dead of Belgrade might have found some comfort in revenge when it later became apparent that the Yugoslavian diversion had fatally set back Hitler's timetable for the Russian invasion. The month lost proved critical, perhaps making the difference between victory and defeat when the onset of Russia's early winter denied Moscow to the German panzer armies mired in ice and mud within sight of the Kremlin's spires.

One witness to Stalin's days of trial was Nikita Khrushchev, even then an important functionary on the edges of power. Khrushchev's testimony, as it appeared in the so-called Glasnost Tapes dictated toward the end of his life, is revealing.[47] Khrushchev claimed that Stalin knew very well that Hitler had designs on Soviet territory and understood the basic elements of Hitler's plan to invade the USSR, although he did not known when. As Khrushchev put it, "Sparrows chirped about it at every crossroad."

Hitler's signature on the treaty of "friendship and nonaggression" with Russia was, in Khrushchev's opinion, a political ruse. By keeping Stalin out of play, the Führer hoped to convince Britain to accept Germany's seizures of Poland and France—that is, to abandon the war on terms not unlike those France had been forced to accept. According to Khrushchev, Stalin believed that Hitler wanted to come to terms with the West so that he could then redraw the map and take back territories Germany had lost in World War I. For his part, Stalin signed the pact to keep Hitler focused on the West and thus buy time badly needed by the Russians.

Khrushchev believed that the military purges of the later 1930s deprived the Red Army of the trained officer cadres it desperately needed to face Hitler in 1941, but the time bought by the nonaggression pact had not been put to good use. Having lost confidence in the Red Army by its poor showing in the Finnish campaign, Stalin did not believe he could cope with a German invasion, so he chose instead to appease Hitler, assiduously avoiding any actions that might provoke the Führer to attack sooner rather than later.

Khrushchev recalled that he and General Semyon K. Timoshenko urged Stalin to mobilize several hundred thousand collective farmers to dig antitank trenches and otherwise fortify the frontier, but Stalin, fearful of provoking Hitler, refused to take such precautions. He stepped up shipments of grain and oil needed badly by German armies to appease his treacherous neighbor.[48] Yet territorial buffer areas would be important in defending the USSR from German aggression, so Stalin, on June 26, 1940 suddenly demanded of Romania the return of Bessarabia and the surrender of Bukovina. The next day the USSR invaded Romania. Germany, Russia's ally, had not been consulted, and Romania had been given only twenty-four hours to comply. Russian occupation of Romanian territory close to the rich oil fields at Ploesti was considered a provocative act by Hitler, who in warning sent two armored divisions and ten infantry divisions into neighboring Poland (and on October 7 seized Romanian oil fields).[49] General Halder's diary of June 25 records his attitude and that of the High Command: "The issue of the Bukovina raided by Russia is new and *goes beyond our agreements with the Russians* [author's italics]. In any event, it is imperative for our interests that there should be no war on the Balkans."[50]

Stalin had earlier annoyed Hitler when, in October 1939, he had pressured the Baltic states into permitting Soviet troops to be stationed on their land. Then, two months later, Soviet Russia had invaded Finland. While the secret protocol of the German-Soviet nonaggression pact had divided Eastern Europe into spheres of influence, Stalin, taking advantage of sometimes ambiguous language, had moved forward with what Hitler thought was unseemly haste. On the same day that France fell, Stalin insisted on occupying Lithuania and soon afterward moved into Latvia and Estonia as well in what proved to be an act of annexation. Hitler now had abundant evidence to conclude that Stalin had predatory instincts that would clash with his own plans of aggression. Hitler realized that if he did not strike first, Stalin would seize the initiative as soon as he felt strong enough to do so.*

Stalin was no less conscious of Hitler's ambitions in Eastern Europe. As early as 1939, on the eve of Germany's invasion of Czechoslovakia, Canaris's Abwehr had been busy arousing pan-Ukrainian sentiment, using the Carpatho-Ukraine, Ruthenia, as a laboratory to create a "jewel in the Ukrainian crown"[51] and inciting a wave of Ukrainian nationalism that slopped over into Poland. The potential implications of this for the Soviet Ukraine must have been painfully obvious to Stalin, whose grip on that state was at best precarious.

While concerned by Hitler's actions and perceived intentions, Stalin now believed that because of Russia's military unpreparedness, he had no alternative to appeasement. Anxious not to appear in violation of the secret agreement establishing Soviet and German spheres of influence under the nonaggression pact,[52] and desperate to keep Hitler from attacking the

---

*Another act that the Germans could construe as being provocative was an agreement reached at Istanbul in January 1941, calling for Czech President Beneš to establish anti-German liaison between the Czech Intelligence Service and the Soviet GRU (military intelligence). By April 1941 Czech intelligence officer Heliodore Pika had reached Moscow to begin the relationship.

A Czech legion of some fifteen hundred fighting men sent to Poland struck out for Romania when Germany invaded Poland. The unit was intercepted by the Soviets, however, and barracked in a monastery near Susdal, where, in collaboration with the Russians, it began training in guerrilla warfare. A select group was given parachute training, although later Soviet efforts to drop the guerrillas in Czechoslovakia to harass the Germans misfired when they all landed far off target. The operations of the Czechs (called the Polish Legion because of their original destination) were supposed to be secret, but there is little doubt that the Germans had learned something about them from their spies and collaborators in Prague—a former Free Czech intelligence officer who had served in the Moscow Czech intelligence liaison mission and was witness to the parachute training program that had been so badly managed by the Soviets.

Soviet Union, he even discussed with Foreign Minister Molotov and Secret Police Chief Beria on October 7, 1940, the possibility of letting the
Germans determine the fate of the Baltics, Moldavia, Byelorussia, and the
western Ukraine.[53]

A long-delayed Soviet disclosure shedding light on Stalin's reactions
to Barbarossa's buildup appeared in an article written by the late Marshal Georgi Zhukov in the September 1987 issue of the Soviet publication *Military History Journal.* Zhukov remembered a communication
that Stalin had sent Hitler in 1941 in which the Soviet dictator complained about heavy German troop concentrations in Poland and concluded that this must be a harbinger of invasion. Hitler replied with a
very personal letter to mollify Stalin. He explained that he had moved
troops to Poland to avoid British air strikes that were taking a heavy toll
because they had been vulnerable to RAF attacks. Zhukov concluded
that Stalin had been satisfied with Hitler's dissembling response as he
clutched at straws of hope.

General Zhukov believed that Stalin had been isolated from ominous
news of German intentions by subordinates who feared to alarm him. One
such yes-man was General F. I. Golikov, chief of the GRU (Soviet military
intelligence), who typically informed Stalin that he had received intelligence that Germany had massed one hundred divisions in Poland but
diplomatically dismissed the report as having been planted by British
agents in an effort to provoke the Soviet Union to rash actions. To avoid of-
fending Stalin, Golikov regularly fed Stalin such watered-down pabulum.

On the eve of the invasion, as military dispatches poured in describing
German border violations and provocative Luftwaffe air reconnaissance,
Stalin began to acknowledge the danger facing the Soviet Union. But even
then Stalin could hope; Directive No. 1, sent to all forces, warned his
troops to "avoid provocative actions of any kind which might produce
major complications."[54] Not until noon on June 23, the day after the actual
invasion, did Moscow announce a state of war.

Russian intelligence estimates may have been toned down to avoid en-
raging Stalin, but the Soviet dictator knew how critical the situation was
despite his resort to various excuses for apparent lack of action. He had argued in closed sessions with his advisers that Germany's massed armor
would not move before it had the traditional artillery support; Germany
would not be foolish enough to conduct a two-front war; Germany must
first dispose of the British, by either force or peace agreement; and the
most used argument of all: Hitler would not attack without first issuing an
ultimatum as he had before he moved against Poland, and this would provide an opportunity to bargain further with him.

One expert on Russia wrote that Stalin's apparent indifference to the flood of reports reaching him during the early spring of 1941 "testified less to his gullibility than it did to his poor sense of timing."[55] Stalin knew that Germany would attack, but he did not think it would occur until the autumn; only then, he believed, would Britain have been knocked out of the war and would Hitler feel confident that he could take on the Soviet Union.

Things looked more hopeful when crucial intelligence supplied by Sorge suddenly made it clear that Japan had decided to move on Southeast Asia, not against the Soviet Union, despite its alliance with Hitler.* Stalin could then transfer a large number of Far Eastern troops to the German front.† But for the moment he could only hope to appease Hitler, reach some further accommodation in order to gain as much time as possible. To make aggressive preparations for war would have done little good

---

*One theory of the Sorge operation was that it provided a cover attribution by which Soviet cryptanalytical successes could be protected. After Sorge's arrest by the Japanese on October 18, 1941, a Japanese message, telegram 27 in November 1941 from Tokyo to the Japanese ambassador in Berlin, which may have been deciphered by Moscow as well as by the United States, stated: "Explain to Hitler that the main Japanese efforts will be concentrated in the South and that we propose to refrain from deliberate operations in the North [USSR]"—ed. Keith Neilson and B. J. C. McKerchor (Westport, Conn.: Praeger, 1992), p. 7. Christopher Andrew, "The Nature of Military History," *Go Spy the Land*.
†Confirming an earlier message that he had sent on September 14, 1941, Sorge sent his definitive message on Japanese intentions to strike southward instead of attacking the USSR on October 4, although it had been written and dated on September 26. The welcome message stated: "The Soviet Far East may be guaranteed against Japanese attack"—Gordon Prange, *Target Tokyo* (New York: McGraw-Hill, 1984), p. 406.
Other reports from Sorge elaborated: "German High Command began moves [of troops] from the Far East as early as May 26, 1941—almost a full month before Russo-German War broke out"—Ibid., p. 407.
Diplomats accredited to the Soviets were evacuated from Moscow with the Soviet government as the Germans approached in October. En route to the new temporary capital farther east, some Soviet Far Eastern units, notably Kazakh cavalry, were observed moving west toward the front—a Czech officer, who was in the diplomatic convoy moving eastward.
In May an old friend of Sorge's, the German officer Lieutenant Colonel Friedrich von Schol, en route to his post as military attaché in Bangkok, passed through Tokyo, where he gave secret instructions to German Military Attaché Ott regarding a German-Russian war predicted to occur on June 20 or possibly a few days later. Schol reported to Ott that a German force of 170 to 180 divisions, all mechanized, were poised to strike toward Moscow, Leningrad, and later the Ukraine. War would begin without a declaration by Germany or issuance of an ultimatum of any kind. Sorge's radio operator, Max Clausen, sent a message containing Schol's information on May 21—Prange, *Target Tokyo*, pp. 339, 340.

anyway and, he feared, might simply have provoked Hitler to strike sooner than he had planned to. Certainly any provocative move by the Red Army would preclude reaching a deal, perhaps one calling for more raw materials to be shipped from the USSR to Germany—or even further territorial concessions.

Hitler, however, did not want a deal; he wanted to conquer the Soviet Union. He was convinced the German Army could do it quickly, and he was almost right. What he failed to estimate correctly was the power of sheer human mass deployed in the vast, unbounded spaces of Russia and Stalin's willingness to sacrifice human beings on the battlefield regardless of the cost. He also neglected the lesson taught Napoleon that Russian winters are formidable barriers for an advancing army. Hitler was frustrated by Great Britain, annoyed by a people who "did not see they were beaten." While he would have preferred to extort a peace agreement from the British, as he had done from the French, he knew they would not attack Germany on its western front with France so long as the Wehrmacht occupied the critical areas of France and controlled all of it.

Winston Churchill later commented that June 22, 1941, the day Hitler invaded Soviet Russia, was one of the two critical dates of World War II. On that day, he said, "I knew we would not lose the war."

The other critical day Churchill had in mind was December 7, 1941, when Japanese carrier aircraft bombed Pearl Harbor in Hawaii and brought the United States into the War. Britain would no longer fight the Axis alone. With the United States, the Soviet Union, and Japan now involved, the struggle had become a world war of immense proportions.

TWENTY

Tricycle and
Pearl Harbor

MI-6 CHIEF MENZIES AND ABWEHR CHIEF CANARIS HAD FOUND THEIR PRO-
fessional lives as spymasters intertwined on many occasions since World
War I. One of the more interesting duels of the game concerned the quick-
witted Yugoslav double agent Dusko Popov, code name Tricycle. He was
one of Canaris's best spies, who, unknown to the Abwehr, was actually
controlled by MI-5, British Security Intelligence Twenty Committee,
which ran the Double-Cross (XX) system—i.e., double agents who reported to Germany what their British masters wanted them to report.
Popov's own account of his convoluted espionage career, *Spy Counter-
Spy*,[1] tells how he allowed himself to be recruited by the Abwehr for espionage duties in London but, having second thoughts, secretly revealed his
new role to the British MI-6 representative in Belgrade, to whom he offered his services. After duly checking on Popov, British Secret Intelligence chief Stewart Menzies personally recruited him as a double agent
during a weekend house party outside London. At least that is Popov's
story. Menzies allegedly gave Popov instructions to report on the Abwehr,
particularly on its senior officers close to Canaris. Menzies suggested that
he knew that Canaris was opposed to Hitler and harbored like-minded
officers in the Abwehr, such as Oster and Dohnanyi. For this reason
Menzies explained that he was interested in finding out all that he could
about them.

Popov had many professional adventures—and even more personal adventures involving beautiful women. But the story becomes more interest-

ing to Americans when, in August 1941, the Abwehr assigned him to the United States to rebuild its intelligence network, crippled when its leader was run over and killed in a New York City taxicab accident.

Recognizing its agreement not to operate in the United States, the British turned Popov over to the FBI. Unfortunately FBI chief J. Edgar Hoover and Popov were cut from quite different cloth. The *bon viveur* Popov offended the prim Hoover, who was particularly shocked to learn that upon arrival in New York, Popov took up with an old flame, a famous film star—among others. Hoover could not abide an agent who regularly "carried on," particularly if he broke the Mann Act by transporting a woman across state lines "for immoral purposes." He was even more outraged to hear gossip (quite apocryphal) that the British had assigned Popov the code name Tricycle because of his penchant for bedding down two women at the same time. If an FBI man ever did such a thing, he would at the least be transferred to Butte, Montana—to quote one FBI man's metaphor for being punished by the service.

More serious, Popov and his British masters were dismayed to learn later that Hoover had ignored the most significant intelligence yet produced by Popov: a detailed requirement list of various targets that he was told to cover, including targets in Hawaii given the Germans by the Japanese. This suggested that the U.S. Pacific fleet anchored at Pearl Harbor was a target for aerial bombing.[2] Hoover showed little interest, perhaps because he considered it a routine catchall list and because he did not trust the double agent. He refused to permit Popov to proceed to Hawaii in fulfillment of his mission, as his German case officer had instructed him. That of course put Popov into the difficult position of trying to explain to his German controller why he would not carry out his mission as ordered.

The British Double-Cross chairman, Sir John Masterman, charged with the supersecret exploitation of intercepted German messages for counterespionage purposes, stated that upon reading Popov's Japanese questionnaire, he had concluded: "It was . . . a fair deduction" that Pearl Harbor would be their first target of attack in the event the Japanese went to war and that "plans for such an attack must, therefore, have been far along by August 1941."[3] Moreover, Popov made reference to intense Japanese interest in the British raid on the Italian Navy at Taranto, the first occasion of the war to test in combat the vulnerability of warships to air attack from low-level torpedo-carrying aircraft.

Within intelligence circles an argument has raged ever since about whether Hoover was careless, if not culpable, in neither recognizing the significance of Popov's questionnaire nor taking seriously his analysis of why Japan studied Taranto so assiduously.[4] In this author's opinion, the questionnaire alone was not enough to ring alarms at Pearl Harbor. But whether or not the FBI should have been more alert than it seems to have been, Hoover mishandled an important agent, used to good advantage before and after his abortive assignment in the United States.[5] Prudence dictated that as a double agent, Popov should have been, and was, treated with caution. The beauty of the Double-Cross system was that the German agents being doubled could be controlled because their cipher text messages back to Germany—and Abwehr traffic in general—were systematically intercepted and read by the British. Moreover, the agents knew that the wages of cheating on the British could be death. In the case of Popov, his reliability prior to his being sent to the United States must have been tested by a variety of other means by the British before they gave him a clean bill of health and put him in touch with the FBI. While Hoover might have been justified in considering Popov's exhaustive German questionnaire covering a variety of targets simply part of a pro forma effort to keep the Japanese ally happy, not a specific indication of Japanese plans, his excessive suspicions of Popov were probably not justified and were debilitating to the agent.

Postmortems on Pearl Harbor are still being written. Somehow they all point to a phenomenon as old as human history: Governments, like individuals, find it difficult to accept that which does not fit preset conclusions, however solid the evidence. In the case of Pearl Harbor the American naval establishment simply did not believe that Japanese aircraft carriers could get within bombing range of Hawaii regardless of intelligence that said they could or the results of a U.S. Navy war game in the Pacific years past that indicated that it was possible.

The significance of the Tricycle case is simply that it was one more of many warnings ignored, one that seemed to mark Hawaii as a possible Japanese first-strike target, but its mention in a questionnaire of this kind was diluted by being included in a long list. Perhaps an even more egregious case of U.S. unpreparedness followed on the heels of Pearl Harbor. How could General MacArthur have been so unmoved by the cataclysmic Pearl Harbor attack that in its wake he and the key officers under his command failed to protect American aircraft at Clark Field in the Philippines from certain attack? From eight to ten hours after Pearl Harbor the Japanese destroyed American aircraft at Clark that they had found neatly parked wingtip to wingtip, stoically awaiting their destruction.

The unfortunate events at Pearl Harbor and Clark Field have been compared with Joseph Stalin's failure to take precautions prior to the German invasion of the Soviet Union despite multiple warnings that had reached him. The difference may be that Stalin, even if aroused to more energetic counteraction, could have done less about the imminent German attack than the United States might have done in Hawaii to prepare itself for a Japanese attack. Any way one looks at it, the United States was guilty of a profound intelligence failure. "Pearl Harbor" became a synonym for American unwatchfulness as well as for Japanese infamy.

TWENTY-ONE

Donovan's People[1]

WHEN WAR WITH JAPAN EXPLODED IN THE PACIFIC, BRINGING THE UNITED States into the European war with Germany and Italy as well, good intelligence became an even more urgent requirement for U.S. forces. Pearl Harbor dramatized, as no other event could have, the dangers of being taken by surprise and the pitfall of conventional wisdom. As the reasons for this catastrophic setback to the American strategic position in the Far East became more apparent, the need for an objective estimative body capable of quickly sifting evidence and predicting the possibilities of the "impossible" happening became apparent.

That President Roosevelt anticipated this need some five months before Pearl Harbor, when he asked William "Wild Bill" Donovan to prepare the groundwork for a new strategic intelligence agency, is a tribute to his foresight and perhaps an indication of how sure he had been that the United States would enter the war. Thus was born the Office of Coordinator of Information (COI), soon to be defined more specifically and renamed the Office of Strategic Services, or the OSS. (The functions of public affairs and overt propaganda were broken out of the COI to become the Office of War Information.) The United States had lost its innocence with Pearl Harbor and embraced secret intelligence and covert operations with the same enthusiasm that it had rejected them during the interwar period of isolationism. "Wild Bill" was the right man to be in charge of this new game and bring to it the gusto it must have to be successful.

The OSS would need something else: talented people worthy of its leader. It needed paladins capable of performing an array of unconventional missions essential to modern war: espionage, counterespionage, deception, black propaganda, behind-the-lines guerrilla warfare, partisan liaison, covert political action, sabotage, maritime operations, and related technical support tasks. That such talent was quickly found, screened, trained, deployed, and, above all, inspired was Donovan's greatest contribution to the war. The Allied supreme commander, General Dwight Eisenhower, said after the Normandy landings that the OSS's covert contributions had been worth a division in Europe.

That the OSS on such short notice acquitted itself well during World War II has a moral: It was not burdened with the baggage of preconception and bias that had characterized so many serious intelligence failures in history. Its formula for success, while illusive and perhaps accidental, must also include its innovative assessment and training program. Its men and women were, above all, taught to look at problems anew, not allow old ways to guide them.

The OSS fitted no mold. However amateurish at times, it was not the product of a civil service mentality, nor did it suffer from the suffocating rigidity of a military force. Its people, whether tall, short, aristocratic or plebeian, white, black, yellow, or red, right, left, or center in political persuasion, shared one goal: Win the war and do it with imagination—outwit the enemy! War is by nature a violent activity, and the OSS did its share of selective killing, but killing was not the object; knowing the enemy and outsmarting him were its mission. Surprises like Pearl Harbor must not happen again.

Much has been written about the OSS, thoughtful, insightful books and entertaining memoirs. Donovan is the subject of several biographies and countless articles. Relatively little, however, has been written about how the OSS was put together in record time. Governments, wherever they may exist, are never happier than when they are organizing themselves except when they are reorganizing themselves. In intelligence agencies, however, success depends on finding the "right stuff," to use the phrase the author Tom Wolfe applied to America's space exploration program, not on organizational wiring diagrams so dear to the hearts of personnel officers who vainly try to define graphically on paper how organizations work.

A glimpse of the OSS screening center called Station "S" gives some idea of how OSS personnel were tested for suitability. The assessment process at Station "S" was to many a splendid lark—a sort of English country house party except for the phalanx of clinical psychologists scrutinizing every move. And even they seemed more like recreation directors on a cruise ship than inquisitors. On arrival at the old Willard family place in Fairfax County, Virginia, the OSS applicants, who had survived a preliminary screening and security check, were swept into a three-day swirl of activity calculated to take their measure. Each was privately and sternly admonished to stick to a cover story and keep his or her true identity secret despite efforts made by the staff to ferret it out. Everyone—staff and subjects alike—had to be eternally vigilant.

The candidates were split into teams. One team, called Team B, was a disparate group, to say the least, but then, most teams were. It included the president of a prominent American bank in prewar Paris, a male ballet dancer, a disc jockey, a college professor, and a giant who had played pro football before the army inducted him and passed him on to the OSS—all of course with suitable cover identities to hide their pasts.

The battery of written aptitude tests may not have been very exciting to those itching for action, but the live exercises were challenging and sort of fun. The Brook Test, an exercise in teamwork, was a favorite. In this test Team B, like other teams before it, was faced with a large boulder sitting heavily beside a small stream. The monitor explained to the team that its performance would be timed. This sent its members scampering to organize themselves and make the best use of the boards and pulleys strewn about to move the boulder to the other side of the stream. But before anyone could stop him, the football hero grabbed the huge rock, hugged it to his chest as he would some sort of outsize, overweight football, and leaped nimbly to the other side for a touchdown. A time record had been broken, but the monitor was crushed with disappointment since none of the attributes of teamwork, ingenuity, or organizational skill had been tested. Rock carrying, after all, is not a frequently used technique in normal intelligence work. But the moral of this case is that in wartime the quickest, most direct solution may be the best one. "School solutions" are no substitute for on-the-spot ingenuity.

In the Behind the Barn Test each team with the help of two assistants provided by management, took turns at trying to erect a giant Tinkertoy-like cube. It soon became clear that the two "helpers," known as Kippy and Buster, were intent on sabotaging the effort, not helping it. This test, presumably designed to measure patience, or perhaps unshakable good nature, evoked a variety of responses. Well-adjusted persons took it in the spirit of high humor, even joined in the high jinks, turning it into a sort of impromptu Three Stooges routine. Others, of course, let their frustrations show. Rumors were rife at the time that the only student to complete the Tinkertoy in the face of such purposeful sabotage had been a strapping

Texan who flattened Kippy and Buster with two well-aimed blows. As a result, the Texan became a sort of folk hero at the station, perhaps symbolic proof that we could win the war after all so long as we had problem solvers like that.

The Liquor Test was presumably based on the adage *In vino veritas.* Under the guise of a relaxing farewell party all were plied with liquor, presumably so that the testers could catch them with their guards down. An interesting approach, but in this case it produced uncertain results. The college professor announced that he never touched the stuff. The linebacker poured more than his share into his generous paunch without its appearing to have the slightest effect. The disc jockey, exhausted by his rather physical weekend, fell asleep promptly while the Paris bank president shrewdly switched to French, which went over the heads of the observers who couldn't tell a drunken slur from a Paris accent. The ballet dancer, aghast at it all, simply looked as inconspicuous as possible.

The OSS's membership list was long. It read like a who's who of America. Many of the young and untried later rose to prominence. It would be interesting to see the assessment profiles of Arthur Goldberg, David Bruce, Ralph Bunche, Walt Rostow, Julia Child, Sterling Hayden, Stewart Alsop, Lucky Luciano, John Gardner, Douglas Dillon, and Paul Mellon—or, for that matter, the big-league baseball star Moe Berg.

Not that Team B was necessarily a typical microcosm of the OSS, but it acquitted itself well in later real action. The disc jockey with few apparent warlike talents distinguished himself behind the lines in France. The somewhat musty professor did magnificently in North Africa. The pro ball star never surpassed his accomplishment of getting the rock across the stream, but he did well in the Far East. The Paris banker served gloriously with the French underground and was among the first to enter liberated Paris in triumph. The ballet dancer also served with flair, tracking down German agents among French villagers as the Wehrmacht retreated.

The OSS's accomplishments were many although it would be ridiculous to claim that there were no failures. On the estimative side, OSS analysts, particularly Donovan himself, on the basis in large part of Allen Dulles's reporting from Switzerland, were quick to spot our ally the Soviets as our postwar enemy and adopt new targets accordingly as war neared its end. On the operational side, America's counterespionage effort has never been better than it was during the war, and countless books of the now-it-can-be-told genre came out after the war to chronicle espionage and underground guerrilla feats of derring-do. Women distinguished themselves as well as men and in ways more cerebrally than Mata Hari had in World War I. Yet clinical psychologists after the war could find little correlation between the performances of OSS officers and their Station "S" records. Most OSS men and women were encouraged by the thought that by surviving the Station "S" trial, they had been determined by scientific testing to be capable of winning the war. In fact, the Station "S" assessment record revealed that it was only 14 percent more accurate in picking good officers than would have been the case had the screening been turned over to a roulette wheel in Las Vegas. Still, the experiment was a brave effort, and at least it dramatized how the OSS, by expecting its people to win, encouraged them to perform a little beyond their usual limits. High morale and self-confidence were the OSS's greatest weapons. Certainly, no civil service examination or corporate screening application form could have produced a body of men and women such as were found among Donovan's people.

While America's OSS struggled to fit itself for battle with the enemy by making warriors for the unseen war, Germany's two major intelligence organizations, the General Staff's Abwehr and the SS's Sicherheitsdienst, devoted a disproportionate amount of time fighting with each other. Skirmishes for supremacy between the two rival organizations were to thrust Admiral Canaris and Reinhard Heydrich, once friends, into an adversarial relationship that had deadly results.

TWENTY-TWO

The Assassination of
Reinhard Heydrich

RADIO PRAGUE'S SPECIAL BROADCAST ON FRIDAY, MAY 29,1942, STARTLED
Europe with the announcement that Reinhard Heydrich, Nazi overlord of
Bohemia and Moravia, was a victim of an assassin's grenade. His frightened charges, the Czechoslovakian people, did not mourn him, nor did
the peoples of Germany, Poland, Eastern Europe, the Ukraine, and western Russia who had suffered at his hands in the wake of the German invasions. His reputation for cruelty had preceded his assignment to Prague,
and true to prediction, he had begun his regime amid grave apprehension.
As Heydrich lay dying, attended by the best physicians Hitler could provide, Czechs were torn by two emotions: relief that the "Butcher of
Prague" would soon be dead and terror that Hitler would exact a terrible
revenge on the populace for his death. Two villages, one, the town of
Lidice (near Prague), which became an international symbol of Nazi bar-
barism, the other, Lezhaky in southwestern Bohemia, were leveled and all
able-bodied men killed, while women and their children were separated
and sent to separate concentration camps. A massive search for the assassins went on for weeks, but with every passing day, more Czechs paid with
their lives the price of Nazi rage and frustration.[1]

Admiral Canaris must have wondered how Heydrich's death would affect his already uneasy relationship with the SD and Gestapo, a rivalry that
had become progressively more debilitating for the Abwehr, more inhibiting for the Resistance, and more dangerous to himself. Two weeks before
Heydrich was struck down by the assassins, Canaris had met with him in

Prague. Heydrich had kept his control of the Sicherheitsdienst (SD), se-curity intelligence arm of the SS, and the Gestapo despite his assignment in September 1941 as *Reichsprotektor*, or proconsul, of Bohemia and Moravia. Canaris had been summoned to Prague to work out final details of an agreement between them, a revision of the original so-called Ten Commandments, which had defined their relationship since 1936.[2]

On this occasion Admiral and Frau Canaris had been houseguests of the Heydrichs in Prague. Despite the depressing consequences of an agreement that weakened the Abwehr, Canaris maintained a façade of friendliness with the man whom he had once befriended when they were shipmates on the warship *Berlin* two decades ago but who now stealthily gathered evidence with which to ruin him.

Implicit in Heydrich's presentation during his meeting with Canaris was the threatening promise that he would ultimately replace "inept, po-litically unreliable" Abwehr officers with SS-trained experts in security. While the admiral may have wondered about what suspicions Heydrich harbored, he could conclude that his own power, if not physical well-being, was ultimately doomed at the hands of "his old friend." Canaris and Heydrich, whose relationship was ambivalent, could reminisce about bet-ter times despite the undercurrent of their rivalry and mutual distrust. Hey-drich's widow, Lina Heydrich, looking back on their reunion in Prague with Admiral and Frau Canaris, commented nostalgically after the war, "Ah yes, they were happy days."[3] Perhaps she even meant it.

Walter Schellenberg, SD chief, with whom Canaris frequently dealt, particularly after Heydrich moved to Prague, was more realistic about the relationship between Canaris and Heydrich. While Schellenberg had re-spect for Canaris, he was wary. Not long before his death Heydrich advised Schellenberg not to let himself "be lulled to sleep" by Canaris. He warned, "You won't get anywhere by handling him with kid gloves."[4] According to Schellenberg, Heydrich had more than suspicions: He "felt certain that Canaris had betrayed the date of the [German] attack in the West," but he seemed to want to hold off for some reason.[5] Schellenberg well remem-bered Canaris's state of mind on the eve of his final meetings with Heydrich to update their agreement: "I noticed now for the first time signs of an inner weariness in Canaris." He wrote that the admiral "was worn out by the con-tinual internecine conflict. . . . He felt insecure and restless, and something like a physical fear of Heydrich." Schellenberg claimed that Canaris had said to him, "Things can't go on this way much longer."[6]

Canaris rushed back to Prague when he received the news of Heydrich, but the stricken man had not yet regained consciousness. Himmler too called on Heydrich in the hospital. Because of Heydrich's condition, their conversation was brief. Himmler reported that the dying man had only energy enough to quote a favorite passage from an opera which his father used to sing: "Yes, the world is but a barrel organ, which our Lord God turns himself, and each must dance to the tune. . . ."[7]

When Heydrich finally succumbed to his wounds on June 4, the official state funeral, staged in Berlin as a pagan extravaganza with all the pomp and panoply the Nazis could muster for their "martyr," was well attended by the party faithfuls and those who were expected to attend for protocol reasons.

In greeting Walter Huppenkothen of the Gestapo at the funeral, Canaris allegedly had tears in his eyes.[8] Historians have since wondered at this demonstration of sorrow: Why would he grieve for an evil man and archrival? Canaris perhaps had two conflicting emotions: great relief, on one hand, that his nemesis was gone and, on the other, fear of a Gestapo in the charge of a new zealot whose hostility would be unleavened by a long relationship and past favors, as Heydrich's relationship had been, someone whose dossier hidden in Canaris's safe held no useful incriminating information that could be used to restrain him. Canaris surely realized that although Heydrich's death gave him a reprieve from SD hostile plotting, he was still a target for removal by Himmler's men.

TO UNDERSTAND CANARIS'S RELATIONSHIP WITH HEYDRICH, IT IS NECESsary to go back many years and watch it evolve. When Canaris took over as head of the Abwehr on January 15, 1935, his predecessor, Konrad Patzig, gave him one piece of advice: Beware of Reinhard Heydrich. The departing Abwehr chief had reason to hate Heydrich; he could blame him for losing his job. Heydrich, it seems, had lodged a complaint with his boss, Reichsführer Heinrich Himmler, accusing Patzig of not cooperating with the SD and Gestapo.* Neither Admiral Raeder, commander in chief of the navy, nor his superior, Minister of War von Blomberg, felt strongly enough or had the courage to oppose Himmler; both men were thoroughly "browned," as the expression of the day went—i.e. cowed by Hitler and his brown-shirted entourage.[9]

But in 1935 Heydrich was no stranger to Canaris; their relationship had begun in 1922, when Heydrich was a mere cadet aboard the training ship *Berlin* who looked upon Canaris as his mentor and friend.[10] Canaris had

---

*Among other things, Patzig had offended Hitler by ignoring an order to stop spying against Poland. Hitler, at that particular moment, did not want to offend Poland, with which he had concluded a treaty of friendship in 1934 that contained a secret clause banning espionage—Colvin, *Canaris*, pp. 13–15.

been kind to this fledgling officer who was struggling in his new career. Heydrich had then been a strange one. The tall and stringy cadet with his long neck, long face, and slightly upward-slanting eyes, looked as though he had been somehow stretched. A large aquiline nose protruded from high cheekbones, and the slits that were his eyes darted about as he spoke. Bad teeth were revealed when he smiled—not often. His otherwise athletic build was spoiled by plumpish, almost feminine hips.

As a schoolboy Heydrich was often teased by his mates, who made fun of his high-pitched voice. That he played the violin when other boys were playing outside at sports set him apart. It was no wonder he loved music; his father had been a music teacher and operatic tenor. A loner with a permanent chip on his shoulder, young Heydrich would walk down a street with a strange gait caused by his keeping one foot in the gutter, the other on the curb, and would shove aside any boy who did not get out of his way, providing a glimpse of the bully he became as an adult.

Heydrich's mother, an actress named Sarah, was thought to have been half Jewish, although the family always denied this. Rumors of Jewish ancestry were enough, however, to threaten young Heydrich among Jew-baiting Nazis. Childhood taunting was replaced by official scrutiny as he grew older, and during his early career he more than once had to prove his Aryan origins before "racial purity" hearings.[11] While still a teenager Heydrich was swept up by the Nazi movement and joined the Freikorps, where he became well schooled in the arts of street fighting.[12]

When Heydrich joined the navy and was posted aboard the frigate *Berlin* as officer cadet, he felt out of place. His shipmates, amused by his high-pitched voice, called him Goat and joked about his passion for music. He alternated between arrogance and obsequiousness to the annoyance of almost everyone.[13] Canaris, an officer on the *Berlin* at the time, took pity on this young man who had no friends and made an effort to befriend him. Frau Erika Canaris, herself a musician, liked the young man and welcomed him in their home, where he could be easily persuaded to play the violin in duets with her. While Canaris had no particular love for music—"Music is for musicians," he would say—he enjoyed the company of this lonesome soul who was clearly brilliant, if not well balanced.

While serving as signals officer on board the Baltic fleet flagship *Schleswig-Holstein* in 1929, Heydrich was ousted from the navy as the result of a sex scandal. In violation of a strict navy code of behavior for "gentlemen" in the service, he had broken an engagement with a woman whom he had made pregnant. Bound by his double standard toward sex, he refused to marry her on the excuse that a woman who gave herself freely to a man was "not worthy of being his wife."

Making matters worse for Heydrich, the woman he wronged was the daughter of a director of I. G. Farben, the industrial giant that held several important navy contracts. When her outraged father complained to Admiral Raeder, Heydrich lied and tried to pin the blame on the hapless daughter.[14] Raeder gave him an ultimatum: Either marry the woman or resign. Since Heydrich chose to resign, the naval board of review had no choice but to separate him from the service,[15] as it did on April 31, 1929.

At about the same time as Heydrich was disengaging himself from the impregnated daughter of an I. G. Farben director, he was falling in love with a striking "Nordic" woman, Lina Mathilde von Osten, whom he had come to know after rescuing her in a sailing accident. If his partner in profane love had enjoyed the protection of an influential father in the business world, Miss von Osten, more relevant to an ambitious young man like Heydrich, enjoyed good contacts with the upper strata of the Nazi party. Heydrich wooed and won her, becoming betrothed in December 1930.[16]

Being unemployed in 1931, the midst of the Great Depression, was hard to bear, particularly for someone as ambitious as Heydrich. Within two months of leaving the navy, Heydrich joined the SS. How he made such a rapid transition from disgrace to distinction, albeit evil distinction, strains credulity. If one is to believe available records, young Heydrich, with an introduction from his well-connected new wife, Lina, and from a friend in the SS, Baron Friedrich Karl von Eberstein,[17] visited Reichsführer Himmler at his Waldtrudering chicken farm. Asked for his views on how counterespionage should be organized and managed, Heydrich scribbled off a written blueprint in twenty minutes. Greatly impressed, Himmler dubbed it "Sicherheitsdienst des Reichsführer" (Secret Service of the Reichsführer) and hired his visitor on the spot to implement it. In a telegram to Nazi party headquarters in Hamburg, dated October 5, 1931, Himmler ordered: "Party member Reinhard Heydrich, Hamburg, Membership number 544916, with effect from October of this year, be carried on the strength of Party HQ as a member of the staff of the Reichsführer SS Himmler with rank of Sturmführer SS."[18] Thus Himmler hired a navy reject whom he had never seen before to become his deputy and head an office destined to become one of the most powerful and most feared in the Third Reich. This off-key Cinderella story is a commentary on the total inanity of the fledgling Nazi establishment, or there is more to the story than appears, or both.

Hans Gisevius, who had served in the Gestapo under Himmler before transferring to the Abwehr to work for Canaris and join the Black Orchestra Resistance movement, writes in his postwar memoir that early in 1934: "Himmler had become a subject of gossip."[19] Mary Bancroft, an assistant to Allen Dulles, OSS station chief in Bern, who maintained contact with

Gisevius and helped him prepare his memoir, quoted him in her own postwar autobiography as saying, "[T]he real bond between Himmler and Heydrich was that they had once been 'involved with each other.' " By way of explanation Gisevius added that this kind of involvement, by surviving the breakup of an "original affair," was indestructible, "just like a similar heterosexual relationship."[20]

Certainly, Heydrich's promiscuous sex life more than once attracted unfavorable attention, or so claimed his subordinate Walter Schellenberg. In a postwar memoir Schellenberg describes Heydrich's insatiable sexual appetite as a serious character weakness: "He would surrender himself without inhibition or caution."[21] Another author claims that Heydrich, in the throes of a drinking binge with close friends, sometimes dressed up as a woman.[22]

In Berlin Heydrich gained a certain notoriety for his womanizing. Perhaps in order to create his own, more controlled environment for debaucherie, he set up a house of prostitution with Gestapo funds, justifying it as a "honeypot" with which to ensnare unsuspecting foreign diplomats. In fact Heydrich himself seemed to have been the best customer of Salon Kitty—as it was called.[23] The prostitutes allegedly dreaded his visits; he usually insisted on humiliating his partners in some way. When drunk, he was dangerously sadistic.

Whatever his sexual proclivities, Heydrich prospered in his new career. Having made a spectacular score by using pilfered and forged German military documents to plant on Stalin, providing him with evidence with which to launch his terrible purge of the Red Army in 1937, Heydrich turned his attention to the German Army, which he suspected of harboring pro-Soviet elements. He saw this as a way to humble the Wehrmacht and bring it more firmly under Hitler's control. In March 1937 he arrested a friend of General Hans von Seeckt's named Ernst Niekisch, who had been one of the drafters of the secret military training agreement of 1926 between Soviet Russia and Germany. Like Seeckt, Niekisch had felt a close professional bond with the Red Army, but he may not have been legally guilty of treason.* He had also been a friend of Karl Radek, the Soviet Comintern leader who had done time in a German jail for his role in the abortive pro-Bolshevik Spartacus revolt of 1919 in Berlin, and under Hitler such friendships were suspect.

The Niekisch case, badly bungled by the prosecution, accomplished nothing by way of breaking the power of the Wehrmacht. It was then that

---

*In 1946 it was discovered that Niekisch had survived the war and had been liberated from a German prison camp by Red Army troops as they overran eastern Germany in 1945.

Himmler and Heydrich had involved themselves in the Blomberg and Fritsch affairs in an effort to strike a blow against the Wehrmacht by defaming two of its leaders. These episodes, particularly the Fritsch affair, disgusted Canaris. It strengthened his commitment to the Black Orchestra and revealed to him again that his onetime friend Heydrich was a diabolical adversary. Canaris had been right in 1935, when he commented to one of his officers that the man was "a brutal fanatic with whom it will be most difficult to collaborate frankly and with confidence."[24]

Since becoming chief of the Abwehr, Canaris had devoted much of his time to keeping Heydrich and the burgeoning SD and Gestapo at bay. The admiral had one basic advantage from the outset: On October 17, 1933, soon after the Nazis came to power, Hitler had issued a decree granting the Wehrmacht full and exclusive power in matters having to do with counterespionage and countersabotage affecting the armed forces.* This was a strong charter. The Abwehr, moreover, had its own passport office, which could issue passports and other travel documents at will and was not subject to racial purity screening. Nor was the Gestapo allowed to investigate it.

Heydrich, however, had also maneuvered adroitly. On June 9, 1934, Rudolf Hess declared the Sicherheitsdienst (SD) to be the Nazis' only political intelligence service.[25] For all their long association, Canaris now instinctively feared Heydrich, whom he once described as "that most clever beast."[26] As insurance against Heydrich's predatory intentions, Canaris kept in his files what he considered proof of Heydrich's Jewish blood, and he may have had hidden away other compromising information describing his rival's aberrant sexual promiscuity.

When he assumed office in 1935, Canaris, in pursuit of good relations with Heydrich, sought a treaty delimiting each service's jurisdiction. But he knew that Heydrich, one of Germany's best fencers, would be a worthy opponent in bureaucratic fencing as well; he would have to move carefully. As before, the two families, now neighbors in a Berlin suburb, often saw each other socially. Besides Frau Canaris's weekly musicales, in which she and Heydrich played violin duets, the admiral presided as chef at cookouts or organized croquet games on their lawn. Such pleasantries set an ostensibly congenial, if not sincere, atmosphere. Heyrich must also have remembered how Canaris had prevailed with Admiral Raeder in his

---

*Hitler's edict stated: "The Reichswehr Minister shall take all steps essential to the preservation of National Security and of interests relating to military policy in the field of counterespionage and propaganda. He will set out the requisite guidelines which shall be observed by Reich departments and the land authorities concerned"—Heinz Höhne, *Canaris* (Garden City, N.Y.: Doubleday, 1976), pp. 180, 181.

behalf to restore some of his navy privileges taken from him when he was cashiered. Thanks to Canaris, he could, for example, wear his uniform on certain formal occasions. But Heydrich probably did not like to be beholden to his mentor at this stage of his career, and despite past kindnesses, frictions invariably intruded on their relationship.

By the terms of Canaris's agreement with Heydrich, signed in 1936 and nicknamed the Ten Commandments, the Abwehr was to confine itself to purely military intelligence and pass to the SD any political intelligence it incidentally picked up. Conversely, the SD would pass to the Abwehr any military intelligence it gathered. Counterespionage was the Abwehr's business, although Canaris had to rely on the Gestapo for executive action, such as arresting foreign agents and bringing them to trial.[27] While the agreement did not give Canaris all the authority that he would have liked to have had, the Abwehr still retained preeminence in espionage and counterespionage.[28] Heydrich was of course not satisfied with the agreement and by 1941 was pressing Canaris for more concessions. This was a good time to go after Canaris; events on the eastern front were causing dangerous stresses. Resentment in high places of Canaris's pessimistic attitude combined with intelligence failures on the eastern front put the admiral's authority at risk.

Canaris had made enemies by his role as naysayer. He was revolted by the atrocities of the SS in general and the actions of Heydrich's SD and Gestapo agents in particular. Hitler's grisly intentions had become evident. Canaris and many other military officers were appalled as they came to realize fully that this was not only war but a campaign of systematic genocide against the "Jewish-Bolshevik intelligentsia." This policy was embodied in Hitler's order of March 3, 1941, and in his speech before two hundred officers promising the most barbarous war of military history. Heydrich, the Grim Reaper who carried out this policy, is remembered for his announcement at the end of the Polish campaign that no more than 3 percent of the Polish upper classes still survived. He meant to better this achievement in the Russian campaign. As reward for diligence, Himmler made Heydrich chief of the RSHA, the entire security intelligence apparatus of the SS. With some three thousand troops at his disposal, Heydrich rounded up the "subhumans," as he called Bolsheviks, Jews, and Russian intellectuals. His target was no less than the estimated five million Jews in Russia.

Canaris saw unfolding the crime of the century that would result in not only the death of thousands of noncombatants but, in the end, the destruction of Germany. What depressed him the most was his inability to do anything to stop it; the German invasion juggernaut, bent on total de-

WILHELM CANARIS, ARCH-INTRIGUER

Suspected of espionage and fomenting unrest among French North African tribes in World War I, Wilhelm Canaris, future German military intelligence chief in World War II, was rescued by the German submarine *U-35* only minutes before the French submarine *Opale* closed in to capture him, as shown here in a later photograph.

In 1920 Canaris, while second in command of the training ship *Berlin*, was active off duty in anti-Communist street demonstrations led by monarchist agitator Wolfgang Kapp.

In World War II, Admiral Canaris led a double life as head of Military Intelligence (Abwehr) and as an activist in the German Resistance. But he considered himself a German patriot whose actions were justified by the enormity of Hitler's crimes.

In 1936 Canaris talks with Reichsführer Himmler, as Propaganda Minister Göbbels, between them, looks on. Although Canaris and Himmler were fiercely competitive in intelligence matters, the Abwehr chief long seemed immune to action against him by the Gestapo despite growing evidence linking him with the Resistance. Himmler, also guilty of anti-Hitler plotting, likely feared him.

ALLEN DULLES, SUPERSTAR

Allen Dulles served as intelligence officer for the U.S. consulate in Bern in World War I.

Gero von Schulze-Gaevernitz, a German-American later to become an OSS agent assisting Allen Dulles in Bern, contemplates a less-real challenge of wits over a chessboard in Zermatt, Switzerland, in 1941. From 1942 he played an important role in OSS European operations, including the German surrender in Italy.

ANGUS THUERMER

Allen Dulles as director of the CIA. Like Canaris, Allen Dulles served as an intelligence officer in both world wars. In World War II his operations penetrating the Reich for OSS from Bern were very successful. Less welcome in Washington, but in retrospect most prescient, was his forecasting of Stalin's intention to dominate Eastern Europe after the war.

VENLO:
PERPETRATOR . . .

Walter Schellenberg

SD officer Walter Schellenberg helped Heydrich provide impetus to Stalin's prewar purge of the Red Army by planting forged evidence incriminating the cream of the Soviet officer corps, and would soon attempt to subvert the Duke of Windsor. But as Western Europe braced for German attack Schellenberg made his mark with a sting operation that destroyed British intelligence networks there.

The Backus Café

The trap was baited in early November 1939 at the Backus Café near the Dutch town of Venlo on the German border, where the two British MI-6 officers and a Dutch intelligence officer waited for their contact. Schellenberg, pretending to be an emissary of a cabal of German officers conspiring against Hitler, arrived reinforced by a commando squad for the denouement. After a shoot-out worthy of an American Western, the Dutch officer was dead and the two Englishmen, Stevens and Best, prisoners. The British network would soon be in ruins.

AND VICTIMS

Major Richard Stevens

Nazi propaganda tried to link the Venlo prisoners, Stevens and Best, with a bomb explosion in a Munich beer hall during an anniversary celebration of Hitler's 1923 abortive putsch, thereby justifying their kidnapping. (Hitler escaped death by leaving the hall early.) The real culprit, George Elser, was caught, but, despite intensive interrogation, refused to admit having had accomplices.

Captain Sigismund Payne Best   *George Elser*

HESS, MISGUIDED NAZI ZEALOT

It was a version of this aircraft, the Messerschmitt 110, equipped with extra gas tanks, that Hitler's trusted deputy Rudolf Hess flew to Scotland on his ill-fated attempt to meet and discuss peace with the Duke of Hamilton.

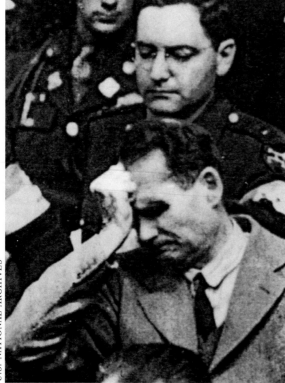

Hitler probably did not know that Hess planned to make a black flight to Scotland and personally play peacemaker, although he seemed to have encouraged Hess to seek indirect contact with appeasement-minded Englishmen.

Hess's prior letters to the Duke of Hamilton were intercepted by British intelligence and answered in the Duke's name, perhaps in an attempt to lure a Hess emissary into a trap. Stalin, however, could never be dissuaded from believing that Hess was acting in secret collusion with the British in preparation for Germany's attack on Russia.

DONOVAN, FOUNDER OF OSS

William "Wild Bill" Donovan seemed to spend as much time overseas visiting his stations as he did in headquarters, one key to the devotion his OSS men and women felt for him. In his travels he not only urged OSS to outscore the Axis enemy but, sensing trouble with Stalin, he argued fervently that in a postwar rush to normalcy the United States should not jettison its new strategic intelligence capability.

OPERATION TORCH

Eisenhower and staff plot the North African landings, code-named Torch—the first major offensive launched with the benefit of Ultra intelligence gleaned from deciphered German radio traffic. The Allies had also misled the Germans as to the true landing areas through doubled agents in Operation Double-Cross.

Torch Supreme Commander Dwight D. Eisenhower, General Mark Clark, and Robert Murphy at a twenty-fifth reunion in Washington of the "Canoe Club," commemorating Clark and staff's secret landing in Algiers by submarine and dinghy.

Clark, representing Eisenhower, and Murphy, principal U.S. representative in Algiers, led the Allied delegation that met secretly on October 20, 1942, at a rendezvous on the Algerian coast with French representatives of General Henri Giraud to work out details of the imminent Allied landings in North Africa.

Canaris's Abwehr colleague Colonel Lahousen sits on the right of the Grand Mufti of Jerusalem at a Berlin meeting in 1941.

Canaris, friend of the Grand Mufti, could not convince Ribbentrop to back the influential cleric in raising French North African tribes to revolt with promises of independence.

Canaris, shown in slouch hat and upturned collar somewhere in Spain, enjoyed traveling incognito in this strategically located country. But despite his good intelligence apparatus there and close friendship with Franco, he had not alerted Hitler to the nearby Allied landings, one cause of his fall from grace.

STALIN'S SPIES

The Rote Drei, Switzerland-based branch of the Soviet espionage net known as the Red Orchestra, provided Stalin with much-needed military information on the Eastern Front. Rudolf Roessler, code-named Lucy, was its star performer.

The Englishman Alexander Foote was the Rote Drei's wireless operator. After the war he made the claim, unsubstantiated by the British, that he had really been a British-controlled double agent used by them to insinuate Ultra intelligence into the Soviet network so that Stalin, who distrusted the British, would not know the true source.

Before being caught by the Japanese, Richard Sorge proved his worth to his Soviet masters with timely reports indicating that the Japanese had decided to invade southward into Southeast Asia rather than attack the Soviet Union. This enabled Stalin to transfer troops from the Far East in time to save Moscow from the Germans.

Harold Adrian ("Kim") Philby, recruited by Soviet intelligence after Communist cultivation at Cambridge University, was able to join the British Secret Service during World War II. He thus provided the Soviets with an invaluable window on the most secret aspects of the British war effort. The Soviets paid tribute to him after his death by issuing a commemorative stamp *(right)* in his honor.

СОВЕТСКИЙ РАЗВЕДЧИК

КИМ ФИЛБИ
1912—1988
5 к ПОЧТА СССР 1990

ASSASSINATION OF HEYDRICH

Canaris and RSHA chief Reinhard Heydrich at a banquet of German armed forces and SS officers in Berlin, 1936.

Although Canaris had befriended Heydrich when the latter was a naval cadet, by World War II an intense professional rivalry had developed between them. As Nazi proconsul for occupied Czechoslovakia in 1942 Heydrich was determined to take over the Abwehr and fire Canaris.

As a lever against Canaris, Heyrich used the case of Paul Thümmel, an Abwehr officer discovered to have been spying for Czech intelligence in Prague since 1936. When Prague fell, the Czech government in London exile shared Thümmel with MI-6. Heydrich would probably have moved against Canaris and taken over the "unreliable" Abwehr had he not been assassinated by the British and Czechs.

This bend in the road required Heydrich's driver to slow, providing an opportunity for Heydrich's assassin to toss a lethal grenade especially made by Britain's SOE. Treachery in the ranks of the underground permitted the Gestapo to capture the assassination team.

Total destruction of the Czech town of Lidice and the massacre of its inhabitants by the Gestapo as reprisal for Heydrich's assassination so inflamed world opinion that the name Lidice became a metaphor for Nazi terror. This is one of several sketches submitted by the noted artist William Gropper to the U.S. Office of War Information to illustrate a pamphlet condemning the atrocity.

AXIS AT RISK

More than a score of assassination attempts had threatened Hitler when, on July 20, 1944, his closest call, the Resistance plot code-named Valkyrie, failed, provoking mass arrests. Hitler had earlier almost lost his life on a flight between Smolensk and Rastenburg when a bomb disguised as a Cointreau bottle prepared by General Henning von Tresckow, chief of staff of the Central Army Group, failed to explode.

Mussolini had not been as lucky as Hitler. A beaten man, he greets Ribbentrop as Hitler enters the reception room at Rastenburg headquarters to console him for his ouster by Badoglio. The Führer was unaware that his intelligence chief, Canaris, had known about the plot in advance and had, moreover, encouraged the head of Italian Intelligence to talk Badoglio into quitting the war.

OPERATION SUNRISE

General Karl Wolff, SS commander in Italy, having become disillusioned with Hitler and his war, sought out OSS officer Dulles in Bern to discuss the surrender of German forces in Italy. He secretly negotiated unconditional surrender on April 29, 1945.

Since RSHA chief Ernst Kaltenbrunner (shown here at the Nuremberg trials) had fronted for Himmler in making secret contact with Dulles in 1945, he did not welcome Wolff's initiative with the OSS and tried to discredit him as a traitor in Hitler's eyes.

Allen Dulles's secret negotiations with Wolff provoked Stalin, revealing the depth of his suspicion that the Western Allies intended to exclude the USSR from postwar German and East European affairs. Code-name Sunrise, meant to herald the dawn of world peace, instead illuminated the foreboding features of an incipient "cold war."

MARTYR

Ulrich von Hassell, former German ambassador to Italy and important leader of the anti-Nazi Resistance, was apprehended and executed with many others in the wake of the July 20, 1944, bomb plot against Hitler. He stands before his accusers at the Nazi "People's Court" to receive an inevitable sentence of death.

struction, drowned out all voices of reason in this atmosphere of terror. Only three days earlier, on September 12, Canaris with his assistant Lahousen in attendance had spoken up in protest to the bombardment of Warsaw, only to be slapped down by the chief of the OKW, Keitel, who dismissed him by denying any responsibility.[29]

Canaris did sign a memorandum dated September 15, 1941, prepared by Count Helmuth von Moltke, and sent it to General Keitel objecting to a harsh OKW regulation concerning the handling of prisoners of war. It had no effect; Keitel cynically admitted that such objections may be in accord with soldierly conceptions of a chivalrous war, but Germany was intent on destroying an ideology.

Abwehr views were rejected for another reason: They described the futility of the campaign by chronicling the deteriorating German military situations in the East. As a fiercer than usual Russian winter began to grip the eastern front in 1941, German Army Group Center drew close to Moscow, so close that the Soviet government and the diplomatic corps fled eastward in anticipation of the capital's fall. The peripatetic Canaris was at the front, warning all who would listen that occupation of the Soviet capital was impossible. His message was confirmed by the half-frozen soldiers and vehicles mired in snow and mud that labored in vain to reach Moscow. But the bearer of bad news is never welcome.

British intelligence was a more receptive audience. On his way back to Berlin in October 1941 Canaris stopped off to see Halina Szymanska in Switzerland and confided in her his estimate of the Soviet offensive, which of course he knew she would pass on to the British Secret Service. His prediction was glum but accurate: "If the Russian Army is disorganized and exhausted, so are we too." He was concerned that the Germans had outrun their supplies: "Our resources in transport are wholly inadequate to maintain such large formations so far forward."[30] He added: "If the situation of Russia is bad, it can hardly be worse than ours." This grim estimate, which must have reached London almost immediately, was welcomed by the British, who were planning military aid to Russia, a much-needed ally for all its ideological differences and past fickleness.

Before the invasion Hitler had promised General von Runstedt that the Red Army was too demoralized to fight: "You have only to kick in the door and the whole rotten structure will come crashing down." It did Canaris no good to have been right and Hitler wrong. Canaris's Nazi detractors also criticized the inadequacy of Abwehr intelligence, a charge very likely true of an organization that did not have its heart in the kind of war Hitler was waging. As the Wehrmacht pushed into Russia, where on-the-spot damage assessment and tactical communications interception became possible, it was apparent that the Abwehr intelligence had been inaccurate. Canaris thus had been right in his predictions but wrong in his facts.[31]

Criticized by some in the Resistance for not protesting more loudly against Hitler and Nazi inhumanity in Russia, Canaris had learned that ranting and roaring were useless. If he offered to resign, Hitler would be only too glad to oblige, and then where would the Resistance be? To speak out more stridently against Hitler would have been to court his own destruction and with it the destruction of the Resistance movement. To go further than he already had gone in serving as critic of the eastern campaign would only play into Heydrich's hands. The solution to Hitler's atrocities and obsessive plunge toward disaster was not shriller protest but his removal from power.

Canaris was fast losing any influence he may have had with Hitler or his accolytes. And circling for the kill was Heydrich, who, to enlarge his empire at Abwehr expense, would wage his bureaucratic battle with Canaris ever more ferociously. Heydrich took the first initiative in his power struggle with Canaris. In December 1941 he formally appealed to the chief of operations, General Jodl, to find a new formula defining the powers and jurisdictions of the Abwehr and RSHA.[32] Canaris met with Heydrich in early 1942, each with his advisers.

To Heydrich's surprise, Canaris readily accepted the proposition made to him. It was agreed that the RSHA would also have counterespionage authority, while the Abwehr would otherwise satisfy itself with military, not political, intelligence reporting. This represented a substantial loss to Canaris and the Abwehr. But when the Abwehr committed the agreement to paper in a counterdraft, nearly all of Canaris's concessions were omitted. This provoked an outraged Heydrich to cry "bad faith" and break off relations with the admiral. Only because Keitel intervened did the two antagonists reach a mutually acceptable compromise.

On March 1, 1942, Canaris and Heydrich in behalf of their respective agencies signed a document entitled "Implementation Directives" relating to official dealings between them.[33] This represented a victory for Heydrich; Canaris's wings were clipped although he could still fly. It was now the time for the two rivals to ratify the agreement with as much grace as they could muster. The conference, which was convened on May 17, was a charade of conciliation as both parties ceremonially signed the accord. Canaris may have been grateful for this apparent relief from Heydrich's relentless stalking, but he realized that the days of the Abwehr as he knew it were numbered. Heydrich savored his victory, but only briefly; his days were also numbered.

Within little more than a week Heydrich would be dead of an assassin's grenade. The manhunt provoked by Heydrich's assassination was intense. The Nazis proclaimed martial law for Bohemia and Moravia with a dusk-to-dawn curfew in force. Himmler appointed former Sudetenland leader Karl Hermann Frank, now acting *Reichsprotektor*, to oversee systematic reprisals. In Prague Frank made mass arrests and conducted executions with no regard for legal niceties. After the war the Allies estimated that at least five thousand Czechs, three thousand or more of whom were Jews, had been killed by the Nazis as revenge for Heydrich's death.

The reign of terror was meant to intimidate the Czechs and demoralize the underground Resistance, not to administer justice, but this meat-ax approach did not flush out the assassins from their hiding place. Even Frank's threat to massacre the population of Prague if the culprits were not produced had no immediate effect. But a prize of one million reichsmarks for information leading to their arrest did achieve results.

On June 24, Radio Prague announced cryptically that the assassins, Jan Kubiš and Josef Gabčik, and two other members of the Czech Resistance, Lieutenant Adolf Opálka and Sergeant Josef Valčik, were found hiding out in the catacombs of the Orthodox Church of Karel Boromaeus, near the center of Prague. The report inaccurately added that all four had been killed in a gunfight resisting arrest.

As later reconstructed by British and Czech intelligence, the two assassins had carefully planned their attack on Heydrich. Having cased the route he customarily took to work, they lay in ambush on the morning of May 27 at a place midway between the village of Brezany and Prague. This particular spot was selected because a sharp curve in the road would force Heydrich's vehicle to slow perceptibly, providing the assassins with an opportunity to strike with maximum accuracy. As Heydrich's chauffeur-driven green Mercedes cabriolet and motorcycle escort passed on schedule, Jan Kubiš's Sten gun jammed as he tried to fire, but Gabčik was able to throw under the auto a grenade that exploded with telling effect. Despite a hail of bullets, some fired by a badly wounded Heydrich himself, the two men were able to escape on their bicycles in the confusion.

Kubiš and Gabčik were sheltered by several members of the Czech Resistance before they found sanctuary in the Orthodox church under the protection of a brave and patriotic Czech priest. The fugitives were discovered, however, as a result of a tip to the police by a Judas in the Resistance, one Sergeant Karel Čurda, who found the million-mark bounty irresistible, or so he said at his trial after the war. In his testimony Čurda claimed to have been present at the capture; he described a spirited gunfight that drove Kubiš and Gabčik, as well as two other Resistance fighters who had holed up in the church, to an underground vault. After the police found a way to insert a hose and begin flooding the vault, the two assassins killed themselves rather than surrender or be drowned. An unrepentant Čurda, in admitting his betrayal, confronted his Resistance accusers with the question: Which was the greater crime, to kill two men or to kill several thousand innocent people, victims of reprisals, as had the Czech Resistance by their murder of Heydrich?[34]

At the end of World War II a Communist partisan accused Colonel František Moravec, Beneš's link with the Czech Resistance, of being a toady of the British; Czech heroes in the postwar era, he promised, would be Communists, not wartime Resistance fighters who had served the British.[35] Czech Communists aside, there were others who found Beneš's London government-in-exile to blame for provoking the catastrophic German reprisals. R. T. Paget, a member of the British House of Commons, later stated that the Czech Resistance "often deliberately provoked reprisals in order that hatred of the occupier may be intensified and more people can be induced to resist." Freely admitting the British role in the operation, he added: "This was our general idea when we flew in a party to murder Heydrich."[36] These tactics predictably did not work; not only were German reprisals a terrible burden for the Czech people to endure, but the Czech underground was virtually destroyed.

The Nazi German Security Office in Prague reported to Hitler that the reaction of the populace in Czechoslovakia to Heydrich's assassination had been at first "malicious joy," but as the seriousness of the situation (i.e., German reprisals) became apparent, "the worker's populace condemned, with few exceptions, the *Attentat* [attempted assassination]. . . . They were grateful to him [Heydrich] for many social measures." The "intelligentsia and broad masses of the Czech middle class," however, "expressed satisfaction over the *Attentat*." But after Lidice there was "general consternation, even among workers."[37]

With allowances made for bias in this German report, it did seem to be true that the German occupation, intent on keeping the workers happy and busy producing armaments for the Wehrmacht, widened the split in Czech society between the laborers on one side and the middle class as well as the intelligentsia on the other.

A POSTMORTEM IS IN ORDER; IT IS WORTH EXAMINING MORE CLOSELY HOW the operation to kill Heydrich had come about in order to understand better what British motives there may have been, other than the simplistic one of removing a man whose dreadful deeds cried out for punishment.

Eduard Beneš, Free Czech president in London, was chagrined that the Czech Resistance had not been as effective as the British had hoped it would be. Perhaps this could be attributed to the fact that Heydrich had suddenly switched tactics, modifying his reign of terror with certain benefits calculated to win over the working class and isolate the intelligentsia. It was important for the Germans to keep Czech labor satisfied enough to produce armaments vital to Germany's war effort. When the Czech president proposed to his intelligence chief, František Moravec, an assassination operation to kill some prominent pro-Nazi collaborator, he hoped to overcome the Czech underground's reputation for passivity and stimulate a more widespread upheaval against the German occupiers by the people—and thus motivate the British to provide his movement with maximum moral and material assistance.

This represented a change of attitude that seemed to have owed its origin to both British and Soviet pressure. In mid-August 1941 the Soviets, who had recently recognized Beneš's government in London exile, were in a desperate situation and pressed the Czechs for sabotage operations against oil, rail, and industrial targets vital to the Nazis. At the time Beneš expressed himself frankly to his friend and champion within the British government Robert Bruce Lockhart, head of the Political Warfare Executive. He made it clear that the Czech underground army should not be put at risk of German reprisals that could destroy them and leave Czechoslovakia vulnerable to Communist influence.[38] Beneš then believed that a national uprising should be reserved for a time chosen by the London Czechs, not the Russians.* But the British too were making it clear to Beneš that the Czech Resistance was making a pallid effort, compared with the Resistance movements in France and the Netherlands.

Beneš's original instincts can also be seen from an even earlier conversation with Lockhart in October 1940, soon after Beneš's exodus from Prague. Beneš had then realized the problem of German reprisals when he told Lockhart that Resistance activity should be confined to undetectable acts, passive sabotage (industrial slowdowns, etc.), and intelligence gathering. Above all, open challenges to the Nazis should be avoided until the Reich was on the verge of collapse.[39]

Why, then, did Beneš change his attitude? It is likely that under implied pressure he had come to believe that a more aggressive Resistance would not only please the British and Soviets but also increase his own

---

*Soviet pressure on Beneš continued throughout the war. Lockhart, who was close to Beneš, having been British liaison man with him at the time the Czech government-in-exile was first established in London, discussed *Pravda* criticism of the lack of Czech Resistance activity (November 3, 1944). Beneš realized that the events following Heydrich's assassination had, for all practical purposes, brought an end to effective Czech resistance—Diaries of Robert Bruce Lockhart, War Notebook 54, 1954, House of Lords Record Office, File 313.

popularity and put his party in a stronger position to assume the reins of government in the restructuring of Czechoslovakia after the war—that is, of course, if Germany lost the war.

In August 1941, nearly two months before Konstantin von Neurath was replaced in Prague by Heydrich as *Reichsprotektor* (German proconsul), exiled President Beneš, for all his previously expressed reluctance to challenge the Germans, seemed to have changed his mind. He sent a secret message to Professor Ladislav Vaněk, an on-the-spot leader of the Czech Resistance in Prague, describing a daring plan meant to boost Czech morale by assassinating either Karl Hermann Frank, number two Nazi administrator in Prague, or, even better, the Czechoslovakian quisling minister, General Emanuel Moravec (not to be confused with the exile intelligence chief František Moravec in London).[40]

When Heydrich replaced Neurath in Prague, Beneš changed the target. Heydrich, whose image was infinitely more infamous, would instead be the target for assassination in what was called Operation Salmon. His death, Beneš hoped, would surely stir the Czechs to greater resolve.

Others felt differently: Beneš's message announcing his decision to proceed prompted an anguished protest from Vaněk and other Resistance leaders, who realized that the killing of a man of Heydrich's exalted position in the Nazi hierarchy would trigger serious German reprisals. Beneš, however, was undeterred, and planning in London with British SOE (Special Operations Executive) went forward.*

Careful British and Czech screening of expatriate Czechs produced the would-be assassins, Kubiss and Gabčik, as well as a trained radio operator named Bartos, all collectively now known by the team cryptonym An-

---

*Colonel Moravec in his memoir claimed to have warned Beneš that Heydrich's death at the hands of a Resistance assassin would result in heavy German reprisals: The "price would be high." Beneš, he claimed, insisted that this operation was "necessary for the good of the country"—František Moravec, *Master of Spies* (Garden City, N.Y.: Doubleday, 1975), p. 197.

President Beneš later reacted defensively to criticism that the assassination of Heydrich would bring terrible reprisals without achieving any useful results. Beneš in fact may have shifted the blame by announcing that General Moravec had planned and supervised the assassination.—R. C. Jaggers, "The Assassination of Reinhard Heydrich," *Central Intelligence Agency Studies in Intelligence* (Winter 1960), p. 14.

In fact, Moravec's protests were peremptorily cut off by Beneš's chief of staff, General Sergěj Ingr, who insisted that the decision had been made and could not be further questioned. Moravec was mystified, unable to account for this judgment—Zdenek Kordina, "Assassination of Reinhard Heydrich," *On All Fronts*, ed. Lewis White, (Boulder, Colo.: East European Monographs 442, distributed by Columbia University Press, 1995), p. 152.

thropoid. Selected from the twenty-five-hundred-man Czech brigade attached to the British armed forces, they were given special training in Scotland carried out under the supervision of a team of British SOE experts headed by a Colonel Wilson.[41]

From Prague by clandestine radio, Vanék continued to protest the operation. Beneš's responses seemed designed to relieve himself of responsibility if things went wrong; he implied that the Czech government in London was under British pressure to carry it out.[42] The Czech intelligence chief, Colonel Moravec, describes his dependency on the British in his memoir, *Master of Spies*, explaining that he had worked "almost exclusively with British Intelligence"* and had little ability to maneuver on his own.

The British had reacted strongly to Moravec's warning that Heydrich was closing in on the Czech Resistance and its intelligence apparatus. Of concern was Paul Thümmel (A-54), long of value to both Czech and British intelligence in his capacity as a senior officer of the Abwehr. British concerns, however, may have been much deeper; MI-6 had become alarmed by indications that Heydrich might soon force Canaris to relinquish much of his authority to the SD, if not to step down altogether and turn the Abwehr over to the SD. The exposure of Thümmel would deprive the British and the Czechs of one of their best agents—he had given advance notice of almost every major event of the war—but more significant, his capture would give Heydrich an excellent example of Abwehr "corruption," providing an excuse he needed to make his move against Canaris. It was in this atmosphere that the British Joint Intelligence Committee must have authorized the mission to kill Heydrich.[43]

Moravec remembered delivering the message from Vanék to Beneš and MI-6 chief Stewart Menzies. Moravec claimed to have learned after the war that it had been Menzies who insisted that the assassination operation proceed despite Vanék's objections.—Callum MacDonald, *The Killing of SS Obergruppen-Führer Reinhard Heydrich* (New York: Collier Books/Macmillan, 1989), p. 158, from Stanislav Berton, "Who Ordered the Assassination of R. Heydrich and Why," unpublished, p. 16.

*The operation targeting Heydrich for assassination was managed in London by the Special Operations Executive (SOE), although MI-6 obviously had an important interest in it. MI-6 chief Menzies, however, had little use for SOE. In a January 20, 1943, conversation with Robert Bruce Lockhart, who by this time was head of the Political Warfare Executive (PWE), Menzies told of his suspicions that the London Czechs were adulterating, or even inventing, intelligence reports from Czechoslovakia. He also suspected that SOE might be responsible for this state of affairs. Menzies went so far as to describe the SOE's Czech intelligence operations as false. The SOE, he believed, had not only achieved nothing but had even compromised MI-6 agents. In his opinion, the SOE consisted of a bunch of amateurs in political affairs—Diaries of Robert Bruce Lockhart, War Notebook 48, 1943, House of Lords Record Office, File 313.

IN PRAGUE HEYDRICH SPARED NO EFFORTS TO FIND BRITISH/FREE CZECH agent Paul Thümmel, whose existence the Gestapo now knew of but whose identity was still a mystery. The Gestapo referred to him as Traitor X. A Gestapo special squad dedicated to finding "X" included two officers, Will Leimer and "Commissar" Nachtmann, who in reality were Soviet NKVD agents who had connections in the Czech Resistance as well as had infiltrated the Gestapo in Prague. Their usefulness to the Soviets was in betraying members of the Czech underground since Stalin for political reasons did not like the fact that a Czech Resistance movement was guided by Beneš's London-based Czech government-in-exile.

Leimer and Nachtmann, using their Soviet resources, were able to discover X's hiding place and tipped off the Gestapo. X was arrested on October 13, 1941.[44] Gestapo interrogations of X, or Thümmel, revealed that he had met secretly with British agents Best and Stevens in Holland before they were captured at Venlo in 1939. Now known to be a British agent as well as working for the Free Czech movement in exile, X was even a bigger catch than the Gestapo first realized.

Positive identification of X as Thümmel and his Venlo linkage with British agents Best and Stevens was the handiwork of Gestapo agent Willi Abendschön, who had been the interrogator of the two kidnapped British officers as well as Thümmel so could spot the relationship.[45]

On being apprehended by the Gestapo, Thümmel nimbly claimed that he had played along with the Czech Resistance so that he could unravel its networks and bring about its demise—all part of his job with the Abwehr. When Canaris intervened in Thümmel's behalf, Heydrich agreed to release him to pursue his "quarry," Czech Resistance agents. But Thümmel was kept on a short tether and under constant surveillance. Finally, convinced of his guilt, the Gestapo jailed him again on March 2, 1942, only two months before Canaris and Heydrich were due to meet and ratify their new agreement. This action could well have been timed by Heydrich to keep pressure on Canaris during the course of their negotiations. Heydrich now had a lever with which to force Canaris to relinquish some of his authority.

Faced with the prospect of death, Thümmel through Czech Resistance radio contact had pleaded with his London masters to rescue him. The Anthropoid team was air-dropped in Czechoslovakia by a British RAF bomber piloted by Czech Captain Anderle on 15 April, but Thümmel by then was probably beyond saving, and anyway, the Anthropoids would not have been allowed to jeopardize the success of their mission to kill Heydrich by a complicating diversion to rescue Thümmel. The doomed agent paid the price of his elaborate games of deception.[46] He was executed by a firing squad on April 20, 1945, at the fortress prison of Theresienstadt.[47] His death deprived British intelligence of perhaps its best human source of the war and seriously endangered the Czech Resistance.

Thümmel's capture and interrogation were one more incident with which to fatten Heydrich's dossier proving Abwehr incompetence and perhaps disloyalty on Canaris's part, but this aside, the British had reason enough to worry about the Abwehr chief's continuing viability in light of the new agreement, the revision of the Ten Commandments signed under Heydrich's pressure. It was a harbinger of worse to come. While the unmasking of Thümmel was bad enough, Heydrich almost certainly knew of or suspected other scandals within the Abwehr with which to discredit Canaris.

BY SEPTEMBER 1942 THERE WOULD BE ANOTHER SCARE WHEN AN AMERICAN newspaper ran a sensational article revealing that Admiral Canaris himself was in a conspiracy against Hitler.[48] Ian Colvin, in his book on Canaris, told of a conversation he had held in the autumn of 1942 with a very senior British "intelligence officer," whom he described but did not name. When the American press printed its allegation that Canaris was plotting against Hitler, Colvin recalled his MI-6 friend's sadness and concern, lamenting that "Every time we build something up, something like this . . . destroys what we have built." Well acquainted with the German public psychology, Colvin made a suggestion: Through planted British press attacks against Canaris indicate to the Nazis the depths of British revulsion toward the admiral. In December 1942 this apparently was done. In what seemed to be an upwelling of British press vilification, Canaris was accused of being an evil genius of the Reich, an enemy of Britain, and a cold-blooded assassin—among other epithets.[49]

The prospect of Canaris and his relatively benign Abwehr's disappearing under Heydrich's relentless pressure must have been extremely worrisome to the British for a compelling and very specific reason. Facing the British was the terrible possibility that such a development would seriously put at risk Double-Cross, its control of the Abwehr's agent networks and their deception product so artfully crafted by British writers to mislead the Germans at every turn. If this capability were to be lost, the British not only would be deprived of a defensive counterespionage weapon of awesome effectiveness but would lose irreplaceable conduits for deception needed by the Allies to ensure a successful landing in France.

The truth of such speculation must await release of British intelligence files, but logic would suggest that this may have been the real reason why Heydrich had to die. While his death in Prague would not save the

Abwehr from eventual RSHA absorption, it did buy the British critically needed time and preserved the Double-Cross system, whatever Britain's motive may have been.

British MI-5 (security intelligence), responsible for protecting the Double-Cross system, considered any disruption of Abwehr agent nets to be one of the greatest threats to a successful landing in France. Heydrich's ambition to become czar of all German intelligence and counterintelligence, which could be realized only by getting rid of Canaris, would certainly disrupt the Abwehr. Contributing to this danger was the ever-increasing likelihood of defection by Abwehr officers, discrediting Canaris and his organization and leading to a thorough housecleaning that would likely sweep out Canaris's British-doubled agents on which Double-Cross depended, as well as Canaris himself.[50] John Masterman, a prime mover of Double-Cross, realized how precarious Abwehr stability was; in his post-war book on the Double-Cross system he admitted: "The margin of safety for our Double-Cross system was very small."[51] With the elimination of the Heydrich threat to the Abwehr, its demise was postponed by a crucial few months until other problems finally overwhelmed it. Describing Abwehr officer Erich Vermehren's defection in Turkey, used by Hitler as the ostensible excuse for firing Canaris in February 1944, Masterman wrote: ". . . we [Double-Cross] just and only just survived long enough."[52]

The astonishing British achievement in breaking German ciphers, the Ultra interceptions of German radio traffic, saved Great Britain from what might have been even worse aerial attacks during the Battle of Britain and fatally suffocating merchant marine losses to U-boat attack in the Battle of the Atlantic. But no less important were the so-called ISOS* interceptions made possible by breaking the Abwehr ciphers.[53] The cryptanalytical wizardry at Bletchley Park plus the inspired labors of the Twenty Committee, which designed deception scenarios according to the Double-Cross system, successfully misled the Germans about the forthcoming Allied landing sites in France. Simply described, the Double-Cross operations began with the interception and breaking of clandestine German spy radio transmissions, particularly within the British Isles, soon after the fall of France in 1940. Sophisticated methods of locating enemy agent transmitters—DFing (directional finding), as it was called—led Britain's internal security agency, MI-5, to German agent hideouts. But rather than incarcerate or kill all the captured agents, MI-5 induced some agents to maintain radio contact with Germany on schedule as though nothing had happened. In

---

*ISOS stands for Intelligence Service Oliver Strachey. Oliver Strachey, in his wartime vocation, was the brain behind the breaking of Abwehr ciphers at Bletchley Hall.

fact, they transmitted only what the British gave them to send. This built up a pattern of information with enough truth in it to maintain the agents' credibility but laced with deception designed to suit Allied purposes. The scriptwriting was done by a body of extremely talented specialists called the Twenty Committee; hence the symbol XX.[54] This deception system's greatest triumph was to convince the Germans that the Allies in Operation Overlord would launch their invasion at Pas-de-Calais, not the Normandy locations actually chosen. If the Germans had not been totally deceived about the site of the Allied landings, thanks to Double-Cross, the casualties at Normandy would have been dramatically higher and the invasion might even have failed.

Masterman, a member of the Twenty Committee and one of the most important players in the Double-Cross game, described their end objective: "to influence enemy plans by the answers sent to the enemy" by controlled German agents and "to deceive the enemy about our plans and intentions."[55] To the uninitiated who assume that counterespionage means the unmasking and incarceration of enemy spies, the Double-Cross system served as a vivid demonstration that the principal purpose of this fine art is to manipulate the enemy—an espionage jujitsu in which the enemy's guile and cleverness are turned against him. In this case Masterman could boast that the British Double-Cross operations "for the greater part of the War . . . did much more than practice a large-scale deception though double agents; [they] actively ran and controlled the German espionage system."[56]

It is important to realize that the British had an early start; they had broken the Abwehr hand ciphers at the beginning of 1940 and were able to read Abwehr machine ciphers beginning in 1942.[57] Note that the machine cipher breaking took place just before Canaris was made to sign the new agreement with Heydrich putting Abwehr independence in jeopardy. It would be understandable if the British considered this development to be ominous enough to warrant assassinating Heydrich to save a controlled Abwehr.

Plans for the invasion of North Africa, Operation Torch, were well under way during 1942, and Double-Cross was intended to play a major role in disguising the landing locations or even the fact that North Africa was the target. This was no time to see the status, much less the agent roster of the Abwehr, changed. Then, from 1944, the Allies devoted most of their energies to preparing for the Normandy landings when strategic deception would prove to be the keystone of their success. Masterman admitted that at some critical moment all the double agents feeding false intelligence into the Abwehr estimative machine might have to be "blown sky high in carrying out the grand deception," but this one great effort "would both repay us many times over for all the efforts of the previous years and bring our war to an end."[58]

The British surely did not want to see Canaris thrown out of his job and replaced by a Nazi zealot, such as Heydrich, who would eliminate all legacies of the Canaris regime, including the matrix of agents so carefully doubled and nurtured by the British. As Masterman categorically states in his book, the Double-Cross system would have been "endangered from internal changes in the German service."[59]

AFTER HEYDRICH'S FUNERAL ADMIRAL CANARIS THROUGH SPANISH CONtacts was emboldened to seek a personal meeting with MI-6 chief Menzies, possibly in neutral Portugal. Since World War I Menzies had followed Canaris's strange career and to the extent possible kept current on his activities with the German Resistance. He admired Canaris and had long wanted to meet him. The Allied invasion of North Africa provided Menzies with cover excuses to visit Mediterranean countries, including Portugal. He is believed to have had visions of reaching agreements with the Resistance through Canaris that could significantly shorten the war.[60]

Menzies had perceived the fine hand of the admiral in many otherwise unexplainable wartime happenings. Now Britain's mysterious benefactor wanted to see him face-to-face. The temptation was great, and Menzies was willing to risk it, but Anthony Eden would not hear of it. The foreign secretary feared it would alarm the paranoid Stalin, who never ceased to worry about a British effort to seek a separate peace with Germany at Russian expense. As would be discovered many years after the war, Stalin had Soviet spy Kim Philby, of high rank in MI-6, primed to keep him closely informed on this subject. The possibility of an Allied-German peace settlement excluding the Soviet Union was in fact Philby's top priority for the NKVD in World War II.

In his 1968 book *The Philby Affair*, Hugh Trevor-Roper writes that Canaris had made repeated visits to Spain during the early course of the war and had "indicated a willingness to treat with us: he would even welcome a meeting with his opposite number, 'C' [Menzies]."[61] An MI-6 study of Canaris and the German Resistance, very positive in tone, had been written in late 1942 by Trevor-Roper with the help of a specialist on Germany, Stuart Hampshire. The study concluded that clandestine collaboration with Canaris would be very useful and could be accomplished without violating agreements with Russia or Britain's unconditional surrender pledge. Trevor-Roper and Hampshire recommended that such collaboration should be attempted. Philby, however, objected to the study on the nebulous grounds it was "speculative." But his real reason, probably dictated to him by his NKVD control officer, was that an uprising against Hitler by the German Resistance would interfere with Stalin's plans to install a Soviet-controlled Communist puppet government in Germany after the war.

To what extent, if any, Philby's objections to dealing with Canaris were a factor in Foreign Secretary Eden's veto of Menzies's proposal to meet with Canaris is not apparent. It did, however, cast a pall within MI-6 on any idea of having a more dynamic relationship with Canaris. At least Heydrich's death provided Canaris with a respite from unwelcome harassment and kept the Abwehr from being absorbed by the SD for a critical period before the invasion of North Africa and while the Western Allies prepared for their ultimate assault on Europe, Overlord, the second front on which ultimate victory depended.

In this first major test of the British Double-Cross system, vital in itself and a useful learning experience in preparation for the later Normandy landings in France, the Western Allies went on the offensive. The North African landings were important in the context of Britain's North African campaign against General Rommel's Suez-bound Afrika Korps, but it would also make possible later Allied landings planned for Sicily, the Italian mainland, and southern France and bolster Spain's resolve to keep German troops out of Spain. Defensively the landings prevented German control of North Africa from Gibraltar to Suez and kept the Mediterranean Sea from becoming a German lake. And even if Stalin refused to concede its value to him, it did take at least some German pressure off the USSR along the eastern front and made possible a supply line to Russia by way of the Mediterranean and Iran.

From the American point of view, Operation Torch, the North African invasion, was the first major involvement of U.S. forces in the European war.

TWENTY-THREE

Operation Torch:
Allied Invasion of North Africa

THE ALLIED INVASION OF NORTH AFRICA CAME AS A RUDE SURPRISE TO Hitler. The reputation of the Abwehr and, tied to it, the personal fortunes of Admiral Canaris went into decline when Hitler learned with shock of the U.S.-British landings on November 8, 1942.

The German Kriegsmarine (Navy) reported at the end of October that a large Allied convoy had been sighted in the Atlantic approaching Africa but speculated that it was headed for Dakar, far south of Gibraltar on the western bulge of Africa. Earlier reports reaching the Germans of Allied invasion plans suggested that a major offensive could occur in a number of places. The British orchestration of misinformation, relying on double agent deception—the Double-Cross system—had thoroughly confused the enemy about Allied intentions. Heydrich was dead, but his heirs within the RSHA could take satisfaction in Canaris's failure, realizing it could be their gain in the ceaseless rivalry between the SD and the Abwehr.

The Führer's first news of Allied action in the Mediterranean reached him in his private railway car on November 7, as he sped toward Munich to participate in an anniversary of his abortive 1923 beer hall putsch. A teletype flashed the word at daybreak that an Allied fleet was entering the Strait of Gibraltar. General Jodl, chief of Hitler's personal military staff, whose intelligence files now bulged with Allied Double-Cross misinformation, had just concluded wrongly that the reported Allied convoy was probably headed for Malta.

Operation Torch, Allied code name for the North African landings, was a success. The German Army had been taken by complete surprise, although some Vichy French officials had nursed suspicions that it was imminent, and a very few knew where it would occur. The deception had been masterful: No significant German Army units had been rushed to the south to meet the landings, and German Mediterranean airpower remained concentrated far to the east, out of striking distance of Allied forces. The deception plan for Torch was the first major use of Double-Cross by the Western Allies[1] and served as an effective rehearsal for the later, climactic landings in Normandy.

Churchill had convinced Roosevelt that for all Stalin's pressure, the Allies were not yet ready to risk an invasion of metropolitan France. A North African landing in late 1942 was not what Stalin wanted, even though it would relieve some of the pressure on the Red armies fighting for their existence along the eastern front. The Soviet leader wanted the Western Allies to launch a full and definitive invasion of metropolitan France itself. From the British point of view, Torch would be important not only to secure North Africa and control the Mediterranean but to involve the United States actively in the war against Hitler rather than allow it to focus exclusively on the Pacific war with Japan.

It had been with some reluctance that the United States joined the British. At the Arcadia Conference held in Washington from December 22, 1941, to January 14, 1942, Churchill and Roosevelt had planned the Allied grand strategy: The United States and Great Britain agreed to keep the Germans out of North Africa, dominate the Mediterranean, and, by a preemptive invasion of the northwestern African coast, provide a launching ground for an assault on Italy, Europe's soft underbelly, as Winston Churchill referred to it. Torch would also provide another claw with which to trap Rommel's retreating Afrika Korps in a pincer.

ALLIED STRATEGIC THINKING IN JANUARY 1942 CANNOT BE FULLY UNDERstood unless viewed against a backdrop of developments in North Africa and the Middle East that began to unfold a year earlier. In view of the lackluster performance of Italian troops in Libya, Mussolini agreed to Hitler's proposal to send the broad-gauged General Erwin Rommel with a German armored and motorized expeditionary force to provide punch for Axis efforts to invade Egypt from Libya. The Afrika Korps, as it was known, was created in February 1941. Rommel's mission was to seize the Suez Canal, cutting off the British from their Near East bases and their Indian empire beyond. A critical part of this strategy concerned oil, badly needed by Germany, whose tanks and aircraft depended on it. The road to the oilfields of Iran and Iraq was Suez.

In coordination with Rommel's Libyan and Egyptian campaign, the Germans planned to push through the Balkans, cutting across Turkey to reach the Mosul oilfields in northern Iraq. While German troops handily took Bulgaria in March, Turkey was a tougher problem; German Ambassador Franz von Papen in Ankara warned that Turkey would not permit the Germans to cross its territory and would fight to prevent it. But if the Turks could not be easily brought into the German camp, they were relatively permissive in permitting German intelligence operations aimed at the Near and Middle East to be run from Turkey.* The Turks were to prove equally hospitable to covert activities run from Turkey into the Balkans by the British and later by the Americans.

Admiral Canaris placed Paul Leverkühn in Ankara to head Abwehr operations in Turkey and the Middle East. Canaris calculated that not only was Leverkühn a capable operator, but his background as a man known to the OSS's Donovan since prewar days in Washington would well suit Canaris's secret Resistance agenda after the Americans joined the war and set up their own intelligence apparatus in Istanbul. Canaris valued Leverkühn not only as a friend but as someone who felt as he did about the Nazis. Leverkühn was, moreover, close to Helmuth von Moltke, the prominent member of the Kreisau Circle of the Resistance.

Operating in competition with Leverkühn's Abwehr nets was the SD station chief, L. C. Moyzisch, who made intelligence history as the case handler of the British ambassador's Albanian butler, Elyesa Bazna, better known by his code name, Cicero. Bazna nightly rifled Ambassador Hughe Knatchbull-Hugessen's safe for valuable Allied secrets of war. Papen as usual stood balanced on a tightrope, ready to leap in whatever direction the fortunes of war indicated.

Canaris exploited his several good contacts in the Near and Middle East in pursuit of Germany's objectives. However much he secretly opposed Hitler's war aims, he had to give a credible performance as Germany's military intelligence chief if he was to stay in his job, and staying in his job was vital to the Resistance.

*American descriptions of Japanese messages, known by the code word Magic, shed considerable light on events in Europe, thanks to the cipher traffic generated by the well-informed Japanese ambassador in Berlin, Hiroshi Oshima, and other Japanese diplomats in Europe. A cable sent in early 1942 by the ambassador reported on Russian plans to expand Communist influence throughout Asia. A Japanese diplomat in Sofia reported more specifically on increasing Russian interest in Iran. Iran had already virtually handed over control of two of its northern provinces to the USSR, and the Soviets were intriguing among the Kurds, urging them to establish an autonomous state of Kurdistan. The Japanese minister in Sofia warned Tokyo of Russia's plan to control the Near East and India and urged speed in bringing India under Japanese control. A German advance into the Near East was seen as a necessary adjunct to the Japanese effort.—Bruce Lee, Marching Orders, the Untold Story of World War II (New York: Crown Publishers, 1995), pp. 26–28.

Canaris arranged to have his close friend Hadji Amin al-Husseini, the Grand Mufti of Jerusalem, the most influential Muslim cleric at this time, invited to Berlin on occasion. They would talk of "holy war" against the British in the Near East. In Iraq another Canaris friend, Rashid Ali al-Gaylani, in mid-May staged an anti-British coup d'état and installed a short-lived pro-German government in Baghdad that seized the Mosul oil-fields from the British.

In February 1941 Canaris sent Abwehr officer Berthold Schulze-Holthus to Iran, where he was to recruit agents in Azerbaijan for assignments to the USSR's oil-rich Baku on the west coast of the Caspian Sea. Later Schulze-Holthus intrigued with some of the southern tribes of Iran within stalking distance of the British oil installations in the Abadan area. The SD too had an agent in Iran, Franz Mayr, who worked the area closer to Teheran and Isfahan in a curious competition with the Abwehr.

Iran, divided between a British sphere of interest in the south and a Soviet sphere in the north, was a important hunting ground for German agents since its ruler, Shah Reza Pahlevi, was sympathetic toward Germany—a posture designed to hold at bay both his northern neighbor Russia and his southern neighbor the British Raj in India. Now that these two giants were allied, the traditional Iranian game of playing them off against each other would no longer work. Germany was the shah's only hope as a benign patron and, he hoped, a protector if it proved successful in its campaigns against the USSR.

The British, always sensitive to their Near Eastern strategic position as well as dependent on Middle East oil to fuel their navy, watched with dismay as the German Army moved southward, first against Yugoslavia and Greece in April. Syria too had fallen under German influence as a French-mandated country controlled by Vichy; in view of Turkey's obstinance, Syria loomed large in the German scheme of things as an alternative route to Iraq's oil.

British and Free French forces in a little-known campaign ousted the Vichy French from Syria on July 12, 1941. Then, to protect its oil interests in Iraq and Iran, as well as to gain access to trans-Iran road and rail routes that would soon be used by the American Army to supply the USSR from the Persian Gulf, Rashid Ali was turned out of Iraq. As part of this strategy, the British on August 25 invaded Iran from the Persian Gulf while the Soviets descended on Iran from the Caucasus. The British exiled Shah Reza Pahlevi for his pro-German bias, replacing him on the throne by his more pliable young son.

The British had at first not been as successful in the eastern Mediterranean and Egypt. The strategically important British-occupied island of Crete was attacked by a German airborne invasion on May 14, 1941. While the Germans succeeded in taking Crete, it was a costly campaign, one that almost failed. The Germans lost some four hundred aircraft and nearly sixteen thousand troops killed in action.

The battle for Crete was significant, not only because Britain lost a key bastion in the Mediterranean but because it was one of the earliest battles in which the British had the benefit of Ultra. While the Germans narrowly won the Crete campaign, they were astonished and dismayed by the defenses put up by their enemy. Moreover, the German ships and planes lost at Crete had been needed for a planned invasion of Syria to preempt its capture by the British and Free French. Without them the campaign could not and did not take place.

The Germans never seemed to have realized that their enemy's uncanny ability to foresee their every move and react accordingly might have been made possible by British cipher traffic interceptions. British security to protect Ultra in this engagement had been so strict that even the British commanding officer, General Bernard Freyberg, was not made fully aware of the source of his remarkable battle order intelligence. Had he realized the utter reliability of his information, he might have acted more boldly, conceivably turning back the Germans in this close-run battle.

At least one German, a veteran signals officer experienced enough to realize that Britain's unerring accuracy in tactical decisions on Crete could have been only the result of signals interceptions, went unnoticed. The Ultra secret survived this early test of its security; the Germans concluded that the British must have had some exceptional agent penetration of the German High Command.[2]

This demonstration of Ultra's value in combat made a profound impression on Churchill, who later announced enigmatically before the House of Commons that the British had been fully informed of the impending German battle plan for Crete.[3]

In the western end of the Mediterranean, Torch depended on Ultra. U.S. forces had to slip through submarine-infested Atlantic waters for forty-five hundred miles and coordinate their attack with the British and American assault force sailing from Britain. Unfortunately the operation coincided with a period when Ultra naval intercepts had been temporarily cut off, blinding the Admiralty to German U-boat deployment. On the brighter side, a string of technically sophisticated listening posts maintained by Canaris's Abwehr along the Mediterranean coastline in Spain to monitor British shipping were shut down by Franco under intense Allied diplomatic pressure.

The breaking of Abwehr Ultra ciphers (Operation ISOS) in December 1941 gave the SIS several months in which to uncover Canaris's Abwehr operational structure throughout Iberia. Of particular worry in reference to the upcoming Torch landings were the Abwehr's station in Algeciras, which monitored ship movements through the Strait of Gibraltar, and substations at Tangier and Ceuta on the African side, from which British convoy movements could also be watched. Most dangerous of all was an Abwehr operation code-named Bodden begun in the autumn of 1941 by which infrared and shortwave devices as well as special night telescopes mounted in fourteen strategic locations could monitor British convoys at night and during low-visibility days.[4] Abwehr-instigated sabotage conducted against British shipping and shore facilities at Gibraltar in cooperation with the Spanish Army also posed a significant threat to the planned invasion. All this was a more technically advanced rerun of Canaris's World War I actions against the Western Allies. It was now important that the British for the sake of Torch convince the "neutral" Spanish and the Portuguese that aid and comfort to the Germans must stop.

In early 1942 the British with American help undertook a diplomatic offensive in Madrid and Lisbon. British MI-6 evidence of Abwehr activity in Iberia, based mainly on intercepts of Abwehr messages (ISOS), convinced Franco that he should intervene with the Abwehr, forcing it to dismantle its monitoring sites. It should be noted that it had been the British turncoat Kim Philby who had artfully camouflaged the true source of the evidence in order to protect ISOS before Ambassador Hoare passed it on to Franco.[5] It must therefore be assumed that Philby's masters in Moscow could and would carefully follow these developments. Antonio de Oliviera Salazar of Portugal also took action against the more flagrant Abwehr anti-British operations.[6]

The Abwehr special surveillance devices were finally dismantled by Canaris under pressure from Franco, who explained that he wanted to avoid any pretext for the Allies to invade Spain.[7] Canaris must have found it difficult to lodge anything more than pro forma objections to this decision in view of his own past advice to the Caudillo that he should avoid provoking the Western Allies.

The real significance of British action against Bodden, from an intelligence point of view, was that it represented the first rebuff of Canaris in Spain by his friend Franco; more broadly it was a reflection of Franco's recognition that in view of probable Allied landings in North Africa, he would do well to continue resisting continuing German efforts to get him into the war.

Kim Philby, while visiting Spain in 1942, played a role in the Bodden affair. From his exile in Moscow, long after his flight from Beirut in January 1963, he wrote in his book *My Silent War* that he had masterminded Sir Samuel Hoare's protests to Franco. The British ambassador's démarche was drafted by Philby in such a way as to reveal that not only were the British on to Bodden, but they had thoroughly penetrated the Abwehr networks in Spain. Franco tipped off Canaris to this, as was hoped and expected, with the result that the Abwehr became defensive and realized it would be futile to argue with Franco over Bodden.[8]

In the latter part of 1942 Philby received another ISOS intercept that caught his attention: Canaris, during his visit to Spain, planned to drive to Seville, spending a night en route in a town named Manzanares. Knowing Spain well from his Civil War days as a correspondent, Philby guessed that Canaris would put up at the only decent inn, the Parador. In view of his standing instructions from Moscow to do all he could to discredit Canaris and cripple the Abwehr, Philby shot off a message to SIS London urging that the action lads at the SOE be tasked to murder Canaris by throwing a grenade through his hotel window after he had gone to bed.[9]

While MI-6 deputy chief Felix Cowgill approved the operation, it was immediately vetoed by his boss, Menzies. Things had changed since World War I, when Allied counterintelligence had tried to capture Canaris off the Spanish coast to prevent him from doing what he was doing now. In this war Canaris was too valuable to the Allies in his Resistance role and probably for other services rendered more indirectly. Particularly because he was a Soviet agent, Philby saw Canaris as a menace; he was a threat to Stalin. But Menzies saw the Abwehr chief as a boon to the Western Allies because of his hostility toward Hitler. Later, when Philby had the occasion to question Menzies about his refusal to have Canaris murdered, the MI-6 chief replied enigmatically, "I've always thought we could do something with the Admiral."[10] And indeed, it had been a disappointment to Menzies that Foreign Secretary Eden had not allowed him to respond positively to Canaris's request for a face-to-face meeting in Spain or Portugal. Philby claimed to have learned later that Menzies "was in touch with Canaris via a cut-out in Sweden." This must have been most interesting to Stalin when he heard about it from Philby; it certainly would have fed his festering suspicion that the British would ultimately make common cause with Germans against him.

It is worth noting that MI-6 officer Desmond Bristow in a 1993 memoir of his war experiences describes a trip to Algeciras in Spain on the eve of Torch, during which he was informed of a pending visit by Canaris to the area. Discovering that the admiral would be staying at the Hotel Reina

Christina, Bristow claims that he radioed London suggesting that he "have a go" at capturing him. As in Philby's similar story, London's reply made it clear that under no circumstances should Canaris "be threatened in any way whatsoever." In his book Bristow suggests that MI-6 feared that if the Abwehr chief were captured, all the German ciphers would be changed, nullifying the Ultra advantage.[11] Here again, as in the Heydrich case, is a suggestion that MI-6 feared grave problems concerning the survival of Ultra if Canaris were removed from play.

THE BRITISH DECEPTION PROGRAM SPECIFICALLY IN PREPARATION FOR Torch was managed in London by the newly formed security body called the London Controlling Section, headed by Major Sir Ronald Wingate, Flight Lieutenant D. Y. Wheatley (better known as the British mystery writer Dennis Wheatley), and H. L. Petavel. The object of this group was to keep the Germans confused about Allied intentions. Through misinformation transmitted by British-controlled German agents, false rumor campaigns, and other devious means, it was first made to appear that the Allies intended to invade the Continent somewhere along the Norwegian coast (Operation Solo I) or the French coast (Operation Overthrow) in the area of Pas-de-Calais. Hitler, who had long been nervous about possible Allied action in Norway, was easy to convince. He would not hear of depleting German forces that might be needed for the defense of Norway, and Field Marshal von Rundstedt, commander in chief, West, kept his forces tied down in France for some two months rather than risk an Allied invasion in this sector.

By the time it became obvious that nothing would occur in Europe, a new British deception campaign made it appear that Allied forces were pointing toward the Middle East. Word was put out that a Gibraltar buildup, difficult to hide, was a forerunner of an operation to rescue a beleaguered Malta. To confuse things more, a concentration of landing craft in Gibraltar was described in agent misinformation reports as intended for an invasion of Dakar, French West Africa.[12]

A British-intercepted Abwehr message dated October 5 from Madrid quoted a report from the Spanish ambassador in London also warning that a Dakar landing was momentarily expected.[13] Then, as D Day neared, the Germans were further confused when they heard that the Allies were planning an imminent invasion of Sicily and the foot of the Italian boot. These latter reports neatly accounted for sightings of Alled convoys actually entering the Strait of Gibraltar.[14] In the meantime German U-boats had been thrown off the scent by a British convoy of empty ships deadheading it to the U.K. from Sierra Leone in West Africa. Dealing with this target of opportunity distracted the Germans, preventing their wolf packs from spotting the North Africa–bound armada.[15]

The Allied invasion convoys had been able to enter the Mediterranean without interference. By the time sightings were made, the German OKW still believed that they were headed for Sicily: "If it is intended to break through the Sicilian Channel, having regard to the strength and make-up of the formation, we must take into account the possibility of a landing being made in the Tripoli-Benghazi area, in Sicily or Sardinia, apart from supplying Malta."[16] Rome Radio interrupted programs to warn the people of Sicily and Calabria of probable Allied landings.[17] The Germans, it was later discovered, also feared a Libyan and Tunisian landing to catch Rommel's army as it fell back from El Alamein.

The effectiveness of British Double-Cross deceptions was a product of uncommon skill on the part of those writing the disinformation scenarios and those orchestrating the efforts of a half dozen or so controlled double agents. Success was assured by Ultra intercepts of German military traffic that told the British what the Germans were believing—or not believing—as a result of the deception programs. The success of Ultra's role in Torch was not only that the desired misinformation was effectively planted on the Germans but that the real plan was never suspected. From Ultra the British could tell that the November 8 landings had been an unqualified surprise.

Admiral Canaris, supposedly Germany's Mediterranean expert, was of course the butt of criticism within Hitler's High Command. The Abwehr suffered accordingly from this colossal intelligence failure. When news of the landings first arrived, Jodl erupted in anger: "Once again, Canaris had let us down through his irrationality and instability."* But the admiral had not been as poorly informed as he was made out to be.

"Noise," a superabundance of conflicting reports, most of which had been sent by Double-Cross, had been a problem for the Wehrmacht, as the British meant it to be. Indications of Allied landing sites had ranged from Norway to Dakar as well as Sicily and Malta, yet Canaris could point to certain of his reports that had been on or close to the mark. Why had the OKW not listened to him? An early report from Abwehr sources in the Vat-

---

*Not all the generals were as ill informed. A month or so before the Allied invasion Field Marshal Albert Kesselring radioed Berlin that he was sure that the invasion would be in North Africa, Sicily, or Sardinia. This was not a very precise estimate, but the Marshal used it to justify troop reinforcements for Sicily and southern Italy, where they would be nearer to the scene of action. At the same time Rommel radioed Kesselring that he intended to retreat back to El Agheila at the Tripolitanian border in the expectation of a possible Allied North African landing—J. C. Masterman, *The Ultra Secret* (London: Weidenfeld & Nicolson, 1974), p. 93.

ican, for example, predicted an October American landing in Dakar coinciding with a British landing in Algiers.[18] That was close.* And Canaris's man in Hamburg, Captain Herbert Wichmann, had sent a highly rated report to the OKW stating that there would be an Allied landing in French North Africa.[19]

One of the more intriguing stories involving Canaris's prior knowledge of Torch involved an interesting cast of characters. In mid-1942 Colonel Franz Seubert, Abwehr representative with the Western Army Command, met in Rome with the pro-German Muslim leader Hadji Amin al-Husseini, Grand Mufti of Jerusalem, and received from him a startling report meant for Canaris. The Grand Mufti had been a friend as well as professional contact of the admiral's since 1938, when they had met in Baghdad at a time when German intrigues against British influence in Mesopotamia were gaining momentum. The Mufti fled Iraq after the collapse of an anti-British uprising led by the Arab nationalist leader Rashid Ali al-Gaylani and found asylum in Rome under Mussolini's protection. From there he continued his Middle East machinations in behalf of the Axis.

The Japanese ambassador in Rome, always alert to intelligence concerning Asia, reported to Tokyo that the Grand Mufti and Rashid Ali had requested written guarantees from the Germans and Italians that when the Axis won the war, the Arab countries of the Middle East would be granted real independence. Count Ciano, Italian foreign minister, and Ribbentrop, Germany's foreign minister, in response gave them secret letters promising to support the independence of those Arab countries currently under British jurisdiction.[20] Germany obviously did not find it politic to promise independence for Arabs under French rule.

What the Grand Mufti now showed Seubert in greatest confidence was an amazingly detailed report on the imminent Allied invasion of North Africa. The Grand Mufti would not at first disclose the origin of the report, but the letter told of an Allied landing scheduled for early November, probably between the fifth and tenth of that month. The strength of the invading force would be nine American divisions transported from the United States and five from the United Kingdom. This operation would precede an invasion of Italy.

---

*In a British intercept of September 28, 1942, a German agent reported that he had heard from Vatican contacts that the American invasion force would make a landing in Dakar in mid-October while the British with the help of Gaullist French troops would attempt a landing in Algiers. The report was in part accurate in predicting this would be followed by Allied invasions of Sicily, Sardinia, and southern France in the area of Toulon and Nice—Piece 932, dated September 28, 1942, British Public Record Office, Kew, HW 1.

Colonel Seubert finally cajoled the Grand Mufti into revealing his source by promising not to tell anyone but Canaris. The Grand Mufti's caution was justified: The information came from no less a personage than Muhammad V, the Sultan of Morocco, who had joined with Moroccan nationalists in plotting with the Germans against French rule but, hedging his bets, was at the same time on good terms with the British and Americans whose great secret he was nonetheless divulging.

Seubert's information excited Canaris; it fitted with other agent reports of a strong British naval force anchored off Gibraltar.[21] Without giving away the sultan's identity, the Abwehr chief showed Keitel the report, only to have him ridicule it. In an effort to humiliate Canaris even more, Keitel reported to him that Hitler too scoffed at it. Both were by now convinced that Sicily and Sardinia were the targets of the Allied naval task force.

Hitler had commented to Keitel: "Canaris is a fool. He swallows everything the Americans feed him. Give me a rest from Abwehr reports which are always defeatist and always wrong."[22] Had Canaris revealed the sultan of Morocco as his source, Keitel's and Hitler's reaction might well have been quite different. It is easy to speculate that Canaris purposely did not do so. Colonel Heinz of the Abwehr stated after the war that Canaris had deliberately downplayed advance reports of the North African landings.[23]

Operation Torch marked the beginning of a period of crisis leading to the fall of the Abwehr. Its failure to forecast the Allied landings correctly, or at least convincingly, followed by similar failures in predicting Operation Husky, the Allied invasion of Sicily in July 1943, and the fall of Mussolini would contribute to the growing fragility of Canaris's position.[24]

THE ALLIES, TO THE CONTRARY COULD BATHE IN THE SUCCESS OF THE landings, which had been so successfully kept secret from the German High Command. But problems enough, political as well as military, still faced the Allies. Canaris received an agent report on November 11, three days after the invasion, that the Moroccans were becoming disillusioned with the Americans, who were making statements favoring continued support for French rule over the country. Realizing this, the OSS attempted to send out American broadcasts aimed at mollifying the Riff tribesmen and Berbers of Morocco by holding out hopes for postwar independence from France. The broadcasts were produced by one of Bill Donovan's men, anthropologist Carleton Coon of Harvard, who was well acquainted with the Riff. This talented operator turned out near-poetic rhetoric calculated to soften the hearts of the most cynical natives: "Behold, We the American Holy Warriors have arrived. Our numbers are as the leaves on the forest trees and as the grains of sand in the sea. We have come here to fight the great Jihad of Freedom. We have come to set you free."[25]

There were, in fact, signs that Roosevelt, certainly no imperialist, was still open-minded on the matter. At a dinner with the sultan during the Casablanca meetings Roosevelt, to Churchill's dismay, seemed to encourage Morocco's would-be ruler by promising American aid with which to develop his realm—without reference to Charles de Gaulle.

A free-flowing conversation about the war and forthcoming Allied military objectives found its way to Canaris by way of a letter sent in secret by the sultan. Sharing some of the information it contained with Hitler, Canaris sought to convey a pessimistic picture of the Axis military position in the Mediterranean now that the United States and Great Britain had gained a foothold in North Africa. The forthcoming battle for Tunisia would be critical to German fortunes.

Canaris met in person with his friend the Grand Mufti on December 9, 1942, in Rome. In the presence of Abwehr officers Seubert and Lahousen, the Arab leader asked Canaris to use his resources in backing rebellion against France in Algeria, French Morocco, and Tunisia. Almost certainly connected with this was a December 11 Abwehr message, probably from a special detachment in Wiesbaden, querying a person in the Control Inspectorate, Africa in Tunisia for an estimate of how quickly and successfully Tunisians could be incited to insurrection through the influence of the Grand Mufti.[26] Influenced by a cautious Ribbentrop, Hitler vetoed such operations. German official policy had to be more circumspect. The Germans did, however, agree to having the Tunisian nationalist leader Habib Bourguiba, released from a French jail. But Bourguiba took haven in Egypt rather than risk problems with the Free French in Tunisia.* While in Egypt, Bourguiba became friendly with another Canaris contact, Anwar al-Sadat, destined one day to become president of Egypt.[27]

IT OFTEN SEEMED THAT THE LOGISTICAL AND SECURITY INTRICACIES of the North African invasion were exceeded in complexity by French politics. The original problem for the Allies had been to seize French North Africa without provoking Vichy hostility and, preferably, to gain Vichy French forces as allies to facilitate the landings. In the spring of 1941, well in ad-

---

*Bourguiba also visited the United States, where he lobbied for Tunisian independence. Generally ignored by American officialdom, the financially strapped Bourguiba was grateful for free room and board offered by a medium-grade Arab-American naval officer who felt sorry for him and put him up in his modest flat in Arlington, Virginia.

vance of the landing, Robert Murphy, second in charge of the U.S. mission in Vichy, had been sent to Algiers in an effort to negotiate with General Maxime Weygand, then Vichy's "delegate," or governor, in charge of North and West Africa, for the importation of badly needed American foodstuffs and other goods. The terms of the agreement permitted the United States to station "vice-consuls" in Casablanca, Algiers, Tunis, Ora, Bizerte, and Safe, who would monitor the trade and see to it that American goods were not being transshipped to the Germans in occupied France. In fact, the vice-consul/monitors, known as Murphy's twelve apostles, were Donovan's intelligence agents,[28] directed to master the political-military complexities of North Africa and otherwise do what was necessary to prepare the way for Torch.

There were those who thought Murphy made too many secret concessions to men who had collaborated with the Germans. Certainly Free French leader Charles de Gaulle in London looked glumly on this American sortie into French politics and wanted nothing to do with Vichy, however expedient it may have seemed. In the subterranean world of French North African politics, people opposing Murphy spread salacious gossip linking him romantically with the Princesse de Ligne, an agent of the comte de Paris, pretender to the long-defunct French throne and an active player in the North African struggle for power. This reinforced Murphy's critics in their opposition to him.

The twelve apostles had done their jobs well, but they could not promise uncontested landings. Further negotiation was necessary. On October 22 Major General Mark Clark, deputy commander of Torch under Eisenhower, made a daring landing by submarine near Cherchel on a lonely beach west of Algiers so that he could be introduced by Murphy to the chief of staff of French forces in North Africa and five other anti-German conspirators. The American choice of General Henri Honoré Giraud, recently escaped from German detention, was generally accepted as a rallying point for French forces if he could be exfiltrated from France and brought to North Africa in time for the landings. But the French conferees were by no means certain that all French forces would take orders from General Giraud, particularly if his appointment was suddenly sprung on them during the invasion.

As a foreshadow of unforeseen problems that would bedevil the North African enterprise, the conferees at the remote farm on the beach suddenly received word that the police, obviously tipped off, were on their way to see what was going on. Since discovery of this secret meeting would be disastrous, there was a mad scramble to disperse. General Clark and his men stuffed themselves into a hidden wine cellar, while the French principals left for Algiers. Once General Clark and his party under cover of darkness managed to escape to a waiting submarine, the farm's owner, Jacques Teissier, convinced the local police commissioner that the American Murphy and some friends had only been enjoying a few days with some "ladies"—nothing more sinister than a rather rowdy *bamboula*. According to press stories that eventually came out, the only casualty of the whole affair had been General Clark's pants, lost to the high seas as he furiously paddled through the surf to the submarine.*

It soon became clear that Giraud would not be able to arrange a complete French cease-fire during the Allied invasion. But a fortuitous coinci-

---

*The clandestine rendezvous of American officers and key Frenchmen dedicated to planning a successful Allied landing in North Africa was later described in all its breathless drama by the owner of the meeting site and courageous host, Jacques Teissier. Isolated and close to the beach, Teissier's farm, called Sitges, was ideally near Algiers, some twenty kilometers west of Cherchel. To prevent inopportune interruptions, Teissier had arranged that two cooperative members of the coast guard serve as guards. Lieutenant Le Nen and Cadet Michel were enlisted to patrol the neighborhood on the lookout for unwelcome intruders.

The first rendezvous date, October 19, 1942, was missed. Alerted that the American emissaries would be landed from submarine and paddle ashore in canoes (dinghies) the following night at ten, plans were again made to receive them securely at Sitges. By 7:00 P.M. on the twentieth, Henri d'Astier de la Vigerie, Jean Rigaud, and Lieutenant Colonel Louis G. M. Jousse, representing the French, arrived. Chief of the French mission General Charles Emanuel Mast arrived early the following morning along with Lieutenant Colonel A. S. van Ecke and Captain Watson. Robert Murphy and Ridgway Knight, in charge of American onshore planning for the North African landings, drove in from Algiers by auto a few minutes later.

All went well as four dinghies came ashore from the Allied submarine. General Mark Clark leaped ashore to embrace a relieved Robert Murphy. The rest of his party included Brigadier General Lyman Lemnitzer, Colonel A. M. Hamblen, Colonel Julius Holmes, and Captain Wright. Three British officers, not named by Teissier in his description of events, were also in the party.

The morning and early afternoon of October 21 were taken up with detailed negotiations regarding the imminent Allied landing forces. But the late afternoon brought near disaster. Two local painters, it seemed, had by chance come upon Teissier's farm and witnessed the arrival of Murphy and Knight and reported it to the police. This unsettling news was learned by the guard Michel when he encountered Cherchel's police commissioner in the nearby village of Gouraya that afternoon while reconnoitering the area.

Michel was able to make a quick phone warning to the group at Sitges farm. The fast-thinking cadet managed to forestall a raid by the police, promising to investigate the matter himself and report more definitively on what was going on. After Michel's call the farm was a scene of confusion while everyone burned incriminating maps and papers. The French participants left quickly by auto for Algiers, but high seas prevented an immediate departure by Clark and his group. Clark himself and his aide were hidden in

dence occurred—if it was a coincidence. Vichy's Admiral Jean François Darlan, next in rank to Pétain in French military authority and the one man who could command the French forces in North Africa with conviction and have them obey, had arrived in North Africa on the eve of the invasion to see his son, stricken by sudden illness. He was prevailed upon by the Allies to use his authority and declare a general cease-fire by the French.

A German intelligence message from Vichy to Berlin in mid-September claimed that Darlan and Pétain had recently reached agreement that German demands on the French should be resisted. The message, deciphered by the British, also referred to General Weygand's continuing unyielding attitude toward the Germans and a belief within the Vichy government that he had reached an understanding with the Americans on matters bearing on the defense of North Africa.[29]

Darlan, one of Admiral Canaris's many contacts, may well have had him to thank for advance knowledge that the Allies were poised to invade although this is only conjecture. Having long secretly opposed Hitler's plans to occupy Spain, Canaris understandably would have been appre-

---

a wine cellar while the others in his party hid in the woods or dragged out the dinghies for departure as soon as the weather would permit.

Murphy and Knight, on the advice of their host, Teissier, converted the dining room to a tableau of debaucherie: wine bottles strewn about and general disorder suggesting hard partying. The two Americans with Teissier and Lieutenant Le Nen positioned themselves at a poker table and prepared to act appropriately drunk should the police arrived.

At nine-thirty that night Michel finally arrived, one jump ahead of a police contingent preparing to raid the farm. He was appalled that Clark and party had not yet left. To buy time until the seas subsided, Murphy and Teissier instructed Michel to return to the police commissioner and hold him off by saying that "there were some Americans on the farm, but that it was Murphy and Knight who were simply having a raucous party with some women from Algiers and were completely drunk." In an appeal to his sense of honor, the police chief was to be advised that it would not be right for him to see "representatives of a great nation in such a state." The ruse worked, and the police agreed not to send an investigating party until the following morning.

Not until just before dawn on the twenty-second did General Clark and party finally navigate the heavy surf and make their getaway. One of the dinghies overturned, giving rise to the oft-repeated press story that Clark had lost his pants and dollar-stuffed wallet to the sea. But all hands made it to the waiting submarine just in time. By 5:00 A.M. a relieved Jacques Teissier and coastguardsmen Michel and Le Nen had cleaned up any remaining evidence of the night's drama. Murphy and Knight returned safely to Algiers, remembered by the local constabulary only for their epic *bamboula*, as the local folk referred to the American orgy—Jacques Teissier, "Notes sur la Mission du General Clark en Afrique du Nord." Private library.

hensive about a botched Allied landing in North Africa that would provide time and excuse for German troops to occupy Spain and seize Gibraltar whether Franco wanted it or not. He may have realized that only Darlan could ensure an unopposed and quick Allied landing.

In the campaign for Tunisia, follow-up to the invasion of Algeria and Morocco, Eisenhower and Clark were very aware of the danger of a German attack through Spain, outflanking the Allies. Thanks to a series of operations conducted during the spring of 1942, when the OSS burgled the Spanish Embassy in Washington, stealing ciphers essential to British efforts to read Spanish traffic at Bletchley Park, the United States was alerted to this possibility. And a British intercept of an August German message stated that Darlan had then been willing to facilitate the passage of German troops through Tunisia.[30]

SPAIN'S ATTITUDE WAS IMPORTANT TO AN ALLIED SUCCESS. A DECIPHERED Spanish message revealed that Foreign Minister Ramón Serrano Súñer, Franco's pro-Nazi son-in-law, was pressing for active Spanish participation in the war on Germany's side. Then an OSS agent in Lisbon acquired a Spanish merchant marine instruction dated July 1, 1942, warning Spanish ships to avoid nonfriendly ports—i.e., Allied ports—and be prepared for sudden hostilities. Despite such provocative reports, Spanish diplomatic traffic broken by the British at Bletchley revealed that Franco did not intend to join Hitler in the war unless the Allies attacked him.[31] There were, however, internal schisms within Spain that threatened dangerous volatility.

The Allies were able to gain considerable insight into the politics of Spain during those critical days preceding the North African landings by intercepting diplomatic traffic from such interested observers as the Turkish Embassy. In October the Turkish minister in Madrid learned of an inflammatory report written for Franco's benefit by the influential General Espinosa de los Monteros, former Spanish ambassador in Berlin. The report, circulated among the higher ranks of the army as well, accused Serrano Súñer of conduct "amounting to high treason" during a recent visit to Germany. According to Espinosa, Serrano Súñer had involved Spain in matters going well beyond his instructions.

What seemed certain was the likelihood of Serrano Súñer's removal as foreign minister. The Turkish minister did not believe that the army would go so far as to demand the disbanding of the Falange party, but Franco's efforts at conciliation by cabinet changes or changes in the Army command would be only temporary fixes. In the Turkish minister's opinion, the course of foreign and domestic policies within Spain could lead to a serious, even violent crisis between the Falange and the Spanish military.[32]

The American political and diplomatic role in Spain had an important bearing on Allied fortunes in the Mediterranean. When the United States found itself at war, its instincts had been to put pressure on "pro-Nazi" Spain. A general embargo slapped on Spain, among other necessary commodities, deprived it of oil. Closer to the scene and with much at stake in Gibraltar, the British objected to this policy on the ground that it would drive Franco completely into Hitler's camp and complicate Britain's interests in Spain. The Caudillo's desire was to remain neutral, benefit by trade with both sides, avoid the ravages of war and the consequences of being on the losing side when the war ended. He also feared the prospect of a German occupation of North Africa.

It was ironic that while Canaris had been secretly attempting to keep Franco neutral and out of Hitler's clutches, American policy toward Spain could have had the opposite effect. The American Embassy in Madrid, however, saw the folly of what appeared to be the direction of U.S. policy and warned Washington of its political and military implications. In March 1942 Undersecretary of State Welles agreed and convinced President Roosevelt that he should at least lift the crippling oil embargo. He also sent Carlton Hayes, a distinguished historian and strong Catholic, to Madrid as U.S. ambassador. In reciprocation Franco replaced, Ramón Serrano Súñer, with the more acceptable General Gómez Jordana as Spanish foreign minister. Falling in line with British policy toward Spain, the United States benefited by gaining access to Spanish tungsten, much needed for the production of certain kinds of armaments, particularly in the aircraft industry. This policy also ensured a more friendly environment in Spain three months before the Allied landings in North Africa.

Two days after the Torch landings, November 10, 1942, a nervous Spanish foreign minister informed his ambassador in Washington that Franco had been assured in writing by Roosevelt that the Western Allies would respect the territorial integrity of Spain and its colonies.[33] With regard to U.S. fears of German pressure on Spain to secure passage through Spain for the purpose of attacking Gibraltar, Madrid's message to the Spanish ambassador in Washington denied that Gibraltar was at risk and instructed him to explain to the U.S. government that "really and truly, Spain is complete mistress of her sovereignty. . . ." The foreign minister confided in the ambassador his astonishment at how badly informed the U.S. government seemed to be with regard to Spain's relationship with the Axis; U.S. fears of Spanish-German collusion were not merely false but devoid of "verisimilitude."[34]

In a follow-up cable the Spanish ambassador in Washington was instructed to give verbally to the U.S. government Spain's appreciation for assurances that the North African landings were not meant to threaten Spanish interests.[35]

Thanks to Ultra intercepts confirming the sincerity of Spanish démarches to the United States, it had become evident that Spain would not succumb to German pressure on it to enter the war or permit German troops to enter its territory so long as the United States made no hostile military moves. Yet the United States did not fully trust Franco, nor could German actions in Spain be dismissed solely on the basis of Franco's word. The OSS accordingly busied itself with efforts to destabilize Franco despite contrary British and U.S. policy in this matter and Roosevelt's promises to respect the Caudillo's position.

The OSS and the British SOE paramilitary agents secretly tried to widen the schism between Franco and certain of his generals. By July 1942 thirteen million dollars had been budgeted for this purpose.[36] On one embarrassing occasion the OSS representative in Madrid was caught red-handed in a hotel room as he was making subvention payments to certain Spanish generals. Whether the generals who accepted OSS largess would in fact have rebelled against Franco if called upon to do so was never put to the test.

Following Torch, the OSS also ran serious risks in Spain by other ill-advised, reckless agitation against Franco, vaguely justified as keeping the Germans preoccupied with Spain so they would be less inclined to interfere with a planned Allied invasion of Italy. American operations of this sort were nonetheless at odds with promises made to Franco by British Ambassador Sir Samuel Hoare and U.S. Ambassador Carlton Hayes, not to mention those of President Roosevelt. They were conducted without their knowledge by a flamboyant OSS operative, Donald Downes, who had earlier worked as a MI-6 agent.

Downes tried to infiltrate several agents into Spain to stir up opposition in the Málaga area as part of Operation Bananas. Eight of Downes's "Banana Boys," as they were known in-house, were killed by Spanish soldiers while 10 others were captured, only later to be killed after revealing under torture some 261 members of an anti-Franco underground.[37] Spanish Foreign Minister Gómez Jordana, having replaced Serrano Súñer, had been cooperative with U.S. Ambassador Hayes (and helpful to Canaris in his secret efforts to keep Spain out of the war) but had to protest vigorously such a flagrant disregard of Spanish sovereignty.* Ambassador Hayes protested to

---

*A recently published book (New Haven: Yale University Press, 1995) by Harvey Klehr, John Earl Haynes, and Fridrikh I. Firsov, entitled *The Secret World of American Com*

Donovan, who unconvincingly replied that Downes's actions were known to the 5th Army and were intended to protect the army's flank. Downes's operation gave the lie to Roosevelt's and Sumner Welles's promises in writing to respect Franco's position and his country's territorial integrity.

In November Hayes was still uneasy about the OSS, and insisted that it formally agree to refrain from conducting espionage against the Spanish.[38] Donovan, out of loyalty to his men, defended Downes as best he could and opposed Hayes's draconian recommendations.[†] An American OSS officer serving in Spain recalled that OSS operatives in Madrid existed by the grace of Ambassador Hayes, who was doing everything in his power to get rid of them. By August 1945 Hayes finally prevailed, and Washington ordered the immediate return of all OSS employees in Spain and the closing of all their agent networks.[39]

---

munism, describes ninety-two documents dealing with secret Comintern operations in the United States.

During World War II the American Communist party secretly assisted Soviet intelligence and facilitated "channels into the OSS." Milton Wolff, commander of the Lincoln Brigade veterans of the Spanish Civil War and staunch Communist, met with Colonel William Donovan in November 1941, according to this book. Donovan at the time proposed selecting veterans of the brigade for war operations, including operations utilizing Spanish veterans (pp. 260, 261). A relationship was arranged between Wolff and the OSS after the United States entered the war, but in mid-1942, on orders from Moscow sent through the American Communist party, Wolff shut down his OSS recruiting operation. He stated in 1992 that without the Communist party's assistance, it would have been "very difficult to continue to recruit International Brigade veterans." He stressed, however, "the decision was a personal one stemming from his irritation with the OSS because it was not, as he had expected, planning to operate against the Franco regime in Spain" (p. 271). Wolff reconsidered his decision in 1943 and talked Donovan into reinstating him as an OSS agent in Italy, where he worked with a number of Lincoln Brigade veterans whom he had originally recruited for the OSS (p. 272).

[†]An OSS message dated March 22, 1943, TOR 3122143 101-43, from Donovan to William Eddy, 126 (National Archives, RG-226, Entry 88, Box 613) states:

> Recommendation of American Ambassador in Spain, informally concurred in by State Department, proposed establishing joint agency in Madrid for coordination and control of intelligence agencies of War, State, Navy and OSS, which later to be under War Department direction. Put OSS representative now operating independently under control of Military Attaché.
>
> Donovan: Do not regard control in neutral countries appropriate to status of OSS.

In reply Eddy stated on March 25, 1943, in message 196: "His [the ambassador's] attitude prevailing would prevent both our planting clandestine cells against improbably but ever-possible German occupation [of Spain] and coordination of our work from Spain and from this theater with France."

The rough-riding tactics of Donald Downes aimed at getting rid of Franco, if successful, could have undone Canaris's long-running efforts to keep the Caudillo in power but firmly in opposition to German war aims in Spain. The Western Allies could perhaps have been grateful that the OSS in this case slipped on its own banana, and the "Downes syndrome," as one former OSS wag put it, lost out to the "Canaris factor."

IF SPAIN HAD POSED KNOTTY PROBLEMS FOR THE UNITED STATES, THE problems facing it in North Africa with all its confusing currents and cross-currents were just as troublesome. Immediate combat imperatives were in conflict with long-range postwar considerations that had to take into consideration strong native independence movements and French politics. And it would not be easy to resolve the political gulf that separated the various French factions vying for postwar power.

French industrialist Jacques Lemaigre-Dubreuil, deeply involved in anti-Vichy intrigues and a friend of America's advance man Robert Murphy, was party to the escape of Henri Giraud from the maximum-security Königstein fortress-prison, high in the hills of Saxony, where Giraud had languished as a prisoner of war since his capture by the Germans in 1940.

Lemaigre-Dubreuil was to become a controversial figure. He was later suspected of leaking foreknowledge of Torch preparations to French banking contacts so that he and his friends could make a killing on currency fluctuation after the invasion. And there were those who considered him essentially a Nazi collaborator despite opportunistic cooperation with the Allies. After the war, on July 12, 1953, his machinations caught up with him when he was murdered by an unknown assailant. But whatever his motives in the war, he seemed to have been helpful to Giraud.

Despite his sixty years and physical infirmities, Giraud let himself down from the so-called escapeproof fortress by a wire-filled rope smuggled to him in cans of ham. He fled to the Château de Froments near Lyons provided by a friendly French businessman, where Lemaigre-Dubreuil met him and explained the plan he had worked out with Murphy for French participation in the forthcoming Allied invasion of North Africa.

Giraud named General Charles Emmanuel Mast, a friend and for a while a fellow prisoner at Königstein, to be chief of staff of the French XIX Corps in Algeria after the Allies liberated it. It was probably Mast who had engineered Giraud's escape with the help of secretly anti-Vichy members of the Deuxième Bureau, intelligence arm of the French Army of the Armistice who, according to plan, were to join Giraud's entourage in North Africa.

Spiriting Giraud to Morocco by submarine at the time of the Allied landings was a hazardous enough undertaking, but more threatening had been a German effort before that to find and assassinate him after his escape from Königstein. Canaris had been under orders from Hitler to spare no effort in tracking down Giraud and having him killed before he could cause difficulties for Vichy and the Germans. This project was known as Operation Gustav. But despite prodding from General Keitel and a bounty of one hundred thousand marks offered to the public by Hitler for information of Giraud's whereabouts, the French fugitive was able to evade capture by the Abwehr.

Canaris in fact had no intention of capturing Giraud. From the beginning he would not be party to the French general's assassination and let Keitel know that the operation was not the sort of thing the Abwehr would undertake.[40] He protested that unlike the SD, his organization was not a band of assassins. Canaris had, however, made an effort to discover the general's intentions before he made his escape. Because of Hitler's intense interest in this matter, the Abwehr dispatched an agent to get in touch with Giraud and try to ascertain whether the general believed the Americans and British would try to land somewhere in North or northwestern Africa in early 1943 and whether he intended to play any significant role in the future. The agent was also instructed to discover and comment on the prospects of French resistance to such landings.

Churchill showed great concern about Giraud when this German message, broken at Bletchley in late September 1942, was shown to him. He scrawled in the margin of the text that Giraud should be duly warned he might be questioned by a German-sent agent about his knowledge of Allied intentions to open a second front and his own intentions in French North Africa.[41]

Canaris was playing a dangerous game in defying and evading Hitler's order to kill Giraud. His inaction could not be easily explained if he were found out, but he seized on Heydrich's death to lie to Keitel, telling him that he had turned over the operation to the late SD chief. It had therefore been Heydrich, now unable to defend himself, who had to bear responsibility for letting Giraud slip through the SS dragnet and collaborate with the Allies in North Africa.[42]

Canaris's close friend and Abwehr associate General Erwin Lahousen gave testimony at the Nuremberg trials that revealed some of Canaris's role in the North African affair. Among other things, Lahousen mentioned under oath that the Abwehr chief used a Cagoulard (pro-Nazi French organization) activist named Eugène Deloncle as an intermediary to maintain contact with Darlan. Deloncle, who was close to Darlan, had been a former commander of the French brigade of anti-Soviet, pro-Nazi volunteers in the German Army. According to British writer Richard Deacon,[43] Canaris, after the North African landings, tried unsuccessfully to arrange a meeting between Deloncle and British Ambassador to Spain Hoare to discuss the possibility of dealing with the Resistance to reach a compromise peace. (Deacon claimed that Deloncle later met a violent end in his Paris apartment when he was gunned down by the Gestapo.[44])

GIRAUD'S ROLE AS HEAD OF FRENCH FORCES IN NORTH AFRICA WAS MADE difficult from the beginning by the fact that he had little influence, and as an expediency Darlan had been recognized as the top French official in North Africa. Further complicating the problem of authority, Hitler had called for the implementation of Operation Attila, renamed Anton, the German occupation of Vichy France contrary to the armistice promises made at the time of France's surrender. Hitler's order validating Attila, Directive No. 19, was issued secretly on December 10, 1940. Its terms were unequivocal. It specified: "In the event that those areas of the French colonial empire now under General Weygand were to show any signs of making a move toward defection, the immediate occupation of the still unoccupied territory of the French mother country is to be prepared." It added: "At the same time, moves must be made to secure the French home fleet and the elements of the French air force which are located on domestic airfields, at the least to prevent their going over to the enemy side."[45]

On November 10, only two days after the Allied invasion, German and Italian troops implementing the plan took over Vichy France; whatever pretenses of independence and whatever authority Vichy had preserved for itself under the terms of the armistice were now completely gone. This prejudiced Allied plans to occupy Tunisia, whose Vichy government remained loyal to the German occupation regime and was now beyond Darlan's control. The Germans were able to rush troops to Tunisia and secure its airfields in anticipation of an Allied effort to seize them. The Allied offensive became much more difficult without local French support, particularly because Rommel's hard-hitting Afrika Korps was expected to make its last stand in North Africa there.

Not only would this German show of force complicate the Tunisian campaign, but it put at risk the French fleet at Toulon, which, if captured by the Germans, would seriously tip the naval balance of power in the Mediterranean in favor of the Germans. But an effort by the Germans to seize the fleet miscarried; as German armor forced its way into the port area of the important Toulon naval base at dawn that day, French Admiral Jean de Laborde scuttled the French fleet at anchor, denying Hitler his prize.*

HITLER'S REACTION TO THE ALLIED LANDINGS IN NORTH AFRICA ALSO REvived Operation Felix, now named Ilona. A prescient Canaris had warned Franco earlier in 1942 that Hitler had not given up on Gibraltar. Taking to heart Canaris's tip, Franco erected concrete barriers on the roads leading to Spain through the Pyrenees—a pointed precaution duly reported to Hitler by Schellenberg's SD agents in Spain. It was clear that if Hitler were to move into Spain, he would have to do so by force, a difficult objective now that Allied forces were in North Africa and Rommel's forces were in retreat.[†]

While the Allies and their French partners prepared their offensive against a German-reinforced Tunisia, Hitler remained convinced that the next Allied target would be Spain. In a conference with Keitel and Ribbentrop, the Führer ordered Canaris to visit his friend Franco and determine what the Caudillo's reaction would be to an Anglo-U.S. landing in Spain. Significantly, nothing was said to Canaris about Operation Ilona, which called for German preemptive occupation of Spain to forestall an Allied invasion. Ilona had been hatched behind his back, although the wily Canaris knew all about it and dreaded it as another Hitler blunder aborning. He rushed off to Madrid, intending again to frustrate Hitler's design on Spain.

With the faithful Lahousen in attendance, Canaris was determined to find a formula by which Spain could stay out of the war without provoking Hitler to strike. Backdrop for the trip was the imminent defeat of Field Marshal Friedrich Paulus's 6th Army at Stalingrad and Rommel's delaying battles to permit an evacuation of the Afrika Korps from Africa—hardly omens suggesting to an anxious Franco that he should cooperate more closely with Germany.

---

*When France surrendered, Darlan had agreed to keep the French fleet out of Allied hands. But faced with the imminent seizure of the fleet at Toulon and having compromised his position with the Germans anyway by his assistance to the Allies in the North African landings, Darlan ordered it to be scuttled.—Lee, *Marching Orders*, p. 32, fn. 14.
[†]By November 2, 1942, following the second Battle of El Alamein in October, Ultra intercepts revealed to British General Montgomery that the Afrika Korps was in bad shape and that Rommel was pleading with Hitler to permit him to retreat. Hitler's response was: "You can show your troops no other road than to victory or to death." After Rommel again asked permission to fall back, Hitler and Mussolini agreed that this was the only course, thus ending the German offensive in North Africa.—Lee, *Marching Orders*, p. 41.

In Madrid Lahousen watched Canaris draft a telegram describing Spanish Foreign Minister Gómez Jordana's reaction to a German occupation of Spain, this before the Abwehr chief had even seen Gómez Jordana, much less had the benefit of his views. Canaris's purely invented text told how the Spanish foreign minister, speaking for Franco, would agree to play host to a German army only if the Wehrmacht's eastern front held firm and if Tunisia were kept out of Allied hands, conditions unlikely to be met.[46] A few hours later Canaris met Gómez Jordana over tea and showed him the text he had drafted for his approval. Lahousen was astonished to hear later from Canaris that Gómez Jordana had endorsed the predrafted rhetoric without changing a word, and the negative views attributed to him by Canaris were sent off by telegram to an irate Hitler.

An intercepted message from the Japanese minister in Madrid to his Foreign Ministry contained an analysis of Spain's position as written by José María Doussinaguey Texidor, chief of the Political Affairs Office within the Spanish Ministry of Foreign Affairs. This had been shown to the Japanese minister in confidence during a November 15 interview with the new Spanish foreign minister, Gómez Jordana. Of particular importance was the statement that Spain had accepted the guarantees given it by the Western Allies respecting Spanish sovereignty and promises to keep their trade relations as they had been. Allegedly neither the Germans nor the Italians had formally made suggestions concerning Spain's entering the war on the side of the Axis, but even if they had, Spain was still too exhausted from its Civil War days to comply; Spain would continue its friendship with the Axis only in a nonbelligerent capacity.[47] On November 19 the Japanese minister to Spain confided in his diplomatic colleague the Swedish minister that the Allied victory in North Africa had been a bad blow for Germany and had put an end to long-held plans envisioning a meeting of German and Japanese armies in India and the Persian Gulf.[48]

The Allies had no designs on Spain but did invade Tunisia; Hitler's dream of conquering Egypt and the Suez Canal evaporated with Rommel's retreat from Libya. As the author of a 1992 Central Intelligence Agency retrospective monograph on the first years of World War II puts it, Canaris had found satisfaction in "putting sand in his own gas tank" when he frustrated Hitler's ambitions in Spain and the Mediterranean.[49] So could the Western Allies find satisfaction in these developments, prompting Winston Churchill after the war to express his gratitude for Franco's "inestimable advantages" to Great Britain.[50]

Stalin, however, was not so pleased, believing that his "allies" were using the North African invasion to stall for time, putting off a definitive invasion of France so that the Soviet Union and Germany would cancel each other out in their bloody engagements on the eastern front. Stalin saw the Western Allies as hoping to inherit global power once the Soviet Union and Germany had bled themselves white.

That Stalin thought in such terms is not surprising. He had secretly enunciated a mirror-image war strategy at a meeting of the Politburo on August 19, 1939, when he promised that after the Axis and the Western Allies exhausted each other, he would throw the power of the Red Army into the balance to conquer Europe.[51] Things had not worked out his way; to the contrary, Germany had not invaded Britain. Stalin now feared that instead the Wehrmacht and the Red Army were locked in deadly embrace while the Western Allies purposely held back from major engagement letting the Soviet Union bear the main burden of the European war.

ANOTHER PLAYER WATCHED EVENTS IN NORTH AFRICA WITH DISMAY. Charles de Gaulle, leader of the Free French, did not like the Vichy Frenchmen with whom the United States and Great Britain were dealing in North Africa. Darlan's call for French surrender may have saved the day when Allied troops hit the beaches in North Africa, but his continuing presence as French high commissioner had struck de Gaulle as unconscionable. De Gaulle's rage became greater when it was suggested that he accept the position of vice president of an Imperial Council. Not only was he infuriated, but in Great Britain there had been an upwelling of anger that the Allies were dealing with the archcollaborator who had thoroughly aligned himself with Hitler while the British fought for their very survival. As the United States and Great Britain tried to fight a war, secret plots and political maneuvering became the order of the day in French North Africa.

One group of plotters, the monarchists led by Henri d'Astier de la Vigerie, contemplated a coup d'état against Darlan designed to replace him with France's pretender to the defunct throne, Prince Henri d'Orléans. Eisenhower vetoed the scheme, fearing it would cause disturbances distracting to his forthcoming campaign against Tunisia.

The British hoped for an alliance of de Gaulle's supporters with those of Giraud. Suddenly a de Gaulle man, Henri d'Astier de la Vigerie's brother, General François d'Astier de la Vigerie, deputy commander of the Free French in London, arrived in Algiers. This created political turmoil. Robert Murphy, still tied to Darlan, and, of course, Darlan himself tried to win over General d'Astier, but when the two men met, Giraud in attendance, the atmosphere was highly charged with mutual animosity. Nothing was accomplished. Not only had d'Astier been uncivil to Darlan, but the general's suite at the Aletti Hotel bristled with anti-Darlan plotters—particularly Gaullists.

Eisenhower and Murphy still clung to Darlan as a welcome convenience in holding the Algerian administration together, but they realized that with opposition growing he could not indefinitely remain in power. Darlan himself told Murphy that there were four plots against his life simmering just under the surface.

IT WAS CHRISTMAS EVE WHEN ALGIERS, APPARENTLY TRANQUIL WITH HOLY reverence, became the scene of a very untranquil, un-Christian act. A young Frenchman, barely twenty, slipped into the High Commissariat. As he waited for Darlan and his entourage to arrive, no one seemed to notice him. When Darlan reached his office, a shot rang out; mortally wounded, the French leader slumped to the floor. The young assassin fled but was almost immediately caught.[52] He was identified as a royalist and a Gaullist named Fernand Bonnier de la Chapelle, who was serving as a trainee in an Allied special forces camp at Aïn-Taya. On the night before his execution, Bonnier made his confession—two confessions, to be exact: one confession, probably the true one, and a second, revised confession in which he claimed to be solely responsible for his act.

It is one of those coincidences of history that the MI-6 chief Menzies and Georges Ronin, chief of counterespionage for the Army of the Armistice in France, were lunching together only a few houses away from the scene of the assassination. But was it a coincidence?* Ronin had just escaped from France and arrived in Algiers, where he was met by Menzies to discuss the formation of a Free French intelligence organization under Giraud to replace the Vichy service in North Africa. The two men and a few of their underlings, when informed of Darlan's murder, expressed little concern; no one seemed to miss Darlan.[53]

At the hurriedly held inquest the original confession, which implicitly involved certain royalists, was produced as evidence. Bonnier had scrawled, "I affirm having killed Admiral Darlan, High Commissioner in French Africa, after having told the Abbé Cordier in a [church] confession that I would do so. It was the Abbé who gave me the plan of offices at the Commissariat and of the office of the Admiral; it was through him that I was able to obtain the pistol and shells which I used to execute the mission I had assigned myself . . . to dispose of the Admiral."[54] The second and

*A wartime British intelligence office (MI-14), Noel Annan in a recent book has this intriguing comment to make relevant to the Darlan affair: "The wife of the family on whom I was billeted was as charming as her Vichyssois husband was not. Did I not know, he said—I assuredly did know but would not admit it—that Admiral Darlan . . . had been assassinated on the orders of the British in 1942?"—Annan, *Changing Enemies*, p. 114.

revised confession, in which Bonnier denied having any accomplices, seemed to have been extracted from him under pressure.

Abbé Cordier, a young army chaplain, was close to the group of conspirators headed by Lemaigre-Dubreuil and including Henri d'Astier de la Vigerie, who had organized the anti-Vichy movement in Oran in late 1941, before the Allied landings. D'Astier had maintained close contact with Robert Murphy at that time in an effort to negotiate for American arms with which to seize power after the landings. The group had hoped to persuade General Weygand to head a new North African regime, but the old leader begged off with the excuse that he was too old to become "a rebel."[55] Assassin Bonnier seemed to have been inspired and helped by Abbé Cordier, who had given absolution to Bonnier in a hurriedly conducted street corner confession immediately before the assassin struck.* Whether involved or not, d'Astier and his collaborators applauded Bonnier's act, and there were those among the Allies who were glad that fate, if nothing else, had intervened to rid them of the Darlan embarrassment. General Mark Clark, Eisenhower's deputy and an architect of Torch, stated in his postwar memoirs that Darlan's death had been "an act of Providence." The general probably reflected the opinions of a great many others when he wrote that Darlan "had served his purpose, and his death solved what could have been the very difficult problem of what to do with him in the future." Clark concluded: "Darlan was a political investment forced upon us by circumstances, but we made a sensational profit in lives and time through using him."[56]

By 1942 Darlan, a man resented by many French patriots for his collaboration with the Nazi-formed Vichy regime, probably had realized that he had chosen the wrong side. Things looked much different to Darlan once Soviet Russia and the United States were arrayed against Hitler. Motivated by self-serving expediency, Darlan before the invasion had sent secret probes to Admiral William Leahy, the U.S. mission chief in Vichy, hinting that deals could be made. And when he suddenly appeared in North Africa on the eve of the landings, he must have hoped that he could leap onto a new and winning bandwagon by serving the Allies. This at least would be better than becoming their captive.

On November 11 Darlan sent Pétain a message giving his rationale for collaborating with the Western Allies. The admiral stated that he had pro-

---

*The Paris newspaper *Figaro* on December 24, 1945, reported that exactly three years earlier on the fateful Christmas Eve of 1942, a witness, who remained anonymous, claimed to have overheard Abbé Cordier at the next table to him in a restaurant as the latter discussed the forthcoming attempt on Darlan's life with a companion.

posed to the American invaders an armistice throughout North Africa. Wey-gand, he claimed, had made a similar overture to the British. At a crisis meeting of Vichy's Council of Ministers, Pétain rejected Darlan's armistice proposal and ordered him to continue resistance to the Allies. This provoked Darlan to reply that he had accordingly canceled the armistice request and thereafter considered himself an Allied prisoner of war.[57]

The German intelligence officer, who reported this exchange between Darlan and Pétain, commented that the admiral had probably been trying to preserve the sovereignty of the Vichy French administration in North Africa by "negotiating" with the Americans. In connection with Darlan's comment that Weygand too had proposed an armistice, it is noteworthy that Weygand was soon arrested on his way to southern France and sent to Germany under armed guard.[58]

As for the Allies' rationale for dealing with Darlan, Churchill explains in his memoir *The Second World War* when commenting candidly on the French admiral's sudden death: "Darlan's murder, however criminal, re-lieved the Allies of their embarrassment at working with him, and at the same time left them with all the advantages he had been able to bestow during the vital hours of the Allied landings."[59]

With Darlan out of the picture, Giraud took his place as high commis-sioner, but his power struggle with de Gaulle continued. This could be only resolved by Roosevelt and Churchill.

THE HISTORIC CASABLANCA CONFERENCE IN JANUARY 1943 BROUGHT DE Gaulle and Giraud physically together, but it was to be an uneasy rela-tionship that Roosevelt and Churchill imposed on them. Roosevelt had never liked de Gaulle, but he had also developed serious reservations about Giraud, who he believed had been vastly overestimated by Robert Murphy. And Churchill, famous for his memorable comment on de Gaulle "The Cross of Lorraine is the heaviest I have had to bear," played willing host to his Free French movement based in Britain.

It had not been easy to lure de Gaulle to Casablanca. While the po-litical maneuvering went on, Roosevelt cabled Secretary of State Hull, "We produced the bridegroom, General Giraud, who cooperated very nicely on the proposed nuptials. . . . Our friends [the British], how-ever, could not immediately produce de Gaulle, the temperamental bride [who] . . . shows no intention of getting into bed with Giraud."[60] Churchill finally produced the shy bride, but not before he had primed Foreign Secretary Eden to make the ultimate threat to have de Gaulle removed as head of Free French forces if he did not cooperate. A carrot was also extended when Churchill promised de Gaulle that he would be declared coequal with Giraud on the French Committee of National Liberation.

At Casablanca de Gaulle and Giraud were encouraged to have a heart-to-heart discussion. According to Churchill, acting as matchmaker, the two rivals talked for two or three hours. They seemed to get along. De Gaulle buried his pride long enough to meet Roosevelt as well. The American president's critical views of de Gaulle were well known, but Churchill was slightly encouraged by their meeting. Roosevelt, it seemed, thought the Free French leader had a "spiritual look in his eyes," even if he could not picture him as a "living representative of Joan of Arc," as de Gaulle liked to claim to be.[61]

THE CASABLANCA CONFERENCE WAS EXTREMELY IMPORTANT AND TO SOME controversial. Roosevelt's and Churchill's enunciation of the doctrine of unconditional surrender, made without Churchill's prior concurrence, thereafter seriously inhibited both the OSS and MI-6 in any dealings with the German Resistance, whose aim was to make a deal with the Western Allies that denied the Soviets any role in the occupation of Germany and the peace process to follow. Such a deal would henceforward be in violation of the Western Allies' agreement with the Soviet Union forbidding separately arranged peace agreements with the Germans. But short of reaching any secret understandings with the Resistance and all the complications that would entail, the Allies were inhibited by the policy of unconditional surrender in practice from negotiating in the field surrender of any specific German units. Lives could be needlessly lost before a definitive, formal three-power surrender of all German forces could be arranged.

Arriving in Switzerland just as the Torch landings ended, one American official, the OSS intelligence officer Allen Dulles, found ways to skirt the inhibiting injunction of unconditional surrender in dealing with the German Resistance and finally actually negotiated the surrender of German forces in Italy. In doing so, he infuriated Stalin, but he also provided insights, little appreciated in Washington, revealing Stalin's postwar Cold War intentions.

TWENTY-FOUR

Allen Dulles:
OSS Superstar

ALLEN DULLES BEGAN OPERATIONS IN BERN WITH AN ASTONISHING LACK OF subtlety. Whatever his official title in the American Legation, he was known around town as the special representative of the president of the United States. He did not live modestly or inconspicuously, as spy chiefs are classically supposed to do: He rented a deluxe ground-floor apartment in a distinguished mansion at 23 Herrengasse Street with discreet access for night visitors. It did not escape the attention of the Swiss police that he had unscrewed the bulb from the streetlamp in front of his apartment, obviously to make entry and egress easier for his "clients." The police apparently did not complain; Swiss intelligence was content to let Dulles arrange his stage lighting in any way he wanted since he would be under careful surveillance anyway and darkness hides the watcher as much as it does the watched.

Dulles, however, was neither a fool nor a dilettante in the business of spying; he had spied before in this very town only one war ago. He realized that he was known as an intelligence officer and would be carefully watched, but more to the point, efforts would be made to provoke his agents and penetrate his networks by every espionage service in Bern. That was where the danger would be, not in shrouded figures lurking in the shrubbery. (Dulles later discovered that his cook was a German SD agent.[1]) In fact there was merit in his hanging out a shingle: It would quickly attract business, and Dulles did not have time to creep up slowly on his targets if he was to help pave the way for the grand invasion and final defeat of the Third Reich.

At age forty-nine Dulles was admirably suited for his role in Bern. A worldly-wise man, he was experienced in international law and foreign affairs. He had also taught school in a missionary school in India when first out of college. Dulles was wellborn, well bred and, above all, from a professional point of view, well connected. His natural disguise as a bluff, jovial, pipe-smoking extrovert made him instantly accepted in Swiss society and hid a subtle mind. He had all the ingredients for success in his trade, but he got off to a bad start.

Dulles's product was rigidly cross-checked in headquarters against Ultra and ISOS intercepts. His chief, Bill Donovan, warned him in late April 1943 with a deflating telegram that read: "All news from Bern these days is being discounted 100% by the War Department."[2] Similar criticism followed although Donovan tried to make allowances for operating conditions in Switzerland, that oasis in the midst of war, whose currency was "tendentious intelligence, plants and peace-feelers." Nonetheless, as Donovan pointed out, "your information . . . is now given a lower rating [i.e., less reliable] than any other source [on Germany]."[3]

Stung to greater enterprise by such barbs, Dulles redoubled his efforts. But it was luck that changed his fortunes. A remarkable person, destined to be called by some "the best Allied agent of the War," volunteered his services as a spy against the Germans. While serving Dulles in the OSS from 1943 to 1945, this agent produced some sixteen hundred valuable, highly secret German documents.[4]

Dulles's new agent, best remembered in the OSS by his wartime code name, George Wood, was in real life Fritz Kolbe, a German Foreign Ministry official assigned as aide to Ambassador Karl Ritter, who conducted liaison between the Foreign Ministry and the German High Command. His access to important information was phenomenal. And since the Foreign Ministry had been relocated to Salzburg to avoid Allied bombing, he did not have far to travel to reach Switzerland and deliver his stolen papers. Nor was it difficult for him to volunteer for the German diplomatic courier run to Switzerland, thereby giving him cover for his trips.

Before meeting Dulles, Kolbe had made contact with the British Legation in Bern on August 17, 1943. Despite a portfolio filled with highly significant documents, the British Secret Service chief in Switzerland, Count Frederick vanden Heuvel, refused to accept them. Nor would the British military attaché have anything to do with him. Kolbe had explained his anti-Hitler sentiments, but the British could not believe that a high-ranking German Foreign Ministry official would make such a bold, direct contact with the enemy and risk smuggling highly classified documents across the border to Switzerland.

Badly burned at Venlo and confused by the Hess episode, the British had since been shy about overtures from German dissidents. Churchill had forbidden contact with the Resistance after Venlo.[5] The Allied unconditional surrender agreement signed at Casablanca had put an effective cap on opposition political operations out of concern that they would evoke strong Soviet reactions. But Kolbe's willingness to be helpful was not contingent upon meeting German Resistance demands; he wanted to help the Allies with information for his own idealistic reasons.

Allen Dulles saw the British military attaché, Colonel Henry Cartwright, at a social engagement the same day as Kolbe had called at the British Legation. Cartwright, in passing, quaintly reported as an item of gossip that "A cove with a funny name" had approached him. The attaché added, "He'll undoubtedly turn up at your shop in due course."[6] Sure enough, Dulles was alerted the next day by a legation colleague, Gerald Mayer of the Office of War Information (OWI), who had received secondhand a feeler from Kolbe. A meeting was arranged, and Kolbe gave Dulles sixteen telegrams that seemed both interesting and authentic.

A forty-three-year-old man who had worked at the German Foreign Ministry since 1925, Kolbe was described by Dulles as being five feet seven inches, balding, with prominent ears. His son had been in the care of a former housekeeper in South Africa ever since his mother, Kolbe's wife, died in 1936. At the moment Kolbe was being divorced from a second wife and had a fiancée waiting in the wings.

The documents Kolbe brought were significant. One message described a plot to free a captured German agent in Dublin; another report led to the identification of a German spy who had been present at an important conference held by Sir Stafford Cripps in London. Most important, Kolbe warned Dulles of Allied cipher systems that had been broken by the Germans.[7]

Kolbe's messages, known collectively in the OSS as the Boston Series, were thereafter checked with British intelligence, which was in a position to authenticate them by comparing his information with Ultra traffic. Sir Claude Dansey, number two in MI-6, dismissed Kolbe's product out of hand as faked. He called the material "obviously a plant."[8] Dansey, who disliked the OSS in general and Allen Dulles in particular, was not prepared to admit that this freewheeling American now had a first-class source, one whom MI-6 had cavalierly rejected. Kim Philby, then head of the Iberian Section of MI-6, also scoffed at Kolbe's product. This of course can now be understood in the context of Philby's postwar exposure as a longtime Soviet agent intent on sabotaging MI-6, particularly its contacts with the German Resistance. At the time, however, his word as a counterespionage expert carried considerable weight.[9]

Sustained comparisons with Ultra traffic indicated that Kolbe's material was authentic; the British finally acknowledged: "Both the material and the source had stood the test and are thought to be of great value."[10] The OSS nonetheless continued to check the Boston Series carefully in the fear it might be part of a buildup for passing damaging deception at a later, critical time once confidence had been established with accurate but expendable information. Dulles had expressed his confidence in Kolbe by a telegram sent on December 29, stating: "I now firmly believe in the good faith of Wood [Kolbe] and I am ready to stake my reputation on the fact that these documents are genuine."[11] Donovan agreed and gave his blessing to the agent. Even then a three-man panel formed by the OSS but headed by Colonel Alfred McCormack, chief of the Special Branch of military intelligence and U.S. custodian of British Ultra material, insisted on a cautionary caveat: "[A] good deal of the material is second-hand information upon subjects on which first-hand information is available." This was an example of a maddening maxim often invoked in the intelligence world: "If the intelligence looks good, there must be something wrong with it." In the case of the Boston Series, time proved its worth, and skeptics were left looking foolish or bureaucratically timid.

In a batch of two hundred documents Kolbe brought to Bern in late December 1943, there was a report on a new German supersonic fighter aircraft, a jet fighter that briefly saw service before the war ended. There was another equally fascinating report of a new "secret weapon under development" soon to be identified—and suffered in London—as the devastating cross-Channel V-2 rocket.

There was a startling document dated November 4, 1943, from German Ambassador von Papen in Ankara, Turkey, which began with the statement "A number of [official British] documents have come to us from SD officer, Moyzisch [in Ankara]. I shall designate the source: 'Cicero.' "[12] The source of the Cicero reports, it will be recalled, was the Albanian butler, paid by the German SD to burgle the personal safe of his employer, British Ambassador Sir Knatchbull-Hugessen. Kolbe's reports on this matter were disseminated to the British, causing MI-6 to take a renewed interest in the once-ignored "walk-in" Fritz Kolbe.

It was difficult to tell how receptive official U.S. customers would be to the Kolbe product; they were at first not allowed to see it. While Donovan tried to provide summaries of the Boston Series messages to the top leaders of the Army, Navy, and State Department, Colonel McCormack blocked their dissemination. A collection of particularly important Kolbe reports routed to the president by Donovan were also stopped by McCormack, who was still skeptical of their authenticity.

McCormack thought that his caution was vindicated when Kolbe reported that the German command in Italy had ordered electrical power plants in Rome and the bridges crossing the Tiber to be demolished in the event the Allied advance in Italy forced the Germans to evacuate the Eternal City. McCormack insisted that only Hitler could issue such an order. But by Eastertime, April 11, 1944, Dulles could gleefully cable Washington that Kolbe had brought in "more than 200 highly valuable 'Easter eggs.'" "What a bunny," Washington enthusiastically responded. Still, there were those like McCormack who feared deception despite the "increasingly significant character of the data . . . proportionately more damaging to German interests." Military intelligence's Special Branch, favorably impressed with some reporting from German military attachés in Tokyo, finally gave up and promised that further Boston Series reporting would be daily disseminated. The reports would, moreover, be enshrined in the "top list" of the eleven highest-ranking officials in Washington—this after nine months of squelching highly significant material from Kolbe.[13]

The absence of laudatory feedback demoralized Kolbe; he once complained, "When are you going to wake up?"[14] He was also dispirited by the failure of Resistance military officers in their attempts to kill Hitler. In the mass pogrom of suspects that followed the July 20, 1944, bomb attack he himself had narrowly avoided arrest. During his next trip to Bern in October, Dulles urged him to avoid active participation in the Resistance, which by now had become extremely vulnerable, and concentrate instead on less dangerous intelligence collection. As Dulles put it, what he was doing for the Allies in bringing them critical information was infinitely more important than plotting against Hitler.

During his Bern debriefing Kolbe described a significant development. He told of a confidential conversation he had had with Resistance activist Peter Kleist, an Eastern expert in the Foreign Ministry, revealing that Foreign Minister Ribbentrop, possibly influenced by Germany's critical defeat at Kursk, had sent him to Stockholm in early September 1943, the last of a series of trips to extend peace feelers to Soviet representatives there.* How much, if any, of this trip was sanctioned by Hitler was not made clear.

---

*When German Field Marshal Erich von Manstein launched his crucial attack on Kursk in July 1943, the Red Army defeated German forces with the help of British Ultra order of battle intelligence secretly provided to Moscow by its spy John Cairncross, then employed by Britain's top secret cipher-cracking installation at Bletchley Park. It is a measure of Stalin's distrust of the British that he did not believe essentially the same Ultra material (suitably disguised as to source) disseminated to him through the British Embassy in Moscow because he feared it had been adulterated to deceive him— Annan, *Changing Enemies*, p. 73.

Ribbentrop of course did not realize that Kleist was a Canaris man and secret member of the Resistance Black Orchestra who was alert to peace
possibilities that would bypass Ribbentrop, Hitler, or other Nazis.[15] While
Russian representatives were not willing to see Kleist this time, similar efforts were still being made through the German Embassy in Stockholm to
reach the Soviets.[16]

McCormack's Special Branch reacted to Kolbe's reporting on this critical matter cautiously: "Report #426 regarding German negotiations with
Russia is . . . of great importance, if it is true. . . . Military Intelligence Service is inclined to doubt its credibility, in view of the fact that the Germans
are known to have told Japanese not to make overtures on their behalf to
the Russians."[17] If Stalin was too quick to suspect the Western Allies of trying to make a deal with the Germans behind his back, much of the U.S.
military intelligence establishment was too slow to suspect the Soviets of
themselves trying to reach a deal with the Nazis.

The situation had become too hot for Kolbe in Germany, so it was
agreed that when he next came out to Switzerland in March 1945, he
would remain. A last mother lode of documents was photographed in the
offices of a Resistance friend, psychologist Adolphe Jung, whose offices
were on the third floor of Chirurgische Universtätsklinik in Berlin. This
was the University Hospital directed by a prominent surgeon, Dr. Ferdi-
nand Saurerbruch, who had once included Hitler among his patients but
was a friend and Resistance collaborator of Kolbe's and whose secretary,
Maria Fritsch, was Kolbe's fiancée and mistress. Jung, a native of Alsace,
was a secret Gaullist who had joined the German Resistance in his zeal to
work against Hitler so that France could be liberated. Kolbe used his office
as a storage place to keep purloined Foreign Ministry documents until he
could photocopy them for Dulles.

Following the war, Jung's remembrances of superspy Fritz Kolbe provide a rare and close-up glimpse of an agent at work under severe pressure
in the surreal atmosphere of a dying Berlin: "He was judicious, deliberate
and prudent. . . . He was very much aware of all the dangers. He was en-
dowed with a lively imagination which enabled him to see, as though revealed in a flash of lightning, the right solution or the right reply in the
most difficult situations. . . .

"After the raid we [he and his fiancée] often looked out at the fires raging all around and marvelled that our building once again had not been
touched. When would it be?"

Jung recalled: "In March 1945, he came to the Klinik one last time. He
had been assigned a trip to Switzerland . . . and he was going to stay there.
All night long we photographed documents. Everything that could still be

of importance to the U.S. embassy we pinned up in front of the camera. . . . He was tired and nervous. He left us knowing that soon Berlin would be literally wiped out. . . . His fiancée wept."[18]

Kolbe and his fiancée survived and found sanctuary in Switzerland. He had done his part in winning the war.

DULLES WAS FORTUNATE IN HAVING AS HIS TOP ASSISTANT A TALENTED German of recent American citizenship, Gero von Schulze-Gaevernitz, whom he had known since World War I. Gaevernitz, son of a well-respected economist, was connected with a prominent Rhenish family named Stinnes (his sister had married a Stinnes) and had access to Germany's old elite. Having providentially settled in Switzerland just as war broke out, he was on the spot, burnishing old contacts within Germany that opposed Hitler, when Dulles arrived in November 1942.[19]

While intelligence gathering was vital, Dulles considered political operations his top priority. He was to establish contact with Resistance elements of every kind, from left to right in the political spectrum, although he concentrated on the military-weighted Black Orchestra, whose activities bore the best promise of hastening the disintegration of the Third Reich.[20] Dulles saw the problem as more than gaining victory over the Nazis; he was rare among American senior officials in his concern for the political nature of the postwar world. More specifically, Dulles was concerned about Germany's future and the role that the Soviet Union would arrogate to itself throughout Eastern Europe. Generally Donovan shared Dulles's concerns; both men discovered, however, that their views were not always welcome in Washington. President Roosevelt, imbued with the spirit of a crusade against Nazi Germany and impressed with the sacrifices endured by the Soviet Union in the fight against Hitler, seemed unconcerned with the threat posed by Stalin after victory was won. "Uncle Joe," the president naïvely believed, could become a long-range and valued ally in the postwar era; there were few problems he thought, that could not be solved by the two of them sitting down together and talking them out.

Dulles in his Swiss oasis of peace in war-torn Europe had a ringside seat from which to watch the unfolding drama of Europe, a drama that vitally affected the United States for another generation or more. Observing at close quarters the political currents of Europe beginning to wash about him, Dulles could foresee the future torrents from the east that were to engulf the Western world.

This was frustrating. When two months after his arrival in Bern, Roosevelt and Churchill announced the doctrine of unconditional surrender at the Casablanca summit, Dulles recognized that in effect it promised

postwar humiliation and dismemberment of Germany, the sole benefi-
ciary of which would most likely be the Soviet Union. This did not augur
well for establishing and maintaining contact in Bern with German Resistance representatives who opposed Hitler but recoiled at the specter of a
viscerated Germany and captive Eastern Europe ruled by Stalin. The Resistance was looking for a secret understanding with the Western Allies in
which the overthrow of Hitler and surrender in the West would be rewarded by a commitment to help a new, democratic German government
keep Russia out of Germany.[21]

In January 1943 Adam von Trott zu Solz of the German Foreign Min-
istry sought out Dulles in Bern for discussions on behalf of the Resistance.
Trott's contacts with the West had begun in 1931–33, when he studied at
Oxford. As Germany began to fall under Hitler's spell, he had secretly allied himself with Moltke and the Kreisau Circle—"philosophers" of the
Resistance. Dulles knew that in 1939, when war threatened, Trott had
made contact with certain influential Britons, the historian John Wheeler-
Bennett among others, and discussed with them their Resistance objec-
tives and their efforts to prevent Hitler from provoking war.

In his meeting with Dulles, Trott protested the apparent arm's length
attitude of the Western Allies toward the Resistance since the Casablanca
pronouncements on unconditional surrender. He warned Dulles of the
Soviet threat to postwar Europe if the United States and Britain continued
to remain passive in this matter.[22]

While linked with the Black Orchestra and the military participants in
the Resistance, the Kreisau group led by Moltke looked to its own ideological platform to guide action decisions; this was reflected in its overtures to OSS. In mid-June 1943 the circle held its third major meeting at
Moltke's Kreisau estates, a critical time in Germany's inexorable slide toward defeat.

It was here that Trott, international expert for the group, presented his
views on foreign policy in a post–world war era. He talked of high-minded
purpose: "A just and durable peace cannot be based on force. It can only
be achieved through commitment to the divine order which upholds
man's inward and outward existence." There was nothing about realpolitik
in this kind of statement. He added: "Only when it is possible to make this
order the measure of the relationship between nations will it be possible to
overcome the moral and material confusion of our time and to establish a
genuine peace." Still nothing was said of a balance of power or other traditional formulas for European coexistence. Trott's soaring idealism continued: "The special responsibility and loyalty that everyone owes to his
nation, his language and the spiritual and historical traditions of his peo-

ple must be respected and protected. It must, however, not be abused for the benefit of the amassing of political power and for the degradation, persecution and oppression of foreign peoples. The free and peaceful development of national cultures is incompatible with the retention of absolute sovereignty by each individual state." Before he was through, however, Trott came to the question of Germany's fate, the real crux of the problem. "Germany," he believed, must "accomplish its own regeneration as a result of spontaneous initiative, not pressure from the big powers."[23]

He believed that Germany must be able to mediate between the "revolutionary East" and the "restorative West." He opposed the "outworn forms of individual liberalism" represented by the United States. But Trott was aware that all this represented an impossible dream for a country by now considered a pariah in the community of nations as a result of its leaders' unprovoked aggression, cruelty in waging war, unmitigated folly, and apparent insistence on self-destruction.

Trott, Moltke, and the others at Kreisau would not, however, find it difficult under the circumstances to fall back from high-flown ideological concepts to direct, even ruthless action. While they were morally opposed to terrorism, it would soon become evident that all they stood for depended on the destruction of Hitler *before* an Allied victory was won; a humiliating surrender would destroy what little bargaining power still remained.

Discouraged by Dulles's inability to act more dynamically despite his personal sympathy for the Resistance cause, the Kreisau Circle now looked to Turkey as a place to make contact with the West, specifically with Moltke's good friend the American ambassador to Cairo Alexander Kirk. While a new generation of military men within the Resistance began to make plans to assassinate Hitler and stage a coup d'état, Trott and Moltke persisted in trying to interest the Americans in helping them.

TWENTY-FIVE

Moltke's Mission

THERE WAS A NOTE OF DESPERATION IN PEACE OVERTURES MADE TO THE Americans by the Resistance in late 1943. Either naïveté or false hope may have accounted for offers that the United States could not possibly have accepted because of Roosevelt's commitment to unconditional surrender. Political motives, sometimes cynical, often drive international relations, but in World War II the United States considered itself on a crusade that tolerated no compromise with principle: Germany and Japan must be totally beaten by force of arms. Ominous intelligence revealing Soviet postwar intentions that reached Allen Dulles, intelligence at odds with Roosevelt's utopian dream of lasting harmony, was rarely read, much less seriously considered in Washington.

Seeds of the Cold War to come were already sprouting. The German Resistance had always believed that Hitler's terrible adventures in war were doomed to fail. By now, however, there was no doubt about the outcome of the war: Germany would lose. The questions were: How many horrors must be endured before the war ended, and what then was in store for Germany? The nemesis facing Germany—and the rest of the world, for that matter—continued to be Joseph Stalin. The problem was trying to convince the United States of this fact and doing so before it was too late.

However futile it seemed, desperation made the Resistance persist in trying to alert the United States to postwar reality. The Kreisau Circle of the Resistance was in the forefront of Resistance planning for the future,* and it had not yet given up on the Americans. Count Helmuth James von Moltke,† scion of a distinguished Prussian family, was chosen as its emissary. As a friend of Canaris as well as Abwehr legal adviser and secret head of the Kreisau Circle, he was deeply involved in determining Kreisau strategy and defining its philosophy. In 1943, as the Third Reich crumbled, Moltke and like-minded members of the Resistance felt a sense of particular urgency about reaching peace before the German Army ceased to exist as a viable fighting force, but it was peace with the Western Allies, at the exclusion of the Soviets, that they wanted. To put it more starkly, they wanted Western protection against the Red Army's inexorable advance, a logical, if impractical, objective.

In midsummer 1943 the Kreisau group looked toward neutral Turkey as a place of contact with the West. It was one thing to agree among themselves on a set of high-principled plans for a post–Nazi Germany; it was another to interest the Western Allies, now certain of victory through sheer force of arms and committed to the unconditional surrender of Germany, to consider any negotiations whatsoever with the enemy. President Roosevelt, who seemed to have faith in Stalin's good intentions, would be hard to convince.

Kreisau member Adam von Trott zu Solz, whose Foreign Ministry position provided him with legitimate reasons to travel abroad, had been sent to Turkey in May 1943 with Canaris's blessing on a hidden mission to persuade Germany's ambassador in Ankara, Franz von Papen, to cooperate with the Resistance. While Papen was known since World War I for his

---

*The Kreisau Circle was particularly active in July 1941, May and October 1942, and June 1943.

Count von Moltke's Kreisau Circle was dedicated to making plans for the rebirth of Germany after its inevitable fall under Hitler. The Resistance leaders of this group were an eclectic assemblage that included Adam von Trott zu Solz of the German Foreign Ministry; Father Lothar König, a theologian; Theodor Haubach, a Social Democrat; Father Augustin Rosch, regional prefect of the Jesuit order in Munich; Theodor Steltzer, a Socialist and General Staff officer; Hans Lukaschek, governor of Upper Silesia; and civil servant Count Peter Yorck von Wartenburg.

Two prominent Socialist leaders of the Resistance, Julius Leber and Wilhelm Leuschner, a trade unionist, collaborated closely with Moltke and the Kreisau Circle. Most of the Moltke group, however, believed strongly in Christian precepts and family values as a basis for German society.

Seven members of the Kreisau Circle, charged with participation in the July 20, 1944, bomb plot against Hitler, were executed by hanging. They were: Moltke himself, Count Peter Yorck von Wartenburg, Adam von Trott zu Solz, Hans Bernd von Häften, Father Augustin Rosch, Alfred Delp, Dr. Theodor Haubach, and Socialist Dr. Julius Leber.

†Helmuth von Moltke was the great-grandnephew of the famous Prussian field marshal who distinguished himself in the Franco-Prussian War of 1870–71.

self-serving political intrigues, he could be useful if he chose to be. But despite Trott's long talks with him in the German chancery, Papen held himself aloof from the Resistance. He doubtless knew that he must be cautious. His close call with death in February 1942 at the hands of a bomb-throwing assassin on the streets of Ankara was troubling.*

Long before Trott's visit to Turkey, Canaris seems to have focused on Istanbul as a likely site for Resistance contact with the Americans. Whether or not he personally involved himself is open to question, but Canaris's early biographer Heinz Höhne claims that the admiral's Turkey station chief, Paul Leverkühn, had put his friend Baron Kurt von Lersner, distinguished former German diplomat, in contact with Commander George Earle, assistant U.S. naval attaché in Istanbul. Earle's reputation as something of a free-booter during his assignment as ambassador to Bulgaria preceded him. Nonetheless, Earle was of understandable interest to Leverkühn because of his close relationship with President Roosevelt. Höhne alleges that Canaris himself in one brief encounter during January 1943 met Earle in Istanbul's Park Hotel and conveyed the Resistance's hoped-for formula for action: armistice with the West (after removal of Hitler) and joint Allied-German war against Stalin in the East.[1] Nothing came of this.

Moltke traveled to Turkey in early July 1943. Unlike Trott, he did not bother seeing Ambassador von Papen, whom he considered an "absolutely deplorable" person. Having Canaris's backing for the mission, he called instead on the Abwehr chief of station Leverkühn. He knew Leverkühn well; they had been law partners in Berlin during the years 1938 and 1939. Leverkühn had been co-opted for the Resistance by Canaris in the hope he might at some point be useful as a clandestine contact with Western intelligence. Leverkühn's friendship with Donovan began long before the war, when he served in Washington with the German Reparations Committee. In 1937 and 1938 he visited New York in connection with the famous Anastasia case, in which a young refugee claimed to be the youngest daughter of Czar Nicholas II and to have survived the massacre of Russia's royal family by Bolsheviks at Ekaterinburg. These trips provided Donovan occasions on which to renew his friendship with Leverkühn and discuss with him the looming Nazi threat.

Moltke also established contact in Istanbul with a German expatriate, Professor Hans Wilbrandt, employed by the Turkish government, and a

---

*While it has been widely recognized that the Soviets were behind the attempt on Papen's life in Ankara, senior SD officer Wilhelm Hoettl embraced the theory that the real villain was Heydrich. The "Butcher of Prague" had kept Papen on his list of enemies from the early days of Hitler's rise to power, according to Hoettl.

German economist, Alexander Rustow, both of whom were connected with the OSS through a clandestine operation known by the code designation Dogwood. While Moltke had several brainstorming sessions with Wilbrandt and Rustow on how the Resistance should proceed in establishing contact with the Americans, he was cautious when it came to risking more direct contact with the OSS. He wanted to deal only with someone whom he personally knew and trusted. The person he had in mind was Alexander Kirk, whom he had known well in Berlin when the latter was the American chargé d'affaires in the early months of the war. Now Kirk was in Cairo as ambassador to Egypt.

Moltke left Istanbul with the firm intention of soon returning; he hoped that in the meantime a meeting with Kirk could be set up, in either Istanbul or Cairo. He also left Istanbul imbued with Rustow's opinion that the United States could not deviate from the terms of its unconditional surrender agreement with Britain and Soviet Russia and that any peace terms agreed to by the Western Allies would be harsh as long as the German Army was still intact. Rustow insisted that the only condition that the Resistance should discuss was that Russia not be allowed to occupy any part of Germany.

OSS Istanbul passed on to Donovan Moltke's message with a thoughtful analysis. The message caught Wild Bill's attention enough to bring him in person to Istanbul, where he met secretly with his old friend Leverkühn. The fruits of their meeting included a significant memorandum given Donovan by Leverkühn, acting in behalf of the German Resistance. The memorandum, bearing the letterhead of the German Embassy, stated unequivocally that German military commanders would not resist an invasion of France by the Western Allies. With this in hand, the OSS chief could hope to interest President Roosevelt.[2] Donovan's discussion with the president on this matter, however, did not take place until after the July 20, 1944, bomb attempt against Hitler,[3] by which time the situation had radically changed.

Papen appears briefly again when in October 1943 he had a brief encounter with an American in Ankara, Theodore Morde, correspondent for *Reader's Digest* and OSS agent. When they met, Papen professed to be anti-Hitler and willing to cooperate in overthrowing him if President Roosevelt would be willing to make terms attractive enough to "his friends" in the German Resistance.*

*In an OSS message to headquarters dated April 18, 1943, Morde, presumably on OSS instructions but not with White House authority, sought out Papen, introducing himself as being on a presidential mission. Morde proposed that Papen arrange somehow to oust Hitler and spark an anti-Nazi revolt in Germany. Again without any high-level

Bill Donovan was intrigued by this overture, but it came to nothing. For one thing, Robert Sherwood, head of the Office of War Information (OWI), had neither liked nor trusted Morde when he had served briefly with the OWI. Sherwood's suggestion that Morde be prevented from continuing his contact with Papen was acted upon by Assistant Secretary of State Adolf Berle, who lifted Morde's passport. More important, President Roosevelt would have nothing to do with the scheme, fearing it would violate the Allied agreement to observe unconditional surrender as the only basis for peace.[4] He probably also feared it would upset Stalin.

On December 11, 1943, Moltke again visited Istanbul, where he hoped Kirk would be waiting for him, but he was disappointed to find that the American ambassador was not there. OSS contacts explained to him that security was too tenuous in Istanbul, where intrigue lurked in every byway, and a secret trip to Cairo was out of the question. The truth of the matter was that Kirk did not want to see him since for policy reasons he was not in any position to encourage Resistance initiatives. Moltke had to be satisfied with a conversation in Ankara with the U.S. military attaché, Brigadier General Richard G. Tindall, that was as annoying as it was inconclusive. All Moltke got out of the talk was a promise to send Kirk the Kreisau Resistance proposal entitled "Exposé on the Readiness of a Powerful German Group to Prepare and Assist Allied Military Operations Against Nazi Germany."[5]

The proposal was based on the desire not only to end the war with the Western Allies but to ensure a rapid occupation of Germany and active Allied assistance in establishing a new German border in the East and a new post-Nazi democratic government. These conditions of surrender were intended to keep Soviet troops out of Germany and deny Stalin participation in the final peace negotiations determining Germany's fate.

---

policy authority, he made it clear to the German ambassador that "a reaction might set in in the U.S. such as was occasioned when Mussolini was suddenly removed from the Italian scene" and that "he could count on every assistance from America"—OSS message to Washington from Cairo, dated April 18, 1943, National Archives, RG 226, entry 134, box 251, folder 1519.

Papen's response was to promise support for such an idea if "President Roosevelt was prepared to offer him a promise of peace that would be attractive enough to 'his friends,'" something concrete that promised a future for Germany—ibid.

Donovan enthusiastically endorsed the idea in a memorandum to President Roosevelt suggesting that if the plan worked, unconditional surrender would not be violated and "it would strengthen your position morally at the peace table"—Folder OSS/Donovan, 1941–43, Franklin D. Roosevelt Library, PSF, Box 167. Also see Christof Mauch, "Dream of a Miracle War, the OSS and Germany, 1942–1945," Prologue, vol. 27, no. 2 (Summer 1995), pp. 137–138.

Moltke's letter to Ambassador Kirk, which also asked for a secret rendezvous at which he could discuss a German surrender to the Western Allies, was significant for its recognition that "The political post-armistice world would have to be touched." As he put it, this issue "constitutes part of the diagnosis of the present situation."[6] Whatever Germany's fate, there must not be a repeat of the Italian fiasco, in which, through lack of planning, only chaos replaced Mussolini's fall from power.

A December 29 transmittal letter written by a German expatriate, Alfred Schwarz, an important OSS secret agent known by his code name Dogwood, was also given to the U.S. military attaché General Tindall. The letter explained why Moltke had insisted on dealing with Kirk, a man who knew Europe well but, above all, was trustworthy. That was extremely important; during previous overtures to the Western Allies "flagrant breaches of security occurred which jeopardized the entire [Resistance] organization and caused the execution of important members for high treason." Schwarz explained that since Moltke could not make it to Cairo to see Kirk while on this brief trip to Istanbul, he was enclosing a memorandum explaining the conditions under which further talks could proceed. This he hoped would reach President Roosevelt, General Marshall, and OSS chief General Donovan so that a conference of their representatives could be held to discuss the matter thoroughly with Resistance plenipotentiaries no later than January 1944.[7]

The Moltke memorandum contained several specific requests. It called for a quick British-American occupation of Germany "on the largest possible scale . . . eastward to an unbroken line from Tilsit to Lemberg," including most of Poland, forestalling any "overpowering threat from the East." The plan envisioned a provisional German democratic government that would include strong left-wing Social Democrats and labor representatives so as to "steal the thunder" of the Soviets.

In analyzing the current Resistance situation in Germany, the memorandum sketched the two competing, irreconcilable groups: Moltke's own group seeking a "Western solution"—i.e., collaborating with the Western Allies—and those looking toward the Soviet Union for an "Eastern solution."

The drafters of Moltke's analysis described the "Eastern" group as the stronger, having a considerable following in the Wehrmacht and Luftwaffe, where "it rules supreme." The military connection had its roots in the distant past: "The driving force behind the Eastern wing is the strong and traditional conviction of a community of interests between the two mutually complementary powers, Germany and Russia, which led to the historical cooperation between Prussia and the Russian monarchy, and between the German Republic and Soviet Russia in the Rapallo period [1922] when the Reichswehr and the Red Army concluded a far-reaching understanding regarding military collaboration and reciprocal training facilities."

The memorandum noted that the "Eastern" sentiment was also encouraged by the impressive resilience of the Red Army in revitalizing itself after near defeat. The formation of the German Officers' League at Moscow with its complement of outstanding and widely respected military figures (although as POWs they were under implicit, if not explicit, Soviet pressure to cooperate) was cited as an example of the attraction some German officers had for Russia. With obvious reference to the Soviet-controlled spy network Rote Kapelle, the memorandum seemed to be impressed with the wireless contact that had been maintained with the Soviet Union by German officers who clandestinely passed valuable intelligence to Moscow until they were uncovered and killed in 1943.[8]

There would be those postwar analysts who believed that Moltke's "Exposé" reflected Wilbrandt's and Rustow's views more than those of Moltke and the Kreisau Circle. Specifically tailored by these two OSS agents to attract the Americans, it exaggerated the "Eastern" orientation of the German military. It did not, however, attract Alexander Kirk, whose reply to his old friend Moltke, was almost rudely brief: "I would always be glad to see you but I do not see that any good purpose would be served by our meeting now as it is my personal conviction that nothing short of unconditional surrender of the German armed forces will terminate the war in Europe."[9] Kirk's message did not even give Moltke the satisfaction of promising that his message would be referred to higher authority in Washington, nor did he even pass on this offer of capitulation and peace to the State Department.

In a covering note the American ambassador explained frankly to General Tindall in Ankara, through whom he passed his reply to Moltke: "I am enclosing my reply . . . which I am making on my responsibility, without consulting with anyone." Kirk went so far as to ask Donovan to see to it that his name did not appear in any of the correspondence on this subject, known by the code name Herman Plan.[10] It will be recalled that Kirk in 1939 had elected not to tell Washington about urgent intelligence that he had received from Associated Press correspondent Louis Lochner that World War II was about to begin; now he apparently did not feel it necessary to let Washington know that the Resistance had made a serious, if not acceptable, bid to end hostilities.

While bound by the policy of unconditional surrender, which Kirk thought "should remain our slogan," he saw no need even to keep Washington informed about Resistance activities. Colonel David Bruce, OSS station chief in London with European responsibilities, noted in his post-war diary: "Lunched with Alex Kirk. . . . He is a queer fellow, uncoopera-tive and seemingly uninterested in intelligence matters. His mind is quick, his wit mordant, but he is ill-attuned to the times, particularly to matters pertaining to war."[11]

Kirk's basis for rejection was his conviction "that the war must end by the military defeat of the German Armed Forces and not by any dickering on our part with factions within Germany."[12] He did not seem to consider the possibilities and advantages of early surrender by the German armed forces such as that which soon occurred in Italy.

If Kirk was not willing at least to encourage discussion on the Moltke ini-tiative, William Donovan was. He not only urged his Istanbul station chief to send his views but asked for several other opinions, particularly with re-gard to the Soviet threat referred to by Moltke. The OSS's chief analyst, Professor William Langer of Harvard, in response to Donovan betrayed a woeful ignorance of the German Resistance movement. Allen Dulles in Bern was keeping well abreast of Resistance operations through Gisevius and other contacts, so it is strange that the fruits of his labors, the so-called Breaker Reports, did not seem to have made an impression on Langer's an-alytical offices in the OSS in Washington. The professor wrote that his staff's study of December 1943 showed "no evidence to support the con-tention that there is a fairly large, well organized and influential opposition group." Langer apparently found it difficult to believe that an opposition as described by Moltke really existed. As for the Soviet threat, Langer gave his unduly optimistic conviction that the "present Russian Government is *pre-pared to play ball* [author's italics], but is equally prepared and determined to execute a volte-face if the British and Americans do not play fair."[13]

Langer recommended playing fair by informing the Russian govern-ment that "we have been approached in this way but do not propose to commit ourselves, except in agreement with the Allied Powers."[14] Ignoring evidence of Soviet unilateral designs for postwar Europe, Langer recom-mended remaining on good terms with the Moltke group with a view to using it later as nucleus for a post-Nazi government—"if agreeable to Rus-sia and Britain."[15]

Another Donovan referent, Captain Fritz Oppenheimer, also recom-mended submitting Moltke's plan to Russia while at the same time asking for information from Stalin about the Soviet controlled German Officers' League. And with a more positive approach than Langer's, Oppenheimer believed that the OSS "should do . . . whatever might increase the differ-ences inside Germany and thus strengthen the opposition to the regime."[16]

A German expert, Professor Karl Brandt of the New School of Social Research, when queried by Donovan, assessed Moltke's Resistance leaders as a "highly select and strategically located group . . . more worthy of full consideration than any other so-called underground movement" and one that was "the only practicable and politically permissible way to keep Russia out of Central Europe." He recommended that the OSS "start to work out with them the complete strategy for the key action" proposed by Moltke.[17]

The British were aware of Moltke's December 1943 visit to Istanbul. In *The Cadogan Diaries*, a fleeting reference is made to an approach made by Ambassador von Papen that same month. Papen apparently suggested that Germany maintain the Austrian Anschluss and "rent" Danzig and the Polish Corridor from Poland. But the British were even less interested in a deal than Roosevelt, even if the Nazis could be overthrown. No deal would be acceptable "until the military balance had tilted much more heavily against the Axis,"[18] ensuring unconditional surrender

Recognizing that the Moltke plan was certain to enrage Stalin, something Roosevelt was loath to do, and lacking enough information about the group's capabilities, the OSS Planning Group recommended to General Donovan on April 3, 1944, that it should not be transmitted to the Joint Chiefs of Staff for action "at this time." If this was not enough to kill the Moltke plan, an OSS telegram from Dulles in Bern, dated March 5, 1944, was. It reported that intelligence acquired from within the Abwehr revealed that Helmuth von Moltke had been arrested by the Gestapo on charges of treason in January 1944.

Moltke's demise came about because of a social connection with a group of conspirators, known as the Solf Circle. Ever seeking evidence that would incriminate the Abwehr and his rival Canaris, Schellenberg learned of the Solf Circle from an SD agent provocateur who had penetrated the group. Frau Anna Solf, widow of the last foreign minister of Imperial Germany, was well known in Berlin for her elegant salons. These affairs often provided cover for meetings of like-minded people long united by their opposition to Hitler. Despite a hurried warning by one of Canaris's Abwehr officers, a Gestapo raid on a Solf Circle meeting netted more than sixty persons, the cream of Berlin's society. Interrogations conducted before their executions compromised Moltke as well as many others. Following the abortive bomb plot against Hitler in July 1944, Moltke was hanged.[19]

Almost certainly there had been more than the Solf affair to explain Moltke's unmasking and subsequent execution. For one thing, the OSS discovered that its important agent Alfred Schwarz, or Dogwood, who had handled the contact with Moltke in Istanbul, had been running an espionage net thoroughly penetrated by the Germans. The OSS dissolved the Dogwood organization in late July 1944 and fired Schwarz, but the damage had already been done.

Another Abwehr official who came under Gestapo suspicion as a result of the Solf affair, if not from other chinks in the Resistance armor, was Erich Vermehren, who served Canaris in Istanbul as Leverkühn's assistant. Rather than return to Berlin for questioning and almost certain death, Erich Vermehren and his wife, Elisabeth, defected to the British and were given asylum in Cairo. In the wake of the Vermehren scandal, still another Abwehr agent and his wife, the Kleczkowskis, defected to the Americans and fled to Cairo one step ahead of the Gestapo.[20]

These events reflected badly on Paul Leverkühn, who was already suspected by the Gestapo of maintaining clandestine contact with the Americans in Istanbul (Istanbul was not a city in which secrets were easily kept). He was asked to return to Germany but managed to avoid Moltke's fate by stalling until the German collapse and the end of the war.

The Vermehren affair, capping a series of other Abwehr embarrassments, provided Schellenberg and Himmler with an excuse to take over the Abwehr—a long-sought objective. This meant the end of Canaris's career and ultimately a violent end to his life.

TWENTY-SIX

Images of Treachery

THE INHUMANITY OF NATIONAL SOCIALISM AND THE PROMISE OF INFAMY early recognized in Hitler provided motives for the German Resistance. Hitler had to die if Germany was to live. Less estimable is the spectacle of perfidy among the Nazi leaders, the keepers of the faith, whose concern for the glory of the Third Reich was exposed as a sham, masking in most cases blind devotion to self rather than to their Führer, behind whose back they intrigued.

As we have seen, Göring's proclivity for treachery revealed itself to the British on the eve of the Polish invasion; he resented war because it would interfere with his self-satisfying life of pomp and power. Others, principally Heinrich Himmler, Martin Bormann, SD chief Walter Schellenberg, and Gestapo chief Heinrich Müller, secretly committed high treason well before war's end in frantic realization that Germany was losing the war and they stood to forfeit their lives unless they could plea-bargain with the victors.

There was also lack of trust and faith among the partners of the Grand Alliance. Stalin considered his partnership with the Western Allies an arrangement of convenience until Hitler could be disposed of. He did not trust either the British or Americans, who he believed had purposely stalled on opening a second front in France so that Germany and Russia would destroy each other. Nor did Britain look forward to the postwar Soviet Union, ravaged by war but eager to exploit Germany's defeat and ruin to dominate Europe. In the meantime a hypersuspicious Stalin was obsessed by his fear that despite their commitments to the doctrine of unconditional surrender, the Western Allies would join with Germany to gang up on him.

Stalin's moles within British intelligence—Philby, Blunt, and Cairncross—had certainly kept Soviet intelligence informed of early British contacts with the Resistance as well as Dulles's later machinations with German Abwehr agents in Bern, all of which nourished Stalin's political paranoia.

The Soviets were well aware of MI-6's bias. Comments such as those of Frederick Winterbotham, British chief of air intelligence, who commiserated with Menzies when Anthony Eden forbade the MI-6 chief from meeting with Canaris in late 1942, were probably typical. Referring to the Soviets, Winterbotham mused: "Why we should fall over backwards to appease those who were, and are, pledged to destroy our life, I shall never understand."[1]

Stalin did not trust the British Secret Service, which—Resistance games aside—he believed not only was behind Hess's flight to Scotland on May 10, 1941, but had as its purpose reaching a peace agreement with Hitler himself on the eve of Germany's attack on Russia. Certainly there were appeasers and defeatists in Britain's establishment, including the Duke and Duchess of Windsor, with whom German agents flirted. For that matter, the British Foreign Office often looked askance at the Secret Intelligence Service with its bulging bag of tricks and informed all British diplomatic and Consular missions abroad to reject any and all overtures for peace by the Germans.[2]*

Stalin later grumbled about alleged plots hatched behind his back by his Western Allies, but his own diplomats and NKVD agents were certainly feeling out the Germans about a separate peace as early as September 1941. In Russia's hour of peril, Canaris's Abwehr received indications from Sweden that a thoroughly worried Stalin was beginning to consider overtures to Hitler. Edgar Klaus, one of Canaris's agents in Stockholm, had been taking soundings since the spring of 1941; specifically he had established close relations with the Soviet minister to Sweden, Madame Aleksandra Mikhailovna Kollontay, a longtime Bolshevik revolutionary

---

*German defector Wolfgang zu Putlitz, not yet unmasked by the British as a secret Soviet agent, advised that a postwar German government dominated by German Resistance leaders, particularly active survivors of the Social Democrat party, would be dangerous. Kim Philby's influence within British intelligence was also a factor since he had consistently screened out approaches to MI-6 by Abwehr chief Admiral Canaris and otherwise done all he could to discredit the German Resistance. But however gratifying Philby's and Putlitz's actions may have seemed to Stalin, the hypersuspicious Soviet leader could not erase from his mind a profound fear that Churchill (and Roosevelt), acting with German Resistance, would double-cross him in the end.

closely connected with the centers of power in Moscow. Klaus had made a name for himself as a Russian expert and, it was suspected by the Abwehr, had sold his services to both the French and Soviet intelligence services before Canaris hired him.[3] Klaus was nothing if not versatile.

At frequent bridge games with Klaus, Kollontay anguished over Soviet defeats during those first black months of Germany's blitzkreig. By late June 1941 Klaus was convinced that Mme. Kollontay was really looking to save herself in what she feared would be a Soviet collapse, although she professed to have an official mandate from Moscow to explore formulas for peace. She confided in Klaus that she would consider defecting to Germany if she were given certain guarantees and rewarded financially.

Canaris passed this interesting development to Foreign Minister Ribbentrop, who informed Hitler: "The Russian minister in Stockholm, Mme. Kollontay, intended to break with the Soviet Government and come to Germany. . . ."[4] Hitler personally sent back word that the lady should be "generously accommodated"[5] although the matter of her defection seemed to have become dormant, if it had been genuine in the first place.

While Kollontay's frame of mind may have been a symptom of the despair felt by Russians as German panzers smashed swiftly into their country, it was in the summer of 1942 that Stalin gave concrete signs of being ready to bargain. The Allied landings in North Africa, code-named Torch, had not been welcomed by Stalin. In the Soviet dictator's opinion, this was a useless diversion; it was not the definitive landings on the Continent that Stalin desperately needed to relieve the pressure on the Soviet Union. Stalin believed he could not rely on the Allies to rescue him.

By late 1942 Canaris's agent Klaus reported: "I guarantee you that if Germany agrees to the 1939 frontiers, you can have peace in a week."[6] On November 11 the Finnish ambassador to Germany had heard from Soviet Minister Kollontay in Stockholm that Stalin was considering a Finnish-Soviet peace formula calling for a return to the 1939 prewar Soviet-Finnish borders.* But the Soviet message made it clear that any such agreement

---

*A message from the Japanese minister at the Vatican to the Japanese Foreign Ministry in Tokyo on September 23, 1942, deciphered under the Magic program, stated in part that the Italians had forbidden the press to publish anything about U.S. Ambassador to the Vatican Myron Taylor's return to the Vatican and audience with the Pope. This message was concerned with rumors of a separate peace between Finland and the USSR in which Finland hoped to make peace with the USSR under an American guarantee through the mediation of the Vatican. The German ambassador to the papal court believed that even if rumors of Finland's making a separate peace should materialize, it would be only Western propaganda calculated to split the ranks of the Axis (Public Record Office, Kew. File HW-1, 929).

with Finland would be dependent on a German-Soviet settlement. Realizing that the Germans were the real object of Stalin's initiative, the German Foreign Ministry asked the Finns to abandon their contacts with the Soviets as a complicating distraction.[7]

The Japanese, who still maintained relations with the Soviets despite their alliance with Germany, also let Berlin know in the fall of 1942 that the Soviets would probably be willing to negotiate. The Red Army's military position at this time was precarious; a quick German victory still seemed entirely possible.[8] Indications that a change of Soviet policy was perhaps in the offing caused Ribbentrop to send his Eastern European expert Peter Kleist to Stockholm in early December 1942 to investigate. Ribbentrop did not realize that Kleist was secretly one of Canaris's men and a Resistance collaborator. But, whatever bias Kleist may have wanted to express in furtherance of Resistance objectives and however much Canaris himself would have liked to sabotage détente between Germany and Soviet Russia, it was Ribbentrop who was calling the shots. The German foreign minister would have been livid with rage had he realized that his representative, Kleist, and the Soviet go-between, Klaus, with whom Kleist would be working, both were Canaris agents.[9]

Klaus showed Kleist a specific peace proposal given him by Soviet Minister Kollontay and Andrei Aleksandrov, a Soviet intelligence officer; on July 7, 1943,* he met with the latter to discuss the plan, which called for a return to the 1939 frontiers in Eastern Europe.[10] Then in September Kleist met with Mme. Kollontay and her counselor of legation, Vladimir Semy-

---

*When the German 6th Army investing Stalingrad was defeated on January 30/31, 1943, the power equation on the eastern front changed dramatically. The German eastern offensive had been stopped. There were those in Britain who believed that this momentous development required a new look at policy. For example, William Cavendish-Bentinck, the chairman of the Joint Intelligence Committee charged with estimating and planning, wrote a frank memorandum in which he acknowledged that before the German defeat at Stalingrad British strategy had correctly called for maximum military effort to keep German pressure off Russia. Moreover, he realized that Russia's heroic defense had had British public opinion rooting for the Russian underdog. But things were now different, and when one looked at the situation hardheadedly, a victorious Russia would prove to be a postwar threat to Britain. Thus now it was in British interests to let the Germans and Russians tear each other to shreds, implying that a second front in France during 1943 might be premature despite "however sentimental the British people might be about her [Russia]"—Annan, *Changing Enemies*, pp. 61, 62.

Despite his influential position, Cavendish-Bentinck's indiscreet excursion into *realpolitik* did not translate into official British policy. Still, well-positioned Soviet spies, such as Philby and Cairncross, almost certainly reported that these views were being authoritatively expressed within the Joint Intelligence Committee, and this was enough to cause Stalin to fear the worst from his partners in the Grand Alliance.

onov.¹¹ When Ribbentrop presented the plan to Hitler, the Führer, in a particularly bad mood, erupted in anger at the thought of negotiating for peace: Soviet capitulation, yes; a negotiated peace, never!

The anti-Bolshevik Canaris may have been relieved that a negotiated peace with the Soviet Union, surely a Faustian deal at best, seemed out of the question. He must also have been pleased that the peace negotiations, having gone farther than Hitler realized, reflected badly on Ribbentrop's judgment. In Canaris's opinion, and in the opinion of most other high officials in Hitler's government, Ribbentrop was a fool who always seemed to make the wrong decision. Yet there would be other apparent Nazi zealots ready to bargain with one or another enemy behind Hitler's back in an effort to find a haven after the inevitable deluge.

FOLLOWING HEYDRICH'S DEATH ON JUNE 4, 1942, HIMMLER'S AIDE SS Obergruppenführer Karl Wolff assembled senior officers of the RSHA to hear an inspirational talk from Heinrich Himmler. The usual platitudes, such as "My fatherland, right or wrong," and the SS credo "My honor is loyalty" were delivered with a straight face to his "obedient" audience. Curiously he admitted that the SD was still inferior to the vaunted British Secret Service, but with hard work and buoyed by a sacred memory of Heydrich, it should soon close the gap.¹²

Not long afterward a private conference between Schellenberg, temporarily filling in for the dead Heydrich, and Himmler took place on quite another note. According to Schellenberg's account of an August meeting held at Himmler's advance field headquarters at Zhitomir in the Ukraine—not far from Hitler's headquarters at Vinnitsa—the Reichsführer rambled on about such incongruous subjects as pending operations in Tibet, Indian philosophy, the history of German witchcraft, and the magical powers of his personal physician, Dr. Felix Kersten (who dabbled in the occult and who was suspected by Schellenberg of having sold out to the British). When he could bring Himmler back to matters at hand, Schellenberg on instinct asked him an exceedingly indiscreet question: "In which drawer of your desks have you got your alternative solution for ending this war?"¹³

In his postwar memoir Schellenberg professed to have lost faith in the concept of German "total victory" as early as the summer of 1942. While Hitler's war juggernaut was still rolling forward, there were imminent dangers on the horizon. The Wehrmacht was overextended, and the United States with its war production capability would soon turn the tide of war in favor of the Allies. Germany logically should bargain with the West while it could still do so from a position of strength. Assuming Himmler too foresaw the defeat of the Reich, Schellenberg would not find it strange that he would seek insurance. Schellenberg knew that Himmler's lawyer, Karl Langbehn, had ties with the West, and he suspected that Himmler's physician was also hedging his bets. If Himmler dealt leniently with Albrecht Haushofer in the wake of the Hess affair, it was because he believed that the young man might soon prove useful as a contact with the West.

Schellenberg's blunt question caught Himmler by surprise; the Reichsführer shouted, "Have you gone mad?" When he finally calmed down, Himmler admitted that only the "idiot" Ribbentrop was encouraging Hitler to pursue a lost cause and admitted that he himself was indeed considering alternatives. As they discussed the matter, Himmler asked Schellenberg to look into the possibilities for establishing secret contacts with the West in such a way that it could not be construed as an act of weakness on Germany's part. He concurred with Schellenberg that the matter should be handled discreetly through the SD, so if things went wrong, he would not be implicated. Himmler believed that step one should be to get rid of Ribbentrop. After discussing the possible terms of a settlement and how they would apply to the various concerned nations of Europe, the meeting broke up at three in the morning. It had been a long and fateful night from which Schellenberg emerged with authority to proceed down a dangerous path, but with the ominous warning that the least misstep would force Himmler to drop him "like a hot coal."[14] No intelligent Nazi leader in a position to know what was going on in mid-1943 could believe that Germany would be able to win the war. The true ideological members of the Resistance, the members of the Black Orchestra, had put their lives on the line, plotting against Hitler from the moment it appeared that he was headed for war, if not before. While there were late joiners, no less genuinely opposed to Hitler, there were also opportunists who simply knew when to jump off a lagging bandwagon. Himmler was one of the latter, whose fears were reinforced by Schellenberg, a persuasive man who in effect had gained a measure of protection from the Gestapo by making a secret pact with his Reichsführer but who proceeded to carry out his own plans in the knowledge he was taking great risks. Schellenberg knew well that the Western Allies would never consider any agreement with Himmler, the perpetrator of unspeakable crimes against humanity, so he did not want to be inextricably linked with him. It was odd that Himmler himself seemed undismayed by the odium in which he was held.

Schellenberg was not the only one to work on Himmler to defect. Professor Johannes Popitz, former Prussian minister of state and finance and currently an active member of the opposition, sought out Himmler at Langbehn's instigation. Himmler's aide SS General Karl Wolff, also newly in contact with the opposition, invited Langbehn to eavesdrop on Popitz's conversation with Himmler from an anteroom (Wolff had Himmler's office bugged). They heard Popitz give his opinion that Germany was heading for defeat or, at best, stalemate; the war could not be won. But Popitz added that the British and the Americans, recognizing the dangers of bolshevism, were probably ready to negotiate with an alternative German government. Langbehn became more explicit in his own subsequent conversation with Himmler, making it clear that Hitler must be removed before any accommodation with the Allies would be possible. Himmler seemed to take such frank talk without flinching.[15]

Unfortunately an incriminating Allied message from Switzerland, quoting Langbehn's account of his meeting with Himmler, was intercepted and broken by the German cryptanalytical experts. (Both the British and Americans denied sending the message.) Gestapo head Heinrich Müller, who was actively scheming against Himmler, seized this opportunity to give the intercepted message to his accomplice in this Machiavellian palace intrigue, Martin Bormann, who in turn saw to it that it reached Hitler. To clear himself, Himmler pinned the whole thing on Langbehn and had him arrested.[16] Popitz somehow escaped Langbehn's fate, but this incident obviously slowed down Himmler's flirtation with the Resistance. It was typical of him to have played both sides, loyal defender of Hitler and intriguer with the Resistance, keeping his options open so that he could jump in whatever direction developments dictated.

This story, casting Bormann and Müller as the villains as far as Himmler was concerned, requires a closer look at them both. They too had their plans for the ultimate fall of the Third Reich. Gestapo chief Heinrich Müller had secretly allied himself with Martin Bormann, who had guided him in looking "eastward" and convinced him to conspire against Himmler. Both reasoned that the Soviets were less scrupulous than the Allies about maintaining a common front against Germany and had their own agendas for Germany after the war. The Soviets also seemed less squeamish about dealing with Nazis tainted by the excesses of the Gestapo.

Müller had played a role in uncovering the Soviet-directed espionage net in Germany Rote Kapelle (Red Orchestra), and the implacable Gestapo chief had earned the reputation of being the quintessential Nazi bully, blindly loyal to Hitler and uncompromising in his opposition to Bolshevism. Schellenberg was therefore startled one day in the spring of 1943 when Müller made strange remarks about the Rote Kapelle, remarks not consistent with his usual anti-Bolshevik phobia.

According to Schellenberg, a slightly tipsy Müller emerging from a get-together of foreign-posted "police attachés," or Gestapo officers, engaged him in a conversation that veered precariously toward treason. While he considered the Rote Kapelle an unequivocal manifestation of Soviet influence, Müller thought it went beyond the working class and involved the more educated German classes as well. Perhaps, he mused, this represented an inevitably historical development, considering the "spiritual 'anarchy' of Germany's Western culture." Müller added that the Nazi ideology was "nothing more than a sort of dung on this spiritual desert" in contrast with the Communists' offer of a "positive electrical charge to Western negativism."[17] This coming from Müller was out of character, an astonishing display of political blasphemy. When he accused Hitler of lacking wisdom, his remarks sounded dangerously seditious to Schellenberg. "Somehow," Müller added, "Stalin does things better." He described Stalin as a leader with whom the Germans should reach an agreement as soon as possible. That would be a "blow which the West with their damned hypocrisy would never be able to recover from."[18]

Müller topped off his strange monologue with some laudatory comments about Bormann that were wholly inconsistent with earlier disparaging remarks he had made about Hitler's deputy. Müller thought Himmler's feud with Bormann was unseemly, "like a couple of snakes fighting," but placed the blame on Himmler. The Reichsführer, in Müller's opinion, would "have a tough job to come out on top" in this quarrel.[19]

Schellenberg thought that Müller spoke from some genuine conviction, but if he was simply trying to provoke the SD chief, he failed. Playing it safe, Schellenberg dismissed the conversation with friendly joshing: "All right, 'Comrade' Müller, let's all start saying 'Heil Stalin'—perhaps our little father Müller will become head of the NKVD!"[20]

SS intelligence officer Wilhelm Hoettl writes in his memoir that in early 1944 "Schellenberg had suspected that Müller was using 'turned' [doubled] radio operators to make a real and sincere contact with the Russians." Schellenberg claimed to have had proof of his allegation from a surveillance of those involved in the radio operations.[21] Strangely, Heydrich's successor, Kaltenbrunner, paid no attention to Schellenberg's accusations, even when the latter threatened to reveal at some future date that Müller, "head of the Gestapo, had worked for the Russians."[22] After the war Schellenberg never produced evidence to prove his allegation although it may well have been true. His own situation was precarious enough for him not to alienate the Soviets, equal partners in the ongoing war crimes trials, by making such allegations.

But where did Bormann stand in what seemed to be an underground scramble for postwar patrons and protectors? Not only Schellenberg but

Canaris was convinced that he had sold himself to the Soviets. Canaris referred to Bormann as "the Brown Bolshevik."[23] In this connection it's worth looking at the saga of a German double agent deception operation run against the Soviets by the Gestapo through captured Red Orchestra members who were forced to collaborate and allow themselves to be used by the Gestapo to send disinformation to the Soviets.

This classic deception operation was a Gestapo version of the British Double-Cross Operation against the Abwehr. Gestapo officer Heinz Pannwitz, who had been Heydrich's deputy in Prague and had organized the massive reprisals in response to Heydrich's assassination, personally assumed control of the doubled Red Orchestra spy network with a team referred to as the Sonderkommando, a special task force devoted exclusively to playing the "radio game." The Sonderkommando prepared scripts that laced legitimate and often very good intelligence on Germany, the purpose of which was to establish credibility, with deception material and was transmitted by radio to Moscow, the Center. There was one thing wrong with the operation: The victim knew he was being victimized so discounted the German-prepared material meant to deceive. Moreover, some of the Rote Kapelle members who had been forced to cooperate with the Sonderkommando, including its "Big Chief," Leopold Trepper, managed to let their masters in Moscow know of their predicament through alternate channels still undiscovered by the Germans and warn them to ignore their controlled transmissions.

Originally the radio game, as it was sometimes known by the Germans, with Heinrich Müller in operational charge, was Himmler's brainchild. He hoped eventually to exploit the Sonderkommando facilities to establish a credible link with the West, as well as the East, in which he would reveal his interest in attempting to negotiate some kind of peace agreement in which he, not Hitler, would lead Germany. In the meantime he had Müller feed *Funkspiel*—in this case meaning deception material embedded in good intelligence—as bait. Himmler had covered his treacherous intent by telling Hitler that his deception program was intended to mislead the enemy with false information.[24]

Himmler knew how important it was to establish credibility by supplying sound and useful intelligence over this radio link to mask the misinformation calculated to deceive the enemy, but it was not always easy to shake loose such treasures from security-minded donor agencies. Ribbentrop's office was particularly reluctant to risk Foreign Ministry secrets in this way. Canaris too was opposed to allowing Germany's secrets to be sacrificed for this dubious enterprise. The bickering became so fierce that Hitler told Bormann to adjudicate the disputes.

As Himmler feared, his rival, the hated Bormann, used his position to move in on the *Funkspiel* operation. And as Hitler's favorite he had little trouble in attracting the opportunistic Müller as an ally.[25] Bormann finally threw Himmler out altogether and assumed control of the Operation for his own purposes. Bormann and Müller could now proceed to play their own radio games, which meant establishing personal contact with the Soviets. What shines through the evidence, for all its complications, is the conclusion that Himmler and Bormann were seeking traitorous contact with their Führer's enemy. This did not go unnoticed by Canaris.

We have the word of Paul Leverkühn, Canaris's friend and chief of station in Istanbul—also involved in the Black Orchestra—for a reflection of the Abwehr chief's suspicions about Bormann. In his postwar memoir Leverkühn writes: "He [Canaris] was extremely worried about the situation revealed by the exposure of the Rote Kapelle. . . . He firmly believed that the threads of this organization stretched outwards and upwards to Hitler's own headquarters and to his deputy, Martin Bormann, himself."[26]

Reinhard Gehlen, Soviet expert and chief of Germany's *Bundesnachrichtendienst* (BND), the Abwehr's postwar successor, claimed that Canaris had long suspected Bormann of Soviet connections and considered him "Moscow's most prominent informant from the very moment the campaign against Russia started." Canaris was in fact convinced that Bormann was committing espionage in behalf of the Soviets. Bormann may have covered himself with Hitler by claiming that his purpose was to feed disinformation to the Russians by clandestine radio or, conceivably, that he was attempting to cause a split between the Western Allies and the USSR, a solution for which the Führer hoped as his prospects of victory dimmed. Whatever the case, efforts by Canaris to investigate were blocked by Hitler.

Schellenberg's memoir contains this categoric statement: ". . . having a very clear idea of the general situation and being quite aware of the danger he [Bormann] was running, he was one of the first to try to go over to the East." Significantly Schellenberg made it clear that Bormann's Eastern connection had occurred before the end of 1943, prior to the general scramble by Nazis to make secret accommodation with the enemy before the Third Reich collapsed.[27]

Allen Dulles's commentary on Bormann's and Himmler's plans at this stage of the war was sent to Washington in February 1944. Their opportunism is revealed in Dulles's statement: "It is my opinion . . . that some rivalry exists between Bormann and Himmler, and that Bormann is more positively committed than Himmler to the possibility of a Soviet orientation of Nazi policy." It was made clear by Dulles that both men were thinking in terms of saving their respective skins by making the best deal they could with one or another enemy rather than by any motive that could be considered helpful to the Axis war effort. Dulles's specific concern was that such overtures to the Soviets could lead to a fracturing of the Grand Alliance: "In the last few months, there has been an increase in the strength of groups who would rather surrender to the Russians than the Anglo-Saxons when the crash comes. Even though overtly Nazi policy and propaganda is bitterly opposed to the Soviet Union, there are a number of realists within Germany who are aware that Germany must surrender, sooner or later."[28]

Another commentator on the Bormann connection with the Soviets was Leopold Trepper, the "Big Chief" of the Soviet Rote Kapelle spy ring. In his memoir, *The Great Game*, Trepper recalls that during the summer of 1943, "even Martin Bormann—the Führer's right arm—became keenly interested in the project [Gestapo doubling of the Rote Kapelle communications and playing back disinformation to Moscow]. Not only did he appoint a group of experts to prepare the material that would be used in the Great Game, as Trepper referred to the *Funkspiel*, but he wrote the despatches with his own hand." Trepper added significantly that Hitler was aware of the deception operation as a sophisticated instrument of war, "but certainly was not aware of his lieutenant's real intentions"—i.e., his objective to establish a personal, traitorous link to the Soviets.[29]

When appointed head of the Gestapo Sonderkommando, Heinz Pannwitz (real name Heinz Paulson) also saw this as a golden opportunity to make his own arrangements with the Soviets. Like his Gestapo boss Müller, who seemed to be unaware of his plans, Pannwitz was clearly defecting to the Soviets. According to Trepper, Pannwitz's assignment heralded a more aggressive policy; "radio games" were not enough. To serve his own plans of establishing closer links to the Soviets, he recommended that an emissary be sent to Moscow to establish a face-to-face connection. He obviously had in mind that he or someone he could trust would be that emissary. Pretending to be sent by an important secret cabal of high-ranking German military officers, the emissary would not simply discuss the intelligence role of the Rote Kapelle in keeping the Soviets informed of German moves but in this plot within a plot also propose a putsch to depose Hitler and negotiate a surrender. In order to impress the Soviets with the urgency of this matter, he would present the Center—i.e., NKVD headquarters—with "proof" that there were other German officers on the verge of reaching a peace agreement with the Western Allies aimed at excluding Soviet participation in a postwar peace process.

Pannwitz's idea of establishing personal contact was vetoed by wiser counsel as too dangerous. Instead he sent a letter to the Center asking for physical contact in Paris. As Trepper observes, "The wolf donning the shepherd's cloak, the butcher of Prague, was playing peacemaker with Moscow."*[30]

Moscow did not bite. No emissary was sent to Paris although the Center continued to levy intelligence requirements on the Rote Kapelle by radio and received in return confidence-building accurate information from it. Pannwitz was particularly generous in sharing with Moscow counterespionage material exposing German anti-Nazi dissidents who were beating a path to Allen Dulles's door in Bern.[31]

While Russia was attracting individual German opportunists such as Bormann, Müller, and Pannwitz, a symptom of Hitler's impending defeat, Stalin was forging ahead with his postwar plans with regard to Germany. In 1993, as the Russian archives were releasing bits and pieces from their World War II records, Swedish documents held in Moscow revealed that Stalin had discussed the post–World War II division of Germany as early as December 1941.[32] Stalin's master plan called for a German National Committee (formed in Moscow after the Soviets defeated the Germans at Stalingrad) to provide the basis for a Communist German puppet government to take over at war's end. It was for this reason that Moscow did not like German Resistance groups that could complicate the National Committee's efforts.[33]

Dulles could see that the Soviet Union was rapidly shifting its sights to a different Europe that would present itself after the Germans were beaten. The Cold War was beginning. As the tide of war on the eastern front shifted in favor of the Soviets after the Battle of Stalingrad at the end of January 1943, Moscow lost interest in German peace overtures.

*Heinz Pannwitz, or Heinz Paulson, became a Soviet prisoner of war and was flown to Moscow at war's end (*The Central Intelligence Agency, Counter-intelligence Staff, The Rote Kapelle, a Survey Report*, vol. I [December 1973], originally classified Secret, declassified September 27, 1976, p. 406). He tried unsuccessfully to justify his role during the period when he was serving as a Gestapo architect of deception in charge of the Sonderkommando, Paris. A twenty-five-year prison sentence was nonetheless his fate. He was released early in 1954.

"Gestapo" Müller's story did not end with the fall of Berlin if we are to believe the testimony given by Josef Frolik, a defector from the postwar Communist Czech Intelligence Agency. Müller was not apprehended when the war ended and was presumed to have been killed. At least a tombstone indicated this. A search for Müller began when Czechoslavakia's postwar minister of the interior, Rudolf Barak, on a hunch had his grave dug up only to find, as he suspected, Müller's remains were not in it. According to Frolik's sources, a very much alive Müller was tracked in 1955 to South America, where he was living under an assumed name. Barak, eager for information about pro-Nazi Czechs—i.e., anti-Soviet Czechs—that might still be relevant, had Müller kidnapped and brought back to Prague for incarceration and interrogation— Josef Frolik, *The Frolik Defection* (London: Leo Cooper, 1975), pp. 21, 22, 29.

The Soviets at the same time assembled the survivors of Field Marshal Paulus's 6th Army, captured at Stalingrad, to create a League of German Officers as a military adjunct to the free Germany movement, headed by the National Committee for a Free Germany. The league was led by General Walther von Seydlitz-Kursback, a corps commander during the Battle of Stalingrad.[34] While General Paulus did not want to join the league, he gave in to Stalin's pressure after the July 20, 1944, bomb plot debacle and supported it; although still a prisoner of war in Russia, he now enjoyed a palatial villa near Moscow.

The Committee for a Free Germany, clearly a Soviet front, issued a "manifesto" on July 19, 1944—one day before the bomb meant to kill Hitler was exploded—promising that the German Army would play an important role in the struggle for liberation from Hitler. Shades of the Rapallo Treaty of 1922, the League of German Officers endorsed a close alliance between the German and Soviet military, ironically the combination that had provoked a suspicious Stalin to conduct his Red Army purges of 1937.

Not only was this development a mockery of Soviet agreements with its Western Allies, but it revealed Stalin's cynicism in protesting Allied contacts with the German Resistance. Moscow had formed the National Committee for a Free Germany without consulting its Western Allies. Molotov's explanation after the fact was that this was simply a propaganda maneuver was unconvincing. This was Soviet political action, not simply propaganda, and was a portent of Stalin's intention to control postwar Germany. Rather than cause a breach in the Grand Alliance at a critical time, Britain and the United States looked the other way.

President Roosevelt was particularly eager to sustain what he believed to be an enduring friendship with Stalin, needed to steady a ravaged Europe after the war. The Big Three Teheran Conference in late November and early December 1943, in which the United States and Britain promised a Western invasion—Operation Overlord—in May 1944, papered over their differences for the moment. Stalin's suspicions of the Western Alliance was not, however, assuaged, nor did Soviet Russia cease its own covert political games designed to give it a power edge in Eastern Europe following the war. If anything, Stalin became more suspicious of the Allies, reasoning that they too must surely be unilaterally preparing for a postwar period. He saw the aggressive OSS clandestine activities of Allen Dulles in Bern as evidence of this. The Soviet dictator not only worried about Dulles's Resistance contacts—certainly made known to him by Philby or other Soviet penetrations of the Allies—but was suspicious of Allen Dulles's so-called Crown Jewel inventory, a secret list of worthy Germans who might be considered by the Western Allies acceptable leaders in a postwar Germany.

THE PRO-WESTERN ADAM VON TROTT ZU SOLZ VISITED ALLEN DULLES IN January 1943. Dulles was cordial and interested but, contrary to Stalin's suspicions, stopped well short of making political commitments to the Resistance. A secret meeting by Trott with British contacts in Sweden in the fall of 1943 had also been discouraging to him; the British seemed to fear the emergence of post-Nazi militarism in the wake of the war. Resistance members would have been even more discouraged had they realized that the Western Allies and the Soviets were making plans for the dismemberment of Germany and its division into zones of occupation once the war was over.

In September 1943 Dulles reported to Washington that influential Resistance leaders were divided between the Eastern and Western "solutions."[35]

The German Resistance, however, reacted cautiously to secret Soviet overtures despite its frustration in trying to deal with the Western Allies. General Beck distrusted the Soviets. Ulrich von Hassell did not feel comfortable in dealing with the Russians although he recorded in his diary that if need be, he would "consider an agreement" with them.[36] Count von der Schulenburg, however, was pro-Soviet and seemed to favor aligning the internal Resistance with the expatriate Free Germany Committee and General von Seydlitz-Kursback's League of German Officers in Russia.[37]

He even expressed his willingness to be smuggled into Russia and meet with his old friend Stalin to discuss Hitler's ouster and a negotiated peace! But even if most Resistance members stopped short of dealing seriously with the Soviets, they saw advantage in holding out this possibility to the Western Allies in order to pressure them into being more accommodating.

TWENTY-SEVEN

An Unraveling

THE PRINCIPAL OCCUPATIONAL HAZARD OF ALL INTELLIGENCE AGENCIES IS failure. The wonder of the Abwehr was that it did not unravel sooner than it did. The beginning of the end of the Abwehr is a cautionary tale of how little mistakes can undermine mighty edifices. It is also a story that concerns Abwehr Resistance officers Hans Bernd Gisevius and Eduard von Waetjen in Bern, Switzerland, who provided Allen Dulles with a window on the drama being played out in Berlin, and the drama itself, in which brave men struggled to survive when caught out. Finally and most strangely, the story reveals undertones of uncharacteristic restraint exercised by a relentless adversary: Reichsführer Himmler, the devil himself.

IT WAS INEVITABLE THAT ALLEN DULLES WOULD MEET HANS BERND GISEvius, the Abwehr representative under German consular cover in Zurich and a secret member of the Black Orchestra. Canaris had assigned Gisevius to Zurich at the onset of war expressly to maintain contact with persons of interest to the Resistance. Dulles first met Gisevius through Gaevernitz. It had not been simple to arrange a secret meeting with this six-foot-four-inch giant of a man with an arresting mien, but the critical first meeting took place without incident in early 1943 on the front steps of the World Council of Churches building in Bern. This furtive rendezvous proved to be the beginning of a fruitful association, another point of access to the Black Orchestra.

Much earlier Gisevius had been in touch with the British Secret Intelligence Service (MI-6), which had found him useful as a link with the Resistance. He rebelled, however at being exploited as a "spy" when British policy precluded political discussions with the Resistance; the relationship ultimately withered.

As previously described, one of Gisevius's tasks in Zurich following the fall of Poland had been to guide Canaris's friend the Polish widow Halina Szymanska in her role as link between British Secret Intelligence and Canaris. The fact that the strapping Prussian had allied himself with the Nazi movement in 1933—though he had not joined the party—and had worked for the Gestapo may have given the British pause. Gisevius, however, had long since broken with the Gestapo after a disagreement with its chief at that time, Rudolf Diels. He had then joined the Ministry of the Interior, but when war broke out, he had been recruited for the Abwehr—and the Black Orchestra—by Oster and Dohnanyi.[1]

Gisevius's relations with British intelligence had also been affected by the Venlo incident in November 1939, in which British agents Best and Stevens were arrested in Holland by the SD in a deception operation that seriously crippled MI-6's European operations. Lieutenant Colonel Claude Dansey, architect of the supersecret "Z" espionage organization within MI-6 and mastermind of the misbegotten Venlo affair, thereafter became suspicious of Gisevius.[2] Dansey reasoned that if SD officer Schellenberg had duped the British at Venlo by pretending to be a representative of German military dissidents, Gisevius might well be part of a similar SD sting in Switzerland.

Gisevius, from his vantage point, expressed himself on the British attitude in his postwar memoir of the Resistance: "It had hitherto proved impossible to maintain permanent political contact with the enemy. There had been only occasional meetings because the Allies restricted themselves largely to pure espionage. . . . The British, above all, stuck to the old fashioned scheme in which the 'enemy' was considered solely as an object of espionage. It was saddening to observe how this point of view hindered them from drawing any political advantage from the existence of a German Underground."[3]

Dulles apprised Washington of his contact with Gisevius, whom he touted as a valuable source on the Resistance. Knowing that Gisevius had been a British asset, the OSS checked him out with MI-6. This provoked Dansey to warn the Americans. The London OSS station in turn cautioned Dulles in Bern: "It is believed by the British that you should stop seeing 512 [code designation used by OSS for Gisevius] as they think he is untrustworthy."[4] But Dulles was not persuaded. Gaevernitz, a man whose judgment he trusted, had rated Gisevius highly. More convincing, one of Gisevius's first offerings was proof that German cryptanalysis had broken both the U.S. State Department and British Foreign Office cipher links to

Switzerland. This was not the kind of intelligence the Germans would "dangle" (i.e., throw away) to establish Gisevius's bona fides as a double agent if they were controlling him.

The British too must have used this reasoning since Dansey had a change of heart. OSS London cabled Dulles: "Our British friends now tell us that they have heard that he [Gisevius] has probably burned his bridges in Germany. His talks may, therefore, be even more interesting and they hope the talks will go on."[5] Gisevius's reporting had also caught British attention when he gave details of the V-1 and V-2 rockets as well as their launching pads at Peenemünde on the Pomeranian coast, a secret kept by the Germans since 1937, when the project had first begun. Allied bombings of these installations were of major importance in curtailing British civilian casualties, which nevertheless reached 8,588 dead, 47,838 wounded, and some 30,000 houses destroyed.[6]

Dulles was able to gain good information as well on the German Resistance through Gisevius, who was not only currently reporting on events in Germany but, with the help of Dulles's helpmeet Mary Bancroft, was writing a retrospective memoir of his experiences in the Resistance. Gisevius's Abwehr assistant Eduard von Waetjen, also well known to Gaevernitz, was a Resistance member and had his own contacts within Germany, from whom he kept abreast of developments. He too became part of Dulles's rapidly expanding roster of assets.

By the spring of 1943 there were developments that would radically change the fortunes of the Black Orchestra and bring several of its members, including Gisevius, within the crosshairs of Gestapo sights. It was more a question of Gisevius's bridges' being burned rather than his burning them, as the British had put it. But Gisevius's compromise, serious as it was, paled in significance when compared with other events set in motion by an unraveling of the Abwehr. The fate of Canaris was at stake.

TROUBLE CAME UNEXPECTEDLY. DR. WILHELM SCHMIDHUBER, PORTUguese honorary consul in Munich, who secretly worked for Canaris as both an Abwehr agent and a Resistance activist, had come under suspicion for illegal foreign currency transactions during the summer of 1942. He had tried to avoid arrest by remaining in Italy, where he had traveled on duty, but was extradited and forced to return to Germany. To save himself, he had given evidence that implicated others in the Abwehr.

Earlier it had been Schmidhuber who introduced Josef Müller to Canaris and had been active in Rome with Müller in behalf of the Black Orchestra in enlisting the Pope in secret negotiations with the British to forestall a German invasion of France. When interrogated about his irregular currency transactions, Schmidhuber denied that he had sought personal gain; he claimed that this had all been part of an Abwehr clandestine operation to fund secret agents abroad and, in some cases, fund Jewish refugees whom the Abwehr had helped escape from Germany.[7]

The Gestapo wanted to take advantage of this chink in the Abwehr's armor but had to hand over the case to the Wehrmacht. This meant that it would be the ferretlike inquisitor Dr. Manfred Röder, of the judge advocate general's department, no less suspicious of Canaris's organization than the Gestapo, who would instead relentlessly mount the attack. Gisevius believed that it had been Göring who had persuaded Hitler to let Röder investigate the case since it had been Röder who had so efficiently broken the Russian Rote Kapelle espionage net within the Luftwaffe. Now, Göring hoped, it would be the army's turn to be humiliated by a Röder-style inquisition, thus shifting the focus away from his Luftwaffe.[8] Röder submitted his case to the military court for indictment.

Schmidhuber was bitter that Canaris and the Abwehr had not rushed to rescue him. Canaris in fact did not like the man. But when Schmidhuber's evidence in court threatened to implicate such other Resistance luminaries as Dohnanyi, Oster, Josef Müller, and Bonhoeffer, Canaris heard alarm bells ringing. At the same time Canaris had learned from fellow Resistance member Arthur Nebe, head of the Criminal Investigation Department, that the Gestapo was sharpening its knives for another assault on the Abwehr. Bonhoeffer had already joined Schmidhuber in Tegel Prison when Canaris began his damage control efforts. Having been tipped off by Nebe that a raid on Abwehr offices was imminent, Canaris warned Oster to destroy all documentary evidence that might incriminate him and other Resistance members. According to comments made after the war by Munich Resistance veteran Karl Süss, "In our files there was proof of certain political activities by Admiral Canaris, as well as support given to Jews escaping abroad."[9] Canaris had been well advised by Nebe to take all possible precautions; unfortunately Oster was sloppy in carrying out the admiral's order. This was to prove calamitous.

Röder ordered Gisevius to Berlin from Zurich to give evidence. Röder reasoned that as Abwehr representative in Switzerland Gisevius should know about any Abwehr underground railway helping Jews escape. Gisevius endured two days of ferocious cross-examination but wriggled out of harm's way by claiming that Keitel had forbidden him to testify on classified Abwehr operations. Gisevius went to Chief Magistrate Dr. Karl Sack, a Resistance collaborator, to get help. According to Gisevius's memoir, Sack "intervened at once and secured a twenty-four-hour postponement of the warrant for my arrest." On Sack's advice, Gisevius in haste "dictated a detailed complaint" demonstrating that the questions Röder had put to him "were directed against neither Dohnanyi, Oster, nor Canaris, but in reality against Field Marshal Keitel himself in his capacity as supreme chief of the Abwehr."[10] This gambit provided Gisevius with a much-needed respite, and he beat a hasty retreat to Switzerland and safety. Others, however, remained in serious jeopardy.

Dietrich Bonhoeffer's widow, Christine, after the war provided some background on her husband's precarious situation, describing how he had helped his boss, Minister of Justice Franz Gürtner, to save various Jewish lawyers from Nazi pogroms. In 1942, as the plight of the Jews grew even more desperate, Bonhoeffer sought help from Canaris. The Abwehr chief was sympathetic, and he "employed" a certain number of the Jews to serve as "Abwehr intelligence agents" so that he could send them abroad out of harm's way. This was called Operation Seven because there had been seven Jews thus saved in the first group expatriated. Canaris, with a straight face, had told Gestapo chief Müller of "this operation," although the latter knew full well that the old, infirm, or frightened Jews who made up the group were a most unlikely-looking cast of spies.[11] Canaris was obviously guilty of politically incorrect philanthropy, if not of a felony under Nazi law.

When Canaris went to Himmler to rescue Bonhöffer's seven Jews, he shrewdly took the offensive, accusing the Gestapo of interfering with Abwehr counterespionage operations. "How do you expect me to carry on with the Abwehr, Herr Reichsführer, if your people arrest my agents?" he asked.[12] Canaris then quickly told Oster, "You had better teach them a code or two, for I have claimed them as my agents."[13]

Canaris continued to permit his officers to rescue individual Jews from Nazi persecution, provided some plausible rationale could be made to explain why they were "hired" by the Abwehr. In March 1941 the admiral helped some five hundred Jewish residents of Holland escape through the good offices of the Amsterdam Abwehr representative, Major Walter Schulze-Bernett.[14] Arrangements were made to send these Jews to various places of safety in South America. But such things did not escape Himmler's notice. When on one occasion the *Reichsführer* hinted at Canaris's sympathy for the Jews in conversation with Hitler, the admiral had a difficult time explaining to the Führer that any Abwehr use of Jews was justified for operational purposes.[15]

Dohnanyi's arrest had come about as a result of the raid on his office, just as Nebe had warned. On April 5, 1943, Röder, accompanied by Gestapo Inspector Franz Xavier Sonderegger, descended on the Abwehr headquarters on the Tirpitzufer. With Canaris and Oster in tow the raiders entered Dohnanyi's office and proceeded to search the safes. At first they uncovered nothing very incriminating. As Canaris and Oster stood nervously in attendance, Dohnanyi's eyes stared at his desk while Röder shuffled through the papers on it. Dohnanyi knew that among them were such highly incriminating material as Bonhoeffer's secret talks with the British bishop of Chichester and, worse, the dossier on Project X, the Resistance link with the British through the Vatican.

Dohnanyi caught Oster's eye and managed to point out the damaging papers with his darting glances. Oster grasped the problem and maneuvered himself next to the table, where he quickly slipped the files beneath his coat. But Oster had not been quick enough; Sonderegger saw his furtive movement and barked, "Halt!" Röder demanded that the papers be handed over.[16]

Canaris could only watch with dismay as Röder seized the keys to Dohnanyi's safe, where the V-7 file reposed, describing the seven Jews recently sent to Switzerland in terms that left little doubt that this had been an act of forbidden compassion, not a legitimate Abwehr intelligence operation.[17] Within hours Dohnanyi was in prison. On April 5 Müller was also arrested and forced to endure some 160 hours of interrogation. Other documents seized by Röder implicated Count von Moltke, Bonhoeffer, and Oster. Canaris too inevitably came under suspicion.

Canaris was shaken by the whole affair, but he had not lost his cunning. He intervened with Himmler to have the case involving his men handled exclusively by a military court and kept away from the Gestapo. He insisted that all the evidence revealed only legitimate Abwehr operations, typical of the kinds of tricks used by all intelligence agencies. Without argument Himmler stated that in fact he did not want to be responsible for the investigations. Once again Himmler had backed away from a confrontation with Canaris. Notwithstanding the damning evidence, he had restrained his Gestapo from pouncing on the admiral, however profound their rivalry.[18]

Canaris's fine hand could be seen within the military as well. By July Röder had been ordered to abandon his case for treason against the Abwehr officers. In August 1943 Dohnanyi, Schmidhuber, and Oster all were relieved of their indictments and let off with minor charges of "inefficiency." Schmidhuber was declared to have engaged in simple currency violations—nothing more sinister—and his self-serving accusations against fellow Abwehr officers were not found to be credible.[19]

Oster, while spared prosecution, was relegated to the Service Reserve. This was a terrible blow to Canaris and the Resistance; Oster had been one of the most aggressive of the Resistance leaders and would be missed by his colleagues. Third-ranking Abwehr officer Hans Piekenbrock was also edged out of the Abwehr. But Röder accepted defeat in this denouement and was shifted out of play by being given a face-saving promotion, although he continued to nurse his well-developed suspicions about Canaris. He remained convinced that he had uncovered a conspiracy, at the apex of which Canaris stood. He was right.

The Abwehr edifice was crumbling, and it would not take much more to topple Canaris himself, for all his adroit maneuvering and despite Himmler's mysterious indulgence of him.

HAVING QUICKLY RETURNED TO SWITZERLAND, GISEVIUS WAS SPARED THE harassment suffered by his colleagues as a result of the Schmidhuber affair, but while he was safe for the moment, he was under suspicion and no longer permitted to serve in the German consulate in Zurich. His official place as vice-consul—and Abwehr representative—was taken by Eduard von Waetjen while Captain Theodor Strünck replaced Waetjen as Abwehr number two. In January 1944 Waetjen, known in OSS correspondence as Gorter or No. 670, became Dulles's secret contact with the Abwehr Resistance circle, the Black Orchestra.

Through his sister, the wife of J. Sterling Rockefeller of the prominent New York family, Waetjen was well connected in the United States. His mother in fact was an American; his father had made a name for himself as a prosperous banker in Germany. Dulles actually felt closer to Waetjen than he had to Gisevius. Both Dulles and Waetjen were lawyers, and both had traveled in the same international circles. While Waetjen had joined the Nazi party in 1931, he soon became disillusioned and quit. His later devotion to the Resistance led him to Canaris, as both a source of information and a secret member of the Resistance.[20]

Waetjen conscientiously counseled Dulles on the political intricacies of the Resistance. Dulles cabled the OSS on January 27, 1944, that through Gorter (Waetjen) he had "secured a line to Breakers [the Resistance] which we think can be used now for staying in close touch with events."[21] "For a number of reasons," Dulles wrote, "I have not talked with Zulu [the British] about the Breakers situation at this particular time and . . . I recommend that you also refrain from doing so. . . ."[22]

As Waetjen saw it, there were three general groups within the Resistance. As it became obvious that Nazi Germany would lose the war, there were people who saw merit in letting Hitler remain in power so that there could be no doubt that he was responsible for the catastrophe. Those inclined toward the left favored an Eastern solution, by which the Resistance could seek a secret alliance with the Soviet Union. The third group, to which Waetjen, like Canaris, belonged, wanted an alliance with the West-

ern Allies in expelling Hitler and joining in common cause against the Soviet Union.[23] Waetjen, like Moltke in his letter to Alexander Kirk, believed
that the United States was making a mistake by not collaborating with the
Resistance; Allied victory and German unconditional surrender would not
alone serve Allied postwar needs. Consideration had to be given to the
kind of Europe that they wanted.

Dulles, during his first year in Bern, took the view that the Resistance
was an uncoordinated assemblage of church groups, labor unions, Socialists, civil service officials, and military leaders divided equally between
those inclined toward the East and those inclined toward the West.[24] He
blamed Gestapo terror for keeping the opposition off-balance. On the basis
of conversations with Prince Max Eugen zu Hohenlohe-Langenburg, a
contact of Himmler's and a sometime collaborator of the Resistance who
wandered through the never-never land of ambiguous politics, he thought
that Himmler might be amenable to an accommodation with the West
without Hitler.[25]

By January 1944, however, Dulles was regarding the Resistance as a
more cohesive opposition coalition. Much of his traffic, the Breakers Series, was thereafter concerned with this movement, which he now described as military, government, intellectual, and church dissidents who
sought foreign help and internal services, particularly communications
services, from the Abwehr. The Resistance took new life from the German
reversals on the eastern and Mediterranean fronts. Nazi Germany was
clearly headed for defeat and national destruction.

On April 6, 1944, Dulles received more detailed information on the Resistance from Gisevius after the harassed Abwehr officer hurriedly exited
Germany. General Beck, Gisevius reported, was eager to stage a coup but
needed help from the Western Allies. Generals Rundstedt and Falken-
hausen, he claimed, were ready to facilitate the landings of Allied paratroopers in designated zones on the western front and otherwise assist the
U.S. and British invasion so long as the German Army was allowed to continue to fight the Russians on the eastern front.[26]

Dulles was intrigued by these overtures and continued to bombard
Washington with news of Resistance actions and plans in the Breakers
cable series. But always casting its long shadow over Dulles's operations
were the restraints of the unconditional surrender doctrine. On a more
personal level Dulles was depressed by a telegram from Donovan dated
February 27, 1944, in response to his query about helping his contacts find
postwar sanctuary, a customary reward given agents who risked their lives
in their work. This message warned that the president feared "carrying out
such guarantees [of asylum] would be difficult and probably widely mis-

understood both in this country and abroad [read "Soviet Russia"]."²⁷ Roosevelt's further reference to those "who should properly be tried for war crimes" reflected a tendency by some American officials to discount the Resistance as composed of either feckless dreamers or rats lining up to jump ship.

There were indeed the late joiners, opportunists who tried to take out insurance by joining the Resistance. And there were those military leaders who opposed Hitler but found it difficult to take part in a rebellion at the same time as they led their troops in battle against the enemy or who were restrained by the sacred oath of loyalty to their country that all German officers had to take. But there were also those, military and civilian alike, who felt strongly enough about the catastrophe facing Germany and the atrocities perpetrated by the Nazis that they were prepared to give their life for the cause—and most would do so. Canaris, who had been secretly fighting Hitler in his own way since before the war, was one of the latter. He had already survived a series of narrow escapes, but time was running out for him. Intrigues in Italy and Turkey would next test his mettle and his luck.

TWENTY-EIGHT

Exit Canaris

As in Spain, Canaris had made a special effort to develop useful contacts in Italy. While Hitler had banned German espionage operations against his ally Mussolini, Canaris could justify his activities in Italy under the rubric liaison. In the course of his official activities he had gained the confidence, even friendship of General Mario Roatta and his successor, General Cesare Amé, Italy's top intelligence chiefs (military intelligence of the Military High Command, or SIM). He had in fact stretched these associations well beyond the usual boundaries of formal liaison: Both Italians had become assets of considerable value to Canaris, useful as confidential informants on backstage political developments in Rome. He confided in his Abwehr colleague Hans Piekenbrock that he had found Roatta and Amé sincere men with whom he could "exchange confidences."[1] Canaris's professional contact with Roatta went back at least to August and September 1936, just before the siege of Madrid in the Spanish Civil War, when he and his Italian colleague conferred secretly with Franco in Cáceres with regard to German and Italian military assistance.[2] Canaris's and Roatta's exploratory conversations on that occasion were in fact the genesis of German-Italian military cooperation, the first seeds of the Axis, as the Nazi-Fascist alliance was to be known.

Canaris was able to benefit from Roatta's and Amé's views on morale in Italy and the secret intrigues of Il Duce's son-in-law, Count Ciano, who favored Italy's withdrawal from the war, a matter of great concern to Germany. Through Italian intelligence friends Canaris heard strong rumblings of dissent as early as the autumn of 1941. Count Ciano was among the Grand Council of Fascism leaders who were to repudiate Mussolini.[3] The German ambassador to Rome, Ulrich von Hassell, an activist in the Resistance, records in his diary at the time that SIM officers told Canaris frankly that Italian Army officers "would and must overthrow Mussolini."[4]

Mussolini himself was not always happy about his role within the Axis. Ciano's diary entry of July 6, 1941, makes mention of German action threatening Italian interests in the South Tyrol area, which provoked Il Duce to comment, "I foresee an unavoidable conflict arising between Italy and Germany."[5] In November Ciano wrote in his diary that Mussolini had complained that the Germans, "both in military and political fields, have always acted without his knowledge."[6]

Then, early in 1943, Canaris informed his Abwehr colleague Colonel Erwin Lahousen that "the acute crisis in Italy could lead to serious upheavals." This was very different from the rosy picture given Hitler by Himmler on June 23, 1943, describing Il Duce's loyalty to Germany as something that "cannot be doubted . . . a split between the officers and the Duce need not be feared."[7] Canaris, who had little respect for Keitel, resented the fact that the field marshal had ignored Abwehr reporting on Italy, often refusing to pass on Canaris's information to Hitler because he thought it "would unnecessarily annoy the Führer."[8]

Himmler, like Keitel, probably did not want to upset Hitler with bad news, but the SD in Rome, like the Abwehr, could sense the trouble brewing. Despite Hitler's order banning intelligence activities in Italy, Schellenberg had quietly posted in Rome an SD (Amt VI) officer, Wilhelm Hoettl, who in April 1943 reported increasing opposition to Mussolini. Hitler, however, paid little attention to such warnings.[9]

An American message from Bern, intercepted and deciphered by the Germans, enabled Canaris to confirm that high officials in the Italian Foreign Ministry, including Ciano himself, were secretly talking with the Americans about withdrawal from the war. This intelligence, given the German High Command on June 25, proved accurate when Ciano and a majority of the Italian Grand Council came out openly in opposition to Mussolini. Mussolini was arrested on July 25, and Marshal Badoglio formed a new government.

Hitler was shocked; he immediately called a meeting with his senior officers, who held differing views on how Germany should deal with this potentially calamitous setback. An optimistic Kesselring was certain that Badoglio would stay the course with the Germans. But a skeptical Hitler ordered Canaris to assess the situation on the spot in Italy.

The Abwehr chief saw Cesare Amé in Venice for two days, August 2 and August 3. Amé's postwar account of their meeting, as related to André Brissaud, a French biographer of Canaris, is revealing. Canaris startled Amé when he greeted him saying, "My warmest congratulations; we also hope that our 25 July will come quickly."[10] Their mutually agreed-upon official memorandum of the meeting was of course circumspect and politically correct, with Italy vowing to continue the war staunchly beside its German ally. But in the course of a long walk on the Lido the two exchanged candid confidences. Both agreed that Italy would soon quit the war. It was indicative of their close relationship that Canaris confided in Amé his opinion that Hitler had to be overthrown as well and that Germany must end its war with the Western Allies. Such talk was dangerous; the admiral swore Amé to secrecy and reminded him to support the official party line of German-Italian unity in continuing the war when reporting to his government. Canaris, however, left his friend with a confidential warning against German efforts to make Italy captive to its doomed war effort: "Take my advice and allow as few German troops into Italy as possible. Otherwise you will regret it."[11]

Now that Germany's ally was in crisis, Schellenberg's RSHA was full of wild schemes to "liberate" Mussolini, kidnap the King, even remove the Pope to German territory "for security reasons." Tipped off by fellow Resistance activist Arthur Nebe, *Reichskriminaldirektor* (director of the Criminal Department), Canaris warned Amé to be alert for such plots.[12] Reference to removing the Pope must have been particularly shocking to Canaris, a staunch Roman Catholic.* Amé concluded, "It is evident that at this time Canaris had abandoned every precaution . . . this was high treason!"[13] Throughout the summer of 1943 Hitler exhorted the SD to find and rescue Mussolini. On September 12 Otto Skorzeny of the SD with a few paratroopers did "liberate" Il Duce from a ski lodge on the Gran Sasso in the Apennines, stimulating Hitler to develop grand plans to restore Il Duce to power.[14]

Thanks to Amé, Canaris was not taken by surprise when on September 3, 1943, Badoglio's government signed an armistice agreement with the Western Allies—at the very moment that the marshal was reassuring the German ambassador to Italy of his intention to remain at war. On October 13 Italy under Badoglio declared war on Germany.

The capitulation of Italy sent Canaris's friends Amé and Roatta scurrying for cover. Amé hid out near Venice while Roatta fled to Brindisi with

---

*After the war General Erwin Lahousen, close associate of Admiral Canaris's in the Abwehr, confided in Ian Colvin, the British Foreign Office German expert, that the admiral had made his trip to Venice in August 1943 specifically to warn Amé, and through him, the Italian government of the Führer's intention to kidnap the Pope and the king of Italy—Ian Colvin, *Canaris, Chief of Intelligence*, p. 191.

the Italian king. The OSS in Italy reported that Roatta's escape had been organized by the royal family. But he was permitted to escape only after he had threatened to release "sensational" information regarding Badoglio's government that would seriously incriminate the king.[15]

Canaris had to worry about Italian intelligence files that might bring to light his own activity in Italy. He did his best to seize all files that could reveal his special relationship with the two intelligence chiefs, but the SD nonetheless found evidence that tended to incriminate him.

When Schellenberg gave Himmler the file on Canaris's suspicious discussions with Amé, the *Reichsführer's* reaction was surprising. He looked troubled and promised to show it to Hitler, but there was no further conversation about the matter. Schellenberg was convinced that Himmler in fact did not share the information with the Führer or otherwise follow up. Schellenberg was certain that at one time or another Canaris had learned something compromising, making Himmler vulnerable to Canaris's implied blackmail.[16] Schellenberg, who already had dossiers linking Canaris to Dr. Müller's Resistance negotiations with the Vatican in 1940, his role with Franco in keeping the Caudillo out of Hitler's war, and the Resistance activities of Abwehr officers Dohnanyi and Bonhoeffer revealed by the Schmidhuber currency case, had now produced evidence of Canaris's treachery in his liaison relationships with Italian intelligence. Yet Himmler had done nothing further about it. Why not?

THE SCENE SHIFTS TO TURKEY, WHERE DEVELOPMENTS WERE ABOUT TO make Canaris's official position untenable and his ability to help the Resistance negligible. His luck was fast running out. On February 24, 1944, Dulles got wind of trouble brewing and reported that Himmler was about to fire Canaris and take over the Abwehr, incorporating it within the SD.[17] The trouble erupted when Erich Vermehren, Paul Leverkühn's assistant, defected to the British in Istanbul and sought asylum. Before the British could keep OSS Istanbul fully informed of developments there, Dulles in Bern reported that the status of the entire Abwehr had been "seriously jeopardized" by the Vermehren affair, and "the possibility that Vermehren may make certain disclosures concerning present relations between Turkish and Nazi intelligence is a matter of grave concern to the Nazis."

The Solf affair, in which a Resistance meeting had been raided by the Gestapo in Berlin and led to Moltke's incrimination, had also implicated Erich Vermehren. Rather than return to Berlin for questioning about his Resistance links Vermehren and his aristocratic wife, Elisabeth, the former Countess Plettenberg, defected to the British and reached Cairo in February 1944.[18]

Dulles was seriously disturbed by the likelihood that his important Abwehr informants would be lost by any major shift of power within the Abwehr. He notified Donovan that because it was likely that the SD would take over and shake up the Abwehr, the OSS should encourage several of its more important Abwehr contacts to refuse any order to report to Berlin. This, however, provoked Donovan to take a different view and notify all concerned OSS stations to be cautious in encouraging Abwehr defections that could only intensify SD housecleaning of the whole Abwehr apparatus.[19]

But even more important than this, the demise of the Abwehr under Canaris's leadership could disrupt its overseas agent nets on which the Double-Cross operation depended to pass misleading information about the site of the forthcoming Allied invasion of France. Recall Heydrich's accusation that Canaris's agents were corrupt and inefficient; if the RSHA chief, before his death, had not trusted Canaris, he probably would not have trusted his agents, particularly after the A-54 experience in Prague.

British MI-5, with its stake in the Double-Cross system, feared Abwehr instability and a stampede by Abwehr agents abroad to seek Allied protection as the two greatest dangers to this magnificent mechanism through which the Allies virtually controlled the Wehrmacht order of battle information. The saving of Double-Cross, according to its principal architect, John Masterman, depended on winning a race against time. Masterman later wrote, "Had the Abwehr begun its collapse six months sooner," denying the Allies the ability to draw the Germans off target, "the Normandy landings would have failed."[20]

In the wake of the Vermehren scandal, news of which had generated considerable publicity in Germany, another Abwehr agent, Karl Kleczkowski, and his wife fled to Cairo, one step ahead of the Gestapo, as did a lesser member of the Turkish Abwehr establishment, the Austrian Willi Hamburger. These events reflected badly on Paul Leverkühn, probably already under Gestapo suspicion because of his prewar links with Donovan[21] as well as his suspected current clandestine contact with the Americans in Turkey. Ankara and Istanbul were not cities in which secrets were easily kept. Leverkühn was asked to return to Germany for questioning but managed to avoid Moltke's fate by stalling until the German collapse and end of the war.

Another Nazi setback that discredited Canaris in Hitler's eyes had been Argentina's diplomatic break with Germany under American pressure on January 26, 1944, which, as Dulles reported, precipitated the arrests of "a large number of Nazi spies"—Canaris's spies—in Buenos Aires.[22]

These events provided SD chief Schellenberg with the excuse he had been waiting for to discredit Canaris and take over the Abwehr. Himmler could no longer avert his eyes to the accumulating evidence implicating Canaris, and the Führer was no longer in a mood to listen to Canaris's excuses. It seemed to be the admiral's unceasing pessimism about the eastern front that enraged Hitler the most; the Vermehren case and other Abwehr defections were lesser irritants, only symptoms of the defeatism that had infected Canaris and the Abwehr.

Double agent Dusko Popov, controlled by the British but working within the Abwehr as a penetration, saw the fall of Canaris from an insider's perspective. According to his story, Hitler summoned Canaris to Berchtesgaden to hear his latest assessment of the German offensive in Russia. After getting an unvarnished description of the problems besetting the Wehrmacht, an outraged Hitler knocked over a table standing between them and grabbed the "tiny admiral by his lapels."

"Are you trying to tell me I [have] lost the war?" Hitler exploded. Canaris protested that he was only passing on what his agents were telling him. Hitler, afroth with rage, shouted, "Are your Russian agents as trustworthy as the Vermehrens?"[23]

It was Ribbentrop, however, not Himmler, who administered the professional coup de grâce to Canaris. The foreign minister had long complained that Abwehr sabotage of British shipping in Spanish ports was interfering with his conduct of relations with Spain although in fact it was probably his jealousy of Canaris's power in Spain that really troubled him. On February 8, 1944, Hitler obligingly decreed that the Abwehr would cease sabotage operations in Spain. Only three days later the Abwehr blew up a British ship in the harbor of Cartagena; at least Ribbentrop claimed that it had been the Abwehr that committed the act. Enraged by what he considered Canaris's defiance of his order, Hitler made the final decision to have the Abwehr joined with the SD in a unified service headed by Himmler. The terms of the merger, negotiated by Kaltenbrunner, Gestapo chief Müller, and Schellenberg in behalf of Himmler and by Keitel for the OKW, were solemnized in a document issued on February 18.[24] Intelligence was now under Himmler and Schellenberg; Canaris was out of work.

Canaris was not arrested, however, nor were charges made against him; he was dismissed from office, ostensibly at least simply for lack of performance. Such leniency was perhaps motivated by Hitler's wish to dampen speculation that the shake-up in the intelligence establishment was indicative of serious internal dissension within the beleaguered Third Reich. But it is easy to conclude that Canaris's fairly painless retirement was another case of Himmler's reluctance to treat the admiral harshly. For all his resentment of Canaris as a rival in the intelligence business, Himmler still seemed bent on protecting him from the wages of high treason.[25]

Waetjen duly informed Dulles of events connected with the shake-up within the Abwehr, including the somewhat reassuring news that Colonel Georg Hansen, Canaris's replacement but now subordinate to Schellenberg, "was sympathetic to the German resistance, and [would allow] the organization to continue to be a refuge for the anti-Nazi elements." Dulles reported, with what seems to be a telegraphic wink, that the new Abwehr chief "is taking care of the matter" of allowing Canaris to take "extended leave."[26]

Canaris was at first forced to live a cloistered life at a government-controlled castle in Franconia, and by April he was formally retired from the service, but in June he was revived and given his make-work job as chief of economic warfare within the Wehrmacht and permitted to live fairly normally in his own villa at Schlachtensee. But for security reasons and because the Resistance was coming under the influence of a younger generation of military officers with whose activist philosophies he did not wholly agree, Canaris had to distance himself from involvement in the anti-Hitler plotting.

Despite Hansen's pro-Resistance stewardship, Canaris's removal and the withering of the Abwehr under overall SD command gave cause for grave worry on the part of the Western Allies. The assassination of Heydrich by British and Czech intelligence had given Canaris a brief but crucial reprieve from SD seizure and preserved controlled Abwehr intelligence nets feeding disinformation to the German High Command, so crucial to the success of the Normandy landings. But if Heydrich's timely death had spared Canaris, the admiral could also be grateful that he had survived other assaults on his position and had dodged the dangers constantly stalking him as a Resistance patron. The question nags: Why did Himmler not use the abundant evidence he had in his files to imprison Canaris and have him rigorously interrogated, particularly since he was surely aware that the Resistance was continually plotting to destroy Hitler and Nazidom? Why did he continue to protect Canaris from arrest, even now?

Ironically Canaris's undoing had been the result of serial intelligence failures, not suspicions of high treason. The admiral's drumbeat warning that military defeat in the East was inevitable obviously never sat well with Hitler nor with many military commanders, who grew tired of Canaris's pessimism, in effect a form of disparagement. But when Canaris's defeatist predictions began to come true, Hitler and some of his generals in their frustration blamed him for Abwehr "intelligence failures" on the eastern front. The bearer of bad tidings had not been welcome, but he was doubly despised by Hitler when the tidings came to pass.

Then there was the Abwehr "failure" to predict the site of an American-British invasion of the Axis southern flank. The Ultra/Double-Cross triumph of Allied intelligence in support of Torch would conversely be the Abwehr's disgrace. But of course it may be demanding too much of an intelligence agency whose leadership was dedicated to overthrowing its government to be very efficient in carrying out its obligations to provide a shield against its enemies.

As seen in the North African landings, the British Double-Cross operation, as brilliant a piece of counterespionage jujitsu as ever devised, provided the Western Allies with the incredible capability to script their enemy's intelligence product to suit their strategic and tactical needs. Luck had been with the Allies, but this happy state of affairs, which in good part depended on a benign and stable Abwehr under Canaris, could not last forever. That it had lasted longer than the Allies had any right to expect—long enough to see the Allies through the Normandy landings—may have been due to more than just luck.

TWENTY-NINE

Canaris and Himmler:
An Odd Couple

CANARIS'S ABILITY TO SURVIVE AS LONG AS HE DID IS A PHENOMENON DIFFIcult to understand. His apparent immunity to charges of high treason reveals his genius in keeping Himmler at bay. A chronicle of the Abwehr chief's career tells much about the man although there may always remain an aura of unresolved mystery surrounding him. It is certain, however, that from well before World War II he saw in Hitler a threat to Germany's wellbeing, even its very existence. From his high office as a guardian of the state's security, he paradoxically devoted the war years to undermining it—that is, to undermining Adolf Hitler, who considered himself, like Napoleon, to be the state.

By conspiring against the Führer in every way he could, Canaris hoped to save Germany. He wielded his formidable weapon of guile with subtlety and sophistication, but it is difficult to believe that his wits alone protected him from the power and omniscience of Hitler's police state. There had to be a reason or reasons why Reichsführer Himmler, commander of the SS, the SD security-intelligence arm of the SS, and the dreaded Gestapo, for so long spared Canaris from those instruments of repression that so relentlessly stalked him as an enemy of the Third Reich. The mystery of Himmler's remarkably restrained attitude toward Canaris is particularly curious in view of the SD's marathon intrigues to gain primacy over the Abwehr rather than allow it to exist as a troublesome rival.

Organizational control of the Abwehr, however important to Himmler—and of course to eager subordinates, such as Heydrich, Schellenberg, and "Gestapo" Müller—had to play second place to Himmler's own ambitions, which seemed to have required Canaris variously as an appeased rival and a potential ally, depending on how things worked out. So long as Canaris posed a threat to Himmler because of what he had on him, some of which was perhaps documented in Canaris's diary (which did not survive the war) or, conversely, because he might become a valuable ally in a grab for supreme power at Hitler's expense, he must be allowed to survive. In fact Canaris would never have allowed himself to become Himmler's ally, but the *Reichsführer's* political fantasies were useful to him; he could play on such vulnerabilities. Until apparent Abwehr failures, culminating in Canaris's Italian intrigues and the Vermehren defection, provoked Hitler himself to repudiate Canaris and demand his removal, Himmler had consistently frustrated the efforts of his ambitious top lieutenants to oust the admiral and seize control of his Abwehr. Complicating things further was Canaris's own sometimes manipulative, sometimes defensive relationships with two would-be heirs apparent to Himmler: Heydrich and Schellenberg.

Himmler's suspicions concerning Canaris's opposition to Hitler probably went a long way back. If in 1934 Spain's self-made magnate Juan March and the international arms dealer Basil Zaharoff, both British agents, spotted Canaris as a secret opponent of the newly installed Third Reich,[1] others must surely have noted this tendency as well. Canaris, a veteran of World War I German naval intelligence, spent the chaotic interwar years in Germany honing his talents in intrigues no less than those of war. Between the wars he built the network of friends that was to serve him—and protect him—for nearly a decade as Abwehr chief from 1935 until his death by execution in 1945. He also made many enemies who would seek to destroy him. His defenses depended on his ability to control his enemies more than invoke his friendships.

Hugh Wilson, a prominent American prewar diplomat who served many years in Germany, dredged his memory in 1942 to paint for the OSS a word picture of the Canaris he had heard about in Berlin. While his impressions, dating back to the days of the Weimar Republic, were simplistic and overdrawn, those of an incompletely informed outsider, they correctly portrayed Canaris as a politically conscious, somewhat Machiavellian man.

According to Wilson, Canaris, financed by rich German industrialists, had "established in the early '20s a sort of industrial detective agency," which probed for industrial and economic secrets. During the chaotic period of the Weimar Republic, a regime that his royalist heart could not abide because of its weak and feckless nature, he pursued his own aims as well as those of the German Navy, amassing an "enormous collection of discreet and secret knowledge, blackmailing whenever it served his purpose."[2]

Such information proved useful in the political free-for-all that was the Weimar Republic. It was probably not ambition that drove Canaris; it was love of Germany, self-defense—and a love of the "game." British World War II Secret Service expert Hugh Trevor-Roper wrote after the war: "Canaris was envisaged, as the heads of secret services are so often envisaged, as a master spy, an impersonal genius at the center of an invisible spider's web."[3]

There was nothing particularly strange about Canaris's political activities as a naval officer, including his involvement in the show trial that acquitted the murderers of Liebknecht and Luxemburg. As Trevor-Roper observed, "The German armed forces were a political party in the Weimar years."[4] Nor was it out of character for Canaris to play an active role in secretly rebuilding the German Navy in contravention of the Versailles Treaty and to help broker massive German assistance to Franco during the Spanish Civil War. But these were the kinds of activities that gave rise to the Canaris legend.

Heinrich Himmler, chicken farmer made chief inquisitor and high executioner of the Nazi party, was among those who held Canaris in considerable awe—and probably fear. While the admiral became his archrival in intelligence and security matters, Himmler respected Canaris. Canaris's early biographer Heinz Höhne went so far as to write: "Himmler was wedded to Canaris by an almost grotesque over-estimation of his professional ability."[5] But what exactly made Himmler's estimate of Canaris "grotesque"? What was the anatomy of a relationship that caused him to handle the admiral with such care at the same time he intrigued against him?

To understand this standoff between two deadly rivals, it is worth briefly revisiting some of the several situations in which Himmler seemed to have protected Canaris and look through the Canaris dossier once again in search of clues.

Project X, the Resistance efforts to enlist Pope Pius XII as intermediary with the British to warn the Western Allies of an imminent invasion of the Lowlands and France and to negotiate a peace behind Hitler's back, became known to Heydrich in January 1940. Evidence concerning the secret activities of Abwehr agent Josef Müller in behalf of Resistance at the Vatican was convincing enough for Heydrich and his deputy, Schellenberg, to open a special Black Orchestra Abwehr file and by May 1940 to begin intense investigations.[6] In fact as early as 1936 Heydrich had suspected Müller's Vatican connections. And in 1940 an erratic, ambitious Benedictine monk named Hermann Keller, who had worked for the SD but was enlisted by the Abwehr when war broke out, leaked the story of Project X.

He took it upon himself to reveal the details to a journalist in Switzerland, who wrote a story predicting that certain generals, including Franz Halder and Erwin von Witzleben, were about to stage a coup d'état against Hitler and sue for peace. When questioned by Heydrich personally, Keller accused Müller of being a confidential courier for the Pope.[7]

Only by putting his personal prestige on the line was Canaris able to save Müller, Dohnanyi, and Oster, whose connections in this affair were suspected by the SD. The admiral assured Heydrich that the story was wildly distorted; he claimed that Müller was an Abwehr "penetration" agent targeted against the Vatican, not its secret collaborator, and that it was preposterous to believe that a military coup d'état was being planned. Heydrich backed off, but his information, saved for future reference, swelled the ever-growing Black Orchestra file in his office. Since this case had attracted so much attention within the SD, it must be assumed that Himmler had been kept fully informed. It may also be assumed that the hard-charging, obsessive Heydrich would not have dropped the case without orders to do so from Himmler.

Canaris had a closer call when his wrecking role in Operation Felix leaked to Himmler. Because of his friendship with Franco, Canaris had been sent to Madrid in the late summer of 1940 to gain Franco's cooperation in a plan to seize Gibraltar, but as will be recalled, he instead convinced the Caudillo that Spain should not admit German troops or be a party to an assault on Britain's important bastion of Gibraltar, controlling the strategically vital strait. Perhaps even more dangerously, Canaris tipped off Franco to the highly secret forthcoming German invasion of Soviet Russia, making it impossible for the Wehrmacht to spare troops to force its will on Spain should he prove uncooperative. Moreover, recall that Canaris assured Franco that Germany was doomed to defeat in the war, a startling admission coming from the head of German military intelligence, the man who should know, at the height of Hitler's military successes.

Canaris was directly and dangerously exposing himself by his extraordinary sabotage of Hitler's policy in Spain. Franco's foreign minister and brother-in-law Ramón Serrano Súñer, revealed after the war (March 1958) to the historian and former OSS analyst Harold C. Deutsch that Franco had several times commented to him on "how amazed he was that, despite the dramatic Nazi march of victory, Canaris kept insisting to him that Germany would lose the war in the end."[8]

That Canaris's real role in Operation Felix reached Himmler's ears is suggested in statements made after the war by former SS group chief Walter Huppenkothen of the Nazi RSHA. Huppenkothen testified under oath that the RSHA had incriminating evidence from "an official at the German embassy in Madrid [that] Canaris had divulged military secrets to Franco and advised him against entering the war on Germany's side in 1940."[9] Himmler also had the benefit of accusations made by Spanish General Muñoz Grandes, commander of the Spanish Blue Division of "volunteers" fighting with the Germans on the Russian front, who claimed that Canaris had persuaded Franco to stay out of the war. Muñoz Grandes's comments, included in a report on Canaris prepared for. Himmler by Huppenkothen, strangely drew no response nor stimulated any action from the *Reichsführer*.[10] This evidence was produced at Canaris's drumhead hearing moments before he was strung up by piano wire to die a slow, suffocating death just as the war was ending. If Himmler was in possession of such damning evidence implicating Canaris, why didn't he exploit it earlier?

One of the Gestapo's most expert investigators, Franz Xavier Sonderegger, revealed during his postwar debriefing by the Allies that in 1942 Abwehr officer Nicolas von Halem had been apprehended in connection with a conspiracy against Hitler's life. During his interrogation Halem had mentioned that fellow Resistance activist Dohnanyi had paid him twelve thousand reichsmarks for the explicit purpose of funding the assassination of Hitler. Moreover, authorization for this plot seemed to originate with Canaris. To Sonderegger's consternation, Himmler called a halt to the proceedings and ordered all references to Canaris in the Gestapo report to be removed from the record.[11] Sonderegger also testified about another plot to kill Hitler involving Abwehr agent Mumm von Schwarzenstein. Again Himmler intervened to block further investigation.[12] In still another instance a Resistance cell formed by a district court counsel named Strassmann at the direction of Abwehr officer Dohnanyi had been discovered by the Gestapo in early 1942. The Gestapo in this case was instructed to cease all inquiries directed toward the Abwehr. Sonderegger testified, "My investigations disclosed that the relevant orders had in each case come from Himmler."[13]

Another version of the Strassmann case was described by Canaris's admirer Dr. Karl Abshagen. In his postwar book on Canaris, Abshagen claimed that the revelations of the Strassmann case marked the first occasion in which Canaris's right-hand man Hans Oster was caught out by the Gestapo dabbling in domestic political affairs in violation of the agreement delimiting duties reached by the Abwehr and SD. Despite Strassmann's confession of having acted on orders from Abwehr officers within Oster's division, SD chief Heydrich did nothing to follow through with this case.[14] Considering Heydrich's usual zeal in attacking the Abwehr, Himmler would have been the most likely, if not the only one, who could have stopped him.

Himmler's strange solicitude toward Canaris cannot be fully fathomed without including Heydrich in the equation. Canaris had of course known Heydrich well since the latter's fledgling days in the navy and had tried to get along with him when they later found themselves rivals in the German intelligence community. But Canaris, a searcher of dark closets, had nonetheless kept a dossier on Heydrich that included evidence of Jewish ancestry, which could be a dangerous black mark on his record. What else Canaris had on Heydrich is not a matter of surviving record, but the young SD officer had certainly led a promiscuous private life.

The deadly game played by the two men would not have admitted explicit blackmail. But each knew much about the other; there probably was a tacit, unspoken realization that frontal attacks would be mutually dangerous. Moreover, Heydrich had Himmler to contend with; so long as the *Reichsführer* was unwilling to provoke a showdown with Canaris, Heydrich's hands were tied.

While still under Himmler, Heydrich had, however, achieved considerable power in his own right when he became *Reichsprotektor* (German proconsul) of Czechoslovakia. In this capacity he could report directly to Hitler. Whether or not Himmler could or would have tightened the leash on his ambitious protégé had he not been killed will never be known. There were indications that Himmler had feared Heydrich, whose mental agility and force of will far exceeded his own.[15] Schellenberg once referred to Heydrich as "the hidden pivot around which the Nazi regime revolved."[16]

Peter Padfield, a biographer of Himmler, writes: "Himmler and Heydrich were a partnership . . . they knew each other's strengths and weaknesses and each his position vis-à-vis the other as intimately as the partners in a marriage. . . ."[17] There may or may not have been truth in Gisevius's gossipy remark to Mary Bancroft, the OSS officer in Bern, when he said to her: "The real bond between Himmler and Heydrich was that they had once been 'involved' with each other. . . . The relationship, just like a similar hetrosexual relationship, was indestructible."[18] But there had definitely been a close bond between the two men even though Himmler distrusted his subordinate. Gisevius was more restrained in his own memoir, writing only that in 1934 "Himmler had become a subject of gossip. . . ."[19] If there was substance to allegations of personal misconduct of any kind by Himmler and Heydrich, Canaris surely had taken note of it.

Just before his assassination in 1942 Heydrich did turn the screws on Canaris when the SD unmasked Abwehr officer Paul Thümmel (aka agent

A-54) as a Czech Resistance collaborator. While Heydrich used the Thümmel case as a lever to extract concessions from Canaris as they negotiated a new agreement dividing intelligence responsibilities, he did not go after Canaris personally. He even let Canaris talk him out of taking immediate action against Thümmel despite the overwhelming evidence against him.

Another influence on Himmler who played a role in determining Canaris's fate, particularly after Heydrich's death, was Walter Schellenberg, whose star had risen rapidly. Investigating Canaris's activities in Italy, Schellenberg found Himmler curiously unresponsive to the evidence against the admiral that came to light. Schellenberg claimed after the war that he had been aware of Canaris's confidential relationship with the Italian intelligence chief Amé. He knew specifically about Canaris's and Amé's compromising conversation in Venice and had told Himmler: "It would have been better if Admiral Canaris had carried out his duties in Italy instead of taking part in these sessions with General Amé." Himmler only squirmed uncomfortably and promised to show the dossier to Hitler, but he never did.[20] This kind of experience caused Schellenberg to conclude "that at one time or another Canaris had discovered something compromising about Himmler."[21] The SD chief was convinced that Canaris "had a hold over Himmler, perhaps some odious episode in the Reichsführer's background or ancestry."[22]

If Canaris's control over Himmler was possible because of some incriminating information about him that, if leaked, could bring down Hitler's wrath, it probably did not concern salacious gossip. More likely it concerned Himmler's acts of high treason, his peace overtures to the Western Allies, which were discovered by Hitler only shortly before committing suicide in the Berlin command bunker. The Führer, at the end, became enraged when he heard that Himmler had opened negotiations with Sweden's Count Folke Bernadotte toward achieving an armistice with the Western Allies.[23] In the dying hours of Nazi Germany, Hitler issued a warrant for Himmler's arrest and execution. The genesis of Himmler's treason, however, goes back at least to 1942, perhaps earlier, when it became evident to him that Germany could not win the war. Schellenberg's reminiscence of his fateful meeting with Himmler in the early summer of 1942, when the two men agreed to work secretly together in making approaches to the West, is not only significant of itself but noteworthy because it marks Schellenberg's emergence as Himmler's éminence grise.

K. H. Abshagen in his biography of Canaris describes Himmler's use of his lawyer Karl Langbehn in December 1942 to maintain contact with the OSS chief in Stockholm, Bruce Hopper.[24] Hopper reported this development to the Resistance; thus Canaris heard about it. This episode also revealed that "in Himmler's entourage" the concept of removing Hitler and "of putting the *Reichsführer* in his place" had been toyed with at least since the failure of the offensive against Moscow in the early winter months of 1941.[25]

In May 1943 Langbehn first approached Himmler's chief of staff, Karl Wolff, to arrange for the former finance minister of Prussia and current Resistance collaborator Johannes Popitz to meet with Himmler and discuss the need to "restructure" a German government so that it could reach a peace agreement with the Western Allies. Langbehn stressed the obvious—Germany could not win the war—and he pointed out that Dr. Popitz would be a valuable person in reaching the West.[26]

Wolff made an appointment for Popitz to meet with Himmler on August 26. In his conversation Popitz, using the euphemism "reducing Hitler's powers," did not explicitly talk of removing Hitler. But he left little doubt that Hitler must be removed altogether. And since it had been Wolff who had made the arrangements for this sensitive conversation, he too was clearly a party to Langbehn's and Popitz's plan.

When Langbehn went to Switzerland to make contact with the OSS through Dulles's assistant Gaevernitz,[27] his designs were known not only by Wolff but almost certainly by Himmler, himself. In his testimony during the Nuremberg trial, Gaevernitz stated that he had been intrigued by Langbehn's proposition to enlist the SS as a force against Hitler and promised to pass it on to Allen Dulles.[28] Popitz had become aware that Himmler was very well informed about the Resistance and concluded optimistically that the *Reichsführer* SS would be willing to protect the movement in the hope that he could survive Hitler after the war ended and use it to secure power for himself.[29]

Resistance members, however, rejected the idea of collaborating with the SS, particularly with Himmler. General Beck was furious with Popitz for approaching Himmler without consulting the other conspirators since this could not only wreck their plans but endanger them. Popitz was in effect ostracized and left out of the July 20, 1944, assassination planning.[30] Aside from the physical jeopardy in which planners had been placed, Beck feared that Langbehn's and Popitz's efforts could discredit the Resistance as true ideological opponents of nazism. This would be an unacceptable price to pay for operational expediency.

Himmler was hardly a man whom anyone could trust, but at least Himmler's compromising association with Langbehn and Popitz provided Canaris with a point of leverage against the *Reichsführer* should it be needed. Schellenberg continued to have contact with some Resistance members in order to interest them in collaboration with elements of the SD in bringing about Hitler's fall. He also continued to flirt with the OSS as insurance against a grim future as a war criminal. Canaris, no admirer of Himmler, whom he blamed for untold SS atrocities, and distrustful of the self-serving Schellenberg, was not surprised to see this sign of rot within the Nazi hierarchy.

Himmler's awareness of Resistance Western contacts provided him with a rationale for his own secret efforts to communicate with the enemy. He did not want to move precipitously against the Abwehr. It would better suit his purposes to let the Abwehr and its Wehrmacht collaborators overthrow Hitler, then move in with his SS to preserve order and negotiate an honorable peace with the Western Allies. As "savior" of Germany he would take charge.[31] That in brief was Himmler's grandiose and quite unrealistic objective—one that made him extremely vulnerable. When Langbehn's secret contacts with the United States were blown to the Gestapo through German intercepts of Allied cipher traffic, Himmler had to sacrifice him to save himself. He did not relish having Canaris and the Abwehr actively investigated by his Gestapo. To unmask the Abwehr could reveal Himmler's own intrigues and compromising connections.[32]

Before he died, Schellenberg confided in the French journalist André Brissard, then writing his biography of Canaris, that it was likely that Admiral Canaris had evidence revealing Himmler's endorsement of Langbehn's overtures to the Americans.[33] Himmler's subordinate, Gestapo chief Heinrich Müller, also came into possession of details concerning the Langbehn case connecting the *Reichsführer* with certain members of the Resistance. Himmler had naturally not been eager to pursue the matter. But when he could stall no longer and Langbehn was finally brought to trial, Himmler instructed Ernst Kaltenbrunner, chief of the SD, "to see to it as a practical matter that the public be excluded from the proceedings." Himmler added, "I shall despatch about ten of my collaborators to make up an audience."[34] It was no wonder that Himmler had been relieved to learn of Langbehn's execution in October 1944 since his old "friend" knew too much and had seen too much at close range. To Himmler he looked better in a wooden box than he would have looked in a witness box.

The Austrian Wilhelm Hoettl, who served under Schellenberg in Branch VI of the Nazi SD, was very much at home in the labyrinthine world of European intelligence. His opinion of Canaris, while probably tinged with bias, is nonetheless interesting in trying to understand the Abwehr chief's seeming immunity to arrest. Hoettl writes in his wartime memoir of his astonishment that Canaris kept his job as Abwehr chief until February 1944, a long run for a conspirator against Hitler leading a double life.

The Gestapo files fairly bulged with incriminating reports on Canaris.*
According to Hoettl, SD chief Kaltenbrunner, soon after his appointment
in 1943, urged Himmler to move against Canaris on the basis of evidence
already on file. Hoettl thought it strange at the time that the *Reichsführer*
refused, saying only that he had good reasons for not doing so. Moreover,
Himmler made it clear to Kaltenbrunner that any such initiatives should
not be taken. Kaltenbrunner was left to conclude that Canaris, obviously
linked somehow to anti-Hitler plots, had nonetheless been left alone because he had something on Himmler.[35]

The Schmidhuber case, in which a simple currency violation bal-
looned into a serious investigation of Abwehr senior officers suspected of
assisting Jews to escape Germany, cast a long shadow over Canaris himself.
While Canaris escaped catastrophe by nimble maneuvering, he could be
grateful to Himmler for divesting himself of the case and willingly hand-
ing it over to the military justice system. Himmler, in possession of enough
evidence to indict Canaris and almost the entire senior echelon of the Abwehr, did not do so. Gestapo ace investigator Franz Sonderegger was convinced he had an airtight case and was dismayed to receive a note in
Himmler's own handwriting saying, "Kindly leave Canaris alone."[36] While
the Schmidhuber crisis did cause the removal of key Abwehr officers and
in effect crippled its subterranean Resistance efforts, the Abwehr itself survived—at least briefly. Himmler had not wanted to open completely the
Abwehr Pandora's box.

The Vermehren defection set off a chain of events that finally made it
impossible for Canaris to remain as chief of the Abwehr. But this was a
symptom of or perhaps an excuse for, not the root cause of, Hitler's dissatisfaction with Canaris. The basic problem was that the disease of defeatism had become epidemic, at least among officers, military and
civilian, in a position to know what was really going on. And Canaris had
become a symbol of this disease in Hitler's eyes. Moreover, the Führer
had concluded that Canaris's Abwehr was incompetent; it had not called
the main events of the war during and since the Allied North African
landings—at least in Hitler's opinion. While Himmler had protected Canaris despite the growing dossier of highly suspicious actions, the Vermehren case with its attendant publicity made it impossible for him to
save the admiral's job—nor did he now want to. This was a golden oppor-

*In his memoir *The Secret Front*, Wilhelm Hoettl writes that among the GRS
(Geheime Reichssache, or State Secret Documents archive) files provided by the
Gestapo there were several volumes devoted to alleged misdeeds of the Abwehr and
Canaris. This material was not used against Canaris when he was removed from office
in 1944—*The Secret Front* (New York: Praeger, 1954), p. 75.

tunity to take over the Abwehr, long his objective. Schellenberg, who could not wait to get his hands on the Abwehr, was prodding Himmler to get rid of Canaris. Just as Heydrich had used the Thümmel case to get at Canaris, so Schellenberg used the Vermehren case in 1944 to discredit him. Most compelling of all, Hitler himself insisted on firing Canaris. There was nothing Canaris could do to defend himself; he was finally checkmated.

In summary there had been a standoff between Canaris and Himmler, an equilibrium that both found useful. Canaris had been well informed about Himmler's treachery in making indirect overtures to the West, and Himmler knew of Canaris's long involvement with the Resistance as well as his indirect contacts with the Americans. But with the rush of events and Hitler's exasperation, the equilibrium could no longer be maintained.

As the war drama approached its climax and Hitler, racked by poor health and faced with the terrible prospects of defeat, waited in vain for a collapse of the enemy coalition, a break between the Western Allies and Soviet Russia, Himmler hoped to use the Resistance as an unwitting cat's-paw, paving the way for a Western solution to Germany's fate featuring himself. By mid-1944 he was in secret competition with Soviet-leaning Bormann, who was equally unrealistic about his own possibilities of becoming Germany's cotrustee—i.e., Stalin's German puppet.

Allen Dulles could thank Eduard von Waetjen, Abwehr Resistance contact in Bern, for still another insight into Himmler's strange role. As the OSS station chief summarized it in a March 1944 message to Washington, "It is not because of any partiality to England or the U.S. that Himmler is pursuing a policy of so-called Western orientation, but because of purely selfish reasons." Waetjen was convinced that Himmler, "correctly or incorrectly, believes that he would be completely out of the picture in a German policy directed toward the East for the reason that Stalin would insist on his execution." Remembered as the Nazi who arbitrarily declared their ally the Japanese to be Aryans, Himmler nursed a hopelessly unrealistic ambition to secure Western blessing to lead a post-Hitler "Japanese-German attack on Russia as part of a compromise peace settlement with the Western powers. . . ."[37]

The best-laid plans of patriots, traitors, opportunists, and nervous war criminals alike were to go awry when the Western Allies invaded France on June 6, 1944, and six weeks later a young Wehrmacht colonel, Count Klaus Schenk von Stauffenberg, tried unsuccessfully to assassinate Hitler with a bomb hidden in his briefcase. Hitler's merciless retribution, with the full force of Himmler's security apparatus, killed all who were tainted with the slightest suspicion.

Yet some months before the July 20 bomb episode Canaris had been told directly by Himmler that "he knew very well influential circles within the Army were hatching plans for a rebellion." Himmler told Canaris that he would "not let it get that far" but would "put a stop to it in time."[38] Himmler in fact correctly named General Ludwig Beck and Carl Goerdeler as among his prime suspects. And on July 17, three days before the bomb went off, Resistance activist Arthur Nebe, head of the criminal branch of the Gestapo, tipped off Goerdeler that a warrant had been issued for his arrest and that he must go into hiding immediately.[39] It is significant that Himmler saw fit to warn Canaris but apparently did not issue the kind of alert or take the range of precautions that might have prevented the explosion that nearly killed Hitler.

THIRTY

Operation Valkyrie

TOWARD THE END OF JULY 1941, AS GERMAN TROOPS WERE INVADING THE Ukraine, Major General Hans Henning von Tresckow, chief of staff of the German Central Army Group at Smolensk, took the lead in secret Resistance planning on the eastern front. He had worked on his superior officer, Field Marshal Günther von Kluge, commander of Army Group Center, finally convincing him—he thought—that Hitler was leading the German Army toward destruction and must be thrown out of power. Kluge was cautious, however, and seemed to need continual reassurances from both Tresckow and Tresckow's personal staff officer, Fabian von Schlabrendorff, also a Resistance activist. Kluge, whose resolve was fragile at best, sent Schlabrendorff back to Berlin from time to time to test the mettle of the movement. He wanted to know if the Black Orchestra was in fact "crystallizing" and was "ready to act."

In September Schlabrendorff met with fellow conspirator Ulrich von Hassell of the Foreign Ministry to discuss Resistance matters. Kluge, it seemed, unrealistically insisted on guarantees that "England would make peace soon after a change of regime was effected." Hassell later commented: "With what naïveté the generals approach this problem."[1]

Tresckow worked out an operational plan in which Hitler would be shot when he made a visit to Kluge's headquarters at Smolensk on March 13, 1943. Under cover of holding an intelligence conference, Canaris himself visited Kluge on the eastern front with a group of his Abwehr senior officers—all coconspirators—on the eve of the Führer's visit. Erwin

Lahousen, Hans Piekenbrock, Egbert von Bentivegni, and Hans von Dohnanyi were present with Canaris to firm up the plan. Schlabrendorff, in behalf of Tresckow, made an eloquent case for killing Hitler rather than simply detaining him as prelude to a Resistance uprising. With evident fervor Schlabrendorff insisted: "Only Hitler's death will put an end to this mad slaughter of people in the concentration camps and in the armies fighting this criminal war."[2]

Canaris, a staunch Catholic who had always opposed assassination as a weapon in his profession, finally agreed, but because of his scruples, he said that he did not want to be part of the detailed planning process—a fine point of morality.* The Abwehr chief had a long talk with Kluge, after which he had doubts as to whether the marshal would in the end play his role. "Our generals have cold feet" he confided to Lahousen and Dohnanyi.[3] Tresckow's and Schlabrendorff's assassination plan had to be abandoned at the last minute when the field marshal lost his nerve—just as Canaris had predicted.

Before returning to Berlin, Canaris joined his comrades for a last drink. When he casually dropped a comment that he had to get back to see Himmler, the others protested; one or two in the heat of the moment declared that they "would no longer be able to shake hands with Canaris" if he persisted in meeting with that "swine." Canaris only grinned in his enigmatic way, perhaps pleased that his friends felt close enough to him to indulge in such histrionics or perhaps because he was confident that they would soon learn that his mission to Himmler was to save some of their colleagues, including Dohnanyi, who were caught up in the Schmidhuber case.[4] Canaris was troubled by the deepening threat to the Abwehr posed by the RSHA, the Schmidhuber scandal being only the most recent symptom of Kaltenbrunner's determination to take over his organization. The time was coming when discreet appeals to Himmler might not be enough.

Having failed to receive Kluge's cooperation in anything as daring as assassination, Tresckow and Schlabrendorff on the spot worked out an alternate plan not requiring his help or knowledge. This called for placing a bomb in Hitler's aircraft, timed to go off in midair while the Führer was en route back to Rastenburg from Smolensk. The Abwehr had provided two

*In another fine point of morality, many in the Resistance made a distinction between "high treason," defined as conspiracies against the state or plots to assassinate its leader, and "treason against the state," such as spying for a foreign country. High treason was ennobling if the nation's leadership was criminally corrupt or debilitating for the fatherland, while espionage was debasing. Canaris, however, had strong objections to assassination and believed that it should be used only in an exceptional case.

time bombs, British-made plastic explosives disguised as square Cointreau bottles, which would be smuggled aboard the aircraft and hidden in the baggage. The bombs were successfully placed, but to the dismay of the plotters, they failed to work; Hitler arrived back in Rastenburg without incident. Schlabrendorff had the unenviable job of hurriedly retrieving the "Cointreau" bottles before anyone could discover their true purpose. This was discouraging, but just as there had been attempts to kill Hitler in the past, there would be other efforts in the future.

It was not surprising that there had been so many attempts on the Führer's life; what is strange is that none of them succeeded. In 1935 a Jewish medical student from Switzerland named Felix Frankfurter, intent on killing Hitler, failed to get close enough so he shot Wilhelm Gustloff, Nazi leader in Switzerland, instead. A Swiss Catholic theological student, Maurice Bavand, planned to shoot Hitler in 1938 on the occasion of a parade celebrating the abortive Nazi putsch in 1923 but could not find the opportunity. Exactly one year later, as will be recalled, Georg Elser, leftist laborer, planted a bomb in the Munich beer hall where Hitler and his followers were to hold another commemorative reunion in celebration of the same event. The bomb went off with a resounding explosion, killing several Nazi functionaries, but missing Hitler, who had just left the hall.

In February 1943, before Tresckow planted bombs in the aircraft carrying Hitler from Smolensk to Rastenburg, several officers in the Kharkhov area, appalled by German casualties suffered on the eastern front, vowed to kill Hitler when he visited Army Group B at Poltava. The Führer suddenly changed his plans, however, and visited Army Group South headquarters at Saporozhe instead. Then, on March 21, 1943, soon after the Smolensk failure, an officer named Baron Rudolph Cristoph von Gersdorff of Army Group Central was brought back to Berlin to escort Hitler through an exhibition in honor of a Heroes' Memorial Observation ceremony, during which he would kill him. Tresckow had helped Gersdorff strap explosives with ten-minute delay fuses to his body so that he could blow up the Führer—as well as himself—but Hitler swept through the exhibition so fast that Gersdorff had no time to arm his bombs. Both men survived.

The Schmidhuber case and the arrest of Resistance leaders Dohnanyi, Müller, and Bonhoeffer had made it clear that the Abwehr circle of the Resistance had lost most of its leadership. Oster's removal from office and Canaris's forced retirement from the service in February 1944 were particularly crippling developments. If any doubts about the Abwehr predicament persisted, Arthur Nebe, the Resistance man within the CID, removed them with a warning that Kaltenbrunner was closing in. The Allied entry into Rome on June 4, 1944, and, above all, the Allied invasion of

Hitler's Europe at Normandy on June 6 also lent urgency to the situation. The Resistance had no time to lose.

The Resistance, or what was left of it, paid close attention to a statement made by Clement Attlee in the British Parliament to the effect that the Germans themselves should rid their country of the "criminal government." Churchill was even more blunt when he called upon the German people to overthrow the Nazis. Allen Dulles believed that such comments helped stimulate new Resistance planning despite the long drought of encouragement from their British contacts and despite repeated but unsuccessful efforts to get in touch with the British. In a message to Washington, Dulles recommended that the United States issue similar statements. Anything to stir up the Breakers Group, his code name for the Resistance, might at least shorten the war.[5]

The Resistance's resolve to act was revived when Colonel Count Klaus Schenk von Stauffenberg, a maimed veteran of the North African campaign, joined the Resistance in May 1943. Stauffenberg believed he had a mission to destroy Hitler and went about it with uncommon determination. As chief of staff to General Friedrich Olbricht, a fellow Resistance member in Berlin's command center, Stauffenberg threw himself into this enterprise.* This would be the Resistance's last chance.

WHILE STILL RECOVERING FROM CRIPPLING WOUNDS IN A NORTH AFRICAN military hospital, Stauffenberg had told his uncle Count von Uxkull, "Since the generals have so far done nothing, the colonels must now go into action against Hitler."[6] Stauffenberg's enthusiasm was not shared by Canaris, who by now was a very discouraged man. Nor could Canaris muster much enthusiasm for Stauffenberg himself. However brilliant the young officer was, the anti-Soviet admiral disapproved of what he perceived to be Stauffenberg's "Eastern" political inclinations. For his part, Stauffenberg disliked Canaris and thought that his chronic hesitancy to act decisively had been the reason for the Resistance's lack of success. The new generation of coup leadership was certainly at odds with the political views of Canaris, Oster, and most of the others who had hitherto taken the lead in the Resistance.

---

*Stauffenberg's opposition to Hitler and the Nazis had manifested itself as early as July 1942. In a meeting with Field Marshal Manstein he gave his opinion that Germany could not win the war. The young officer tried to convince Manstein to seize command of the army in a putsch and negotiate a peace invoking the precedent of Tauroggen, where in 1812 General Yorck von Wartenburg broke Prussia's alliance with Napoleon Bonaparte and changed sides. Manstein's icy response was "Prussian field marshals do not mutiny"—Annan, *Changing Enemies*, p. 109.

OSS officer Allen Dulles in his postwar account of the Resistance writes that in June 1944, when it became clear that the American and British troops had established their foothold in France, Stauffenberg looked for support from the left and "proposed that the Communists be taken into the coalition."[7] When the Gestapo on July 4 arrested the Socialist Julius Leber, the capability of the left was greatly diminished for the duration of the war, but those who opposed Stauffenberg within the Resistance feared that a Red peril would present itself again after the war if he were to survive and achieve a position of influence in a post-Hitler government.

When Goerdeler met in Stockholm with Jakob Wallenberg, who sometimes served as an intermediary between the Resistance and the Western Allies, he was worried about Stauffenberg's left-leaning proclivities and sent word encouraging the West to make a deal with the Resistance before the Soviets did. This had of course been the line given by Moltke to American Ambassador Kirk. Gisevius's conviction that Stauffenberg had "swung eastward," perhaps acquired from his friend Goerdeler, was obviously passed on to Allen Dulles in Bern,[8] although it should be kept in mind that Gisevius's views were influenced by his hatred of Stauffenberg, a feeling that was reciprocated. Stauffenberg also distrusted Goerdeler and would have rejected him as chancellor, probably choosing the Socialist Leber instead for inclusion in a postcoup government.[9]

Dulles's suspicions about Stauffenberg may have been exaggerated; Dulles may have wrongly believed that Stauffenberg was ideologically motivated when he was simply being pragmatic. Stauffenberg maintained that the Western Allies could not help the Resistance so long as they were committed to unconditional surrender. That left only the less scrupulous but possibly more realistic Soviets to work with. Whatever Stauffenberg's motivation may have been, Dulles perhaps cannot be blamed for seeing in his position foreshadows of a postwar Cold War in which the Soviets would control Germany and Eastern Europe through Soviet puppets. Like Donovan, Dulles was convinced that the United States had given little thought to the political problems facing the United States in Europe, particularly Eastern Europe.

General Jaroslav Kašpar-Páty, a top officer of Czech intelligence, who continued to report on German affairs from Yugoslavia after France fell and who then served with Czech Colonel Heliodore Pika as a top intelligence officer with the Czech mission in Moscow after May 1941, had some well-informed and prescient views on Soviet intentions. In a report submitted on July 6, 1943, to Colonel František Moravec, intelligence chief with Beneš's London government-in-exile, Kašpar-Páty commented on the long-range Soviet "idea of world revolution and conquest of Europe." He wrote: "Today when it is clear that the USSR cannot win the war without the Allies, the plans of the nearest Soviet expansion are reduced to these concrete objectives: control of Central Europe and the Balkans, a leading role in Asia, and access to the Persian Gulf."[10]

Most German generals by mid-1944 were more concerned with the here and now than with a future they hated to think about. They were worried about Hitler's fantasies, his apparent refusal to face up to the immediate catastrophe facing Germany as Allied and Soviet armies closed in. Field Marshal Rommel, now commander in chief of Army Group B on the western front, whom Canaris in North Africa had earlier tried to recruit into the Resistance, was finally sympathetic to their cause. He would be crucial to any effort to reach an armistice with the West. An honest man, he saw the futility of further fighting and, moreover, had the courage to tell this to Hitler: "The troops are fighting heroically everywhere, but the unequal struggle is nearing its end. I must beg you to draw the political conclusions without delay. I feel my duty as C-in-C of the Army Group to state this clearly."[11] This only aroused Hitler's ire and made Rommel politically vulnerable.

Stauffenberg and his coconspirators had a more direct solution to Hitler's Götterdämmerung complex. In mid-June 1944 General von Tresckow assured Stauffenberg that he still favored killing Hitler. "The assassination must be attempted at any cost," he wrote, "even if it is doomed to fail." He added: "We must prove to the world and to future generations that the men of the German Resistance movement dared to take the decisive step and to hazard their lives on it."[12] He also urged Stauffenberg to see Rommel's chief of staff, Lieutenant General Haus Speidel, a sympathizer of the Resistance, to arrange somehow, "by a deliberate blunder if necessary," that the western front be opened for a quick Allied breakthrough.

At the end of June Tresckow sent Lieutenant Colonel von Böllager to Field Marshal von Kluge, now commander in chief of the West with a similar request. Kluge demurred, responding helplessly that the British and Americans were about to break through anyway.[13] While Kluge had agreed with Dr. Goerdeler in November 1943 that Hitler had to be assassinated, he now had second thoughts. On July 3, 1944, soon after arriving in France, he had a violent argument with Rommel on this issue. A week later the German hero of the North African campaign told Resistance members that he was ready to surrender the troops under his command in western France whether Kluge agreed or not.

The Luftwaffe was nowhere to be seen, and critical supplies were not reaching the rapidly thinning troops; the situation was, in short, hopeless.

Kluge finally agreed with Rommel that it was unreasonable to continue fighting. When he took Rundstedt's place on the western front, he discovered that Hitler had deceived him about the true situation. The general was outraged and declared himself ready to act,[14] but as events proved, he could not bring himself to defy Hitler. Fate also let the Resistance down when Rommel, the last hope for a surrender in the West, was wounded on July 17 by aircraft fire and had to be medically evacuated.

Within two days Kluge assumed personal command of the forces that had been under Rommel and prepared to fight to the end in the West. His loyalty to Hitler and Hitler's lost cause would not save him from the Führer's wrath when the front collapsed. His "defeatist" attitude in talks with Rommel and earlier more compromising conversations with Tresckow and Schlabrendorff on the eastern front could not be hidden during a later rigorous investigation. His vacillation only left him in a purgatory of his own devices: He could neither ascend to a pantheon of martyrs in death nor live by the grace of Hitler in a hell of disgrace.

Allen Dulles in Bern watched the buildup of the July 20 bomb plot mainly through Gisevius's eyes, although General Beck personally made contact with the OSS station chief toward the end of June. It was important for the general to get some last-minute idea of how the Americans would respond if the Germans put down their arms on the western front. As ever, the response was and had to be that Germany's surrender must be unconditional.[15] No deal was possible—much less one that excluded Stalin. And by now the certainty of German surrender by the fortunes of war alone made the issue moot.

Gisevius reported that the Resistance was badly split: Stauffenberg's clique, strongly influenced by Stauffenberg's brother Berthold, included a group that leaned toward the Eastern solution. In this group were Fritz-Dietlof von der Schulenburg, a general staff officer, and field officers Count Peter Yorck von Wartenburg, and Count Ulrich Schwerin von Schwanenfeld. Most disconcerting to the likes of Goerdeler and Canaris was Stauffenberg's close friendship with the Socialist Julius Leber, who aspired to be chancellor in a post-Hitler government and counseled coalition with the German Communists. Canaris, Oster, and others in the Abwehr circle of Resistance fighters were by now virtually out of play, having one way or another attracted serious Gestapo suspicion. The military Resistance stalwarts were gathered under the central figures of retired Colonel General Beck and his civilian right arm, Goerdeler. They included Major General Hans Henning von Tresckow, Field Marshal von Witzleben, ambiguously assigned to the "Supreme Command Reserve," and General Friedrich Olbricht, chief of the General Army Office in the

OKW and deputy commander of the Reserve Army—a very useful position from the Resistance's point of view.

During the last week of June the liberal Kreisau Circle, headed by Count von Moltke and Stauffenberg's close friend Peter Yorck von Wartenburg, went so far as to hold a secret conference with the German Communist party to discuss postcoup politics. A second such meeting ended in disaster when the Gestapo raided it; one of the members of the Communist Central Committee, it seems, had been a Gestapo informer.

Other Gestapo reports had noted Stauffenberg's meetings with various people, including Hermann Maass, director of German youth movements prior to Hitler's accession in 1933, who dreamed of a new social order based on socialist trade unionism. The Gestapo may also have taken note of Stauffenberg's contacts with Wolf von Helldorf, a vital cog in the Resistance plan because of his strategic position in the capital as president of the uniformed police. Helldorf had long been devoted to the cause of overthrowing Hitler.[16]

Many, if not most, of the Resistance collaborators were unaware of the depth of the schism between the Beck-Goerdeler leadership and Stauffenberg, but it would probably have become a major factor had the coup succeeded.[17] Time was of the greatest importance; the vital secrets of Operation Valkyrie, as the plan was named,[18] could not be kept much longer. In the meantime Stauffenberg's energies were concentrated on the bomb plot, in which he, as architect and self-designated assassin, would be the prime player. The plotters quickened their efforts without resolving the political differences within their ranks. It was now all action, very little deep thought, and certainly no agreement on the shape of a postcoup government to be if they succeeded.

On July 6, the day after his friend Dr. Leber was arrested by the Gestapo, Stauffenberg was summoned to a routine briefing with Hitler at his Obersalzberg retreat. A Gestapo report, prepared as a postmortem of the events that fateful July, told how Stauffenberg had then carried with him to the conference a bomb earmarked for the Führer. As he left his office for the meeting, he mentioned to General Helmuth Stieff, who was in on the plot and usually accompanied him to briefings, "I have got the whole bag of tricks with me."[19] Stauffenberg did nothing, however, since Himmler was not in attendance. As Stauffenberg's brother Berthold later explained under interrogation, "my brother hoped to be able to carry out the assassinations at a briefing conference attended also by Himmler and Goering."[20] Himmler with the powerful SS at his disposal and Göring with his Luftwaffe were competing powers to be seriously considered in the event of Hitler's demise.

The coup plotters suddenly notified Gisevius to remain in Switzerland, preferably in hiding. His associate in Bern, Theodor Strünck, had heard from Berlin that Hansen and Nebe were already being closely questioned by Kaltenbrunner; Gestapo chief Müller wanted to grill Gisevius as well. This was the second time Gisevius had been summoned to Berlin for questioning. Strünck also reported to Gisevius that Abwehr chief Hansen had notified him that the Allied invasion of Normandy and the collapse of German Army Group Center in Russia had convinced the Resistance that it must act as soon as possible. Dulles sent this news quickly to Washington.[21] The plot, code-named Breakers, was rapidly coming to a head.

Gisevius was determined not to be left out of the action, whatever dire consequences might befall him in Germany. He left a note for Dulles, telling him of his plans and leaving the OSS station chief to worry about the fate of his headstrong collaborator.

Gisevius and Strünck entrained on July 10, but Gisevius had no intention of running into a Gestapo welcoming committee, so he exited before Berlin at Potsdam to make his way as inconspicuously as possible by local shuttle to Zehlendorf, where he intended to see police chief Helldorf. In his discussions with Helldorf in Berlin police headquarters—and what safer place could there be to hold conspiratorial talks?—Gisevius learned that Stauffenberg had passed up another opportunity to bomb Hitler on July 11 since again neither Himmler nor Göring would be present. Helldorf sketched out the operational highlights and commented frankly on Stauffenberg. The police chief clearly had little faith in the plot. "The old crew was no longer around," he complained, and it was difficult to have confidence in Stauffenberg and his clique. He did not believe that the German people, apathetic in their despair, would rise in support of the coup.[22]

Gisevius saw Goerdeler, who was also disappointed with the way things were working out. Gisevius's old friend complained that he could maintain contact with Stauffenberg only through Beck. The policy split within the Resistance, if anything, had become more pronounced. Stauffenberg sought a military-controlled Germany that would become socialist, something that sounded very much to Goerdeler like what they now had under Hitler but with a new cast of characters.[23] Unrealistically Stauffenberg aimed at creating an authoritarian nation that could keep its national integrity and freedom despite being sandwiched between two victorious enemies, the Western Allies and Soviet Russia. It also appeared to Goerdeler that Stauffenberg intended to stage a coup within a coup, in this way eliminating Goerdeler and Beck from power in Stauffenberg's hour of triumph. Once power was achieved, Stauffenberg would jettison all the old

Resistance players, the spine of the movement, whose political orientation was not to his liking. Instead he would base his regime on the militant left, including the Communists. Goerdeler's dream of a democracy with a grand coalition of all political factions except the Nazis would be doomed.

Given Goerdeler's bias against Stauffenberg, he may have been overly pessimistic about the shape of things to come, but Stauffenberg's policy statement, drawn up in September 1943, was revealing: "The liberal-minded German working class together with the Christian Churches will lead and represent those popular forces upon which reconstruction can be based."[24]

In response to his critics within the Resistance, Stauffenberg claimed that he had not yet made up his mind. In discussing what appeared to be leftist views, he claimed he was only playing the "devil's advocate." He also claimed to be a pragmatist: There was nothing to be gained by trying to come to an agreement with the Western Allies, rigidly committed as they were to unconditional surrender. Realistically the Soviet Union would dominate Germany at the end of the war; all political action must therefore be oriented toward the east. In a 1992 biography of Stauffenberg and his brothers by Peter Hoffmann,[25] Berthold von Stauffenberg denied that his brother favored the Soviet-sponsored Free Germany Committee and the League of German Officers, as sometimes claimed by Soviet historians. Berthold stated that Klaus believed that Germany should not surrender on either its western or eastern front; so long as the German Army was able to fight, there was hope that the West and East could be played off against each other to Germany's benefit.

According to Berthold, Klaus von Stauffenberg acknowledged that the danger of Bolshevism was too great to permit a deal with the devil,[26] but he had been discouraged by the refusal of the Western Allies to negotiate a surrender and was definitely overoptimistic in his hope that once the invading Soviet Army inundated eastern Germany, the Western Allies would come to their senses and be willing to deal with the Resistance in stopping the common threat from the East. Those who condemned Stauffenberg as too pro-Russian probably did him an injustice. Toward the beginning of 1944 he refused categorically to work with the Soviet-organized Free Germany Committee, claiming, "What I am doing is treason against the government, but what they are doing is treason against the country."[27]

July 20 was the final date set for Valkyrie. This time the operation would proceed whether or not Himmler and Göring were present. A tense Stauffenberg accompanied by General Stieff and Lieutenant Werner von Hüften arrived in the morning at Hitler's forward headquarters, the Wolfsschanze near the East Prussian town of Rastenburg to attend a meeting presided over by the Führer. Stauffenberg barely had time to "freshen up," his excuse to disappear into a bathroom and activate his bomb's detonating device with the only remaining three fingers of his maimed left hand, before the meeting began. An attendant, Sergeant Major Vogel, who had been sent to summon Stauffenberg, later testified that he had glimpsed him in the dressing room laboriously putting an object wrapped in brown paper into his briefcase:[28]

Accompanied by Field Marshal Keitel, chief of the German High Command, Stauffenberg walked rapidly to the map hut, a flimsy temporary structure used for such briefing sessions. He clutched his briefcase containing the bomb, reluctant to have Keitel's aide carry it for him. The bomb was timed to explode in fifteen minutes. There was little margin for error.

The meeting was in session when Stauffenberg arrived at the meeting. He and Keitel with two other officers entered after Hitler had begun the proceedings. By now there remained only moments before the bomb was timed to go off. Introduced by Keitel, Hitler greeted Stauffenberg as he was seated at the heavy oak conference table next to Lieutenant General Adolf Heusinger. Stauffenberg managed to place the briefcase with its lethal contents under the table close to Hitler before excusing himself to "take a phone call." As Heusinger sat down, he shoved the briefcase out of the way, farther under the table, so that he would have more room for his feet.

Once having escaped the doomed room with only seconds to spare, Stauffenberg joined fellow conspirator Major General Erich Fellgiebel, chief of army signals, in a nearby building, shelter 88, to await the imminent blast. Everything was prepared for his getaway, including a car and driver to rush him to the airport, he hoped before alarms were sounded and the gates sealed.

In the midst of a presentation on Army Group North's predicament on the eastern front, General Heusinger was saying, "If the army group does not now withdraw from Lake Peipus, a catastrophe will—"[29] He never finished the sentence; his talk was interrupted by another more immediate catastrophe as the bomb went off with a deafening roar, hurling the stunned conferees to the floor like so many rag dolls.

Stauffenberg's attention was riveted on the mayhem unfolding before his eyes in the briefing hut next door, which he had just left. Fellgiebel helped him into the car, which sped off toward the airport. As he drove by the remains of the devastated briefing hut, Stauffenberg was convinced that Hitler could not still be alive. With only minor delays he was able to board his plane and be airborne before the flustered guards were able to organize security procedures to cope with what had occurred.

What in fact happened inside the briefing room, packed with twenty-four personages of high rank, defies imagination: Despite the shattering explosion, the Führer was not killed or even seriously hurt. Luftwaffe General Bodenschatz, Göring's liaison officer with Hitler, remembered hearing the sharp crack of an explosion and being blinded by its flash before losing consciousness. The force of the blast hurled SS General Hermann Fegelein and Major Otto Gunscke across the room while others either lay screaming from their injuries or numb with shock amid the debris. Smoke and flame filled the room, hiding for a while the full extent of the damage, as men rushed to the rescue and tried to administer first aid.[30] Four were to die from their wounds.

The bomb had ripped an eighteen-inch hole in the floor beneath it. Despite the proximity of the bomb, Hitler was saved by the massive conference table on which he was leaning when the explosion occurred. Since the room was of flimsy construction and the windows and walls were easily shattered, the force of the blast was dissipated more than it would have been in a more substantial room. Hitler's two eardrums were smashed, and his legs and one elbow bruised. As he was led to safety, covered with plaster and black with smoke, he was conscious enough to scream, "Some swine has thrown a grenade."

Within less than an hour Hitler was shouting orders to search the area and demanding that Kaltenbrunner and a Gestapo investigative team be rushed to Rastenburg. More remarkably, he prepared himself to meet Mussolini for a long-scheduled visit within a few hours of the explosion. Despite advice from his doctors, he refused to call off the event.

General Friedrich Dollmann, who escorted Mussolini to Hitler's Rastenburg headquarters on July 20, remembered vividly how the Führer greeted his ally. "I've just had the greatest piece of luck I've ever had," he told Il Duce as he pointed out the scene of destruction left by the explosion meant for him.

The reception for Mussolini was truly a Mad Hatter's tea party. General Dollmann's firsthand description of it, given a year later under Allied interrogation, cannot be improved upon:

All began arguing and shouting at one another, each one putting blame on the other. . . . Ribbentrop raved against the generals, because "they had betrayed us to England." Doenitz raved against the generals and the generals raved against Ribbentrop and Doenitz! The Führer had kept pretty quiet the whole time and Mussolini was very reserved too. . . . All of a sudden the Führer leapt up in a fit of frenzy with foam on his lips, and yelled out that he would be revenged on all traitors, that Providence had just shown him once more that he had been chosen to make world history, and shouted about terrible punishments for women and children, all of them would have to be put inside concentration camps! He shouted about an eye for an eye and a tooth for everyone who dared to set himself against Divine Providence. It was awful, and it went on for about a half an hour! I thought to myself, the man must be mad. I don't know why I didn't go over to the Allies there and then. Mussolini found it most unpleasant. Meanwhile more tea was served by the footmen in white gloves. . . .

When a call came through from Berlin saying that order had not yet been restored, the Führer [on the telephone] started yelling again, and gave full powers for shooting anyone they liked. [He asked] why Himmler wasn't there yet, and so on. Then came the lovely bit: "I'm beginning to doubt if the German people are worthy of my great ideas."

Everyone began to describe their own devotion to Hitler: Doenitz told him about the blue-eyed boys in blue — damned rubbish — and Goering started having a row with Ribbentrop and Ribbentrop shouted back at him: "I am still the foreign minister and my name is *von* Ribbentrop!" Goering made a pass at him with his field marshal's baton. I'll never forget that scene. The Führer was in a very peculiar state at the time. It was the time when his right arm began to develop tremors. He sat there almost the whole time eating his colored pastilles [medicine]. He had pastilles of all kinds of colors in front of him and kept on eating them. He would be quiet for a time, and then suddenly he'd break out like a wild animal, and wanted to put everyone, women and children too, into a concentration camp. He was the one Providence had chosen![31]

If Mussolini found this unseemly exhibition "most unpleasant," as Dollmann said, the Resistance found it a harbinger of disaster. It meant the end of their cause and, for most, the end of their lives. The anti-Hitler activists, almost to a man, were tracked down, tortured during interrogation, and summarily executed; many others met the same fate even though they had not been involved in the Resistance. Even the families of those found guilty were killed.

THIRTY-ONE

Reprisal and Retribution

THE FAILED ATTEMPT ON HITLER'S LIFE TRIGGERED A MASSIVE GESTAPO roundup of suspects, peremptory executions, drumhead trials, and mass manhunts for suspects — and their kin — who had gone into hiding. Among the conspirators there were different reactions. Some went to their deaths like martyrs, resigned to their fate; others fled or hid; a few sought to evade charges by turning state's evidence or making hypocritical oaths of loyalty to Hitler. Some committed suicide rather than endure the pain of torture or the agony of being forced to implicate friends.

Valkyrie conspirators paid dearly for their lack of planning for the contingency that Hitler would survive the explosion. When Stauffenberg's collaborators learned that Hitler had somehow escaped death in the explosion, they had two courses of action: Abort the plot and go into hiding, or proceed with the putsch, hoping that their army confederates would seize power soon enough to prevent a countercoup. But resolute action of either kind was lacking.

Signals chief Major General Erich Fellgiebel had alerted fellow conspirators in Berlin as to what had occurred but thereafter failed to cut the communications link from Rastenburg as planned, enabling Hitler to go on the air and rally his forces. Moreover, communications from Berlin to outlying commands were not used soon enough to stimulate action in support of the uprising; key people seemed mired in inaction. Fellgiebel's chief of staff, Lieutenant General Fritz Thiele, who, according to the plan, was responsible in Berlin for signaling orders to key army units in on the plot, did not appear when needed. Filling in for Thiele, Colonel Albrecht Mertz von Quirnheim, of the General Staff, tried desperately to goad General Friedrich Olbricht, chief of the General Section of the Ministry of War, into action. In frustration Quirnheim sent the critical orders out in Olbricht's name. Later the general complained: "Mertz has railroaded me."[1] Not until late that afternoon did Olbricht take the reins himself and circulate the teleprinter orders necessary to carry out the coup. Although he was fully aware that Hitler was very much alive, his message was that the Führer had been assassinated, official denials notwithstanding, and that the Wehrmacht would henceforth be responsible for maintaining order under the command of Field Marshal Erwin von Witzleben. No closer to reality was the announcement that Colonel General Ludwig Beck, former chief of the German General Staff, had assumed supreme power in Germany.[2] He had not.

The Bendlerstrasse offices of the War Department, nerve center of the Resistance, restlessly awaiting Stauffenberg's return from Wolfsschanze to hear at first hand details of the debacle. On hand were Beck, Colonel General Erich Höpner, Hans Gisevius, Otto John, Friedrich Werner von der Schulenburg, Dr. Eugen Gersteinmaier of the Foreign Ministry, Lieutenant Peter Yorck von Wartenburg, and others who drifted in and out during the course of the afternoon. Olbricht had left the group long enough to talk to Colonel General Frederich Fromm who, as commander in chief of the Home Army, was being relied upon to play a pivotal role in the uprising. A doubting Fromm, however, was hesitant to act; he insisted on checking first with Field Marshal Keitel. When Keitel testily told him that reports of Hitler's death were totally false, the fainthearted Fromm took fright, and when the field marshal asked about Stauffenberg's whereabouts, Fromm could only conclude with despair that the secret was out.[3]

Stauffenberg arrived from Rastenburg in late afternoon on that fateful day. He and Olbricht both confronted Fromm in the latter's office. Stauffenberg admitted that he had personally placed the bomb and swore that Hitler was dead despite Keitel's denial. "Keitel is lying, as usual," Stauffenberg shouted. "I, myself, saw Hitler being carried out dead."[4]

Fromm could not be convinced and was livid with anger when Olbright informed him that Valkyrie alert messages had been sent out without his knowledge. He accused the two officers of "insubordination, revolution and treason," for which they could be shot. He told Stauffenberg that he had only one option: Kill himself! When Stauffenberg countered this challenge by arresting him on the spot, the raging Fromm lunged at him with fists flying. Only when Kleist and Häften drew their pistols could Fromm be restrained. He was then locked in an office with a guard posted at the door.

Olbricht and Höpner finally marshaled a battery of teletypes and telephones to spread the word among the outlying commands, not yet informed, that the regime's new commander in chief was Field Marshal von Witzleben. Hitler was dead, they lied, and the action plan called for under Valkyrie should be carried out. All posts were warned that SS officers, who had begun to attack the Wehrmacht, should be arrested, and key points defended.[5]

At about four in the afternoon of the twentieth, General Paul von Hase in support of the uprising began to surround government buildings in Berlin with his guards battalion, but other military units on which the coup depended were alarmingly slow to act or never responded at all. Berlin's police chief, Wolf von Helldorf, dutifully placed the capital's uniformed police under army control, but doubts about Hitler's death had infected other key officers, and the discipline needed for revolt rapidly faded.

The little group of conspirators in their Bendlerstrasse command center was in a state of considerable confusion, and spirts plummeted as the gravity of the situation became apparent. There was also turmoil at the field commands.

Fabian von Schlabrendorff was at Army Group Center's headquarters on the eastern front on July 20, when he first heard by phone that the assassination had taken place, but official radio news bulletins made it apparent that the attempt had failed and Hitler still lived. By midday Hitler himself delivered an address by radio. When Schlabrendorff roused Major General von Tresckow from deep sleep to hear the news, the general calmly announced to his intimates, "I am now going to shoot myself." He realized that he would be found out "and then they will try to extract the names of others."[6] The next day Tresckow drove out to the 28th Rifle Division, and from its lines he walked into no-man's-land along the front and blew himself up with a hand grenade. To make it appear that he was killed in an enemy firefight, he shot off a few rifle shots before he took the fatal step.

The most important regional command from the conspirators' point of view was that of Field Marshal von Kluge, commander west, now locked in combat with Allied invaders pushing their way inland from Normandy. Stauffenberg sent a message to Kluge during the evening of the twentieth, despite knowledge of Hitler's escape from death, urging him to seize control of all German forces on the western front in the name of the "new government." Burdened by his officer's oath to Hitler and disillusioned by what had been obviously a botched effort at a coup, Kluge sent word back: "The attempt on Hitler's life failed . . . [and it is] over." He shared his pessimism with his chief of General Staff, General Günther Blumentritt. "It is of no avail," he moaned. "Hitler is the God of the masses; as long as he lives there is nothing one can do. . . ."

Having overpowered and jailed SS and Gestapo officers in Paris, General Karl Heinrich von Stülpnagel, military commander of France, had been summoned to Kluge's headquarters at La Roche-Guyon to account for his actions. Stülpnagel pleaded with the field marshal to assume leadership of the coup in the West and surrender to the Allies, but Kluge only stormed at him for taking "treasonous" action in Paris and peremptorily relieved him of his command. Kluge contemptuously advised Stülpnagel to "get into civilian clothes and disappear somewhere."[7] The field marshal's righteous attitude was hardly consistent with his own guilt. Despite his vacillation, Kluge had been a collaborator of the Resistance. Moreover, he had known in advance that there was a plot against Hitler's life; as accessory he had been guilty of high treason.

Ignoring Kluge's advice, Stülpnagel returned to Paris, arriving at his own headquarters sometime soon after midnight. He immediately ordered the release of the SS officers he had arrested and in a surprisingly civil atmosphere made his peace with Hitler's powerful proconsul in Paris, Otto Abetz, and SD chief Lieutenant General Karl Oberg over drinks at the Hôtel Raphael. It was all dismissed by both sides as a mistake made in the confusion of the times. Best forgotten were both the illegal revolt of the army in Paris and the lackluster showing of the SS in allowing its forces to be captured. Abetz, in fact, had reacted suspiciously like someone who found it expedient to switch sides, making it more understandable why he had surrendered so easily.

Ordered to return to Berlin by an irate Hitler and realizing what lay ahead for him, Stülpnagel drove to Verdun, where he had fought for the fatherland in World War I, and shot himself. After finding him crumpled on the banks of the Meuse River, seriously wounded but still alive, his driver rushed him to a hospital. Stülpnagel, blinded and dying, was revived enough to be tortured and hanged on August 30 for his crime.[8]

Kluge was also depressed by military reverses on the western front. Hitler had not allowed him to withdraw from the Seine and had in fact ordered the beleaguered commander to counterattack on August 7. Overwhelmed on the ground and mercilessly strafed by Allied airpower, the field marshal believed he had no choice but to defy orders and retreat. Ultra intercepts of the traffic between Hitler and Kluge just before and during the disastrous Battle of Falaise, in which much of the German Army of the West was destroyed, was one of Ultra's greatest triumphs. Kluge's agony had been monitored with great precision.[9] Hitler's reaction to this monumental defeat was swift: He relieved Kluge of his command.

On August 17, Field Marshal Walther Model, whom Hitler had appointed as Kluge's successor, phoned Kluge to pass on Hitler's decision. The message, starchily referring to Kluge in the third person, stated: "The stress of battle was too great for the field marshal and a change in command seemed desirable."

Disgraced militarily and certain to be ultimately linked with the conspirators, Kluge wrote Hitler a last letter pleading with him to stop the war: "The German people have suffered so much that it is time to end this horror."[10] As he prepared to leave his command, Kluge said his farewells to General Blumentritt. "Let's say good-bye now," he said with evident emotion; then suddenly he added, "Blumentritt, believe me, it's not so hard." Blumentritt testified during his postwar interrogation that he had not understood at the time what Kluge meant, but later events revealed that "of course, he meant dying."[11] Kluge poisoned himself on board an aircraft bound for Metz and died.[12]

Kluge's code of propriety allowed him to promise cooperation with the coup if Hitler were first disposed of, but so long as the Führer lived, he could not bring himself to act against him. Fear played a role, of course, and perhaps he felt beholden to Hitler not only because of his officer's oath of loyalty but because Hitler had in effect bribed him in the past, as he had certain other officers, with handsome gifts of land. And he now certainly had little incentive to join a coup effort that had obviously failed.

As the coup fizzled, discipline broke down within the ranks of the conspirators, and the Nazi chain of command was reconstituted once Hitler proved he was alive and well. At about 9:00 P.M. Himmler was appointed commander in chief of the Replacement Army in Berlin, and Fromm was rescued from his dispirited captors, who had already permitted him to return to his quarters. He strode back to his office and confronted Stauffenberg, General Beck, Colonel von Quirnheim, Lieutenant von Häften, General Olbricht, and General Höpner, who had so briefly forcibly detained him. Fromm announced triumphantly: "Well, gentlemen, I am now going to do to you what you did to me this afternoon."[13] Thereupon he put them all under arrest.

Beck asked to keep his pistol. Knowing that the old general meant to kill himself, Fromm let him do so but ungraciously ordered him to "make it quick." Beck's effort at suicide failed; despite a shot to the temple, he was still alive. A second shot also failed to kill him. Not until Fromm ordered an officer of the guards battalion to administer a coup de grâce did Beck finally die.

Olbricht's frantic efforts to defend the Bendlerstrasse dissolved in a shoot-out in which Stauffenberg was hit in the left forearm. The wounded man was heard to mumble dejectedly, "They've all left me in the lurch."[14] After an on-the-spot "court-martial" proceeding found all present guilty of high treason, Stauffenberg announced that he assumed responsibility for the actions taken against the government; the others had only followed orders. This brave but futile effort was unsuccessful. A ten-man firing squad was quickly assembled in the courtyard. Höpner, after a quick private consultation with Fromm, was for some reason spared death for the moment but ordered to prison.

General Olbricht, target of the first volley, was the first to die. Stauffenberg, next to be placed before the firing squad, shouted, "Long live Holy Germany!" As the rifles cracked, Häften was killed instantly when he lunged in front of Stauffenberg to protect him. Stauffenberg was killed moments later, however, by a second volley. Quirnheim was the last to die; the coup of July 20, 1944, was over. Hitler's revenge took much longer, but in the end it killed all but a few of those who had risked so much for a cause in which they believed.

Beck's way out had been to kill himself, but what of the other giant of the Resistance, Karl Goerdeler? On July 18, two days before the coup attempt, he had dropped from public sight, having been tipped off by Nebe that the Gestapo was after him and had offered a bounty of one million marks to anyone who could provide information leading to his arrest. Despite moving constantly from one hideout to another, Goerdeler was found by the Gestapo on August 12 and jailed for high treason. Unlike the several hundred others who had been peremptorily killed following the July 20 failure, Goerdeler was kept incarcerated for five months before being executed, and then he was hanged without any pretense of a trial.

Otto Ohlendorf, RSHA secret police official, notorious for his ruthlessness, singled Goerdeler out for special handling. Taking advantage of Goerdeler's skills as an administrator, Ohlendorf set him to work writing learned monographs on administrative matters, although no one was really interested in them. It was as though Ohlendorf and Himmler with this contrivance were trying to keep Goerdeler from the gallows for a while. Conscious of his fate when the Allies overran a defeated Germany, Ohlendorf may have seen in Goerdeler someone who could vouch for his moderation if the occupying authorities put him on trial. Himmler, however, had a more complicated agenda.

Recall Himmler's secret collaboration with Schellenberg in seeking some kind of deal with the West. There had also been Himmler's use of Langbehn and Popitz to build a bridge to the Allies—a misfired initiative for which Langbehn had been sacrificed. And since the spring of 1943 he had sought contact with the Swede Jakob Wallenberg for the same purpose.[15] Now, in late 1944, Himmler intended to exploit Goerdeler as a conduit to Wallenberg and the Zionist leader Chaim Weizmann, both of whom Himmler hoped could be used to convince Churchill that some kind of negotiated end to the war would be in British interests.

Goerdeler's friendship with Wallenberg went back a long way. In November 1941 the Swedish businessman had learned from Goerdeler of Germany's inability to take Moscow. Then again, in February 1942, Goerdeler disclosed Hitler's court-martial and ouster of the officers he considered responsible for this setback. In April 1942 Goerdeler asked Wallenberg to make contact with Churchill in behalf of the Resistance, and in March 1943 he told Wallenberg of the plans for a putsch. All this information had been passed on to the British by Wallenberg, as Goerdeler intended. Goerdeler also kept the Swede fully informed of the fact that Himmler through intermediaries had made contact with the United States during the summer of 1943. After Goerdeler was arrested in connection with the July 20 1944, bomb plot against Hitler, Wallenberg received word from him that Himmler would like to see him. He refused because he feared the *Reichsführer* would ask him "to perform for his account the assignment [making contact with the Western Allies] which I had accepted for Goerdeler."[16]

This should be seen in the context of Himmler's almost desperate efforts to establish connections with the Western Allies. Since early 1944 Dr. Franz Six of the Foreign Ministry had been sending out feelers to the Allies on behalf of Himmler. June 16, 1944, saw Six in Stockholm, and it was he who recommended to Himmler that Resistance activist Trott not be killed but be kept on tap for possible peace negotiations with the Western Allies.[17] Himmler favored the idea, but Hitler was consumed by his bloodletting orgy and insisted that all Resistance suspects be hanged.

Himmler hit upon the idea of bartering Jews for badly needed foreign exchange and equipment, thinking that he could in this way ingratiate himself with the West while covering his self-serving actions as being beneficial to Germany in the event Hitler and Bormann heard of them.[18] Himmler was also trying to reach Churchill through Göring's friend the ubiquitous Swedish engineer Birger Dahlerus. The Dahlerus contact only infuriated Churchill, who had no intention of dealing with Himmler and all too accurately feared that Stalin would learn of this. Himmler even considered the wildly impractical idea of promising to repatriate Frau Gluck, American-born sister of Mayor La Guardia of New York, trapped in Germany during the war, if Roosevelt would agree to negotiations.[19]

At Himmler's behest, Goerdeler wrote a letter to Wallenberg in which he stated, "Europe, the world, humanity and civilizations" must be saved from Russian Bolshevism even if Britain had to put up with National Socialism in Germany.[20] This unrealistic plea, sent to Stockholm by the Swedish minister, was surely a sorry compromise with his own hatred of Nazism. Perhaps he rationalized that National Socialism minus Hitler and diluted by an involvement by the democratic Western Allies would be a more palatable devil's brew than anything that Stalin could cook up were the Russians to occupy Germany.

In the course of his questioning, Goerdeler made fuller admissions and disclosures than some believed necessary. But it took a very exceptional person to withstand Gestapo interrogation. Goerdeler's last days, a time of agony, personal and intellectual, were also marred by unrealistic fantasies. Always overoptimistic about the chances of Allied help to the Resistance, Goerdeler was badly misjudging Britain and the United States in believing they might deal with Himmler. It was ignoble of him to have lent his name to such overtures. Within the context of the Soviet Union's chronic distrust of its Western Allies, the ever-suspicious Stalin would predictably draw dark conclusions about any approach to the West, however unrequited, that might prove threatening to the Soviet Union.

As the twilight of the gods was rapidly turning to darkest night, Himmler incurred Hitler's wrath for trying to negotiate a peace through Swedish Count Folke Bernadotte, with whom Schellenberg had put him in touch. Hitler never seemed to have heard about the many earlier efforts by Himmler to make secret deals with the West but had growing suspicions about Göring. In his last political testament, dictated shortly before his death, Hitler stated: "Göring and Himmler, quite apart from their disloyalty to my person, have done immeasurable harm to the country and the whole nation by secret negotiations with the enemy, which they were conducting without my knowledge and against my wishes and by illegally attempting to seize power . . . for themselves."[21]

Himmler in his actions had been driven by some mix of political delusion and desperate self-preservation. Conversely, Goerdeler, for all his unrealism, had selflessly and consistently striven to save Germany, first in the 1920s to spare the fatherland from the suffocating restraints of the Versailles Treaty, then from Hitler's criminal excesses during the Nazi era, and finally to prevent a Soviet occupation following the war. It was February 2, 1945, when Goerdeler forfeited his life by hanging as Nazi Germany itself was expiring.

WHEN ALLEN DULLES HEARD THAT STAUFFENBERG'S COUP HAD FAILED, HE was desolate. He had sustained his faith in the Resistance. He excitedly reported to Washington, "Apparently Breakers are breaking."[22] Tresckow had told Stauffenberg, "[T]he main purpose of a coup attempt by the Resistance was to prove to the World and for the records of history that the men of the Resistance movement dared to take the decisive step."[23] But Dulles, more pragmatically and reflecting American, not German, interests, had hoped that a quick surrender of German forces on the western front as the result of a coup would at least save Allied lives and permit a more rapid advance through Germany, giving the Allies a postwar advantage in their negotiations with the Soviet Union. He saw no value in the failure of the coup attempt; to the contrary, he realized that it meant the end of any organized resistance to Hitler and virtually no survival of anti-Nazi moderates who could prove important in a postwar German government. This was prescient thinking in contrast with the naïve political miasma of the Roosevelt administration.

Washington was not interested in the Resistance, much less in proving to the world that the Resistance had dared to take a decisive step, nor did it concern itself with achieving a better bargaining position with the Soviets. Roosevelt naïvely believed he could handle "Uncle Joe." The war would be won by Allied power, and peace would be achieved without negotiating with the Germans.

Not only had Dulles believed that there would be value in a Western-oriented and successful German Resistance movement culminating in the overthrow of Hitler, but so had Bill Donovan. Wild Bill was as distressed as Dulles that the Stauffenberg bomb plot had failed. He feared that Hitler's retributive pogrom of Resistance moderates would ultimately "increase the influence of Russia in Germany and somewhat decrease the influence of the West."[24]

Following the failure of the July 20 coup attempt, Donovan endorsed Dulles's ideas and recommendations and sent them to Roosevelt in a memorandum entitled "Suggested Lines of Action,"[25] but the president showed no interest in either Dulles's ideas or, for that matter, how close Hitler had come to death. A directive issued by President Roosevelt to the European theater headquarters went so far as to forbid mention of anything concerning the failed coup attempt or the German Resistance in press handouts or other publications.[26] This order remained in force for some time after the war.

The OSS's Research and Analysis branch, headed by William Langer, reported that the Resistance was made up of "bankrupt generals and nationalistic intellectuals," whose activities could have no bearing on a postwar political renewal of Germany. And the American psychiatrist Walter Langer, William Langer's brother and author of a psychiatric assessment of Hitler done for the OSS, produced an astonishingly farfetched report giving his opinion that the July 20 episode had been a "set-up, a Nazi fake."[27] Brothers Langer were out of step with Donovan and reflected Roosevelt's lack of interest.*

The American press, despite the news black-out in the Allied theater headquarters, had the story from leaks but seemed for the most part uninterested, even hostile to Resistance efforts to kill Hitler. *The New York Times* described the officers of the Resistance as victims of the "atmosphere of a gangster's lurid underworld," adding that "one does not win wars with soldiers who cheer the death of their top leaders."[28] *The New York Herald Tribune* was simplistic about the whole affair, wondering why Americans should feel sorry that the bomb plot failed: "Let the generals kill the corporals or vice versa, preferably both."[29]

The British expert on Germany John W. Wheeler-Bennett believed that Britain was "better off" for the failure of the July 20 bomb plot; had Hitler been killed and the putsch succeeded, he believed, Germany would have been in a better position to extract a settlement from the Allies less constraining than unconditional surrender. In his comments, perilously close to genocidal in tone, he even favored Hitler's massive purge of dissidents following the bomb plot failure on the ground that "the killing of Germans by Germans will save us from future embarrassments of many kinds."[30] Oliver Harvey, British acting assistant secretary of state, took a similar line: "If Hitler had died, we would have had a surge to make peace with the generals. . . . Our enemies are both the Nazis and generals; we should make peace with neither."[31]

On August 2 Winston Churchill had his say in a speech before the House of Commons that seemed to make no moral distinction between the Nazi and the Resistance causes: "The highest personalities in the Reich are

---

*While supporting Dulles, Donovan seemed defensive about his emphasis on the Resistance and the July 20 bomb plot in his reporting. The OSS director, for example, did not inform the State Department of Dulles's Resistance contacts and Breakers reporting for nearly four months, although when he finally sent a memo to Secretary of State Hull on May 16, 1944, a month before the bomb went off, he defended Dulles's thesis that German Resistance actions could be of use to the Allied war effort even though it might disturb the Soviets. Donovan also feared that the British would be skittish about the political implications of Bern Station reporting lest it suggest that Dulles was "negotiating" with the Resistance, an activity proscribed by the Allies. Prompting Dulles on the right line to take, Donovan told him to inform his British contacts that he should admit to being involved "only in passively receiving information about the desire of the Breakers to find a solution," certainly not in conducting negotiations of any kind—Jürgen Heideking and Christof Mauch, *The USA and the German Resistance: Analysis and Operations of the American Secret Service in World War II* (Tübingen: A. Franke Verlag, 1993).

murdering one another, or trying to, while the avenging armies of the Allies close upon the doomed and ever-narrowing circle of their power."[32] To the great annoyance of Foreign Secretary Anthony Eden, Minister of Propaganda Brendan Bracken, like Langer in the United States, went so far as to announce that the July 20 episode was a Nazi propaganda plot.[33]*

In the Soviet Union *Pravda* reflected Marxist class doctrine as might be expected. The men of the Resistance, the newspaper stated, wanted to kill Hitler only to preserve their "position and money."[34] Strangely less doctrinaire, Radio Moscow honored the "brave men who stood up to Hitler."[35] Indicating a conflict between a strict Marxist-Leninist line and the parochial position of the Soviet puppet National Committee for a Free Germany, the latter praised the "brave men" who fought Hitler and declared: "Every blow against the Hitler system, whoever may strike it, is a blow against the mortal enemy of our nation."[36] By August 16 Moscow's theoreticans had established an orthodox, doctrinaire party position: A German Communist speaker delivered a diatribe meant to convince a Free Germany Committee audience that the plot was simply "a palace revolution," not a true people's revolt.

ADMIRAL CANARIS, LANGUISHING IN HIS MAKE-WORK ECONOMIC WARFARE job, had not been involved in the July 20 plot, but he knew all about it, as he knew about most things. He doubtless knew the reasons for his having been given his comfortable sinecure rather than having been tried for high treason on the basis of compelling information held in Himmler's safe. He surely realized that the wages of Stauffenberg's failure would spark mass arrests ordered by an unforgiving and rabidly outraged Führer, and this time he would be one of the victims.

July 20 found Canaris relaxing with a friend at his Schlachtensee house. According to one story, Stauffenberg had called him on the telephone to tell him that Hitler had been killed by a bomb. Another version of the story had it that an aide of Stauffenberg, not the assassin himself, had called. Whoever alerted Canaris had committed a dangerous indiscretion since Canaris's phone was being monitored, as usual, by the Gestapo. The quick-witted admiral immediately replied to his caller: "Who did it? The Russians?"[37] Canaris's artful guile, however, would not save him when his turn came to face his tormentors.

---

*Worst of all, a BBC broadcast commenting on the bomb plot, according to Noel Annan in his book *Changing Enemies* (p. 110), revealed the names of certain Resistance members not yet known to the Gestapo who were promptly arrested and put on trial.

He knew well that if Hitler survived, his enemies in the RSHA would eventually get him despite his influence with Himmler. His fears were borne out sooner than he expected when at five in the afternoon he heard that the Führer was very much alive. Canaris's doubts about the efficacy of Stauffenberg's plot were vindicated, but he found no comfort in this. Nor was he happy about sending a message to Hitler as demanded by protocol—and discretion—congratulating the Führer on having survived. On Sunday, July 23, one of Canaris's former aides tried to call him, but no one answered the phone. By then he was in jail.

Unluckily for Canaris, certain files captured by the Gestapo in the course of their investigations revealed Resistance relationships with the Vatican and the Western Allies that implicated him. Some of the more compromising passages in his own diaries may not have been discovered, having been hidden by a person entrusted with them, but enough evidence was unearthed to warrant his imprisonment.[38]

In his memoirs Schellenberg wrote that he personally made the arrest of Canaris. In his description of this experience, Schellenberg claimed that "Canaris was very calm when confronted at his home and said: 'Somehow, I felt it would be you. . . .' "

The SD chief, now also in overall charge of the Abwehr—at least what remained of it—then told Canaris in a manner more formal than their long association would have suggested: "If the Herr Admiral wishes to make other arrangements, then I beg him to consider me at his disposal. I shall wait in this room for an hour, and during that time you may do what you wish. My report will say that you went to your bedroom in order to change."

Canaris allegedly replied to the effect, "No, dear Schellenberg, flight is out of the question for me. And I won't kill myself either. I am sure of my case . . . and have faith in the promise you have given me [to intervene with Himmler in my behalf]."[39] Canaris added, "We'll get over this." He reiterated, "You must promise me faithfully that within the next three days you will get me an opportunity to talk with Himmler, *personally* [author's italics]. All the others, Kaltenbrunner and Müller are nothing but filthy butchers out for my blood."[40] Canaris then "embraced me with tears in his eyes," recalled Schellenberg, and said, "Well then, let us go."

Schellenberg claimed to have passed on Canaris's request for a meeting to Himmler, but events moved too fast and too far for special intervention. In commenting in his memoirs on why Himmler had not long before moved against Canaris, on whom he had considerable compromising evidence, Schellenberg writes: "Himmler obviously did not wish to be burdened with the responsibility." As with Heydrich, Canaris "seemed to have learned something incriminating against Himmler, for otherwise there is no possible explanation of Himmler's reaction to the material I placed before him."[41]

When Canaris asked for an interview with Himmler as he was being arrested, Schellenberg must have realized that he intended to try to use once more what leverage he had on the *Reichsführer* to save himself. But as Allied and Soviet troops closed in on a rapidly dying Germany, it was too late for maneuver. In the chaos of Germany's death throes, Himmler was so enmeshed in trying to reach a deal with the West contrary to Hitler's wishes that he could not save even himself.

In war's finale drawing near was Germany's day of reckoning, when retribution would be meted out by its outraged enemies. Canaris was a dangerous liability to all Nazi leaders whose atrocities he had systematically chronicled from the beginning. Himmler certainly had nothing to gain now and much to lose by saving Canaris's life. It is little wonder that no real trial was ever held for Canaris in which a host of embarrassing facts concerning the *Reichsführer* could be revealed and enshrined in the record for the victorious Allies to act upon.

THIRTY-TWO

Dulles Plays
the Field

ALLEN DULLES HAD AN ECLECTIC ARRAY OF AGENTS AND USEFUL CONTACTS in Bern. In this fast-moving war, strict security at OSS's Bern station took second place to quick results; Dulles used whomever he could to further his intelligence mission even if some of his agents may have been of dubious political persuasion. One such person was the American expatriate Noel Field, a Communist but a longtime acquaintance of Allen Dulles, who arrived in Switzerland at about the same time as he. Dulles hoped that Field could use his Communist connections in Switzerland and Germany to shed light on Stalin's postwar objectives in Europe, a subject that concerned Dulles even if Washington was not yet particularly interested. Yet for all his reservations about Stalin's sincerity, Dulles had not yet given up hope that the German Communists might play a cooperative, constructive role in the postwar rebirth of a democratic Germany, rather than serve as a fifth column intent on carving out a Soviet puppet state under the protection of an occupying Red Army.

Dulles had first met Noel Field in Zurich in 1918 at the home of Field's father. Even then the young Field was outspoken in his criticism of the American government as a "toady" of capitalism. They saw each other often again in Washington where both worked at the Department of State. Active in various liberal causes, Field was by then a member of the American Communist party although the Department of State, in its then casual approach to security, was unaware of it.[1]

In retrospect the question arises: Was Dulles justified in using an avowed Communist and Soviet apologist, vulnerable to NKVD recruitment, as an intelligence link to the Communist world? The answer was probably yes in the context of World War II *if* Dulles understood the limits beyond which Field should not be trusted and *if* Field was treated as a very short-term agent of expediency, kept isolated from other operations. There were those, however, who believed that Dulles was naïve with regard to Field. Certainly OSS officer Arthur Schlesinger, Jr., thought so in late 1944, when Dulles recommended Field to the OSS Research and Analysis station in Paris. Schlesinger and a colleague, Bert Jolis, rejected Dulles's suggestion that OSS subsidize a left-wing organization, the Comité Allemagne pour l'Ouest, in which Field seemed to have been involved.[2]

Some in the OSS believed that the Grand Alliance of the war must be salvaged if a lasting peace were to be achieved; many others, including Dulles, mistrusted Stalin and saw a postwar U.S. break with the Soviets as inevitable. Dulles, the consummate intelligence operator, felt justified in using Field as "liaison" with the German Communists, either to help shepherd them toward some kind of German national unity government or, if that was not possible, at least to gain insight into future Soviet moves. One cannot spy on the devil without paying an occasional visit to hell.

What Dulles did not realize was the extent to which Field had become a tool of Soviet espionage. Field's biographer Flora Lewis refers to his having done "furtive chores of espionage" for the Soviets, although she denies unconvincingly and somewhat naïvely that he had ever "performed as a spy."[3] The difference is difficult to see.

In a scholarly paper delivered at New York University in 1993, a knowledgeable Hungarian historian, Maria Schmidt, revealed that newly released Hungarian records quoted Field as saying that he knew Alger Hiss, the high State Department officer, to have been a Soviet agent as early as 1935. Field claimed under Hungarian police interrogation that Hiss "wanted to recruit me for espionage for the Soviet Union; I did not find the right answer and carelessly told him that I was already working for Soviet intelligence."[4]

Allen Dulles also may not have known during the war that in 1939 a Soviet defector General Walter Krivitsky, former high official of Soviet intelligence, testified before the U.S. House of Representatives Un-American Affairs Committee that Field was disloyal to the United States. Before Krivitsky could say more on the subject, he was found dead in a Washington, D.C., hotel room, probably a victim of an NKVD assassination operation to shut him up. Then Hede Massing, former Soviet agent, serving as witness for the prosecution during the Hiss trial, testified under oath that she and her Soviet agent husband, Paul Massing, had been Noel Field's handlers in a Soviet spy ring located in Washington.[5]

Dulles's employment of Noel Field's foster daughter, Erika Glaser, was also unwise from a security point of view. Born in Germany, Glaser lived in Spain throughout the Civil War with her father, a German physician. Suspected by Franco's police of Communist sympathies, she moved to France in 1939 after the Civil War ended. The French kept her in custody for a while but released her after Field intervened through friends. As World War II engulfed Europe, Glaser moved to Switzerland with the Fields.

Erika Glaser was among those hired in Switzerland by Allen Dulles to help out on his OSS island in the sea of war where regular American employees from the United States could not be sent. As the war ended and Allen Dulles moved his seat of German operations to Wiesbaden, Glaser became interpreter for Gerhard von Arkle, OSS German trade union expert.[6] Unbeknown to Arkle, she joined the Communist party in Germany. She also offered her services to the party as a spy willing to report on the OSS. Apparently too suspicious to get into a double agent game with her, the Communist party insisted that she leave her American employment before she joined the party. In 1948 she married an American army captain and moved with him to Paris.

In an effort to track down her foster parents Noel and Herta Field, who had disappeared at war's end in Eastern Europe, Glaser began her search in Berlin. She was arrested there and imprisoned by hypersuspicious Communist East German authorities who were convinced she had become a U.S. spy. The Soviets arrested her on the same charge and transferred her to a Moscow jail. She was not released until 1955, when Nikita Khrushchev granted amnesty to certain political prisoners. She was at first denied a U.S. visa because of her Communist background, but finally, in 1957, was permitted to enter the United States, where she joined her husband in Warrenton, Virginia.[7]

Dulles claimed that Field had been useful because of his Communist connections. Among other things, Dulles was able to establish contact through Field with two pro-Tito Yugoslav Communists. This helped the United States establish a relationship with Tito and his partisans behind German lines in Yugoslavia.[8] While there were those who saw in Tito a stalking-horse for Stalin in the Balkans, his defection from the Soviet bloc following the war proved him a man with an independent mind. But what was important to the Allies during the war was, of course, Tito's ability to create a partisan army capable of tying up a significant number of German troops.

After the war revelations of Field's past as a Soviet agent, not just a youthful liberal, must surely have been unsettling to Dulles. Field's true colors came out in the famous Alger Hiss trial, when his name was linked with Hiss's prewar Soviet espionage cell in Washington. It came to light that Noel and Herta Field had sought refuge from U.S. investigation and probable indictment on charges of Soviet espionage by escaping behind the Iron Curtain to Hungary. Ironically the couple were put behind bars for many years by the Hungarian Communist government, which believed them to be American spies because of Field's wartime connection with Dulles. While held under Soviet control in Hungary, Stalin used Field as a convenient whipping boy in the trials of the Czech leader Rudolf Slansky and other East European Communists who were being pruned from the more fiercely loyal Stalinist cadres within the Hungarian government. Noel and Herta Field were finally released from Soviet incarceration in 1954, but despite all they had been put through by the Communists, they elected to remain in Hungary, where Noel died fourteen years later.

ANOTHER PERSON OF QUESTIONABLE ALLEGIANCES IN CONTACT WITH Dulles in Switzerland during the war was Dr. Josef Wirth, who had been chancellor of Germany from May 1921 to November 1922. During Wirth's administration, sometimes wistfully referred to by his supporters as the "Government of Fulfillment," he created an ambiance that made possible the Treaty of Rapallo, reestablishing German-Russian diplomatic relations after World War I. Rapallo in turn spawned the so-called Spirit of Tauroggen, which brought close collaboration between the Red Army and the German Army and led to German military training programs conducted in secret on Soviet soil in violation of the Versailles Treaty.

When Hitler gained power in 1933, Wirth left Germany and settled in Lucerne, Switzerland, convinced that in Germany "the enemy is on the right." It may have been more than coincidence that Rudolf Rössler, or Lucy, his code designation within the Rote Drei (Swiss segment of the widely ramified Soviet intelligence network Rote Kapelle), moved to Lucerne at about the same time as Wirth did.[9] As time went on, it became evident that Wirth had a close relationship with the Soviet Union. He headed a leftist group of Germans in Switzerland who plotted to establish a postwar socialist German government that, with help from the Soviets, would take power in Germany.

Dulles, who was willing to use almost anyone who could keep him informed on Germany, however politically ambidextrous he or she might be, found Wirth useful. Dulles writes in his postwar book *Germany's Underground*: "After the attack on Norway [April 9, 1940] but before the invasion of the Lowlands and France [May 10, 1940], the military conspirators on the initiative of General Beck . . . asked Wirth to make use of certain Anglo-French contacts he had to ascertain the intentions of the Western powers in the event a military putsch succeeded in overthrowing Hitler."[10] As an emissary of Stauffenberg's July 20 coup group, Wirth established contact with Dulles in 1944. If Wirth was useful to the Soviets as even a cloudy window on Allen Dulles's contacts with the German Resistance, it may be no wonder that the hypersuspicious Stalin saw in the OSS Bern operations an indication that the Americans intended to deal out the Russians and work unilaterally with the German underground in disregard of the unconditional surrender agreement.

Wirth also maintained contact with SD senior officer Walter Schellenberg, who by mid-war was convinced that Germany would lose and had encouraged his boss, Himmler, to plot against Hitler with the intent of taking his place and suing for peace with the Western Allies. Schellenberg, like Beck, saw Wirth as a possible conduit to the West. The SD officer used as his point of contact with Wirth one of his agents, Richard Grossman (code-named Director). It is significant that Grossman later described Wirth as a double agent, also in touch with the Soviets. Wirth's Soviet coloration emerged more clearly after the war, in 1951, when he went to East Germany for political conversations with Soviet representatives as well as with high East German officials. A year later he saw Secret Police Chief Lavrenti Beria in Berlin.[11]

After digging into Wirth's background, CIA's voluminous postwar study on the Rote Kapelle suggests that he had become a Soviet "agent of influence" in the early 1920s, a year or two after the signing of the Treaty of Rapallo, and had made several trips to the USSR in connection with the German military training program in Russia.[12] During World War II he provided information to the Soviets. While he may or may not have told Schellenberg about his Soviet relationship, he probably gave advance warning to the Soviets of the July 20, 1944, bomb plot against Hitler. This again raises the question: How much did Himmler himself know in advance about that fateful affair? In March 1944, some four months before the July 20 event, Captain Ludwig Gehre of Oster's Abwehr staff was unmasked by the Resistance as a Gestapo penetration of their secret ranks.[13]

The CIA's postwar Rote Kapelle survey draws the following conclusion, which bears on this confused picture of relationships and allegiances: "There are clear indications in the record that he [Himmler] envisioned himself as Hitler's successor. He once told Canaris that he knew perfectly well the identities of all the anti-Hitler plotters. In short, if Wirth and others were betraying the conspiracy to Schellenberg, they were also being double-crossed by a Himmler who *hoped that the plan to assassinate the*

Führer would succeed [author's italics for emphasis]."[4] Of course, if it did not, the perpetrators would be ruthlessly punished.

Another view of Himmler had been given Dulles in late 1943 by Carl Burckhardt, International Red Cross head in Switzerland. Recognizing that Dulles was interested in Himmler's secret plans, Burckhardt believed that the *Reichsführer's* power was increasing and that his capacity for switching sides in the interest of expediency was infinite. On the basis of Burckhardt's information, Dulles reported that if "Himmler is persuaded, at last, that there is no hope of making a deal with the Anglo-Saxons, he may flop over, although at the present time he does not favor the Russian solution." Burckhardt gloomily predicted: "The odds are heavily in favor of Communism arising in Germany. The only force which keeps the people together is Hitler and if he should vanish, rapid degeneration would follow accompanied by war among would-be successors, all of which would be followed by Bolshevism."[5]

Dulles was perched precariously in the middle of this wilderness of mirrors obscured by clouds of smoke made the more opaque by shifting allegiances, double agents, and other devices adopted in the interest of survival. Resistance fighters, who found their overtures to the West unrequited, in some cases felt justified in searching for another patron: the USSR. Even Hans Gisevius, Dulles's trusted contact with the Resistance, or Breakers, as Dulles referred to it, was not beyond suspicion. Certainly the British for a while suspected him of being a German provocation after the Venlo affair; if "Venlo" could happen in Holland, something similar could happen in Switzerland. But any suggestion that Hans Gisevius was one of Rössler's (or Lucy's) sources within the Soviet-run Rote Drei would have been protested by Dulles, and the accusations that Gisevius may have had insidious connections with the Abwehr's rival, the SD, RSHA, would also have provoked denials by the OSS Swiss station chief.[6]

The CIA's December 1973 Rote Kapelle survey report summarizes its conclusions about Gisevius: "We know that Gisevius had intelligence contacts with the Western Allies. Rössler (Lucy), essentially a mercenary working for several clients, for all his Soviet Rote Drei affiliations, listed Gisevius as a source," and "there are also valid indications that despite the confidence which Hans Oster, Goerdeler and others in the 20 July group seem to have accorded him, he may have been an RSHA agent too. Some interrogations of German intelligence officers included their comments that Ernst Kaltenbrunner, RSHA chief and Schellenberg's superior, received reports from Gisevius as late as April 1945. The record contains other references to links between Gisevius and Heydrich as well as between Gisevius and Schellenberg."[7] But since Gisevius had originally been affiliated with the Gestapo before he switched to the Abwehr, such links could well have been natural and innocent. How innocent depended on what kind of "reports" had been passed on. Moreover, Gisevius as a Resistance operator had in effect license to beat the bushes—any bushes—in pursuit of intelligence or helpful connections. Gisevius, for all his help, never claimed to be an American agent or wanted to be considered one. He was a member of the Resistance *in liaison* with the Americans. As the CIA retrospective report admits, "Such reports . . . are likely to be unreliable; some denunciations were inspired by rancor [particularly just after the war, when Gisevius testified before the Nuremberg tribunal in behalf of the prosecution], therefore seem highly improbable."

Whatever dubious friends and contacts Gisevius may have had while working with Dulles, it was probably all part of the game. Gisevius, more than most, understood the limitations faced by the United States in making commitments to the Resistance because of the unconditional surrender agreement with its allies yet was willing to help Dulles. As Dulles's main contact with the Resistance, he was of considerable value to the OSS. U.S. Justice Robert Jackson at the Nuremberg trials described Gisevius as "the one representative of democratic forces in Germany to take this stand to tell his story."[8] The CIA report, written in the cool light of history, nearly thirty years later, concludes: "On balance then, it is considered that Gisevius had intelligence contacts with the Americans, the British, the Swiss and probably with the Soviets, but not with Nazi Germany, except for his major role in the Resistance."[19]

Of all of Dulles's activities, perhaps the most memorable was his success in bringing about an unconditional surrender of German forces in Italy. This was an example of covert political action at its most intricate and was an exhibition of both his skill and the OSS's versatility. It is only unfortunate that the process of neutralizing German forces in Italy could not have been swifter. In part the delay was caused by political complications, particularly by acute Soviet suspicions of Allied intentions. The sudden death of President Roosevelt and the succession to office by a hurriedly briefed Harry Truman perhaps also contributed to the delay. Operation Sunrise was the code designation given the German surrender in Italy by Allen Dulles, who could hope, if not believe, that this would be the first dawn of a new and brighter day. Instead it proved to be an opening Soviet salvo in what became nearly a half century of Cold War, in which Dulles also played an important role.

THIRTY-THREE

Sunrise

As imminent defeat faced Germany, certain Nazi leaders became progressively more frantic in trying to reach some kind of accommodation with their enemies in order to save themselves from wrathful retribution. A few military officers sought an honorable surrender to spare their troops needless death. Despite being bound by a near-sacred officer's oath of loyalty, such men saw the criminal folly of sending troops to their destruction on the orders of an unbalanced, obsessive tyrant. Allen Dulles's OSS station in Switzerland was the magnet that attracted all variety of plotters, whether they were sincere in their convictions or simply self-serving.

As the end of the war drew nearer, a succession of secret emissaries descended on Dulles, hoping to interest him in a deal unrealistically based on presumed common opposition to Stalin and international Communism despite the U.S. promise of solidarity with the USSR, which they dismissed as the product of temporary expediency. Many of those in the Resistance, who had from an early time deplored Hitler as an evil Pied Piper leading Germany inexorably toward disaster, had become discouraged by the Western Allies' commitment to unconditional surrender. But Dulles at least was a sympathetic listener with a sense of pragmatic politics. He seemed to realize that the postwar enemy of both Germany and the Western Allies would most likely be the Soviet Union, even if this was not a subject for discussion welcomed in Washington. The basic flaw in the German Resistance, Dulles believed, was the reluctance of the military to act. Loyalty was the root of an officer's credo, however now misplaced.

Dulles walked a tightrope between strict observance of policy restrictions and keeping a window open to the genuine Resistance. But after the failure of Stauffenberg's bomb plot on July 20, 1944, the Resistance, as he had known it, was obliterated. Nearly all its participants—and some who were not—had been rounded up and killed. The men were shot or hanged; the women, killed by the guillotine. Dulles had watched this tragedy unfold mainly through his Bern contacts, Abwehr officers Eduard von Waetjen and Hans Gisevius. The latter had at great risk returned to Germany from Switzerland so that he could participate in the putsch. When it failed and the mass roundup of suspects began, Gisevius, despite his conspicuous size and presence, managed to hide out until Dulles could send him false identification papers with which to escape from Germany and return to Switzerland.

Dulles sent a memorable telegram to Washington on July 22, breaking the news of the July 20 debacle, predicting that this demise of the Resistance would work to the benefit of those survivors who favored accommodation with the Soviets. The details of what had occurred and how the plot had failed as received by Dulles provided the OSS with an intelligence scoop of commendable proportions.[1]

A path to Dulles's door at Herrengasse 23 in Bern would now be beaten by those who came late to the game and attempted to defect in belated hope that their own existence as well as that of their country could be preserved by making accommodation with one or another member of the Grand Alliance, Western or Eastern, whichever offered the best prospects. Dulles was wary now because most of the feelers seemed to be coming from SS rather than army officers.[2] The Catholic Church was anxious to see the end to a war whose outcome was by now predictable. Too many lives had already been given in what fared to be the most destructive conflict in history.

In November 1944 a Catholic Church official in Switzerland told Dulles that an Italian industrialist, Franco Marinotti, in behalf of certain German officers in Italy, had made peace overtures to the British. The deal offered was the standard one: The German Army would surrender to the Western Allies if the Allies would join forces against the invading Red Army. The British rejected the approach out of hand, but a less inhibited Dulles probed more deeply, hoping to find a formula that would not violate the spirit of unconditional surrender but could at least be explored. The person behind Marinotti seemed to be an SS police general, Wilhelm Harster, although Marinotti claimed that Heinrich Himmler himself had inspired the approach. Schellenberg too seemed to be in on it.[3]

Another approach, this one from the Reverend Giuseppe Bicchierai, secretary to Ildefonso Cardinal Schuster of Milan, presented a proposal that the German Army would promise to spare Italian industry if the Italian partisans, now working with the Allies, agreed not to harass the German Army in retreat. This was predictably vetoed by the Italian partisans, who insisted on being in on the kill and wanted to see some of the credit for defeating the Germans go to the Italians. While unacceptable, the cardinal's approach was interesting since by implication, SS General Karl Wolff, ranking SS officer, and Wehrmacht Field Marshal Kesselring, top German commanders in Italy, must have given it their approval.[4]

In December 1944 Dulles's assistant Gero von Gaevernitz, discovered that the German consul in Lugano, Switzerland, Alexander von Neurath,[5] was searching for channels to the Western Allies. Gaevernitz reported that Neurath claimed to be in close contact with Marshal Kesselring and SS Generals Wolff and Harster in Italy.

Kesselring was cautious but had at least given Neurath a green light to work things out through German officers less conspicuous and of lower rank than himself. The field marshal steered him specifically to German Generals Siegfried Westphal and Johannes Blaskowitz. Wolff, who turned out to be lead player in this drama, was the senior SS and German police officer in Italy and previously Himmler's influential chief of staff in Berlin.[6]

Dulles was intrigued by the possibilities of arranging an early peace even though the prospects were still unclear. Among other things, he felt hamstrung by a presidential order sent him on December 18, 1944, stating that no promises could be given to Germans willing to collaborate with the West.[7] Donovan explained to Dulles that the president "considers that the carrying out of such guarantees would be difficult and probably widely misunderstood both in this country and abroad." By "abroad" the president had in mind Stalin, who was becoming increasingly suspicious of Allied intentions. Recognizing that "an increasing number of Germans will try to save themselves by coming over to our side at the last moment," Roosevelt added, "there will be some who should properly be tried for war crimes or at least arrested for participation in Nazi crimes against humanity."[8]

In late February 1945 feelers originating with Himmler and SD chief Kaltenbrunner were received by Dulles. This time Kaltenbrunner, with Himmler's blessing, sent an SD officer, Wilhelm Hoettl, and an Austrian industrialist, Fritz Weston, to talk with the OSS Bern chief. Their pitch was to the effect that it was Martin Bormann who had been and was still the warmonger; Himmler, to the contrary, wanted to reach agreement with the West for peace. Apparently unable to grasp the depth of Allied hatred of him and believing that his control of the SS and RSHA security apparatus could be an appealing bargaining chip, Himmler to the end continued to court the Allies, particularly through the Swedish nobleman Count Bernadotte. Dulles was under no illusions and realized he could not deal with these men, high on the list of German war criminals, but he believed that they and their actions could for the moment be exploited to sow dissension within Hitler's rapidly decaying regime.[9]

In Hoettl's version of his contact with Dulles in late February, he emphasized the danger of a Soviet occupation of Germany but introduced a new talking point calculated to frighten the Western Allies into reaching agreement. This dealt with alleged plans for a Nazi redoubt in the Italian and Austrian Alps that would harbor German guerrilla forces known as "werewolves" so that they could wage prolonged partisan warfare against Allied occupying forces.[10] This essentially mythical threat never materialized, but at the time his principals hoped that it would provide a lever by which better surrender terms could be pried out of the Allies.

Hoettl claimed to have support from German Generals Alexander Löhr, who had just retreated from Greece, and Colonel General Lothar Rendulic, commander in chief of the army group on the Austro-Hungarian frontier. Kesselring, commander in chief of Army Group South, and Field Marshal von Rundstedt on the western front were described as generally supporting the plan to surrender, provided that negotiations were conducted with the Western Allies, not the Soviets.

In March Hoettl visited Switzerland with the Polish Count Potocki, through whom he made contact with Dulles's assistant Gaevernitz. Hoettl had gained the impression that the Americans, in their desire to keep Soviet influence in Austria to a minimum, were interested in setting up an Austrian government in competition with the Soviet-sponsored one about to be established in Vienna. The Austrian Kaltenbrunner, who had full authority in southern Europe, was discussed as a likely player in an Allied-sponsored Free Austrian movement.

In April Hoettl described to Kaltenbrunner his conversations in Switzerland and urged him to meet with Dulles at some mutually agreed-upon place, perhaps at Feldkirch in Austria. Events moved too rapidly, however, and Kaltenbrunner abandoned his political aspirations, eventually fleeing to an Alpine retreat at Altaussee rather than risk capture by either advancing American or Russian troops.[11]

By April Dulles was treated to another interesting approach, this one by SS General Walter Schellenberg, whose colorful career with the Nazi SD (Amt VI of the RSHA), as we have seen, included the Venlo sting and the attempted defection of the Duke and Duchess of Windsor in Spain. Schellenberg tried to make contact with Dulles through General Roger Masson, a senior officer in Swiss intelligence whom Dulles included among his many contacts in Bern. Schellenberg's improbable gambit was to claim that the rapid Soviet approach from the East was the result of a deal made with Stalin in which German troops would hold firm against the Allied advance in the West but allow the Soviets to enter Germany without opposition. If the Western Allies were prepared to abandon their commitment to unconditional surrender and join forces with Germany against Stalin, the Germans would agree to a cease-fire on the western front instead. Dulles frostily let Schellenberg know that the Allies did not need his help in their invasion of Germany; the German forces were already on the run.[12]

Schellenberg revealed in his postwar memoir that after his fateful 1942 agreement with Himmler in which they agreed to seek secret contacts with the enemy, he had made indirect overtures to the Soviets as well as to the Western Allies through Switzerland and Sweden. Unlike the West, rigidly bound by its unconditional surrender commitment, the Soviets "were genuinely interested in negotiations" behind the backs of their Western Allies toward ending hostilities. He claimed that thanks to Ribbentrop's "short-sighted clumsiness and incredible conceit and optimism," his efforts had been wrecked; the bigoted foreign minister "demanded proof that the Soviet representatives were not of Jewish origin."[13] Ribbentrop was probably still smarting from his misbegotten efforts to talk peace with the Soviets in July 1943 and again in September of that year, when the Soviet envoy to Sweden, Mme. Kollontay, presented a plan that required the return to the 1939 frontiers in Eastern Europe. (Recall that this had been the occasion when Hitler scolded Ribbentrop for going too far in his peace initiative in Sweden.) In the Kollontay negotiations the Soviet go-between, Klaus, secretly a double agent reporting to Canaris as well, was Jewish, therefore offensive to Himmler. Schellenberg acknowledged that the apparent Soviet willingness to talk may have been only a tactic to put pressure on the Western Allies to launch a second front in France.

Soon after the July 20, 1944, bomb plot failure, Schellenberg, now czar of all German intelligence, was called to Ribbentrop's headquarters to discuss a fantastic idea. According to Schellenberg, the foreign minister sketched a plan in which "a conference will be arranged with Stalin, and it will be my mission to shoot down the Russian leader."[14] Then, to Schellenberg's horror, he added: "I named you [Schellenberg] as my accomplice." Realizing that he was talking to "a determined fanatic" with "a neurotic and overstrained mind," Schellenberg pointed out that after their experience in dealing with the Russians in Stockholm, it was unlikely that Stalin would agree to a face-to-face meeting.[15] According to Schellenberg, the idiotic plan was fortunately abandoned and never brought up again.

Another idea, this one promoted by Hitler's propaganda chief, Josef Goebbels, was more successful. Its essence was to frighten the Allies into a reasonable peace settlement by warning them of a German guerrilla war to harass their occupation armies. The Nazi plan to withdraw all troops to an Alpine redoubt from which werewolves, the mythology-based, somewhat romantic name for guerrillas, could indefinitely harass the armies of occupation, was imagined by the Americans as more than just a *Götterdämmerung* fantasy. Thanks to master propagandist Goebbels, the Americans feared that the Nazis would make a determined last stand in the Alps as a means of buying time in the conviction that an exploitable breach in the Grand Alliance between the Western Allies and the Soviets was inevitable as they quarreled over the fate of Germany and Eastern Europe.

Consideration had been given to adopting some such strategy by the German General Staff, but ironically its inspiration may have originated in an intercepted American message. The message, based on an American agent report from Zurich, described vast fortifications being constructed in the Alps as housing for an SS redoubt army. The report was fanciful. While the German High Command was exploring fallback defensive preparations in the Alps that might accommodate German troops retreating from the boot of Italy, there was no large-scale construction anticipated, as described in the American report.

It was obvious that massive fortifications and the stocking of vast quantities of supplies to support such an army could not be accomplished in time before the flood of invading American, British, and Russian troops overwhelmed Germany, Austria, and Italy. The embryonic OKW idea, perhaps one of several contingency studies routinely made, was eagerly embraced by an imaginative regional gauleiter, one Franz Hofer, who tried to push it. Although some minor construction actually took place, the grander but fanciful concept was exploited by Goebbels for propaganda purposes. Goebbels knew a good lie when he saw one.

A *New York Times* article datelined London, November 12, 1944, broke the story with the headline HITLER'S HIDEAWAY. This stimulated a rash of similar articles by newspapers hungry for sensational war developments. A series run by the Communist party New York *Daily Worker* on the subject had almost certainly been planted by the Soviets who leaped at the chance to keep U.S. attention focused on the south while they won the race to Berlin and staked out their claim for occupation rights in East Germany. The *Daily Worker* of December 15 blew the story out of all proportion as it trumpeted Wehrmacht and SS plans to fight to the "last drop of German blood."

Delighted with such hype and recognizing its potential for splitting the Western Allies from the Soviets, Goebbels's ministry fanned the flames by planting stories telling of impenetrable bastions housing V weapons and even an advance rocket dubbed V-3 with which to make Allied occupation of Germany an expensive proposition. Dulles sent long telegrams quoting from the German and other European press. The SS press organ *Das Schwarze Korps*, for example, threatened that any German collaborating with the occupying powers "would not last more than a month because the partisans would liquidate such collaborators."[16]

General Eisenhower in September 1944 had announced, "The main target is, of course, Berlin." But by March 31, 1945, he seemed to have been taken in by national redoubt propaganda, fanned by credulous Allied informants anxious to earn their pay and a gullible foreign press. He notified British General Montgomery: ". . . you will have noticed that I have not mentioned Berlin at all. That place is no more than a geographical definition to me . . . pure theater, that may safely be left to the Russians."[17]

On March 28, 1945, Eisenhower unveiled a new military plan in which Western forces would strike south aiming toward the alleged German Alpine redoubt instead of driving on to Berlin.[18] The prize had been abandoned to the Russians. General Montgomery telegraphed Churchill complaining that a "terrible mistake" had been made by Eisenhower; while the American supreme commander dismissed Berlin as a strategically unimportant target, Stalin was hurling 2.5 million of his best troops at the German capital.[19]

Goebbels must have thought he had reason to exult. In a September 7, 1945, diary entry the propaganda minister wrote: "Our Werewolf activity is now being taken extraordinarily seriously in Anglo-American circles, so seriously that Eisenhower is said to be toying with the idea of using gas against Werewolf detachments." He added: "The British realize that the Werewolf could be the germ of an extraordinarily dangerous instrument of German resistance to be maintained at any cost and for an unpredictable time. . . . The Werewolf in particular is regarded as the germ of . . . a development [chaos in Germany] which would, of course, upset the entire Anglo-American war concept."[20]

It has never been wholly clear why Eisenhower clung so tenaciously to the national redoubt myth, perhaps at the expense of better positioning the Allied armies astride the western approaches to Berlin and reaching a better occupation deal with the Soviets. Intent on his efforts to bring about the surrender of German troops in Italy, Dulles may have been partially responsible for a significant intelligence failure in not seeing through the German redoubt disinformation campaign. But one wonders why aerial reconnaissance had not been brought to bear or why it was not evident that logistical support for such a massive undertaking and troop concentrations in the Austrian Alps would have been virtually impossible.[21]

THE STORY OF OPERATION SUNRISE,[22] THE GERMAN SURRENDER IN ITALY, reveals Allen Dulles's enterprise and skill in trying to shorten the war, saving lives that would otherwise be needlessly lost on both sides. It would also prevent scorched-earth destruction in northern Italy as the Germans retreated or massive trespassing on Swiss territory by German troops trying to escape. While unanticipated, Sunrise also shed its rays of light on the difference in war aims pursued by the Western Allies and the Soviet Union. It starkly revealed Stalin's fundamental distrust of his allies and provided them with a chilling initiation to the Cold War that was to dominate international relations for more than a generation to come.

Karl Wolff, top SS officer in Italy, accompanied by a representative from General Kesselring's army staff, arrived in Lugano, Switzerland, on March 8, 1945. Dulles reported that they were "allegedly prepared to make definite commitments in regard to terminating German resistance in North Italy."[23] Dulles saw this as an opportunity to save lives by shortening the war. He also realized that Wolff was in command of SS units deployed behind the front whose surrender would make it difficult, if not impossible, for the German Army in Italy to fall back to some Alpine redoubt.

This sounded intriguing but also dangerous. The SS was Hitler's ultimate bastion of loyalty. What was Wolff up to, and how valid were his intention and ability to surrender his forces to the Allies? Wolff had crossed Hitler before. During the summer of 1943, soon after Mussolini's fall, he had derailed a mad plan hatched by Hitler in a fit of rage to kidnap the Pope and loot the Vatican. In fact Wolff's relations with the Vatican to warn the Pope and pledge his secret support pointed a way to reach Dulles and ultimately to surrender the German Army in Italy. It is useful to be aware of this little-known episode featuring Wolff before following the drama of the surrender.

WHEN IN 1940 HIS HOLINESS PIUS XII ACTED AS INTERMEDIARY FOR CANaris's Resistance circle and the British ambassador in an effort to arrange a military putsch against Hitler and find peace, he had shown his willingness to take risks. Recall that Project X, as this plot was known in the Abwehr, did not prosper because the Venlo incident had frightened off the British, and the German Army had become too occupied with Western campaigns to make possible any revolt within its ranks. But it was significant that the Pope had throughout been willing to give encouragement to the German Resistance at great risk to himself and the church.

The restoration of peace was a goal toward which the Pope consistently worked, even if unrealistically at times and despite apparent lack of interest by the Western Allies committed to winning a war. Shortly before the Allied invasion of North Africa, the Portuguese Foreign Ministry sent its ambassador in Madrid intelligence concerning a mission to the Vatican undertaken by Myron Taylor in behalf of President Roosevelt. According to this, Taylor was to explain America's war policy based on unconditional surrender of Axis forces and head off any effort by His Holiness [to negotiate peace] that could lessen the fighting spirit of the Allies. As for any concern the Pope might have regarding the Soviet Communist peril, Taylor was to express his conviction that this would not become a problem.[24] The State Department would hardly have described Taylor's mission in quite this way, but like Britain, the United States had not been receptive to peace initiatives with the Germans, even the Resistance, that could complicate relations with the Soviets or interfere with Allied military plans to conquer Germany.

Grave problems faced the Vatican on July 25, 1943, when Mussolini was forced to resign and was arrested by Marshal Badoglio's new regime. With his ally forced from power and American forces now in Sicily what would Hitler do and how would it affect the Vatican? The Pope's concern was well founded. At 12:25 A.M., on July 26, Hitler met in emergency session with some of his officers to discuss the crisis and determine what action could be taken to restore Mussolini or at least to prevent Badoglio from allying himself with the Allied forces and what should be done about Pope Pius XII, whose complicity in this affair was definitely suspected.

Walter Hewel, liaison officer between the Foreign Ministry and Hitler, raised the question of the Vatican, suggesting that the exits to the Vatican be blocked, preventing flight by the Pope or other Vatican officials. Hitler's reaction was more forceful: "I'll go right into the Vatican. Do you think the Vatican embarrasses me? We'll take that over right away. For one thing the entire diplomatic corps are in there. It's all the same to me. That rabble is in there [meaning Jews given sanctuary in the Vatican]. We'll take that bunch of swine out of there. . . . Later we can make apologies. . . ."

When Hewel raised the matter of Vatican documents, Hitler ranted on: "Yes, we'll get documents. The treason [presumably the suspected Vatican involvement in the Badoglio takeover] will come to light. . . . A pity that Foreign Minister [Ribbentrop] isn't here. How long will it take him to draft the directive for Ambassador Mackensen [German ambassador to Italy]?"[25]

By later in the morning of July 26 Hitler had been joined by Himmler and Göring. Then Field Marshal von Kluge came in from the eastern front to discuss with Hitler the effect of Mussolini's fall from power on his command. Later Dönitz for the Navy and Rommel, who had flown in from Salonika in Greece, took part in the discussions.

When Ribbentrop joined the talks, he immediately objected to the involvement of the Vatican in German operations against Badoglio. Goebbels too objected, presumably fearing the adverse affect it would have on Germany's image. As a result, Hitler's impulsive idea to invest the Vatican and seize the Pope seemed to have been abandoned. And because of fears that Germany's forces in Italy could be threatened by precipitous action, Hitler's military advisers, Jodl, Dönitz, and Rommel, talked the Führer out of doing anything for the time being. Until German forces in Italy could be augmented, no effort would be made to unseat the new government. In the light of the American campaign in the south of Italy and the Wehrmacht's drive toward Kharkov on the eastern front launched on August 3, this counsel made sense. The Army was stretched too far to risk large-scale civil unrest in Italy. Hitler's plan to overthrow Badoglio and take reprisals of any kind against the Vatican appeared to be shelved.[26] But was it really?

Enjoying the Führer's favor was a sometime thing. As much time and effort were devoted to maneuvering and scheming by Hitler's closest courtiers as were devoted to doing their jobs. The chosen few at the top were incessantly intriguing; Göring, Himmler, Goebbels, Bormann, and Ribbentrop all hated one another, or so said Himmler's masseur, Felix Kersten, who called Hitler's court "a true theater of the absurd."

The next echelon down was also infected with the virus of internecine strife. Waffen SS General Karl Wolff as Himmler's chief of staff was the keeper of the gate, a position of enormous influence, but he was tired of the charade and suffered from bad health. Moreover, Wolff and Himmler had squabbled over Wolff's request to divorce his first wife and marry another. When Himmler turned him down, Wolff appealed to Hitler, who gave his blessing. That his chief of staff would go over his head rankled Himmler; it suggested that Wolff might have stronger influence with Hitler than he did. That would never do.

After the German defeat at Stalingrad in February 1943, it was obvious to most close to the seat of power that Germany could not win the war. Wolff, looking to the future, could see advantage to distancing himself from Himmler, who was surely a prime candidate for Allied punitive action. Thus he was not regretful when Himmler shipped him off to Italy to command the Waffen SS units there. He was also pleased that Hitler personally promoted him to a new title created just for him: "Highest Ranking SS and Police Chief." He would be a powerful man in Rome.

The German position in Italy radically changed after Mussolini was deposed; Badoglio had agreed to an Italian Army cease-fire and, for all intents and purposes, had cast his lot with the Western Allies. As the American and British fought their way northward and anti-Fascist Italian partisans became more active in the north, Wolff as SS commander and Kesselring as army commander were faced with a difficult, actually hopeless situation.

Hitler was dismayed by the accession of "that traitor" Badoglio and the demise of his Axis partner Mussolini, now a fugitive under German protection. He summoned Wolff to his East Prussian headquarters on September 12 and, to the general's astonishment, gave him an assignment that would have had terrible consequences had he carried it out. Now only slightly more than two weeks after Hitler's idea to kidnap the Pope had been shot down by his top advisers, the persistent Führer, it seems, had not given up on it after all. As Wolff reconstructed his story in an interview with the German newspaper *Neue Bildpost* in April 1974, more than thirty years later, Hitler said to him: "I have another special assignment for you, Wolff, which, because of its worldwide implications, I am personally conveying to you and you alone. I make it your duty to speak to no one about this matter without my concurrence. Himmler, whom I have just initiated, is the one exception."

What Hitler had in mind came as a shock to Wolff: "I want you to use your troops to occupy the Vatican and Vatican City, immediately if possible, to secure the Vatican's fabulous archives and art treasures as well as the Pope's Curia [the official body that governs the Catholic Church]. Bring [the Pope] north so he does not fall into the hands of the Allies or under their political influence. I want the Pope brought to Germany, if possible, or, depending on political and military developments, to neutral Liechtenstein. How soon can you carry out this assignment?"[27]

Aside from Hitler's strong suspicions that Pius XII had been part of the plot that ousted Mussolini, he knew the Vatican was being used to harbor a considerable number of refugees, principally persecuted Jews. He probably also believed that the Pope had been in secret contact with anti-Hitler elements trying to find a formula for peace with the Western Allies. Wolff was dumbfounded by the enormity of Hitler's command. Stalling for time, he told the Führer he needed at least four to six weeks to draw up plans.

Hitler was impatient; he would prefer "clearing out the Vatican immediately," but he gave Wolff the time he needed, provided he reported progress every two weeks. Horrified by the project, Wolff was determined to find some way to have it abandoned. In the meantime, to "show progress"—which he did not intend to make—he had drawn up a blueprint for action that called for two thousand SS troops to occupy the Vatican, spirit the Pope and cardinals off to Liechtenstein by armored car, and arrest the Jewish refugees hiding within the Vatican. Experts would be charged with packing and removing the art treasures and some half million rare books and documents for shipment to Germany.

Wolff took into his confidence Dr. Rudolf Rahn, German ambassador to Italy, and Ernst von Weizsäcker, ambassador to the Vatican—and secretly a Resistance collaborator. (Both these men testified after the war in Wolff's behalf, describing his role in frustrating Hitler's plans.) Rahn was instrumental in introducing Wolff to Father Pankretius Pfeiffer, head of the Salvatorian Ecclesiastical Order and, through Weizsäcker, to Dr. Ivo Zeiger, rector of the German Theological College in Rome.

Surprised and suspicious that the top SS general in Italy wanted to talk to them, both men were astonished when they heard Wolff disclose, in all its frightening detail, Hitler's plan. They soon came to trust Wolff, however, and believe that he was sincere in his promise to block it. In early December 1943 Wolff sent to Pius his personal pledge that the Germans would not threaten His Holiness or violate the Vatican.[28]*

When Wolff saw Hitler in December, the Führer was growing impatient with the apparent lack of progress. The general vividly remembered pleading with the Führer to drop the whole thing: "If we attack the Vatican now, we will no longer be able to contain the population. We will then have unrest, acts of violence, strikes and mass demonstrations to contend with. It will then be impossible to guarantee Field Marshal Kesselring the supplies he needs [for this southern campaign against the advancing Allies]. . . . The Pope's abduction would lead to extremely negative consequences for us regarding not only German Catholics at home and on the front, but also all Catholics around the world. . . . Have confidence in me to resolve the problem with my positive approach."

On one of the rare occasions Hitler accepted opposition to his schemes, he concurred with Wolff and agreed to drop the plan. It had been a close call.[29]

---

*There had been rumors that Pius XII might flee the Vatican to avoid a Nazi attempt to kidnap him. And an unsubstantiated report spoke of arrangements for His Holiness to seek asylum in Spain. Pope Pius believed it necessary to squash such rumors and is supposed to have said: "Rumors of Nazi intentions to kidnap me are not flights of fancy but must be taken seriously. However, I will never leave Rome nor the Vatican unless I am chained and taken away by force"—Richard Lamb, *War in Italy, 1943–1945* (New York: St. Martin's Press, 1993), p. 45, based on Georgio Garibaldi, *Pio XII, Hitler e Mussolini: Il Vatican fra le Dittature*, pp. 206, 207, 217, quoting General Wolff to the Tribunal for the Beatification of Pius XII, and Wolff's interrogations as an Allied prisoner per British Foreign Office document, FO 371/46787.

On May 10, 1944, Wolff claimed to have met in secret with Pope Pius XII after being introduced by Father Pfeiffer. What transpired, or even that a meeting took place, is not believed to be a matter of record in the Vatican. But according to Wolff, the Pope promised he would "do everything in his power under reasonable and honorable circumstances to curtail this unholy war against the West." But His Holiness feared that the Allied insistence on unconditional surrender of the Germans might be "an obstacle to peace."[30]

The only awkward moment in an otherwise successful meeting, was at the moment of departure when Wolff gave the pontiff the Nazi salute with straight arm outstretched; it was a matter of habit.

After the war Wolff described his meeting with the Pope to the Milan newspaper *Tempo*:

> His Holiness Pius XII had been duly informed by cardinals and bishops of the way I carried out my duties, my efforts to avoid pointless harshness, and my efforts toward shortening the war. He then had me invited to come to an audience with him, provided this would not involve too many difficulties in connection with my position. And thus, early in May 1944, Pius XII received me in private audience.... His Holiness showed an astonishing familiarity with the most secret circumstances and the most minor problems. During the course of this meeting—an unforgettable one for me—I declared my readiness to do whatever was in my power for the rapid conclusion of the war, should an honorable opportunity present itself.[31]

Wolff had hoped to meet again with Pope Pius XII, but before he could get to it, the Allies occupied Rome (June 4). The SS commander had to set up a new headquarters on Lake Garda in Gardone, where by year's end he had established indirect clandestine contact with Dulles in Bern with the object of surrendering his forces in Italy.

WOLFF'S INITIATIVE IN SEEKING OUT DULLES CAN BE CREDITED TO THE urging of Cardinal Schuster of Milan. An Italian businessman, Baron Luigi Parilli, who was close to the Pope, also urged Wolff to do so. This approach was also related to the early February meeting in which Alexander von Neurath, German consul in Lugano, met with Field Marshal Albert Kesselring and General Wolff. Neurath, whom Dulles knew well, had been surprised that Hitler was not planning to begin to withdraw troops from Italy, despite the pressing need for them as reinforcements on the eastern front. The consul general could only speculate that the army was being saved for use in protecting the southern flank of an "inner fortress," or redoubt area, in the Bavarian and Austrian Alps.[32] It was reports like this that fueled Dulles's belief in the possibility of a German last stand in the Alps, a belief that might have been more plausible had it not been for the fact that total German collapse was clearly imminent. The Battle of the Bulge in the Ardennes in December 1944 had been the Wehrmacht's last gasp.

Two weeks later, on February 24, Dulles heard that Kesselring and German Ambassador Rahn were prepared to surrender—and possibly "fight against Hitler, if the Allies can make it worth their while."[33] Then on February 26, Neurath at the urging of Marshal Kesselring, met on the western front with Lieutenant General Siegfried Westphal, Rundstedt's chief of staff, and Marshal Johannes Blaskowitz, commander of Army Group G in the West, to discuss the possibility of opening the western front as well as the Italian front to the Allies. Such an action would have to be preceded by assurances that the officers involved would not be tried as war criminals. These meetings, which could easily arouse the suspicions of the Gestapo and SD working levels if discovered, were made in strictest secrecy. But somehow word began to leak out: A *London Daily Dispatch* article of February 24, datelined Bern, reported that Kesselring had offered secretly to make an uncontested withdrawal from Italy, leaving the cities intact.[34]

In early March Dulles and his right-hand man Gaevernitz separately arrived at an OSS safe house in Zurich to meet with Professor Max Husmann, who was acting as go-between with Wolff. The next step, in the interests of security (Dulles was still wary of Wolff's initiative and feared treachery), was for Gaevernitz and Dulles to visit discreetly a Zurich medical clinic where they met two men disguised as patients, both Italian patriots and members of the Italian underground. Ferruccio Parri, one of the chiefs of the Italian Resistance, destined soon to become premier of Free Italy, and Antonio Usmiani, a contact of Dulles's also captured by the Germans, had just been freed as promised. But only by meeting physically with them could Dulles be convinced that Wolff had been as good as his word in having them released as an earnest of his intentions. Satisfied, Dulles and Gaevernitz returned to their safe house for a meeting with Wolff.

Sitting around a cozy fire in the fireplace, a standard prop used by Dulles in making his contacts "less inhibited," the two men awaited General Wolff's and Professor Husmann's arrival. They arrived promptly at 10:00 P.M. Gaevernitz, who greeted the general at the door, tried to put him at ease; this was a tense situation for both men. As Dulles relates in his account of the event, Gaevernitz reminded the general that they had a "good friend in common, a beautiful German Countess," who had once intervened with Wolff to save Romano Guardini, Catholic philosopher, from the clutches of the Gestapo.[35] According to Gaevernitz, Wolff did, indeed, appear to relax at the mention of their mutual lady friend.

The long meeting went well. Wolff made it clear that what he was doing was on his own initiative, and he was making no demands for personal immunity. Himmler, as far as he knew, was not aware of his actions. The key to success, they all agreed, was Kesselring; he must be convinced to cooperate. Wolff had already discussed with the field marshal this matter, but the latter was uncertain; while not opposed to the plan, Kesselring was not yet willing to commit himself.[36]

Wolff was convinced that Germany should abandon the war "to end useless human and material destruction," and he would be willing to surrender his SS troops in Italy. To prove his sincerity, he also offered to perform several other acts, such as issuing with Kesselring a joint appeal to all Germans and German commanders to terminate hostilities and disassociate themselves with "Himmler-Hitler control." He was also willing to announce the end of hostilities in Italy, free certain Italian partisans captured by the Germans, end the warfare against the partisans, release several hundred Jews held in northern Italy, and guarantee good treatment of British and American POWs at Mantua. If he could convince Kesselring to act with him, Wolff believed "Hitler and Himmler [would be] powerless to take effective countermeasures." Total surrender on the western front would follow.

By this time Allied forces headquarters in Caserta, Italy, had become interested in these developments but wanted more details, particularly concerning Kesselring's willingness to negotiate with the Allies. There was, however, the problem of the Soviet Union. Both British and Americans believed that Stalin not only would have to be informed of these developments but must be invited to send a representative to the surrender ceremony.

Molotov was informed on March 11 and responded to U.S. Ambassador Harriman in Moscow the next day, saying that the Soviets did not object to providing three Soviet officers who would join the talks. But this introduced a complicating dimension: The State Department replied that it would not be appropriate for Soviet officers to attend what were at this stage essentially only exploratory conversations in a purely Anglo-U.S. theater of war.

It was this response that set off the ensuing explosion in Moscow. In what escalated to become the most serious split within the Grand Alliance, Molotov handed Harriman a testy letter in which American actions were described as "unexpected and incomprehensible." He demanded that all negotiations be stopped.

The Department of State responded minimally to the effect that conversations with Wolff had taken place on March 19, but nothing had come of them.[37] In essence this was true. At the meeting, held in a villa owned by Gaevernitz near Ascona on Lake Maggiore in the Italian area of Ticino, Dulles was joined by Major General Lyman Lemnitzer and the British major general Terence Airey, both of Allied Commander Field Marshal Alexander's staff at Caserta. Wolff briefed the group on developments on his side. Special interest focused on the prospects for obtaining Kesselring's cooperation for a surrender of all German troops in Italy. While he had just been transferred to the western front, his attitude would have an important bearing on the success of any plan. There were still many problems to iron out. Nothing definitive had come out of the meeting, but it was a hopeful beginning.

Since Kesselring by this time had been temporarily assigned to Rundstedt's command on the western front, Wolff would have to act alone unless he were able to bring on board Kesselring's replacement, Field Marshal Heinrich von Vietinghoff. Without Vietinghoff, Wolff would have under his direct command only ten thousand men plus some fifty-five thousand unreliable service and supply troops. The best course, Wolff thought, was to convince Kesselring himself to make every effort to join him in common action.[38]

None of this was very encouraging, but downright alarming was the firestorm blowing up in U.S.-Soviet relations. On March 23 Molotov shot off a note to the British and Americans strenuously objecting to their negotiations with the Germans "behind the back of the Soviet Government which is bearing the brunt of the War against Germany." Molotov threatened to stay away from the scheduled San Francisco Conference to launch the United Nations,[39] centerpiece in Allied post-war planning.

Admiral William Leahy observed at the time, "An open break between Russia and her Anglo-Saxon allies would be the only miracle that would prevent the speedy collapse of the German armies."[40]* German forces were retreating rapidly, and surrender was imminent; nothing must spoil this. But Stalin was still worried by the possibility that the Western Allies, perhaps with a newly constructed German government without Hitler, would find common cause against the Soviet Union. He would settle for no less than the destruction of the German Army and the occupation of Berlin and East Germany by Red Army forces.

---

*Soviet intelligence may have known that Mussolini had tried to make an approach to the Vatican through Cardinal Schuster of Milan in early March 1945, in the hope that he could use the Pope's good offices to make a deal with the Americans. Even though the Vatican rejected the overture, this episode, however embryonic, could have further inflamed Stalin's suspicions — Lamb, *War in Italy,* p. 296.

On March 24 Roosevelt sent an urgent message to Stalin. Regretting any misunderstanding, he sternly asserted that the United States would not agree to suspending talks that might lead to the possibilities of German surrender. Such talk, he made it clear, had no "political implications whatever, and no violation of our agreed principle of unconditional surrender." He regretted that the "surrender conversations" had developed "an atmosphere of fear and distrust."

On April 3 Stalin replied in what must be considered disrespectful and unacceptably rude language by any standard of diplomatic intercourse. He agreed with Roosevelt that "negotiations" by the Anglo-American command in Bern or some other place "has developed an atmosphere of fear and distrust deserving regrets" but added sarcastically; "It may be assumed that you have not yet been fully informed." Stalin continued: "As regards my military colleagues, they, on the basis of data which they have on hand, do not have doubts that negotiations have taken place and that they have ended in an agreement with the Germans on the basis of which the German commander on the Western Front . . . has agreed to open the front and permit the Anglo-American troops to advance to the east, and the Anglo-Americans have promised to ease for the Germans the peace terms."[41] Stalin then inserted a broadside against Churchill by referring to the "silence of the British, who have allowed you [Roosevelt] to correspond with me in this unpleasant manner."

Stalin's next accusation was as stunning as it was inaccurate for what it portended: "As a result of this, at the present moment the Germans on the Western Front in fact have ceased the war against England and the United States. At the same time the Germans continue the war with Russia."[42] Dulles understandably drew the conclusions from Stalin's letter that the Soviet dictator had somehow been briefed on the secret discussions with Wolff in a distorted fashion and was extremely worried that U.S. troops might reach Trieste and Venezia Giulia before the Red Army did.[43]

Roosevelt returned the fire in a message to Stalin expressing "astonishment" and suggesting that Soviet sources must have been Germans who were trying to create dissension between them. Roosevelt stated: "Frankly, I cannot avoid a feeling of bitter resentment toward your informers, whoever they are, for such vile misrepresentation of actions . . . of my trusted subordinates."[44]

Stalin's informants referred to by Roosevelt, we now know, included turncoat Kim Philby who, long after the war, wrote in his self-serving memoir, *My Silent War:* "It would have been dangerous for the Russians to think we [the Western Allies] were dickering with Germans. The air was opaque with mutual suspicions of separate peace feelers."[45] Considering Philby's placement in the heart of British intelligence and his Soviet instructions to concentrate on Allied-German machinations above all others, it is probably safe to assume that Stalin had been kept well informed on Dulles's contacts, including his contact with Wolff.[46] And considering the Soviet leader's suspicious nature, it was too much to hope that he would understand that the British-American motive was mainly to shorten the war and save lives—or perhaps also avoid a German last-ditch effort from an Alpine redoubt.

Churchill sent a stiff telegram refuting Stalin's accusations. It was Roosevelt's message to Churchill of April 6, however, that suggests the depths of disillusionment experienced by the president as a result of this nasty exchange, which had twisted events out of context. Roosevelt, who thought he could handle "Uncle Joe" and had high hopes for a continuation of the Grand Alliance, now expressed himself as being "in general agreement" with Churchill's suggestion that the Western Allies try to meet the Red Army as far to the east as they could and, if possible, be the first to take Berlin. Roosevelt reminded Churchill: "Our armies will in a very few days be in a position that will permit us to become tougher than has heretofore appeared advantageous to the war effort."[47]

What may have hurt Roosevelt the most in this episode was a telegram from Stalin accusing the United States of having furnished deceptive intelligence to the Red Army in February, placing some of its units in jeopardy.[48] The Grand Alliance did not now look so grand. As victory was almost at hand, serious cracks in the alliance could yet give Hitler hope that Allied disunity might provide Germany with an opportunity to play the East off against the West. As it turned out, nothing interfered with the inevitable Allied victory. But as events revealed, nothing would prevent Soviet domination of East Germany and the rest of Eastern Europe.

Roosevelt had cause for disillusionment with Stalin as a result of the Big Three Yalta Conference, which had been held from February 4 to 11, 1945, during which the Soviet dictator insisted on being Poland's master at war's end. But another tip-off of Soviet intentions toward Poland occurred in March, when sixteen Polish leaders, who had gone to Moscow under written guarantee of their safety to discuss the formation of a postwar all-party government, disappeared, never to be heard from again. On April 5 Sir Alexander Cadogan, undersecretary of the British Foreign Office, had the sad task of informing Count Raczynski, Polish government-in-exile representative in London, that no news had been received concerning the fate of the sixteen delegates. Cadogan confessed that the Foreign Office "did not understand what the Russians were driving at."[49]

With access to newly released Averell Harriman papers, William Larsh writes in a University of California scholarly journal, *Eastern European*

Politics and Society,[50] that Harriman, America's wartime ambassador in Moscow, had secretly negotiated an agreement with Stalin that in effect permitted Stalin to install a Soviet-picked Communist puppet government in Warsaw when the war ended rather than turn over power to the Polish government-in-exile in London, recognized by the Western Allies. Rhetoric that the Moscow-blessed Poles would enjoy "self-rule" predictably proved meaningless. Symptomatic of this secret understanding was the widely publicized episode in which advancing Red Army troops halted outside Warsaw until the retreating German forces were able to destroy Poland's national uprising in which underground Poles had manned the barricades in anticipation of imminent liberation by the Soviets. There remained no coherent group to contest the Soviet-chosen puppet regime. According to Russian expert George Kennan, Harriman was "shattered" by this. Such blatant rejection of Polish will and denial of Polish independence, the professed cause for which Britain and France had gone to war in the first place, was devastating for Harriman; he belatedly realized his mistake in trusting Stalin to grant self-rule for Poland.

The question lingers to this day: Did Roosevelt himself only see the light in his last days of life as a result of the several angry communications from Stalin protesting the Allied surrender discussions with Wolff? Or was Roosevelt under no illusions about Stalin, and did he simply ignore the likely adverse long-term political significance of Stalin's many actions in preparation of imposing Soviet hegemony over Eastern Europe and Germany — perhaps because of the short-term imperative of winning the war with Germany so America could concentrate its strength against Japan? Harriman's personal papers, as reported by Larsh, contain a significant statement that perhaps bears on this question: "On one occasion in May [1944] the president had told me [Harriman] that he didn't care whether the countries bordering Russia became communized." Harriman's note protested: "At that time, I did not have a chance to indicate my views."[51]*

TO RETURN TO DULLES'S SURRENDER TALKS, WOLFF WAS ENCOUNTERING complications in his efforts to arrange a German surrender. Ernst Kaltenbrunner, using his authority as chief of the Nazi security police and security intelligence service (SD), frantically tried to wave off Wolff in mid-March, complaining that the latter's contact with the Allies would

---

*According to a column in *The Washington Post* of November 26, 1993, by Stephen S. Rosenfeld, Harriman later authorized Herbert Feis to write up his Moscow assignment, but because Feis's account was such a "sharply critical evaluation" of Harriman on Poland, Larsh claims that it was suppressed.

upset his plans. These referred to his and Himmler's late February efforts
to make contacts with Dulles in Switzerland through SS officer Hoettl[52]
and their pending attempt to arrange an early meeting with Carl Burckhardt, retiring president of the International Red Cross, who had maintained long-standing contacts with Foreign Ministry members of the
Resistance. Himmler was also trying to get word to the Vatican that Germany wanted peace and was willing to open the country to Western, but
not Soviet, forces.[53] Clearly Himmler had reason to be disturbed by Wolff's
initiatives.

Dulles did not hear from Wolff until the end of March, by which time
Kesselring had encouraged Wolff to proceed with his plan for Italy but regretted that he could do nothing about arranging a surrender on the western front. Wolff explained that his delay in returning to Italy was caused
by Himmler and told of the *Reichsführer's* suspicions and how he wiggled
out of accusations he had made about him. Despite Kaltenbrunner's
warning to Wolff that he must remain in Germany and certainly not
revisit Switzerland, the SS general had flown back to his command
in Italy.[54]

An April 10 OSS memorandum for the President from Donovan reported that Wolff seemed to have things under control. General von Vietinghoff, now commander of German forces in Italy, was willing to join
Wolff in surrendering "unconditionally" so long as the surrender would be
"dressed up" to appear consistent with "military honor" and he would not
be cast as a "traitor."

By mid-April Wolff found that his relationship with Himmler, the man
with whom he had once been close, was becoming tense. In a communication to Dulles expressing sorrow for the April 12 death of President Roosevelt, Wolff described how Himmler had summoned him to Berlin. He
would go, he said, fearing that if he did not, he would be summarily replaced and declared a deserter. This state of affairs disturbed Dulles, who
reported to Washington, "Himmler apparently plans either to eliminate
Wolff or to use him to establish his own contact with the Allies."

Dulles had other reasons for being disturbed when he received on
April 20 a message from the U.S. Joint Chiefs of Staff directing him to
terminate all contact with German emissaries. This decision was the
result of a Combined Chiefs of Staff message to the supreme Allied commander, Mediterranean theater, pointing out that the German commander in chief in Italy did not intend to surrender on acceptable terms,
and probably more important in the disheartening decision, there had
been complications. Truman's accession to the presidency had an important effect on it; he must surely have been disheartened by the

prospect of inheriting Roosevelt's quarrel with Stalin over the surrender talks initiated by Dulles.

Since Roosevelt's death Truman had quickly focused his attention on vital foreign policy issues. Flanked by Secretary of State Edward Stettinius, former Ambassador to Japan Joseph Grew, and Russian authority Charles "Chip" Bohlen, Harriman briefed the new president on the precarious state of U.S.-Soviet relations. Bohlen predicted that despite differences with Stalin, the Soviet dictator would not break with the United States. Stalin knew he needed financial assistance after the war, and the United States was the most likely place to find it.[55]

Roosevelt, for so long an apologist for "Uncle Joe," may have begun to face reality on this matter just before his death. He told Anne O'Hare McCormick of *The New York Times* that he had concluded that Stalin was not one whose word could be trusted.[56]

IN BERLIN WOLFF FACED AN IRATE HIMMLER, WHO HE FEARED WOULD accuse him of treason. In anticipation of this, Wolff armed himself with a letter from Rahn, the cooperative German ambassador to the rump Italian government in northern Italy, who justified Wolff's activities with an ambiguous statement to the effect that the general had contacts with the Allies pursuant to Hitler's wish to hold up, if possible, their offensive in Italy.[57]

Kaltenbrunner was not so easily put off; he waved sheaves of paper allegedly incriminating Wolff as he accused him of conspiracy. Wolff went on the offensive and insisted on seeing Hitler. This terrified Himmler, who was holding secret peace talks with the Swedish intermediary Folke Bernadotte in an effort to halt the war and assume leadership of a defeated Germany. Kaltenbrunner was no less tainted with guilt and grudgingly agreed to accompany Wolff to Hitler's bunker. Wolff made sure that Kaltenbrunner would not say anything compromising him in front of Hitler by threatening to reveal his secret Allied contacts which Kaltenbrunner and Himmler had maintained.

Kaltenbrunner, however, had already briefed Hitler on Wolff's activities in such a way as to suggest inappropriate action—if not worse. Hitler therefore greeted Wolff with the charge that he had exhibited a "colossal disregard for authority" in his approaches to the Allies. Wolff shrewdly protested that because he had not invoked Hitler's authority in his talks with Allen Dulles, the Führer could deny all knowledge if things went wrong and make him the scapegoat.[58] Wolff also argued that by the very act of coming to see the Führer, he could not possibly be guilty of treachery. To make his activity seem more in line with Hitler's limited authorization to talk with the West, Wolff claimed that his aim was to persuade the Americans to join forces with the Germans against the Soviets. Apparently mollified, Hitler said farewell to Wolff with a simple admonishment to "go back to Italy, maintain your contacts with the Americans, but see that you get better terms."[59]

What perhaps saved Wolff was Hitler's state of exhaustion. He was a beaten man. He simply was not all there as he stumbled around in the confusion of the bunker. That he had no intention of fleeing to some Bavarian or Austrian mountain redoubt gave the lie to that much-inflated canard. Hitler vowed to hold out in Berlin against both the East and West for six to eight weeks, hoping that Wolff too would stand firm in Italy. Hitler's only remaining hope was that a serious split between the Western Allies and the Soviets would develop, at which time he would join the side that gave him the best terms.[60] This was far different from the Wagnerian climax of his earlier fantasies. The show was over, and Hitler, reeling from his adversity, probably realized it in his more lucid moments.

Wolff had faced down Himmler, proved himself immune to Kaltenbrunner's tattling, and convinced Hitler he was still on his side. But he would surrender his troops in Italy, and nothing, he thought, could stop him from it.

Having survived his Berlin ordeal, Wolff returned to Italy on April 19 undiminished in his determination and confident that he had agreement from the army commander in Italy, Vietinghoff, to act with him. But when he made contact with Dulles in Switzerland, he was dumbfounded to face a wholly unexpected obstacle. Dulles had the unenviable task of telling the general's emissary—curiously in the presence of Swiss intelligence officers—that the matter was no longer of interest to the Allies. This presented a surreal situation in which Wolff, determined to surrender unconditionally, was rebuffed by the Allies, who said they would not accept it. There are not many precedents in history in which an army has refused to accept the surrender of a beaten adversary.

Within a week (April 26), however, reason returned; Dulles was instructed to reestablish contact with Wolff and make arrangements for him and Lieutenant Colonel Viktor von Schweinitz, authorized to act for army commander Vietinghoff, to proceed to Allied forces headquarters in Caserta, Italy, for the surrender-signing ceremony.[61] Before this could occur, however, Dulles faced still another obstacle. He bombarded Washington and Caserta with messages to support British Field Marshal Alexander's efforts to obtain Whitehall's approval. At stake were not only soldiers' lives but, as the Allies pushed northward in Italy, the real danger that the German Army would destroy Italian industry and infrastructure in the wake of its retreat.

Faced with Allied delays, Wolff was under considerable pressure. Himmler sent a message to him stating that the Italian lines should hold firm and "no negotiations . . . should be undertaken."[62] Clearly Himmler did not want Wolff's efforts to spoil his own self-serving negotiations through Bernadotte. But Wolff would not allow himself to be deterred by Himmler's order, however threatening it sounded.

Dulles sent Gaevernitz off to find Wolff and take whatever steps he could to protect the general from another threat, that now posed by the Italian partisans who looked for a chance to humiliate the Germans in Italy. Dulles's assistant caught up with the general in Lugano, Switzerland, and persuaded him to return to Bolzano in Italy, where partisan strength was minimal. As a precaution against the partisans, Wolff directed his SS troops to avoid engagements with them. Gaevernitz, exceeding his orders, took steps to shepherd Wolff through Italian lines.

The SS general received an unexpected windfall when Marshal Rodolfo Graziani, Italian minister of war, deeded to him full power in his behalf to negotiate with the Allies a surrender of Italian forces. When Mussolini learned of the German plans to surrender, he exploded in wrath, accusing them of "always treating us like servants" and "at the end betraying me."[63] Knowing he was powerless, he fled, only to be picked up on April 28 by Italian partisans, who dragged him from his automobile and shot him and his mistress, Clara Petacci, before stringing them both up by their heels for all to see.

On April 29, 1945, Colonel von Schweinitz for the German Army and Major Wenner, deputized by Wolff to act on behalf of the SS, signed the surrender documents at Allied headquarters in the Royal Summer Palace in Caserta. A million German and Italian troops put down their arms. Dulles and Gaevernitz broke out a bottle of champagne to celebrate when they received the news. The last few days preceding the ceremony had been tense for Dulles. Many things could have gone wrong in orchestrating the surrender, and one thing did when on April 28 Kesselring, newly appointed commander in chief in the south—including Italy—backed down from his earlier commitment, refusing to give the order for surrender. On April 30 Kesselring relieved Vietinghoff and Röttiger of their SS and Army commands respectively and ordered Röttiger to report to army groups headquarters, where court-martial charges faced him for signing the surrender order. Kesselring notified Wolff that because he was an SS officer, his "treasonous" acts were being referred to Kaltenbrunner for punitive action.

At the eleventh hour, after much backing and filling, indecision and histrionics on the part of those involved, most of the SS officers ordered their troops to surrender despite orders to the contrary, but the army waited for Kesselring to make up his mind. On May 2 the field marshal finally returned Wolff's frantic phone calls; after two hours of pleading by Wolff, Kesselring gave in. Wolff's arguments that Hitler's death relieved Kesselring of his officer's oath to the Führer and that a cease-fire in Italy would give the Western Allies a better chance to stop the Soviets in their drive into Germany had been convincing.

Goebbels, propagandist to the end, delivered a flaming speech on April 19, Hitler's birthday, threatening a terrible "flood of bolshevism," in a desperate attempt to cause the Western powers to turn on their Soviet Allies. Goebbels's biographer Ralf Georg Reuth thinks that unlike Himmler, who looked westward, Goebbels believed that Stalin was "more realistic than the English-American runners amok" and "it was more likely that something could be accomplished in the East."[64]

While Goebbels's ranting made no impression on the Western Allies, it probably served once more to rattle Stalin, who could not be dissuaded from his conviction that the West would make a separate peace with the Nazis and join forces with the German Army against the USSR. Soviet intelligence had been well aware of General Wolff's negotiations with Dulles all along and knew that Himmler and Schellenberg in the end were trying desperately to make a deal with the West through Bernadotte's good offices. Ribbentrop too had sent out probes to the West through Stockholm.[65]

In newly occupied Vienna Soviet loudspeakers shrieked warnings of the coming "greatest betrayal in world history," in which the capitalist powers would join the Nazis in a struggle against democracy. The Austrian people were exhorted by the Russians to "come over to us."[66]

Dulles's and Gaevernitz's labors were finally rewarded. The war in Italy was over. Even though this had not occurred until the final days of the war, a last-gasp defense by retreating German troops in Italy could have been costly in terms of lives and destruction. The collapse of German forces in Italy also ended any possibility that they could find sanctuary in the fastness of the Alps and from there conduct a guerrilla campaign that could have complicated the occupation of Germany—not that this was ever very likely.[67]*

---

*British Major General Terence S. Airey, commander of British and American forces, Trieste, stated in a sworn affidavit in support of Wolff, signed in Trieste on October 4, 1948:

Dulles's daring initiatives, which may at times have skirted U.S. policy limits, provoked expressions of Stalin's fundamental animosity toward the Western democracies and revealed his intentions to pursue postwar policies hostile to the United States as well as democratic Europe. Dulles's operations were surely provocative and triggered the strong Soviet reaction, but they illuminated rather than caused the inevitable discord within the Grand Alliance. Sunrise had provided an early glimpse backstage before the curtain went up on a Cold War drama that dominated international affairs for a long time to come.

The Surrender of the German armies in Italy was due to the initiative of Karl Wolff who contacted Allied Forces while the war was still in progress and consequently against the wishes and declared policy of the Nazi government and at great risk to himself. His actions led to the abandonment of a fighting withdrawal . . . into Austria and must necessarily have saved the lives of a large number of German soldiers, Austrian and Italian civilians, and avoided useless destruction. . . .
Sworn at Trieste on the 4th day of October 1948 before me, J. Stewart Reakes, Major R.S.F., Deputy Chief Legal Officer, HQ. Allied Military Government.

Signed

From a private collection

THIRTY-FOUR

Sundown

ALLEN DULLES HAD BROUGHT OFF A COMPLICATED AND VERY USEFUL OPERation in Sunrise, even though the entire German war machine would soon give up under the weight of American, British, and Soviet force of arms. He could take pride in his part of this accomplishment.

In contrast, Canaris would have cause for sorrow, not jubilation, in the way things had turned out for him and for Germany. He had fought his own war, a war against Hitler, in an effort to bring his nation back to sanity so it could rejoin the European family of nations without having to be battered into submission. He had lost his war and was about to lose his life. Soon there would be for him no more sunrises, no more tomorrows. As World War II drew to a close, he would doubtless try to savor memories of a family and country he had loved before a last sundown saw the cruel end to his most uncommon life.

Canaris was obviously a very special prisoner in Flossenburg prison. Kaltenbrunner had seen to it that the once-respected and sometimes feared Abwehr chief, the man who had kept the book on Nazi atrocities, was closely supervised. Since his arrest Canaris had not been allowed to contact, much less confront Himmler. The *Reichsführer* obviously did not want to be confronted; he had his own survival to worry about and was frantically busy with unrealistic schemes for making a deal with the Western Allies.

Since February 1945 Himmler had been secretly in contact with Swedish intermediary Count Bernadotte in a futile efforts to save himself from Allied prosecution. Whatever mix of fear, favor, and rivalry had defined his relationship with Canaris in the past, he was now too busy to think about the admiral's predicament. But he must have been concerned by what Canaris might say to incriminate him if he were put on public trial. Himmler was all consumed by the crisis he himself faced in Berlin as the Nazi edifice came tumbling down.

The death rattles of Nazi Germany had changed the pattern of power within the party. Hitler was doomed; the challenge for high bureaucrats was no longer how to stay in his favor. The new arbiters of favor or disfavor, the conquerors, would soon occupy Germany and in all likelihood mete out retributive punishment. The game was how to ingratiate oneself in advance of defeat with the imminent victors—or, more specifically, with the victor—Western or Eastern, more likely to be lenient. Himmler preferred the "Western solution," still apparently underestimating the extent of British-American rage and revulsion felt toward him. Himmler could not hope to survive.

Any semblance of German legal procedures that may have survived Nazi rule had long since disappeared in the orgy of executions following the failure of the July 20 plot on Hitler's life. Certainly Canaris, who had secretly documented the atrocities committed by Nazi leaders, particularly Himmler, could not be allowed to testify at any postwar crimes trial. The fate of Canaris thus determined, there remained in question only the circumstances under which he would die.

Canaris would not be among those liberated by the Allies. Nor would Oster and the two other Abwehr officers, Josef Müller and Liedig, be rescued. One by one they found themselves in Flossenburg prison near Pilsen for further interrogation and, as it turned out, "disposal." Canaris suspected that his betrayer had been Colonel Georg Hansen, his successor as Abwehr chief but now subordinate to Kaltenbrunner. Hansen was, however, a secret member of the Resistance and knew many of its secrets. If Canaris's fears were true, he had probably been broken under severe pressure by his interrogators. He had been under no illusions about Hansen's ability to resist Gestapo interrogation if unmasked as a member of the Resistance. When arrested by Schellenberg, Canaris had inquired, "Have they found anything in writing from that fool, Hansen?"[1]

Hans Oster too was said to have incriminated Canaris under torture. Secret Resistance documents, seized by Huppenkothen's men, had laid bare Oster's leading role in the Black Orchestra, including his warnings to the Allies of Case Yellow, the plan for invasion of the Lowlands and France.

At Flossenburg Canaris's guards were under orders from Kaltenbrunner to keep him in a lighted cell and prevent him from talking with other prisoners. But the Abwehr chief found occasions to exchange furtive whispers and somehow cajoled guards to keep him abreast of the state of the war. Given the code name Caesar, Canaris was placed in cell 22, hands cuffed and ankles shackled to the wall. Camp Commandant Starvitski was under strict orders to keep the prisoner in good enough shape to endure "vigorous" interrogation. It soon became apparent to Canaris that someone familiar with details of his actions for the Resistance had talked too much since documents he believed to have been destroyed were quoted. An old report from the German Embassy in Madrid had accused him of advising Franco not to enter the war, as Hitler demanded in 1940, and of leaking to the Caudillo classified German military information.[2] This probably referred to Canaris's tip-off to Franco that Hitler planned to invade the Soviet Union.

What is interesting is why such damning evidence against Canaris remained unused in his RSHA dossier for so long. This was one more indication of Himmler's reluctance to bring Canaris to trial for his conspiratorial activities, however persuasive the evidence against him had been. The most damning evidence implicating Canaris was contained in his voluminous diaries, found by General Walter Buhle when he was rummaging through the former Abwehr premises at the OKW headquarters. Canaris had given orders for his diaries to be destroyed, but at least part of them had apparently been left untouched in a deserted safe, where Buhle found them.[3] When Hitler was made aware of this discovery, he was predictably enraged at the treachery of his former Abwehr chief and demanded his blood.

Significantly Canaris's diaries were not used as evidence in the drumhead hearing given him at Flossenburg. They revealed too much. Kaltenbrunner had in fact ordered Huppenkothen to destroy them.[4] Nor were charges of betraying military secrets made. Canaris was accused of having been aware of Resistance plans for a putsch since 1938 and of having protected the subversive activities of Oster and other Resistance activist within the Abwehr. He was also charged with knowing about Josef Müller's secret role in enlisting Vatican assistance in establishing Resistance contact with the British government.[5]

Hans Oster, who preceded Canaris to the gallows by a few minutes, was briefly brought face-to-face with his old boss. Obviously under tremendous strain, Oster was again forced to denounce his friend and patron as having played an active role in the Resistance. Canaris, more hurt than angry by his betrayal, did not deny Oster's charges and stoically listened to his sentence of death by hanging.[6]

Probably the best witness to what then occurred at Flossenburg during Admiral Canaris's imprisonment was fellow prisoner Lieutenant Colonel

H. M. Lunding, formerly of the Danish General Staff and chief of Danish military intelligence. Having established espionage links into Germany as early as 1937, he had come under SD suspicion in August 1943. Canaris had tried to protect Lunding by having placed him under the protection of the Abwehr station in Copenhagen, but eventually the hapless Dane was imprisoned by the Gestapo despite Canaris's best efforts to prevent it.

When not darning sweaters to keep himself occupied at Flossenburg, Lunding kept watch on developments as seen through a crack in the door of his cell, number 21. By Lunding's tally, between seven hundred and nine hundred executions took place no more than twenty yards from his cell. Those who were not shot in the napes of their necks while kneeling were hanged.[7]

Lunding was particularly interested in Canaris, now in cell 22, next to his. The Dane knew that Canaris had tried to protect Danish intelligence offices from abuse by SS forces in Denmark and generally lessened the severity of SS occupation wherever he could. It is significant that Canaris's interference with Himmler's repressive policies in Denmark had become known to Lunding and presumably other Danish intelligence figures during the war; surely Himmler must have been aware of it as well but chose not to make an issue of it.

Lunding remembered that Canaris dressed smartly in his own business suit, not in prison garb, and often could be seen wearing a tweed overcoat to keep out the cold. But like all prisoners, he was shackled with chains around his hands and feet that clanked along the concrete floor as he walked. Lunding managed to maintain communications with Canaris, thanks to the indulgence of a warden who enjoyed small bribes and promises in exchange for such services. He also set up a wall-tapping code with Canaris by which they were able to maintain a limited dialogue. Throughout Canaris maintained his innocence in his wall talks with Lunding.

Canaris had been subjected to frequent interrogations over a period of several weeks. In late March RSHA chief Kaltenbrunner himself questioned his old adversary, but there is no evidence that Canaris revealed any more to him than he had to the others—and that was essentially nothing.[8] In early April Canaris conveyed to Lunding that he was being subjected to physical torture.[9]

Prince Philip of Hesse of Hessen-Nassau, once a confidant of Hitler's, found himself imprisoned at Flossenburg for his suspected ambivalence toward the Nazis and testified after the war that a top official of the camp was "something of a sadist who hanged his victims slowly." To satisfy a morbid curiosity about death, he would let them down and revive them when they were almost strangled so that he could ask them what it felt like to die. Only then would he finally kill them![10]

On April 9, early in the morning after returning from interrogation, Canaris tapped out a message for Lunding's benefit, saying, "I think that was the last one." He also indicated that during the interrogation his nose had been broken. Huppenkothen, head of Amt IV-B RSHA, flown in from Berlin to preside over a summary court proceeding, had given the authority to schedule Canaris's execution. The admiral seemed to know that death was near and conveyed to Lunding a "last statement": "I die for my country and with a clear conscience. You, as an officer, will realize that I was only doing my duty to my country when I endeavored to oppose Hitler and to hinder the senseless crimes by which he had dragged down Germany to ruin. I know that all I did was in vain, for Germany will be completely defeated. I knew that she would be as far back as 1942."

After a final message for Lunding to pass to his wife if he was able to do so, Canaris spent what must have been a difficult night. At 6:00 A.M. he was roused and escorted from his cell. Lunding could hear the clank of metal as his shackles were taken off and the peremptory order "Strip" followed by the command "March." Lunding could faintly see the naked Canaris through the crack in his cell door. Five minutes later the command "Next" told him that Canaris was dead, hanged slowly by wire, not rope, from a meat hook. It has been said that he took nearly a half hour to die.

Questioned by Allied interrogators in May 1945, Kaltenbrunner denied any direct responsibility for Canaris's execution but considered the admiral's death justified on the basis of "irrefutable" evidence of his "treasonous" activities as described in his diary and the certainty that he knew about the July 20 plot on Hitler's life even if he had not been part of it.[11] Kaltenbrunner was executed by the Allies following the Nuremberg trial, in which he was charged with complicity in the murder of Canaris and other Resistance figures.

Lunding survived his imprisonment and was liberated by advancing units of the U.S. Army, units that would have freed Canaris as well had he lived but a few days more. Lunding testified after the war that ashes from the cremation of Canaris's body and the bodies of others who met the same end that fateful day were wafted on the wind across the prison courtyard.

Source Notes

Chapter 1. Genesis

1. David Kahn, *Hitler's Spies* (New York: Macmillan, 1978), p. 227.
2. Roger Manvell and Heinrich Fraenkel, *The Canaris Conspiracy* (New York: David McKay, 1969), pp. 252, 253. From Captain von Arnauld's report to the German Admiralty, as provided by the captain's niece.

    Nigel West, *A Thread of Deceit* (New York: Random House, 1985), pp. 26–29.
3. William Henhoeffer, *The Intelligence War in 1941* (Washington D.C.: CIA Center for the Study of Intelligence, 1992) p. 18.
4. William M. Henhoeffer, "Donovan's Allies in World War I," *Studies in Intelligence* (Winter 1986).
5. Peter Hopkirk, *On Secret Service East of Constantinople* (London: John Murray, 1994), pp. 387–399.
6. Peter Wright, *Spycatcher* (New York: Dell, 1988), pp. 410–416. Ellis's confession is described on p. 415.
7. William Stevenson, *A Man Called Intrepid* (New York: Harcourt Brace Jovanovich, 1976), pp. xxi, 49, 412 n.

    William Stevenson, *Intrepid's Last Case* (New York: Villard Books, 1983), pp. xi, 73, 238–256, 305.

    West, *A Thread of Deceit*, pp. 127–143.
8. Leonard Mosley, *Dulles* (New York: Dial Press, 1978), pp. 47, 48.
9. *The Trust*, Sr. ed. Pamela K. Simkins (Arlington, Va., Security and Intelligence Foundation, 1989). Originally written by the U.S. Central Intelligence Agency, which supervised the editing of this published reprint.

Chapter 2. Interwar

1. "Memorandum For: Mr. George K. Bowden from Mrs. Murray." OSS Report 11679–1030, October 30, 1942. Georgetown University Lauinger Memorial Library, Special Collections Department, Anthony Cave Brown Collection, Box 4.

2. James H. Belote, "The Lohmann Affair," *Studies in Intelligence* (Spring 1960), pp. A31–A38. Article based on a variety of German sources in the custody of the U.S. Navy Division of Naval History, the U.S. State Department, the U.S. National Archives, and the Library of Congress.

3. U.S. Naval Attaché Report from Berlin, dated June 8, 1928, transmitting a German press article from *Weltbühne*, May 22, 1928.

4. Ian Colvin, *Canaris, Chief of Intelligence* (Maidstone, England: George Mann, Publishers, 1973), p. 31.

5. Colvin, *Canaris*, p. 31.

6. Richard Deacon, *A History of British Secret Service* (London: Panther/Grenada, 1980), p. 310. The London *Times Literary Supplement* reviewer of this book found the author's comments about Zaharoff "outside of reality." George Constantinides, in his monumental *Intelligence and Espionage* (Boulder, Colo.: Westview Press, 1983), describes Deacon's book as "spotty in reliability."

   Also see Donald McCormick (aka Richard Deacon), *Pedlar of Death* (London: Macdonald, 1965), for the Zaharoff story.

   Anthony Cave Brown, *Bodyguard of Lies* (New York: Quill/William Morrow, 1991), pp. 144, 145, 153, 154, 212–215.

7. Deacon, *History of British Secret Service*. According to Deacon, March also advised the British to cultivate General von Kleist of the German High Command and the German industrialist Baron von Thyssen.

8. Deacon, *History of British Secret Service*, pp. 168, 169.

9. André Brissaud, *Canaris* (New York: Grosset & Dunlap, 1974), p. 19.

10. Colvin, *Canaris*, p. 44.

11. Colvin, p. 31.

12. Colvin, p. 32.

13. Colvin, p. 33.

14. Colvin, pp. 33–35. Based on interviews with Richard Protze, an Abwehr II-F officer.

15. As a gesture of reciprocation for Hitler's having sent the Condor Legion to Spain to fight in the civil war, Franco sent the Spanish Blue Legion to fight on Germany's eastern front against the Soviet Union.

16. John Costello and Oleg Tsarev, *Deadly Illusions* (New York: Crown Publishers, 1993), pp. 170, 171.

17. Brian R. Sullivan, "A Highly Commendable Action: William J. Donovan's Intelligence Mission for Mussolini and Roosevelt, December 1935–February 1936," *Intelligence and National Security*, vol. 6, no. 2 (April 1991), pp. 395–417.

Chapter 3. Enigma

1. Paul Paillole, *Notre Espion chez Hitler* (Paris: Éditions Robert Laffont, 1985), p. 27.
2. Paillole, p. 39
3. Paillole, pp. 39–41.
4. F. H. Hinsley, E. E. Thomas, C. F. Ransom, and R. S. Knight, "The Polish, French and British Contributions to the Breaking of Enigma," in *Its Influence on Strategy and Operations,* 2d ed., vol. 1 of *British Intelligence in the Second World War* (London: Her Majesty's Stationery Office, 1986).
5. Paillole, *Notre Espion,* pp. 103, 104.
6. Paillole, p. 107.
7. David Irving, ed. *Breach of Security* (London: William Kimber, 1968), p. 16.
8. Paillole, *Notre Espion,* p. 148.
9. Gustave Bertrand, *Enigma ou La Plus Grande Enigme de la Guerre, 1939–1945* (Paris: Libraire Plon, 1973), pp. 59–60.
   Patrick Beesly, *Very Special Intelligence* (New York: Ballatine Books, 1981), pp. 78, 80.
   Marian Rejewski, "How Polish Mathematicians Deciphered the Enigma," tr. Jean Stepenske, *Annals of the History of Computing,* vol. 3, no. 3 (July 1981).
   Richard A. Woytak, *On the Border of War and Peace* (New York: Columbia University Press, 1979), pp. 88, 89.
10. Frederick W. Winterbotham, *The Ultra Secret* (London: Weidenfeld & Nicolson, 1974), p. 25.
    J. C. Masterman, *The Double-Cross System in the War of 1939 to 1945* (New Haven: Yale University Press, 1972).
11. William Henhoeffer, *The Intelligence War in 1941* (Washington D.C.: CIA Center for the Study of Intelligence, 1992), p. 8.
12. Christopher Andrew, *Her Majesty's Secret Service* (New York: Viking Penguin, 1986), pp. 448–486.

Chapter 4. German-Soviet Relations: Friendly Enemies

1. Gero v. S. Gaevernitz, *They Almost Killed Hitler* (New York: Macmillan, 1947), p. 10.
   Paul Blackstock, *The Secret Road to World War II* (Chicago: Quadrangle Books, 1969), pp. 253–255.
2. John Erickson, *The Soviet High Command* (London: 1962), p. 157. Cited in Blackstock, *The Secret Road.*
3. F. L. Carsten, *Reichswehr and Politics, 1918–1933* (Oxford: Oxford University Press, 1966), p. 359.
   Blackstock, *The Secret Road,* pp. 255–265.
4. Ernest L. Woodward and Rohan Butler, eds., *Documents on British Foreign Policy, 1919–1939,* 2d Series II (London: Her Majesty's Stationery Office, 1947), pp. 520–521.

5. G. M. Gathorne-Hardy, *A Short History of International Affairs* (London: 1950), p. 357. Cited in Blackstock, *The Secret Road.*
6. John Lukacs, *The Duel* (New York: Ticknor & Fields), p. 39.
7. Blackstock, *The Secret Road*, p. 262.
8. Erickson, *Soviet High Command*, pp. 346–348.
9. Walter G. Krivitsky, *In Stalin's Secret Service*, 2d ed. (New York: Harper & Brothers, 1939).
10. Stephen Koch, "The Dimitrov Conspiracy," *The New York Times*, January 22, 1994, p. 21.
11. Jane Degras, ed., *Soviet Documents*, vol. 3 (London: 1953), p. 70. Cited in Blackstock, *The Secret Road.*
12. Erickson, *Soviet High Command*, p. 416.
13. Walter Schellenberg, *Hitler's Secret Service*, tr. Louis Hagen, 2d ed. (New York: Pyramid, 1962), pp. 30–32. Schellenberg was involved in the operation under Heydrich.
14. George F. Kennan, *Russia and the West Under Lenin and Stalin* (Boston: Little, Brown, 1961), p. 308.
15. Blackstock, *The Secret Road*, pp. 338, 339.
16. Ibid.
17. U.S. Embassy, Paris, Dispatch no. 1267, November 23, 1937. File 861.00/11705, National Archives.
18. Ibid.

Chapter 5. Exit General von Fritsch

1. Peter Hoffmann, *German Resistance to Hitler* (Cambridge: Harvard University Press, 1988), p. 34
2. Walter Schellenberg, *Hitler's Secret Service*, tr. Louis Hagen, 2d ed. (New York: Pyramid, 1962), pp. 22, 23.
3. "The German Intelligence Branch and the 20 July Plot," Georgetown University Lauinger Memorial Library, Special Collections Department; Anthony Cave Brown Papers, Box 4. This document transcribes the interrogation of Franz Maria Liedig, arrested by the Gestapo after the 20 July 1944 bomb plot against Hitler because of his close association with Admiral Canaris (hereinafter referred to as Liedig interrogation).
4. Annedore Leber, ed., *The Conscience in Revolt* (Munich: v. Hase and Koehler, 1994), p. 128.
5. Leber, *Conscience in Revolt*, p. 128.
6. Liedig interrogation.
7. Ibid.
8. Leber, *Conscience in Revolt*, pp. 110–112.
9. Liedig interrogation.
10. Callum MacDonald, *The Killing of SS Obergruppen-Führer Reinhard Heydrich* (New York: Collier/Macmillan, 1989), p. 36.

11. Ian Colvin, *Canans, Chief of Intelligence* (Maidstone, England: George Mann, Publishers, 1973), p. 13.
12. Schellenberg, *Hitler's Secret Service*, p. 23.

Chapter 6. Munich

1. Hans Bernd Gisevius, *To the Bitter End* (Boston: Houghton Mifflin, 1947), p. 228.
2. Harold C. Deutsch, *The Conspiracy Against Hitler in the Twilight War* (Minneapolis, University of Minnesota Press, 1968), p. 30.
3. Trial of the German War Criminals, *Proceedings of the International Military Tribunal*, vol. 12 (Washington: U.S. Government Printing Office, 1947–1949), p. 237.
4. Roger Manvell and Heinrich Fraenkel, *The Canaris Conspiracy* (New York: David McKay, 1969), pp. 33, 34.
5. Ian Colvin, *Canaris, Chief of Intelligence* (Maidstone, England: George Mann, Publishers, 1973), p. 55.
6. Ibid.
7. Colvin, p. 58.
8. Manvell and Fraenkel, *Canaris Conspiracy*, pp. 36, 37, 38.
9. Ibid.
10. Ibid.
11. Ibid.
12. Klemens von Klemperer, *German Resistance Against Hitler* (Oxford: Oxford Clarendon Press, 1992), p. 99. From minute by Sir Ivo Mallet, August 22, 1938, FO-371/21732/C 8520/1941/18, British Public Records Office.
13. Deutsch, *Conspiracy Against Hitler*, pp. 19–22.
14. Sir Alexander Cadogan, *The Diaries of Sir Alexander Cadogan, 1938–1945*, ed. David Dilks (New York: G. P. Putnam's, 1972), p. 95. Diary entry for Wednesday, September 7, 1938.
15. Manvell and Fraenkel, *Canaris Conspiracy*, pp. 41, 42, 43.
16. Brian R. Sullivan, "A Highly Commendable Action: William J. Donovan's Intelligence Mission for Mussolini and Roosevelt, December 1935–February 1936," *Intelligence and National Security*, vol. 6, no. 2 (April 1991), p. 356.

    David Kahn, "United States Views of Germany and Japan, 1941," *Knowing One's Enemies*, ed. Ernest R. May (Princeton, N.J.: Princeton University Press, 1984), p. 493.

    "Colonel Donovan Says Reich Is Prepared to Equip Another 1 Million in Few Months—9000 War Planes Ready," *The New York Times*, October 2, 1938.
17. Manvell and Fraenkel, *Canaris Conspiracy*, pp. 41–43.
18. Deutsch, *Conspiracy Against Hitler*, pp. 19–22.
19. Deutsch, pp. 305–309. From Carl J. Burckhardt, *Meine Danziger Mission, 1937–1939* (Munich: 1960).
20. Deutsch, pp. 23, 24.
21. Ibid.

22. Manvell and Fraenkel, *Canaris Conspiracy*, pp. 41–43.
23. William Manchester, *The Last Lion* (Boston: Little, Brown, 1988), p. 349, fn. 253, 254.
24. Terence Prittie, *Germans Against Hitler* (Boston: Little, Brown, 1964), p. 61.
25. Theodor Prochazka, *The Second Republic* (Boulder, Colo.: East European Monographs, distributed by Columbia University Press, 1981), p. 10.
26. Prochazka, p. 11.
27. Manchester, *The Last Lion*, p. 258.
28. Winston Churchill, *The Gathering Storm*, vol. 1 of *The Second World War* (London: Reprint Society, 1954), p. 265.
29. Colvin, *Canaris*, p. 70.
30. Hans Rothfels, "The German Resistance in Its International Aspects," Record of the General Meeting held at Chatham House, London, p. 488, March 14, 1958.
31. F. H. Hinsley, E. E. Thomas, C. F. G. Ransom, and R. C. Knight, *Its Influence on Strategy and Operations*, 2d ed., vol. 1 of *British Intelligence in the Second World War* (London: Her Majesty's Stationery Office, 1986), p. 56.
32. John Dryden, *Oedipus*, Act III, sc. i.

Chapter 7. Case White: Hitler Invades Poland

1. Christopher Andrew, *Her Majesty's Secret Service* (New York: Viking/Penguin, 1986), p. 417, fn. 22.
2. Sir Alexander Cadogan, *Diaries of Sir Alexander Cadogan*, ed. David Dilks (New York: G. P. Putnam's, 1972), p. 141.
3. Cadogan, p. 143.
4. Lewis Carroll, "The Walrus and the Carpenter," stanza 1.
5. Winston Churchill, *The Gathering Storm*, vol. 1 of *The Second World War* (London: Reprint Society, 1954), p. 271.
6. Andrew, *Her Majesty's Secret Service*, p. 413. From fn. 5: Admiral John H. Godfrey, unpublished memoirs, vol. V, Part I, p. 7; vol. VII, pp. 41, 42. Private information.
7. Andrew, *Her Majesty's Secret Service*, p. 413.
8. F. H. Hinsley, E. E. Thomas, C. F. G. Ransom, and R. C. Knight, *Its Influence on Strategy and Operations*, 2d ed., vol. 1 of *British Intelligence in the Second World War* (London: Her Majesty's Stationery Office, 1986), p. 58. A disclaimer printed in each volume of this series of histories states: "The authors of this, as of other official histories of the Second World War, have been given free access to official documents. They alone are responsible for the statements made and the views expressed."
9. Janusz Piekalkiewicz, *Secret Agents, Spies and Saboteurs* (New York: William Morrow, 1973, p. 142.
10. Andrew, *Her Majesty's Secret Service*, p. 415, fn. 13: Memorandum by Vansittart, January 16, 1939, "Summing Up of Information from Secret Sources," dated January 1939, FB (36) 74. British Public Record Office, CAB 27/267.

11. Mario Toscano, "Machiavelli: Views on World War II Intelligence," *International Journal of Intelligence and Counter-intelligence*, vol. 1, no. 3 (1986). From *Pagine di Storia Diplomatica Contemporanea* (Milano: Dott. A. Guiffre, 1963).
12. Hinsley et al., *Influence on Strategy and Operations*, p. 46.
13. Alex de Jonge, *Stalin and the Shaping of the Soviet Union* (New York: Quill/William Morrow, 1986), pp. 360, 361.
14. Allan Clark, *Barbarossa* (New York: Quill/William Morrow, 1985), p. 25.
15. John Weitz, *Hitler's Diplomat* (New York: Ticknor & Fields, 1992), p. 214. *The Washington Post*, January 22, 1993, p. A-24.
16. Klemens von Klemperer, *German Resistance Against Hitler* (Oxford: Oxford Clarendon Press, 1992), p. 131.
17. Roger Manvell and Heinrich Fraenkel, *The Canaris Conspiracy* (New York: David McKay, 1969), p. 55.
18. Hans Bernd Gisevius, *To the Bitter End* (Boston: Houghton Mifflin, 1947), p. 373.
19. Nikita Khrushchev, *Khrushchev Remembers*, ed. Jerrold Schecter and Vyacheslav V. Luchkov (Boston: Little, Brown, 1990), pp. 50–55.
20. Khrushchev, pp. 50–55.
21. Klemperer, *German Resistance*, p. 132.
22. Klemperer, p. 153., fn. 364: David Dilks, "Appeasement and Intelligence," *Retreat from Power* (London: 1981), pp. 162–164.
23. Klemperer, p. 133. From Letter from Sir George Ogilvie-Forbes to Mr. Kirkpatrick, Berlin, August 25, 1939, DBFP 3/vii pp. 257–260.
24. Manvell and Fraenkel, *Canaris Conspiracy*, p. 52.
25. William Manchester, *The Last Lion* (New York: Little, Brown, 1988), p. 405, fn. 89.
26. Churchill, *The Gathering Storm*, p. 284.
27. Richard M. Kechum, *The Borrowed Years, 1938–1941* (New York: Random House, 1989), p. 184.
28. William L. Shirer, *The Nightmare Years, 1930–1940*, vol. 2 of *20th Century Journey* (New York: Bantam Books, 1992), p. 362.
29. Klemperer, *German Resistance* p. 132. From DBFP 3/v, p. 433.
30. Manvell and Fraenkel, *Canaris Conspiracy*, p. 54.
31. Ibid.
32. Ibid.
33. Churchill, *The Gathering Storm*, p. 280.
34. Weitz, *Hitler's Diplomat*, p. 214.
35. "May 15 1945 interrogation of Bodenschantz," Document CS DIC GG Reports, SRGG 1219 (C). Georgetown University Lavinger Memorial Library, Special Collections Department, Anthony Cave Brown Papers, Box 3.
36. Donald Cameron Watt, "British Intelligence and the Coming of the Second World War in Europe," *Knowing One's Enemies*, ed. Ernest R. May (Princeton: Princeton University Press, 1984), p. 248.
37. David Irving, *Göring* (New York: Avon Books, 1990), p. 256.

Chapter 8. The Göring Connection

1. Birger Dahlerus, *The Last Attempt* (London: Hutchinson, 1945), pp. 18, 19.
2. David Irving, *Göring* (New York: Avon Books, 1989), p. 257.
3. Irving, p. 258.
4. Franz Halder, *The Halder War Diary 1939–1942*, ed. Charles Burdick and Hans-Adolf Jacobsen (Novato, Calif.: Presidio Press, 1988), pp. 19–23.
5. Ian Colvin, *The Chamberlain Cabinet* (New York: Taplinger, 1971), p. 234.
6. Irving, *Göring*, p. 259.
7. Colvin, *Chamberlain*, pp. 234, 235.
8. Dahlerus, *Last Attempt*, p. 53.
9. Dahlerus, pp. 58, 59.
10. Dahlerus, p. viii, 62.
11. Dahlerus, pp. 62, 63.
12. Dahlerus, p. 64.
13. Dahlerus, pp. 67, 68.
14. Dahlerus, p. 74.
15. Dahlerus, pp. 78, 79.
16. Ulrich von Hassell, *The Von Hassell Diaries* (Garden City, N.Y.: Doubleday, 1947), p. 53.
17. Sir Nevile Henderson, *Failure of a Mission* (New York: G. P. Putnam's, 1940), p. 284.
18. Dahlerus, *Last Attempt*, p. 88.
19. Ibid.
20. Dahlerus, p. 94.
21. Dahlerus, p. 127.
22. Dahlerus, p. 129.
23. Ibid.
24. Heinz Höhne, *Canaris* (Garden City, N.Y.: Doubleday, 1979), pp. 339, 353.
    John Weitz, *Hitler's Diplomat* (New York: Ticknor & Fields, 1992), p. 219.
25. Lauran Paine, *The Abwehr* (London: Robert Hale, 1984), p. 42.
26. Hassell, *Diaries*, p. 95.
27. Allen Dulles, *Germany's Underground* (New York: Macmillan, 1947), pp. 76, 78.
28. "The German Intelligence Branch and 20 July Plot." Georgetown University Lavinger Memorial Library, Special Collections Department, Anthony Cave Brown Papers, Box 4. Extract from Number 14, December 17, 1945. Interim interrogation of Franz Maria Liedig, Naval Intelligence Branch, Abwehr, arrested by the Gestapo following the July 20, 1944, attempted assassination of Hitler.
29. Dulles, *Germany's Underground*, pp. 76, 78.
30. Dulles, p. 77.
31. Annedore Leber, ed. *The Conscience in Revolt*, re-ed. Karl Dietrich Bracher (Munich: v. Hase & Koehler, 1994), p. 372.
32. Harold C. Deutsch, *The Conspiracy Against Hitler in the Twilight War* (Minneapolis: University of Minnesota Press, 1968), pp. 291–293.
33. Deutsch, p. 293.

34. Ibid.
35. Klemens von Klemperer, *German Resistance Against Hitler* (Oxford: Oxford Clarendon Press, 1992), p. 169.
36. Hassell, *Diaries*, p. 84.
37. Dahlerus, *Last Attempt*, p. vii.
38. Dahlerus, p. viii.
39. Dahlerus, p. vii.
40. Gero v. S. Gaevernitz, ed., *They Almost Killed Hitler* (New York: Macmillan, 1947), pp. 25, 26.
41. Winston Churchill, *The Gathering Storm*, vol. 1 of *The Second World War* (London: Reprint Society, 1954), p. 285.
42. Telford Taylor, *The Anatomy of the Nuremberg Trials* (New York: Knopf, 1992), pp. 188, 189.
43. Allan Clark, *Barbarossa* (New York: Quill Morrow, 1985), p. 25, fn. 26.
44. Roger Manvell and Heinrich Fraenkel, *The Canaris Conspiracy* (New York: David McKay, 1969), p. 80.
45. Manvell and Fraenkel, *Canaris Conspiracy*, p. 80.

Chapter 9. A Polish Lady

1. Klemens von Klemperer, *German Resistance Against Hitler* (Oxford: Oxford Clarendon Press, 1992), p. 193. From fn. 272, p. 214, Most Secret Report by Victor A. L. Mallet (British Foreign Office), September 1, 1944, FO 371/43503/N 56131/ 767/42.
2. Nigel West, *MI-6* (New York: Random House, 1983), pp. 116, 117.
3. Anthony Read and David Fisher, *Colonel Z* (New York: Viking Press, 1985), p. 241.
4. Read and Fisher, p. 117.
5. Ian Colvin, *Canaris, Chief of Intelligence* (Maidstone, England: George Mann, Publishers, 1973), pp. 88–90.
6. Colvin, pp. 91, 92.
7. *Sunday Times* of London, October 16, 1983.
8. West, *MI-6*, pp. 116, 117.
9. Nigel West, *A Thread of Deceit* (New York: Random House, 1985), pp. 37, 38.

Chapter 10. Operation X: The Vatican Connection

1. Christopher Sykes, *Troubled Loyalty* (London: Collins, 1968).
2. A good picture of Trott is drawn in Marie Vassiltchikov, *Berlin Diaries 1940–1945* (New York: Vintage Books, 1988). See index for diary references to him.
3. Louis L. Snyder, *Hitler's German Enemies* (New York: Berkley Books, 1992), pp. 156, 157.
4. Peter Hoffmann, *The History of the German Resistance 1933–1945* (Cambridge, Mass.: Harvard University Press, 1988), p. 115.

5. Hoffmann, p. 115.
6. Hoffmann, p. 119.
7. Hoffmann, p. 121. From Weizsäcker trial documents based on discussions between Resistance member Theo Kordt and Philip Conwell Evans in Bern, October 25–29, 1939.

   Also see Harold C. Deutsch, *The Conspiracy Against Hitler in the Twilight War* (Minneapolis: University of Minnesota Press, 1968), pp. 160–163.
8. Deutsch, p. 112.
9. Roger Manvell and Heinrich Fraenkel, *The Canaris Conspiracy* (New York: David McKay, 1969), p. 74. From Groscurth Papers.
10. Anthony Cave Brown, *Bodyguard of Lies* (New York: Quill/William Morrow, 1991), p. 181.
11. Ibid.
12. Sir Alexander Cadogan, *The Diaries of Sir Alexander Cadogan, 1938–1945*, ed. David Dilks (New York: G. P. Putnam's, 1972), p. 255.
13. Manvell and Fraenkel, *Canaris Conspiracy*, pp. 73–75.
14. Brown, *Bodyguard of Lies*, pp. 184, 185.

Chapter 11. The Venlo Incident

1. Christopher Andrew, *Her Majesty's Secret Service* (New York: Viking Press, 1986), p. 434. From: Beaumont-Nesbitt to Jebb, June 30, 1939, enclosing "Records of Conversation and Other Details of Von Schwerin"; Public Record Office Foreign Office Nr. 371/22974, published in *Documents on British Foreign Policy*, 3d Series, vol. 6.
2. F. H. Hinsley, E. E. Thomas, C. F. G. Ransom, and R. C. Knight, *Its Influence on Strategy and Operations*, 2d ed., vol. 1 of *British Intelligence in The Second World War* (London: Her Majesty's Stationery Office 1986), pp. 55, 56.
3. Hinsley et al., pp. 47, 48.
4. Ibid.
5. Anthony Read and David Fisher, *Colonel Z* (New York, Viking Press, 1983), p. 211.
6. Read and Fisher, pp. 206, 207.
7. Hinsley et al., *Its Influence on Strategy and Operations*, pp. 56, 57.
8. Sir Alexander Cadogan, *The Diaries of Sir Alexander Cadogan 1938–1945*, ed. David Dilks (New York: G. P. Putnam's, 1972), pp. 224, 225.
9. Cadogan, p. 226.
10. Andrew, *Her Majesty's Secret Service*, p. 435.
    Read and Fisher, *Colonel Z.*, p. 212.
11. Andrew, p. 437, fn. 102. From: S. Payne Best, *The Venlo Incident* (London, Hutchinson, 1950), pp. 11, 12.
12. Cadogan, *Diaries*, p. 228.
13. Andrew, *Her Majesty's Secret Service*, p. 437, fn. 103,
    Cadogan, pp. 228, 229.
14. Andrew, pp. 438, fn. 107.
15. David Irving, *Göring* (New York: Avon Books, 1989), p. 256.

16. Ibid.
17. Irving, p. 254.
18. Louis C. Kilzer, *Churchill's Deception* (New York: Simon & Schuster, 1994), p. 152. From Trial of the German War Criminals: *Proceedings of the International Military Tribunal*, vol. 9 (Washington: U.S. Government Printing Office, 1947–1949), p. 237.
19. Irving, *Göring*, pp. 274, 275.
20. Irving, p. 274.
21. Irving, p. 275. Irving's source was given as Joachim Hertslet's postwar interrogation by the Americans: SAIC/PIR/194 of July 19, 1945, and SAIC/FIR/43, September 11, 1945. See fn. p. 529.
22. Irving, p. 275.
23. Irving, p. 529; fn. for p. 276.
24. Cadogan, *Diaries*, p. 237.
25. Walter Schellenberg, *Hitler's Secret Service*, tr. Louis Hagen, 2d ed. (New York: Pyramid, 1962), p. 54.
26. Cadogan, *Diaries*, p. 226.
27. Cadogan, p. 227.
28. American Embassy telegram no. 1607, from chargé Alexander Kirk in Berlin to the secretary of state, dated November 9, 1939.
29. Ibid.
30. Charles Whiting, *The Spymasters* (New York: E. P. Dutton Saturday Review Press, 1976), pp. 38, 39.
31. Cadogan, *Diaries*, pp. 230, 231.
32. Hugh Trevor-Roper, *The Philby Affair* (London: William Kimber, 1968), p. 72.
33. Ibid.
34. Lord Dacre of Glanton (Hugh Trevor-Roper), "Sideways into S.I.S.," *In the Name of Intelligence*, ed. Hayden B. Peake and Samuel Halpern (Washington, D.C.: NIBC Press, 1994), p. 255.
35. Otto John, *Twice Through the Lines* (New York: Harper & Row, 1969), p. 62.
36. Ulrich von Hassell, *The von Hassell Diaries* (New York: Harper & Row, 1972), pp. 88, 89.
37. André Brissaud, *The Nazi Secret Service* (New York: W. W. Norton, 1974), pp. 271, 276.

Chapter 12. Hitler Goes West

1. Walter Schellenberg, *The Schellenberg Memoirs* (London: André Deutsch, 1956), pp. 68, 69.
2. Klemens von Klemperer, *German Resistance Against Hitler.* (Oxford: Oxford Clarendon Press, 1992), p. 209, fn. 194.
3. David Dilks, "Flashes of Intelligence: The Foreign Office, the SIS and Security Before the Second World War." *The Missing Dimension*, eds. Christopher Andrew and David Dilks (Urbana: University of Illinois Press, 1984), p. 123.

4. Harold C. Deutsch, *The Conspiracy Against Hitler in the Twilight War* (Minneapolis: The University of Minnesota Press, 1968), p. 247.
5. Deutsch, p. 248
6. Ibid.
7. Deutsch, p. 137.
8. Klemperer, *German Resistance*, p. 179.
9. *The New York Times*, February 10, 1940.
10. Klemperer, *German Resistance*, p. 189.
11. Ulrich von Hassell, *The von Hassell Diaries* (Garden City, N.Y.: Doubleday, 1947), pp. 120, 121.
12. Klemperer, *German Resistance Against Hitler*, p. 190.
13. Hassell, *Diaries*, p. 121.
14. George F. Kennan, *Memoirs, 1925–1950* (Boston: Little, Brown, 1967), p. 122.
15. Klemperer, *German Resistance*, p. 180.
    Deutsch, *Conspiracy Against Hitler*, pp. 336, 337.
16. David Thompson, *Journal of Military History*, vol. 57, no. 2 (April 1993), pp. 343, 344. Book review of Karl Rommetveit, ed., *Narvik 1940* (Oslo: Norwegian Institute for Defense Studies, 1991).
    Franz Halder, *The Halder War Diary, 1939–1942*, ed. Charles Burdick and Hans-Adolf Jacobsen (Novato, Calif.: Presidio, 1988).
    David Irving, *Göring* (New York: Avon Books, 1989), p. 285.
17. Ian Colvin, *Canaris, Chief of Intelligence* (Maidstone, England: George Mann, Publishers, 1973), pp. 107–109.
18. Colvin, *Canaris*, p. 110.
19. Ibid.
20. F. H. Hinsley, E. E. Thomas, C. F. G. Ransom, and R. C. Knight, *Its Influence on Strategy and Operations*, 2d ed., vol. 1 of *British Intelligence in the Second World War* (London: Her Majesty's Stationery Office, 1986), p. 127.
21. Irving, *Göring*, p. 285.
22. Irving, p. 286.

Chapter 13. Case Yellow: German Invasion of France

1. Roger Manvell and Heinrich Fraenkel, *The Canaris Conspiracy* (New York: David McKay, 1969), p. 82.
2. Manvell and Fraenkel, p. 85.
3. Franz Halder, *Hitler as Warlord* (London: 1950), pp. 27, 28. Cited in Correlli Barnett, ed., *Hitler's Generals* (New York: Grove Weidenfeld, 1989), p. 123.
4. Barnett, pp. 106, 107.
5. One contact was probably Theo Kordt. Klemens von Klemperer, *German Resistance Against Hitler* (Oxford: Oxford Clarendon Press, 1992), p. 197, fn. 296.
6. Franz Halder, *The Halder War Diary*, ed. Charles Burdick and Hans-Adolf Jacobsen (Novato, Calif.: Presidio Press, 1988), pp. 90, 91. January 20, 1940 entry.
7. Ibid.

8. Heinz Höhne, *Canaris* (Garden City, N.Y.: Doubleday 1979), pp. 415–421.
9. David Irving, *Göring* (New York: Avon Books, 1989), p. 180.
10. Irving, *Göring*, p. 180.
11. F. H. Hinsley, E. E. Thomas, C. F. G. Ransom, and R. C. Knight, *Its Influence on Strategy and Operations*, vol. 1 of *British Intelligence in The Second World War* (London: Her Majesty's Stationery Office, 1979), pp. 133–135.
12. Hinsley et al., p. 131.
13. William L. Shirer, *The Nightmare Years, 1930–1940*, vol. 2 of *20th Century Journey* (New York: Bantam, 1992), pp. 482, 483.
14. Frederick W. Winterbotham, *The Ultra Secret* (London: Weidenfeld & Nicolson, 1974), p. 31.
15. Winterbotham, p. 32.
16. Winston Churchill, *The Gathering Storm*, vol. 1 of *The Second World War* (London: Reprint Society, 1954), p. 530.
17. Martin Gilbert, *The Second World War*, rev. ed. (New York: Henry Holt, 1989), p. 59.
18. Winterbotham, *The Ultra Secret*, p. 32.
19. Harold C. Deutsch, "The Matter of Records," *Journal of Military History*, vol. 59, no. 1 (January 1995), pp. 141, 142.
20. "Summary of Principal Peace Feelers, September 1939–March 1941." FO 371/26542/C 4216/610/G, FO 371/26542/C 610/324/P, British Public Records Office.

Chapter 14. France Falls: Britain Stands Alone

1. B. H. Liddell Hart, *The German Generals Talk* (New York: Quill, 1979), p. 133.
2. Earl F. Ziemke, "Rundstedt," *Hitler's Generals*, ed. Correlli Barnett (New York, Grove Weidenfeld, 1989), p. 191.
3. Liddell Hart, *German Generals*, p. 133.
4. William L. Shirer, *The Nightmare Years*, vol. 2 of *20th Century Journey* (New York: Bantam, 1992), pp. 504, 505.
5. John Keegan, *The Second World War* (New York: Viking Press, 1989), p. 81.
6. Liddell Hart, *German Generals*, pp. 134, 135, 136.
7. Franz Halder, *The Halder War Diary 1939–1942*, ed. Charles Burdick and Hans-Adolf Jacobsen (Novato, Calif.: Presidio Press, 1988), p. 65.
8. F. H. Hinsley, E. E. Thomas, C. F. G. Ransom, and R. C. Knight, *Its Influence on Strategy and Operations*, 2d ed., vol. 1 of *British Intelligence in the Second World War* (London: Her Majesty's Stationery Office, 1986), p. 148.
   John Costello, *Ten Days to Destiny* (New York: William Morrow, 1991), p. 191.
9. Costello, p. 175.
   Brian Bond, ed., *Chief of Staff: The Diaries of Sir Henry Pownell* (London, 1972), p. 175. May 24, 1940.
10. Costello, p. 188. From November 7, 1939, Büro Staatsekretär England, Politisches Archiv A.A.B.

11. Costello, p. 329. From Cadogan's diary.
12. Peter Padfield, *Hess* (London: Weidenfeld & Nicolson, 1991), p. 126.
13. Henry J. Taylor, "The Story Told in Kent Stolen Document Case," *New York World-Telegraph*, September 5, 1944.
14. Ibid.
15. Costello, *Ten Days*, pp. 124, 125.
16. *London Observer*, July 4, 1971. From James Lutze, ed., *The Journal of General Raymond E. Lee, 1940–41* (London: 1971).
17. *The Economist* (July 3–9, 1993), p. 86.
18. Gore Vidal, "Screening History," *American Heritage* (September 1992, p. 72.
    Anthony Read and David Fisher, *Colonel Z* (New York: Viking Press, 1985), pp. 176–180.
19. Sir Alexander Cadogan, *The Diaries of Sir Alexander Cadogan, 1938–1945*, ed. David Dilks (New York: G. P. Putnam's, 1971), entry for August 8, 1941.
20. H. Montgomery Hyde, *Secret Intelligence Agent* (New York: St. Martin's Press, 1982), p. 162.
21. Hyde, p. 164.
    H. Montgomery Hyde, *The Quiet Canadian* (London: Hamish Hamilton, 1962), pp. 183, 184.
22. Lee A. Gladwin, "Hollywood Propaganda, Isolationism and Protectors of the Public Mind, 1917–1941," *Prologue* (Winter 1994), pp. 241–244.
    Propaganda in motion pictures: Hearings before a Subcommittee of the Committee on Interstate Commerce, U.S. Senate, 77th Congress, First Session, on S. Res. 152 (September 9–26, 1941), p. 33.
23. Nicholas John Cull, *Selling War* (New York: Oxford University Press, 1995), pp. 169, 170.
24. Gerhard L. Weinberg, *A World at Arms* (Cambridge, England: Cambridge University Press, 1994), p. 242.
25. William Stevenson, *A Man Called Intrepid* (New York: Harcourt Brace Jovanovich, 1976).

Chapter 15. A Friendly Connection

1. F. H. Hinsley, E. E. Thomas, C. F. G. Ransom, and R. C. Knight, *Its Influence on Strategy and Operations*, 2d ed., vol. 1 of *British Intelligence in The Second World War* (London: Her Majesty's Stationery Office, 1986), p. 312.
2. William Henhoeffer, *The Intelligence War in 1941* (Washington D.C.: CIA Center for the Study of Intelligence, 1992), p. 27.
3. F. H. Hinsley et al., *Its Influence on Strategy and Operations*, p. 312.
    Brian R. Sullivan, "A Highly Commendable Action: "William J. Donovan's Intelligence Mission for Mussolini and Roosevelt, December 1935–February 1936," *Intelligence and National Security*, vol. 6, number 2 (April 1991), p. 358.
4. John Lukacs "The Transatlantic Duel: Hitler vs. Roosevelt," *American Heritage*, special edition, *Battles and Leaders* (1994), p. 40.

5. John Costello, *Ten Days to Destiny* (New York: William Morrow, 1991) p. 379.
6. Anthony Cave Brown, *The Last Hero* (New York: Times Books, 1982), p. 152. From William J. Donovan Miscellaneous Collection (of correspondence and files), U.S. Army War College, Carlisle Barracks, Pa.
7. Ibid.
8. Anthony Cave Brown, *"C"* (New York: Macmillan, 1987), pp. 364, 365.
    U.S. War Department Strategic Services Unit, *War Report of the OSS*, vol. 2, intr. Kermit Roosevelt (Washington, D.C.: Carrollton Press; New York: Walker; 1976), pp. 3–7.
9. Bradley Smith, "Admiral Godfrey's Mission to America, June, July 1941," *Intelligence and National Security*, vol. 3 (September 1986), pp. 441–450.
10. Henhoeffer, *The Intelligence War in 1941*, pp. 27, 28.
    Bradley Smith, "Admiral Godfrey's Mission to America," pp. 441–450.
11. Richard Dunlop, *Donovan* (New York: Rand McNally, 1982), p. 290.
12. Tom Troy, "The Coordinator of Information and British Intelligence," *Studies in Intelligence* (Spring 1974).
13. Thomas Troy, *Donovan and the CIA*, 2d ed. (Frederick, Md.: University Publications of America, 1984), p. 83.
14. Bruce Lee, *Marching Orders* (New York: Crown, 1995).
    Carl Boyd, *Hitler's Japanese Confidant* (Lawrence: University of Kansas Press, 1993).
15. David Kahn, *Hitler's Spies* (New York: Macmillan, 1978), pp. 329–331.
    Bradley F. Smith, *The Shadow Warriors* (New York: Basic Books, 1983), p. 22.
16. Cordell Hull, *Memoirs of Cordell Hull* (New York: Macmillan 1948), vol. 1, p. 821.
17. H. Montgomery Hyde, *Secret Intelligence Agent* (New York: St. Martin's Press, 1983).
18. Hyde, pp. 157, 158.
    The full Belmonte letter, translated into English, appeared in *The Christian Science Monitor*, August 22, 1941.
19. Hyde, p. 159.
20. Hyde, p. 160.
21. Sumner Welles, *Seven Major Decisions* (London: 1951), p. 101.
22. Henhoeffer, *The Intelligence War in 1941*, p. 28.
23. Henhoeffer, pp. 24, 27.
24. Nicholas John Cull, *Selling War* (New York: Oxford University Press, 1995), pp. 174, 175.
25. Peter Wright, *Spycatcher* (New York: Dell, 1988), p. 414.

Chapter 16. Felix Foiled: How Gibraltar Was Saved

1. Roger Manvell and Heinrich Fraenkel, *The Canaris Conspiracy* (New York: David McKay, 1969), p. 90.
2. André Brissaud, *Canaris* (New York: Grosset & Dunlap, 1974), p. 191.
3. Brissaud, p. 194.

4. John Costello, *Ten Days to Destiny* (New York: William Morrow, 1991), pp. 358, 359. From Item 6, War Cabinet Minutes (171), June 18, 1940, Cab. 657, Public Record Office microfilm.
5. Costello, p. 359.
6. John Lukacs, *The Duel* (New York: Ticknor & Fields, 1990), p. 151.
7. Ibid.
8. K. H. Abshagen, *Canaris* (London: Hutchinson, 1956), p. 213.
9. Sir Alexander Cadogan, *The Diaries of Sir Alexander Cadogan*, ed. David Dilks (New York: G. P. Putnam's, 1972), p. 287.
10. Brissaud, *Canaris*, p. 191.
11. William Henhoeffer, *The Intelligence War in 1941* (Washington, D.C.: CIA Center for the Study of Intelligence, 1992), p. 19.
12. Manvell and Fraenkel, *Canaris Conspiracy*, p. 195.
13. Jacques de Launay, *Secret Diplomacy of World War II* (New York: Simmons-Boardman, 1963), pp. 38, 39.
14. Abshagen, *Canaris*, pp. 212, 213.
15. Winston Churchill, *Their Finest Hour*, vol. 2 of *The Second World War* (London: Reprint Society, 1953), p. 468.
16. Brissaud, *Canaris*, p. 196.
17. Franz Halder, *The Halder War Diary 1939–1942*, ed. Charles Burdick and Hans-Adolf Jacobsen (Novato, Calif.: Presidio Press, 1988), p. 247.
18. Halder, pp. 252, 255.
19. Ian Colvin, *Master Spy* (New York: McGraw-Hill, 1951), p. 149.
20. Halder, *Diary*, p. 262.
21. Paul Preston, *Franco* (New York: Basic Books/HarperCollins, 1994), p. 394.
22. Ernst von Weizsäcker, *Die Weizsäcker Papiere, 1933–1950* (Frankfurt, 1974), p. 24. Diary entry October 21, 1940. Cited in Preston, *Franco*, p. 400.
23. Halder, *Diary*, p. 263.
24. Halder, pp. 263, 264.
25. Preston, *Franco*, p. 396.
26. Ian Colvin, *Canaris, Chief of Intelligence* (Maidstone, England: George Mann, Publishers 1973), p. 67.
27. Colvin, *Canaris*, pp. 130, 131.
28. Churchill, *Their Finest Hour*, p. 420.
29. Launay, *Secret Diplomacy*, p. 44. From Sir Samuel Hoare, *Ambassadeur en Mission Speciale* (Paris: Vent du Large, 1946), p. 157.
30. Colvin, *Canaris*, p. 127.
31. Colvin, *Canaris*, p. 128.
32. Mary Ellen Reese, *General Reinhard Gehlen* (Fairfax, Va.: George Mason University Press, 1990). From conversations with Eric Waldman.
33. Reese, p. 132.
34. Cadogan, *Diaries*, p. 340.
35. Cadogan, p. 340.
36. Abshagen, *Canaris*, pp. 212, 213.
37. Churchill, *Their Finest Hour*, p. 416.
38. Ibid.

39. Churchill, pp. 420, 421.
40. Henhoeffer, *The Intelligence War*, p. 19. Publisher's note states: "The views expressed do not necessarily represent those of any U.S. Government entity."

Other sources given in the CIA study by Henhoeffer are: Anthony Cave Brown, *Bodyguard of Lies* (New York: Quill, 1975), pp. 137–147, 212–215; Ian Colvin, *Canaris, Chief of Intelligence* (London: Victor Gollancz, 1951), p. 217; Reese, *Gehlen*, p. 86.

Chapter 17. A Reluctant Sea Lion and an Errant Duke

1. B. H. Liddell Hart, *The German Generals Talk* (New York: Quill, 1979), p. 146.
2. Liddell Hart, pp. 146, 147.
3. Peter Fleming, *Operation Sea Lion* (New York: Simon & Schuster, 1957), p. 179.
4. John Costello, *Ten Days to Destiny* (New York: William Morrow, 1991), p. 345.
5. Minute by Frank Roberts on the Burckhardt and Hohenlohe telegrams, July 16, 1940, FO 371/2440 7, Public Record Office.
6. Costello, *Ten Days*, pp. 203, 204. From Diary of W. L. Mackenzie King, May 24, 1940, and Hugh Keenleyside, *Memoirs* (Toronto, 1982), vol. 2, pp. 34, 35.
7. Lothian to foreign secretary, July 24, 1940, FO 371/24408, Public Record Office, quoted in Costello, p. 347.
8. Costello, p. 348.
9. Costello, pp. 398–341.
10. Costello, pp. 362, 363. From Stohrer to Berlin, July 2, 1940, Documents on German Foreign Policy (DGFP) no. 86.
11. Pell to Secretary, July 20, 1940, Pell Papers, FDR Library.
12. Michael Bloch, *Ribbentrop* (New York: Crown Publishers, 1992), p. 290. From DGFP, D/X, no. 152.
13. Ibid.
14. Ibid.
15. Michael Bloch, *Operation Willi* (New York: Weidenfeld & Nicolson, 1986), pp. 103–110. Serrano Gúñer interview. Cited in Bloch, *Ribbentrop*.
16. Bloch, *Operation Willi*, pp. 103–110.
17. Walter Schellenberg, *Hitler's Secret Service*, tr. Louis Hagen, 2d ed. (New York: Pyramid, 1962), p. 68.
18. Schellenberg, p. 71.
19. Peter Allen, *The Crown and the Swastika* (London: Robert Hale, 1983).
20. Allen, pp. 212, 213. From Bundesarchiv document no. R SS/1236.
21. Leo Kessler, *Betrayal at Venlo* (London: Leo Cooper, 1991), p. 158.
22. Allen, *Crown and Swastika*, p. 213. From Bundesarchiv document no. E 147120. Allen also refers to a conversation with Hugh Thomas, author of *Murder of Rudolf Hess*, whose research for his book led him to an SS officer who claimed, "Hess met the Duke of Windsor in Lisbon."
23. Bloch, *Operation Willi*, pp. 192–198.
24. Anthony Cave Brown, "C" (New York: Macmillan, 1987), pp. 676, 677, 678.

25. Schellenberg, *Hitler's Secret Service*, p. 77.
26. Bloch, *Ribbentrop*, p. 295. From DGFP D/X, no. 274.

Chapter 18. The Hess Mission:
Quixotic Adventure, Secret Diplomacy or British Sting?

1. James Douglas-Hamilton, *Motive for a Mission* (New York: Paragon House, 1986), p. 160. Letter from Albrecht Haushofer to the duke of Hamilton, datelined Lisbon, September 23, 1940.
2. From an originally secret report of an interview of Hess by the duke of Hamilton after the German had parachuted to earth in Scotland on May 10, 1941: "Report on Interview with Herr Hess by Wing Commander, the Duke of Hamilton, on Sunday, 11 May, 1941," Georgetown University Lauinger Memorial Library, Special Collections Department; Father Edmund A. Walsh, SJ, Papers, Box 10, Folder 640.
3. Based on Diaries of Robert Bruce Lockhart, British House of Lords Record Office, Files 313, War Notebook 48, 1943.
4. John Costello, *Ten Days to Destiny* (New York: William Morrow, 1991).
5. Klemens von Klemperer, *German Resistance Against Hitler* (Oxford: Oxford Clarendon Press, 1992), pp. 36, 37.
6. Klemperer, pp. 221, 222. From Letter from Dr. Karl Haushofer to Dr. Albrecht Haushofer, Munich, September 3, 1940, *Akten zür deutschen auswartigen Politik, 1918–1945*, Serie D (1937–1949) (Bonn, 1964), vol. 11, pp. 13–15.
7. Klemperer, p. 223.
8. Peter Padfield, *Hess* (London: Weidenfeld & Nicolson, 1991), p. 161.
9. Walter Schellenberg, *Hitler's Secret Service*, tr. Louis Hagen, 2d ed. New York: Pyramid, 1962), pp. 106–109.
10. Peter Padfield, *Himmler* (New York: Henry Holt, 1990), p. 326.
11. Klemperer, *German Resistance*, p. 224.
12. Ulrich von Hassell, *The von Hassell Diaries* (Garden City, N.Y.: Doubleday, 1947), p. 194.
13. Hassell, pp. 240, 241.
14. Hassell, p. 193.
15. Douglas-Hamilton, *Motive for a Mission*, p. 160.
16. Douglas-Hamilton, pp. 163, 165.
17. Costello, *Ten Days*, p. 13.
18. Douglas-Hamilton, *Motive for a Mission*, p. 144.
19. Hassell, *Diaries*, p. 193.
20. Wilhelm F. Flicke, *War Secrets in the Ether*, ed. Sheila Carlisle (Laguna Hills, Calif.: Aegean Park Press, 1994), vol. 1, p. 108.
21. Douglas-Hamilton, *Motive for a Mission*, p. 188. From J. R. Rees, ed., *The Case of Rudolf Hess* (Surrey, England, Heinemann: 1947), pp. 137–139.
22. Franz Halder, *The Halder Diary, 1939–1942*, ed. Charles Burdick and Hans Adolf Jacobsen (Novato, Calif.: Presidio Press, 1988), p. 387.
23. Halder, pp. 386, 387.

24. Schellenberg, *Hitler's Secret Service*, pp. 106, 107.
25. Costello, *Ten Days*, p. 436.
26. Genrikh Borovik, *The Philby Files* (Boston: Little, Brown, 1994), p. 184.
27. Costello, *Ten Days*, p. 437, fn 2 from File no. 20566, Hess-Black Bertha Kam., KGB Moscow.
28. Costello, *Ten Days*, p. 437.
29. Winston Churchill, *The Grand Alliance*, vol. 3 of *Second World War* (London: Reprint Society, 1953), p. 49.
30. Phillip Knightly, *The Master Spy* (New York: Knopf, 1989), pp. 106, 107.
31. William Henhoeffer, *The Intelligence War in 1941* (Washington, D.C.: Center for the Study of Intelligence, 1992), pp. 2, 3.
32. Halder, *Diary*, p. 298.
33. Ibid.
34. B. H. Liddell Hart, *The German Generals Talk* (New York: Quill, 1979), p. 149.

Chapter 19. Barbarossa

1. Allan Clark, *Barbarossa* (New York: Quill/Morrow, 1985), p. 24.
2. Franz Halder, *The Halder War Diary, 1939–1942*, ed. Charles Burdick and Hans-Adolf Jacobsen (Novato, Calif.: Presidio Press, 1988), p. 244.
3. Wesley K. Wark, "British Intelligence and Operation Barbarossa, 1941: The Failure of the F.O.E.S." *In The Name of Intelligence*, ed. Hayden B. Peake and Samuel Halpern (Washington, D.C.: NIBC Press, 1994).
4. Janusz Piekalkiewicz, *Secret Agents and Saboteurs* (New York: William Morrow, 1973), p. 143. From a firsthand account of A-54 provided by Free Czech Colonel Fryc, who handled him from Paris.
5. Barton Whaley, *Codeword Barbarossa* (Cambridge, Mass.: MIT Press, 1973), p. 234.
6. F. H. Hinsley, E. E. Thomas, C.F.G. Ransom, and R.C. Knight, *Its Influence on Strategy and Operations*, 2d ed., vol. 1 of *British Intelligence in The Second World War* (London: Her Majesty's Stationery Office, 1986), p. 429.
7. John Costello and Oleg Tsarev, *Deadly Illusions* (New York: Crown Publishers/Random House, 1993), p. 82. (Taken from *Frankfurter Zeitung*, December, 19, 1931; archives of the Security Service, I. G. Farben Leverkusen.)
8. Alexander Foote, *Handbook for Spies* (London: Hart-Davis, 1976).
9. John Keegan, *The Second World War* (New York: Viking Press, 1989), p. 180.
10. Cordell Hull, *Memoirs of Cordell Hull* (New York: Macmillan, 1948), vol. 2, pp. 968–969.
11. Sam Woods's memorandum (undated), Cordell Hull Papers, U.S. Library of Congress, p. 6.
    Respondek's "Personal, Confidential Report" for Cordell Hull of May 1946 from Thomas B. Stauffer Papers, Cordell Hull Papers, Library of Congress, p. 4. Respondek, however, did not receive a copy of Hitler's Directive no. 21, issued December 18, 1940, which ordered a quick defeat of the USSR before Britain was defeated.

12. Military attaché, Berlin, Report no. 17, 815.
13. Breckinridge Long's diaries, entry of February 21, 1941, p. 28. Box 5, Breckinridge Long Papers, U.S. Library of Congress.
14. Hull, *Memoirs*, p. 968.
15. Telegram, Hull to Steinhardt, March 1, 1941. Record Group 59, no. 240,740,0011, E. W. 1939/8656, National Archives.
16. *Pacific Historical Review*, vol. 50, no. 1 (February 1981), p. 83. From Carl Boyd, *Hitler's Japanese Confidant* (Lawrence: University of Kansas Press, 1993), p. 206, fn. 7.
17. Warren F. Kimball, *The Juggler* (Princeton N.J.: Princeton University Press, 1991), pp. 23, 209–210, fn. 5. From: National Archives, Record Group 457, Records of the National Security Agency, document no. SRH–252 (regarding Japanese ciphers 1930–1945), by John B. Hurt (declassified).
18. Alex de Jonge, *Stalin and the Shaping of the Soviet Union* (New York: Quill/Morrow, 1986), p. 373. From M. Lissan, "Stalin the Appeaser," *Survey*, no. 76 (1970), p. 172.
19. John Costello, *Ten Days to Destiny* (New York: Morrow, 1991), p. 436. (A May 14, 1941, Soviet message from London discusses information obtained from Kim Philby.)
20. Ibid.
21. Record of a British interview with Hess on May 13. The document was in the files of HM secretary of state for foreign affairs, January 22, 1946, Nürnberg Documents, State Archive Nürnberg, M-117.
22. For information on the Rote Kapelle, see CIA monograph *Rote Kapelle*, vol. 1, *The CIA's History of Soviet Intelligence and Espionage Networks in Western Europe, 1936–1945* (Washington, D.C.: University Publications of America, 1979).
23. Costello and Tsarev, *Deadly Illusions*, p. 436, 437. Costello drew on a filmed interview with cooperating KGB officer Oleg Tsarev at KGB headquarters, Moscow, in February 1991.
24. Costello, *Ten Days*, p. 441.
25. Costello, p. 442.
    James Douglas-Hamilton, *Motive for a Mission* (New York: Paragon House, 1986), pp. 159, 160.
26. James Lutze, ed., *The London Journal of General Raymond E. Lee, 1940–41* (Boston: Little, Brown, 1971).
27. Costello, *Ten Days*, p. 453. From NKVD file, no. 09764, dated September 1941, items 1–3 on Hess, containing Leopold Schwarzchild, "Captive inattendue de Hess dans un piège tendu par le secret service," *Gazette de Montréal*, August 4, 1941.
28. Douglas-Hamilton, *Motive for a Mission* (New York: Paragon House, 1986), p. 127.
29. Klemens von Klemperer, *German Resistance Against Hitler* (Oxford: Oxford Clarendon Press, 1992), p. 92.
30. Klemperer, p. 163. From Christie's notes, "I met my friend on Wednesday, November 15, 17, 1939," Christie Papers, Churchill College, Cambridge: Group Captain Malcolm Grahame Christie [CHRS] 180/1/33.

31. Peter Padfield, *Hess* (London: Weidenfeld & Nicolson, 1991), p. 165.
32. Ibid.
33. Padfield, p. 166.
34. Padfield, p. 167.
35. John Lukacs, *The Duel* (New York: Ticknor & Fields, 1990), pp. 28, 29.
36. Halder, *Diary*, p. 104. Diary date, February 26, 1940.
37. Lukacs, *The Duel*, p. 29.
38. Diaries of Robert Bruce Lockhart, War Notebook No 48, 1943. British House of Lords Record Office, 313 files.
39. Phillip Knightly, *The Second Oldest Profession* (New York: W. W. Norton, 1986), pp. 188, 189.
40. Klemperer, *German Resistance*, p. 151, fn.
41. Jonge, *Stalin and Shaping of Soviet Union*, p. 374.
    Ulrich Blennemann, "Stalin and the Start of Operation Barbarossa," *Command* (March–April 1993), p. 60.
42. Roger Manvell and Heinrich Fraenkel, *The Canaris Conspiracy* (New York: David McKay, 1969), pp. 111–112.
43. Nigel West, *A Thread of Deceit* (New York: Random House, 1985), pp. 37, 38. From Andrew King, retired British Secret Intelligence Service officer, "who had been privy to details of her [Szymanska's] case." According to West, London *Sunday Times* journalists Barrie Penrose and Simon Freeman published a story on this in the *Sunday Times* on October 16, 1983.
44. Donald Cameron Watt "British Intelligence and the Coming of the Second World War," *Knowing One's Enemy*, ed. Ernest May (Princeton, N.J.: Princeton University Press, 1984), p. 248.
45. David Irving, *Göring* (New York: Avon Books, 1989), pp. 318, 319. Irving gave Dahlerus's wife as the source of this.
46. Irving, pp. 318, 319. Irving's footnotes provide useful source information:
    Göring had summoned Dahlerus to Berlin, where, according to the latter's passport, he remained from June 9 to June 16.
    British Foreign Office commentary based on Ambassador Mallet's reporting described Göring's June 9 message to Dahlerus about the imminent invasion. See British Public Record Office file, FO 371/29482.
    With regard to Dahlerus's tips to the Americans, Undersecretary Sumner Welles informed British Ambassador Lord Halifax of this late on June 9.
47. Nikita Khrushchev, *Khrushchev Remembers*, ed. Jerrold Schecter and Vyacheslav V. Luchkov (New York: Little Brown, 1990).
48. Khrushchev, pp. 52, 54, 55.
49. B. H. Liddell Hart, *History of the Second World War* (New York: Perigee/G. P. Putnam's, 1982), p. 143.
50. Halder, *Diary*, p. 217.
51. Heinz Höhne, *Canaris* (Garden City, N.Y., Doubleday, 1979), p. 320.
52. John Erickson, "Threat Identification and Strategic Appraisal by the Soviet Union, 1930–1941." *Knowing One's Enemies*, ed. Ernest R. May (Princeton: Princeton University Press, 1984), p. 413.
53. Ulrich Blennemann, "Stalin and the Start of Operation Barbarossa," *Command*, issue 21 (March-April 1993).

54. Ibid.
55. V. H. Dippell, "Jumping to the Right Conclusion: The State Department Warning on Operation Barbarossa," *International Journal of Intelligence and Counter-Intelligence*, vol. 6, no. 2 (Summer 1993).

Chapter 20. Tricycle and Pearl Harbor

1. Dusko Popov, *Spy/Counter-Spy* (Greenwich, Conn.: Fawcett, 1975).
   Other accounts of the Popov story include: Ewen Montagu, *Beyond Top Secret Ultra* (New York: Coward, McCann and Geoghegan, 1978), pp. 74–76, 78–79; Winston Churchill, *The Grand Alliance* (Boston: Houghton Mifflin, 1950), p. 603; William Stevenson, *A Man Called Intrepid* (New York: Harcourt Brace Jovanovich, 1976), pp. 256, 258; Nigel West, *MI-6* (New York: Random House, 1983), p. 29; Richard Powers, *Secrecy and Power* (New York: Free Press, 1989), pp. 245, 246; J. C. Masterman, *The Double-Cross System in the War 1939–1945* (New Haven: Yale University Press, 1972), Appendix 2, pp. 196–198.
2. Masterman, *The Double-Cross System*, pp. 196–198.
3. Ibid.
4. Thomas Troy, "The British Assault on J. Edgar Hoover: The Tricycle Case," *International Journal of Intelligence and Counter-Intelligence*, vol. 3, no. 2 (1989), pp. 169–209.
5. F. H. Hinsley and C. A. G. Simkins, *Security and Counter-Intelligence*, vol. 4 of *British Intelligence in the Second World War* (New York: Cambridge University Press, 1990), p. 183. Regarding Popov's loyalty to the British as checked by the ISOS intercept material in the Double-Cross system.

Chapter 21. Donovan's People

1. This chapter is based on the CIA-published *Studies in Intelligence* (Fall 1979), sidebar by the author, John H. Waller, entitled "Guinea Pig," accompanying an article, "The OSS Assessment Program," by Dr. Donald Mackinson. National Archives.

Chapter 22. The Assassination of Reinhard Heydrich

1. U.S. National Archives and Record Service, Part VI, Amt Ausland/Abwehr, Office of Foreign Counter-Intelligence. See German circular giving regulations for sentencing and executing persons suspected of aiding the enemy in connection with the assassination attempt of SS Obergruppenführer Heydrich. OKW 1763, Roll 1443, 1st frame 895.
2. Heinz Höhne, *Canaris* (Garden City, N.Y.: Doubleday, 1979), p. 471 and fn. 297.
3. Höhne, p. 471.

4. Roger Manvell and Heinrich Fraenkel, *The Canaris Conspiracy* (New York: David McKay, 1969), p. 105, citing as source: Walter Schellenberg, *The Schellenberg Memoirs* (London: André Deutsch, 1956), pp. 403, 404.

5. Manvell and Fraenkel, p. 106, citing as source: Schellenberg, *The Schellenberg Memoirs*, pp. 405–406.

6. Manvell and Fraenkel, p. 107.

7. Paul Padfield, *Himmler* (New York: Henry Holt, 1990), p. 380, fn. 8.

8. Höhne, *Canaris*, p. 471.

9. K. H. Abshagen, *Canaris* (London: Hutchinson, 1956), p. 95.

10. OSS document, SA-8560, July 9, 1942, Hugh R. Wilson (former U.S. diplomat, Berlin, now in OSS) to Colonel Butler, OSS. Georgetown University Lauinger Memorial Library, Special Collections Department. Anthony Cave Brown Papers, Box 4.

11. R. C. Jaggers, "The Assassination of Reinhard Heydrich," *Studies in Intelligence* (Winter 1960), p. 2.

12. Jaggers, p. 1.

13. Höhne, *Canaris*, p. 86.

14. Anthony Cave Brown, *Bodyguard of Lies* (New York, Quill/William Morrow, 1991), p. 157.

15. Jaggers, "Assassination of Heydrich," p. 1.

16. Brown, *Bodyguard of Lies*, p. 157.

17. André Brissaud, *The Nazi Secret Service* (New York: W. W. Norton, 1974), p. 24.

18. Brown, *Bodyguard of Lies*, p. 158.

19. Hans Bernd Gisevius, *To the Bitter End* (Boston: Houghton Mifflin, 1947), p. 139.

20. Mary Bancroft, *Autobiography of a Spy* (New York: William Morrow, 1983), p. 191.

21. Walter Schellenberg, *Hitler's Secret Service*, tr. Louis Hagen, 2d ed. (New York: Pyramid, 1962), pp. 21, 22.

22. Charles Whiting, *The Spymasters* (New York: E. P. Dutton/Saturday Review Press, 1976), p. 32, fn. 5.

23. Peter Norden, *Madam Kitty* (London: Abelard-Schuman, 1973).

24. Abshagen, *Canaris*, p. 102.

25. Höhne, *Canaris*, p. 163, fn. 179.

26. F. H. Hinsley and C. A. G. Simkins, *Security and Counter-Intelligence*, vol. 4 of *British Intelligence in the Second World War* (New York: Cambridge University Press, 1990), Appendix 1, p. 300.

27. Hinsley and Simkins, Appendix 1, p. 300.

 Abwehr document 4218/12.36, December 23, 1936, signed by Canaris's officer on his behalf, Oberstleutnant Bamler, which contains the ten points to which Canaris agreed. This document is in the U.S. National Archives in its Abwehr collection.

28. Höhne, *Canaris*, p. 181.

29. Manvell and Fraenkel, *Canaris Conspiracy*, p. 65.

30. Ian Colvin, *Canaris* (Maidstone, England: George Mann, Publishers, 1973), pp. 90, 91.

31. Wilhelm F. Flicke, *War Secrets in the Ether*, ed. Sheila Carlisle (Laguna Hills, Calif.: Aegean Park Press, 1994).

32. Hinsley and Simkins, *Security and Counter-Intelligence*, Appendix 1, p. 300.
    Höhne, *Canaris*, p. 469.

33. "Correspondence between Heydrich and Canaris showing controversy between them and the Armed Forces Intelligence and Police, and an agreement signed by Heydrich and Canaris for cooperation of the Security Police and the SD (Security Service) entitled '10 Gebote' with the Armed Forces Intelligence Service [Abwehr]." U.S. National Archives and Record Service. Records of the German Armed Forces High Command, Part VI, No. 80. Item No.: OKW 2410, Roll 1513, 1st Frame, 540.

34. Jaggers, "Assassination of Heydrich," p. 17.

35. Jaggers, p. 19.

36. Herbert Molloy Mason, Jr., *To Kill the Devil* (New York: W. W. Norton, 1978), p. 71, fn.

37. Josef Korbel, *The Communist Subversion of Czechoslovakia, 1938–1948* (Princeton, N.J.: Princeton University Press, 1959), pp. 60–62.

38. Diaries of Robert Bruce Lockhart, War Notebook 54, 1954. File 313, House of Lords Record Office.

39. Callum MacDonald, *The Killing of SS Obergruppen-Führer Reinhard Heydrich* (New York: Collier/Macmillan, 1989), pp. 80, 81.

40. Whiting, *The Spymasters*, p. 71.

41. Whiting, p. 72.

42. Whiting, p. 71, fn. 6.

43. Whiting, p. 71.
    Also see George C. Constantinides, *Intelligence and Espionage* (Boulder, Colo.: Westview Press, 1983), p. 201.

44. Whiting, p. 68.

45. Whiting, pp. 68–70.

46. Whiting, p. 72. Whiting's source for the assertion that British pressure played a major role in carrying out the Heydrich assassination operation was a postwar defector from Czech intelligence, identified only as Major F., who had served seventeen years in this service. It is possible that Whiting's source was Czech intelligence officer Josef Frolik, who defected to the West in 1968. See Constantinides, *Intelligence and Espionage*, pp. 201, 202.

47. Janusz Piekalkiewicz, *Secret Agents, Spies and Saboteurs* (New York: William Morrow, 1973), pp. 148, 149.

48. Colvin, *Canaris*, p. 148.

49. Ibid.

50. J. C. Masterman, *The Double-Cross System in the War of 1939–1945* (New Haven: Yale University Press, 1972), pp. 149–155.
    Timothy Naftali, "X-2 and the Apprenticeship of American Counter-espionage," 1993 dissertation, Harvard University (UMI Dissertation Service, Ann Arbor, Michigan, 1994), p. 512. Acquired by permission of the author.

51. Masterman, p. 152.

52. Ibid.

53. F. H. Hinsley and Alan Stripp, *Code Breakers* (New York: Oxford University Press, 1993), pp. 123–131, 205.

54. William Henhoeffer, *The Intelligence War in 1941* (Washington, D.C.: CIA Center for the Study of Intelligence, 1992), pp. 11–13.

55. Masterman, *The Double-Cross System*, p. xiv.

56. Ibid.

57. Hinsley and Stripp, *Code Breakers*, pp. 123–131.

58. Masterman, *The Double-Cross System*, p. 145.

59. Masterman, p. 151.

60. Richard Deacon, *A History of the British Secret Service* (London: Panther/Granada, 1984), pp. 321, 322.

    Höhne, *Canaris*, pp. 481, 482.

61. Hugh Trevor-Roper, *The Philby Affair* (London: William Kimber, 1968), pp. 78, 79.

Chapter 23. Operation Torch:
Allied Invasion of North Africa

1. "Masterman Revisited," *Studies in Intelligence* (Spring 1974), p. 32.

2. Wilhelm F. Flicke, *War Secrets of the Ether*, ed. Sheila Carlisle (Laguna Hills, Calif.: Aegean Park Press, 1994), p. 108.

    Frederick L. P. White, "Old Secrets Revealed," *International Journal of Intelligence*, vol. 7, no. 3 (Fall 1994), pp. 395, 396.

3. Flicke, p. 108.

4. F. H. Hinsley and C.A.G. Simkins, *Security and Counter-Intelligence*, vol. 2 of *British Intelligence in the Second World War* (New York: Cambridge University Press, 1981), Appendix 15, p. 719 ff.

5. Anthony Cave Brown, *Treason in the Blood* (New York: Houghton Mifflin, 1994), pp. 286–288.

6. Hinsley and Simkins, *Security and Counter-Intelligence*, pp. 161, 162.

    Brown, pp. 286–288; 293–294.

7. Hinsley and Simkins, p. 721.

8. Kim Philby, *My Silent War* (New York: Grove Press, 1968), pp. 69–71.

    Phillip Knightly, *The Master Spy* (New York: Knopf, 1989), p. 105.

9. Knightly, p. 106.

10. Klemens von Klemperer, *German Resistance Against Hitler* (Oxford: Oxford Clarendon Press, 1992), p. 397, fn. 7.

11. Desmond Bristow with Bill Bristow, *A Game of Moles* (London: Little, Brown, 1993), pp. 26, 27.

12. Piece 932, September 20, 1942. British Public Record Office, Kew, HW–1, German military intelligence (Abwehr) also reported rumors of Allied plans for landings in the Canary Islands and Azores in preparation for a landing in Dakar, French West Africa.

13. Piece 958, October 8, 1942, British Public Record Office, Kew, HW–1.

14. Michael Howard, *Strategic Deception*, vol. 5 of *British Intelligence in the Second World War* (New York: Cambridge University Press, 1990), pp. 55–60.

15. Anthony Cave Brown, *Bodyguard of Lies* (New York: Harper & Row, 1975), p. 233.
16. Howard, *Strategic Deception*, p. 60.
17. Howard, *Strategic Deception*, p. 61.
18. Howard, *Strategic Deception*, p. 62.
19. Brown, *Bodyguard of Lies*, p. 234.
20. HW–1. Piece 555, British Public Record Office, Kew.
21. André Brissaud, *Canaris* (New York: Grosset & Dunlap, 1974), p. 281.
22. Brissaud, p. 284.
23. Roger Manvell and Heinrich Fraenkel, *The Canaris Conspiracy* (New York: David McKay, 1969), p. 91.
24. Hinsley and Simkins, *Security and Counter-Intelligence*, p. 301.
25. Anthony Cave Brown, *The Last Hero* (New York: Times Books, 1982), p. 252. Carleton S. Coon, *A North African Story* (Ipswich, Mass.: Gambit, 1980), p. 14.
26. HW–1, Piece 1729, British Public Record Office, Kew,
27. Brissaud, *Canaris*, p. 287.
28. They were in Donovan's short-lived coordinator of information (COI) organization, a predecessor of the OSS.
29. HW–1, Piece 79, September 18, 1941, British Public Record Office, Kew.
30. Ibid.
31. Brown, *The Last Hero*, p. 230.
32. Piece 162, British Public Record Office, Kew, HW 1.
33. Spanish telegrams, Madrid to Washington, number 613, November 10, 1942. OSS, General Donovan Papers, Carlisle Barracks, Pennsylvania.
34. Brown, *The Last Hero*, p. 231.
35. Ibid.
36. Robin W. Winks, *Cloak and Gown* (New York: William Morrow, 1987), p. 194. Also see Brown, *The Last Hero*, p. 225; Norman Holmes Pearson Papers, Beinecke Library, Yale University; Record Group 226, Entry 115, Box 35, Folder 1[3], OSS Archives, National Archives.
37. Winks, p. 202.
38. Winks, p. 198.
39. Aline, Countess of Romanoes, "The OSS In Spain During World War II," *The Secrets War*, ed. George Chalou (Washington, D.C.: U.S. National Archives Trust Fund Board, 1992).
40. Record Group 226, Entry 128 A, Giraud, National Archives.
41. HW–1, Piece 932, September 1942, British Public Record Office, Kew.
42. Brissaud, *Canaris*, p. 274. From Lahousen's testimony at the Nuremberg International War Crimes Tribunal.
43. Richard Deacon, *A History of the British Secret Service* (London: Panther/ Grenada, 1980), pp. 420, 421.
44. Deacon, p. 421.
45. Special Collections Department, Anthony Cave Brown Papers, Box 4. Georgetown University Lavinger Memorial Library, Washington, D.C., Directive No. 19, Operation Attila, Top Secret, Eyes Only (declassified), "The Supreme

Commander of the Wehrmacht, Fuehrer Hqs, 10 December, 1940, OKW/ WFSt/Abt. L NR, 33 400/40 g.k. Chefs."

46. Brissaud, *Canaris*, p. 291.

K. H. Abshagen, *Canaris* (London: Hutchinson, 1956), pp. 214, 215.

47. HW–1, Piece 929, July 23, 1942, British Public Record Office, Kew.

48. HW–1, Piece 1137, British Public Record Office, Kew.

Bruce Lee, *Marching Orders* (New York: Crown Publishers, 1995), p. 46, describing how the "hinge of fate" turned at the Battle of Stalingrad, ending Germany's and Japan's plan to "divide the world."

49. William Henhoeffer, *The Intelligence War in 1941* (Washington, D.C.: CIA Center for the Study of Intelligence, 1992), pp. 17, 19.

50. Brissaud, *Canaris*, p. 231.

51. Havas, French News Agency, August 20, 1939.

52. Peter Tompkins, *The Murder of Admiral Darlan* (New York: Simon & Schuster, 1965), pp. 185, 187.

53. Frederick W. Winterbotham, *The Ultra Secret* (London: Weidenfeld & Nicolson, 1974), p. 99.

54. Winterbotham, p. 216.

55. Winterbotham, pp. 28, 29.

56. Mark Wayne Clark, *Calculated Risk* (New York: Harper & Brothers, 1950), p. 130.

57. HW–1, Piece 1078, British Public Record Office, Kew.

58. HW–1, Piece 1137, British Public Record Office, Kew.

59. Winston Churchill, *The Hinge of Fate*, vol. 4 of *The Second World War* (London: Reprint Society, 1954), p. 519.

60. Tompkins, *The Murder of Admiral Darlan*, p. 236.

61. Churchill, *Hinge of Fate*, p. 547.

Chapter 24. Allen Dulles: Superstar

1. Allen Dulles, *The Craft of Intelligence* (New York: Harper & Row, 1963), p. 203.

2. Donovan Papers, OSS telegram 8/9, Donovan to Dulles, April 29, 1943, OSSDC (OSS Director Cables), per Anthony Cave Brown, *The Last Hero* (New York: Times Books, 1982), p. 277.

3. Brown, *The Last Hero*, p. 277, from the Donovan Papers.

4. Neal H. Petersen, "From Hitler's Doorstep: Allen Dulles and the Penetration of Nazi Germany," *The Secrets War*, ed. George C. Chalou (Washington D.C.: National Archives Trust Fund Board 1992), p. 278.

5. Phillip Knightley, *The Master Spy* (New York: Knopf, 1989), p. 106.

6. Anthony Quibble, "Alias George Wood," *Studies in Intelligence* (Winter 1966).

7. Record Group 226, OSS telegram 651–652, August 25, 1943, Box 273, Entry 134; Record Group 226, OSS telegram 654–657, August 26, 1943, Box 339, Entry 134; National Archives.

8. Brown, *The Last Hero*, pp. 278, 279.

9. Petersen, "From Hitler's Doorstep," p. 278.
10. Brown, *The Last Hero*, p. 279. From the Donovan Papers, Memo F.L. Belin to William Donovan, October 12, 1943, in Belin Reports 12,784, October 12, 1943, OSSDF (Office of the Director of the COI and OSS, William Donovan).
11. Brown, *The Last Hero*, p. 280. From the Donovan Papers, Telegram 1477/79, December 29, 1943, OSSDC (OSS Director Cables).
12. Quibble, "Alias George Wood," p. 77.
13. Quibble, p. 82.
14. Quibble, p. 84.
15. Klemens von Klemperer, *German Resistance Against Hitler* (Oxford: Oxford Clarendon Press, 1992), p. 246.
16. Quibble, "Alias George Wood," p. 85.
    Roger Manvell and Heinrich Fraenkel, *The Canaris Conspiracy* (New York: David McKay, 1969), p. 174.
17. Quibble, "Alias George Wood," p. 85.
18. Quibble, pp. 86, 87.
19. Anthony Cave Brown, *Bodyguard of Lies* (New York: Quill/William Morrow, 1991), p. 310.
20. Allen Dulles, *Germany's Underground* (New York: Macmillan, 1947), p. 127.
21. Records Group 226, Entry 134: Telegram 723, January 31, 1943, Box 171; and Telegram 967, February 11, 1943, Box 307; National Archives.
22. Manvell and Fraenkel, *Canaris Conspiracy*, p. 174.
23. Klemperer, *German Resistance*, p. 327.

Chapter 25. Moltke's Mission

1. Heinz Höhne, *Canaris* (Garden City, N.Y.: Doubleday, 1979), pp. 483, 484.
2. Höhne, p. 484. From Peter Hoffmann, *Widerstand, Staatsstreich, Attentat* (Munich: 1970), pp. 278.
3. Klemens von Klemperer, *German Resistance Against Hitler* (Oxford: Oxford Clarendon Press, 1992), p. 333.
4. Jürgen Heideking and Christof Mauch, *The USA and the German Resistance* (Tübingen, Germany: A. Franke Verlag, 1993), as reviewed and excerpted in *World Intelligence Review*, vol. 13, no. 6 (1994), p. 5.
5. Record Group 226, Entry 180, A 3304, Roll 68, National Archives.
6. RG 226, Entry 190, M–1462, Roll 52, Frame 307, National Archives.
7. RG 226, Entry 190, M–1462, Roll 52, Frames 314–319, National Archives.
8. Ibid.
9. RG 226, Entry 190, M–1642, Roll 52, Frame 320, National Archives.
10. RG 226, Entry 190 M–1462, Roll 52, Frame 321; Document 4a, Kirk to Tindall, January 10, 1944; National Archives.
11. David K. E. Bruce, *OSS Against the Reich*, ed. Nelson D. Lankford (Kent, Ohio: Kent State University, 1991), p. 30.
12. Ibid.
13. RG 226, Entry 110, Box 47, Folder 3, Document 14, National Archives.

14. Ibid.
15. Ibid.
16. RG 226, Entry I90, A-3304, Roll 68, National Archives.
17. RG 226, Entry 190, M-1462, Roll 52, Frame 3, 47–350, National Archives.
18. Sir Alexander Cadogan, *The Diaries of Sir Alexander Cadogan, 1938–1945*, ed. David Dilks (New York: G. P. Putnam's, 1972), p. 562.
19. André Brissaud, *Canaris* (New York: Grosset & Dunlap, 1974), pp. 314, 315.
20. Timothy J. Naftali, "X-2 *and the Apprenticeship of American Counter-espionage, 1942–1944*, vols. 1 and 2, dissertation, Harvard University, 1993, pp. 489–502 (Ann Arbor: UMI Dissertation Service, 1994).

Chapter 26. Images of Treachery

1. Frederick W. Winterbotham, *Secret and Personal* (London: William Kimber, 1969), p. 162.
2. R. Harris Smith, *OSS* (Berkeley: University of California Press, 1972), pp. 210, 211.
3. Heinz Höhne, *Canaris* (Garden City, N.Y.: Doubleday, 1979), pp. 338, 339.
4. Höhne, p. 340. From Bernd Martin, *Friedensinitiativen und Macht Politik im Zweiten* (Düsseldorf: 1974).
5. Höhne, p. 343.
6. Höhne, p. 346.
7. Ulrich Blennemann, "German-Soviet Peace Talks, 1941–44," *Command*, issue 22 (May–June 1993), p. 9.
8. Klemens von Klemperer, *German Resistance Against Hitler* (Oxford: Oxford Clarendon Press, 1992), p. 245.
9. Klemperer, p. 479.
10. Höhne, *Canaris*, p. 480.
11. Klemperer, *German Resistance*, p. 245.
12. Walter Schellenberg, *Hitler's Secret Service*, tr. Louis Hagen, 2d ed. (New York: Pyramid, 1962), pp. 148, 149.
13. Schellenberg, pp. 158, 159.
14. Schellenberg, p. 163.
15. Peter Padfield, *Himmler* (New York: Henry Holt, 1990), pp. 416, 427.
16. Padfield, p. 427.
17. Walter Schellenberg, *Hitler's Secret Service*, p. 166.
18. Schellenberg, p. 167.
19. Ibid.
20. Ibid.
21. Wilhelm Hoettl, *The Secret Front* (London: Weidenfeld & Nicolson, 1953), p. 302.
22. Hoettl, p. 302. From Gilles Perrault, *The Red Orchestra* (New York: Schocken Books, 1969).
23. Perrault, p. 442.
24. Perrault, p. 439.

25. Ibid.
26. Paul Leverkuehn, *German Military Intelligence* (New York: Praeger, 1954), p. 197.
27. Walter Schellenberg, *The Labyrinth* [aka *Hitler's Secret Service*] (New York: Harper & Brothers, 1956), pp. 316–321.

   Reinhard Gehlen, *The Service* (New York: World Publishing, 1972), pp. 70, 71.
28. OSS Document 170 (3-29), Bern Station telegram 2183-85, February 24, 1944. National Archives.
29. Leopold Trepper, *The Great Game* (New York: McGraw-Hill, 1977), p. 264.
30. Trepper, pp. 264–267.
31. Trepper, p. 46.
32. *International History Project from the Russian Archives*, issue 3 (Fall 1993), pp. 76, 77. Cites R. C. Raad, "Stalin Plans His Post-War Germany," *Journal of Contemporary History*, vol. 28 (1933), pp. 52–73.
33. Phillip Knightly, *The Master Spy* (New York: Knopf, 1989), p. 109. From MI-5 officers in 1988 who based their information on comments made by turncoat "Kim" Philby.
34. FO/371/34414/ C 8626/29/18 and FO/372/34416/ C 14723/29/18, British Public Record Office.
35. RG 226, Telegrams 763–767, September 21, 1943, Box 273. Entry 134, National Archives.
36. Klemperer, *German Resistance*, pp. 174, 175.
37. Klemperer, p. 248.

Chapter 27. An Unraveling

1. Allen Dulles, *Germany's Underground* (New York: Macmillan, 1947), pp. 126, 127.

   Also refer to: Jozef Garlinski, *The Swiss Corridor* (London: J. M. Dent 1959), pp. 84–97.

   Klemens von Klemperer, *German Resistance Against Hitler* (Oxford: Oxford Clarendon Press, 1992), p. 193.

   Ian Colvin, *Canaris, Chief of Intelligence* (Maidstone, England: George Mann Publishers, 1972), pp. 90–92.
2. Anthony Read and David Fisher, *Colonel Z* (New York: Viking Press, 1985), p. 241.
3. Hans Bernd Gisevius, *To the Bitter End* (Boston: Houghton Mifflin, 1947), pp. 480, 481.
4. Anthony Cave Brown, *The Last Hero* (New York: Times Books, 1982), p. 288. From OSS Telegram 181, London to Bern, July 31, 1943, OSSDC, Donovan Papers, Carlisle Barracks, Pa.
5. Ibid. From OSS telegram 198, London to Bern, August 11, 1943, OSSDC.
6. Brown, p. 290.
7. Karl Bartz, *The Downfall of the German Secret Service* (London: William Kimber, 1956), pp. 96–129.

8. Gisevius, *To the Bitter End*, p. 476.
9. Roger Manvell and Heinrich Fraenkel, *The Canaris Conspiracy* (New York: David McKay, Inc., 1969), p. 136.
10. Gisevius, *To the Bitter End*, p. 478.
11. Manvell and Fraenkel, *Canaris Conspiracy*, pp. 148, 149.
    Bartz, *Downfall of German Secret Service*, pp. 113–119.
12. Fabian von Schlabrendorff, *The Secret War Against Hitler* (New York: Pittman, 1965), p. 169.
13. Schlabrendorff, *Secret War*, p. 169.
14. Heinz Höhne, *Canaris* (Garden City, N.Y.: Doubleday, 1979), p. 466.
15. Höhne, *Canaris*, p. 466.
16. Gisevius, *To the Bitter End*, p. 477.
17. Bartz, *Downfall of German Secret Service*, pp. 115–117.
    Manvell and Fraenkel, *Canaris Conspiracy*, pp. 149–151.
18. Manvell and Fraenkel, p. 163.
19. Ibid.
20. Klemperer, *German Resistance*, p. 320.
21. Record Group 226, Document 134, Telegram 1890–93, January 27, 1944, National Archives.
22. Ibid.
23. RG 226, Telegram 1890–1893, January 27, 1944, Box 2, Entry 138; Telegram 1965–1966, February 4, 1944, Box 228, Entry 134; Flash Message, February 19, 1944, Box 273, Entry 134, National Archives.
24. RG 226, Telegram 1023–1028, November 9, 1943, Box 341, Entry 134, National Archives.
25. Ibid.
26. RG 226, Telegram 2714–2716, April 6, 1944, Box 307; Telegram 2718–2722, April 7, 1944, Box 228; Telegram 2423–3431, May 31, 1944, Box 228, Entry 134; National Archives.
27. RG 226, Entry 138, B–2, February 27, 1944, National Archives.

Chapter 28. Exit Canaris

1. André Brissaud, *Canaris* (New York: Grosset & Dunlap, 1973), p. 305.
2. Charles Foltz, Jr., *The Masquerade in Spain* (Boston, Cambridge: Houghton Mifflin/The Riverside Press, 1948), p. 49.
3. Howard Smyth, "The Ciano Papers: Rose Garden," *Studies in Intelligence* (Spring 1969).
4. K. H. Abshagen, *Canaris* (London: Hutchinson, 1956), p. 217.
5. Smyth, "The Ciano Papers."
6. Ibid.
7. Brissaud, *Canaris*, p. 306.
8. Abshagen, *Canaris*, pp. 220, 221.
9. Wilhelm Hoettl, *The Secret Front*, tr. R. H. Stevens (New York: Frederick A. Praeger, 1954), pp. 221, 223.
10. Brissaud, *Canaris*, p. 308.

11. Brissaud, p. 309.
12. Abshagen, *Canaris*, pp. 220, 221.
13. Ibid.
14. Smyth, "The Ciano Papers."
15. Record Group 226, Entry 124, Box 22, 3/7/45 title: OSS HQ Detachment, 2677 Regt. Italian Division, SI MEDTO. National Archives.
16. Brissaud, *Canaris*, p. 312.
17. Record Group 226, Telegram 2173–2175, February 24, 1944, Box 274, Entry 134, National Archives.
18. RG 226, Entry 134, Telegram 2173–75, February 24, 1944, National Archives.
19. RG 226, OSS Donovan to OSS, X-2 Stations, March 1, 1944, Entry 121, Box 4, National Archives.
20. J. C. Masterman, *The Double-Cross System in the War of 1939–1945* (New Haven: Yale University Press, 1972), pp. 149–155.
21. Klemens von Klemperer, *German Resistance Against Hitler* (Oxford: Oxford Clarendon Press, 1992), fn. 134, p. 406.
22. RG 226, Entry 134, Box 275, telegram 2160, February 22, 1944, National Archives.
23. Dusko Popov, *Spy/Counter-Spy* (Greenwich, Conn.: Fawcett, 1975), p. 232.
24. Peter Padfield, *Himmler* (New York: Henry Holt, 1990), p. 480.
25. Heinz Höhne, *Canaris* (New York: Doubleday, 1976), pp. 509, 510.
26. RG 226, Entry 134, Telegram 2173–75, February 24, 1944, National Archives.

Chapter 29. Canaris and Himmler: An Odd Couple

1. Richard Deacon, *A History of the British Secret Service* (London: Granada/Panther, 1982), p. 310.
2. OSS message SA-8560, from Hugh R. Wilson to Colonel Butler dated July 9, 1942, Georgetown University Lauinger Memorial Library, Special Collections Department, Anthony Cave Brown Papers, Box 4.
3. Hugh Trevor-Roper, *The Philby Affair* (London: William Kimber, 1968), p. 104.
4. Trevor-Roper, p. 108.
5. Heinz Höhne, *Canaris* (Garden City, N.Y.: Doubleday, 1979), p. 509.
6. André Brissaud, *Canaris* (New York: Grosset & Dunlap, 1974), pp. 181–183.
7. Harold C. Deutsch, *The Conspiracy Against Hitler* (Minneapolis: University of Minnesota Press, 1968), pp. 129–134.
8. Deutsch, p. 355, fn. 7.
9. Höhne, *Canaris*, p. 589, per fn. 187. From remarks made by Huppenkothen, February 4, 1951, during his postwar trial.
10. Ian Colvin, *Canaris, Chief of Intelligence* (Maidstone, England: George Mann, Publishers, 1973), p. 132.
11. Höhne, *Canaris*, p. 508. From Franz Xaver Sonderegger deposition, Aug. 31, 1950, vol. 9, p. 299. L St A, pp. 246, 248, 250, 299.
12. Höhne, *Canaris*, p. 508. From Josef Müller, *Biz sur letzten Konsequenz*, p. 214.
13. Höhne, p. 508.
14. K.H. Abshagen, *Canaris* (London: Hutchinson, 1956), p. 228.

15. Peter Padfield, *Himmler* (New York: Henry Holt, 1990), p. 360.
16. Padfield, p. 360, fn. 52.
17. Padfield, p. 361.
18. Mary Bancroft, *Autobiography of a Spy* (New York: William Morrow, 1983), p. 191.
19. Hans Bernd Gisevius, *To the Bitter End* (Boston: Houghton Mifflin, 1947), p. 139.
20. Brissaud, *Canaris*, p. 312.
21. Ibid.
22. Lord Moran, *The Diaries of Lord Moran* (Boston: Houghton Mifflin, 1966), p. 141.
    William B. Breuer, *Hoodwinking Hitler* (Westport, Conn.: Praeger, 1993), p. 20.
23. Gilles Perrault, *The Red Orchestra* (New York: Schocken Books, 1969). p. 443 fn.
24. Klemens von Klemperer, *German Resistance Against Hitler* (Oxford: Oxford Clarendon Press, 1992), p. 326; fn. 77, p. 402.
25. Abshagen, *Canaris*, p. 229.
26. Allen Dulles, *Germany's Underground* (New York: Macmillan, 1947), pp. 157, 158.
27. Klemperer, *German Resistance*, p. 402, fn. 78
28. Ibid, fn. 79.
29. Annedore Leber, ed. *The Conscience in Revolt*, re-ed. Karl Dietrich Brocher (Munich: v. Hase & Koehler, 1994), p. 372.
30. Dulles, *Germany's Underground*, p. 161.
31. Abshagen, *Canaris*, p. 229.
32. Höhne, *Canaris*, p. 510.
    Brissaud, *Canaris*, p. 248.
33. Brissaud, *Canaris*, p. 249.
34. Dulles, *Germany's Underground*, pp. 162, 163. Dulles's source of this information was given as a conversation with Langbehn's friend Marie-Louise Sarre.
35. Wilhelm Hoettl, *The Secret Front* (New York: Praeger, 1954), pp. 74, 75.
36. Höhne, *Canaris*, pp. 508, 509.
37. Record Group 226, OSS Official Dispatch from Bern dated March 6, 1944, National Archives.
38. Fabian von Schlabrendorff, *The Secret War Against Hitler* (London: Hodder and Stoughton, 1966), p. 273.
39. Dulles, *Germany's Underground*, p. 4.

Chapter 30. Operation Valkyrie

1. Roger Manvell and Heinrich Fraenkel, *The Canaris Conspiracy* (New York: David McKay, 1969), pp. 96, 97. From: Ulrich von Hassell, *The von Hassell Diaries* (Garden City: Doubleday, 1947), pp. 219, 220.
2. André Brissaud, *Canaris* (Garden City, N.Y.: Grosset & Dunlap, 1974), p. 297.

3. Ibid.
4. Fabian von Schlabrendorff, *The Secret War Against Hitler* (London: Hodder & Stoughton, 1966), p. 228.
5. Allen Dulles, *Germany's Underground* (New York: Macmillan, 1947), pp. 140, 141.
6. Anthony Cave Brown, *Bodyguard of Lies* (New York: Quill/William Morrow, 1991), p. 301.
7. CIA Counter-Intelligence staff, *The Rote Kapelle*, vol. 1, December 1973.
8. Joachim Kramarz, *Stauffenberg* (New York: Macmillan, 1967), pp. 176–178.
9. Kramarz, p. 9.
10. Yaroslav Kaspar-Páty, "Report of a Major of the General Staff, Yaroslav Kaspar-Páty," *Today*, weekly magazine section of the Prague daily newspaper *Young Front Today*, January 20, 1994. (As submitted during the war to colonel of the General Staff, F. Morevec, in London, July 6, 1943.)
11. Kramarz, *Stauffenberg*, pp. 180, 181. From Hans Speidel, *We Defended Normandy* (London: Herbert Jenkins 1951), p. 127.
12. Gero v. S. Gaevernitz, *They Almost Killed Hitler* (New York: Macmillan, 1947), p. 103.
13. Peter Hoffmann, *The History of the German Resistance to Hitler, 1933–1945* (Cambridge, Mass.: Harvard University Press, 1988), pp. 103, 104.
14. Hans Bernd Gisevius, *To the Bitter End* (Boston: Houghton Mifflin, 1947) p. 518.
15. Kramarz, *Stauffenberg*, p. 176.
16. Hoffmann, *German Resistance*, p. 102.
17. Kramarz, *Stauffenberg*, p. 150.
18. There existed an official Nazi plan, code-named Valkyrie, whose purpose was to restore order in Germany in the event of an uprising against Hitler or some other political disorder. The Resistance believed that to use the same name for its planned uprising lent an element of security should some of its documentation fall into the wrong hands.
19. Kramarz, *Stauffenberg*, pp. 176, 177.
20. Kramarz, p. 117.
21. Hoffmann, *German Resistance*, p. 239.
22. Gisevius, *To the Bitter End*, p. 502.
23. Gisevius, p. 503.
24. Kramarz, *Stauffenberg*, p. 129.
25. Peter Hoffmann, *Claus Schenk Graf von Stauffenberg und seine Brüder* (Stuttgart: Deutsche Verlags-Anstalt, 1992), pp. 356, 357.
26. Gisevius, *To the Bitter End*, p. 509.
27. Hoffmann, *German Resistance*, p. 244. From verbal account given the author by Countess Nina von Stauffenberg, August 23, 1969.
28. Hoffmann, *German Resistance*, p. 398.
29. Kramarz, *Stauffenberg*, pp. 186, 187. From Adolf Heusinger, *Befehl im Widerstreit* (Tübingen: Wunderlich, 1950), p. 354.
30. Interrogation of General der Fleiges Bodenschatz, May 15, 1945. Document CSDIC Report SRGG 1219 (c). Georgetown University Lauinger Memorial Library, Special Collections Department, Anthony Cave Brown Papers, Box 4.

31. Interrogation of General Friedrich Dollmann. Document CSDIC, Report SRGG 1219 (c). Georgetown University Lauinger Memorial Library, Special Collections Department, Anthony Cave Brown Papers, Box 4.

Chapter 31. Reprisal and Retribution

1. Peter Hoffmann, *The History of the German Resistance to Hitler, 1933–1945* (Cambridge, Mass.: Harvard University Press, 1988) p. 416.
2. Heinz Höhne, *Canaris* (New York: Doubleday, 1976), p. 566.
3. Hoffmann, *German Resistance*, p. 418.
4. Hoffmann, p. 422, fn. 57.
5. Allen Dulles, *Germany's Underground* (New York: Macmillan, 1947), p. 184.
6. Fabian von Schlabrendorff, *The Secret War Against Hitler* (New York: Pittman, 1965), p. 294.
7. Hoffmann, *German Resistance*, p. 475, fn. 73.
8. Dulles, *Germany's Underground*, p. 188 fn.
9. Frederick W. Winterbotham, *The Ultra Secret* (London: Weidenfeld & Nicolson, 1974), p. 158.
10. Otto E. Moll, *The German Generalfieldmarshals, 1934–1945*, rev. Wolfgang W. Marek (Frankfurt: Erich Pabel, 1991).
11. "Account of the Twentieth of July Putsch by One of the Minor Conspirators, 2 May 1945, CS/2222, General of Infantry Blumentritt, BRGG 1347." Interrogation of General Blumentritt, CSDIC. Georgetown University Lauinger Memorial Library, Special Collections Department, Anthony Cave Brown Papers, Box 4.
12. Dulles, *Germany's Underground*, p. 188.
13. Hoffmann, *German Resistance*, p. 503.
14. Hoffmann, Chapter 45, fn. 117. From Heinz Buchholz, "Das Attentat auf Adolf Hitler am 20 July 1944," typescript, Berchtesgaden Interrogations, University of Pennsylvania Library 46M–25.
15. Klemens von Klemperer, *German Resistance Against Hitler* (Oxford: Oxford Clarendon Press, 1992), p. 394.
16. Dulles, *Germany's Underground*, pp. 145, 146.
17. Marie Vassiltchikov, *Berlin Diaries 1940–1945* (New York: Vintage Books, 1988), p. 211.
18. Peter Padfield, *Himmler* (New York: Henry Holt, 1990), p. 545.
19. Padfield, pp. 545–547.
20. Klemperer, *German Resistance* p. 395.
21. Dulles, *Germany's Underground*, p. 164.
22. Klemperer, *German Resistance*, p. 38, fn. 437
    Breakers series of reports from USS Bern, Record Group 226, Cable 4199–4200 01-02, National Archives.
23. Klemperer, *German Resistance*, p. 384.
    Schlabrendorff, *Secret War*, p. 227.
24. Klemperer, *German Resistance*, p. 386, fn. 473. From William J. Donovan, director, memo for the secretary of state (also to FDR and Marshall), July 24, 1944. Record Group 226, Entry 99, Box 14, National Archives.

25. William J. Donovan, director, memorandum for the president, July 22, 1944, FDR Library, DSF 168.
26. Louis Lochner, *Always the Unexpected* (New York: Macmillan 1956), p. 294.
27. Record Group 226, Entry 092, Box 51, Folder 08, National Archives.
28. *The New York Times*, August 9, 1944.
29. "International Swine," *The New York Herald Tribune*, August 9, 1944.
30. Klemperer, *German Resistance*, p. 387, fn. 484.
31. Baron Oliver Harvey, *The War Diaries of Oliver Harvey 1941–1945*, ed. John Harvey (London: 1978), p. 368.
32. Parliamentary Debates, 5th Series, vol. 402, House of Commons, 8th volume of session, 1943/44 (London: 1944), col. 1487.
33. Diaries of Robert Bruce Lockhart, War Notebook, 1944. Index # 176, File 313, House of Lords Record Office.
34. "International Review," *Pravda*, July 23 and 30, 1944.
35. Klemperer, *German Resistance*, p. 390, fn. 505.
36. Ibid.
37. K. H. Abshagen, *Canaris* (London: Hutchinson, 1956), p. 242.
38. Roger Manvell and Heinrich Fraenkel, *The Canaris Conspiracy* (New York: David McKay, 1969), pp. 241, 242.
39. Manvell and Fraenkel, pp. 194, 198, fn. 8.
40. Manvell and Fraenkel, p. 195.
41. Manvell and Fraenkel, p. 197.

Chapter 32. Dulles Plays the Field

1. Leonard Mosley, *Dulles* (New York: Dial Press, 1978), p. 73.
2. Arthur Schlesinger, Jr., "The London Operation," *The Secrets War*, ed. George C. Chalon (Washington D.C.: National Archives Trust Fund Board, 1992), p. 65.
3. Flora Lewis, *Red Pawn* (Garden City N.Y.: Doubleday, 1965), p. 266.
4. Jeffrey A. Frank, "The Unending Trial of Alger Hiss," *The Washington Post*, October 29, 1993, p. B-4.
   Maria Schmidt, "The Hiss Dossier," *The New Republic*, vol. 209, no. 19 (November 8, 1993), pp 7–20.
   Sam Tanenhaus, "Hiss: Guilty as Charged," *Commentary*, vol. 95, no. 4 (April 1993) pp. 32–7.
   Sam Tanenhaus, "Hiss Case, Smoking Gun?" *The New York Times*, October 15, 1993, p. A-35, op-ed.
5. Tanenhaus, "Smoking Gun?"
   Lewis, *Red Pawn*, p. 59.
6. Lewis, *Red Pawn*, pp. 184, 185.
7. Erika Glaser Wallach died on December 24, 1993. *The Washington Post*, obituaries, December 24, 1993, p. B-5.
8. Lewis, *Red Pawn*, pp. 160, 161.
9. CIA Counter-Intelligence Staff, "The Background of Joseph Wirth," *Rote Kapelle*, vol. 9, chap. 21, December 1973.

10. Allen Dulles, *Germany's Underground* (New York: Macmillan, 1947), pp. 59, 60.
11. CIA Counter-Intelligence Staff, "The Background of Josef Wirth," pp. 209–213.
12. CIA Counter-Intelligence Staff, p. 222.
13. Joachim Kramarz, *Stauffenberg* (New York: Macmillan, 1967), p. 150.
14. CIA Counter-Intelligence Staff, "Joseph Wirth," p. 222.
15. Record Group 226, OSS document 70, telegram from Bern to Washington no. 1151–53, National Archives.
16. CIA Counter-Intelligence Staff, "Joseph Wirth," p. 223.
17. Ibid.
18. Allen Dulles, *Germany's Underground*, p. 25.
19. CIA Counter-Intelligence Staff, "Joseph Wirth," p. 223.

Chapter 33. Sunrise

1. Gisevius's accounts of the July 20 bomb plot, transmitted by Dulles to Washington OSS, can be found in the National Archives, Record Group 226, Box 14, Entry 99. Some of the other Dulles messages on this subject are identified as follows: Record Group 226: Telegram 847–848, July 21, 1944, Box 276; Flash Message, July 21, 1944, Box 273; Telegram 4199–4202, July 22, 1944, Box 228; Flash Message, July 22, 1944, Entry 134, Box 273.
2. Allen Dulles, *The Secret Surrender* (New York: Harper & Row, 1966), p. 43.
3. Dulles, pp. 44, 45.
4. Dulles, pp. 45, 46.
5. Alexander Neurath was the son of Baron Konstantin von Neurath, former foreign minister, preceding Ribbentrop in Hitler's cabinet.
6. Documents in the National Archives bearing on subject include Record Group 226: Telegram 1757, December 5, 1944, Box 277, Entry 134; Telegram 2769, Janaury 19, 1945, Box 7, Entry 90; Telegram 360, February 9, 1945, Box 60, Entry 139. Box 19, Entry 21.
7. Memorandum for General Donovan from President Roosevelt of December 1944, RG 226, National Archives.

   John Goshko, "Roosevelt Memo Barred Protection for Nazis," *The Washington Post*, May 28, 1987.

   Memorandum for the President from William Donovan, December 1, 1944. Declassified from Secret on May 26, 1987, MND-750120. RG226, National Archives.

   Washington Office Director of OSS microfilm M-1642, Roll 81.
8. Record Group 226, Telegram Donovan to Dulles, of February 27, 1944, Entry 138, Box 2, National Archives.
9. Record Group 226: Telegram 6097, February 28, 1945, Box 228, Entry 134, Telegram 6209, March 2, 1945, Box 6, Entry 190. Telegram 6210, March 4, 1945, Box 7, Entry 90. National Archives.
10. Wilhelm Hoettl, *The Secret Front*, tr. R.H. Stevens (New York: Praeger, 1954), pp. 284, 285.
11. "Kaltenbrunner's Last Days," *Studies in Intelligence* (Spring 1960), p. A-27.

12. Telegram 8139, April 5, 1945. Record Group 226, Box 2, Entry 110, National Archives.
13. Walter Schellenberg, *Hitler's Secret Service*, tr. Louis Magen, 2d ed. (New York: Pyramid, 1962), p. 193.
14. Schellenberg, p. 195.
15. Schellenberg, p. 196.
16. OSS Dispatch 221 of October 5, 1944, from Bern. National Archives, RG 226.
17. Neal H. Petersen, "From Hitler's Doorstep: Allen Dulles and The Penetration of Germany." *The Secrets War*, ed. George C. Chalon (Washington, D.C.: National Archives Trust Fund Board, 1992), p. 293. See footnote 54 for a list of Dulles cables on the redoubt held in the National Archives.
18. Janusz Piekalkiewicz, *Secret Agents, Spies and Saboteurs* (New York: William Morrow, 1973), p. 514.
19. Piekalkiewicz, p. 515.
20. Joseph Goebbels, *Final Entries 1945*, ed. Hugh Trevor-Roper (New York: G. P. Putnam's, 1978), p. 311.
21. Record Group 226 sources on the German National Redoubt plan: Telegram 6761, October 29, 1943, Box 273, Entry 134; Telegram 4471-4473, August 12, 1944, Box 191, Entry 134; Flash, January 18, 1945, Box 1, Entry 160; Flash, January 22, 1945, Box 1, Entry 160; Flash, February 13, 1945, Box 1, Entry 160; Flash, March 3, 1945, Box 1, Entry 160; Flash, March 16, 1945, Box 1, Entry 160; Flash, March 17, 1945, Box 1, Entry 160; Telegram 8349, April 6, 1945, Box 7, Entry 90; Flash, April 18, 1945, Box 1, Entry 160. National Archives.
    "Memorada for the President," *Studies in Intelligence* (Spring 1963). Intelligence cables covering the capitulations of the Nazi armies in northern Italy.
    Michael Howard, *Strategic Deception*, vol. 5 of *British Intelligence in the Second World War* (New York: Cambridge University Press, 1990), pp. 194–195.
    Joseph E. Persico, *Piercing the Reich* (New York: Viking Press, 1979), pp. 281–297.
    Dulles, *Secret Surrender*, pp. 149–151.
    George C. Chalou, ed. *The Secrets War* (Washington D.C. National Archives Trust Fund Board, 1992), p. 286.
    Hoettl, *Secret Front*, pp. 281–294.
22. The British designation was Operation Crossword.
23. "Memoranda for the President," p. 78. See memorandum dated March 8, 1945.
24. HW-1, No. 942, "Portuguese Report on Mission of Myron Taylor to Vatican," September 28, 1942, British Public Record Office, Kew.
25. Felix Gilbert, annotator, *Hitler Directs His War* (New York: Oxford University Press, 1950), p. 53. From manuscripts in the University of Pennsylvania Library
26. Gilbert, p. 71.
27. Georg Giese, "Wolff, I Want the Vatican," *Neue Bildpost*, May 5, 1974, p. 6. Based on interviews with Karl Wolff.
28. Ibid.

29. Georg Giese "The Man Who Was to Abduct the Pope," *Neue Bildpost*, May 12, 1974.
30. Ibid. Also see Richard Lamb, *War in Italy* (New York: St. Martin's Press, 1993), pp. 44–46.
31. Dulles, *Secret Surrender*, pp. 61, 62. From (Milan) *Tempo*, vol. 13, no. 8 (February 24, 1951).
32. Dulles, *Secret Surrender*, p. 63.
33. Dulles, pp. 63, 64.
34. Dulles, p. 77.
35. Dulles, p. 96.
36. Dulles, pp. 96, 97.
37. Dulles, pp. 147–149.
38. "Memoranda for the President." Donovan memorandum for the President, dated March 21, 1945.
39. Dulles, *Secret Surrender*, p. 149.
40. Lamb, *War in Italy*, p. 296.
    Dulles, *Secret Surrender*, p. 149.
41. Anthony Cave Brown, "*C*" (New York: Macmillan, 1987), p. 658.
42. Prem 3 198/2, telegram Roosevelt to Churchill, April 5, 1945. British Public Record Office, Kew.
43. Dulles, *Secret Surrender*, p. 150.
44. Ibid.
45. Kim Philby, *My Silent War* (New York: Grove Press, 1968), p. 102.
    Also see Hugh Trevor-Roper, *The Philby Affair* (London: William Kimber, 1968), pp. 78, 79.
46. Phillip Knightly, *The Master Spy* (New York: Knopf, 1989), pp. 107–109.
47. Brown, "*C*", p. 659.
48. Brown, "*C*", pp. 659, 660.
49. Sir Alexander Cadogan, *The Diaries of Alexander Cadogan; 1938–1945*, ed. David Dilks (New York: G. P. Putnam's, 1972), p. 726.
50. Stephen S. Rosenfield, "An Earlier Tilt Toward Moscow," *The Washington Post*, November 26, 1993, p. A 31. From an article by William Larsh in *Eastern European Politics and Societies*, Journal of the University of California at Berkeley, 1993. Based on Harriman's hitherto unreleased personal papers.
51. Ibid.
52. "Memoranda for the President," pp. 84, 85. From William Donovan, dated March 13, 1945.
53. "Memoranda for the President," p. 85.
54. "Memoranda for the President," pp. 84, 85.
55. OSS File, April 2, 1945, Harry S Truman Library, Independence, Mo.
56. David McCullough, *Truman* (New York: Touchstone/Simon & Schuster, 1992), p. 372.
57. Dulles, *Secret Surrender*, p. 170.
58. Dulles, p. 173.
59. Dulles, p. 178.
60. Dulles, p. 177.

61. "Memoranda for the President." From William Donovan, dated April 28, 1945.
62. Dulles, *Secret Surrender*, p. 183.
63. Dulles, p. 195.
64. Ralf Georg Reuth, *Goebbels* (New York: Harcourt, Brace, 1990). p. 347. From Goebbels diary entry, March 8, 1945.
65. Reuth, p. 354.
66. *Frankfurter Allgemeine Zeitung*, April 11, 1945.
67. Record Group 226, Entries 90, 110, 139, 165, National Archives.

Chapter 34. Sundown

1. Walter Schellenberg, *The Labyrinth* [aka *Hitler's Secret Service*] (New York: Harper & Brothers, 1956), p. 357.
2. Assize Court, Munich, Judgment against Walter Huppenkothen, February 16, 1951, p. 33; archives of Kammergericat, Berlin. From Heinz Höhne, *Canaris* (New York: Garden City, N.Y.: Doubleday, 1979), p. 589.
3. Will Grosse, "Im Hintergrund der Admiral Canaris," Grosse Estate. From Höhne, *Canaris*, p. 591.
4. Huppenkothen deposition transcript, p. 193, Munich Judgment.
5. Munich Judgment II, p. 11. From Höhne, *Canaris*, p. 594.
6. Munich Judgment II. From *Die Welt*, February 14, 1951.
7. K. H. Abshagen, *Canaris* (London: Hutchinson, 1956), pp. 248, 249.
8. Abshagen, p. 254.
9. Ibid.
10. "Interrogation of Prince Philip of Hesse," OSS declassified document dated July 2, 1945, Georgetown University Lavinger Memorial Library, Special Collections Department, Anthony Cave Brown papers, Box 4.
11. Clinton Gallagher, review, *Studies in Intelligence* (Fall 1957), p. 130. Review of Walter Schellenberg's memoirs by Clinton Gallagher, who had interrogated Schellenberg after the war.

Bibliography

Archives

UNITED STATES

Georgetown University: Joseph Mark Lauinger Memorial Library, Special Collections. Washington, D.C.
—Father Edmund A. Walsh, SJ, Papers
—Russell J. Bowen Collection (Intelligence Literature)
—Anthony Cave Brown papers
Military History Institute, U.S. Army War College, Carlisle Barracks, Carlisle, Pa.
William J. Donovan Papers
National Archives and Records Administration.
—Record Group 226; the Records of the Office of Strategic Services
—Records of the German Armed Forces High Command (microfilmed),
Part IV, No. 80, Item: OKW 2410, Roll 1513
—Record Group 263, Military Reference Branch, Textual Reference Division; Central Intelligence Agency; *Studies in Intelligence.*
Index: 1955–1992
Vol. 36, Nr. 5, 1992; Vol. 37, Nr. 5, 1994
Princeton University, Mudd Library, Allen W. Dulles Papers

UNITED KINGDOM

Public Record Office, Kew
—File HW-1: Government Code and Cipher School (Bletchley; site of
wartime Ultra decipherments). Messages passed to the Prime Minister,
Winston Churchill, by "C" (head of MI-6)
—House of Lords Record Office File 313, Diaries of Robert Bruce Lockhart,
War Notebooks

GERMANY

Bundesarchiv
—Documents on German Foreign Policy, 1918–1945, Series C–D.

Publications

Aarons, Mark, and Loftus, John. *Unholy Trinity: The Vatican, The Nazis, and Soviet Intelligence.* New York: St. Martin's Press, 1991.

Abshagen, K. H. *Canaris.* London: Hutchinson, 1956.

Accoce, Pierre, and Quet, Pierre. *The Lucy Ring.* London: W. H. Allen, 1967.

Allen, Peter. *The Crown and the Swastika: Hitler, Hess and The Duke of Windsor.* London: Robert Hale, 1983.

Andrew, Christopher. *Secret Service: The Making of the British Intelligence Community.* London: Heinemann, 1985.

———. *Her Majesty's Secret Service: The Making of the British Intelligence Community.* New York: Viking/Penguin, 1986.

———, and Dilks, David, eds. *The Missing Dimension: Governments and Intelligence Communities in the Twentieth Century.* London: Macmillan, 1984. Urbana, Ill., University of Illinois Press, 1984.

———, and Gordievsky, Oleg. *KGB: The Inside Story of Its Foreign Operations from Lenin to Gorbachev.* New York: HarperCollins, 1990.

———, and Noakes, Jeremy, ed. *Intelligence and International Relations, 1900–1945.* Exeter, England: Exeter University Publications, 1987.

Annan, Noel. *Changing Enemies.* London: HarperCollins, 1995.

Bailey, Geoffrey. *The Conspirators.* New York: Harper's, 1960.

Balfour, Michael. *Propaganda in War, 1933–1945.* London: Routledge and Kegan Paul, 1979.

Bamford, James. *The Puzzle Palace: A Report on America's Most Secret Agency.* Boston: Houghton Mifflin, 1982.

Bancroft, Mary. *Autobiography of a Spy.* New York: William Morrow, 1983.

Barker, A. J. *Dunkirk: The Great Escape.* New York: David McKay, Inc., 1977.

Barnett, Correlli, ed. *Hitler's Generals.* New York: Grove Weidenfeld, 1989.

Bartz, Karl. *The Downfall of the German Secret Service.* London: William Kimber, 1956.

Bar-Zohar, Michael. *Arrows of the Almighty.* New York: Macmillan, 1985.

Bazna, Elyesa, with Hans Nogly. *I Was Cicero.* New York: Harper & Row, 1962.

Bearse, Ray, and Read, Anthony. *Conspirator: The Untold Story of Tyler Kent.* New York: Doubleday, 1991.

Beesly, Patrick. *Very Special Intelligence: The Story of the Admiralty's Operational Centre.* New York: Ballantine Books, 1981.

Belote, James H. "The Lohmann Affair," *Studies in Intelligence* (Spring 1960).

Bennett, Ralph. *Ultra and Mediterranean Strategy.* New York: William Morrow, 1989.

Bertrand, Gustave. *Enigma ou La Plus Grande Enigme de la Guerre.* Paris: Libraire Plon, 1973.

Best, S. Payne. *The Venlo Incident.* London: Hutchinson & Co., 1950.

Bethell, Nicholas. *The Last Secret.* New York: Basic Books, 1974.

Black, Peter. *Ernst Kaltenbrunner: Ideological Soldier of the Third Reich.* Princeton, N.J.: Princeton University Press, 1984.

Blackstock, Paul W. *The Secret Road to World War II: Soviet Versus Western Intelligence, 1921–1939.* Chicago: Quadrangle Books, 1969.

Bloch, Michael. *Operation Willi: The Nazi Plot to Kidnap the Duke of Windsor.* New York: Weidenfeld & Nicolson, 1986.
———. *Ribbentrop:* New York: Crown Publishers, 1992.
Bokun, Branko. *Spy in the Vatican, 1941–1945.* New York: Praeger, 1973.
Bonhoeffer, Dietrich. *Letters and Papers from Prison.* London: S.C.M. Press, 1953.
Bonhoeffer Family. *Last Letter of Resistance.* Philadelphia: Fortress Press, 1986. In General Collection, Library of Congress.
Boorstin, Daniel J. *Hidden History.* New York: Vintage/Random House, Inc., 1989.
Borovik, Genrikh. *The Philby Files.* Boston: Little, Brown & Co., 1994.
Boveri, Margaret. *Treason in the Twentieth Century.* New York: G. P. Putnam's, 1963.
Bowen, Russell J. *Scholars' Guide to Intelligence Literature: Bibliography of the Russell J. Bowen Collection in the Joseph Mark Lauinger Memorial Library.* Georgetown University. Frederick, Md.: University Publications, Inc., 1983. Published for the National Intelligence Study Center.
Bower, Tom, *The Perfect English Spy: Sir Dick White and the Secret War, 1935–1990,* London: Heineman, 1995.
Boyd, Carl. *Hitler's Japanese Confidant.* Lawrence: University of Kansas Press, 1993.
Boyle, Andrew. *The Fourth Man: The Definitive Account of Kim Philby, Guy Burgess and Donald Maclean, and Who Recruited Them to Spy for Russia.* New York: Dial Press/James Wade, 1979.
Breuer, William B. *Hoodwinking Hitler: The Normandy Deception.* Westport, Conn.: Praeger, 1993.
Brissaud, André. *Canaris: The Biography of Admiral Canaris, Chief of German Military Intelligence in the Second World War.* New York: Grosset & Dunlap, 1974.
———. *The Nazi Secret Service.* New York: W. W. Norton & Co., 1974.
Bristow, Desmond, with Bill Bristow. *A Game of Moles: The Deceptions of an MI-6 Officer.* London: Little, Brown & Co., 1993.
Bross, John. *Special Operations.* Privately published (concerning the author's OSS experience in World War II).
Brown, Anthony Cave. *Bodyguard of Lies.* New York: Quill/William Morrow, 1991. Originally published by Harper & Row in 1975.
———. *"C": The Secret Life of Sir Stewart Graham Menzies.* New York: Macmillan, 1987.
———. *The Last Hero: Wild Bill Donovan.* New York: Times Books, 1982.
———. *Treason in the Blood.* New York: Houghton Mifflin, 1994.
Bruce, David K. E. *OSS Against the Reich: The World War II Diaries of Colonel David K. E. Bruce,* ed. Nelson Lankford. Kent, Ohio: Kent State University Press, 1991.
Buranelli, Vincent, and Buranelli, Nan. *Spy, Counterspy: An Encyclopedia of Espionage.* New York: McGraw-Hill, 1982.
Burdick, Charles B. *Germany's Military Strategy and Spain in World War II.* Syracuse, N.Y.: University of Syracuse Press, 1968.
Butler, Rohan, and Woodward, Ernest L., eds. *Documents on British Foreign Policy 1919–1939.* 2d Series II. London: 1947.

Cadogan, Sir Alexander. *The Diaries of Sir Alexander Cadogan, 1938–1945*, ed. David Dilks, New York: G. P. Putnam's, 1972.

Calvocoressi, Peter. *Top Secret Ultra*. New York: Pantheon Books, 1980.

———, Wint, Guy, and Pritchard, John. *Total War*. New York: Pantheon, 1989.

Carsten, F. L. *Reichswehr and Politics, 1918–1933*. Oxford: Oxford University Press, 1966.

Central Intelligence Agency. *The Trust*, ed. Pamela K. Simkins. Arlington, Va.: Security and Intelligence Foundation, 1989. Released for public distribution under the Freedom of Information Act.

Central Intelligence Agency Counter-Intelligence Staff. *Rote Kapelle: A Survey Report*, vol. 1 of *The CIA's History of Soviet Intelligence and Espionage Networks in Western Europe: 1936–1945*. December 1973. (declassified September 27, 1976)

———. *Rote Kapelle: A Survey Report*, vol. 1 of *The CIA's History of Soviet Intelligence and Espionage Networks in Western Europe: 1936–1945*. Washington, D.C.: University Publications of America, 1979 (published later).

Chalou, George C., ed. *The Secrets War: The Office of Strategic Services in World War II*. Washington, D.C.: National Archives Trust Fund Board (for National Archives and Records Administration), 1992.

Charmley, John. *Churchill: The End of Glory*. New York: Harcourt Brace & Co., 1993.

Churchill, Winston. *The Second World War*:
Vol. 1. *The Gathering Storm*
Vol. 2. *Their Finest Hour*
Vol. 3. *The Grand Alliance*
Vol. 4. *The Hinge of Fate*
Vol. 5. *Closing the Ring*
London: Reprint Society, 1950–1954. 5 vols. Originally published by Cassell, 1950.

Clark, Allan. *Barbarossa: The Russian-German Conflict, 1941–1945*. New York: Quill/William Morrow, 1985. Originally published New York: Morrow 1965.

Clark, Mark Wayne. *Calculated Risk*. New York: Harper & Brothers, 1950.

Clifford, Alexander. *Conquest of North Africa, 1940–1943*. Boston: Little, Brown, 1953.

Colvin, Ian. *Canaris, Chief of Intelligence*. Maidstone, England: George Mann, Publishers, 1973. First published by Victor Gollancz, 1951, under title *Chief of Intelligence*.

———. *The Chamberlain Cabinet*. New York: Taplinger, 1971.

———. *Master Spy*. New York: McGraw-Hill, 1951.

Conot, Robert E. *Justice at Nuremberg*. New York: Carroll & Graf Publishers, 1983.

Conquest, Robert. *The Great Terror: Stalin's Purge of the Thirties*. New York: Macmillan, 1968.

———. *The Great Terror: A Reassessment*. New York: Oxford University Press, 1990.

Constantinides, George C. *Intelligence and Espionage: An Analytical Bibliography*. Boulder, Colo.: Westview Press, 1983.

Coon, Carleton S. *A North African Story: The Anthropologist as OSS Agent, 1941–1943.* Ipswich, Mass.: Gambit, 1980.

Cooper, Alfred Duff. *The Second World War. First Phase.* New York: 1939.

"Correspondence Between Heydrich and Canaris; Agreement on Relationship between the Abwehr and the SD — 10 Gebote." *Records of the German Armed Forces High Command.* Part IV, No. 80, Item: OKW 2410, Roll: 1513, 1st Frame, 540. National Archives.

Costello, John. *Mask of Treachery.* London: Collins, 1988.

——. *Ten Days to Destiny.* New York: William Morrow, 1991.

Costello, John, and Tsarev, Oleg. *Deadly Illusions.* New York: Crown Publishers, 1993.

Cull, Nicholas John. *Selling War.* New York: Oxford University Press, 1995.

Dahlerus, Birger. *The Last Attempt.* London: Hutchinson & Co., 1945.

Deacon, Richard. *A History of British Secret Service.* London: Panther/Grenada, 1984. First published by Frederick Muller in 1969.

——. *"C": A Biography of Sir Maurice Oldfield, Head of MI-6.* London: Mac-Donald, 1985. See McCormick, Donald.

Deane, John R. *The Strange Alliance: The Story of Our Efforts at Wartime Cooperation with Russia.* New York: Viking Press, 1947.

Degras, Jane, ed. *Soviet Documents,* vol. 3. London: 1953.

Deighton, Len. *Blood, Tears and Folly.* New York: HarperCollins, 1993.

De Jonge, Alex. *Stalin and the Shaping of the Soviet Union.* New York: Quill/William Morrow, 1986.

De Launay, Jacques. See Launay, Jacques de.

Delmer, Sefton. *The Counterfeit Spy.* New York: Harper & Row, 1974.

Deutsch, Harold C. *The Conspiracy Against Hitler in the Twilight War.* Minneapolis: University of Minnesota Press, 1968.

——. "The Matter of Records," *The Journal of Military History,* vol. 59, no. 1 (January 1995).

Dilks, David. "Appeasement and Intelligence." *Retreat from Power: Studies in Britain's Foreign Policy of the 20th Century.* London: 1981.

——, ed. *The Diaries of Sir Alexander Cadogan, 1938–1945.* New York: G. P. Putnam's 1971.

Donhoff, Countess Marion. *Before the Storm: Memories of My Youth in Old Prussia.* New York: Knopf, 1990.

Douglas-Hamilton, James. *Motive for a Mission.* New York: Paragon House, 1986. Originally published London: Macmillan & Co.; New York: St. Martin's Press, 1971.

——. *The Truth About Rudolf Hess.* Albany/Edinburgh: Mainstream Publishing Co., 1993.

Downes, Donald. *The Scarlet Thread: Adventures in Wartime Espionage.* New York: British Book Center, 1953.

Dulles, Allen W. *Germany's Underground.* New York: Macmillan, 1947.

——. *The Craft of Intelligence.* New York: Harper & Row, 1963.

——. *The Secret Surrender,* New York: Harper & Row, 1966.

——. ed. *Great True Spy Stories.* New York: Harper & Row, 1968.

Dunlop, Richard. *Donovan: America's Master Spy.* New York: Rand McNally & Co., 1982.

Eisenhower, Dwight D. *Crusade in Europe.* New York: Doubleday, 1948.

Farago, Ladislas. *The Game of the Foxes.* New York: Bantam Books, 1973.

Feis, Herbert. *Churchill, Roosevelt, Stalin.* Princeton, N.J.: Princeton University Press, 1957.

Fleming, Peter. *Operation Sea Lion,* New York: Simon & Schuster, 1957.

Flicke, Wilhelm F. *War Secrets in the Ether,* ed. Sheila Carlisle, Laguna Hills, Calif.: Aegean Park Press, 1994. 2 vols. 1994.

Foltz, Charles. *The Masquerade in Spain.* Boston: Houghton Mifflin/Riverside Press, 1948.

Foote, Alexander. *Handbook for Spies.* London: Hart-Davis, 1976.

Ford, Corey. *Donovan of OSS.* Boston: Little, Brown & Co., 1970.

Fraenkel, Heinrich. See: Manvell, Roger.

Friedhoff, Herman. *Requiem for the Resistance.* London: Bloomsbury, 1993.

Frolik, Josef. *The Frolik Defection.* London: Leo Cooper, 1975.

Fuller, Major General J. F. C. *A Military History of the Western World.* New York: Funk and Wagnalls Co., 1956. 3 vols.

Funk, Arthur Layton. *The Politics of Torch: The Allied Landings and the Algiers Putsch 1942.* Lawrence: The University Press of Kansas, 1974.

Gaevernitz, Gero v. S, ed. based on personal account of Fabian von Schlabrendorff. *They Almost Killed Hitler.* New York: Macmillan, 1947.

Garlinski, Jozef. *The Swiss Corridor.* London: J. M. Dent, 1959.

Gathorne-Hardy, G. M. *A Short History of International Affairs.* London: 1950.

Gehlen, Reinhard. *The Service: The Memoirs of General Reinhard Gehlen.* New York: World Publishing Co., 1972.

Gelb, Norman. *Dunkirk.* New York: Quill, 1989.

Gellman, Irwin F. *Secret Affairs: Franklin Roosevelt, Cordell Hull, Sumner Welles.* Baltimore: Johns Hopkins University Press, 1995.

Gilbert, Felix, annotator. *Hitler Directs His War: The Secret Records of His Daily Military Conferences.* From the manuscripts in the University of Pennsylvania Library. New York: Oxford University Press, 1950.

Gilbert, Martin. *Churchill, a Life.* New York: Henry Holt, 1991.

———. *The Second World War,* rev. ed. New York: Henry Holt, 1989.

Gill, Anton. *An Honourable Defeat.* New York: Henry Holt, 1964.

Gisevius, Hans Bernd. *To the Bitter End.* Boston: Houghton Mifflin, 1947.

Giskes, Herman J. *London Calling North Pole.* New York: British Book Centre, 1953.

Gladwin, Lee A. "Hollywood Propaganda, Isolationism and Protectors of the Public Mind; 1917–1941," *Prologue* magazine (Winter 1994). National Archives.

Glantz, David M. *The Role of Intelligence in Soviet Military Strategy in World War II.* Novato, Calif.: Presidio Press, 1990.

Goebbels, Joseph. *The Goebbels Diaries,* ed. Louis P. Lochner. Garden City, N.Y.: Doubleday, 1949.

———. *Final Entries 1945: The Diaries of Joseph Goebbels,* ed. Hugh Trevor-Roper, New York: G. P. Putnam's 1978.

Great Britain Naval Intelligence Division. *Algeria*, vol. II. Geographical Handbook Series, May 1944.

Grose, Peter. *Gentleman Spy*. New York: Houghton Mifflin, 1994.

Gudmundsson, Bruce I. "The Strategic View: Enterprise Green," *Military History Quarterly*, vol. 7, no. 2 (Winter 1995).

Gun, Nerin. *Hitler's Mistress, Eva Braun*. New York: Bantam Books, 1969.

Halder, Franz. *The Holder War Diary 1939–1942*, ed. Charles B. Burdick and Hans-Adolf Jacobsen. Novato, Calif.: Presidio Press, 1988.

——. *Hitler as Warlord*. London: 1950.

Halpern, Samuel, and Peake, Hayden, eds. *In the Name of Intelligence*. Privately published. Washington D.C.: National Intelligence Book Center Press, 1994.

Hart, B. H. Liddell. See Liddell Hart, B. H.

Hassell, Fey (Pirzio-Biroli) von. *Hostage of the Third Reich*. New York: Scribner's, 1989.

Hassell, Ulrich von. *The Von Hassell Diaries*. London: Hamish, 1947. New York: Doubleday, 1947. Later published: New York: Harper & Row, 1972. German-language edition: *Vom Andern Deutschland*. Zurich: Atlantis Verlag, 1969.

Hayes, Carlton J. H. *Wartime Mission in Spain, 1942–1945*. New York: Macmillan, 1946.

Heiber, Helmut, ed., *The Early Goebbels Diaries*. Introduction by Alan Bullock. New York: Praeger, 1962.

Heideking, Jürgen, and Mauch, Christof. *The U.S. and the German Resistance: Analysis and Operations of the American Secret Service in World War II*, Tübingen: A. Franke Verlag, 1993. German language.

Henderson, Sir Nevile. *Failure of a Mission*. New York: Putnam's, 1940.

Henhoeffer, William. "Donovan's Allies in World War I," *Studies in Intelligence* (Winter 1986).

——. *The Intelligence War in 1941: A 50th Anniversary Perspective*. Washington D.C.: CIA Center for the Study of Intelligence, 1992. National Archives.

Hersh, Burton. *Old Boys*. New York: Scribner's, 1992.

Hinsley, F. H., and Stripp, Alan. *Code Breakers*, Oxford: Oxford University Press, 1993.

Hinsley, F. H., and Simkins, C.A.G. *Security and Counter-Intelligence*, vol. 4 of *British Intelligence in the Second World War*. New York: Cambridge University Press, 1990.

Hinsley, F. H., Thomas, E. E., Ransom C.F.G., and Knight, R.C. *Its Influence on Strategy and Operations*, 2 vols. of *British Intelligence in the Second World War*.

Vol. 1, 2d ed.: London: Her Majesty's Stationery Office, 1986.

Vol. 2: New York: Cambridge University Press, 1981.

Hoare, Sir Samuel. *Ambassadeur en Mission Speciale*, Paris: Vent du Large, 1946. French language.

Hoettl, Wilhelm. *The Secret Front: The Story of Nazi Political Espionage*, tr. R. H. Stevens. London: Weidenfeld & Nicolson, 1953. New York: Praeger, 1954;

Hoffmann, Peter. *Claus Schenk Graf von Stauffenberg und seine Brüder*. Stuttgart: Deutsche Verlags Anstaft, 1993. German language.

――――. *The History of the German Resistance, 1933–1945.* Cambridge, Mass.: Harvard University Press, 1988. First published with title: *Widerstand, Staatsstreich, Attentat*, 1964, R. Piper & Co., 1970.

Höhne, Heinz. *Canaris.* Garden City, N.Y.: Doubleday, 1979.

――――. *Codeword: Direktor: The Story of the Red Orchestra.* New York: Coward, McCann & Geoghegan, 1971.

――――. *The Order of the Death's Head: The Story of Hitler's S.S.*, tr. by Richard Barry, 4th ed. New York: Ballantine Books, 1983. Originally published by Secker & Warburg in 1969.

Hopkirk, Peter. *On Secret Service East of Constantinople; The Plot to Bring Down the British Empire* London: John Murray, 1994. U.S. edition: *Like Hidden Fire.* New York: Kodansha, 1994.

Howard, Michael. *Strategic Deception*, vol. 5 of *British Intelligence in the Second World War.* New York: Cambridge University Press, 1990.

――――. *Studies in War and Peace.* New York: Viking Press, 1971.

Hull, Cordell. *Memoirs of Cordell Hull.* New York: Macmillan, 1948. 2 vols.

Hyde, H. Montgomery. *The Quiet Canadian: The Secret Service of Sir William Stephenson.* Foreword by Ambassador David K. E. Bruce. London: Hamish Hamilton, 1962.

――――. *Room 3603: The Story of the British Intelligence Center in New York During World War II.* New York: Farrar, Straus & Co., 1963.

――――. *Secret Intelligence Agent: British Espionage in America and the Creation of the OSS.* New York: St. Martin's Press, 1982.

International History Project from the Russian Archives, issue 3 (Fall 1993). Publication of Woodrow Wilson International Center for Scholars, Smithsonian Institution.

International Military Tribunal Proceedings: Trial of Major German War Criminals. Vol. 12. Washington, D.C.: U.S. Government Printing Office, 1947–1949.

Irving, David, ed. *Breach of Security: The German Intelligence File on Events Leading to the Second World War.* London: William Kimber, 1968.

――――. *Göring.* New York: Avon Books, 1989.

Jaggers, R. C. "The Assassination of Reinhard Heydrich." *Studies in Intelligence* (Winter 1960). National Archives.

James, D. Clayton. "The Other Pearl Harbor." *Military History Quarterly*, vol. 7, no. 2 (Winter 1995).

John, Otto. *Twice Through the Lines; The Autobiography of Otto John.* New York: Harper & Row, 1972.

Kahn, David. *The Code-breakers: The Story of Secret Writing.* New York: Macmillan, 1967.

――――. *Hitler's Spies: German Military Intelligence in World War II.* New York: Macmillan, 1978.

Kalugin, Oleg. *The First Directorate.* New York: St. Martin's Press, 1994.

Karpinsky, Sgt. "Interrogation of German Non-commissioned Officer on Guard 25 meters from Hitler's Conference Room on July 20. 1944." U.S. Army Chief of Staff for Intelligence G-2 Interrogation Reports Correspondence, 1943–1945. U.S. National Archives, Record Group 165, CSDIC/SIR-1583 15w3189E 179.

Katz, Barry M. *Foreign Intelligence Research and Analysis in the Office of Strategic Services, 1942–1945*. Cambridge, Mass.: Harvard University Press, 1989,

Kechum, Richard M. *The Borrowed Years, 1938–1941*. New York: Random House, 1989.

Keegan, John, *The Second World War*. New York: Viking Press, 1989.

Kennan, George F., *From Prague After Munich*. Princeton, N.J.: Princeton University Press, 1968.

———. *Russia and the West Under Lenin and Stalin*. Boston: Little, Brown & Co., 1961.

Kent, Sherman, *Strategic Intelligence for American World Policy*, Princeton, N.J.: Princeton University Press, 1949.

Kersten, Felix. *The Kersten Memoirs, 1940–1945*, tr. Constantine Fitzgibbon and James Oliver. New York: Macmillan, 1954.

Kessler, Leo, *Betrayal at Venlo*. London: Leo Cooper, 1991.

Kettenacker, Lothar, and Klett, Ernest, eds. *Das andere Deutschland ein sweiten Weltkrieg*. U.S. Library of Congress General Collection. German language.

Khrushchev, Nikita. *Khrushchev Remembers*, ed. Strobe Talbott. Boston: Little Brown & Co., 1970. *Khrushchev Rembers: The Glasnost tapes*, eds. Jerrold Schecter, and Vyacheslav V. Luchkov. Boston: Little, Brown & Co., 1990.

Kilzer, Louis C. *Churchill's Deception*. New York: Simon & Schuster, 1994.

Kimball, Warren F. *The Juggler: Franklin Roosevelt as Wartime Statesman*. Princeton, N.J.: Princeton University Press, 1991.

Kimche, Jon. *Spying for Peace*. New York: Roy Publishers, 1961.

Klehr, Harvey; Hayes, John Earl; and Igorevich, Fridrikh. *The Secret World of American Communism*. New Haven: Yale University Press, 1995.

Klemperer, Klemens von. *German Resistance Against Hitler: The Search for Allies Abroad 1938–1945*. Oxford: Oxford Clarendon Press, 1992.

Knightly, Phillip. *The Master Spy: The Story of Kim Philby*. New York: Knopf, 1989.

———. *The Second Oldest Profession*. New York: W. W. Norton, 1986.

Koch, Stephen, "The Dimitrov Conspiracy," *The New York Times*, January 22, 1994.

Konstantin, Prince of Bavaria. *The Pope*. Woerrishoften, 1952.

Korbel, Josef. *The Communist Subversion of Czechoslovakia, 1938–1948*. Princeton, N.J.: Princeton University Press, 1959.

Kozaczuk, Wladyslaw. *Enigma: How the German Machine Cipher Was Broken, and How It Was Read by the Allies in World War Two*. Frederick, Md.: University Publications of America, 1984.

Kramarz, Joachim. *Stauffenberg: The Architect of the Famous July 20th Conspiracy to Assassinate Hitler*. New York: Macmillan, 1967.

Krivitsky, Walter G. *In Stalin's Service: An Exposé of Russia's Secret Policy by the Former Chief of the Soviet Intelligence in Western Europe*. 2d ed. New York: Harper & Brothers, 1939.

Kussinen, Aino. *The Rings of Destiny: Inside Soviet Russia, From Lenin to Brezhnev*. New York: William Morrow, 1974.

Kuzichkin, Vladimir. *Inside the KGB*. New York: Pantheon, 1990.

Lamb, Richard. *War in Italy 1943–1945: A Brutal Story.* New York: St. Martin's Press, 1993.

Lane, Peter B. *The U.S. and The Balkan Crisis of 1940–1941.* New York: Garland Publishing Co., 1988.

Langer, William L. *Our Vichy Gamble.* New York: Knopf, 1947.

Lankford, Nelson, ed. *OSS Against the Reich: The World War II Diaries of Colonel David K. E. Bruce.* Kent, Ohio: Kent State University Press, 1991.

Launay, Jacques de. *Secret Diplomacy of World War II.* New York: Simmons-Boardman, 1963.

Leber, Annedore, ed., *The Conscience in Revolt: Portraits of the German Resistance in 1933–1945*, re-ed. Karl Dietrich Bracher. Munich: v. Hase and Koehler, 1994.

Lee, Bruce. *Marching Orders.* New York: Crown Publishers, 1995.

Leverkuehn, Paul. *German Military Intelligence.* New York: Praeger, 1954.

Lewin, Ronald. *Hitler's Mistakes.* New York: Quill/William Morrow, 1984.

———. *Ultra Goes to War: The First Account of World War's Greatest Secret Based on Official Documents.* New York: McGraw-Hill, 1978.

Liddell Hart, B. H. *The German Generals Talk.* New York: Quill, 1979.

———. *History of the Second World War.* New York: Perigee Books/Putnam, 1982.

Lockhart, Robert H. Bruce. *Comes the Reckoning.* London: Putnam, 1947.

Lockhart, Robin Bruce. *Reilly: Ace of Spies.* Middlesex, England: Penguin, 1967. U.S. edition, New York: Stein & Day, 1967.

Lovell, Mary S. *Cast No Shadow: The Life of the American Spy Who Changed the Course of World War II.* New York: Pantheon, 1992.

Lukacs, John. *The Duel.* New York: Ticknor & Fields, 1990.

Lutze, James, ed. *The Journal of General Raymond E. Lee, 1940–1941.* London: 1971.

MacDonald, Callum. *The Killing of SS Obergruppen-Führer Reinhard Heydrich.* New York: Collier/Macmillan, 1989.

Manchester, William. *The Last Lion: Winston Spencer Churchill, Alone, 1932–1940.* Boston: Little, Brown & Co., 1988.

Manvell, Roger, and Fraenkel, Heinrich. *The Canaris Conspiracy.* New York: David McKay, Inc., 1969.

Mason, Herbert Molloy, Jr. *To Kill The Devil.* New York: W. W. Norton, 1978.

Masterman, J. C. *The Double-Cross System in the War of 1939–1945.* New Haven: Yale University Press, 1972.

May, Ernest, ed. *Knowing One's Enemy.* Princeton, N.J.: Princeton University Press, 1984.

McCormick, Donald (aka Deacon, Richard [pen name]), *Pedlar of Death.* London: Macdonald 1965.

McKale, Donald M., ed. *Rewriting History: The Original and Revised World War II Diaries of Curt Prufer, Nazi Diplomat.* Kent, Ohio: Kent State University Press, 1988.

McLachlan, Donald. *Room 39.* New York: Atheneum, 1968.

Melchior, Ib, and Brandenburg, Frank. *Quest.* Novato, Calif.: Presidio Press, 1990.

"Memoranda for the President." *Studies in Intelligence.* (Spring 1963).

Moll, Oho E. *The German Generalfieldmarshals, 1934–1945,* rev. Wolfgang W. Marek. Frankfurt: Erich Pabel, 1991.

Moltke, Count Helmuth James von. *A German of the Resistance: The Last Letters of Count Helmuth James von Moltke,* Oxford: Oxford University Press, 1948.

Montagu, Ewen. *Beyond Top Secret Ultra.* New York: Coward, McCann & Geoghegan, 1978.

Moran, Lord. *The Diaries of Lord Moran.* Boston: Houghton Mifflin, 1966.

Moravec, General Frantisek. *Master of Spies: The Memoirs of General Frantisek Moravec.* Garden City, N.Y.: Doubleday, 1975.

Mosley, Leonard. *Dulles.* New York: Dial Press, 1978.

———. *On Borrowed Time.* New York: Random House, 1969.

Moyzisch, L. C. *Operation Cicero.* Postscript by Franz von Papen. New York: Coward-McCann, 1950.

Mure, David. *Master of Deception: Tangled Webs in London and the Middle East.* London: William Kimber, 1980.

Murphy, Robert D. *Diplomat Among Warriors.* New York: Doubleday, 1964.

Naftali, Timothy. "X-2 *and the Apprenticeship of American Counter-espionage, 1942–1944*" Dissertation, Harvard University, 1993. Ann Arbor: UMI Dissertation Service, 1994.

Neilson, Keith, and McKerchor, B. J. C., eds. *Go Spy the Land,* Westport, Conn.: Praeger, 1992.

Nicolai, Colonel Walther. *The German Secret Service.* London: Stanley Paul, 1924.

Nicolson, Harold. *Diaries and Letters, 1939–1945,* ed. Nigel Nicolson. London: Collins, 1967.

Nicosia, Frances R., and Stokes, Lawrence, eds. *Germans Against Nazism.* Oxford: Oxford University Press, 1992.

Norden, Peter. *Madam Kitty.* London: Abelard-Schuman, 1973.

Orlov, Alexander. *Handbook of Intelligence and Guerrilla Warfare.* Ann Arbor: University of Michigan Press, 1963.

———. *Secret History of Stalin's Crimes.* New York: Random House, 1953.

O'Toole, G. J. A. *The Encyclopedia of American Intelligence and Espionage.* New York: Facts on File, 1988.

———. *Honorable Treachery.* New York: Atlantic Monthly Press, 1991.

Padfield, Peter. *Hess: Flight for the Führer,* London: Weidenfeld & Nicolson, 1991.

———. *Himmler.* New York: Henry Holt, 1990.

Paillet, Claude. *Le Desastre de 1940: La Guerre Éclair.* Paris: 1985.

Paillole, Paul. *Notre Espion chez Hitler.* Paris: Éditions Robert Laffont, 1985.

———. *Services Spéciaux: 1935–1945.* Paris: Robert Laffont, 1975.

Paine, Lauran. *The Abwehr: German Military Intelligence in World War II.* London: Robert Hale, 1988.

Parrish, Thomas. *The Ultra Americans: The U.S. Role in Breaking the Nazi Codes.* New York: Stein and Day, 1986.

Pendar, Kenneth W. *Adventure in Diplomacy: Our French Dilemma.* New York: Dodd, Mead & Co., 1945.

Perrault, Gilles. *The Red Orchestra.* Peter Wiles. New York: Shocken Books, 1989.

Persico, Joseph E. *Nuremberg: Infamy on Trial*. New York: Viking Press, 1994.

———. *Piercing the Reich: The Penetration of Nazi Germany by American Secret Agents During World War II*. New York: Viking Press, 1979.

Pforzheimer, Walter, ed. *Bibliography of Intelligence Literature*, 8th ed. Washington, D.C. Defense Intelligence College, 1985.

Philby, Kim (Harold A. R.). *My Silent War*, New York: Grove Press, 1968. London: Granada Publishing, 1969. Introduction by Graham Greene, Reprinted 1983.

Piekalkiewicz, Janusz. *Secret Agents, Spies and Saboteurs*. New York: William Morrow, 1973.

Pincer, Chapman. *Too Secret Too Long*. New York: St. Martin's Press, 1984.

Popov, Dusko. *Spy/Counterspy*. Introduction by Ewen Montagu. Garden City, N.Y.: Grosset and Dunlop, 1975. London: Weidenfeld & Nicolson, 1974; Granada, 1977. Greenwich, Conn.: Fawcett Publications, 1975.

Powers, Richard. *Heisenberg's War: The Secret History of the German Bomb*. New York: Knopf, 1993.

———. *Secrecy and Power: The Life of J. Edgar Hoover*. New York: Free Press, 1989.

Preston, Paul. *Franco*. New York: Basic Books/HarperCollins, 1994.

Prittie, Terence. *Germans Against Hitler*. London: Hutchinson, 1964.

Prochazka, Theodor. *The Second Republic: The Disintegration of Post-Munich Czechoslovakia (October 1938–March 1939)*. East European Monographs. Boulder, Colo.: by Columbia University Press, 1981.

Pujol, Juan, with West, Nigel. *Garbo*. London: Weidenfeld & Nicolson, 1985.

Quibble, Anthony. "Alias George Wood." *Studies in Intelligence* (Winter 1966).

Raad, R. C. "Stalin Plans His Post-War Germany," *Journal of Contemporary History* 28 (1933).

Read, Anthony, and Fisher, David. *Colonel Z: The Secret Life of a Master of Spies*. London: Hodder and Stoughton, 1984. New York: Viking Press, 1985.

———. *Operation Lucy*. New York: Coward, McCann, & Geoghegan, 1981.

Reese, Mary Ellen. *General Reinhard Gehlen: The CIA Connection*. Fairfax, Va.: George Mason University Press, 1990.

Reilly, Sidney. *Britain's Master Spy: His Own Story*. New York: Dorset Press, 1985.

Rejewski, Marian. "How Polish Mathematicians Deciphered the Enigma," tr. Jean Stepenske. *Annals of the History of Computing*, vol. 3, no. 3 (July 1981).

Reuth, Ralf Georg. *Goebbels*. New York: Harcourt, Brace, 1990.

Ritter, Gerhard. *The German Resistance: Carl Goerdeler's Struggle Against Tyranny*. London: 1955.

Rogers, James. *The Secret War: Espionage in World War II*. New York: Facts on File, 1991.

Rommetveit, Karl, ed. *Narvik 1940: Five Nations War in the High North*. Oslo: Norwegian Institute for Defense Studies, 1991.

Roosevelt, Kermit. *The Overseas Targets: War Report of the OSS*, vol. 2. Washington, D.C.: Carrollton Press; New York: Walker & Co.; 1976.

Rothfels, Hans. "The German Resistance in Its International Aspects." Proceedings of the General Meeting held by Chatham House, London, March 14, 1958.

Rubin, Barry. *Istanbul Intrigues*. New York: McGraw Hill, 1989.

Sainsbury, Keith. *The North African Landings, 1942: A Strategic Decision.* London: Davis-Poynter, 1976.

———. *Politics and Strategy of The Second World War,* ed. Noble Frankland and Christopher Dowling. London: Davis-Poynter, 1976.

Schecter, Jerrold L., and Luchkov, Vyacheslav eds. See Khrushchev, Nikita.

Schellenberg, Walter. *The Labyrinth: Memoirs of Walter Schellenberg,* tr. Louis Hagen. New York: Harper & Brothers, 1956. Also published as: Schellenberg, Walter. *The Schellenberg Memoirs,* tr. Louis Hagen. London: André Deutsch, 1956.

U.S. paperback edition published as: Schellenberg, Walter. *Hitler's Secret Service: Memoirs of Walter Schellenberg,* ed. and tr. Louis Hagen, 2d ed. New York: Pyramid, 1962.

Schlabrendorff, Fabian von. *The Secret War Against Hitler,* ed. Gero v. S. Gaevernitz. New York: Pittman, 1965. London: Hodder & Stoughton, 1966.

Schulze-Holthus, Bernard. *Daybreak in Iran: A Story of The German Intelligence Service.* London: Staples Press, 1954.

Semelin, Jacques. *Unarmed Against Hitler.* Westport, Conn.: Praeger, 1993.

Senate, U.S., 93d Congress, 1st Session August 1973. *The Legacy of Alexander Orlov.* 1973.

Sheymon, Victor. *Tower of Secrets.* Annapolis: Naval Institute Press, 1994.

Shirer, William L. *The Nightmare Years, 1930–1940,* vol. 2 of *20th Century Journey.* New York: Bantam Books, 1992. Originally published by Little, Brown & Co. in 1984.

Shulsky, Abram N. *Silent Warfare; Understanding the World of Intelligence.* Washington, D.C.: Brassey's (U.S.), Maxwell-Macmillan Inc, 1991.

Smith, Bradley F. "Admiral Godfrey's Mission to America, June, July, 1941." *Intelligence and National Security,* vol. 3 (September 1986).

———. *The Shadow Warriors: OSS and the Origins of the CIA.* New York: Basic Books, 1983.

———. *The Ultra-Magic Deals and the Most Secret Special Relationship, 1940–1946.* Novato, Calif.: Presidio Press, 1993.

Smith, Gaddis, *American Diplomacy During the Second World War, 1941–1945.* New York: John Wiley & Sons, 1966.

Smith, Paul A., Jr. *On Political War.* Washington, D.C.: National Defense University Press, 1989.

Smith, R. Harris. *OSS: The Secret History of America's First Central Intelligence Agency.* Berkeley: University of California Press, 1972.

Smith, Walter Bedell. *Ike's Six Great Decisions, 1944–1945.* London: Longmans Green & Co., 1947.

Smyth, Howard, "The Ciano Papers: Rose Garden." *Studies in Intelligence* (Spring 1969). National Archives.

Snyder, Louis L. *Hitler's German Enemies.* New York: Berkley Books, 1992.

Speer, Albert. *Inside the Third Reich.* London: Weidenfeld & Nicolson, 1970.

State Department, U.S. *Foreign Relations of the United States Papers, 1944,* vol. 3, *The British Commonwealth.* Washington, D.C.: U.S. Government Printing Office, 1965.

Stead, John Phillip. *Second Bureau*. London: Evans Brothers, 1959.

Stevenson, William. *The Bormann Brotherhood*. New York: Harcourt Brace Jovanovich, 1973.

———. *Intrepid's Last Case*. New York: Villard Books, 1983.

———. *A Man Called Intrepid: The Secret War*. Historical note by Charles H. Ellis. New York: Harcourt Brace Jovanovich, 1976.

Stimson, Henry L., and Bundy, McGeorge. *On Active Service in Peace and War*. New York: Harper & Brothers, 1948.

Stoltzfus, Nathan. "Dissent in Nazi Germany." *Atlantic*, vol. 270, no. 3 (September 1992).

Strong, Major General Sir Kenneth W. D. *Intelligence at the Top: The Recollections of an Intelligence Officer*. Garden City, N.Y.: Doubleday, 1969.

Studies in Intelligence. A quarterly in-house publication of the Central Intelligence Agency, begun in 1955, containing classified articles of intelligence relevance. Some articles are now declassified and available through the National Archives. See Belote; Henhoeffer; Jaggers; Quibble; Smyth; and Troy.

Sullivan, Brian R. "A Highly Commendable Action: William J. Donovan's Intelligence Mission for Mussolini and Roosevelt, 1935 February–1936 December." *Intelligence and National Security* vol. 6, no. 2 (April 1991).

Swearingen, Ben E. "Hitler's Family Secret," *Civilization* (March–April 1995).

Sykes, Christopher. *Troubled Loyalty: A Biography of Adam von Trott zu Solz*. London: Collins, 1968.

Taylor, Telford. *The Anatomy of the Nuremberg Trials*. New York: Knopf, 1992.

Thomas, Hugh. *The Last 100 Days*. New York: Simon & Schuster, 1961.

Toland, John. *The Last 100 Days*. New York: Random House, 1966.

Tompkins, Peter. *The Murder of Admiral Darlan*. New York: Simon & Schuster, 1965.

———. *A Spy in Rome*. Preface by Donald Downes. New York: Simon & Schuster, 1962.

Toscano, Mario. "Machiavelli: Views on World War II Intelligence." *International Journal of Intelligence and Counter-intelligence*, vol. I, no. 3 (1986).

Treadgold, D. W. "The Ideology of the White Movement: Wrangel's Leftist Policy from Rightist Hand." *Russian Thought & Politics*. Slavic Studies, Series E, vol. 4, Harvard University. (Cambridge, Mass.: Harvard University Press.)

Trepper, Leopold. *The Great Game: Memoirs of the Spy Hitler Couldn't Silence*. New York: McGraw-Hill, 1977.

Trevor-Roper, H. R., ed. *Hitler's War Directive, 1939–1945*. London: 1964.

———. *The Philby Affair*. London: William Kimber, 1968.

Troy, Thomas. "The British Assault on J. Edgar Hoover: The Tricycle Case." *International Journal of Intelligence and Counter-intelligence*, vol. 3, no. 2 (1989).

Troy, Thomas F., *Donovan and the CIA: A History of the Establishment of the Central Intelligence Agency*. Foreign Intelligence Book Series, Thomas F. Troy, gen. ed. Frederick, Md.: University Publications of America, 1981.

———. "The Coordinator of Information and British Intelligence," *Studies in Intelligence* (Spring 1974). National Archives.

Tuchman, Barbara W. *The Zimmermann Telegram*. New York: Viking Press, 1950.

Vassiltchikov, Marie. *Berlin Diaries 1940–1945.* New York: Vintage Books, 1988. First American edition: New York: Knopf, 1987.

Verrier, Anthony. *Assassination in Algiers: Churchill, Roosevelt, de Gaulle and the Murder of Admiral Darlan.* London: Macmillan, 1990.

Vidal, Gore. "Screening History." *American Heritage* (September 1992).

Volkman, Ernest. *Spies.* New York: John Wiley & Sons, 1994.

Volkogonov, Dmitri. *Lenin.* New York: Free Press, 1994.

Waller, Martha, and Moore, Dan Tyler. *Cloak and Cipher.* Indianapolis: Bobbs-Merrill, 1962.

Warlimont, Walter. *Inside Hitler's Headquarters, 1939–1945.* Novato, Calif.: Presidio Press, 1964.

Watt, Donald Cameron. "British Intelligence and the Coming of the Second World War in Europe." *Knowing One's Enemies,* ed. Ernest J. May. Princeton, N.J.: Princeton University Press, 1984.

Weinberg, Gerhard L. *A World at Arms.* Cambridge, England: Cambridge University Press, 1994.

Weiner, Jan. *The Assassination of Heydrich.* New York: Grossman Publishers, 1969.

Weitz, John. *Hitler's Diplomat: The Life and Times of Joachim von Ribbentrop.* New York: Ticknor & Fields, 1992.

———. *The Time for Decision.* New York: Harper & Brothers, 1944.

West, Rebecca. *The Circus, MI-5 Operations 1945–1972.* New York: Stein & Day, 1983.

———. *GCHQ: The Secret Wireless War, 1900–1986.* London: Weidenfeld & Nicolson, 1986.

———. *MI-6: British Security Operations, 1909–1945.* London: Weidenfeld & Nicolson, 1981.

———. *MI-6: British Secret Intelligence Service Operations.* New York: Random House, 1983.

———. *Seven Spies Who Changed the World.* London: Secker and Warburg, 1991.

———. *A Thread of Deceit: Espionage Myths of World War II.* New York: Random House, 1985.

West, Rebecca. *The Meaning of Treason.* New York: Viking Press, 1945.

———. *The New Meaning of Treason.* New York: Viking Press, 1964.

Whaley, Barton. *Codeword Barbarossa,* Cambridge, Mass.: MIT Press, 1973.

Wheeler-Bennett, John W. *The Nemesis of Power.* London: Macmillan, 1953.

Whiting, Charles. *The Spymasters.* New York: E. P. Dutton & Co./Saturday Review Press, 1976.

Williams, Charles. *The Last Great Frenchman.* New York: John Wiley, 1995.

Winks, Robin. *Cloak and Gown: Scholars in the Secret War, 1939–1961.* New York: William Morrow, 1987.

Winterbotham, Frederick W. *Secret and Personal.* London: William Kimber, 1969.

Winterbotham, Frederick W. *The Ultra Secret.* London: Weidenfeld & Nicolson, 1974; New York: Harper & Row; 1974.

Wohlstetter, Roberta. *Pearl Harbor: Warning and Decision.* Stanford, Calif.: Stanford University Press, 1962.

Woodward, Ernest L., and Butler, Rohan, eds. *Documents on British Foreign Policy, 1919–1939,* 2d Series II. London: 1947.

Woytak, Richard A. *On the Border of War and Peace: Polish Intelligence and Diplomacy in 1937–1939 and the Origins of the Ultra Secret.* New York: Columbia University Press, 1979.

Wright, Peter. *Spycatcher: The Candid Autobiography of a Senior Intelligence Officer.* New York: Viking Press, 1987. Paperback edition: New York: Dell, 1988.

Index

ABOUT THE AUTHOR

A graduate of the University of Michigan, John Waller spent the last two and a half years of World War II in Cairo, as Deputy Middle East Theater Chief of OSS, Counter-espionage. His postwar career with the Foreign Service was spent mostly abroad, serving in the Middle East, South Asia, and Africa. In 1976, he was appointed Inspector General of the Central Intelligence Agency; he retired in 1980 to devote his time to writing and lecturing on military and intelligence history. He has received the National Civil Service League Award and Distinguished Intelligence Medal for outstanding service. He is the author of *Beyond the Khyber Pass*; *Gordon of Khartoum: The Saga of a Victorian Hero*; and *Tibet: A Chronicle of Exploration* (under the pen name John MacGregor).

ABOUT THE TYPE

This book was set in Electra, a typeface designed for Linotype by W. A. Dwiggins, the renowned type designer (1880–1956). Electra is a fluid typeface, avoiding the contrasts of thick and thin strokes that are prevalent in most modern typefaces.